Christian Theology

Praise for previous editions of *Christian Theology: An Introduction*

"This book is an extraordinary achievement, a *tour de force* which will introduce thousands of students to theology as a discipline with a rich heritage, a clear sense of its own methods and norms, and an elusive yet articulate understanding of Christian language." *Reviews in Religion and Theology*

"'*Introduction*' is perhaps too modest a word for a book which gives a basic introduction to almost every aspect of the history and theology of Christianity. It is clearly written, fairly argued, and very reasonably priced. McGrath has set a standard that will not be broken for a very long time." *Theology*

"There is much to admire in Dr McGrath's skill as a pedagogue. The range of issues he deals with is marvellously broad, and he says a great many things which are important, beautiful, true and worth knowing."*Church Times*

"McGrath has surpassed even himself in ... *Christian Theology: An Introduction*. His assumption that the reader has little theological expertise and reads only English, makes the book extremely valuable to beginners in theology ... His purpose is not to pre-scribe but to de-scribe Christian Theology." *Trinity Journal*

"This is an admirable textbook which will soon grace many shelves." *Expository Times*

"[McGrath] lets the Church and its classic traditions speak for themselves, rather than expostulating on his own arguments and opinions. His own constructive work takes the form of addressing, in light of Scripture and tradition, some of the burning issues in the Church today. The happy result is that the shape of the questions is contemporary, while the substance of the answers is deeply traditional." *First Things*

"This publication is a seminal text for the student or teacher of Christian Theology. Its readability and general presentation make it a very accessible text for those with a general interest in this area of academic endeavour. In essence this is a text which would be a useful and valuable resource for the teacher or student of theology. For school-based practitioners it is a very sound teacher reference text. It contains in one volume a very thorough treatment of the key developments in Christian Theology over the past 2000 years." *Religious Education Journal of Australia*

Also by Alister E. McGrath from Blackwell Publishing

The Christian Theology Reader, 3rd edn. (2007)

Christianity: An Introduction, 2nd edn (2006)

The Blackwell Companion to Protestantism (edited with Darren C. Marks, 2003)

The Intellectual Origins of the European Reformation, 2nd edn (2003)

A Brief History of Heaven (2003)

The Future of Christianity (2002)

Christian Literature: An Anthopology (edited, 2000)

Reformation Thought: An Introduction, 3rd edn (1999)

Christian Spirituality: An Introduction (1999)

Historical Theology: An Introduction (1998)

The Blackwell Encyclopedia of Modern Christian Thought (1995)

For a complete list of Alister E. McGrath's publications from Blackwell Publishing, visit our website at www.blackwellpublishing.com/mcgrath

Christian Theology

An Introduction

Fourth Edition

Alister E. McGrath

University of Oxford

Blackwell Publishing

BLACKWELL PUBLISHING
350 Main Street, Malden, MA 02148-5020, USA
9600 Garsington Road, Oxford OX4 2DQ, UK
550 Swanston Street, Carlton, Victoria 3053, Australia

First edition published 1993
Second edition published 1996
Third edition published 2001
Fourth edition published 2007 by Blackwell Publishing Ltd

1   2007

Library of Congress Cataloging-in-Publication Data

McGrath, Alister E., 1953 –
    Christian theology : an introduction / Alister E. McGrath.—4th ed.
        p. cm.
    Includes bibliographical references and index.
    ISBN-13: 978-1-4051-5360-7 (pbk. : alk. paper)
    ISBN-10: 1-4051-5360-1 (pbk. : alk. paper) 1. Theology, Doctrinal. I. Title.

BT65. M34 2007
230—dc22

                                                            2006008996

A catalogue record for this title is available from the British Library.

Set in 10.5 on 12.5pt PhotinaMT
by SPi Publisher Services, Pondicherry
Printed and bound in the United Kingdom
by TJ International Ltd, Padstow, Cornwall.

The publisher's policy is to use permanent paper from mills that operate a
sustainable forestry policy, and which has been manufactured from pulp
processed using acid-free and elementary chlorine-free practices. Furthermore,
the publisher ensures that the text paper and cover board used have met
acceptable environmental accreditation standards.

For further information on
Blackwell Publishing, visit our website:
www.blackwellpublishing.com

Brief Contents

Contents

Illustrations

Preface

The great Swiss theologian Karl Barth offers us a vision of Christian theology at its finest. It is, he suggests, like Tuscan or Umbrian landscapes, which hold us in awe on account of the breathtaking views which they offer. Even the most distant perspectives seem so clear. Barth is but one of many theologians to have stressed the sheer intellectual excitement that the study of Christian theology can bring, not to mention its capacity to bring new depth to the life of faith. This book is written in the conviction that Christian theology is one of the most fascinating subjects anyone can hope to study. As Christianity enters into a new phase of expansion, especially in the Pacific Rim, the study of Christian theology will continue to have a key role to play in modern intellectual culture. It also remains of seminal importance to any concerned to understand the central issues and preoccupations of the Middle Ages or the European Reformation, as well as many other periods in human history.

Yet one major American religious publication noted recently that "most clergy, never mind lay people, have given up reading theology." As a professional teacher of theology at Oxford University over many years, I am painfully aware that this sense of enthusiasm and excitement is rare among university and seminary students of theology. They are more often baffled and bewildered by the frequently confusing vocabulary of Christian theology, the apparent unintelligibility of much recent writing in the field, and its seeming irrelevance to the practical issues of Christian living and ministry. As someone who believes that Christian theology is amongst the most rewarding, fulfilling, and genuinely *exciting* subjects anyone can ever hope to study, I have worked hard to try to remedy this situation. This book, which arises out of more than two decades of teaching theology to undergraduates and seminarians at Oxford University, is a response to that concern.

There is an obvious need for an entry-level introduction to Christian theology. Too many existing introductions make what experience shows to be hopelessly optimistic assumptions about how much their readers already know. In part, this reflects a major religious shift within western culture. Many students now wishing to study Christian theology are recent converts. Unlike their predecessors in past generations, they possess little inherited understanding of the nature of Christianity, its technical vocabulary, or the structure of its thought. Everything has to be introduced and explained. The present volume therefore assumes that its readers know nothing about Christian theology. Everything is introduced clearly, and set out as simply as possible. Simplicity of expression and clarity of exposition are the core virtues that have been pursued in writing this work.

For some, this will mean that the resulting work lacks sophistication and originality. Those qualities are certainly valuable in other contexts. They are not, however, appropriate to a book of this kind. While originality unquestionably has its merits elsewhere, in a work of this kind it is potentially a liability. Originality implies novelty and development; in writing this book, I have deliberately avoided imposing my own ideas as if these were of any interest or importance. Educational considerations have been given priority over everything else. My aim in this work has not been to *persuade*, but to *explain*.

This book is therefore descriptive, not prescriptive. It does not seek to tell its readers what to believe, but rather aims to explain to them what has been believed, in order to equip them to make up their minds for themselves. It does this by describing options available to them, and their historical origins, and enabling them to understand their strengths and weaknesses through a process of analysis and reflection.

Inevitably, this approach means that the discussion of many questions of Christian theology – especially questions of method – is somewhat limited. If my own notes are anything to go by, it would take a volume nearly five times the size of this one to do anything even approaching justice to the complexities of many of the issues raised. Readers therefore need to appreciate that what is being offered is an introduction, a sketch map, in order that they can pursue these questions in greater detail, having at least gained some understanding of what is at stake. My own experience strongly suggests that students stand a far better chance of understanding and appreciating seminal issues if someone is prepared to take trouble to explain the background to the discussion, the nature and significance of the questions being debated, and the terminology being used. I have assumed that the reader knows no language other than English, and have explained and provided a translation of every Latin, Greek, or German word or phrase that has become an accepted part of the theologian's vocabulary.

Sadly, there is not space to discuss every theological development, movement, or writer which one might hope to include in a work of this sort. Time and time again, pressure on space has forced me to leave out some material which many readers will feel ought to have been included, or give a less full account of some questions than I would have liked. I can only apologize for these shortcomings, of which I am only too painfully aware. The selection of matters to be discussed – and the manner in which they have been discussed – is based upon first-hand recent experience of teaching, and careful surveys of student opinion in many countries, to discover both what students think ought to be included in this volume, and what they find difficult to understand, and hence requiring extended explanation. This survey was extended for the purposes of the second and third editions to include a large number of those involved in the teaching of systematic theology; wherever possible, their suggestions for alterations and improvement were included. For the purposes of the fourth edition, this process of consultation was extended still further, and resulted in the rewriting of four chapters. The "Acknowledgments" section details those who were kind enough to assist in this way.

Alister E. McGrath
Oxford University

Mission Statement

This book aims to introduce you to the basics of Christian theology. It assumes that you know nothing about the subject. It introduces and explains the following aspects of Christian theology:

- its leading ideas;
- how those ideas are developed and defended;
- its basic vocabulary, especially technical terms;
- the key debates that have influenced Christian thinking during the last two thousand years;
- the leading thinkers who have shaped Christian theology down the centuries.

After you have worked through this book, you will be able to achieve the following *objectives*:

- read and understand more advanced works of theology, including works by major theologians, and works about major theologians or areas of theology;
- benefit from the growing body of theological material on the Internet – some of which is identified in the "Theological Resources on the Internet" section of the dedicated website linked to this book;
- make sense of lectures and talks dealing with Christian theology;
- make informed contributions to debates and discussions in churches, universities, seminaries, and colleges;
- give accurate and reliable introductory presentations to church and student audiences on many aspects of Christian thought.

To the Student: How to Use this Work

C hristian theology is one of the most fascinating subjects it is possible to study. This book aims to make that study as simple and rewarding as possible. It has been written assuming that you know nothing about Christian theology. Obviously, the more you already know, the easier you will find this volume to handle. By the time you have finished this work, you will know enough to be able to follow most technical theological discussions and arguments, benefit from specialist lectures, and get the most from further reading.

Precisely because this book is comprehensive, it includes a lot of material – considerably more than is included in most introductions of this kind. You must not be frightened by the amount of material that this volume includes; you do not need to master it all. Considerable thought has been given to the best way of organizing the material. Grasping the structure of the work – which is quite simple – will allow it to be used more effectively by both teachers and students. The book is divided into three major sections.

The first section, entitled "Landmarks," deals with the historical development of Christian theology. These four chapters give historical information which introduces key terms and ideas, some of which will not be explained again. This volume works on the basis of "explain it the first time round." To understand fully the key theological issues you will encounter later in this work, you need to know a little about their historical background.

You also need to know something about the debates over the sources and methods of Christian theology – in short, where Christianity gets its ideas from. The second part of the work introduces you to these issues, and will equip you to deal with the material covered in the third part.

The final section of the book, which is also the longest, deals with the major doctrinal issues of Christian theology – what Christians believe about God, Jesus Christ, and heaven, to mention just three important topics. This material is organized thematically, and you should have no difficulty in finding your way to the material appropriate to your needs. The "Contents" pages will give you a good idea where each specific discussion is to be found. If you have any difficulties, use the index.

However, there is no need to read every chapter in this book, nor need you read them in the order in which they are set out. Each chapter can be treated as a more or less self-contained unit. The book includes internal cross-references, which will ensure that you can follow up related matters which arise in the course of each and every chapter. Once more, it must be stressed that you must not let the sheer length of the book intimidate you; it is *long* because it is *comprehensive*, and gives you access to all the information that you will need. It aims to be a one-stop freestanding reference book, which will cover all the material that you are likely to need to know about.

If you are using the book to teach yourself theology, it is recommended that you read the chapters in the order in which they are presented. However, if you are using the book in conjunction with a taught course, you can easily work out which sections of the book relate to the ordering of material used by your teacher. If in doubt, ask for guidance.

If you come across terms which you don't understand, you have three options. First, try the glossary at the end of the work, which may give you a brief definition of the term. Second, try the index, which will provide you with a more extensive analysis of key discussion locations within the volume. And thirdly, you can carry out a search on the Internet for a definition and discussion of the term in question.

Full references are provided to the sources of all major quotations within this work. The "Sources of Citations" section will allow you to track down the quotation, and study it at length in its proper context. Full extracts of many of these texts are provided in the companion volume to this introduction, *The Christian Theology Reader*. Appropriate cross-references will allow you to take things further if you want to, without placing you at a disadvantage if you do not.

Finally, be assured that everything in this book – including the contents of this work, the way in which the material has been arranged, the style of writing used, and the explanations offered – has been checked out at first hand with student audiences and individual readers in Australasia, Canada, Hong Kong, the United Kingdom, and the United States. The work is probably about as user-friendly as you can get. But both the author and publisher welcome suggestions from teachers and students for further improvement, which will be included in later editions of the work. The fourth edition of this work has benefited considerably from such suggestions; we look forward to receiving suggestions for the fifth and subsequent editions.

To the Teacher: How to Use this Book

C hristian theology is a subject which ought to excite students. In practice, both student and teacher find the teaching of the subject to be difficult, and occasionally rather depressing. The student is discouraged by the vast amount of the material it is necessary to grasp before "getting to the interesting bits" – as one Oxford student once put it to me. Teachers find the subject difficult for two main reasons. First, they want to introduce and discuss advanced ideas, but find that students are simply unable to appreciate and understand these, due to a serious lack of background knowledge. Second, they find that they lack the time necessary to introduce students to the substantial amount of basic theological vocabulary and knowledge required.

This book aims to deal with both these difficulties, and to liberate teachers from the often tiring and tedious business of teaching entry-level theology. This book will allow your students to acquire a surprisingly large amount of information in a short time. You may find it helpful to read the advice given to students (p. xxiv–xxv) to get an idea of how the book can be used. From your perspective as a teacher, however, the following points should be noted.

The contents of this book can be mastered without the need for any input on your part. Every explanation which this book offers has been classroom-tested on students in Australasia, Canada, Hong Kong, the United Kingdom, and the United States, and refined until students reported that they could understand the points being made without the need for further assistance. For example, we know that students as young as 16 years are using this work in the United Kingdom, and finding it intelligible and interesting. You should be able to invite students to read this book as essential background to your own teaching, thus enabling you to deal with more advanced and interesting themes in classroom time. The hard work has been done for you, to allow you to enjoy your own teaching.

The work is theologically neutral; it does not advocate any denominational agenda. It reports criticisms made of positions, but does not criticize positions. It does not tell its readers what to think, but tells them what has been thought. My primary goal in this book has been to introduce readers to the themes of Christian theology, and enable them to understand them. This means that I have included discussion of many theological positions that are not my own, and tried to present them as accurately and fairly as possible. Readers of this text who believe that any positions are misrepresented in any way are invited to write to the author or publisher, so that appropriate corrections can be made in future editions.

Because it aims to be fair and balanced, this textbook will allow you, as the teacher, to build your own distinct approach or understanding on the foundations which it lays. Thus the work will help your students *understand* Aquinas (or Barth or Augustine or Luther), but it will not ask them to *agree* with Aquinas (or Barth or Augustine or Luther). The book aims to put you, the teacher, in the position of interacting with the classic resources of the Christian tradition, on the basis of the assumption that your students, through reading this book, have a good basic understanding of the issues.

You may like to note that the first four chapters offer an overview of historical theology; the next four chapters an overview of aspects of philosophical theology and questions of theological method; and the remaining 10 chapters deal with the leading themes of systematic theology. The work aims to include a fair and representative selection of the contributions of Christian theologians over two thousand years.

You will notice that the work includes generous quotations from the original works of theologians. This is a deliberate matter of policy. It is important that your students get into the habit of reading theologians, rather than just reading what has been written about them. The work aims to encourage students to interact with original texts, and offers them help in doing so. If you find this practice valuable, you might like to think of using the companion volume to this work, *The Christian Theology Reader*, now in its third edition. This work offers its readers the opportunity to engage with more than 360 original sources – substantially more than any other such textbook – while providing far more help with this process of engagement than is normally found. Each reading in *The Christian Theology Reader* is provided with its own individual introduction, commentary, and study questions, and is fully sourced so that it can be followed through to its original context without difficulty.

If you are teaching a course on the basic themes of systematic theology it is strongly recommended that you ask students to read the first *eight* chapters before the course commences. This will give them the background knowledge that they will need to get the most from your teaching. You will find the questions at the end of each of those chapters helpful in judging whether the students have understood what they were asked to read – or, indeed, whether they read it at all!

Because this work is introductory, from time to time certain issues are introduced or explained more than once. This is a deliberate matter of policy, resting on the observation that some of its readers skip chapters in their haste to get to the bits that they think are really important – and in doing so, miss out on some relevant material. The book works at its best if the chapters are read in the order in which they are presented; however, it is sufficiently flexible to permit other approaches to using it.

Additional teaching aids for this volume will be provided through its dedicated website, maintained by the publishers, which includes full bibliographies for each chapter, to be updated annually, and links to theological resources on the Internet. This supersedes the older practice of providing printed reading lists, which date quickly, and are often not particularly comprehensive. In addition, this site is being developed to include lecture outlines, test questions and answers. Please visit this site to see if it offers anything that might be useful to you. You are welcome to suggest additional readings, links, or other resources that would make this website more useful.

The author and publishers are committed to ensuring that this work remains as helpful and thorough as possible, and welcome comments or suggestions for improvement. In particular, we welcome being told of any approaches to teaching any aspect of Christian theology that you have found helpful in the classroom.

Resources for Further Study:
Bibliographies and Websites

Previous editions of this work provided bibliographies and lists of theological websites for each chapter. While many readers welcomed this facility, others pointed out that it was not an effective use of space, and rapidly went out of date. A new strategy has therefore been adopted, in line with the rapidly changing shape of theological education. A dedicated website has been established for this work, which includes extensive and detailed bibliographies for every chapter, which will be updated at least once a year. This allows a much wider and regularly updated list of resources to be made available to students than would otherwise be possible. This dedicated web site is not password-protected, and can be used by anyone with access to the Internet.

You are recommended to bookmark this website, and use it in conjunction with your studies in theology. It also includes answers to the study questions provided in this volume. The website address is:

www.blackwellpublishing.com/mcgrath

Acknowledgments

The fourth edition of this work has built on extended classroom use of the first edition (1993), the second edition (1997), and the third edition (2001). These earlier versions were tested against student audiences in Australasia, Canada, Hong Kong, the United Kingdom, and the United States. The author and publisher are especially grateful to students and faculty of Drew University, McGill University, Oxford University, Princeton Theological Seminary, Regent College (Vancouver), Ridley College (Melbourne), Wheaton College (Illinois), and Wycliffe Hall (Oxford) for invaluable comments and suggestions. They also gladly acknowledge the helpful comments of those who have translated earlier editions into Chinese, Dutch, Finnish, German, Italian, Japanese, and Russian for important suggestions concerning the clarity and arrangement of the text.

The author and publisher also wish to thank the following for their invaluable guidance in revising the work for this new edition: Professor David Cherney (Azusa Pacific University); Dr Cheryl Clemons (Brescia University, Owensboro); Professor David Eaton (Bartlesville Wesleyan College); Dr James Francis (University of Sunderland); Dr Scott Hahn (University of Steubenville); Dr Tom Halstead (The Master's College, Santa Clarita); Dr Myron J. Houghton (Faith Baptist Theological Seminary); Professor Mark Johnson (Marquette University); Dr Neil N. Jones (Stillman College); Professor Kathryn A. Kleinhans (Wartburg College, Waverly, Iowa); Dr John C. Klaassen (Calvary Theological Seminary); Professor Glenn Kreider (Dallas Theological Seminary); Dr Phil Long (Grace Bible College); Dr Timothy Maschke (Concordia University, Wisconsin); Dr Clive Marsh (College of Ripon and York); Professor Gerald McCulloch (Loyola University, Chicago); Professor Paul K. Moser (Loyola University, Chicago); Dr Christopher Partridge (University College, Chester); Prof Dr Albert Raffelt (Freiburg im Breisgau); Dr Harvey Solganik (Missouri Baptist College); Dr Robert Song (Durham University); Dr Ian Tutton (University of Cardiff); Dr Robert Wall (Seattle Pacific University); Dr Edward Wierenga (University of Rochester); Professor George Wiley (Baker University); Dr Susan Wood (College of St Benedict and St John's University, Missouri).

The author and publisher are committed to keeping this work up to date. They welcome suggestions for improvements for the fifth edition, which is expected to appear around 2012.

Part I

Landmarks: Periods, Themes, and Personalities of Christian Theology

Introduction

Introduction

Anyone who thinks about the great questions of Christian theology soon discovers that many of them have already been addressed. It is virtually impossible to do theology as if it had never been done before. There is always an element of looking over one's shoulder to see how things were done in the past, and what answers were then given. Part of the notion of "tradition" is a willingness to take seriously the theological heritage of the past. Karl Barth expresses this idea in a pointed form, as he notes the continued importance of the great theological luminaries of the past in today's theological debates:

> With regard to theology, we cannot be in the church without taking responsibility as much for the theology of the past as for the theology of our own present day. Augustine, Thomas Aquinas, Luther, Schleiermacher and all the others are not dead but living. They still speak and demand a hearing as living voices, as surely as we know that they and we belong together in the church.

It is therefore of importance that the reader becomes familiar with the main voices and conversations of the Christian past, which are both interesting in themselves, as well as providing vital reference points for the debates of our own time.

The first part of this work aims to provide an overview of the development of Christian theology. Its four chapters identify the key periods, themes, and personalities which have shaped that process of evolution. Particular attention will be paid to developments since the Renaissance, in that these have had the greatest impact upon modern western theology. Nevertheless, an appreciation of at least some aspects of the development of theology during the patristic and medieval periods is essential background material to the informed study of modern theology. The present work thus aims to survey some of the most important developments associated with these eras, including the following:

- the geographical location of centers of Christian thought;
- the theological issues under debate;
- the schools of thought associated with theological issues;
- the leading theologians of the periods, and their particular concerns.

The following formative periods are considered in this brief survey of the development of Christian theology:

3

- the patristic period, c.100–c.700 (chapter 1);
- the Middle Ages and Renaissance, c.700–c.1500 (chapter 2);
- the Reformation and post-Reformation periods, c.1500–c.1750 (chapter 3);
- the modern period, c.1750 to the present day (chapter 4).

It will be clear that it is difficult to draw firm dividing lines between many of these periods; for example, the relationships between the Middle Ages, the Renaissance, and the Reformation are controversial, with some scholars seeing the latter two as the continuation of the first, and others seeing them as distinct movements in their own right. The reader should appreciate that all divisions of history are prone to a degree of arbitrariness.

1

The Patristic Period, c.100–c.700

Christianity had its origins in Palestine – more specifically, the region of Judea, especially the city of Jerusalem. Christianity regarded itself as a continuation and development of Judaism, and initially flourished in regions with which Judaism was traditionally associated, supremely Palestine. However, it rapidly spread to neighboring regions, partially through the efforts of early Christian evangelists such as Paul of Tarsus.

The Early Centers of Theological Activity

By the end of the first century, Christianity appears to have be come established throughout the eastern Mediterranean world, and even to have gained a significant presence in the city of Rome, the capital of the Roman Empire. As the church at Rome became increasingly powerful, tensions began to develop between the Christian leadership at Rome and at Constantinople, foreshadowing the later schism between the western and eastern churches, centered on these respective seats of power.

In the course of this expansion, a number of regions emerged as significant centers of theological debate. Three may be singled out as

having especial importance, the first two of which were Greek-speaking, and the third Latin-speaking.

1 The city of Alexandria, in modern-day Egypt, which emerged as a center of Christian theological education. A distinctive style of theology came to be associated with this city, reflecting its long-standing association with the Platonic tradition. The student will find reference to "Alexandrian" approaches in areas such as Christology and biblical interpretation (see pp. 130, 286–7), reflecting both the importance and the distinctiveness of the style of Christianity associated with the area.

2 The city of Antioch and the surrounding region of Cappadocia, in modern-day Turkey. A strong Christian presence came to be established in this northern region of the eastern Mediterranean at an early stage. Some of Paul's missionary journeys took him into this region, and Antioch features significantly at several points in the history of the very early church, as recorded in the Acts of the Apostles. Antioch itself soon became a leading center of Christian thought. Like Alexandria, it became associated with particular approaches to Christology and biblical

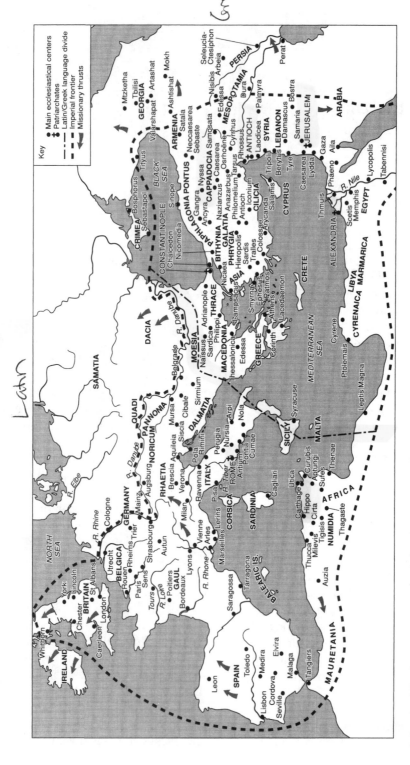

Map 1 The Roman Empire and the church in the fourth century.

interpretation. The term "Antiochene" is often used to designate this distinct theological style (see pp. 130, 287–9). The "Cappadocian fathers" were also an important theological presence in this region in the fourth century, notable especially for their contribution to the doctrine of the Trinity.

3 Western north Africa, especially the area of modern-day Algeria. In the late classical period this was the site of Carthage, a major Mediterranean city and at one time a political rival to Rome for dominance in the region. During the period when Christianity expanded in this region, it was a Roman colony. Major writers of the region include Tertullian, Cyprian of Carthage, and Augustine of Hippo.

This is not to say that other cities in the Mediterranean were not significant centers of Christian life and thought. Rome, Constantinople, Milan, and Jerusalem were also centers of Christian theological reflection, even if none was destined to achieve quite the significance of their rivals.

An Overview of the Patristic Period

The patristic period is one of the most exciting and creative periods in the history of Christian thought. This feature alone is enough to ensure that it will continue to be the subject of study for many years to come. The period is also of importance for theological reasons. Every mainstream Christian body – including the Anglican, Eastern Orthodox, Lutheran, Reformed, and Roman Catholic churches – regards the patristic period as a definitive landmark in the development of Christian doctrine. Each of these churches regards itself as continuing, extending, and,

where necessary, criticizing the views of the early church writers. For example, the leading seventeenth-century Anglican writer Lancelot Andrewes (1555–1626) declared that orthodox Christianity was based upon two testaments, three creeds, four gospels, and the first five centuries of Christian history.

A clarification of terms

The term "patristic" comes from the Latin word *patēr*, "father," and designates both the period of the church fathers, and the distinctive ideas which came to develop within this period. The term is noninclusive; no generally acceptable inclusive term has yet to emerge in the literature. The following related terms are frequently encountered, and should be noted.

- *The patristic period*: This is a vaguely defined entity, which is often taken to be the period from the closing of the New Testament writings (c.100) to the definitive Council of Chalcedon (451).
- *Patristics*: This term is usually understood to mean the branch of theological study which deals with the study of "the fathers" (*patres*).
- *Patrology*: This term once literally meant "the study of the fathers," in much the same way as "theology" meant "the study of God" (*theos*). In recent years, however, the word has shifted its meaning. It now refers to a manual of patristic literature, such as that of the noted German scholar Johannes Quasten, which allows its readers easy access to the leading ideas of patristic writers, and some of the problems of interpretation associated with them.

The theological agenda of the period

The period was of major importance in clarifying a number of issues. A primary task was sorting out the relationship between

Christianity and Judaism. The letters of Paul in the New Testament bear witness to the importance of this issue in the first century of Christian history, as a series of doctrinal and practical issues came under consideration. Should Gentile (that is, non-Jewish) Christians be obliged to be circumcised? And how was the Old Testament to be correctly interpreted?

However, other issues soon came to the fore. One which was of especial importance in the second century is that of *apologetics* – the reasoned defense and justification of the Christian faith against its critics. During the first period of Christian history, the church was often persecuted by the state. Its agenda was that of survival; there was limited room for theological disputes when the very existence of the Christian church could not be taken for granted. This observation helps us to understand why apologetics came to be of such importance to the early church, through writers such as Justin Martyr (c.100–c.165), concerned to explain and defend the beliefs and practices of Christianity to a hostile pagan public. Although this early period produced some outstanding theologians – such as Irenaeus of Lyons (c.130–c.200) in the west, and Origen (c.185–c.254) in the east – theological debate could only begin in earnest once the church had ceased to be persecuted.

These conditions became possible during the fourth century, with the conversion of Constantine, who went on to become the Roman emperor. During his period as emperor (306–37), Constantine succeeded in reconciling church and empire, with the result that the church no longer existed under a siege mentality. In 321 he decreed that Sundays should become public holidays. As a result of Constantine's influence on the empire, constructive theological debate became a public affair. Apart from a brief period of uncertainty during the reign of Julian the Apostate (361–3), the church could now count upon the support of

the state. Theology thus emerged from the hidden world of secret church meetings, to become a matter of public interest and concern throughout the Roman Empire. Increasingly, doctrinal debates became a matter of both political and theological importance. Constantine wished to have a united church throughout his empire, and was thus concerned that doctrinal differences should be debated and settled as a matter of priority.

As a result, the later patristic period (from about 310 to 451) may be regarded as a high-water mark in the history of Christian theology. Theologians now enjoyed the freedom to work without the threat of persecution, and were able to address a series of issues of major importance to the consolidation of the emerging theological consensus within the churches. Establishing that consensus involved extensive debate and a painful learning process, in which the church discovered that it had to come to terms with disagreements and continuing tensions. Nonetheless, a significant degree of consensus, eventually to be enshrined in the ecumenical creeds, can be discerned as evolving within this formative period.

The patristic period is obviously of considerable importance to Christian theology. It is, however, found to be very difficult by many modern students of theology. Four main reasons can be given for this experience.

1   Some of the debates of the period seem hopelessly irrelevant to the modern world. Although they were viewed as intensely important at the time, it is often very difficult for the modern reader to empathize with the issues and to understand why they attracted such attention. It is interesting to contrast the patristic period in this respect with the Reformation era, during which many issues were addressed which are of continuing concern for the modern

8

church; many teachers of theology find that their students are able to relate to the concerns of this later period much more easily.

2 Many of the patristic debates hinge upon philosophical issues, and only make sense if the reader has some familiarity with the philosophical debates of the period. Whereas at least some students of Christian theology have some familiarity with the ideas found in Plato's dialogues, these ideas were subject to considerable development and criticism in the Mediterranean world during the patristic period. Middle Platonism and neo-Platonism differ significantly from one another, and from Plato's original ideas. The strangeness of many of the philosophical ideas of the period acts as another barrier to the study of it, making it difficult for students beginning in theology to fully appreciate what is going on in some of the patristic debates.

3 The patristic period is characterized by a considerable degree of doctrinal diversity. It was an age of flux, during which landmarks and standards – including documents such as the Nicene creed and dogmas such as the two natures of Christ – emerged gradually. Students familiar with the relative stability of other periods in Christian doctrine (such as the Reformation, in which the person of Christ was not a major issue) often find this feature of the patristic period disconcerting.

4 The period saw a major division arise, for both political and linguistic reasons, between the eastern Greek-speaking and the western Latin-speaking church. Many scholars discern a marked difference in theological temperament between theologians of the east and west: the former are often philosophically inclined and given to theological speculation, whereas the latter are often hostile to the intrusion of philoso-phy into theology, and regard theology as the exploration of the doctrines set out in Scripture.

Key Theologians

During the course of this work, reference will be made to a significant number of theologians from the patristic period. The following writers, however, are of especial importance, and deserve to be singled out for special mention.

Justin Martyr (c.100–c.165)

Justin is perhaps the greatest of the Apologists – the Christian writers of the second century who were concerned to defend Christianity in the face of intense criticism from pagan sources. In his "First Apology" Justin argued that traces of Christian truth were to be found in the great pagan writers. His doctrine of the *logos spermatikos* ("seed-bearing word") allowed him to affirm that God had prepared the way for his final revelation in Christ through hints of its truth in classical philosophy. Justin provides us with an important early example of a theologian who attempts to relate the gospel to the outlook of Greek philosophy, a trend especially associated with the eastern church.

Irenaeus of Lyons (c.130–c.200)

Irenaeus is believed to have been born in Smyrna (in modern-day Turkey), although he subsequently settled in Rome. He became Bishop of Lyons around 178, a position which he held until his death two decades later. Irenaeus is noted especially for his vigorous defense of Christian orthodoxy in the face of a challenge from Gnosticism (see pp. 13–14). His most significant work, "Against Heresies" (*adversus haereses*), represents a major defense of the Christian understanding of salvation, and especially of the role of tradition in remaining faithful to the apostolic witness in the face of non-Christian interpretations.

Origen (c.185–c.254)

One of the most significant defenders of Christianity in the third century, Origen provided an important foundation for the development of eastern Christian thought. His major contributions to the development of Christian theology can be seen in two general areas. In the field of biblical interpretation, Origen developed the notion of allegorical interpretation, arguing that the surface meaning of Scripture was to be distinguished from its deeper spiritual meaning. In the field of Christology, Origen established a tradition of distinguishing between the full divinity of the Father, and a lesser divinity of the Son. Some scholars see Arianism as a natural consequence of this approach. Origen also adopted with some enthusiasm the idea of *apocatastasis*, according to which every creature – including both humanity and Satan – will be saved.

Tertullian (c.160–c. 225)

Tertullian was originally a pagan from the north African city of Carthage, who converted to Christianity in his thirties. He is often regarded as the father of Latin theology on account of the major impact which he had upon the western church. He defended the unity of the Old and New Testaments against Marcion, who had argued that they related to different gods. In doing so, he laid the foundations for a doctrine of the Trinity. Tertullian was strongly opposed to making Christian theology or apologetics dependent upon extra-scriptural sources. He is among the most forceful early exponents of the principle of the sufficiency of Scripture, denouncing those who appeal to secular philosophies (such as those of the Athenian Academy) for a true knowledge of God.

Cyprian of Carthage (died 258)

Little is known of Cyprian's early life. He was born, probably around the year 200, to pagan Roman parents in North Africa. He went on become a prominent lawyer and rhetorician of considerable skill. He converted to Christianity around 246, and was elected bishop of the major north African city of Carthage in 248. He was martyred in that city during the Decian persecution of 258. His major essay *On the Unity of The Catholic Church* stresses the importance of visible, concrete unity among Christians, and the role of the bishops in guaranteeing that unity. It is widely regarded as a landmark in the development of Christian understandings of the nature of the church.

Athanasius (c.296–c.373)

Athanasius's significance relates primarily to Christological issues, which became of major importance during the fourth century. Possibly while still in his twenties, Athanasius wrote the treatise *De incarnatione Verbi* ("On the incarnation of the Word"), a powerful defense of the idea that God assumed human nature in the person of Jesus Christ. This issue proved to be of central importance in the Arian controversy (see pp. 16–17), to which Athanasius made a major contribution. Athanasius pointed out that if, as Arius argued, Christ was not fully God, a series of devastating implications followed. First, it was impossible for God to redeem humanity, as no creature could redeem another creature. And second, it followed that the Christian church was guilty of idolatry, as Christians regularly worshiped and prayed to Christ. As "idolatry" can be defined as "worship of a human construction or creation," it followed that this worship was idolatrous. Such arguments eventually carried the day, and led to the rejection of Arianism.

The Cappadocian fathers

This term is widely used in theological literature to refer to three major theologians (two brothers, and a close friend) of the Greek-speaking church, based in the region of Cappadocia, now in modern-day Turkey. The three "Cappadocian fathers" are:

1 Basil the Great (c.330–79), bishop of Caesarea, and the older brother of Gregory of Nyssa;
2 Gregory of Nyssa (c.330–c.395), bishop of Nyssa;
3 Gregory of Nazianzus (329–89), bishop of Sasima and later of Constantinople.

Each of these writers is of considerable important in their own right. However, they collectively made an immense contribution to the development of the doctrine of the Trinity during the fourth century. By emphasizing the idea of "substance" (*hypostasis*), they were able to formulate a stable and relatively coherent concept of the Godhead, consisting of one substance and three persons.

Augustine of Hippo (354–430)

In turning to deal with Aurelius Augustinus, usually known as "Augustine of Hippo" – or just plain "Augustine" – we encounter what is probably the greatest and most influential mind of the Christian church throughout its long history. Attracted to the Christian faith by the preaching of Bishop Ambrose of Milan, Augustine underwent a dramatic conversion experience. Having reached the age of 32 without satisfying his burning wish to know the truth, Augustine was agonizing over the great questions of human nature and destiny in a garden in Milan. He thought he heard a child singing *Tolle, lege* ("take up and read") nearby.

Feeling that this was divine guidance, he reached out for the document nearest to hand – Paul's letter to the Romans, as it happened – and read the fateful words "clothe yourselves with the Lord Jesus Christ" (Romans 13: 14).

Possibly suffering from some form of asthma, Augustine left Italy to return to north Africa, and was made Bishop of Hippo (in modern Algeria) in 395. The remaining 35 years of his life witnessed numerous controversies of major importance to the future of the Christian church in the west, and Augustine's contribution to the resolution of each of these was decisive. His careful exposition of the New Testament, particularly the letters of Paul, gained him a reputation which continues today, as the "second founder of the Christian faith" (Jerome). During the theological renaissance of the early middle ages, Augustine's substantial body of writings would form the basis of a major program of renewal and development, consolidating his influence over the western church.

A major part of Augustine's contribution lies in the development of theology as an academic discipline. The early church cannot really be said to have developed any "systematic theology." Its primary concern was to defend Christianity against its critics (as in the apologetic works of Justin Martyr), and to clarify central aspects of its thinking against heresy (as in the anti-Gnostic writings of Irenaeus). Nevertheless, major doctrinal development took place during the first four centuries, especially in relation to the doctrine of the person of Christ and the doctrine of the Trinity.

Augustine's contribution was to achieve a synthesis of Christian thought, supremely in his major treatise *De civitate Dei*, "On the City of God." Like Charles Dickens's famous novel, Augustine's "City of God" is a tale of two cities – the city of the world, and the city of God (see p. 468). However, in addition, Augustine may also be argued to have made key contributions to three major areas of Christian theology: the doctrine of the church and sacraments, arising from the Donatist controversy (see pp. 394–6); the doctrine of grace, arising from the Pelagian controversy (see pp. 362–7); and the doctrine of the Trinity (see pp. 258–60). Interestingly, Augustine never really explored the area of Christology (that is, the doctrine of the person of Christ), which would unquestionably have benefited from his considerable wisdom and acumen.

Key Theological Debates and Developments

As we have already noted, the patristic period was of immense importance in shaping the contours of Christian theology. The following areas of theology were explored with particular vigor during the patristic period.

The extent of the New Testament canon

From its outset, Christian theology recognized itself to be grounded in Scripture. There was, however, some uncertainty as to what the term "Scripture" actually designated. The patristic period witnessed a process of decision making, in which limits were laid down to the New Testament – a process usually known as "the fixing of the canon." The word "canon" needs explanation. It derives from the Greek word *kanon* meaning "a rule" or "a fixed reference point." The "canon of Scripture" refers to a limited and defined group of writings, which are accepted as authoritative within the Christian church. The term "canonical" is used to refer to scriptural writings accepted to be within the canon. Thus the Gospel of Luke is referred to as "canonical," whereas the Gospel of Thomas is "extracanonical" (that is, lying outside the canon of Scripture).

For the writers of the New Testament, the term "Scripture" meant primarily a *writing of the Old Testament*. However, within a short period, early Christian writers (such as Justin Martyr) were referring to the "New Testament" (to be contrasted with the "Old Testament"), and insisting that both were to be treated with equal authority. By the time of Irenaeus, it was generally accepted that there were four gospels; by the late second century, there was a consensus that the gospels, Acts, and letters had the status of inspired Scripture. Thus Clement of Alexandria recognized four gospels, the Acts of the Apostles, 14 letters of Paul (the letter to the Hebrews being regarded as Pauline), and Revelation. Tertullian declared that alongside the "law and the prophets" were the "evangelical and apostolic writings" (*evangelicae et apostolicae litterae*), which were both to be regarded as authoritative within the church. Gradually, agreement was reached over the list of books which were recognized as inspired Scripture, and the order in which they were to be arranged. In 367, Athanasius circulated his 39th Festal Letter, which identifies the 27 books of the New Testament, as we now know it, as being canonical.

Debate centered especially on a number of books. The western church had hesitations about including Hebrews, in that it was not specifically attributed to an apostle; the eastern church had reservations about Revelation. Four of the smaller books (2 Peter, 2 and 3 John, and Jude) were often omitted from early lists of New Testament writings. Some writings, now outside the canon, were regarded with favor in parts of the church, although they ultimately failed to gain universal acceptance as canonical. Examples of this include the first letter of Clement (an early bishop of Rome, who wrote around 96) and the *Didache*, a short early Christian manual on morals and church practices, probably dating from the first quarter of the second century.

The arrangement of the material was also subject to considerable variation. Agreement was reached at an early stage that the gospels should have the place of honor within the canon, followed by the Acts of the Apostles. The eastern church tended to place the seven "catholic letters" (that is, James, 1 and 2 Peter, 1, 2, and 3 John, and Jude) before the 14 Pauline letters (Hebrews being accepted as Pauline), whereas the western church placed Paul's letters immediately after Acts, and followed them with the catholic letters. Revelation ended the canon in both east and west, although its status was subject to debate for some time within the eastern church.

What criteria were used in drawing up the canon? The basic principle appears to have been that of the *recognition* rather than the *imposition* of authority. In other words, the works in question were recognized as already possessing authority, rather than having an arbitrary authority imposed upon them. For Irenaeus, the church does not *create* the canon; it *acknowledges*, *conserves*, and *receives* canonical Scripture on the basis of the authority which is already inherent to it. Some early Christians appear to have regarded apostolic authorship as of decisive importance; others were prepared to accept books which did not appear to have apostolic credentials. However, although the precise details of how the selection was made remain unclear, it is certain that the canon was closed within the western church by the beginning of the fifth century.

The issue of the canon would not be raised again until the time of the Reformation.

The role of tradition: the Gnostic controversies

The early church was confronted with a major challenge from a movement known as Gnosticism. This diverse and complex movement, not dissimilar to the modern New Age phenomenon, achieved considerable influence in the late Roman Empire. The basic ideas of Gnosticism do not concern us at this point; what is of relevance here is that Gnosticism appeared very similar to Christianity at many points. For this reason, it was viewed as a major challenge by many early Christian writers, especially Irenaeus. Furthermore, Gnostic writers had a tendency to interpret New Testament passages in a manner which dismayed Christian leaders, and prompted questions about the correct manner of interpretation of Scripture.

In such a context, an appeal to tradition became of major importance. The word "tradition" literally means "that which has been handed down or over," although it can also refer to "the act of handing down or over." Irenaeus insisted that the "rule of faith" (*regula fidei*) was faithfully preserved by the apostolic church, and that it had found its expression in the canonical books of Scripture. The church had faithfully proclaimed the same gospel from the time of the apostles until the present day. The Gnostics had no such claim to continuity with the early church. They had merely invented new ideas, and were improperly suggesting that these were "Christian."

Irenaeus thus emphasized the continuity of the teaching and preaching office of the church and its officials (especially its bishops). Tradition came to mean "a traditional interpretation of Scripture" or "a traditional presentation of the Christian faith," which is reflected in the creeds of the church and its public doctrinal pronouncements. This fixing of the creeds as a public expression of the teaching of the church is of major importance, as will become clear in the following section.

Tertullian adopted a related approach. Scripture, he argued, is capable of being understood clearly, provided that it is read as a whole. However, he conceded that controversy over the interpretation of certain passages was inevitable. Heretics, he observed gloomily, can make Scripture say more or less anything that they like. For this reason, the tradition of the church was of considerable importance, as it indicated the manner in which Scripture had been received and interpreted within the church. The right interpretation of Scripture was thus to be found where true Christian faith and discipline had been maintained. A similar view was taken by Athanasius, who argued that Arius's Christological mistakes would never have arisen if he had remained faithful to the church's interpretation of Scripture.

Tradition was thus seen as a legacy from the apostles, by which the church was guided and directed toward a correct interpretation of Scripture. It was not seen as a "secret source of revelation" in addition to Scripture, an idea which Irenaeus dismissed as "Gnostic." Rather, it was seen as a means of ensuring that the church remained faithful to the teaching of the apostles, instead of adopting idiosyncratic interpretations of Scripture.

The fixing of the ecumenical creeds

The English word "creed" derives from the Latin word *credo*, "I believe," with which the Apostles' creed – probably the most familiar of all the creeds – begins: "I believe in God ... ." It has come to refer to a statement of faith, summarizing the main points of Christian belief, which is common to all Christians. For this reason, the term "creed" is never applied to statements of faith associated with specific denominations.

These latter are often referred to as "confessions" (such as the Lutheran *Augsburg Confession* or the Reformed *Westminster Confession of Faith*). A "confession" pertains to a denomination, and includes specific beliefs and emphases relating to that denomination; a "creed" pertains to the entire Christian church, and includes nothing more and nothing less than a statement of beliefs which every Christian ought to be able to accept and be bound by. A "creed" has come to be recognized as a concise, formal, and universally accepted and authorized statement of the main points of Christian faith.

The patristic period saw two creeds achieving increasing authority and respect throughout the church. The stimulus to their development appears to have been the felt need to provide a convenient summary of Christian faith suitable for public occasions, of which perhaps the most important was baptism. The early church tended to baptize its converts on Easter Day, using the period of Lent as a time of preparation and instruction for this moment of public declaration of faith and commitment. An essential requirement was that each convert who wished to be baptized should declare his or her faith in public. It seems that creeds began to emerge as a uniform declaration of faith which converts could use on such occasions.

The *Apostles' creed* is probably the most familiar form of the creed known to western Christians. It falls into three main sections, dealing with God, Jesus Christ, and the Holy Spirit. There is also material relating to the church, judgment, and resurrection. The historical evolution of this creed is complex, with its origins lying in declarations of faith which were required of those who wanted to be baptized. The 12 individual statements of this creed, which seems to have assumed its final form in the eighth century, are traditionally ascribed to individual apostles, although there is no historical justification for this belief.

There are slight differences between the eastern and western versions of this creed; the statements concerning the "descent into hell" and the "communion of saints" (printed below within square brackets) are not found in eastern versions of the work.

The Apostles' creed

1 I believe in God, the Father almighty, creator of the heavens and earth;
2 and in Jesus Christ, his only (*unicus*) Son, our Lord;
3 who was conceived by the Holy Spirit and born of the Virgin Mary;
4 he suffered under Pontius Pilate, was crucified, dead and buried; [he descended to hell;]
5 on the third day he was raised from the dead;
6 he ascended into the heavens, and sits at the right hand of God the Father almighty;
7 from where he will come to judge the living and the dead.
8 I believe in the Holy Spirit;
9 in the holy catholic church; [the communion of saints;]
10 the forgiveness of sins;
11 the resurrection of the flesh (*resurrectio carnis*);
12 and eternal life.

The *Nicene creed* is the longer version of the creed (more strictly known as the "Niceno-Constantinopolitan creed"), which includes additional material relating to the person of Christ and the work of the Holy Spirit. In response to the controversies concerning the divinity of Christ, this creed includes strong affirmations of his unity with God, including the expressions "God from God" and "being of one substance with the Father." As part of its polemic against the Arians, the Council of Nicea (June 325) formulated a short statement of faith, based on a baptismal creed used at Jerusalem.

This creed was intended to affirm the full divinity of Christ against the Arian understanding of his creaturely status, and includes four explicit condemnations of Arian views, as well as its three articles of faith. As the full details of the proceedings of Nicea are now lost, we are obliged to rely on secondary sources (such as ecclesiastical historians, and writers such as Athanasius and Basil of Caesarea) for the text of this creed.

The Nicene creed

We believe in one God, the Father, the almighty (*pantocrator*), the maker of all things seen and unseen. And in one Lord Jesus Christ, the Son of God; begotten from the Father; only-begotten – that is, from the substance of the Father; God from God; light from light; true God from true God; begotten not made; of one substance with the Father (*homoousion tō patri*); through whom all things in heaven and on earth came into being; who on account of us human beings and our salvation came down and took flesh, becoming a human being; he suffered and rose again on the third day, ascended into the heavens; and will come again to judge the living and the dead. And in the Holy Spirit.

As for those who say that "there was when he was not," and "before being born he was not," and "he came into existence out of nothing," or who declare that the Son of God is of a different substance or nature, or is subject to alteration or change – the catholic and apostolic church condemns these.

The development of the creeds was an important element in the move toward achieving a doctrinal consensus within the early church. One area of doctrine which witnessed considerable development and controversy related to the person of Christ, to which we may now turn.

The two natures of Jesus Christ: the Arian controversy

The two doctrines to which the patristic period may be argued to have made a decisive contribution relate to the person of Christ (an area of theology which, as we noted, is generally designated "Christology") and the nature of the Godhead. These two developments are organically related to one another. By 325, the early church had come to the conclusion that Jesus was "of one substance" (*homoousios*) with God. (The term *homoousios* can also be translated as "one in being" or "consubstantial.")

The implications of this Christological statement were two fold: in the first place, it consolidated at the intellectual level the spiritual importance of Jesus Christ to Christians; in the second, however, it posed a powerful challenge to simplistic conceptions of God. For if Jesus *is* recognized as "being of the same substance" as God, then the entire doctrine of God has to be reconsidered in the light of this belief. For this reason, the historical development of the doctrine of the Trinity dates from after the emergence of a Christological consensus within the church. Only when the divinity of Christ could be treated as an agreed and assured starting point could theological speculation on the nature of God begin.

It may be noted that the Christological debates of the early church took place largely in the eastern Mediterranean world, and were conducted in the Greek language, and often in the light of the presuppositions of major Greek schools of philosophy. In practical terms, this means that many of the central terms of the Christological debates of the early church are Greek, often with a history of use within the Greek philosophical tradition.

The main features of patristic Christology will be considered in some detail on pp. 281–91, to which the reader is referred. At this early stage, however, we may summarize the main landmarks of the patristic Christological debate in terms of two schools, two debates, and two councils, as follows.

Schools

The *Alexandrian school* tended to place emphasis upon the divinity of Christ, and interpret that divinity in terms of "the word becoming incarnate." A scriptural text which was of central importance to this school is John 1: 14, "the word became flesh, and dwelt among us." This emphasis upon the idea of incarnation led to the festival of Christmas being seen as especially important. The *Antiochene school*, however, placed a corresponding emphasis upon the humanity of Christ, and attached especial importance to his moral example (see pp. 287–9).

Debates

The *Arian* controversy of the fourth century is widely regarded as one of the most significant in the history of the Christian church. Arius (c.250–c.336) argued that the scriptural titles for Christ, which appeared to point to his being of equal status with God, were merely courtesy titles. Christ was to be regarded as a creature, although nevertheless as pre-eminent among other creatures. This provoked a hostile response from Athanasius, who argued that the divinity of Christ was of central importance to the Christian understanding of salvation (an area of theology known as "soteriology"). Arius's Christology was, he declared, inadequate soteriologically. Arius's Christ could not redeem fallen humanity. In the end, Arianism (the movement associated with Arius) was declared to be heretical. This was followed by the *Apollinarian* debate, which centered on Apollinarius of Laodicea (c.310–c.390). A vigorous opponent of Arius, Apollinarius argued that Christ could not be regarded as being totally human. In Christ's case, the human spirit was replaced by the divine *logos*. As a result, Christ did not possess full humanity. This position was regarded as severely deficient by writers such as Gregory of Nazianzus, in that it implied that Christ could not fully redeem human nature (see pp. 286–7).

Councils

The *Council of Nicea* (325) was convened by Constantine, the first Christian emperor, with a view to sorting out the destabilizing Christological disagreements within his empire. This was the first "ecumenical council" (that is, an assembly of bishops drawn from the entire Christian world, whose decisions are regarded as normative for the churches). Nicea (now the city of Iznik in modern-day Turkey) settled the Arian controversy by affirming that Jesus was *homoousios* ("one in being" or "of one substance") with the Father, thus rejecting the Arian position in favor of a vigorous assertion of the divinity of Christ. The *Council of Chalcedon* (451), the fourth ecumenical council, confirmed the decisions of Nicea, and responded to new debates which had subsequently erupted over the humanity of Christ.

The doctrine of the Trinity

Once the Christological debates of the early church had been settled, the consequences of those decisions were explored. In this intensely creative and interesting period of Christian theology, the doctrine of the Trinity began to emerge in a recognizable form. The basic feature of this doctrine is that there are three persons within the Godhead – Father, Son, and Holy Spirit – and that these are to be regarded as equally divine and of equal status. The coequality of Father and Son was established through the Christological debates lead-

ing up to the Council of Nicea; the divinity of the Spirit was established in the aftermath of this, especially through the writings of Athanasius and Basil of Caesarea.

The main thrust of the trinitarian debates increasingly came to concern the manner in which the Trinity was to be understood, rather than its fundamental validity. Two quite distinct approaches gradually emerged, one associated with the eastern, and the other with the western, churches.

The *eastern* position, which continues to be of major importance within the Greek and Russian Orthodox Churches of today, was developed especially by a group of three writers, based in modern-day Turkey. Basil of Caesarea (c.330–79), Gregory of Nazianzus (329–89), and Gregory of Nyssa (c.330–c.395), known as the *Cappadocian fathers*, began their reflections on the Trinity by considering the different ways in which the Father, Son, and Spirit are experienced. The *western* position, especially associated with Augustine of Hippo, began from the unity of God, and proceeded to explore the implications of the love of God for our understanding of the nature of the Godhead. These positions will be explored in greater detail at the appropriate point in this work (see pp. 257–60).

The doctrine of the Trinity represents a rare instance of a theological issue of concern to both the eastern and western churches. Our attention now shifts to two theological debates which were specifically linked with the western church, and have both come to be particularly associated with Augustine of Hippo.

The doctrine of the church: the Donatist controversy

A major controversy within the western church centered on the question of the holiness of the church. The Donatists were a group of native African Christians, based in modern-day Algeria, who resented the growing influence of the Roman church in northern Africa. The Donatists argued that the church was a body of saints, within which sinners had no place. The issue became of especial importance on account of the persecution undertaken by the emperor Diocletian in 303, which persisted until the conversion of Constantine in 313. During this persecution, in which the possession of Scripture was illegal, a number of Christians handed their copies of Scripture in to the authorities. They were immediately condemned by others who had refused to cave in under such pressure. After the persecution died down, many of these *traditores* – a Latin word which literally means "those who handed over [their Scriptures]" – rejoined the church. The Donatists demanded their exclusion; they had compromised themselves. Augustine argued otherwise, declaring that the church must expect to remain a "mixed body" of saints and sinners, refusing to weed out those who had lapsed under persecution or for other reasons. The validity of the church's ministry and preaching did not depend upon the holiness of its ministers, but upon the person of Jesus Christ. The personal unworthiness of a minister did not compromise the validity of the sacraments. This view, which rapidly became normative within the church, has had a deep impact upon Christian thinking about the nature of the church and its ministers.

The Donatist debate, which will be explored in greater detail elsewhere (see pp. 394–6), was the first to center on the question of the doctrine of the church (known as "ecclesiology"), and related questions, such as the way in which sacraments function. Many of the issues raised by the controversy would surface again at the time of the Reformation, when ecclesiological issues would once more come to the fore (see pp. 59–60). The same may be said of the doctrine of grace, to which we now turn.

The doctrine of grace: the Pelagian controversy

The doctrine of grace had not been an issue of significance in the development of theology in the Greek-speaking eastern church. However, an intense controversy broke out over this question in the second decade of the fifth century. Pelagius, a British ascetic monk based at Rome, argued forcefully for the need for human moral responsibility. Alarmed at the moral laxity of the Roman church, he insisted upon the need for constant self-improvement, in the light of the Old Testament law and the example of Christ. In doing so, he seemed to his opponents – chief among whom was Augustine – to deny any real place to divine grace in the beginning or continuation of the Christian life. Pelagianism came to be seen as a religion of human autonomy, which held that human beings are able to take the initiative in their own salvation.

Augustine reacted forcefully against Pelagianism, insisting upon the priority of the grace of God at every stage in the Christian life, from its beginning to its end. Human beings did not, according to Augustine, possess the necessary freedom to take the initial steps toward salvation. Far from possessing "freedom of the will," humans were in possession of a will that was corrupted and tainted by sin, and which biased them toward evil and away from God. Only the grace of God could counteract this bias toward sin. So forceful was Augustine's defense of grace that he later became known as "the doctor of grace" (*doctor gratiae*).

A central theme of Augustine's thought is the *fallenness* of human nature. The imagery of "the Fall" derives from Genesis 3, and expresses the idea that human nature has "fallen" from its original pristine state. The present state of human nature is thus not what it is intended to be by God. The created order no longer directly corresponds to the "goodness" of its original integrity. It has lapsed. It has been spoiled or ruined – but not irredeemably, as the doctrines of salvation and justification affirm. The image of a "Fall" conveys the idea that creation now exists at a lower level than that intended for it by God.

According to Augustine, it follows that all human beings are now contaminated by sin from the moment of their birth. In contrast to those twentieth-century existentialist philosophies which affirm that "fallenness" is an option which we choose (rather than something which is chosen for us), Augustine portrays sin as inherent to human nature. It is an integral, not an optional, aspect of our being. This insight, which is given more rigorous expression in Augustine's doctrine of original sin, is of central importance to his doctrines of sin and salvation. In that all are sinners, all require redemption. In that all have fallen short of the glory of God, all require to be redeemed.

For Augustine, humanity, left to its own devices and resources, could never enter into a relationship with God. Nothing that a man or woman could do was sufficient to break the stranglehold of sin. To use an image which Augustine was fortunate enough never to have encountered, it is like a narcotic addict trying to break free from the grip of heroin or cocaine. The situation cannot be transformed from within – and so, if transformation is to take place, it must come from outside the human situation. According to Augustine, God intervenes in the human dilemma. God need not have done so, but out of love for fallen humanity God entered into the human situation in the person of Jesus Christ in order to redeem it.

Augustine held "grace" to be the unmerited or undeserved gift of God by which God voluntarily breaks the hold of sin upon humanity. Redemption is possible only as a divine gift. It is not something which we can achieve our-selves, but is some thing which has to be done for us. Augustine thus emphasizes that the resources of salvation are located in God, outside of humanity. It is God who initiates the process of salvation, not men or women.

For Pelagius, however, the situation was very different. Pelagius taught that the resources of salvation are located within humanity. Individual human beings have the capacity to save themselves. They are not trapped by sin, but have the ability to do all that is necessary to be saved. Salvation is something which is earned through good works, which place God under an obligation to reward humanity for its moral achievements. Pelagius marginalizes the idea of grace, understanding it in terms of demands made of humanity by God in order that salvation may be achieved – such as the Ten Commandments, or the moral example of Christ. The ethos of Pelagianism could be summed up as "salvation by merit," whereas Augustine taught "salvation by grace."

It will be obvious that these two different theologies involve very different understandings of human nature. For Augustine, human nature is weak, fallen, and powerless; for Pelagius, it is autonomous and self-sufficient. For Augustine, humanity must depend upon God for salvation; for Pelagius, God merely indicates what has to be done if salvation is to be attained, and then leaves men and women to meet those conditions unaided. For Augustine, salvation is an unmerited gift; for Pelagius, salvation is a justly earned reward.

One aspect of Augustine's understanding of grace needs further comment. As human beings were incapable of saving themselves, and as God gave his gift of grace to some (but not all), it followed that God had "preselected" those who would be saved. Developing hints of this idea to be found in the New Testament, Augustine developed a doctrine of predestination. The term "predestination" refers to

God's original or eternal decision to save some, and not others. It was this aspect of Augustine's thought which many of his contemporaries, not to mention his successors, found unacceptable. It need hardly be said that there is no direct equivalent in Pelagius's thought.

The Council of Carthage (418) decided for Augustine's views on grace and sin, and condemned Pelagianism in uncompromising terms. However, Pelagianism, in various forms, continued to be a point of contention for some time to come. As the patristic era came to its close, with the Dark Ages settling over western Europe, many of the issues remained unresolved. They would be taken up again during the Middle Ages, and supremely at the time of the Reformation (see pp. 371–80).

KEY NAMES, WORDS, AND PHRASES

By the end of this chapter you will have encountered the following terms, which will recur during the work. Ensure that you are familiar with them!

*Apollinarianism	ecumenical council
apologetics	extracanonical
*Arianism	*Gnosticism
canon	*incarnation
canonical	patristic
Cappadocian fathers	patrology
*Christological	*Pelagian
*Christology	*Pelagianism
creed	*predestination
*Donatism	*soteriology
*Donatist	*trinitarian
*ecclesiology	Trinity

Those terms marked with an asterisk (*) will be explored in greater detail later in this work.

QUESTIONS FOR CHAPTER 1

As this is the first chapter of this work that many students will read, two sets of questions are provided. The first group are elementary; the second are pitched at the level found throughout the remainder of this book.

Set 1 Introductory

1 Locate the following cities or regions on map 1 (p. 6): Alexandria, Antioch, Cappadocia, Constantinople, Hippo, Jerusalem, Rome.
2 Now find the Latin/Greek dividing line on the same map. Latin was the main language west of that line, and Greek east of it. Identify the predominant language in each of the cities mentioned in question 1.
3 Which language would you associate with the following writers: Athanasius, Augustine of Hippo, Origen, Tertullian?
4 The following movements were of major importance during the patristic period: Arianism, Donatism, Gnosticism, Pelagianism. Associate the controversies centering on each of these movements with one of the following theologians: Athanasius, Augustine of Hippo, Irenaeus of Lyons. (Note that one of these theologians is associated with more than one controversy.)

Set 2 Standard Level

1 What was the main issue debated during the Arian controversy? Why did Arius's opponents regard this as being of such importance?

2 Why was the introduction of fixed creeds widely regarded as a welcome development by many within the churches?

3 Why was it important to reach agreement on the canon of Scripture? What practical difference would this have made to theological debate at the time?

4 The English historian Thomas Carlyle once suggested that history was basically the biography of great individuals. On the basis of your reading of this chapter, who do you think was the most significant person in relation to the shaping of Christian theology over this period?

5 Why was there relatively little interest in the doctrine of the church in this early period? And why do you think the Donatist controversy broke out in the western, rather than the eastern, church?

2

The Middle Ages and the Renaissance, c.700–c.1500

The Middle Ages represented an immensely creative and innovative period in Christian theology. The courts, monasteries, and later the universities of Europe became centers of excellence for theological reflection, and the forging of new approaches to the relation of Christian thought and life. The period was given an added injection of vitality through the rise of the Renaissance. This dynamic cultural program looked for the reinvigoration of the life and thought of the church and society as a whole through the creative reappropriation of the classical past. As so many theological landmarks date from this period, it is important to identify and reflect on its achievements and contributions to the theological agenda.

On Defining the "Middle Ages"

It is always difficult to be precise about when one era ends, and another begins. Traditionally, accounts of the development of Christian theology proceed directly from the close of the patristic period, marked by the Council of Chalcedon (451), to the great theological renaissance in western Europe during the Middle Ages. This is unsatisfactory for many

reasons. The most obvious of these is that the "Middle Ages" is a cultural development that is specific to western Europe. It overlooks the fact that the Roman Empire in the east was relatively unaffected by the fall of Rome in 410. The development of Byzantine theology does not easily fit the categories of western European history. It also overlooks earlier renewals in Christian theology in the west – for example, the important developments that took place during the reign of Charlemagne, the first Holy Roman Emperor. This "Carolingian renaissance," which began in the eighth century and continued well into the ninth, saw important theological developments, some of which are touched on in this volume.

The terms "medieval" and "Middle Ages" are modern, signifying the period of transition between the intellectual glories of antiquity and those of the modern period. Although phrases similar to "medieval" are encountered in the medieval period itself, their meaning is quite distinct from the modern sense of the term. Thus Julian of Toledo (died c.685) uses the phrase "the middle age" or "the middle of time" (*tempus medium*) to refer to the period between the incarnation and the second coming of Christ. Since the Renaissance, the term has been used in a rather disparaging sense, to meet the somewhat uninteresting period of time separating the intellectual glories of antiquity and their retrieval in the Renaissance.

The expansion of Islam around the Mediterranean in the seventh century led to widespread political destabilization and further structural changes in the region. By the eleventh century, a degree of stability had settled upon the area, three major power groupings having emerged to take the place of the former Roman Empire.

1 Byzantium, centered on the city of Constantinople (now Istanbul, in modern-day Turkey). The form of Christianity which predominated in this region was based on the Greek language, and was deeply rooted in the writings of patristic scholars of the eastern Mediterranean region, such as Athanasius, the Cappadocians, and John of Damascus. A discussion of some distinctive themes of Byzantine theology may be found on pp. 31–3.

2 Western Europe, mainly regions such as France, Germany, the Low Countries, and northern Italy. The form of Christianity which came to dominate this region was centered on the city of Rome, and its bishop, known as "the Pope." (However, for the period known as the "Great Schism," some confusion developed: there were two rival claimants for the papacy, one based at Rome, the other at the southern French city of Avignon.) Here, theology came to be concentrated in the great cathedral and university schools of Paris and elsewhere, based largely on the Latin writings of Augustine, Ambrose, and Hilary of Poitiers.

3 The Caliphate, an Islamic region embracing much of the extreme eastern and southern parts of the Mediterranean. The expansion of Islam continued, with the fall of Constantinople in 1453 sending shock waves throughout much of Europe. By the end of the fifteenth century, Islam had established a significant presence in two regions of the continent of Europe: Spain and the Balkans. This advance was eventually halted by the defeat of the Moors in Spain in the final decade of the fifteenth century, and the defeat of Islamic armies outside Vienna in 1523.

An event of fundamental importance to the history of the church took place during this period. For a variety of reasons, relations between the eastern church based at Constantinople, and the western church based at Rome, became increasingly strained during the ninth and tenth centuries. Growing disagreement over the *filioque* clause in the Nicene creed (see pp. 268–71) was of no small importance to this increasingly sour atmosphere. Other factors also contributed, including the political rivalry between Latin-speaking Rome and Greek-speaking Constantinople, and the increasing claims to authority of the Roman Pope. The final break between the Catholic west and Orthodox east is usually dated to 1054, although this date is slightly arbitrary.

One major result of this tension was that there was little theological interaction between east and west. Although western theologians such as Thomas Aquinas felt free to draw on the writings of Greek fathers, these works tended to antedate this period. The works of later Orthodox theologians, such as the noted writer Gregory Palamas, attracted little attention in the west. It is only in the twentieth century that western theology may really be said to have begun to rediscover the riches of the Orthodox tradition.

The term "medieval theology" is often used to refer to western theology during this era, whereas the term "Byzantine theology" is used to refer to the theology of the eastern church over roughly the same period, prior to the fall of Constantinople in 1453. During this period in western European history, the centers of Christian theology gradually

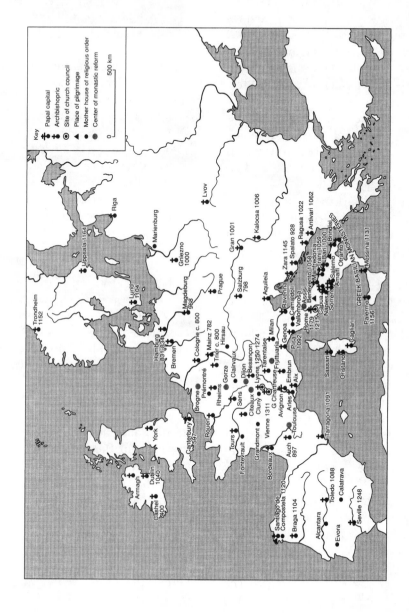

Map 2 Main theological and ecclesiastical centers in western Europe during the Middle Ages

moved northward, to central France and Germany. Although Rome remained a center of Christian power in the region, intellectual activity gradually came to mi grate to the monasteries of France, such as Chartres, Reims, and Bec (in Normandy, now le Bec-Hellouin). With the foundation of the medieval universities, theology rapidly established itself as a central area of academic study. A typical medieval university possessed four faculties: the lower faculty of arts, and the three higher faculties of theology, medicine, and law. In what follows, we shall consider some of these developments in western Europe, before turning to consider developments in Byzantium.

Medieval Theological Landmarks in Western Europe

H istorians have debated for some time the question of when the "Middle Ages" can be said to have begun. The answers given to this question depend, as might be expected, on matters of definition. The practically simultaneous suppression of the Athenian Platonic academy and the establishment of the great monastery at Monte Cassino in 529 are regarded by many as marking, although not in themselves causing, the transition from late antiquity to the medieval period. For some, the medieval period is regarded as having been initiated through Alaric's conquest of Rome in 410, with the resulting gradual shift in the centers of intellectual life from the Mediterranean world to the northern European world of Theodoric and Charlemagne, and later to the abbey and cathedral schools of France, and the universities of Paris and Oxford. We may therefore begin our brief survey of the development of western medieval theology by considering the revival of its fortunes under the first Holy Roman Emperor, Charlemagne (742–814).

The Carolingian renaissance

Under Charlemagne, a concerted effort was directed towards renewing the life of the mind within the church. Perhaps the most important figure in this theological renewal was Alcuin (735–804), who had trained at the cathedral school of York, before becoming its master. At Charlemagne's invitation, Alcuin became abbot of the monastery of St Martin of Tours, which he established as a leading center of learning. A series of imperial decrees established two kinds of theological schools throughout northern Europe. First, there were the monastic schools, which were intended primarily for the instruction of those intending to proceed to monastic vocations. Secondly, there were cathedral schools, set up by the bishop and presided over by a *magister scholarum* or *scholasticus*. One of the results of the Carolingian renaissance was the recognition of the importance of monasteries and cathedrals as seats of learning. The great monastery of Fulda, founded in Germany in 744, became one of the most significant centers of theological and secular learning in the region. Rabanus Maurus, Walafried Strabo, Servatus Lupus, and Otfried of Weissenburg studied there in the eighth and ninth centuries.

In the end, the Carolingian renaissance faltered, due to growing political instability and economic uncertainties. Yet the institutions identified by Charlemagne as central to the tasks of theological education remained, and were able to play a critical role in bringing about the theological renaissance of the twelfth century. We shall consider this development in what follows.

The rise of cathedral and monastic schools of theology

The origins of the monastic movement are generally thought to lie in remote hilly areas of Egypt and parts of eastern Syria during the patristic period. Significant numbers of Christians began to make their homes in these regions, in order to get away from the population centers, with all the distractions that these offered. The theme of withdrawal from a sinful and distracting world became of central importance to these communities. While some lone figures insisted on the need for individual isolation, the concept of a communal life in isolation from the world gained the ascendancy.

During the sixth century, the number of monasteries grew considerably. It was during this period that one of the most comprehensive monastic "Rules" – the "Rule of Benedict" – made its appearance. Benedict of Nursia (c.480–c.550) established his monastery at Monte Cassino at some point around 525. The Benedictine community followed a rule which was dominated by the notion of the unconditional following of Christ, sustained by regular corporate and private prayer, and the reading of Scripture. Benedict's sister, Scholastica, was also active in the monastic movement.

Although the origins of the monasteries is to be traced back to the patristic era, they played a critical role in the development of theology during the medieval period. Most of the great medieval schools of theology are associated with France. One of the most important was linked to the great cathedral of Chartres. Under the leadership of Fulbert (c.960–1028), bishop of Chartres from 1006 until his death, Chartres became one of the most important centers of theological learning in the eleventh century. The Benedictine Abbey of Bec, or Le Bec, in Normandy, provided a base for two of the most important theologians of the eleventh century – Lanfranc (c.1010–89) and Anselm (c.1033–1109).

The great convents of the Middle Ages provided bases for women writers to exercise a significant influence on the thinking of the church. A good example is provided by Hildegard of Bingen (1098–1179), Abbess of Rupertsberg, near the city of Bingen, who established a reputation as a theological and spiritual writer of considerable originality. She is best known for her *Liber Divinorum Operum* ("Book of Divine Works"), which was written over the period 1163–73. Catherine of Siena (1347–80), remembered for a series of theological writings, often in the form of dialogues, was a Dominican tertiary (that is, a layperson who observed a modified version of the Dominican rule).

Not all women theological writers of the Middle Ages were based in convents, however. The English recluse Julian of Norwich (c.1342–c.1415), remembered for her *Revelations of Divine Love*, appears to have led a solitary life. Mechthild of Magdeburg (c.1210?–c.1282) is widely celebrated as one of the most important women spiritual writers of the thirteenth century. She is best known for her *Flowing Light of the Godhead*, which includes her visionary experiences, as well as letters of advice and criticism, allegories, reflections, and prayers. Mechthild was a beguine – that is, a woman with a religious vocation who was not bound by vows, did not live in an enclosed community, and did not totally renounce the possibility of marriage.

The great cathedral of Laon, northwest of Paris, became the site of a very significant school of theology under Anselm of Laon (died 1117), attracting scholars of the caliber of Peter Abelard during its heyday. The Royal Abbey of St Victor, founded in Paris in the twelfth century, became one of the most important centers of theological education, and was of major importance in shaping the theological curriculum at the fledgling University of Paris. Among its twelfth-century luminaries, we may note Hugh of St Victor, Peter Lombard, Andrew of St Victor, and Richard of St Victor.

The rise of importance of these schools is linked with another development, to which we now turn – the emergence of distinctive styles of theology, linked with specific religious orders.

The religious orders and their "schools of theology"

The Middle Ages witnessed the founding of several major new religious orders. In 1097, the Cistercian order was founded at Cîteaux, in the middle of the wild countryside around the River Saône. One of the most noted Cistercian leaders was the great spiritual writer and preacher Bernard of Clairvaux (1090–1153). By the dawn of the fourteenth century, it is estimated that some 600 Cistercian monasteries or convents had come into being.

Two other major orders were founded more than a century later – the Franciscans and Dominicans. The Franciscans were founded by Francis of Assisi (c. 1181–1226), who renounced a life of wealth to live a life of prayer and poverty. He was joined by Clare of Assisi, formerly a noblewoman, who founded the order of "Poor Clares." The Franciscans were often referred to as "Gray Friars," on account of the dark gray habits they wore. The order was distinguished by its emphasis on individual and corporate poverty.

The Dominicans (sometimes referred to as "Black Friars" on account of their black mantle worn over a white habit) were founded by the Spanish priest Dominic de Guzman (1170–1221), with a particular emphasis on education. By the end of the Middle Ages, the Dominicans had established houses in most major European cities, and made a significant contribution to the intellectual life of the church.

From the standpoint of the development of theology, it is important to appreciate that distinct schools of theology came to be associated with monastic orders. Not all religious orders regarded academic theology as being of importance. The Cistercians, for example, placed a particular emphasis on spirituality, rather than more academic forms of theology. Three religious orders may be noted as having had a particularly significant impact on the shaping of medieval theology. In each case, a distinctive style of theology developed within the order, which distinguished it from others.

1   *The Dominicans.* The distinctive theological position of this order was developed by such major writers as Albert the Great, Thomas Aquinas, and Peter of Tarantaise.
2   *The Franciscans.* Three major theologians of the Middle Ages were associated with this order: Bonaventura, Duns Scotus, and William of Ockham.
3   *The Augustinians.* The distinctive theological position of this order was developed initially by Giles of Rome (c.1244–1316), and subsequently by later writers such as Thomas of Strasbourg (c.1275–1357).

The importance of these distinctive schools of theology is evident throughout this period, and continues into the sixteenth century. It is impossible to understand the development of the theological ideas of Martin Luther (originally an Augustinian friar) or the theological debates at the Council of Trent without having some knowledge of these schools.

The founding of the universities

The restoration of some degree of political stability in France in the late eleventh century encouraged the re-emergence of the University of Paris, which rapidly became recognized as the intellectual center of Europe. A number of theological "schools" were established on the Left Bank of the Seine, and on the Ile de la Cité, in the shadow of the newly built cathedral of Notre Dame de Paris.

One such school was the Collège de la Sorbonne, which eventually achieved such fame that "the Sorbonne" came to be a shorthand way of referring to the University of Paris as a whole. Even in the sixteenth century, Paris was widely recognized as a leading center for theological and philosophical study, including among its students such prominent individuals as Erasmus of Rotterdam and John Calvin. Other such centers of study were soon established elsewhere in Europe. A new program of theological development began, concerned with consolidating the intellectual, legal, and spiritual aspects of the life of the Christian church.

The University of Paris soon established itself as a leading center of theological speculation, with such scholars as Peter Abelard (1079–1142), Albert the Great (c.1200–80), Thomas Aquinas (c.1225–74), and Bonaventure (c.1217–74). Initially, the most significant rival to Paris was the University of Oxford, in England. However, the fourteenth and fifteenth centuries witnessed a considerable expansion of the university sector in western Europe, with major new universities being founded in Germany and elsewhere.

Peter Lombard's *Four Books of the Sentences*

The medieval period was characterized by its attempts to accumulate biblical and patristic material considered to be relevant to particular issues of theological interpretation, and by its attempt to develop hermeneutical methods to resolve the apparent contradictions encountered in this process. These collections of patristic "sentences" appear to have been modeled upon the codifications of the canonists, who initially grouped their collected decretals chronologically, and later according to subjects. Prosper of Aquitaine's *Liber sententiarum ex operibus Augustini* ("Book of sentences from the works of Augustine") is an early example of this phenomenon. These collections of patristic "sentences" were largely drawn from the works of Augustine. The most famous of them became a standard medieval theological textbook.

A central resource to the new medieval interest in theology is also linked with Paris. At some point shortly before 1140, Peter Lombard arrived at the university to teach. One of his primary concerns was to get his students to wrestle with the thorny issues of theology. His contribution was a textbook – *Sententiarum libri quattuor* or *Four Books of the Sentences* – which brings together quotations from Scripture and the patristic writers, arranged topically. The work has often been styled an "Augustinian breviary," in that roughly 80 percent of its text is taken up by a thousand citations from Augustine. The task Peter set his students was simple: to construct a theology which was able to reconcile the various quotations he had assembled. The book proved to be of major importance in developing the Augustinian heritage, in that students were obliged to wrestle with the ideas of Augustine, and reconcile apparently contradictory texts by devising suitable theological explanations of the inconsistencies (see pp. 106–7).

Some writers attempted to have the book banned, noting its occasional incautious statements (such as the opinion that Christ did not exist as a person, a view which came to be known as "Christological nihilism"). However, by 1215 the work was firmly established as the most important textbook of the age. It became obligatory for theologians to study and comment on Lombard's work. The resulting writings, known as *Commentaries on the Sentences*, became one of the most familiar theological genres of the Middle Ages. Outstanding examples include those of Thom as Aquinas, Bonaventure, and Duns Scotus. The work was still used in the sixteenth century, and was even annotated by Martin Luther.

The rise of scholasticism

Scholasticism derives its name from the great medieval *scholae* ("schools"), in which the classic questions of theology and philosophy were debated. Although often portrayed negatively, scholasticism needs to be seen in a much more positive light – as an attempt to create a bold and brilliant synthesis of Christian ideas, capable of undergirding every aspect of life. It can be thought of as a "cathedral of the mind" (Etienne Gilson) – an attempt to do with ideas what the great medieval masons did with stones, as they constructed some of the most admired and visited buildings the world has ever known. At its best, scholastic theology is to the world of ideas what those cathedrals are to the world of architecture.

How may scholasticism be defined? Like many other significant cultural terms, such as "humanism" and "Enlightenment," it is difficult to offer a precise definition, capable of doing justice to all the distinctive positions of the major schools within the Middle Ages. Perhaps the following working definition may be helpful: scholasticism is best regarded as the medieval movement, flourishing in the period 1200–1500, which placed emphasis upon the rational justification of religious belief and the systematic presentation of those beliefs. "Scholasticism" thus does not refer to a *specific system of beliefs*, but to a *particular way of doing and organizing theology* – a highly developed method of presenting material making fine distinctions, and attempting to achieve a comprehensive view of theology.

Scholasticism may be argued to have made major contributions in a number of key areas of Christian theology, especially in relation to the discussion of the role of reason and logic in theology. The writings of Thomas Aquinas, Duns Scotus, and William of Ockham – often singled out as the three most influential of all scholastic writers – make massive contributions to this area of theology, which have served as landmarks ever since.

The Italian Renaissance

The French term "Renaissance" is now universally used to designate the literary and artistic revival in fourteenth- and fifteenth-century Italy. In 1546 Paolo Giovio referred to the fourteenth century as "that happy century in which Latin letters are conceived to have been reborn" (*renatae*), anticipating this nomenclature. Certain historians, most notably Jacob Burckhardt, argued that the Renaissance gave birth to the modern era. It was in this era, Burckhardt claimed, that human beings first began to think of themselves as *individuals*. In many ways, Burckhardt's definition of the Renaissance in purely individualist terms is highly questionable. But in one sense, he is unquestionably correct: *something* novel and exciting developed in Renaissance Italy, which proved capable of exercising a fascination over generations of thinkers.

It is not entirely clear why Italy became the cradle of this brilliant new movement in the history of ideas. A number of factors have been identified as having some bearing on the question.

1 Scholastic theology – the major intellectual force of the medieval period – was never particularly influential in Italy. Although many Italians achieved fame as theologians (including Thomas Aquinas and

Gregory of Rimini), they generally lived and worked in northern Europe. There was thus an intellectual vacuum in Italy during the fourteenth century. Vacuums tend to get filled – and Renaissance humanism managed to occupy this particular gap.

2   Italy was saturated with visible and tangible reminders of the greatness of antiquity. The ruins of ancient Roman buildings and monuments were scattered throughout the land, and appear to have aroused interest in the civilization of ancient Rome at the time of the Renaissance, acting as a stimulus to its thinkers to recover the vitality of classical Roman culture at a time which was culturally arid and barren.

3   As Byzantium began to crumble – Constantinople finally fell in 1453 – there was an exodus of Greek-speaking intellectuals westward. Italy happened to be conveniently close to Constantinople, with the result that many such émigrés settled in Italian cities. A revival of the Greek language was thus inevitable, and with it a revival of interest in the Greek classics.

It will be clear that a central component of the worldview of the Italian Renaissance is a return to the cultural glories of antiquity, and a marginalization of the intellectual achievements of the Middle Ages. Renaissance writers had scant regard for the latter, regarding them as outweighed by the greater achievements of antiquity. What was true of culture in general was also true of theology: they regarded the late classical period as totally overshadowing the theological writings of the Middle Ages, both in substance and in style. Indeed, the Renaissance may partly be seen as a reaction against the type of approach increasingly associated with the faculties of arts and theology of northern European universities. Irritated by the technical nature of the language and dis-

cussions of the scholastics, the writers of the Renaissance bypassed them altogether. In the case of Christian theology, the key to the future lay in a direct engagement with the text of Scripture and the writings of the patristic period. We shall explore this matter further shortly (see below).

The rise of humanism

In the modern period, the term "humanism" has come to designate a worldview which denies the existence or relevance of God, or which is committed to a purely secular outlook. This is certainly not what the word meant at the time of the Renaissance. Most humanists of the period were religious, and were concerned to purify and renew Christianity, rather than eliminate it. And how would this process of regeneration take place? By a return to the fountainheads of western thought.

The humanist program was set out in the Latin slogan *ad fontes* ("back to the sources"), which set out the vision of returning to the wellspring and source of modern western culture in the ancient world, allowing its ideas and values to refresh and renew that culture. The classical period was to be both a resource and a norm for the Renaissance. In art and architecture, as in the written and spoken word, antiquity was seen as a cultural resource, which could be appropriated by the Renaissance. In the case of Christian humanism, believers would return directly to simplicities of the New Testament, bypassing the complex theological programs of the Middle Ages. But it would be the original Greek text of the New Testament, not the Vulgate Latin translation, widely used by medieval theologians.

One of the most significant theological developments associated with the rise of humanism is the increased questioning of the reliability of the Vulgate text. If this translation proved unreliable, in the light of an increased understanding of the Greek and Hebrew languages, and an increased recognition of studying the Bible in those original languages, what of the theological ideas that might be dependent on such faulty translations? We shall return to this point later in this chapter (pp. 41–2).

Having thus far concentrated on western Europe, we must now turn to consider some of the important developments that took place in eastern Europe during this period.

Medieval Theological Landmarks in Eastern Europe

Byzantine theology takes its name from the Greek city of Byzantium, which Constantine chose as the site of his new capital city in 330. At this point, it was renamed Constantinople ("city of Constantine"). However, the name of the older town remained, and gave its name to the distinctive style of theology which flourished in this region until the fall of Constantinople to invading Islamic armies in 1453. It must be noted that Constantinople was not the only center of Christian thought in the eastern Mediterranean. Egypt and Syria had been centers of theological reflection for some time. However, as political power increasingly came to be concentrated on the imperial city, so its status as a theological center advanced correspondingly.

During the time of Justinian (527–56) Byzantine theology began to emerge as an intellectual force of some considerable importance. As the eastern and western churches became increasingly alienated from each other (a process which had begun long before the final schism of 1054), so Byzantine thinkers often emphasized the divergence from western theology (for example, in relation to the *filioque* clause: see p. 268), thus reinforcing the distinctiveness of their approach through polem-

ical writings. For example, Byzantine writers tended to understand salvation primarily in terms of *deification*, rather than western legal or relational categories. In addition, they found themselves puzzled by the doctrines of purgatory which were gaining the ascendancy in western Catholic circles. Any attempt to achieve a degree of reunion between east and west during the Middle Ages was thus complicated by a complex network of political, historical, and theological factors. By the time of the fall of Constantinople, the differences between east and west remained as wide as ever.

The emergence of Byzantine theology

In order to understand the distinctive nature of Byzantine theology, it is necessary to appreciate the ethos which lies behind it. Byzantine theologians were not particularly concerned with systematic formulations of the Christian faith. For them, Christian theology was something "given," and which therefore required to be defended against its opponents and explained to its adherents. The idea of "systematic theology" is somewhat foreign to the general Byzantine ethos. Even John of Damascus (c.675–c.749) whose work *de fide orthodoxa* ("On the Orthodox Faith") is of considerable importance in the consolidation of a distinctively eastern Christian theology, is to be seen as an expositor of the faith, rather than as a speculative or original thinker.

Byzantine theology can be regarded as remaining faithful to a principle originally set out by Athanasius, in his writing *de incarnatione* ("on the incarnation"), which affirmed that theology was the expression of the mind of the saints. Byzantine theology (including its modern descendants in both Greek and Russian Orthodoxy) is thus strongly orientated toward the idea of *paradosis* ("tradition"), particularly the writings of the Greek fathers. Writers such as Gregory of Nyssa, Maximus the Confessor, and the writer who adopted the pseudonym "Dionysius the Areopagite," are of particular importance in this respect.

The iconoclastic controversy

Two controversies are of particular importance. The first, which broke out during the period 725–842, is usually referred to as the iconoclastic ("breaking of images") controversy. It erupted over the decision of emperor Leo III (717–42) to destroy icons, on the grounds that they were barriers to the conversion of Jews and Muslims. The controversy was mainly political, although there were some serious theological issues at stake, most notably the extent to which the doctrine of the incarnation justified the depiction of God in the form of images.

John of Damascus played a major role in this controversy. One of his most fundamental arguments in favor of the use of icons was his belief that the material world possesses the capacity to signify and mediate the spiritual world.

> Is not the ink in the most holy gospel book matter? Is not the life-giving altar, from which we receive the bread of life, constructed from matter? Are not gold and silver matter? Yet from them, we make crosses, patens, and chalices. And more importantly than any of these things, are not the body and blood of our Lord matter? Either dispense with the honor and veneration that these things deserve, or accept the tradition of the church and the veneration of images.

The hesychastic controversy

The second controversy, which broke out in the fourteenth century, focused on the issue of Hesychasm (Greek: *hēsychia*, silence), a style of meditation through physical exercises which enabled believers to see the "divine light" with their own eyes. Hesychasm placed considerable emphasis upon the idea of "inner quietness" as a means of achieving a direct inner vision of God. It was particularly associated with writers such as Simeon the New Theologian and Gregory Palamas (c.1296–1359), who was elected as Archbishop of Thessalonika in 1347. Its opponents argued that its methods tended to minimize the difference between God and creatures, and were particularly alarmed by the suggestion that God could be "seen."

In responding to this criticism, Palamas developed the doctrine now generally known as "Palamism," which draws a distinction between the divine energies and the divine essence. The distinction allowed Palamas to defend the Hesychastic approach by affirming that it enabled believers to encounter the divine energies, but not the unseen and ineffable divine essence. Believers cannot participate directly in the divine essence; however, they are able to participate directly in the uncreated energies which are God's mode of union with believers.

Palamas's theology was espoused and developed particularly by the lay theologian Nicolas Cabasilis (c.1320–c.1390), whose *Life in Christ* remains a classic work of Byzantine spirituality. His work has been reappropriated in more recent years by neo-Palamite writers such as Vladimir Lossky and John Meyendorff (see pp. 79–80).

The fall of Constantinople (1453)

The golden era of Byzantine theology came to an end in 1453, when the great city of Constantinople finally fell to the Turks. It was the end of an age. With the fall of Byzantium, intellectual and political leadership within Orthodoxy largely passed to Russia. The Russians had been converted through Byzantine missions in the tenth century, and took the side of the Greeks in the schism of 1054. By the end of the fifteenth century, Moscow and Kiev were firmly established as patriarchates, each with its own distinctive style of Orthodox theology. It was only when Greece, now part of the Ottoman Empire, finally broke free from Turkish rule in 1829 that the renewal of Orthodox theology in that region was able to begin.

It will be clear from the material presented in this chapter that both western and eastern Christian theology underwent significant development during the Middle Ages and Renaissance. Subsequent generations of theologians have regarded the period as being of landmark significance in relation to a number of areas of theological reflection, with a number of its writers being regarded as possessing permanent importance. The rise and fall of Byzantium is of particular importance to a full understanding of the subsequent development of eastern Orthodoxy in Russia and Greece (see pp. 79–80), just as the rise of scholasticism and humanism were of considerable importance to the shaping of western theology.

Key Theologians

Of the many theologians of importance to have emerged during this period of enormous creativity, the following are of especial interest and importance.

John of Damascus (c.675–c.749)

The Syrian theologian known as "John of Damascus" was one of the eastern church's most influential thinkers, and is often regarded as the last of the Greek fathers. At this time, Islam was sweeping through much of north Africa and the Levant, and Syria was firmly under Islamic control. John was brought up within the household of the caliph of Damascus,

Abdul Malek, and succeeded his father as the caliph's chief financial officer. We know little about him, and are dependent upon unreliable later sources for the fragmentary information that has been passed down to us. At some point, probably at some point during the period 726–30, he resigned his position within the caliph's court, and entered the monastery of St Sabas, south-east of Jerusalem.

At an early stage in his career, he was drawn into the iconoclastic controversy, and vigorously opposed those who wanted to destroy icons. Paradoxically, John's position within an Islamic household prevented his many enemies in Byzantium from taking any action against him. His defense of the use of icons involves an appeal to the doctrine of the incarnation, both as a basis of establishing the divine willingness to become visible, and for the use of material forms to represent the divine likeness or convey divine truths.

John is remembered for his work "The Fountain of Wisdom" (pēgē gnōseos), which consists of three parts. The first part deals principally with Aristotle's concept of ontology, apparently on the assumption that this would assist with the understanding of Christian doctrine. The second part is an updated reworking of an earlier work on heresy by Epiphanius. The third part is the most important and interesting. Entitled "A Precise Analysis of the Orthodox Faith," it sets out in detail the fundamentals of the Christian faith, as John has received them from earlier writers. This section of the treatise is often treated as a work in its own right, and is generally referred to simply as "the Orthodox Faith." It was highly regarded by both Latin-speaking and Greek-speaking Christians, and was translated into Latin in 1150 by Burgundius of Pisa. This edition is cited by both Peter Lombard in his *Four Books of the Sentences*, and Thomas Aquinas in his *Summa Theologiae*.

Simeon the New Theologian (949–1022)

Simeon (or "Symeon") was born into a wealthy family in Paphlagonia, Asia Minor, in 949. At the age of 11, he was sent to the great city of Constantinople for further study. His parents had aspirations that he would go on to a political career, but he had a spiritual experience at the age of 20 which convinced him of the importance of a direct encounter with God. Although he did not immediately give up on his political hopes, his ecstatic experience of God as a living presence of radiant light had clearly made a deep impression on him. At the age of 27, he entered the monastery of Studios, and came under the spiritual direction of Symeon the Pious, changing his given name, George, as a mark of respect for his mentor. He subsequently entered the monastery of St Mamas in Constantinople, where he was ordained priest, and eventually became the abbot. During this period, he set about renewing the monastery's life of prayer and meditation, and wrote a number of spiritual treatises, emphasizing the power of contemplative prayer and meditation.

Simeon remains one of the most important theological influences on modern Orthodoxy, reflecting the high regard in which he is held. His theology echoes many of the now-traditional themes of Byzantine doctrine, particularly an emphasis upon the doctrine of the incarnation, and an accentuation on redemption as deification. He is called "Simeon the New Theologian" within Orthodoxy to distinguish him from John the Evangelist (known as "John the Theologian") on the one hand, and Gregory of Nazianzius (known as "Gregory the Theologian" in the Eastern Orthodox tradition).

Anselm of Canterbury (c.1033–1109)

Anselm was born in northern Italy, but soon moved to France, then establishing a reputation as a center for learning. He quickly mastered the arts of logic and grammar, and acquired a formidable reputation as a teacher at the Norman abbey of Bec. Standing at the dawn of the theological renaissance of the twelfth century, Anselm made decisive contributions in two areas of discussion: proofs for the existence of God, and the rational interpretation of Christ's death upon the cross.

The *Proslogion* (the word is virtually untranslatable) was written around 1079. It is a remarkable work, in which Anselm sets himself the task of formulating an argument which will lead to belief in the existence and character of God as highest good. The resulting analysis, often known as the "ontological argument," leads to the derivation of the existence of God from an affirmation of his being "that than which nothing greater can be conceived." Although the argument has been contested since its inception, it has remained one of the most intriguing components of philosophical theology to this day. The *Proslogion* is also of importance on account of its clear appeal to reason in matters of theology, and its appreciation of the role of logic. In many ways, the work anticipates the best aspects of scholastic theology. Anselm's phrase *fides quaerens intellectum* ("faith seeking understanding") has passed into widespread use.

Following the Norman invasion of England (1066), Anselm was invited to become Archbishop of Canterbury in 1093, thus ensuring the consolidation of Norman influence over the English church. It was not an entirely happy period of his life, due to a series of violent disputes between the church and the monarchy over land rights. During one period spent working away from England in Italy, Anselm penned perhaps his most important work, *Cur Deus homo* ("Why God became man"). In this work Anselm seeks to set out a rational demonstration of the necessity of God becoming man, and an analysis of the benefits which accrue to humanity as a result of the incarnation and obedience of the Son of God. This argument, to be considered at length later in this work, remains of foundational importance to any discussion of "theories of the atonement" – in other words, understandings of the meaning of the death and resurrection of Christ, and its significance for humanity. Once more, the work exhibits the characteristics which are typical of scholasticism at its best: the appeal to reason, the logical marshaling of arguments, the relentless exploration of the implications of ideas, and the fundamental conviction that, at its heart, the Christian gospel *is* rational, and can be *shown* to be rational.

Thomas Aquinas (c.1225–74)

Aquinas was born at the castle of Roccasecca in Italy, the youngest son of Count Landulf of Aquino. To judge by his nickname – "the dumb ox" – he was rather portly. In 1244, while in his late teens, Aquinas decided to join the Dominican order, also known as the "Order of Preachers." His parents were hostile to this idea: they rather hoped he would become a Benedictine, and perhaps end up as abbot of Monte Cassino, one of the most prestigious positions in the medieval church. His brothers forcibly imprisoned him in one of the family's castles for a year to encourage him to change his mind. Despite this intense opposition from his family, Aquinas eventually got his way, and ended up becoming one of the most important religious thinkers of the Middle Ages. One of his teachers is reported to have said that "the bellowing of that ox will be heard throughout the world."

Aquinas began his studies at Paris, before moving to Cologne in 1248. In 1252 he returned to Paris to study theology. Four years later he was granted permission to teach theology at the university. For the next three years he lectured on Matthew's Gospel and began to write the *Summa contra Gentiles*, "Summary against the Gentiles." In this major work Aquinas provided important arguments in favor of the Christian faith for the benefit of missionaries working among Muslims and Jews. In 1266 he began the most famous of his many writings, usually known by its Latin title, *Summa Theologiae*. In this work Thomas developed a detailed study of key aspects of Christian theology (such as the role of reason in faith), as well as a detailed analysis of key doctrinal questions (such as the divinity of Christ). The work is divided into three parts, with the second part subdivided into two. Part I deals chiefly with God the creator; Part II – divided into two sections known as the *prima secundae* and the *secunda secundae* (literally, the "first of the second" and the "second of the second") – with the restoration of humanity to God; and Part III with the manner in which the person and work of Christ bring about the salvation of humanity.

On December 6, 1273, Aquinas declared that he could write no longer. "All that I have written seems like straw to me," he said. It is possible that he may have had some sort of breakdown, perhaps brought on by overwork. He died on March 7, 1274. Among Aquinas's key contributions to theology, the following are of especial importance, and are discussed elsewhere in this volume:

- the "Five Ways" (arguments for the existence of God) (see pp. 187–9);
- the principle of analogy, which provides a theological foundation for knowing God through the creation (see pp. 194–5);
- the relation between faith and reason (see pp. 181–2).

Duns Scotus (c.1265–1308)

Scotus was unquestionably one of the finest minds of the Middle Ages. In his short life he taught at Cambridge, Oxford, and Paris, and produced three versions of a *Commentary on the Sentences*. Known as the "subtle doctor" on account of the very fine distinctions which he frequently drew between the possible meanings of terms, he was responsible for a number of developments of considerable significance to Christian theology. Only three can be noted here.

1 Scotus was a champion of the theory of knowledge associated with Aristotle. The earlier Middle Ages were dominated by a different theory of knowledge, going back to Augustine of Hippo, known as "illuminationism," in which knowledge was understood to arise from the illumination of the human intellect by God. This view, which was championed by writers such as Henry of Ghent, was subjected to devastating criticism by Scotus.

2 Scotus regarded the divine will as taking precedence over the divine intellect, a doctrine often referred to as *voluntarism*. Thomas Aquinas had argued for the primacy of the divine intellect; Scotus opened the way to new approaches to theology, based on the assumption of the priority of the divine will. An example illustrates the point. Consider the idea of merit – that is to say, a human moral action which is deemed worthy of reward by God. What is the basis of this decision? Aquinas argued that the divine intellect recognized the inherent worth of the human moral act. It then informed the will to reward it appropriately. Scotus argued along very different lines. The divine will to reward the moral action came before any evaluation of its inherent worth. This approach is of considerable importance in relation to the doctrines of justification and predestination, and will be considered in more detail later.

3 Scotus was a champion of the doctrine of the immaculate conception of Mary, the mother of Jesus. Thomas Aquinas had taught that Mary shared the common sinful condition of humanity. She was tainted by sin (Latin: *macula*) like everyone else, apart from Christ. Scotus, however, argued that Christ, by virtue of his perfect work of redemption, was able to keep Mary free from the taint of original sin. Such was the influence of Scotus that the "immaculate position" (from the Latin *immacula*, "free of sin") became dominant by the end of the Middle Ages.

William of Ockham (c.1285–1347)

In many ways, Ockham may be regarded as developing some of the lines of argument associated with Scotus. Of particular importance is his consistent defense of a voluntarist position, giving priority to the divine will over the divine intellect. It is, however, probably his philosophical position which has ensured his permanent place of note in the history of Christian theology. Two major elements of his teaching may be noted.

1 Ockham's Razor, often referred to as "the principle of parsimony." Ockham insisted that simplicity was both a theological and a philosophical virtue. His "razor" eliminated all hypotheses which were not absolutely essential. This had major implications for his theology of justification. Earlier medieval theologians (including Thomas Aquinas) had argued that God was obliged to justify sinful humanity by means of what was called a "created habit of grace" – in other words, an intermediate supernatural entity, infused by God into the human soul, which permitted the sinner to be pronounced justified. Ockham dismissed this notion as an unnecessary irrelevance, and declared that justification was the direct acceptance of a sinner by God. There was no need for this intermediate step in the acceptance of the individual by God. What Aquinas held to take place by an intermediate entity, Ockham declared to take place directly, without any intermediate such as a "created habit of grace." The way was thus opened to the more personalist approaches to justification such as those associated with the Reformation.

2 Ockham was a vigorous defender of nominalism. In part, this resulted from his use of the razor: universals were declared to be a totally unnecessary hypothesis, and were thus eliminated. The growing impact of the "modern way" in western Europe owes a considerable debt to him. One aspect of his thought which proved to be of especial importance is the "dialectic between the two powers of God." This device allowed Ockham to contrast the way things are with the way things could have been. A full discussion of this follows later; for the moment it is enough to note that Ockham made a decisive contribution to discussions of divine omnipotence, which are of continuing importance today.

Erasmus of Rotterdam (c.1469–1536)

Desiderius Erasmus is generally regarded as the most important humanist writer of the Renaissance, and had a profound impact upon Christian theology during the first half of the sixteenth century. Although not Protestant in any sense of the term, Erasmus did much to lay the intellectual foundations of the Reformation, not least through his extensive editorial undertakings, including the production of the first printed text of the Greek New Testament (see pp. 41–2). His *Enchiridion militis Christiani* ("Hand book of the Christian Soldier") was a landmark in religious publishing.

The *Enchiridion* developed the revolutionary and highly attractive thesis that the church of the day could be reformed by a collective return to the writings of the fathers and the Bible. The regular reading of Scripture is put forward as the key to a new lay piety, on the basis of which the church may be renewed and reformed. Erasmus conceived of his work as a lay person's guide to Scripture, providing a simple yet learned exposition of the "philosophy of Christ." This "philosophy" is really a form of practical morality, rather than an academic philosophy. The New Testament concerns the knowledge of good and evil, in order that its readers may eschew the latter and love the former. The New Testament is the *lex Christi*, "the law of Christ," which Christians are called to obey. Christ is the example whom Christians are called to imitate. Yet Erasmus does not understand Christian faith to be a mere external observance of a moral code. His characteristically humanist emphasis upon inner religion leads him to suggest that reading of Scripture *transforms* its readers, giving them a new motivation to love God and their neighbors.

Erasmus also undertook extensive scholarly projects, two of which are of especial importance to the development of Christian theology:

1 The production of the first Greek New Testament. As noted earlier, this allowed theologians direct access to the original text of the New Testament, with explosive results.
2 The production of reliable editions of patristic works, including the writings of Augustine. Theologians thus had access to the full texts of such major works, instead of having to rely upon second-hand quotations, known as "sentences," often taken out of context. A new understanding of Augustine's theology began to develop as a result, with significant implications for the theological development of the period.

Key Theological Developments

T he major renaissance in theology which took place during the period under consideration focused on a number of issues, of which the following are of especial importance. They will simply be noted briefly at this point; detailed discussion of most of them will take place later in this work. The first six such developments are associated with scholasticism (see p. 29), the last two with humanism (see pp. 30–1).

The consolidation of the patristic heritage

During the theological renaissance of the twelfth century and following, Christian theologians saw themselves as consolidating and extending the rich heritage of theological resources passed on to them from the patristic era. In that the western church was Latin-speaking, it was natural that its theologians should turn to the substantial collection of works by Augustine of Hippo, and take this as a starting point for their own theological speculations. Peter Lombard's *Four Books of the Sentences* may be regarded as a critical compilation of quotations ("Sentences") drawn largely from the writings of Augustine, upon which medieval theologians were required to comment.

The exploration of the role of reason in theology

The new concern to establish Christian theology upon a totally reliable foundation led to a considered exploration of the role of reason in theology, a central and defining characteristic of scholasticism (see p. 29). As the theological renaissance of the early Middle Ages proceeded, two themes began to dominate theological debate: the need to *systematize* and *expand* Christian theology; and the need to *demonstrate the inherent rationality* of that theology. Although most early medieval theology was little more than a replay of the views of Augustine, there was growing pressure to systematize Augustine's ideas, and take them further. But how could this be done? A "theory of method" was urgently needed. And on the basis of what philosophical system could the rationality of Christian theology be demonstrated?

The eleventh-century writer Anselm of Canterbury gave expression to this basic belief of the rationality of the Christian faith in two phrases which have come to be linked with his name: *fides quaerens intellectum* ("faith seeking understanding") and *credo ut intellegam* ("I believe, in order that I may understand"). His basic insight was that, while faith came before understanding, the content of that faith was nevertheless rational. These definitive formulae established the priority of faith over reason, just as they asserted the entire reasonableness of faith. In the preface to his *Monologium* Anselm stated explicitly that he would establish nothing in Scripture on the basis of Scripture itself; instead, he would establish everything that he could on the basis of "rational evidence and the natural light of truth." Nevertheless, Anselm is no rationalist; reason has its limits!

The eleventh and early twelfth centuries saw a growing conviction that philosophy could be an invaluable asset to Christian theology at two different levels. In the first place, it could demonstrate the reasonableness of faith, and thus defend it against non-Christian critics. In the second place, it offered ways of systematically exploring and arranging the articles of faith, so that they could be better understood. But which philosophy? The answer to this question came through the rediscovery of the writings of Aristotle, in the late twelfth and early thirteenth centuries. By about 1270, Aristotle had become established as "the Philosopher." His ideas came to dominate theological thinking, despite fierce opposition from more conservative quarters.

Through the influence of writers such as Thomas Aquinas and Duns Scotus, Aristotle's ideas became established as the best means of consolidating and developing Christian theology. The ideas of Christian theology were thus arranged and correlated systematically, on the basis of Aristotelian presuppositions. Equally, the rationality of Christian faith was demonstrated on the basis of Aristotelian ideas. Thus some of Thomas Aquinas's famous "proofs" for the existence of God actually rely on principles of Aristotelian physics, rather than on any distinctively Christian insights.

Initially, this development was welcomed by many, who saw it as providing important ways of defending the rationality of the Christian faith – a discipline which has since come to be known as "apologetics," from the Greek word *apologia* (defense). Thomas Aquinas's *Summa contra Gentiles* is an excellent example of a work of theology which draws on Aristotelianism as a common philosophy shared by Christians and Muslims, which would allow the attractiveness of the Christian faith to be explained within the Islamic world. At points, Aquinas's argument seems to work like this: if you can agree with the Aristotelian ideas presented in this writing, then you ought to become a Christian. As Aristotle was highly regarded by many Muslim academics of the period, Thomas can be seen as exploiting the apologetic potential of this philosopher.

This development came to be viewed with concern by some late medieval writers, such as Hugolino of Orvieto. A number of central Christian insights seemed to have been lost, according to such critics, as a result of a growing reliance upon the ideas and methods of a pagan philosopher. Particular concern centered on the doctrine of justification, in which Aristotelian ethical ideas came to play a significant role. The idea of the "righteousness of God" came to be discussed in terms of the Aristotelian idea of "distributive justice." Here, "righteousness" (*iustitia*) was defined in terms of "giving someone what they were entitled to." This seemed to lead to a doctrine of justification by merit. In other words, justification takes place on the basis of entitlement, rather than grace. It can be shown without difficulty that this concern lies behind Martin Luther's growing dislike of Aristotle, and his eventual break with scholastic doctrines of justification.

The development of theological systems

We have already noted the pressure to consolidate the patristic, especially the Augustinian, heritage (p. 38). This pressure to systematize, which is integral to scholasticism, led to the development of the sophisticated theological systems which Etienne Gilson, a noted historian of the period, described as "cathedrals of the mind." This development is perhaps best seen in Thomas Aquinas's *Summa Theologiae*, which represents one of the most forceful statements of the comprehensive and all-embracing character of this approach to Christian theology.

The development of sacramental theology

The early church had been somewhat imprecise in its discussion of the sacraments. There was little general agreement concerning either how the term "sacrament" was to be defined, or what items were to be included in a list of the sacraments (see pp. 421–3). Baptism and the Eucharist were generally agreed to be sacramental; sadly, there was relatively little agreement on anything else. However, with the theological renaissance of the Middle Ages, the church was coming to play an increasingly important role in society. There was new pressure for the church to place its acts of public worship on a secure intellectual footing, and to consolidate the theoretical aspects of its worship. As a result, sacramental theology developed considerably during the period. Agreement was reached on the definition of a sacrament, the number of the sacraments, and the precise identity of these sacraments.

The development of the theology of grace

A central element of the Augustinian heritage was a theology of grace. However, Augustine's theology of grace had been stated in a polemical context. In other words, Augustine had been obliged to state his theology of grace in the heat of a controversy, often in response to the challenges and provocations of his opponents. As a result, his writings on the subject were often unsystematic. Occasionally, Augustine developed distinctions in response to the needs of the moment, and failed to lay an adequate theological foundation for at least

some of them. The theologians of the Middle Ages saw themselves as charged with the task of consolidating Augustine's doctrine of grace, placing it upon a more reliable foundation, and exploring its consequences. As a result, the doctrines of grace and justification were developed considerably during the period, laying the foundation for the Reformation debates over these central issues.

The role of Mary in the scheme of salvation

This new interest in grace and justification led to a new concern to understand the role of Mary, the mother of Jesus Christ, in salvation. Growing interest in devotion to Mary, linked with intense theological speculation concerning the nature of original sin and redemption, led to a series of developments relating to Mary. Many of these are linked with Duns Scotus, who placed Mariology (that is, the area of theology dealing with Mary) on a considerably more developed foundation than hitherto. Intense debate broke out between "maculists" (who held that Mary was subject to original sin, like everyone else) and "immaculists" (who held that she was preserved from the taint of original sin). There was also considerable discussion over whether Mary could be said to be "coredemptrix" (that is to say, whether she was to be regarded as a figure of redemption, in a manner similar to Jesus Christ).

Returning directly to the sources of Christian theology

A central element of the humanist agenda was the return to the original sources of western European culture in classical Rome and Athens. The theological counterpart to this element was the direct return to the foundational resources of Christian theology, above all in the New Testament. This agenda proved to be of major significance, as will be seen later (see p. 42). One of its most important consequences was a new appreciation of the foundational importance of Scripture as a theological resource. As interest in Scripture developed, it became increasingly clear that existing Latin translations of this source were inadequate. Supreme among these was the "Vulgate," a Latin translation of the Bible which achieved widespread influence during the Middle Ages. As revision of the translations, especially the Vulgate, proceeded, it became clear that theological revision was inevitable. Some teachings seemed to be based on faulty translations.

The rise of humanist textual and philological techniques was to expose distressing discrepancies between the Vulgate and the texts it purported to translate – and thus to open the way to doctrinal reform as a consequence. It is for this reason that humanism is of decisive importance to the development of medieval theology: it demonstrated the unreliability of this translation of the Bible – and hence, it seemed, of the theologies based upon it. The biblical basis of scholasticism seemed to collapse, as humanism uncovered error after error in its translation. We shall explore this point further in what follows; it is unquestionably one of the most significant developments in the history of Christian theology at this time.

The critique of the Vulgate translation of Scripture

The literary and cultural program of humanism can be summarized in the slogan *ad fontes* – "back to the original sources." The "filter" of medieval commentaries – whether on legal texts or on the Bible – was abandoned, in order for humanists to engage directly with the original texts. Applied to the Christian church, the slogan *ad fontes* meant a direct return to the title-deeds of Christianity – to the patristic writers, and supremely to the Bible, studied in its original

languages. This necessitated direct access to the Greek text of the New Testament.

The first printed Greek New Testament was produced by Erasmus in 1516. Erasmus's text was not as reliable as it ought to have been: he had access to a mere four manuscripts for most of the New Testament, and only one for its final part, the Book of Revelation. As it happened, the manuscript left out five verses, which Erasmus himself had to translate into Greek from the Latin of the Vulgate. Nevertheless, it proved to be a literary milestone. For the first time, theologians had the opportunity of comparing the original Greek text of the New Testament with the later Vulgate translation into Latin.

Drawing on work carried out earlier by the Italian humanist Lorenzo Valla, Erasmus showed that the Vulgate translation of several major New Testament texts could not be justified. As a number of medieval church practices and beliefs were based upon these texts, Erasmus's allegations were viewed with consternation by many conservative Catholics (who wanted to retain these practices and beliefs) and with equally great delight by the reformers (who wanted to eliminate them). Three classic examples of translation errors will indicate the relevance of Erasmus's biblical scholarship.

1 Much medieval theology justified the inclusion of matrimony in the list of sacraments on the basis of a New Testament text which – at least, in the Vulgate translation – spoke of marriage being a *sacramentum* (Ephesians 5: 31–2). Erasmus pointed out that the Greek word (*mysterion*), here translated as "sacrament," simply meant "mystery." There was no reference whatsoever to marriage being a sacrament. One of the classic proof texts used by medieval theologians to justify the inclusion of matrimony in the list of sacraments was thus rendered virtually useless.

41

2 The Vulgate translated the opening words of Jesus's ministry (Matthew 4: 17) as "*do penance*, for the kingdom of heaven is at hand." This translation suggested that the coming of the kingdom of heaven had a direct connection with the sacrament of penance. Erasmus, again following Valla, pointed out that the Greek should be translated as "*repent*, for the kingdom of heaven is at hand." In other words, where the Vulgate seemed to refer to an outward practice (the sacrament of penance), Erasmus insisted that the reference was to an inward psychological attitude – that of "being repentant." Once more, an important justification of the sacramental system of the medieval church was challenged.

3 According to the Vulgate, the angel Gabriel greeted Mary as "the one who is full of grace" (*gratia plena*) (Luke 1: 28), thus suggesting the image of a reservoir full of grace, which could be drawn upon at time of need. But, as Erasmus pointed out, the Greek simply meant "favored one," or "one who has found favor." Mary was one who had found God's favor, not necessarily one who could bestow it on others. Once more, an important feature of medieval theology seemed to be contradicted by humanist New Testament scholarship.

These developments undermined the credibility of the Vulgate translation and opened the way to theological revision on the basis of a better understanding of the biblical text. It also demonstrated the importance of biblical scholarship in relation to theology. Theology could not be permitted to base itself upon translation mistakes! The recognition of the vitally important role of biblical scholarship to Christian theology thus dates from the second decade of the sixteenth century. It also led to the theological concerns of the Reformation, to which we shall turn in the next chapter.

In the following chapter, we turn to explore the emergence of the movement widely known as "the Reformation," which is generally regarded as establishing the distinctive features of modern western Christianity, whether Roman Catholic or Protestant.

KEY NAMES, WORDS, AND PHRASES

By the end of this chapter, you will have encountered the following terms, some of which will recur during the work. Ensure that you are familiar with them!

ad fontes	Middle Ages
apologetics	Ockham's Razor
Byzantine	*ontological argument
*Five Ways	Renaissance
hesychasm	scholasticism
humanism	*theories of the atonement
iconoclastic	* "two powers of God"
immaculate conception	*voluntarism
medieval	Vulgate

Those terms marked with an asterisk (*) will be explored in greater detail later in this work.

QUESTIONS FOR CHAPTER 2

1 What was the language spoken by most western theologians during this period?

2 "Humanists were people who were interested in studying classical Rome." How helpful is this definition of the term?

3 What were the major themes of scholastic theology?

4 What issues were at stake in the iconoclastic controversy?

5 Why do you think there was such interest in the theology of the sacraments during the Middle Ages?

6 What is meant by the slogan *ad fontes*?

3

The Age of Reformation, c.1500–c.1750

Christian theology underwent major development and transformation during the Middle Ages. At its height, the period produced some highly significant contributions to Christian theology. Yet many scholars of this fascinating era detect a sense of tiredness, a loss of intellectual energy, during the fifteenth century. By this time, the Renaissance had consolidated its hold on many centers of theological education and scholarship, creating pressure for new theological paradigms and expressions. The scene was set for a major shift in the methods, concepts, and vocabulary of Christian theology in western Europe. Historically, this paradigm shift began to take place in the early sixteenth century. The movement in question was complex, yet is often referred to in a single phrase – the Reformation.

Introducing the Reformation

A major new period in western Christian theology opened in the sixteenth century. The styles of Christian theology associated with the medieval period gave way to new paradigms. The most significant development was the period of reformation within the western European church, as a result of movements which sought to return the western church to more biblical foundations in relation to its belief system, morality, and structures. As Christianity was virtually landlocked within Europe at this stage in its history, these developments were destined to have a major impact subsequently on the development of Christian theology globally through its expansion into new regions of the world.

The Reformation initially led to the formation of a cluster of Protestant churches in Europe, subsequently to the renewal and reformation of the Catholic church in the same region, and inevitably to conflict between Protestants and Catholics on the one hand, and between the various Protestant churches on the other. For historians, the importance of this period lies in the social and political ramifications of the Reformations; the birth of confessional Europe; the consolidation of the Protestant and Catholic Reformations (often referred to as the "Second Reformation" and "Catholic Reformation" respectively); the so-called radical Reformation; the intensification of religious, social, and sexual discipline on the part of secular and ecclesiastical authorities; and the origins of the Wars of Religion. Yet the period is of pivotal importance to the development of modern Christian theology, as will become clear in this chapter.

A particularly significant development which took place during the later part of this period is the expansion of western Christianity from its European context. The arrival of English Puritan communities in Massachusetts Bay and Spanish and Portuguese missionaries in South America opened the way to a further period of expansion of Christianity, which would become of increasing theological significance during the modern period.

Reformation – or Reformations?

The term "Reformation" is traditionally used by historians and theologians to refer to the western European movement, centering upon individuals such as Martin Luther, Huldrych Zwingli, and John Calvin, concerned with the moral, theological, and institutional reform of the Christian church in that region. More recent scholarship, noting the emergence of reforming movements throughout Europe at this time, has rightly suggested that we should speak of "reformations." The use of the plural form ensures that the significance of the mainline Protestant Reformation is safeguarded, while at the same time recognizing that this same era gave birth to the Catholic Reformation, the radical Reformation, and the movement now generally known as the "Second Reformation."

Initially, up to about 1525, the Reformation may be regarded as revolving around Martin Luther and the University of Wittenberg, in modern-day northeastern Germany. However, the movement also gained strength, independently at first, in the Swiss city of Zurich in the early 1520s. Through a number of complex developments, the Zurich Reformation gradually underwent a series of political and theological modifications, eventually coming to be associated primarily with the city of Geneva (now part of modern-day Switzerland, although then an independent city-state) and John Calvin.

The Reformation movement was complex and heterogeneous, and its agenda went far beyond the reform of the doctrine of the church. It addressed fundamental social, political, and economic issues, too complex to be discussed in any detail in this volume. The agenda of the Reformation varied from one country to another, with the theological issues which played major roles in one country (for example, Germany) often having relatively little impact elsewhere (for example, in England).

In response to the Protestant Reformation, the Catholic church moved to put its own house in order. Prevented from calling a council at an early date due to political instability in Europe resulting from tensions between France and Germany, the pope of the day (Paul III) was eventually able to convene the Council of Trent (1545). This set itself the task of clarifying Catholic thought and practice and defending them against its evangelical opponents.

The Reformation itself was a western European phenomenon, concentrated especially in the central and northern parts of this region, although Calvinism penetrated as far east as Hungary. However, the emigration of large numbers of individuals to North America, which becomes increasingly significant from 1600 onward, led to post-Reformation Protestant and Catholic theologies being exported to that region. Harvard College is an example of an early center of theological education in New England. The Society of Jesus also undertook extensive missionary operations in the Far East, including India, China, and Japan. Christian theology gradually began to expand beyond its western European base and become a global phenomenon – a development which received final consolidation in the modern period, to which we shall turn shortly. Our attention now turns to a consideration of the terminology linked with the Reformation and post-Reformation periods.

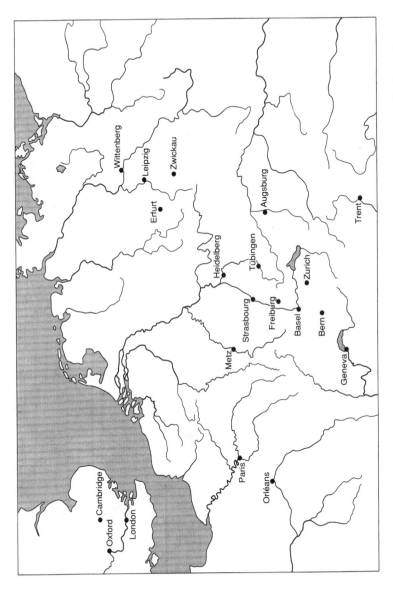

Map 3　Centers of theological and ecclesiastical activity at the times of the European Reformation

The Dynamics of Reformation

Precisely because the movement that is called "the Reformation" is so complex, it is used in a number of different senses. This point is sometimes emphasized by using the plural form "reformations," which draws attention to the undisputable historical fact that there were a number of reforming movements in western Europe at this time, often with different geographical locations and religious agendas. Six meanings of the term are encountered in the literature: the German reformation, which gave rise to Lutheranism; the Swiss reformation, which gave birth to the Reformed version of Christianity often referred to as "Calvinism"; the "radical Reformation," often still referred to as "Anabaptism"; the English Reformation, which gave rise to the distinctive form of Christianity often known as "Anglicanism"; the "Catholic Reformation" (sometimes referred to as the "Counter-Reformation"); and the "Second Reformation" within Protestantism. In its broadest sense, the term "Reformation" is used to refer to all these movements.

The term "Protestant" requires comment. It derives from the aftermath of the Diet of Speyer (February 1529), which voted to end the toleration of Lutheranism in Germany. In April of the same year, six German princes and 14 cities protested against this oppressive measure, defending freedom of conscience and the rights of religious minorities. The term "Protestant" derives from this protest. It is therefore not strictly correct to apply the term "Protestant" to individuals prior to April 1529, or to speak of events prior to that date as constituting "the Protestant Reformation." The term "evangelical" is often used in the literature to refer to the reforming factions at Wittenberg and elsewhere (e.g., in France and Switzerland) prior to this date. Although the word "Protestant" is often used to refer to this earlier period, this use is, strictly speaking, an anachronism.

The German Reformation – Lutheranism

The Lutheran Reformation is particularly associated with the German territories and the pervasive personal influence of one charismatic individual – Martin Luther. Luther was particularly concerned with the doctrine of justification, which formed the central point of his religious thought. The Lutheran Reformation was initially an academic movement, concerned primarily with reforming the teaching of theology at the University of Wittenberg. Wittenberg was an unimportant university, and the reforms introduced by Luther and his colleagues within the theology faculty attracted little attention. It was Luther's personal activities – such as his posting of the famous Ninety-Five Theses, protesting against selling indulgences to raise money for the rebuilding of St Peter's basilica in Rome (October 31, 1517) – which attracted considerable interest, and brought the ideas in circulation at Wittenberg to the attention of a wider audience.

Strictly speaking, the Lutheran Reformation only began in 1522, when Luther returned to Wittenberg from his enforced isolation in the Wartburg. Luther was condemned for "false doctrine" by the Diet of Worms in 1521. Fearing for his life, certain well-placed supporters removed him in secrecy to the castle known as the Wartburg in Eisenach, until the threat to his safety ceased. In his absence, Andreas Bodenstein von Karlstadt, one of Luther's academic colleagues at Wittenberg, began a program of reform at Wittenberg which seemed to degenerate into chaos. Convinced that he was needed if the Reformation was to survive Karlstadt's ineptitude, Luther emerged from his place of safety and returned to Wittenberg.

At this point, Luther's program of academic reform changed into a program of reform of church and society. No longer was Luther's forum of activity the university world of ideas; he now found himself regarded as the leader of a religious, social, and political reforming movement which seemed to some contemporary observers to open the way to a new social and religious order in Europe. In fact, Luther's program of reform was much more conservative than that associated with his Reformed colleagues, such as Huldrych Zwingli. Furthermore, it met with considerably less success than some anticipated. The movement remained obstinately tied to the German territories, and – Scandinavia apart – never gained the foreign power bases which seemed to be like so many ripe apples, ready to fall into its lap. Luther's understanding of the role of the "godly prince" (which effectively ensured that the monarch had control of the church) does not seem to have had the attraction which might have been expected, particularly in the light of the generally republican sentiments of Reformed thinkers such as Calvin. The case of England is particularly illuminating: here, as in the Low Countries, the Protestant theology which gained the ascendancy was Reformed rather than Lutheran.

The Swiss Reformation – the Reformed church

The origins of the Swiss Reformation, which brought the Reformed churches (such as the Presbyterians) into being, lie in developments within the Swiss Confederation (*Confederatio Helvetica* – hence the modern abbreviation "CH" for Switzerland) – in the early sixteenth century. Whereas the German Reformation had its origins primarily in an academic context, the Reformed church owed its origins to a series of attempts to reform the morals and worship of the church (but not necessarily its *doctrine*) according to a more biblical pattern. It must be emphasized that although Calvin gave this style of Reformation its definitive form, its origins are to be traced back to earlier reformers, such as Huldrych Zwingli and Heinrich Bullinger, based in the leading Swiss city of Zurich.

Although most of the early Reformed theologians, such as Zwingli, had an academic background, their reforming programs were not academic in nature. They were directed toward the church as they found it in Swiss cities such as Zurich, Berne, and Basel. Whereas Luther was convinced that the doctrine of justification was of central significance to his program of social and religious reform, the early Reformed thinkers had relatively little interest in doctrine, let alone one specific doctrine. Their reforming program was institutional, social, and ethical, in many ways similar to the demands for reform emanating from the humanist movement.

The consolidation of the Reformed church is generally thought to begin with the stabilization of the Zurich Reformation after Zwingli's death in battle (1531) under his successor, Heinrich Bullinger, and to end with the emergence of Geneva as its power base, and John Calvin as its leading spokesman, in the 1550s. The gradual shift in power within the Reformed church (initially from Zurich to Berne, and subsequently from Berne to Geneva) took place over the period 1520–60, eventually establishing the city of Geneva, its political system (republicanism), and its religious thinkers (initially Calvin, and after his death Theodore Beza) as predominant within the Reformed church. This development was consolidated through the establishment of the Genevan Academy (founded in 1559), at which Reformed pastors were trained. Although Geneva became part of Switzerland in 1815, in the aftermath of the Napoleonic wars, it was an independent city at the time of the Reformation. This means that the term

"Swiss reformation" is being used slightly loosely and anachronistically at this point.

The term "Calvinism" is often used to refer to the religious ideas of the Reformed church. Although still widespread in the literature relating to the Reformation, this practice is now generally discouraged. It is becoming increasingly clear that later sixteenth-century Reformed theology draws on sources other than the ideas of Calvin himself. To refer to later sixteenth- and seventeenth-century Reformed thought as "Calvinist" implies that it is essentially the thought of Calvin – and it is now generally agreed that Calvin's ideas were modified subtly by his successors. The term "Reformed" is now preferred, whether to refer to those churches (mainly in Switzerland, the Low Countries, and Germany) or religious thinkers (such as Theodore Beza, William Perkins, and John Owen) that based themselves upon Calvin's celebrated religious textbook, *The Institutes of the Christian Religion*, or church documents (such as the famous *Heidelberg Catechism*) based upon it.

The Radical Reformation – Anabaptism

The term "Anabaptist" literally means "rebaptizer," and refers to what was perhaps the most distinctive aspect of Anabaptist practice: the insistence that only those who had made a personal, public profession of faith should be baptized. Anabaptism seems to have first arisen around Zurich, in the aftermath of Zwingli's reforms within the city in the early 1520s. It centered on a group of individuals (among whom we may note Conrad Grebel) who argued that Zwingli was not being faithful to his own reforming principles. He preached one thing, and practiced another. Although Zwingli professed faithfulness to the *sola scriptura*, "by Scripture alone," principle, Grebel argued that he retained a number of practices – including infant bap-

tism, the close link between church and magistracy, and the participation of Christians in warfare – which were not sanctioned or ordained by Scripture. In the hands of such thinkers as Grebel, the *sola scriptura* principle would be radicalized; reformed Christians would believe and practice only those things explicitly taught in Scripture. Zwingli was alarmed by this, seeing it as a destabilizing development which threatened to cut off the Reformed church at Zurich from its historical roots and its continuity with the Christian tradition of the past.

A number of common elements can be discerned within the various strands of the Anabaptist movement: a general distrust of external authority; the rejection of infant baptism in favor of the baptism of adult believers; the common ownership of property; and an emphasis upon pacifism and nonresistance. To take up the third of these points: in 1527, the governments of Zurich, Berne, and St Gallen accused the Anabaptists of believing "that no true Christian can either give or receive interest or income on a sum of capital; that all temporal goods are free and common, and that all can have full property rights to them." It is for this reason that Anabaptism is often referred to as the "left wing of the Reformation" (Roland H. Bainton) or the "radical Reformation" (George Hunston Williams). For Williams, the "radical Reformation" was to be contrasted with the "magisterial Reformation," which he broadly identified with the Lutheran and Reformed movements. These terms are increasingly being accepted within Reformation scholarship, and you are likely to encounter them in your reading of more recent studies of the movement.

The English Reformation – Anglicanism

The English reformation took a somewhat different direction than its continental counterpart. Although there was at least some degree of popular pressure for a reform within the church, the leading force for reform was Henry VIII, who ascended the throne in 1509. In 1527, Henry took the first steps to dissolve his marriage to Catherine of Aragon. This decision resulted from Henry's desire to ensure the succession to the English throne. The only child of this marriage, Mary Tudor, was female; Henry wanted a male heir. The pope refused to dissolve or annul the marriage.

It is quite improper to suggest that the English reformation resulted from the pope's refusal to grant Henry his divorce. Nevertheless, it was a factor. Henry gradually appears to have shifted towards a policy which involved the replacement of papal authority in England with his own authority. The creation of an English national church was part of this vision. Henry seems not to have been particularly interested in matters of doctrine or theology, preferring to concentrate upon the practicalities of religious and political power. His decision to appoint Thomas Cranmer (1489–1556) as Archbishop of Canterbury led to at least some Protestant influences being brought to bear on the English church.

When Henry died in 1547, he was succeeded by his son, Edward VI. Edward was a minor on his accession; as a result, real power was exercised by his advisors, who were generally of a strongly Protestant persuasion. Cranmer, who remained in office as archbishop during Edward's reign, was able to bring in noticeably Protestant forms of public worship, and encouraged leading Protestant thinkers (such as Martin Bucer and Peter Martyr Vermigli) to settle in England, and give theological direction to the Reformation. However, Edward died in 1553, leaving the nation in a state of religious flux.

Edward was succeeded by Mary Tudor, who was strongly Catholic in sympathy. She set in motion a series of measures which suppressed Protestantism, and restored Catholicism. Some of the measures were deeply unpopular, most notably the public burning of Thomas Cranmer at Oxford in 1556. Cranmer was replaced as Archbishop of Canterbury by Reginald Pole, a moderate Catholic. At the time of Mary's death in 1558, Catholicism had not yet been entirely re-established. When Elizabeth I succeeded to the throne, it was not entirely clear what direction her religious policies might take. In the event, Elizabeth pursued a complex policy, which seems to have been aimed at appeasing both Protestants and Catholics, while allowing the Queen to have supreme authority in matters of religion. What is usually referred to as "the Elizabethan Settlement" (1558–59) established the national English church as a reformed episcopal church, having broadly Protestant articles of faith with a more Catholic liturgy. Nobody was really entirely satisfied with the outcome, which was widely seen as a compromise; however, it enabled England to emerge from a period of religious tension, and avoid the serious religious conflicts which were raging elsewhere in Europe at the time.

The Catholic Reformation

This term is often used to refer to the revival within Roman Catholicism in the period following the opening of the Council of Trent (1545). In older scholarly works, the movement is often designated the "Counter-Reformation": as the term suggests, the Roman Catholic church developed means of combating the Protestant Reformation, in order to limit its influence. It is, however, becoming increasingly clear that the Roman Catholic Church countered the Reformation partly by reforming itself from within, in order to remove the grounds of Protestant criticism. In this sense, the movement was a reformation of the Roman Catholic Church, as much as it was a reaction against the Protestant Reformation.

The same concerns underlying the Protestant Reformation in northern Europe were channeled into the renewal of the Catholic church, particularly in Spain and Italy. The Council of Trent, the foremost component of the Catholic Reformation, clarified Catholic teaching on a number of confusing matters, and introduced much-needed reforms in relation to the conduct of the clergy, ecclesiastical discipline, religious education, and missionary activity. The movement for reform within the church was greatly stimulated by the reformation of many of the older religious orders, and the establishment of new orders (such as the Jesuits). The more specifically theological aspects of the Catholic Reformation will be considered in relation to its teachings on Scripture and tradition, justification by faith, and the sacraments. As a result of the Catholic Reformation, many of the abuses which originally lay behind the demands for reform – whether these came from humanists or Protestants – were removed.

The Second Reformation – Confessionalization

The period now generally known as the "Second Reformation" attempted to consolidate the insights and achievements of the initial phase of Protestantism. The insights of the reformers were codified and consolidated through the development of a series of systematic presentations of Christian theology. This process is often referred to as "confessionalization," meaning the emergence of forms of Christianity which defined themselves with reference to "Confessions of Faith," such as the Augsburg Confession (1530). As Protestantism grew in strength, tensions between different Protestant groups – above all, Lutheran and Reformed churches – became of increasing

significance, eventually rivaling the older tension between Protestantism and Catholicism.

This can be seen within both Lutheran and Reformed theology. In what follows, we shall focus on the situation within the Reformed church, which is especially illuminating. In the period after Calvin's death a new concern for method – that is, the systematic organization and coherent deduction of ideas – gained momentum. Reformed theologians found themselves having to defend their ideas against both Lutheran and Roman Catholic opponents. Aristotelianism, regarded with a certain degree of suspicion by Calvin, was now seized upon as an ally. It became increasingly important to demonstrate the internal consistency and coherence of Calvinism. As a result, many Calvinist writers turned to Aristotle, in the hope that his writings on method would offer hints as to how their theology might be placed upon a firmer rational foundation.

To appreciate why these developments took place, we need to reflect on the political situation in Europe, especially Germany, in the later sixteenth century. In the 1550s, Lutheranism and Roman Catholicism were well established in different regions of Germany. A religious stalemate had developed, in which further expansion into Roman Catholic regions by Lutheranism was no longer possible. Lutheran writers therefore concentrated upon defending Lutheranism at the academic level, by demonstrating its internal consistency and faithfulness to Scripture. They believed that by showing Lutheranism to be intellectually respectable, they might make it attractive to Roman Catholics, disillusioned with their own system of beliefs.

But this was not to be the case. Roman Catholic writers responded with increasingly sophisticated works of systematic theology, drawing on the writings of Thomas Aquinas. The Society of Jesus (founded in 1534) rapidly established itself as a leading intellectual force within the Roman Catholic church. Its leading writers, such as Roberto Bellarmine and Francisco de Suarez, made major contributions to the intellectual defense of Roman Catholicism.

The situation in Germany became even more complicated during the 1560s and 1570s, as Calvinism began to make major inroads into previously Lutheran territory. Three major Christian denominations were now firmly established in the same area: Lutheranism, Calvinism, and Roman Catholicism. All three were under considerable pressure to identify themselves. Lutherans were obliged to explain how they differed from Calvinists on the one hand, and Roman Catholics on the other. Doctrine proved the most reliable way of identifying and explaining these differences: "We believe this, but they believe that." The period 1559–1622, characterized by its new emphasis upon doctrine, is generally referred to as the "period of orthodoxy." A new form of scholasticism began to develop within both Protestant and Roman Catholic theological circles, as both sought to demonstrate the rationality and sophistication of their systems.

Lutheranism and Calvinism were, in many respects, very similar. They both claimed to be evangelical and rejected more or less the same central aspects of medieval Catholicism. But they needed to be distinguished. On most points of doctrine, Lutherans and Calvinists were in broad agreement. Yet there was one matter upon which they were radically divided: the doctrine of predestination. The emphasis placed upon the doctrine of predestination by Calvinists in the period 1559–1662 partly reflects the fact that this doctrine most sharply distinguished them from their Lutheran colleagues.

The following two developments are of especial importance during this period.

A new concern for theological method

Reformers such as Luther and Calvin had relatively little interest in questions of method. For them, theology was primarily concerned with the exposition of Scripture. Indeed, Calvin's *Institutes* may be regarded as a work of "biblical theology," bringing together the basic ideas of Scripture into an orderly presentation. However, in the writings of Theodore Beza, Calvin's successor as director of the Genevan Academy (a training institute for Calvinist pastors throughout Europe), there can be seen a new concern for questions of method, as noted above. The logical arrangement of material, and its grounding in first principles, comes to assume paramount importance. The impact of this development is perhaps most obvious in the way in which Beza handled the doctrine of predestination, to be noted later.

The development of works of systematic theology

The rise of scholasticism within Lutheran, Calvinist, and Roman Catholic theological circles led to the appearance of vast works of systematic theology, comparable in many ways to Thomas Aquinas's *Summa Theologiae*. These works aimed to present sophisticated and comprehensive accounts of Christian theology, demonstrating the strengths of their positions and the weaknesses of those of their opponents.

Post-Reformation Movements

The Reformations, both Protestant and Catholic, were followed by a period of theological consolidation within both movements. Within Protestantism, both Lutheran and Reformed (or "Calvinist"), the period known as "Orthodoxy" opened up, characterized by its emphasis on doctrinal norms and definitions. Although sympathetic to this doctrinal trend, Puritanism placed considerably greater emphasis on spiritual and pastoral application. Pietism, in contrast, was hostile to this emphasis on doctrine, feeling that the stress on doctrinal orthodoxy obscured the need for a "living faith" on the part of believers. Within post-Tridentine Roman Catholicism (i.e., after the Council of Trent), increasing emphasis came to be placed on the continuity of the Catholic tradition, with Protestantism being viewed as innovative, and hence heterodox.

The consolidation of Roman Catholicism

The Council of Trent (1545–63) represented the definitive response of the Catholic church to the Reformation. The main achievements of the Council may be summarized as follows. First, the Council remedied the problems within the church which had contributed in no small way to the emergence of the Reformation in the first place. Measures were taken to end corruption and abuse within the church. Second, the Council set out the main lines of Catholic teaching on certain central areas of the Christian faith which had become controversial as a result of the Reformation – such as the relation between Scripture and tradition, the doctrine of justification, and the nature and role of the sacraments. (It should be noted that Trent did not address issues such as Christology or the doctrine of the Trinity, precisely because these were not the subject of debate with its Protestant opponents.) As a result, Roman Catholicism was now well prepared to meet the challenges of its Protestant opponents. The final decades of the sixteenth century saw the emergence of a confident, sustained, and significant critique of Protestantism from within the Catholic church.

One of the clearest signs of this new confidence can be seen in Catholic patristic scholarship. The Protestant appeal to the patristic period was initially so effective that some Catholic writers of the middle of the sixteenth century seem to have thought that patristic writers such as Augustine were actually proto-Protestants. However, the final third of the century saw increasing confidence among Roman Catholic writers concerning the continuity between the patristic writers and themselves. The most important work to establish this continuity was Marguerin de la Bigne's *Bibliotheca Patrum* ("Library of the Fathers"), whose eight folio volumes appeared in 1575. This was followed up by major contributions from writers such as Antoine Arnauld and Pierre Nicole.

This new confidence in the continuity of the Catholic tradition led to increasing emphasis being placed upon the constancy of Catholic teaching. The most noted writer to develop this emphasis was Jacques Benigne Bossuet (1627–1704), whose *Histoire des variations des églises protestantes* ("History of the Variations of the Protestant Churches") became a major weapon in the debates between Roman Catholics and Protestants. According to Bossuet, the teaching of the church remained the same down the ages. Protestants had departed from this teaching, either by introducing innovations or by denying some of its central elements. They had therefore forfeited their right to be considered orthodox. The apostles had handed down their successors a fixed deposit of truth, which had to be maintained from one generation to another.

The teaching of the church is always the same. [...] The gospel is never different from what it was earlier. Therefore if anyone at any time should say that the faith includes something which was not said to be "of the faith" yesterday, it is *heterodoxy*, which is any teaching different from *orthodoxy*. There is no difficulty in recognizing false teaching, or argument about it: it is recognized at once, whenever it appears, simply because it is new.

The slogan *semper eadem* ("always the same") thus became a highly significant element of Catholic polemics against Protestantism. For Bossuet, Protestantism was easily shown to be an innovation – and hence heterodox for that very reason.

Puritanism

One of the most important styles of theology associated with the English-speaking world emerged in late sixteenth-century England. Puritanism is probably best understood as a version of Reformed orthodoxy which laid particular emphasis on the experiential and pastoral aspects of faith. The writings of the leading Puritan theologians William Perkins (1558–1602), William Ames (1576–1633), and John Owen (1618–83) are clearly heavily influenced by Theodore Beza, particularly in relation to their teaching on the extent of the death of Christ, and the divine sovereignty in providence and election.

In recent years, particular scholarly attention has focused on the pastoral theology of Puritanism. Early seventeenth-century figures such as Laurence Chaderton, John Dod, and Arthur Hildersam were concerned to bring theology to focus on pastoral issues. The Puritan pastoral tradition is widely regarded as having reached its zenith in the ministry and writings of Richard Baxter (1615–91). Baxter's reputation rests in part on his massive *Christian Directory* (1673), whose four parts set out a vision of theology actualized in everyday Christian life. However, his most celebrated work of pastoral theology remains the *Reformed Pastor* (1656), which addresses ministerial issues from a Puritan perspective.

Although Puritanism was a major theological and political force in early seventeenth-century England, its most significant development took place in the New World. The repressive religious policies of King Charles I forced many Puritans to leave England, and settle on the eastern coastal regions of North America. As a result, Puritanism became a major shaping force in North American Christianity during the seventeenth century. The most significant American Puritan theologian was Jonathan Edwards (1703–58), who combined a Puritan emphasis upon divine sovereignty with a willingness to engage with the new questions being raised through the rise of a rational worldview. Although Edwards was much in demand as a spiritual director, especially in the aftermath of the eighteenth-century "Great Awakening" (in which he played a prominent, and probably decisive, role), his theology found its practical expression particularly in his ethics. His sermon series on 1 Corinthians 13 was published in 1746 as *Charity and its Fruits*.

In some respects, particularly in relation to the issue of Christian experience, Puritanism shows affinities with Pietism, to which we may now turn.

Pietism

As Orthodoxy became increasingly influential within mainstream Protestantism, so its potential defects and weaknesses became clear. At its best, orthodoxy was concerned with the rational defense of Christian truth claims, and a passionate concern for doctrinal correctness. Yet, too often, this came across as an academic preoccupation with logical niceties, rather than a concern for relating theology to the issues of everyday life. The term "Pietism" derives from the Latin word *pietas* (best translated as "piety" or "godliness"), and was initially a derogatory term used by the movement's opponents to describe its emphasis upon the importance of Christian doctrine for everyday Christian life.

The Pietist movement is usually regarded as having been inaugurated with the publication of Philip Jakob Spener's *Pia desideria* ("Pious Wishes," 1675). In this work Spener lamented the state of the German Lutheran church in the aftermath of the Thirty Years War (1618–48), and set out proposals for the revitalization of the church of his day. Chief among these was a new emphasis upon personal Bible study. The proposals were treated with derision by academic theologians; nevertheless, they were to prove influential in German church circles, reflecting growing disillusionment and impatience with the sterility of orthodoxy in the face of the shocking social conditions endured during the war. For Pietism, a reformation of doctrine must always be accompanied by reformation of life.

Pietism developed in a number of different directions, especially in England and Germany. Among the representatives of the movement, two in particular should be noted.

1 *Nikolaus Ludwig Graf von Zinzendorf* (1700–60) founded the Pietist community generally known as the "Herrnhuter," named after the German village of Herrnhut. Alienated from what he regarded as the arid rationalism and barren orthodoxy of his time, Zinzendorf stressed the importance of a "religion of the heart," based on an intimate and personal relationship between Christ and the believer. A new emphasis was placed upon the role of "feeling" (as opposed to reason or doctrinal orthodoxy) within the Christian life, which may be regarded as laying the foundations of Romanticism in later German religious thought. Zinzendorf's emphasis upon a personally appropriated faith finds expression in the slogan "a living faith," which

he opposed to the dead credal assent of Protestant orthodoxy. These ideas would be developed in one direction by F. D. E. Schleiermacher, and in another by John Wesley, who may be regarded as introducing Pietism to England.

2 *John Wesley* (1703–91) founded the Methodist movement within the Church of England, which subsequently gave birth to Methodism as a denomination in its own right. Convinced that he "lacked the faith whereby alone we are saved," Wesley discovered the need for a "living faith" and the role of experience in the Christian life through his conversion experience at a meeting in Aldersgate Street in London in May 1738, in which he felt his heart to be "strangely warmed." Wesley's emphasis upon the experiential side of Christian faith, which contrasted sharply with the dullness of contemporary English Deism, led to a major religious revival in England.

Despite their differences, the various branches of Pietism succeeded in making Christian faith relevant to the experiential world of ordinary believers. The movement may be regarded as a reaction against a one-sided emphasis upon doctrinal orthodoxy, in favor of a faith which relates to the deepest aspects of human nature.

Key Theologians

The Reformation era is widely regarded as one of the most creative in the history of Christian theology. Three theologians are usually singled out as being of particular significance: Martin Luther, John Calvin, and Huldrych Zwingli. Of these, the first two are of especial importance. Although Zwingli is a major figure in his own right, he has been over-shadowed by the creative talent and greater theological impact of Luther and Calvin.

Martin Luther (1483–1546)

Martin Luther was educated at the University of Erfurt, initially studying within the faculty of arts, before beginning the study of theology at the local Augustinian monastery. He gained an appointment as professor of biblical studies at the University of Wittenberg in 1512, and lectured on the Psalms (1513–15), Romans (1515–16), Galatians (1516–17), and Hebrews (1517–18). During this period, Luther's theology can be seen to have gone through a series of developments, especially in relation to the doctrine of justification. His close engagement with biblical texts during this period appears to have led him to become increasingly dissatisfied with the prevailing theological views of the era (which was dominated by the so-called "modern way" or *via moderna*) on the subject. This school of thought emphasized the human need to make an appropriate response to divine grace in order to benefit from it.

Luther first came to public attention in 1517, through the publication of his Ninety-Five Theses on Indulgences. This was followed by the Leipzig Disputation (June–July 1519), in which Luther established a reputation as a radical critic of scholasticism. In 1520 he published three treatises which consolidated his growing reputation as a theological reformer. In the *Appeal to the Christian Nobility of the German Nation* Luther argued passionately for the need for reform of the church. In both its doctrine and its practices, the church of the early sixteenth century had cast itself adrift from the New Testament. His pithy and witty German gave added popular appeal to some intensely serious theological ideas.

Encouraged by the remarkable success of this work, Luther followed it up with *The Babylonian Captivity of the Christian Church*. In this powerful piece of writing, Luther argued that the gospel had become captive to the institutional church. The medieval church, he argued, had imprisoned the gospel in a complex system of priests and sacraments. The church had become the master of the gospel, where it should be its servant. This point was further developed in *The Liberty of a Christian*, in which Luther explored the implications of the doctrine of justification by faith for the Christian life.

Luther was perhaps the most creative of the reformers. Yet his theological impact does not rest upon any major work of theology. Most of Luther's writings were produced in response to some controversy. Only his two Catechisms (1529) can really be thought of as systematic presentations of the basic ideas of the Christian faith. Their largely pastoral role probably disqualifies them from being taken seriously as works of academic theology. Nevertheless, aspects of Luther's theology have had a deep impact upon western Christian thought. For example, his "theology of the cross," set out briefly in a document of 1518 (the *Heidelberg Disputation)*, has had a considerable impact upon twentieth-century theology, as works such as Jürgen Moltmann's *Crucified God* indicate (see p. 213).

Huldrych Zwingli (1484–1531)

The Swiss reformer Huldrych Zwingli was educated at the universities of Vienna and Basel, before taking up parish duties in eastern Switzerland. It is clear that he took a keen interest in the agenda of Christian humanism, especially the writings of Erasmus, and became committed to belief in the need to reform the church of his day. In 1519 he took up a pastoral position in the city of Zurich, where he used the pulpit of the Great Minster, the chief church within the city, to propagate a program of reform. Initially, this program was primarily concerned with the reformation of the morals of the church. However, it soon extended to include criticism of the existing theology of the church, especially its sacramental theology. The term "Zwinglian" is used especially to refer to the belief, associated with Zwingli, that Christ is not present at the Eucharist, which is best seen as a memorial of Christ's death.

Zwingli was of major importance in relation to the early propagation of the Reformation, especially in eastern Switzerland. However, he never achieved the same impact as Luther or Calvin, lacking the creativity of the former and the systematic approach of the latter. The reader will encounter considerable variation in the spelling of Zwingli's forename, with "Ulrich" and "Huldreich" often being used in preference to "Huldrych."

John Calvin (1509–64)

Calvin was born in Noyon, northeast of Paris, in 1509. Educated at the scholasticism-dominated University of Paris, he subsequently moved to the more humanist University of Orléans, at which he studied civil law. Although initially inclined to a career of scholarship, he underwent a conversion experience in his mid-twenties, which led to his becoming increasingly associated with reforming movements in Paris, and eventually being forced into exile in Basel. Eventually, he settled in the city of Geneva, which had achieved its independence, and converted to Protestantism in 1535. By the time of his death in 1564, Calvin had made Geneva the center of an international movement, which came to bear his name. Calvinism is still one of the most potent and significant intellectual movements in human history.

The second generation of reformers were far more aware of the need for works of systematic theology than the first. Calvin, the major figure of the second period of the Reformation, saw the need for a work which would set out clearly the basic ideas of evangelical theology, justifying them on the basis of Scripture and defending them in the face of Catholic criticism. In 1536 he published a small work entitled *Institutes of the Christian Religion*, a mere six chapters in length. For the next quarter of a century Calvin worked away at this, adding extra chapters and rearranging the material. By the time of its final edition (1559), the work had 80 chapters and was divided into four books. By then, it was firmly established as one of the most important religious works of the sixteenth century.

Teresa of Avila (1515–82)

Most of the writers noted in this chapter are systematic theologians. Teresa of Avila represents a quite different approach to theology, which needs to be noted and respected – namely, "mystical theology" or spirituality. For Teresa, theology is about a transformed personal relationship with God, which cannot adequately be expressed in human words. Teresa was a Carmelite, part of the great revival of spirituality which took place in Spain during the second half of the sixteenth century. Her most famous work is *The Interior Castle of the Soul*, in which she uses a fundamentally trinitarian theological framework to explore how God illuminates and transforms the life of the believer. Growth in prayer enables the individual believer to enter into deeper intimacy with God, using the image of a progressive journey through the apartments (or mansions) of the castle from the outermost to the luminous center. Teresa was declared to be a "doctor of the church" by Pope Paul VI in 1970 – the first woman to be accorded this honor.

Theodore Beza (1519–1605)

Beza (also known by his French name "Théodore de Bèze), a noted Calvinist writer, served as professor of theology at the Genevan Academy from 1559 to 1599. The three volumes of his *Tractationes theologicae* ("Theological Treatises," 1570–82) present a rationally coherent account of the main elements of Reformed theology, using Aristotelian logic. The result is a tightly argued and rationally defensible account of Calvin's theology, in which some of the unresolved tensions of that theology (chiefly relating to the doctrines of predestination and atonement) are clarified. Some writers have suggested that Beza's concern for logical clarity leads him to misrepresent Calvin at a number of critical points; others have argued that Beza merely streamlined Calvin's theology, tidying up some loose ends.

Johann Gerhard (1582–1637)

Gerhard was perhaps the most important Lutheran Orthodox theologian. He was appointed professor of theology at the University of Jena in 1616, where he remained for the rest of his teaching career. Gerhard recognized the need for a systematic presentation of Lutheran theology in the face of intense Calvinist opposition. The basic form of Lutheran works of systematic theology had been laid down in 1521, when Philip Melanchthon published the first edition of his *Loci communes* ("Common places"), in which subjects were treated topically, rather than systematically. Gerhard continued this tradition, but felt able to draw increasingly upon Aristotelian works of logic. His *Loci communes theologici* ("Theological Commonplaces," 1610–22) remained a classic of Lutheran theology for many years.

Roberto Bellarmine (1542–1621)

Of the theologians to achieve eminence during the golden period of Catholic theology after the Council of Trent, the most important is probably Roberto Bellarmine, who entered the Society of Jesus in 1560, and subsequently became professor of controversial theology at Rome in 1576. He remained in this position until 1599, when he became a cardinal. His most significant work is generally regarded to be the *Disputationes de Controversiis Christianae Fidei* ("Disputations concerning the controversies of the Christian faith," 1586–93), in which he argued forcibly for the rationality of Catholic theology against its Protestant (both Lutheran and Calvinist) critics.

Jonathan Edwards (1703–58)

It is universally agreed that Jonathan Edwards is America's first great theologian. Although there are some important dissenting voices, many would also argue that he remains America's greatest Christian theologian. Edwards was born at East Windsor, Connecticut, on October 5, 1703. His father was a local pastor, under whose ministry a series of revivals would take place in the 1720s. In September 1716 Edwards entered Yale College, New Haven (now Yale University), where he later served as tutor from 1724 to 1726. When he was around 17 years of age, Edwards underwent a conversion experience. As he read 1 Timothy 1:17, he was overwhelmed by a sense of God's greatness and glory. "As I read the words," he wrote later in his personal journal, "there came into my soul, and it was, as it were, diffused through it, a sense of the glory of the divine Being; a new sense quite different from anything I ever experienced before."

Edwards played a major role in the "Great Awakening," which began in the winter of 1734–5, probably the most significant revivalist movement of its age. In 1757 Edwards was invited to become president of the College of New Jersey, Princeton (now Princeton University). Following an unsuccessful inoculation against smallpox, he died at Princeton on March 22, 1758.

Edwards is remembered as a remarkable theologian. He can be seen as a Puritan writer, giving intellectual and spiritual stamina to a movement often noted for its anti-intellectualism and moral excesses. Perhaps more importantly, Edwards represents a theologian who was aware of the challenges to traditional Christian theology that were emerging from the Enlightenment, and had the foresight and theological acumen to provide an alternative way of conceptualizing and proclaiming the Christian faith within a rationalist culture.

Key Theological Developments

The Reformation was a complex movement with a very broad agenda. The debates of the sixteenth century, which extended into the seventeenth century and beyond, centered in part upon the sources of Christian theology; in part upon the doctrines which resulted from the application of those sources. We shall consider these matters individually.

The sources of theology

The mainstream Reformation was concerned not with establishing a new Christian tradition, but with the renewal and correction of an existing tradition. Arguing that Christian theology was ultimately grounded in Scripture, reformers such as Luther and Calvin argued for the need to return to Scripture as the primary and critical source of Christian theology. The slogan "by Scripture alone" (*sola scriptura*) became characteristic of the Protestant reformers, expressing their basic belief that Scripture was the sole necessary and sufficient source of Christian theology. However, as we shall see later (pp. 138–9), this did not mean that they denied the importance of tradition.

This new emphasis upon Scripture had a number of direct consequences, of which the following are of especial importance:

1   Beliefs which could not be demonstrated to be grounded in Scripture were either to be rejected, or to be declared as binding on no one. For example, the reformers had little time for the doctrine of the immaculate conception of Mary (that is, the belief that Mary, as the mother of Jesus, was conceived without any taint from sin). They regarded this as lacking any biblical warrant, and thus discarded it.
2   A new emphasis came to be placed upon the public status of Scripture within the church. The expository sermon, the biblical commentary, and works of biblical theology (such as Calvin's *Institutes*) came to be characteristic of the Reformation.

The Council of Trent, responding to these developments, insisted that Scripture and tradition were to be given equal weight in theological deliberations. Scripture needed to be interpreted reliably; the Protestants, for writers such as Bellarmine, had made it open to highly subjective individualist interpretations, which would be destructive of both church order and doctrine.

The doctrine of grace

The first period of the Reformation is dominated by the personal agenda of Martin Luther. Convinced that the church had lapsed into an unwitting Pelagianism, Luther proclaimed the doctrine of justification by faith to whomever would listen to him. The question "How can I find a gracious God?" and the slogan "by faith alone" (*sola fide*) resonated throughout much of western Europe, and attracted him a hearing among a substantial section of the church. The issues involved in this doctrine are complex, and will be discussed in detail at the appropriate point later in this volume (see pp. 371–80).

The doctrine of justification by faith is especially associated with the Lutheran Reformation. Calvin, while continuing to honor this doctrine, initiated a trend which became of increasing importance in later Reformed theology: the discussion of grace in relation to the doctrine of predestination, rather than justification. For Reformed theologians, the ultimate statement of the "grace of God" was not to be seen in the fact that God justified sinners; rather, it was to be seen in God's election of humanity without reference to their foreseen merits or achievements. The doctrine of "unconditional election" (see p. 383) came to be seen as a concise summary of the unmerited nature of grace.

The Council of Trent and later Catholic writers regarded such views as a distortion of the teachings of Augustine, and argued vigorously for a return to his ideas. They argued that the Protestant emphasis on justification by faith alone failed to do justice to the New Testament's emphasis on the importance of good works in the Christian life. In addition, they insisted that Protestants had misrepresented Augustine's teaching on what justification actually was, interpreting it to mean "being accounted as righteous," whereas the clear sense of his teaching was "to be made righteous."

The doctrine of the sacraments

By the 1520s the view had become well established within reforming circles that the sacraments were outward signs of the invisible grace of God. This forging of a link between the sacraments and the doctrine of justification (a development especially associated with Luther and his colleague at Wittenberg, Philip Melanchthon) led to a new interest in the theology of the sacraments. It was not long before this area of theology became the subject of considerable controversy, with the reformers disagreeing with their Catholic opponents over the number and nature of the sacraments, and Luther and Zwingli arguing furiously over whether Christ was really present at communion services (see pp. 439–40).

The Council of Trent reaffirmed the traditional teaching concerning the number and identity of the sacraments, while strongly defending the concept of "transubstantiation" against its Protestant critics, both Lutheran and Reformed.

The doctrine of the church

If the first generation of reformers were preoccupied with the question of grace, the second generation turned to address the question of the church. Having broken away from the mainstream of the Catholic church over the doctrine of grace, the reformers came under increasing pressure to develop a coherent theory of the church which would justify this break, and give a basis for the new evangelical churches springing up in the cities of western Europe. Where Luther is especially linked with the doctrine of grace, it is Martin Bucer and John Calvin who made the decisive contributions to the development of Protestant understandings of the church. Those understandings have since become increasingly significant in global Christianity, and will be considered in greater detail later in the present work (see pp. 396–401).

In response to such developments, the Council of Trent emphasized the historical and institutional importance of the church, arguing that Protestants had placed themselves outside its bounds. The church was a divinely ordained and divinely instituted society; salvation was not possible outside its boundaries.

Developments in Theological Literature

The Protestant Reformation of the sixteenth century led to significant developments in theological literature, reflecting the high profile of theological issues at the time. One of the most interesting aspects of the Protestant Reformation was its awareness of the need to communicate and defend its ideas. This led to several important genres of theological literature assuming a significant role at this time.

1 Catechisms: popular presentations of Christian faith, from a Reformation perspective, aimed particularly at educating children.
2 Confessions of faith: statements of the main theological affirmations of a grouping within the Reformation (Lutheran, Reformed, or Anabaptist), aimed at an adult audience.
3 Works of systematic theology, including Melanchthon's *Loci communes* and Calvin's *Institutes of the Christian Religion*, which offered a systematic analysis and defense of Lutheran or Reformed theology.

We shall consider each of these genres of theological literature in what follows.

The catechisms

Although what would now be agreed to be catechisms can be found in the medieval church, it is generally considered that the extensive use of catechisms is especially associated with the Reformation. A visitation of Lutheran churches in Saxony over the period 1528–9 showed that most pastors and just about every layperson were ignorant of basic Christian teachings. Luther was shocked by his findings, and decided to put in place measures to increase public knowledge of basic Christian teachings.

The first result of Luther's new concern in this area made its appearance in April 1529. Although Luther himself termed it a "German Catechism," it is now more generally known as the "Greater Catechism." The work provides a detailed analysis of the Ten Commandments, the Apostles' creed and the Lord's Prayer. These sections were followed by discussions of the two sacraments of the church – baptism and the "sacrament of the altar" (or Communion service). The work does not show Luther at his best. It draws upon earlier sermonical material, and was not written specifically for the purpose of catechizing. As a result, it failed to meet up to its goals.

This was followed in May 1529 by what is now known as the "Lesser Catechism." This work was written specifically for this purpose, and shows a lightness of touch, an ease of communication, and a general simplicity of expression which ensured that it was widely used and appreciated. The work was a remarkable success and was widely adopted within Lutheran institutions. Its question-and-answer format was ideally suited to learning by rote, and the work was widely adopted within the schools of the region. It is important to note that both Luther's 1529 catechisms were written in German, the language of the people. Luther avoided the use of Latin for this purpose, recognizing the severe limitations which the use of this scholarly language would have on the appeal and readership of the works.

To illustrate the approach Luther adopted, we may consider the following passage from the "Lesser Catechism." Note particularly the question-and-answer format, designed to facilitate both teaching and learning.

Q. What is baptism?
A. Baptism is not just water on its own, but it is water used according to God's command and linked with God's Word.
Q. What is this Word of God?
A. Our Lord Christ, as recorded in Matthew 28: 19, said, "Go therefore and make disciples of all nations, baptizing them in the name of the Father and of the Son and of the Holy Spirit."
Q. What gifts or benefits does baptism bring?
A. It brings about the forgiveness of sins, saves us from death and the devil, and grants eternal blessedness to all who believe, as the Word and promise of God declare.
Q. What is this Word and promise of God?
A. Our Lord Christ, as recorded in Mark 16: 16, said, "Anyone who believes and is baptized will be saved; but those who do not believe will be condemned."

The Reformed churches were not slow to appreciate the importance of this literary genre, and the educational advantages which it so clearly offered. After some experimentation, Calvin finally produced the "Geneva Catechism" in French (1542) and Latin (1545). This catechism was widely used within the Reformed constituency until 1563. It was at this point that the "Heidelberg Catechism" made its appearance. The origins of this major work lie in the growth of the Reformed church within Germany, particularly within the Palatinate. Elector Frederick III commissioned two Reformed theologians (Kaspar Olevianus and Zacharias Ursinus) to produce a catechism suitable for use in his churches. The result was a German-language catechism of 129 questions, which could be arranged in 52 blocks of material to permit regular teaching throughout the year.

The extensive Protestant use of catechisms, and the significant results which they achieved, led their Catholic opponents to develop the format. Earlier Catholic catechisms tended to avoid the question-and-answer format, and offered extensive discussions of points of theological importance. An excellent example of this may be found in Johann Dietenberger's 1537 catechism, which takes the form of a discussion of the Apostles' creed, the Lord's Prayer, the Ten Commandments, the "Hail Mary," and the seven sacraments. However, the superiority of the question-and-answer approach became obvious, and was incorporated into Peter Canisius's three catechisms, published over the period 1554–8. This work was published in Latin, as was the more substantial Tridentine Catechism of 1566. While its cumbersome format ensured that it was hardly ever used, the work's appearance in the aftermath of the Council of Trent may be regarded as an important recognition of the significance of the genre.

Confessions of faith

We have already noted how the Reformation placed considerable emphasis upon the authority of Scripture. Yet the Bible needed to be interpreted. As the controversy between the magisterial and radical reformers made clear, there were issues of interpretation that were both divisive and elusive. There was clearly a need for some form of "official" means of setting out the ideas of the Reformation, to avoid confusion. This role was played by the "Confessions of Faith." In view of the importance of these documents, we may consider their place within the thought of the Reformation.

The magisterial Reformation, while placing considerable emphasis upon the authority of Scripture, also recognized a role for the

Christian consensus of the past – an idea usually referred to as "Tradition 1" (see pp. 136–41). In general terms, Protestant theologians can be thought of as recognizing three levels or strata of authority.

1 *Scripture*. This was regarded by the magisterial Reformers as possessing supreme authority in matters of Christian belief and conduct.
2 *The creeds of Christendom*. These documents, such as the Apostles' creed and the Nicene creed, were regarded by the magisterial reformers as representing the consensus of the early church, and as being accurate and authoritative interpretations of Scripture. Although they were to be regarded as *derivative* or *secondary* in terms of their authority, they were seen as an important check against the individualism of the radical reformation (which generally declined to regard these creeds as having any authority). The authority of the creeds was recognized by both Protestants and Catholics, as well as by the various constituent elements within the mainline Reformation.
3 *Confessions of faith*. These documents were regarded as authoritative by specific groupings within the Reformation. Thus the Augsburg Confession (1530) was recognized by early Lutheran churches as possessing authority. Other groups within the Reformation did not, however, regard it in this way. Specific confessions of faith were, for example, drawn up by other groups within the Reformation. Some were linked with the Reformation in specific cities – for example, the First Confession of Basel (1534) and the Geneva Confession (1536).

The basic pattern within the Reformation was thus to acknowledge Scripture as possessing primary and universal authority; the creeds as having secondary and universal authority; and the confessions as having tertiary and local authority (in that such confessions were only regarded as binding by a denomination or church in a specific region). The development of the Reformed wing of the Reformation was complex, with the result that a number of confessions – each linked with a specific region – came to be influential. The following are of particular importance.

Date	Title	Geographical region
1559	Gallic Confession	France
1560	Scottish Confession	Scotland
1561	Belgic Confession	The Lowlands
1563	Thirty-nine Articles	England
1566	Second Helvetic Confession	Western Switzerland

Works of systematic theology

The need for a systematic presentation of the theology of the Reformation was obvious from an early stage. The first work to fill this gap had its origins within the Lutheran Reformation. Philip Melanchthon established the definitive pattern for Lutheran works of systematic theology in 1521, through the publication of his *Loci communes* ("Commonplaces"). In its first edition this work simply treated a number of subjects of obvious relevance to the Lutheran Reformation, including the important theme of justification by faith.

Gradually, however, polemical and educational considerations obliged Melanchthon to expand the work considerably. New issues needed to be addressed, and additional material had to be included to meet the growing demands of its readers. Melanchthon met this challenge in a surprisingly inadequate manner; he merely added additional material, regardless of the impression of lack of a unified structure this created. It soon became evident that this way of handling material was clumsy and disorganized, incapable of achieving the systematic analysis needed for the theological debates of the late sixteenth and seventeenth centuries. The greatest and last work of this kind is *Loci communes theologici* by Johann Gerard, professor at Jena, published in nine volumes (1610–22). It is for this reason that Melanchthon's approach to systematic theology ultimately lost out to the much more organized system of John Calvin, to which we now turn.

Calvin's *Institutes of the Christian Religion* had its origins within the Reformed wing of the Protestant Reformation. The first edition, published in March 1536, was modeled on Luther's "Lesser Catechism" (see pp. 60–1) of 1529. Both its structure and substance indicate the extent to which Calvin has drawn upon this major educational work of the early German Reformation. Its 516 small-format pages comprise six chapters, the first four of which are modeled on Luther's catechism. The second edition of the *Institutes* dates from Calvin's Strasbourg period, and was published in Latin in 1539. The most obvious and important difference in the volume is that of size: the new work is about three times as long as the first edition of 1536, with 17 chapters instead of six. Two opening chapters now deal with the knowledge of God and the knowledge of human nature. Additional material was added on the doctrine of the Trinity, the relation of the Old and New Testaments, penitence, justification by faith, the nature and relation of providence and predestination, and the nature of the Christian life. Although the work retained much material drawn from the earlier edition, it is evident that its character and

status have changed. It is no longer a catechism; it is well on the way to being a definitive statement of the nature of the Christian faith, inviting comparison with the *Summa Theologiae* of Thomas Aquinas.

The work underwent expansion and revision in later editions. The final edition of 1559 had 80 chapters – a vast expansion from the original six chapters of 1536. The material was now distributed among four "books," arranged as follows:

1 the knowledge of God the creator;
2 the knowledge of God the redeemer;
3 the manner of participation in the grace of Jesus Christ;
4 the external means or aids which God uses to bring us to Jesus Christ.

It is possible that Calvin had adapted the fourfold structure of the edition of 1543 to create the new division of material. An alternative explanation, however, is that he had noticed and adapted the fourfold division of material in the *Four Books of the Sentences* of Peter Lombard, a seminal medieval theologian to whom Calvin often refers. Was Calvin setting himself up as the Protestant successor to Peter Lombard, and his *Institutes* as the successor to his great theological textbook? We shall never know. What we do know is that the *Institutes* were now firmly established as the most influential theological work of the Protestant Reformation, eclipsing in importance the rival works of Luther, Melanchthon, and Zwingli.

Part of the process of theological consolidation and renewal within Catholicism after the Council of Trent was the production of numerous works of systematic theology. These took a wide variety of forms. The form of "loci" or theological topics, originally introduced by the Protestant writer Melanchthon, proved attractive to many Catholic writers. The Spanish

Dominican theologian Melchior Cano introduced it, noting its advantages both as a convenient way of presenting Catholic ideas, and also for combating Protestant ideas. Cano's *Loci theologici* was first published in 1563, three years after the author's death, and went into 26 editions: eight in Spain, nine in Italy, seven in Germany, and two in France. Numerous writers during the following century produced works using more or less the same format, such as Seraphimus Ractius (Razzi) (died 1613), and Petrus de Lorca (died 1606).

Most observers regard Catholic theology as being primarily concerned to refute Protestantism at this time, and single out Roberto Bellarmine for developing controversial theology to the point at which it virtually became a form of art. His most famous work is *Disputationes de Controversiis Christianae Fidei adversus hujus temporis hereticos* ("Disputations concerning the controversies of the Christian faith against the heretics of this age"), first published in 1586.

KEY NAMES, WORDS, AND PHRASES

By the end of this chapter you will have encountered the following terms, which will recur during the work. Ensure that you are familiar with them!

*Anabaptism	orthodoxy
Anglicanism	Pietism
*Calvinism	*predestination
Catholic Reformation	Protestant
confessionalization	Puritanism
evangelical	Reformed
Lutheranism	*sola scriptura*
Methodism	

Those terms marked with an asterisk (*) are discussed in more detail elsewhere in this work.

QUESTIONS FOR CHAPTER 3

1 What does the term "Reformation" mean?
2 Which Protestant writer of this period is especially associated with the doctrine of justification by faith alone?
3 How important was humanism to the origins and development of the Reformations?
4 Why did the Protestant reformers come to place such emphasis upon revising existing doctrines of the church?
5 What factors led to the development of (a) confessionalism and (b) Pietism?
6 Why did post-Tridentine Roman Catholic writers (i.e., writers dating from after the Council of Trent) place such an emphasis on continuity with the early church?

4

The Modern Period, c.1750–the Present

In this final historical section, we consider the development of Christian theology in the modern period. During this period, Christianity underwent significant transformation and expansion outside its traditional European homelands, while experiencing considerable difficulties and tensions within them. From 1700 onward, Christian theology moved away from a western European context to become a global phenomenon.

The colonization of North America by western Europeans, especially from Scandinavia, Germany, and England, led to the various schools of Protestant theology – Lutheran, Reformed, and Anabaptist – becoming firmly settled in a North American context. Jonathan Edwards (1703–58), closely linked with the religious revival generally known as the Great Awakening (c.1726–45), is unquestionably the most significant theologian to have operated in such a context. Later waves of immigration, especially from Ireland and Italy, led to Roman Catholic theology becoming of increasing significance.

The establishment of seminaries by various denominations (such as Princeton Theological Seminary by the Presbyterians) consolidated the importance of the United States of America as a leading center of Christian theological teaching and research. However, it was not until the middle of the twentieth century that America came to assume global significance in theological discussions; until that point, German and British theology tended to dominate, partly on account of the continuing immigration of European theologians into the United States. Such theologians, who had trained in European contexts, tended to maintain a European emphasis in their teaching and orientation.

Elsewhere in the world, expansion continued. The enormous impact of Christian missions in Australasia, India, the Far East, and sub-Saharan Africa led to Christian theological seminaries, high schools, and universities becoming established in these regions, and gradually divesting themselves of their western European roots. The development of "local theologies" has become an issue of increasing importance in such regions, particularly as the perceived "Eurocentrism" of much Christian theologizing has been subjected to considerable critical comment on the part of native writers.

This is especially the case in Latin America, where there appears to be a growing reaction against the Roman Catholicism exported to the region with the conquistadores. The rise of liberation theology (see pp. 90–1), with its characteristic emphasis upon the importance of praxis, the prioritization of the situation of the poor, and the orientation of theology toward political liberation, has proved incapable of staunching a severe loss of individuals from the Roman Catholic church. The chief beneficiaries of this trend appear to be evangelicals and charismatics (see pp. 80–2) in the region.

One of the most prominent features of western theology during the modern period has been the intellectual hegemony of German-language theology. The German-speaking lands of Europe, above all Germany and northern Switzerland, have long been the source of a rich and fertile theological tradition. Two leading figures of the Reformation, Martin Luther and Huldrych Zwingli, are witnesses to the importance of this tradition to the development of modern western theology. Since the Enlightenment, the prominence of the German-language tradition has become even more firmly established; a list of the leading theologians of the modern western tradition – including Karl Barth, Rudolf Bultmann, Jürgen Moltmann, Wolfhart Pannenberg, Karl Rahner, and Paul Tillich – has an unquestionably Germanic ring to it.

In recent years, however, this situation has changed. No new generation of German-language theologians of truly global significance has emerged to succeed writers such as Rudolf Bultmann, Jürgen Moltmann, Wolfhart Pannenberg, and Karl Rahner. Instead, there has been a steady increase in the significance of English-language theology, especially that originating from the United States of America. With the increasing role played by English as the *lingua franca* of the world (the parallel with Latin in the Middle Ages being of significance), it seems likely that this development will be consolidated, at least in the opening years of the new millennium.

Given the vast expansion and diversification of Christian theological writing, exploration,

and debate since about 1750, this survey chapter can do little more than note some important trends and developments. Limitations on space mean that a detailed engagement with everything that needs to be covered to gain a comprehensive overview of theology is quite impossible. We shall, however, try to gain something of a bird's-eye view of the contemporary theological landscape, even if we cannot fill in the fine detail that is needed for many purposes.

We begin by surveying some of the many cultural developments which shape the environment in which Christian theology has been done in recent centuries. This is followed by an exploration of some of the denominational distinctives of recent theological debate. Finally, we consider some of the schools of thought or movements which have emerged as important in this period.

Theology and Cultural Developments in the West

The movement which is now generally known as "the Enlightenment" ushered in a period of considerable uncertainty for Christianity in western Europe and north America. The trauma of the Reformation and the resulting Wars of Religion had barely subsided on the continent of Europe, before a new and more radical challenge to Christianity arose. If the sixteenth-century Reformation challenged the church to rethink its external forms and the manner in which it expressed its beliefs, the Enlightenment saw the intellectual credentials of Christianity itself (rather than any one of its specific forms) facing a major threat on a number of fronts. The growing emphasis upon the need to uncover the rational roots of religion had considerable negative implications for Christianity, as subsequent events were to prove.

A good point from which to begin is the movement generally known as "modernism," associated with the rise of the Enlightenment in eighteenth-century Europe.

Modernism: the new intellectual environment for theology

The idea of "modernity," like just about every other term used in this work, is difficult to define. What is characteristic of the "modern" period? When did it begin? And has it now ended? In one sense, "modern" could be understood to mean "most recent," in which case it makes no sense to speak of the "end of modernity." However, for many historians, "modernity" refers to a quite definite outlook, typical of much of western thought since the early eighteenth century, which is characterized by a confidence in humanity's ability to think for itself. Perhaps the classic expression of this attitude is to be found in the Enlightenment, with its emphasis upon the competence of unaided human reason to make sense of the world – including those aspects of that world traditionally reserved for theologians.

The phrase "Age of Reason," often used as a synonym for the Enlightenment, is a little misleading. It implies that reason had been hitherto ignored or marginalized. Yet, as we saw earlier, the Middle Ages was just as much an "Age of Reason" as the Enlightenment; the crucial difference lay in the manner in which reason was used, and the limits which were understood to be imposed upon it. Nor was the eighteenth century consistently rational in every aspect. In fact, the Enlightenment included a remarkable variety of antirational movements, such as Mesmerism and Masonic rituals. Nevertheless, an emphasis upon the ability of human reason to penetrate the mysteries of the world is rightly regarded as a defining characteristic of the Enlightenment.

The Enlightenment critique of traditional theology

The Enlightenment criticism of many traditional Christian beliefs was based upon the principle of the omnicompetence of human reason. A number of stages in the development of this belief may be discerned.

First, it was argued that the beliefs of Christianity were rational, and thus capable of standing up to critical examination. This type of approach may be found in John Locke's *Reasonableness of Christianity* (1695), and within some philosophical schools of thought in early eighteenth-century Germany. Christianity was a reasonable supplement to natural religion. The notion of divine revelation was thus maintained.

Second, it was argued that the basic ideas of Christianity, being rational, could be derived from reason itself. There was no need to invoke the idea of divine revelation. According to this idea, as it was developed by John Toland in *Christianity Not Mysterious* (1696) and by Matthew Tindal in *Christianity as Old as Creation* (1730), Christianity was essentially the republication of the religion of nature. It did not transcend natural religion, but was merely an example of it. All so-called "revealed religion" was actually nothing other than the reconfirmation of what can be known through rational reflection on nature. "Revelation" was simply a rational reaffirmation of moral truths already available to enlightened reason.

Third, the ability of reason to judge revelation was affirmed. As critical reason was omnicompetent, it was argued that it was supremely qualified to judge Christian beliefs and practices, with a view to eliminating any irrational or superstitious elements. This view, associated with Hermann Samuel Reimarus in Germany and many eighteenth-century French rationalist writers (often referred to collectively as *les philosophes*), placed reason firmly above revelation, and may be seen as symbolized in the enthronement of the Goddess of Reason in the cathedral of Notre Dame de Paris in 1793.

Having outlined the general principles of the Enlightenment challenge to traditional Christian thought, it is now appropriate to explore how these impacted on specific doctrinal themes. The rational religion of the Enlightenment found itself in conflict with the following major areas of traditional Christian theology.

The notion of revelation

The concept of revelation was of central importance to traditional Christian theology. While many Christian theologians (such as Thomas Aquinas and John Calvin) recognized the possibility of a natural knowledge of God, they insisted that this required supplementation by supernatural divine revelation, such as that witnessed to in Scripture. The Enlightenment witnessed the development of an increasingly critical attitude to the very idea of supernatural revelation.

The status and interpretation of the Bible

Within orthodox Christianity, whether Protestant or Roman Catholic, the Bible was still widely regarded as a divinely inspired source of doctrine and morals, to be differentiated from other types of literature. The Enlightenment saw this assumption called into question, with the rise of the critical approach to Scripture. Developing ideas already current within Deism, the theologians of the German Enlightenment developed the thesis that the Bible was the work of many hands, at times demonstrating internal contradiction, and that it was open to precisely the same method of textual analysis and interpretation as any other piece of literature.

The identity and significance of Jesus Christ

A final area in which the Enlightenment made a significant challenge to orthodox Christian belief concerns the person of Jesus of Nazareth. Two particularly important developments may be noted: the origins of the "quest of the historical Jesus" (see pp. 310–19) and the rise of the "moral theory of the atonement" (pp. 348–9).

Both Deism and the German Enlightenment developed the thesis that there was a serious discrepancy between the real Jesus of history and the New Testament interpretation of his significance. Underlying the New Testament portrait of the supernatural redeemer of humanity lurked a simple human figure, a glorified teacher of common sense. While a supernatural redeemer was unacceptable to Enlightenment rationalism, the idea of an enlightened moral teacher was not. H. S. Reimarus and others argued that it was possible to go behind the New Testament accounts of Jesus and uncover a simpler, more human Jesus, who would be acceptable to the new spirit of the age. The second area in which the ideas of orthodoxy concerning Jesus were challenged concerned the significance of his death. For orthodoxy, Jesus's death on the cross was interpreted from the standpoint of the resurrection (which the Enlightenment was not prepared to accept as an historical event) as a way in which God was able to forgive the sins of humanity. During the Enlightenment this "theory of the atonement" was subjected to increasing criticism, as involving arbitrary and unacceptable hypotheses such as that of original sin.

Jesus's death on the cross was now reinterpreted in terms of a supreme moral example of self-giving and dedication, intended to inspire similar dedication and self-giving on the part of his followers. Where orthodox Christianity tended to treat Jesus's death (and resurrection) as possessing greater inherent importance than his religious teaching, the Enlightenment marginalized his death and denied his resurrection, in order to emphasize the quality of his moral teaching.

The doctrine of the Trinity

This doctrine was widely ridiculed by Enlightenment thinkers, who held it to be logically absurd. Under the pressure of rationalism, many Christian thinkers de-emphasized the idea, believing that it was impossible to mount an effective defense of the doctrine, given the spirit of the age.

The critique of miracles

Much traditional Christian apologetics concerning the identity and significance of Jesus Christ was based upon the "miraculous evidences" of the New Testament culminating in the resurrection. The new emphasis upon the mechanical regularity and orderliness of the universe, perhaps the most significant intellectual legacy of Newtonianism, raised doubts about the New Testament accounts of miraculous happenings. David Hume's *Essay on Miracles* (1748) was widely regarded as demonstrating the evidential impossibility of miracles. Hume emphasized that there were no contemporary analogs of New Testament miracles, such as the resurrection, thus forcing the New Testament reader to rely totally upon human testimony to such miracles. For Hume, it was axiomatic that no human testimony was adequate to establish the occurrence of a miracle, in the absence of a present-day analog. Similarly, the French rationalist writer Denis Diderot declared that if the entire population of Paris were to assure him that a dead man had just been raised from the dead, he would not believe a word of it.

The rejection of original sin

The idea that human nature is in some sense flawed or corrupted, expressed in the orthodox doctrine of original sin, was vigorously opposed by the Enlightenment. Voltaire and Jean-Jacques Rousseau criticized the doctrine as encouraging pessimism with regard to human abilities, thus impeding human social and political development and encouraging *laissez-faire* attitudes. German Enlightenment thinkers tended to criticize the doctrine on account of its historical origins in the thought of Augustine of Hippo, dating from the fourth and fifth centuries, which they regarded as debarring it from permanent validity and relevance.

The problem of evil

The Enlightenment witnessed a fundamental change in attitude toward the existence of evil in the world. For the medieval period, the existence of evil was not regarded as posing a threat to the coherence of Christianity. The contradiction implicit in the existence both of a benevolent divine omnipotence and of evil was not regarded as an obstacle to belief, but simply as an academic theological problem. The Enlightenment saw this situation change radically: the existence of evil metamorphosed into a challenge to the credibility and coherence of Christian faith itself. Voltaire's novel *Candide* (1759) was one of many works to highlight the difficulties caused for the Christian worldview by the existence of natural evil (such as the famous Lisbon earthquake of 1755). The term "theodicy," coined by the German philosopher Leibniz, derives from this period, reflecting a growing recognition that the existence of evil was assuming a new significance within the Enlightenment critique of religion.

Romanticism and the renewal of the theological imagination

In the closing decade of the eighteenth century, increasing misgivings came to be expressed concerning the arid quality of rationalism. Reason, once seen as a liberator, came increasingly to be regarded as spiritually enslaving. These anxieties were not expressed so much within university faculties of philosophy, as within literary and artistic circles, particularly in the Prussian capital, Berlin, where the brothers Friedrich and August William Schlegel became particularly influential.

"Romanticism" is notoriously difficult to define. The movement is perhaps best seen as a reaction against certain of the central themes of the Enlightenment, most notably the claim that reality can be known to the human reason. This reduction of reality to a series of rationalized simplicities seemed, to the Romantics, to be a culpable and crude misrepresentation. Where the Enlightenment appealed to the human reason, Romanticism made an appeal to the human imagination, which was capable of recognizing the profound sense of mystery which arises from realizing that the human mind cannot comprehend even the finite world, let alone the infinity beyond this.

Romanticism thus found itself equally unhappy with both traditional Christian doctrines and the rationalist moral platitudes of the Enlightenment: both failed to do justice to the complexity of the world, in an attempt to reduce the "mystery of the universe" – to use a phrase found in the writings of August William Schlegel – to neat formulae.

The development of Romanticism had considerable implications for Christianity in Europe. Those aspects of Christianity (especially Roman Catholicism) which rationalism found distasteful came to captivate the imaginations of the Romantics. Rationalism was seen to be experientially and emotionally deficient, incapable of meeting real human needs that were traditionally addressed and satisfied by Christian faith. As F. R. de Chateaubriand remarked of the situation in France in the first decade of the nineteenth century, "there was a need for faith, a desire for religious consolation, which came from the very lack of that consolation for so long." Similar sentiments can be instanced from the German context in the closing years of the eighteenth century.

That rationalism had failed to undermine religion is clear from developments in England, Germany, and North America. The new strength evident in German Pietism and English evangelicalism in the eighteenth century is evidence of the failure of rationalism to provide a cogent alternative to the prevailing human sense of personal need and meaning. Philosophy came to be seen as sterile, academic in the worst sense of the word, in that it was detached from both the outer realities of life and the inner life of the human consciousness.

It is against this background of growing disillusionment with rationalism, and a new appreciation of the importance of human "feeling," that the contribution of Friedrich Daniel Ernst Schleiermacher (1768–1834) is to be seen. Schleiermacher argued that religion in general, and Christianity in particular, was a matter of feeling or "self-consciousness." His major work of systematic theology, *The Christian Faith* (1821, revised 1834), is an attempt to show how Christian theology is related to a feeling of "absolute dependence." The structure of *The Christian Faith* is complex, centering on the dialectic between sin and grace. The work is organized in three parts. The first deals with the consciousness of God, concentrating upon such matters as creation. The second part handles the consciousness of sin and its implications, such as an awareness of the possibility of redemption. The final part considers the consciousness of grace, and deals with such matters as the person and work of Christ. In this way, Schleiermacher is able to argue that "everything is related to the redemption accomplished by Jesus of Nazareth."

The crisis of faith in Victorian England: George Eliot and Matthew Arnold

In his important book *God's Funeral* (2000), A. N. Wilson documents and analyzes the rise of atheism in Victorian Britain. One of the most interesting things about the book is his careful documentation of the ambivalence felt within late nineteenth-century England over its loss of faith. The secular enterprise, begun with great enthusiasm, had achieved substantial successes by the end of the century. Politically and socially, Christianity remained highly significant in national life, and would remain so until after World War I. Yet its ideas were increasingly seen as discredited, unattractive, and outdated by its novelists, poets, and artists. Christianity had been tried and tested at the imaginative and rational levels, and found wanting on both counts. Although it might be thought that this grand retreat from faith would have been greeted with delight and celebration, Wilson brings out the deep sense of emotional loss and confusion which the inexorable elimination of God brought in its wake.

It is difficult to seize on a single figure as illustrating or causing this crisis of faith. However, the novelist George Eliot (the pen-name of Mary Ann Evans, 1819–90) is regularly seen as a major figure in this emerging climate of suspicion and hostility toward religious faith. Many of Eliot's misgivings about Christianity concerned its apparent lack of concern for issues of morality in its own doctrine. Why, Eliot asked, did it devalue human love, except when directed towards the praise of God? We can see here a leading theme of the Victorian crisis of faith – a growing moral revolt against Christianity on account of its leading ideas.

Writers such as J. A. Froude, Matthew Arnold, and F. W. Newman abandoned their Christian faith on account of a growing sense of the immorality of such doctrines as original sin, predestination, and substitutionary atonement.

Eliot, like many others, therefore turned to a "religion of human sympathy" in place of this rather dark and dismal conception of God. Similar patterns of alienation from conventional religion are found throughout her novels, from *Adam Bede* through to *Middlemarch*. The moral aspects of faith can, she believed, be maintained without the metaphysical basics of Christianity. We can be good without God. Indeed, belief in the Christian God can be a significant obstacle to the achievement of "individual and social happiness." These views became the received wisdom of the age, shaping the emerging late Victorian consensus on the ability of humanity to shape its own destiny. While some – Thomas Hardy comes to mind – were more pessimistic about humanity's ability to construct morality without God than Eliot, they were a distinguished minority in this discussion.

The Victorian era is widely regarded as undergoing major changes from about 1870 to 1900, which can be seen as ultimately subverting the values and beliefs of its earlier phases. Many writers of the period were conscious of standing at the threshold of a new age, uncertain of what it might bring, yet suspecting that the old ways of thinking were on their way out. In his *Stanzas from the Grand Chartreuse*, written around this time, Matthew Arnold (1822–88) spoke of being caught …

> Between two worlds, one dead,
> The other powerless to be born,
> With nowhere to lay my head.

Arnold's journey through the Alps is the backdrop against which he explores his sense of displacement, focusing especially on the erosion of faith in his culture – and perhaps even in himself. His once robust faith, he comments, more than a little wistfully, now seems "but a dead time's exploded dream." Arnold expresses a sense of melancholy and sadness over his nation's loss of faith, which he saw pathetically mirrored in the ebbing of the tide on Dover beach:

The Sea of Faith
Was once, too, at the full, and round earth's shore
Lay like the folds of a bright girdle furl'd.
But now I only hear
Its melancholy, long, withdrawing roar,
Retreating, to the breath
Of the night-wind, down the vast edges drear
And naked shingles of the world.

That tide was now ebbing, and Arnold never expected to see it return. It is impossible to read his poem "Dover Beach" without glimpsing something of his pain and bewilderment over his nation's willing loss of its religious soul.

An intellectual rival to Christianity: Marxism

Marxism, probably one of the most significant worldviews to emerge during the modern period, had a major impact upon Christian theology during the twentieth century. The collapse of Marxism as a state ideology in eastern Europe during the final years of the twentieth century has led to a marked reduction in its impact. However, its influence lingers in late twentieth-century theological discussion, especially in Latin American liberation theology and certain "theologies of hope," such as that set out in the 1960s by Jürgen Moltmann. It is therefore important to understand something of this movement, and its implications for Christian theology.

In his 1844 political and economic manuscripts, Karl Marx (1818–83) develops the idea that religion in general (he does not distinguish the individual religions) is a direct response to social and economic conditions. "The religious world is but the reflex of the real world." There is an obvious and important allusion here to Feuerbach's critique of religion, which we shall consider in a later section. Marx argues that "religion is just the imaginary sun which seems to man to revolve around him, until he realizes that he himself is the center of his own revolution." In other words, God is simply a projection of human concerns. Human beings "look for a superhuman being in the fantasy reality of heaven, and find nothing there, but their own reflection."

But why should religion exist at all? If Marx is right, why should people continue to believe in such a crude illusion? Marx's answer centers on the notion of alienation. "Humans make religion; religion does not make humans. Religion is the self-consciousness and self-esteem of people who either have not found themselves or who have already lost themselves again." Religion is the product of social and economic alienation. It arises from that alienation, and at the same time encourages that alienation by a form of spiritual intoxication which renders the masses incapable of recognizing their situation, and doing something about it. Religion is a comfort, which enables people to tolerate their economic alienation. If there were no such alienation, there would be no need for religion.

Materialism affirms that events in the material world bring about corresponding changes in the intellectual world. Religion is thus the result of a certain set of social and economic conditions. Change those conditions, so that economic alienation is eliminated, and religion will cease to exist. It will no longer serve any useful function. Unjust social conditions produce religion, and are in turn supported by religion. "The struggle against religion is thus indirectly a struggle against *the world* of which religion is the spiritual fragrance." Marx thus argues that religion will continue to exist, as long as it meets a need in the life of alienated people. "The religious reflex of the real world can [...] only then vanish when the practical relations of everyday life offer to man none but perfectly intelligible and reasonable relations with regard to his fellow men and to nature." In other words, a shake-up in the real world is needed to get rid of religion. Marx thus argues that when a nonalienating economic and social environment is brought about through communism, the needs which gave rise to religion will vanish. And with the elimination of those material needs, spiritual hunger will also vanish.

The Russian Revolution of 1917 gave Marxism the break it so badly needed. However, although Marxism established itself in a modified form (Marxism–Leninism) within the Soviet Union, it proved unsuccessful elsewhere. Its successes in eastern Europe after World War II can be put down mainly to military strength and political destabilization. The economic failure and political stagnation which resulted when such countries experimented with Marxism in the 1970s and 1980s soon led to disillusionment with this new philosophy. In Europe, Marxism found itself locked into a spiral of decline. Its chief advocates increasingly became abstract theoreticians, detached from working-class roots, with virtually no political experience. The idea of a socialist revolution gradually lost its appeal and its credibility. In the United States and Canada, Marxism had little, if any, social appeal in the first place, although its influence upon the academic world was more noticeable. The Soviet invasion of Czechoslovakia in 1968 resulted in a noticeable cooling in enthusiasm for Marxism within western intellectual circles.

However, Marx's ideas have found their way, suitably modified, into modern Christian theology. Latin American liberation theology can be shown to have drawn appreciatively on Marxist insights, even if the movement cannot really be described as "Marxist." We shall consider liberation theology in a later section (see pp. 90–1).

Postmodernism and a new theological agenda

Postmodernism is generally taken to be something of a cultural sensibility without absolutes, fixed certainties, or foundations, which takes delight in pluralism and divergence, and which aims to think through the radical "situatedness" of all human thought. In each of these matters, it may be regarded as a conscious and deliberate reaction against the totalization of the Enlightenment.

To give a full definition of postmodernism is virtually impossible. In part, this is because there is substantially less than total agreement on the nature of the "modernity" which it displaces and supersedes. In fact, the word "postmodernism" itself might be argued to imply that "modernity" is sufficiently well defined and understood that – whatever it is – it may be said to have ended and been superseded. The problem is particularly acute in the case of literature, where "modernism" has always been a contested notion. Nevertheless, it is possible to identify its leading general feature, which is the deliberate and systematic abandonment of centralizing narratives.

It will thus be clear that there is an inbuilt precommitment to relativism or pluralism within postmodernism in relation to questions of truth. To use the jargon of the movement, one could say that postmodernism represents a situation in which the signifier has replaced the signified as the focus of orientation and value. In terms of the structural linguistics developed initially by Ferdinand de Saussure, and subsequently by Roman Jakobson and others, the recognition of the *arbitrariness* of the linguistic sign and its interdependence with other signs marks the end of the possibility of fixed, absolute meanings.

According to de Saussure, a "sign" consists of three things: the *signifier* (the acoustic image of the spoken words as heard by the intended recipient of the message), the *signified* (the meaning which is evoked in the mind of this recipient through the stimulus of the signifier), and the *unity of these two*. For de Saussure, the unity of the signifier with the signified is a cultural convention. There is no universal or transcendent foundation which relates signifier and signified: it is arbitrary, reflecting the contingencies of cultural conditioning.

Developing such insights, writers such as Jacques Derrida, Michel Foucault, and Jean Baudrillard argued that language was ultimately arbitrary, whimsical, and capricious, and did not reflect any overarching absolute linguistic laws. It was thus incapable of disclosing meaning. Baudrillard argued that modern society was trapped in an endless network of artificial sign systems, which *meant* nothing, and merely perpetuated the belief systems of those who created them.

One aspect of postmodernism which illustrates this trend particularly well, while also indicating its obsession with texts and language, is *deconstruction* – the critical method which virtually declares that the identity and intentions of the author of a text are an irrelevance to the interpretation of the text, prior to insisting that, in any case, no fixed meaning can be found in it. This movement arose primarily as a result of Jacques Derrida's reading of the works of Martin Heidegger in the late 1960s. Two general principles can be seen as underlying this approach to the reading of texts.

1　Anything that is written will convey meanings which its author did not intend, and could not have intended.

2　The author cannot adequately put into words what he or she means in the first place.

All interpretations are thus equally valid, or equally meaningless (depending upon your point of view). As Paul de Man, one of the leading American proponents of this approach, declared, the very idea of "meaning" smacked of fascism. This approach, which blossomed in post-Vietnam America, was given intellectual respect ability by academics such as de Man, Geoffrey Hartman, and J. Hillis Miller. "Metanarratives" – that is, generalizing narratives which claimed to provide universal frameworks for the discernment of meaning – were to be rejected as authoritarian. Far from *discerning* meaning, such narratives *imposed* their own meanings in a fascist manner.

Theologically, the three following developments should be noted as being of especial importance. Although it is not clear what their long-term influence may be, they are likely to remain significant for the next two decades.

Biblical interpretation

Traditional academic biblical interpretation had been dominated by the historico-critical method. This approach, which developed during the nineteenth century, stressed the importance of the application of critical historical methods, such as establishing the *Sitz im Leben*, or "situation in life," of Gospel passages. A number of leading literary critics of the 1980s (such as Harold Bloom and Frank Kermode) challenged such ideas as "institutionally legitimized" or "scholarly respectable" interpretations of the Bible. The notion that there is a meaning to a biblical text – whether laid down by a church authority or by the academic community – is regarded with intense suspicion within postmodernism.

Systematic theology

Postmodernism is, by its very nature, hostile to the notion of "systematization" or any claims to have discerned "meaning." Mark Taylor's study *Erring* (1984) is an excellent illustration of the impact of postmodernism on systematic theology. The image of "erring" – rather than more traditional approaches to theological system-building – leads Taylor to develop an anti-systematic theology which offers polyvalent approaches to questions of truth or meaning. Taylor's study represents an exploration of the consequences of Nietzsche's declaration of the "death of God." On the basis of this, Taylor argues for the elimination of such concepts as self, truth, and meaning. Language does not refer to anything, and truth does not correspond to anything.

Approaches to other religions

The "pluralist" approach to other religions, endorsed by writers such as John Hick, is thoroughly modernist. All religions are defined as saying more or less the same thing, and are forced into the same predetermined mold, ignoring or suppressing their obvious differences. The new approach known as "parallelism" (see pp. 462–3) respects the distinctive identities of each faith, respecting it on its own terms, while at the same time seeking to view it within a Christian framework.

Key Theologians

A close study of works dealing with theology during the last two hundred years demonstrates that a relatively small group of theologians are regularly cited as representing theological benchmarks. Those who feel that

theology is dominated by white European males will, I fear, find many of their concerns confirmed by this finding. It is my hope that this situation will change, and that new names will secure increasing recognition as time passes, so that future editions of this work can respond accordingly.

The purpose of this present section is to introduce the names and agendas of the theologians who have had such an impact in this most recent period of theological reflection. Although many will be discussed in greater detail elsewhere in this volume, readers will find these brief introductions helpful in orientating themselves within the complex landscape of modern theology.

F. D. E. Schleiermacher

Friedrich Daniel Ernst Schleiermacher (1768–1834) is widely regarded as the most important Protestant theologian of the nineteenth century. He rose to fame through his recognition of the need to make Christianity relevant and accessible to its "cultural despisers" of the Enlightenment. His *Christian Faith* (1821–2, revised edition, 1830–1) set out a systematic approach to Christian theology, based on an appeal to the "experience of absolute dependence." Although widely respected for his contributions to the interpretation and criticism of Kant, and his work on hermeneutics, Schleiermacher is best seen as a theologian who laid the intellectual foundations for the rise of liberal Protestantism in the nineteenth and early twentieth centuries.

John Henry Newman

Few English-language theologians have had such an impact as John Henry Newman (1801–90). Newman studied at Oxford University, and went on to become vicar of the

University Church, Oxford. He became a leading figure in the Oxford Movement, which sought to renew the High Church tradition within Anglicanism. In 1845, he was received into the Roman Catholic Church, becoming a cardinal in 1879. Although Newman wrote several works of historical theology, these do not show him at his best. He is remembered for his pioneering work in studying the development of doctrine in his *Essay on the Development of Christian Doctrine* (1845), and his contributions to the clarification of the relation of faith and reason (see especially his *Essay in Aid of a Grammar of Assent* (1870)).

Karl Barth

The Swiss writer Karl Barth (1886–1968) is now virtually universally regarded as the greatest Protestant theologian of the twentieth century, and possibly since the Reformation. Initially brought up within the context of liberal Protestantism, Barth placed an emphasis on divine revelation which forced a re-evaluation of much existing theology. The style of theology associated with Barth was initially termed "dialectical theology" or "neo-orthodoxy," although neither is particularly helpful in understanding his theological agenda. For Barth, theology was an autonomous discipline, whose task was to respond to what it found in God's self-revelation. Although Barth's early writings are often critical, rather than constructive (such as his famous *Romans* commentary of 1919), his *Church Dogmatics* (incomplete at the time of his death) is a positive, constructive presentation of his theological program. Barth has had a major impact on many areas of theology, particularly in relation to the concept of revelation. The twentieth-century renaissance of trinitarian theology is widely put down to his influence.

Paul Tillich

Although Paul Tillich (1886–1965) originally studied theology in Germany, he was forced to resign his teaching positions due to his opposition to Nazism. He emigrated to the United States, and taught at Union Theological Seminary, New York, for the remainder of his career. He became an American citizen in 1940. Tillich can be seen as continuing and extending the theological program of F. D. E. Schleiermacher. His theological agenda can be summarized as an attempt to correlate culture and faith in such a way that "faith need not be unacceptable to contemporary culture and contemporary culture need not be unacceptable to faith." Making extensive use of existentialism, Tillich set out to present and interpret the Christian faith to modern western culture, stressing the "correlation" between the "ultimate questions" of humanity, and the answers provided by the Christian faith. Although this approach is clearly set out in works such as *The Shaking of the Foundations* (1948), it is best studied from his major work, *Systematic Theology* (1951–63).

Karl Rahner

Of the many Roman Catholic theologians to rise to prominence during the twentieth century, the German writer Karl Rahner (1904–84), a member of the Society of Jesus, is generally regarded as the most significant. One of Rahner's most impressive achievements is the rehabilitation of the essay as a tool of theological construction. The most significant source for Rahner's thought is not a substantial work of dogmatic theology, but a relatively loose and unstructured collection of essays published over the period 1954–84, and known in English as *Theological Investigations*. These essays, which extend over 16 volumes in the original German (*Schriften zur Theologie*) and 20 volumes in the English edition, bring out the way in which a relatively unsystematic approach to theology can nevertheless give rise to a coherent theological program. Perhaps the most important aspect of Rahner's theological program is his "transcendental method," which he saw as a Christian response to the secular loss of the transcendence of God. Whereas earlier generations attempted to meet this challenge through liberal or modernist accommodationist strategies, Rahner argued that the recovery of a sense of the transcendent could only be achieved through a reappropriation of the classical sources of Christian theology, especially Augustine and Thomas Aquinas. Rahner's particular approach involves the fusion of Thomism with central aspects of German idealism and existentialism.

Hans Urs von Balthasar

The Swiss Roman Catholic theologian Hans Urs von Balthasar (1905–88) has had a major impact on recent theological debate, especially in relation to questions of beauty. Von Balthasar's chief work, published over the period 1961–9, is entitled *Herrlichkeit* ("The Glory of the Lord"). It sets out the idea of Christianity as a response to God's self-revelation, laying special emphasis upon the notion of faith as a response to the vision of the beauty of the Lord. His analysis of theology in terms of contemplation of the good, the beautiful, and the true has won many admirers. Other major works include his *Theo-Drama: Theological Dramatic Theory*, a five-volume work on what he terms "theodramatics," the action of God and the human response, seen especially in the events of Good Friday, Holy Saturday, and Easter Day; and his *Theo-Logic*, which deals with the relation of Jesus Christ to reality itself.

Jürgen Moltmann

The German Protestant theologian Jürgen Moltmann (born 1926) developed his interest in theology during his time spent in a prisoner-of-war camp near Nottingham, England, where he recalls reading Reinhold Niebuhr's *Nature and Destiny of Man*. After returning to Germany, Moltmann began his career as a theologian. The work which brought him to international attention was his trilogy – *The Theology of Hope* (1964), *The Crucified God* (1972), and *The Church in the Power of the Spirit* (1975). In the first of these, Moltmann addressed the question of hope in dialogue with the Marxist writer Ernst Bloch. *The Crucified God* explored the relevance of Christ to a suffering world, and developed a pioneering approach to the notion of "a suffering God". Although Moltmann has subsequently made landmark contributions to other areas of theology (especially the doctrine of creation, the doctrine of the Trinity, and ecological issues), he is still chiefly remembered for these earlier works.

Wolfhart Pannenberg

The German Protestant theologian Wolfhart Pannenberg (born 1928) rose to prominence during the 1960s on account of his work on "revelation as history." This approach to theology argued that revelation could be discerned within the historical process itself. For Pannenberg, God conducts his self-disclosure through his actions, primarily in the history of Israel, and in the life, death, and resurrection of Jesus Christ. Developing this theme in *Jesus – God and Man* (1968), Pannenberg pointed to the resurrection of Christ as providing the vantage-point from which history could be properly interpreted. Pannenberg's interests include issues concerning theological method (best seen in his early work *Theology and the Philosophy of Science*), which have more recently been extended to include an important discussion of the interaction of Christian theology and the natural sciences. The definitive statement of his mature theology is to be seen in his *Systematic Theology* (1988–93).

Denominational Developments in Theology

Since the time of the Reformation, Christianity has developed in the form of a number of streams, usually referred to as "denominations." In what follows, we shall consider some developments associated with each of these, beginning with the largest – Catholicism, often referred to as "Roman Catholicism" in works of theology.

Roman Catholicism

It is widely accepted that the most significant developments in modern Roman Catholic theology have their origins in the period immediately preceding the Second Vatican Council (1962–5). It would be unfair to inscribe the words "not much happened" against the history of Roman Catholic theology during the eighteenth and nineteenth centuries. Nevertheless, the conditions which the Roman Catholic church encountered in Europe during this period were not particularly suitable for theological reflection. In predominantly Protestant northern Europe, the church often found itself being placed on the defensive, so that polemical rather than constructive theology was of paramount importance. This was even the case during the nineteenth century, when Bismarck launched his *Kulturkampf* ("Culture War") against the German Roman Catholic Church. Yet secularizing forces were also of major importance. The French Revolution and its aftermath posed a powerful challenge to the church, once more placing it on the defensive.

Yet there were also theological reasons for this lack of creativity. Roman Catholicism had been deeply influenced by the ideas of Bossuet, particularly his emphasis on the constancy of the Catholic tradition (see p. 52). Theology was frequently understood in terms of the faithful repetition of the legacy of the past, a trend encouraged by the First Vatican Council (1869–70). One development of particular importance in this respect was Pope Leo XIII's decision to confer a privileged status on the writings of Thomas Aquinas, in effect (if not in intention) establishing Aquinas as normative in matters of theology.

Nevertheless, definite anticipations of the trend toward theological renewal can be discerned in the nineteenth century. German Roman Catholicism was deeply touched by the rise of the idealism of the Romantic movement, which reawakened interest in many aspects of Catholic faith and practice, including its experiential aspects. This new interest in experience can be seen in the rise of the Catholic Tübingen School during the 1830s, when writers such as Johann Sebastian von Drey (1777–1853) and Johann Adam Möhler (1796–1838) began to place an emphasis on the idea of tradition as the living voice of the church. John Henry Newman (1801–90), who was initially an Anglican, also provided a major injection of confidence and theological acumen into later nineteenth-century Catholic theology, even if his influence has arguably been greater in the twentieth century than in his own. Perhaps the most important of his contributions to the development of Catholic theology relate to the areas of the development of doctrine and the role of the laity in the church.

Signs of a major revival in Roman Catholic theology can be seen after World War II (1939–45). One of the most important themes is that of the retrieval of the patristic and medieval heritage of Catholicism, evident in the writings of Henri de Lubac and Yves Congar. The Second Vatican Council promoted interest in the discussion of the nature and role of the church and sacraments, and also established a more positive environment in which Catholic theologians could operate. The writings of Hans Küng, Piet Schoonenberg, and Edward Schillebeeckx illustrate the new vitality within Catholic theology since the Council. The two most significant theologians to emerge within twentieth-century Roman Catholicism are universally agreed to be Hans Urs von Balthasar (1905–88) and Karl Rahner (1904–84).

A document of major importance appeared in 1994. The *Catechism of the Catholic Church* represents a lucid summary of some of the major themes of modern Roman Catholic thought, updated in the light of the Second Vatican Council. This work represents a convenient summary of contemporary Roman Catholic thinking, and will be cited on occasion in the course of this book.

A number of major theological movements within modern Roman Catholicism should be noted. Roman Catholic modernism became of particular importance in England during the early twentieth century (pp. 84–5), as writers such as Albert Loisy and George Tyrell attempted to adapt Catholic dogma to the spirit of the age, provoking considerable debate and dissent in doing so. More recently, a movement emerged within French-speaking Catholicism termed *la nouvelle théologie* ("the new theology") by its opponents, and *la ressourcement* ("returning to sources") by its advocates (pp. 87–8). This movement included writers such as Louis Bouyer, Marie-Dominique Chenu, Yves Congar, and Jean Daniélou. Elsewhere, Latin American liberation theology became a major movement within the Catholic church in that region (pp. 90–1), generating huge interest (and not a little controversy) within the Christian churches at large.

Eastern Orthodoxy

The Byzantine tradition continued to develop after the fall of Byzantium (see pp. 32–3), although in modified forms. With the fall of Constantinople to Islamic invaders, the main centers of eastern Christian thought shifted to Russia, and especially the cities of Kiev and Moscow. Writers such as A. S. Khomyakov (1804–60) and Vladimir Soloviev (1853–1900) did much to develop the intellectual foundations of Russian Orthodox theology during the nineteenth century. The repressive religious policies associated with the Russian Revolution, however, made it impossible for theological education to continue in the homeland of Orthodoxy. Various Russian émigré writers, such as Georges Florovsky (1893–1979) and Vladimir Lossky (1904–58), continued to develop the tradition in exile.

Although the collapse of the Soviet Union has opened the way for the re-establishment of a vigorous tradition of Russian Orthodox theology and spirituality in its homeland, it is likely that the Russian diaspora (from the Greek word for "dispersion," often used to refer to groups of people exiled from their homeland) will continue to be of major importance in this respect, particularly in the United States.

Greece was finally liberated from Turkish rule in the 1820s, thus opening the way to a renewal of this theological tradition within Orthodoxy. However, this renewal did not really get off the ground until the 1960s. Indeed, much Greek theological writing in the nineteenth century shows a considerable degree of dependence on western ideas, largely alien to Greece itself. Since then, writers such as John Zizioulas (born 1931) and Christos Yannaras (born 1935) have provided a major stimulus to the recovery of the distinctive ideas of the eastern Christian tradition. Despite the growing importance of Greek diasporas in cities such as New York and Melbourne, it seems likely that Greece itself will continue to provide a major theological influence within Orthodoxy in the future.

Protestantism

As we noted in the previous chapter, Protestantism came into being as a result of the European Reformation of the sixteenth century. Although initially restricted to western Europe, the movement underwent significant expansion in the modern period. In its first phase of expansion, Protestant émigrés from England, the Netherlands, Germany and other parts of Europe settled in North America, establishing Protestantism as the dominant religious presence in many areas. Jonathan Edwards (pp. 57–8) is widely regarded as one of the most significant theologians during this period. Further expansion took place as a result of missionary work in the eighteenth and nineteenth centuries. Anglican, Lutheran, and Baptist missionary societies were active in parts of Africa, Asia, and Australasia.

The rise of the Enlightenment in Protestant's heartlands during the late eighteenth century was of major importance. Protestant theology often found itself placed on the defensive, responding to cultural developments and agendas happening within the culture around it. The importance of this point is best seen by studying the emergence and development of Liberal Protestantism (pp. 82–4), which is often regarded as one of the most culturally assimilated approaches to theology. Growing anxiety about the extent to which Liberal Protestantism had accommodated its beliefs and norms to secular values prompted the rise of

neo-orthodoxy (pp. 85–7), associated with writers such as Karl Barth. Although this movement continues to be influential, other ways of engaging the liberal heritage have emerged, most notably postliberalism (pp. 92–4) and radical orthodoxy (p. 94).

Yet the second half of the twentieth century has seen two movements within Protestantism generate such momentum that they are best regarded as denominations in their own right – evangelicalism and Pentecostalism. We shall consider both in what follows.

Evangelicalism

The term "evangelical" dates from the sixteenth century, and was then used to refer to Catholic writers wishing to revert to more biblical beliefs and practices than those associated with the late medieval church. It was used especially in the 1520s, when the terms *évangélique* (French) and *evangelisch* (German) came to feature prominently in polemical writings of the early Reformation. The term is now used widely to refer to a transdenominational trend in theology and spirituality, which lays particular emphasis upon the place of Scripture in the Christian life. Evangelicalism now centers upon a cluster of four assumptions:

1 the authority and sufficiency of Scripture;
2 the uniqueness of redemption through the death of Christ upon the cross;
3 the need for personal conversion;
4 the necessity, propriety, and urgency of evangelism.

All other matters have tended to be regarded as what the Protestant reformers termed *adiaphora*, "matters of indifference," upon which a substantial degree of pluralism may be accepted. Of particular importance is the evangelical willingness to be flexible over the question of ecclesiology. Historically, evangelicalism has never been committed to any particular theory of the church, regarding the New Testament as being open to a number of interpretations in this respect, and treating denominational distinctives as of secondary importance to the gospel itself.

A number of evangelical theologians have emerged as significant within the movement since World War II. Carl F. H. Henry (born 1913) is noted for his six-volume *God, Revelation and Authority* (1976–83), which represents a vigorous defense of traditional evangelical approaches to biblical authority. Donald G. Bloesch (born 1928) maintains this emphasis, especially in his *Essentials of Evangelical Theology* (1978–9), setting out an evangelical theology which is distinguished from liberalism on the one hand, and fundamentalism on the other. James I. Packer (born 1926) has also maintained an emphasis on the importance of biblical theology, while pioneering the exploration of the relation between systematic theology and spirituality in his best-selling *Knowing God* (1973). One of evangelicalism's most significant areas of theological activity is the field of apologetics, in which writers such as Edward John Carnell (born 1919) and Clark H. Pinnock (born 1939) have made considerable contributions.

Yet despite the growing theological renaissance within the movement, evangelicalism has yet to make a significant impact on mainline theology. This situation is certain to change during the twenty-first century.

Pentecostal and charismatic movements

One of the most significant developments in Christianity in the twentieth century was the rise of charismatic and Pentecostal groupings, which affirm that modern Christianity can rediscover and reappropriate the power of the Holy Spirit, described in the New Testament and particularly in the Acts of the Apostles.

The term "charismatic" derives from the Greek word *charismata* ("gifts," and particularly "spiritual gifts"), which charismatic Christians believe to be accessible today. The related term "Pentecostal" refers to the events which are described as having taken place on the Day of Pentecost (Acts 2: 1–12), which charismatic Christians see as setting a pattern for the normal Christian life.

The modern rediscovery of spiritual gifts is linked with the movement known as Pentecostalism, generally regarded as the first modern movement to demonstrate clearly charismatic inclinations. In his study of the development of charismatic movements in the twentieth century, *The Third Wave of the Holy Spirit* (1988), C. Peter Wagner distinguishes three "waves" within the movement. The first wave was classic Pentecostalism, which arose in the early 1900s, and was characterized by its emphasis upon speaking in tongues. The second wave took place in the 1960s and 1970s, and was associated with the mainline denominations, including Roman Catholicism, as they appropriated spiritual healing and other charismatic practices. The third wave, exemplified by individuals such as John Wimber, places emphasis upon "signs and wonders."

Although the charismatic movement can be argued to have long historical roots, its twentieth-century development is generally traced back to the ministry of Charles Fox Parham (1873–1929). In 1901 Parham set out the basic ideas which would become definitive for Pentecostalism, including the practice of "speaking in tongues" and the belief that the "baptism of the Holy Spirit" was a second blessing after the conversion of a believer. These ideas were developed and consolidated by Joseph William Seymour (1870–1922), a black pastor who presided over a major charismatic revival at the Azusa Street Mission in downtown Los Angeles during the years 1906–8. Most major North American Pentecostalist groupings, such as the Assemblies of God, trace their origins back to this period.

The new awareness and experience of the presence of the Holy Spirit in the modern church has raised a series of debates over the nature of baptism of the Spirit, and which of the various "spiritual gifts" (*charismata*) are of greatest importance in relation both to personal faith and spirituality, and to the upbuilding of the church as a whole. For such reasons, Pentecostalism has, on the whole, been suspicious of much traditional theology, seeing this as placing too much emphasis on rational reflection on the Christian faith, thereby neglecting its experiential aspects.

Some Recent Western Theological Movements and Trends

I n previous sections of this chapter, we have looked at some of the broader cultural influences on Christian theology in the modern era, as well as noting some denominational issues. In what follows, we shall explore some major recent movements and trends in western theology.

Liberal Protestantism

Liberal Protestantism is unquestionably one of the most important movements to have arisen within modern Christian thought. Its origins are complex. However, it is helpful to think of it as having arisen in response to the theological program set out by F. D. E. Schleiermacher, especially in relation to his emphasis upon human "feeling" (see p. 75) and the need to relate Christian faith to the human situation. Classic liberal Protestantism had its origins in the Germany of the mid-nineteenth century, amid a growing realization that

Christian faith and theology alike required reconstruction in the light of modern knowledge. In England, the increasingly positive reception given to Charles Darwin's theory of natural selection (popularly known as the "Darwinian theory of evolution") created a climate in which some elements of traditional Christian theology (such as the doctrine of the seven days of creation) seemed to be increasingly untenable. From its outset, liberalism was committed to bridging the gap between Christian faith and modern knowledge.

Liberalism's program required a significant degree of flexibility in relation to traditional Christian theology. Its leading writers argued that reconstruction of belief was essential if Christianity were to remain a serious intellectual option in the modern world. For this reason, they demanded a degree of freedom in relation to the doctrinal inheritance of Christianity on the one hand, and traditional methods of biblical interpretation on the other. Where traditional ways of interpreting Scripture, or traditional beliefs, seemed to be compromised by developments in human knowledge, it was imperative that they should be discarded or reinterpreted to bring them into line with what was now known about the world.

The theological implications of this shift in direction were considerable. A number of Christian beliefs came to be regarded as seriously out of line with modern cultural norms; these were dealt with in two ways:

1   They were *abandoned*, as resting upon outdated or mistaken presuppositions. The doctrine of original sin is a case in point; this was put down to a misreading of the New Testament in the light of the writings of Augustine, whose judgment on these matters had become clouded by his overinvolvement with a fatalist sect (the Manichees).

2 They were *reinterpreted*, in a manner more conducive to the spirit of the age. A number of central doctrines relating to the person of Jesus Christ may be included in this category, including his divinity (which was reinterpreted as an affirmation of Jesus exemplifying qualities which humanity as a whole could hope to emulate).

Alongside this process of doctrinal reinterpretation (which continued in the "history of dogma" movement: see pp. 290–1) may be seen a new concern to ground Christian faith in the world of humanity – above all, in human experience and modern culture. Sensing potential difficulties in grounding Christian faith in an exclusive appeal to Scripture or the person of Jesus Christ, liberalism sought to anchor that faith in common human experience, and interpret it in ways that made sense within the modern worldview.

Liberalism was inspired by the vision of a humanity which was ascending upward into new realms of progress and prosperity. The doctrine of evolution gave new vitality to this belief, which was nurtured by strong evidence of cultural stability and progress in western Europe in the late nineteenth century. Religion came increasingly to be seen as relating to the spiritual needs of modern humanity and giving ethical guidance to society.

Many critics of the movement – such as Karl Barth in Europe and Reinhold Niebuhr in North America – regarded liberal Protestantism as based upon a hopelessly optimistic view of human nature. They believed that this optimism had been destroyed by the events of World War I, and that liberalism would henceforth lack cultural credibility. This has proved to be a considerable misjudgment. At its best, liberalism may be regarded as a movement committed to the restatement of Christian faith in forms which are acceptable within contemporary culture. Liberalism has continued to see itself as a mediator between two unacceptable alternatives: the mere restatement of traditional Christian faith (usually described as "traditionalism" or "fundamentalism" by its liberal critics), and the total rejection of Christianity. Liberal writers have been passionately committed to the search for a middle road between these two stark alternatives.

Perhaps the most developed and influential presentation of liberal Protestantism is to be found in the writings of the German émigré Paul Tillich (1886–1965), who rose to fame in the United States in the late 1950s and early 1960s, toward the end of his career, and who is widely regarded as the most influential American theologian since Jonathan Edwards. (Some scholars, however, prefer to refer to Tillich as "neo-liberal," recognizing that his work represents a development, rather than a mere reworking, of classic Liberal Protestant themes). Tillich's theological program can be summarized in the term "correlation." By the "method of correlation" Tillich understands the task of modern theology to be to establish a conversation between human culture and Christian faith. Tillich reacted with alarm to the theological program set out by Karl Barth, seeing this as a misguided attempt to drive a wedge between theology and culture. For Tillich, existential questions – or "ultimate questions," as he often terms them – are thrown up and revealed by human culture. Modern philosophy, writing, and the creative arts point to questions which concern humans. Theology then formulates answers to these questions, and by doing so it correlates the gospel to modern culture. The gospel must speak to culture, and it can do so only if the actual questions raised by that culture are heard. For David Tracy of the University of Chicago, the image of a dialogue between the gospel and culture is controlling: that dialogue involves the mutual correction and enrichment of both gospel and culture. There is thus a close relation between theology and apologetics, in that the task of theology is understood to be that of interpreting the Christian response to the human needs disclosed by cultural analysis.

The term "liberal" is thus probably best interpreted as applying to "a theologian in the tradition of Schleiermacher and Tillich, concerned with the reconstruction of belief in response to contemporary culture" (Tracy), in which form it describes many noted modern writers. However, it must be noted that the term "liberal" is widely regarded as imprecise and confusing.

Liberal Protestantism has been criticized on a number of points, of which the following are representative.

1   It tends to place considerable weight upon the notion of a universal human religious experience. Yet this is a vague and ill-defined notion, incapable of being examined and assessed publicly. There are also excellent reasons for suggesting that "experience" is shaped by interpretation to a far greater extent than liberalism allows.
2   Liberalism is seen by its critics as placing too great an emphasis upon transient cultural developments, with the result that it often appears to be uncritically driven by a secular agenda.
3   It has been suggested that liberalism is too ready to surrender distinctive Christian doctrines in an effort to become acceptable to contemporary culture.

Liberalism probably reached its zenith in North America during the late 1970s and early 1980s. Although continuing to maintain a distinguished presence in seminaries and schools of religion, it is now widely regarded as a waning force both in modern theology and in church life in general. The weaknesses of liberalism have been seized upon by critics

within the postliberal school, to be considered shortly. Much the same criticism can also be directed against a movement known loosely as "modernism," to which we may now turn.

Roman Catholic modernism

The term "modernist" was first used to refer to a school of Roman Catholic theologians operating toward the end of the nineteenth century, which adopted a critical attitude to traditional Christian doctrines, especially those relating to Christology and soteriology. The movement fostered a positive attitude toward radical biblical criticism, and stressed the ethical, rather than the more theological, dimensions of faith. In many ways, modernism may be seen as an attempt by writers within the Roman Catholic Church to come to terms with the outlook of the Enlightenment, which it had, until that point, largely ignored.

Among Roman Catholic modernist writers, particular attention should be paid to Alfred Loisy (1857–1940) and George Tyrrell (1861–1909). During the 1890s, Loisy established himself as a critic of traditional views of the biblical accounts of creation, and argued that a real development of doctrine could be discerned within Scripture. His most significant publication, *L'Évangile et l'église* ("The gospel and the church"), appeared in 1902. This important work was a direct response to the views of Adolf von Harnack, published two years earlier as *What is Christianity?*, on the origins and nature of Christianity. Loisy rejected Harnack's suggestion that there was a radical discontinuity between Jesus and the church; however, he made significant concessions to Harnack's liberal Protestant account of Christian origins, including an acceptance of the role and validity of biblical criticism in interpreting the Gospels. As a result, the work was placed upon the list of prohibited books by the Roman Catholic authorities in 1903.

The British Jesuit writer George Tyrrell followed Loisy in his radical criticism of traditional Catholic dogma. In common with Loisy, he criticized Harnack's account of Christian origins in *Christianity at the Crossroads* (1909), dismissing Harnack's historical reconstruction of Jesus as "the reflection of a Liberal Protestant face, seen at the bottom of a deep well." The book also included a defense of Loisy's work, arguing that the official Roman Catholic hostility to the book and its author has created a general impression that it is a defense of Liberal Protestant against Roman Catholic positions, and that "modernism is simply a protestantizing and rationalizing movement."

In part, this perception may be due to the growing influence of similar modernist attitudes within the mainstream Protestant denominations. In England, the Churchmen's Union was founded in 1898 for the advancement of liberal religious thought; in 1928, it altered its name to the Modern Churchmen's Union. Among those especially associated with this group may be noted Hastings Rashdall (1858–1924), whose *Idea of Atonement in Christian Theology* (1919) illustrates the general tenor of English modernism. Drawing somewhat uncritically upon the earlier writings of liberal Protestant thinkers such as Ritschl, Rashdall argued that the theory of the atonement associated with the medieval writer Peter Abelard was more acceptable to modern thought forms than traditional theories which made an appeal to the notion of a substitutionary sacrifice. This strongly moral or exemplarist theory of the atonement, which interpreted Christ's death virtually exclusively as a demonstration of the love of God, made a considerable impact upon English, and especially Anglican, thought in the 1920s and 1930s. Nevertheless, the events of World War I and the subsequent rise of fascism in Europe in the 1930s, undermined the credibility of the movement. It was not until the 1960s that a renewed modernism or radicalism became a significant feature of English Christianity.

The rise of modernism in the United States follows a similar pattern. The growth of liberal Protestantism in the late nineteenth and early twentieth centuries was widely perceived as a direct challenge to more conservative evangelical standpoints. Newman Smyth's *Passing Protestantism and Coming Catholicism* (1908) argued that Roman Catholic modernism could serve as a mentor to American Protestantism in several ways, not least in its critique of dogma and its historical understanding of the development of doctrine. The situation became increasingly polarized through the rise of fundamentalism in response to modernist attitudes.

World War I ushered in a period of self-questioning within American modernism which was intensified through the radical social realism of writers such as H. R. Niebuhr. By the mid-1930s, modernism appeared to have lost its way. In an influential article in *The Christian Century* of December 4, 1935, Harry Emerson Fosdick declared the need "to go beyond modernism." In his *Realistic Theology* (1934), Walter Marshall Horton spoke of the rout of liberal forces in American theology. However, the movement gained new confidence in the postwar period, and arguably reached its zenith during the period of the Vietnam War.

However, we must now turn back to the opening of the twentieth century, to consider an earlier reaction against liberalism, which is especially associated with the name of Karl Barth: neo-orthodoxy.

Neo-orthodoxy

World War I witnessed a growing disillusionment with, although not a final rejection of, the liberal theology which had come to be associated with Schleiermacher and his followers.

A number of writers argued that Schleiermacher had, in effect, reduced Christianity to little more than religious experience, thus making it a human-centered rather than a God-centered affair. The war, it was argued, destroyed the credibility of such an approach. Liberal theology seemed to be about human values – and how could these be taken seriously, if they led to global conflicts on such a massive scale? By stressing the "otherness" of God, writers such as Karl Barth (1886–1968) believed that they could escape from the doomed human-centered theology of liberalism.

These ideas were given systematic exposition by Barth in the *Church Dogmatics* (1936–69), probably the most significant theological achievement of the twentieth century. Barth did not live to finish this enterprise, so that his exposition of the doctrine of redemption is incomplete. The primary theme which resonates through out the *Dogmatics* is the need to take seriously the self-revelation of God in Christ through Scripture. Although this might seem to be little more than a reiteration of themes already firmly associated with Calvin or Luther, Barth brought a degree of creativity to his task which firmly established him as a major thinker in his own right.

The work is divided into five volumes, each of which is further subdivided. Volume I deals with the Word of God – for Barth, the source and starting point of Christian faith and Christian theology alike. Volume II deals with the doctrine of God, and volume III with the doctrine of the creation. Volume IV deals with the doctrine of reconciliation (or, perhaps one might say, atonement; the German term *Versöhnung* can mean both), and the incomplete volume V with the doctrine of redemption.

Apart from the predictable (and relatively noninformative) term "Barthianism," two terms have been used to describe the approach associated with Barth. The first of these terms is "dialectical theology," which takes up the idea, found especially in Barth's 1919 commentary on Romans, of a "dialectic between time and eternity," or a "dialectic between God and humanity." The term draws attention to Barth's characteristic insistence that there is a contradiction or dialectic, rather than a continuity, between God and humanity. The second term is "neo-orthodoxy," which draws attention to the affinity between Barth and the writings of the period of Reformed orthodoxy, especially during the seventeenth century. In many ways, Barth can be regarded as entering into dialogue with several leading Reformed writers of this period.

Perhaps the most distinctive feature of Barth's approach is his "theology of the Word of God." According to Barth, theology is a discipline which seeks to keep the proclamation of the Christian church faithful to its foundation in Jesus Christ, as he has been revealed to us in Scripture. Theology is not a response to the human situation or to human questions; it is a response to the Word of God, which demands a response on account of its intrinsic nature.

Neo-orthodoxy became a significant presence in North American theology during the 1930s, especially through the writings of Reinhold Niebuhr and others, which criticized the optimistic assumptions of much liberal Protestant social thinking of the time.

Neo-orthodoxy has been criticized at a number of points. The following are of especial importance:

1 Its emphasis upon the transcendence and "otherness" of God leads to God being viewed as distant and potentially irrelevant. It has often been suggested that this leads to extreme skepticism.

2 There is a certain circularity to the claim of neo-orthodoxy to be based only upon divine revelation, in that this cannot be checked out by anything other than an

appeal to that same revelation. In other words, there are no recognized external reference points by which neo-orthodoxy's truth claims can be verified. This has led many of its critics to suggest that it is a form of *fideism* – that is to say, a belief system which is impervious to any criticism from outside its own boundaries.

3 Neo-orthodoxy has no helpful response to those who are attracted to other religions, which it is obliged to dismiss as distortions and perversions. Other theological approaches are able to account for the existence of such religions, and place them in relation to the Christian faith.

Ressourcement, or, *la nouvelle théologie*

During the broad period 1930–50, traditional Roman Catholic theology in western Europe found itself facing a series of challenges that its traditional, rather scholastic approaches were ill-equipped to meet. Many writers in Germany, Italy, Belgium, and the Netherlands attempted to rise to this challenge, developing new approaches to theology which maintained what was good about the tradition, while at the same time allowing it to engage with the questions of the day. Yet it was in France that these questions were pursued with particular energy and insight. The French theological revival of these years included some of the greatest names in twentieth-century Catholic scholarship – writers such as such as Henri de Lubac, Jean Daniélou, Hans Urs von Balthasar, Yves Congar, Marie-Dominique Chenu, and Louis Bouyer.

Why France? Partly because of the urgency of the question in that country. France had a long tradition of secularism, going back to the French Revolution. Yet the theological soul-searching that we see in this movement was sparked off by the publication of Jean Godin's book *France, pays de mission?* ("France – a nation of mission?") in 1943. This book argued that Catholicism was losing its influence on young people and the working classes. The Catholic church was galvanized: the years 1946–7 witnessed an unprecedented level of institutional self-examination and renewal.

And part of that process of renewal was the movement known as *la ressourcement* by its advocates, and *la nouvelle théologie* by its critics (who wished to dismiss it as uncritical innovation). Many regard the manifesto of the movement as being a 1946 article by the young Jesuit writer Jean Daniélou, entitled "The present orientations of religious thought." A chasm, he declared, had opened up between systematic theology and biblical exegesis. The result was inevitable: the church had developed a theology that was divorced from biblical studies on the one hand, and the life and spirituality of the church on the other.

Daniélou's argument was simple, and not unlike that used by Christian humanists of the fifteenth and sixteenth centuries. To equip the church to confront the challenges of the modern age, it must rediscover the riches of the church's two thousand years of history by returning to the very fountainhead of the Christian tradition. The term *ressourcement* encapsulates this program of "rediscovering and reappropriating the original sources of theology."

These theologians did not see this program simply as a repetition of what had been said in the past. Rather, the tradition was interrogated and interpreted in the light of the questions of the present. As Charles Péguy noted, the modern crisis of faith demanded "a new and deeper sounding of ancient, inexhaustible, and common resources." Like the humanists of the Renaissance, the advocates of this reform found themselves advocating what seemed to be a paradox: in order to advance in theology, one first has to go backward. "If theological progress is sometimes necessary, it is never possible unless you go back to the beginning and start all over again" (Etienne Gilson).

Nor did these theologians see theological scholarship as of purely academic importance. The *ressourcement* envisaged and advocated by these writers was not primarily a work of academic scholarship but rather a work of religious revitalization. Indeed, many placed the emphasis on the pastoral orientation of theology, and the need for theology to connect up with the situation of ordinary people. This "primacy of the pastoral" (Yves Congar) extended to worship, addressing the widespread perception that a sense of God's transcendent mystery had been eroded by a rationalistic theology. The recovery of the transcendent in theology was seen as an integral aspect of the program of *ressourcement*, and helps us understand why the movement emphasized the link between theology and spirituality.

Feminism

Feminism has come to be a significant component of modern western culture. At its heart, feminism is a global movement working toward the emancipation of women. The older term for the movement – "women's liberation" – expressed the fact that it is at heart a liberation movement directing its efforts toward achieving equality for women in modern society, especially through the removal of obstacles – including beliefs, values, and attitudes – which hinder that process. Of late, the movement has become increasingly heterogeneous, partly on account of a willingness to recognize a diversity of approaches on the part of women within different cultures and ethnic groupings. Thus the religious writings of black women in North America are increasingly coming to be referred to as "black womanist theology."

Feminism has come into conflict with Christianity (as it has with most religions) on ac-count of the perception that religions treat women as second-rate human beings, both in terms of the roles which those religions allocate to women, and the manner in which they are understood to image God. The writings of Simone de Beauvoir – such as *The Second Sex* (1945) – developed such ideas at length. A number of post-Christian feminists, including Mary Daly in her *Beyond God the Father* (1973) and Daphne Hampson in *Theology and Feminism* (1990), argue that Christianity, with its male symbols for God, its male savior figure, and its long history of male leaders and thinkers, is biased against women, and therefore incapable of being salvaged. Women, they urge, should leave its oppressive environment. Others, such as Carol Christ in *Laughter of Aphrodite* (1987) and Naomi Ruth Goldenberg in *Changing of the Gods* (1979), argue that women may find religious emancipation by recovering the ancient goddess religions (or inventing new ones), and abandoning traditional Christianity altogether.

Yet the feminist evaluation of Christianity is far from as monolithically hostile toward Christianity as these writers might suggest. Feminist writers have stressed how women have been active in the shaping and development of the Christian tradition, from the New Testament onward, and have exercised significant leadership roles throughout Christian history. Indeed, many feminist writers have shown the need to reappraise the Christian past, giving honor and recognition to a large group of faithful women, whose practice, defense, and proclamation of their faith had hitherto passed unnoticed by much of the Christian church and its (mainly male) historians.

The most significant contribution of feminism to Christian thought may be argued to lie in its challenge to traditional theological formulations. These, it is argued, are often patriarchal (that is, they reflect a belief in domination by males) and sexist (that is, they are biased against women). The following areas of theology are especially significant in this respect.

The maleness of God (see pp. 203–5)

The persistent use of male pronouns for God within the Christian tradition is a target of criticism by many feminist writers. It is argued that the use of female pronouns is at least as logical as the use of their male counterparts, and might go some way toward correcting an excessive emphasis upon male role models for God. In her *Sexism and God-Talk* (1983), Rosemary Radford Ruether suggests that the term "God/ess" is a politically correct designation for God, although the verbal clumsiness of the term is unlikely to enhance its appeal.

Sallie McFague's *Metaphorical Theology* (1982) argues for the need to recover the idea of the metaphorical aspects of male models of God, such as "father": *analogies* tend to stress the similarities between God and human beings; *metaphors* affirm that, amidst these similarities, there are significant dissimilarities between God and humans (for example, in the realm of gender).

The nature of sin

Many feminist writers have suggested that notions of sin as pride, ambition, or excessive self-esteem are fundamentally male in orientation. This, it is argued, does not correspond to the experience of women, who tend to experience sin as *lack* of pride, *lack* of ambition, and *lack* of self-esteem. Of particular importance in this context is the feminist appeal to the notion of noncompetitive relationships, which avoids the patterns of low self-esteem and passivity which have been characteristic of traditional female responses to male-dominated society. This point is made with particular force by Judith Plaskow in *Sex, Sin and Grace* (1980), a penetrating critique of Reinhold Niebuhr's theology from a feminist perspective.

The person of Christ

A number of feminist writers, most notably Rosemary Radford Ruether in *Sexism and God-Talk*, have suggested that Christology is the ultimate ground of much sexism within Christianity. In her *Consider Jesus: Waves of Renewal in Christology* (1990), Elizabeth Johnson has explored the manner in which the maleness of Jesus has been the subject of theological abuse, and suggests appropriate correctives. Two areas of especial importance may be noted.

First, the maleness of Christ has sometimes been used as the theological foundation for the belief that only the male human may adequately image God, or that only males provide appropriate role models or analogies for God. Second, the maleness of Christ has sometimes been used as the foundation for a network of beliefs concerning norms within humanity. It has been argued, on the basis of the maleness of Christ, that the norm of humanity is the male, with the female being somehow a second-rate, or less than ideal, human being. Thomas Aquinas, who describes women as misbegotten males (apparently on the basis of an obsolete Aristotelian biology), illustrates this trend, which has important implications for issues of leadership within the church.

In responding to these points, feminist writers have argued that the maleness of Christ is a contingent aspect of his identity, on the same level as his being Jewish. It is a contingent element of his historical reality, not an essential aspect of his identity. Thus it cannot be allowed to become the basis of the domination of females by males, any more than it legitimates the domination of Gentiles by Jews, or plumbers by carpenters.

The relevance of the feminist critique of traditional theology will be noted at appropriate points during the course of this volume.

Liberation theology

The term "liberation theology" could, in theory, be applied to any theology which is addressed to or deals with oppressive situations. In this sense, feminist theology could be regarded as a form of liberation theology, as the older term "women's liberation" suggests. Equally, black theology is unquestionably concerned with the issue of liberation. However, in practice, the term is used to refer to a quite distinct form of theology, which has its origins in the Latin American situation in the 1960s and 1970s. In 1968, the Roman Catholic bishops of Latin America gathered for a congress at Medellin, Colombia. This meeting – often known as CELAM II – sent shock waves throughout the region by acknowledging that the church had often sided with oppressive governments in the region, and declaring that in future it would be on the side of the poor.

This pastoral and political stance was soon complemented by a solid theological foundation. In his *Theology of Liberation* (1971), the Peruvian theologian Gustavo Gutiérrez introduced the characteristic themes that would become definitive of the movement, and which we shall explore presently. Other writers of note include the Brazilian Leonardo Boff, the Uruguayan Juan Luis Segundo, and the Argentinian José Miguéz Bonino. This last is unusual in one respect, in that he is a Protestant (more precisely, a Methodist) voice in a conversation dominated by Roman Catholic writers.

The basic themes of Latin American liberation theology may be summarized as follows.

1 Liberation theology is oriented toward the poor and oppressed. "The poor are the authentic theological source for understanding Christian truth and practice" (Jon Sobrino). In the Latin American situation, the church is on the side of the poor: "God is clearly and unequivocally on the side of the poor" (Bonino). The fact that God is on the side of the poor leads to a further insight: the poor occupy a position of especial importance in the interpretation of the Christian faith. All Christian theology and mission must begin with the "view from below," with the sufferings and distress of the poor.

2 Liberation theology involves critical reflection on practice. As Gutiérrez puts it, theology is a "critical reflection on Christian praxis in the light of the word of God." Theology is not, and should not be, detached from social involvement or political action. Whereas classical western theology regarded action as the result of reflection, liberation theology inverts the order: action comes first, followed by critical reflection. "Theology has to stop explaining the world, and start transforming it" (Bonino). True knowledge of God can never be disinterested or detached, but comes in and through commitment to the cause of the poor. There is a fundamental rejection of the Enlightenment view that commitment is a barrier to knowledge.

At this point, the indebtedness of liberation theology to Marxist theory becomes evident. Many western observers have criticized the movement for this reason, seeing it as an unholy alliance between Christianity and Marxism. Liberation theologians have vigorously defended their use of Marx, on two major grounds. First, Marxism is seen as a "tool of social analysis" (Gutiérrez), which allows insights to be gained concerning the present nature of Latin American society, and the means by which the appalling situation of the poor may be remedied. Second, it provides a political program by which the present unjust social system may be dismantled, and a more equitable society created. In practice, liberation theology is intensely critical of capitalism and affirmative of socialism. Liberation theologians have noted Thomas Aquinas's use of Aristotle in his theological method, and argued that they are merely doing the same thing – using a secular philosopher to give substance to fundamentally Christian beliefs. For, it must be stressed, liberation theology declares that God's preference for and commitment to the poor is a fundamental aspect of the gospel, not some bolt-on option arising from the Latin American situation or based purely in Marxist political theory.

It will be clear that liberation theology is of major significance to recent theological debate. Two key theological issues may be considered as an illustration of its impact.

Biblical hermeneutics

Scripture is read as a narrative of liberation. Particular emphasis is laid upon the liberation of Israel from bondage in Egypt, the prophets' denunciation of oppression, and Jesus's proclamation of the gospel to the poor and outcast. Scripture is read, not from a standpoint of wishing to understand the gospel, but out of a concern to apply its liberating insights to the Latin American situation. Western academic theology has tended to regard this approach with some impatience, believing that it has no place for the considered insights of biblical scholarship concerning the interpretation of such passages.

The nature of salvation (see pp. 353–4)

Liberation theology has tended to equate salvation with liberation, and stressed the social, political, and economic aspects of salvation. The movement has laid particular emphasis upon the notion of "structural sin," noting that it is society, rather than individuals, that is corrupted and requires redemption. To its critics, liberation theology has reduced salvation to a purely worldly affair, and neglected its transcendent and eternal dimensions.

Black theology

"Black theology" is the movement, especially significant in the United States during the 1960s and 1970s, which concerned itself with ensuring that the realities of black experience were represented at the theological level. The first major evidence of the move toward theological emancipation within the American black community dates from 1964, with the publication of Joseph Washington's *Black Religion*, a powerful affirmation of the distinctiveness of black religion within the North American context. Washington emphasized the need for integration and assimilation of black theological insights within mainstream Protestantism; however, this approach was largely swept to one side with the appearance of Albert Cleage's *Black Messiah*. Cleage, pastor of the Shrine of the Black Madonna in Detroit, urged black people to liberate themselves from white theological oppression. Arguing that Scripture was written by black Jews, Cleage claimed that the gospel of a black Messiah had been perverted by Paul in his attempt to make it acceptable to Europeans. Despite the considerable overstatements within the work, *Black Messiah* came to be a rallying point for black Christians, determined to discover and assert their distinctive identity.

The movement made several decisive affirmations of its theological distinctiveness during 1969. The "Black Manifesto" issued at the Inter-Religious Foundation for Community Organization meeting in Detroit, Michigan, placed the issue of the black experience firmly on the theological agenda. The statement by the National Committee of Black Churchmen emphasized the theme of liberation as a central motif of black theology:

> Black Theology is a theology of black liberation. It seeks to plumb the black condition in the light of God's revelation in Jesus Christ, so that the black community can see that the gospel is commensurate with the achievement of black humanity. Black Theology is a theology of "blackness." It is the affirmation of black humanity that emancipates black people from white racism, thus providing authentic freedom for both white and black people.

Although there are obvious affinities between this statement and the aims and emphases of Latin American liberation theology, it must be stressed that, at this stage, there was no formal interaction between the two movements. Liberation theology arose primarily within the Roman Catholic church in South America, whereas black theology tended to arise within black Protestant communities in North America.

The most significant writer within the movement is generally agreed to be James H. Cone, whose *Black Theology of Liberation* (1970) appealed to the central notion of a God who is concerned for the black struggle for liberation. Noting the strong preference of Jesus for the oppressed, Cone argued that "God was black" – that is, identified with the oppressed. However, Cone's use of Barthian categories was criticized: why, it was asked, should a black theologian use the categories of a white theology in articulating the black experience? Why had he not made fuller use of black history and culture? In later works, Cone responded to such criticisms by making a more pervasive appeal to "the black experience" as a central resource in black theology. Nevertheless, Cone has continued to maintain a Barthian emphasis upon the centrality of Christ as the self-revelation of God (while identifying him as "the black Messiah"), and the

authority of Scripture in interpreting human experience in general.

Postliberalism

One of the most significant developments in theology since about 1980 has been a growing skepticism over the plausibility of a liberal worldview. The emergence of postliberalism is widely regarded as one of the most important aspects of western theology since 1980. The movement had its origins in the United States, and was initially associated with Yale Divinity School, and particularly with theologians such as Hans Frei, Paul Holmer, David Kelsey, and George Lindbeck. While it is not strictly correct to speak of a "Yale school" of theology, there are nevertheless clear "family resemblances" between a number of the approaches to theology to emerge from Yale during the late 1970s and early 1980s. Since then, postliberal trends have become well established within North American and British academic theology. Its central foundations are narrative approaches to theology, such as those developed by Hans Frei, and the schools of social interpretation which stress the importance of culture and language in the generation and interpretation of experience and thought.

Building upon the work of philosophers such as Alasdair MacIntyre, postliberalism rejects both the traditional Enlightenment appeal to a "universal rationality" and the liberal assumption of an immediate religious experience common to all humanity. Arguing that all thought and experience is historically and socially mediated, postliberalism bases its theological program upon a return to religious traditions, whose values are inwardly appropriated. Postliberalism is thus *antifoundational* (in that it rejects the notion of a universal foundation of knowledge), *communitarian* (in that it appeals to the values, experiences, and language of a community, rather than prioritizing the individual), and *historicist* (in that it insists upon the importance of traditions and their associated historical communities in the shaping of experience and thought).

The philosophical roots of this movement are complex. Within the movement, particular appreciation can be discerned for the style of approach associated with the philosopher Alasdair MacIntyre, as noted above, which places an emphasis on the relation between narrative, community, and the moral life. In this respect, postliberalism reintroduces a strong emphasis on the *particularity* of the Christian faith, in reaction against the strongly homogenizing tendencies of liberalism, in its abortive attempt to make theory (that all religions are saying the same thing) and observation (that the religions are different) coincide.

Liberal critics of postliberalism have argued that it represents a lapse into a "ghetto ethic" or some form of "fideism" or "tribalism," on account of its retreat from universal norms of value and rationality. Postliberals respond to their liberal critics by arguing that the latter seem unable to accept that the Enlightenment is over, and that any notion of a "universal language" or "common human experience" is simply a fiction, like – to use Hans-Georg Gadamer's famous analogy – Robinson Crusoe's imaginary island.

The most significant statement of the postliberal agenda remains George Lindbeck's *Nature of Doctrine* (1984). Rejecting "cognitive–propositional" approaches to doctrine as premodern, and liberal "experiential–expressive" theories as failing to take account of both human experiential diversity and the mediating role of culture in human thought and experience, Lindbeck develops what he terms a "cultural–linguistic" approach which embodies the leading features of postliberalism.

The cultural–linguistic approach denies that there is some universal unmediated human experience which exists apart from human language and culture. Rather, it stresses that the heart of religion lies in living within a specific historical religious tradition, and interiorizing its ideas and values. This tradition rests upon a historically mediated set of ideas, for which the narrative is an especially suitable means of transmission.

Such ideas can be seen in an earlier work of importance to the emergence of postliberalism – Paul Holmer's *Grammar of Faith* (1978). For Holmer, Christianity possesses a central grammar which regulates the structure and shape of Christian "language games." This language is not invented or imposed by theology; it is already inherent within the biblical paradigms upon which theology is ultimately dependent. The task of theology is thus to discern these intrabiblical rules (such as the manner in which God is worshiped and spoken about), not to impose extrabiblical rules. For Holmer, one of liberalism's most fundamental flaws was its attempts to "reinterpret" or "restate" biblical concepts, which inevitably degenerated into the harmonization of Scripture with the spirit of the age. "Continuous redoing of the Scripture to fit the age is only a sophisticated and probably invisible bondage to the age rather than the desire to win the age for God." Theology is grounded on the intrabiblical paradigm, which it is obliged to describe and apply as best it can. To affirm that theology has a *regulatory* authority is not to imply that it can regulate Scripture, but to acknowledge that a distinctive pattern of regulation already exists within the biblical material, which theology is to uncover and articulate.

Postliberalism is of particular importance in relation to two areas of Christian theology.

Systematic theology

Theology is understood to be primarily a descriptive discipline, concerned with the exploration of the normative foundations of the Christian tradition, which are mediated through the scriptural narrative of Jesus Christ. Truth can be, at least in part, equated with fidelity to the distinctive doctrinal traditions of the Christian faith. This has caused critics of postliberalism to accuse it of retreating from the public arena into some kind of Christian ghetto. If Christian theology, as postliberalism suggests, is intrasystemic (that is, concerned with the exploration of the internal relationships of the Christian tradition), its validity is to be judged with reference to its own internal standards, rather than some publicly agreed or universal criteria. Once more, this has prompted criticism from those who suggest that theology ought to have external criteria, subject to public scrutiny, by which its validity can be tested.

Christian ethics

Stanley Hauerwas is one of a number of writers to explore postliberal approaches to ethics. Rejecting the Enlightenment idea of a universal set of moral ideals or values, Hauerwas argues that Christian ethics is concerned with the identification of the moral vision of a historical community (the church), and with bringing that vision to actualization in the lives of its members. Thus ethics is intrasystemic, in that it concerns the study of the internal moral values of a community. To be moral is to identify the moral vision of a specific historical community, to appropriate its moral values, and to practice them within that community.

Radical orthodoxy

Finally, we may turn to consider a movement that has recently arisen within English-language theology, which has generated some important discussion and debate. The term "radical orthodoxy" is used to refer to a broad approach to theology which emerged

in the 1990s, associated with writers such as John Milbank, Catherine Pickstock, and Graham Ward, all of whom were originally based at Cambridge University. Its ideas are set out in works such as John Milbank's *Theology and Social Theory: Beyond Secular Reason* (1993), and especially the edited volume *Radical Orthodoxy: A New Theology* (1999).

The agenda of the movement is complex and sophisticated, and is perhaps best understood in terms of the need for Christianity to construct its own alternatives to both modernity and postmodernity. Milbank, Pickstock, and Ward hope to articulate a comprehensive Christian perspective that will both supersede and replace secularisms, whether modern and postmodern, finding in writers such as Augustine of Hippo models worthy of emulation. While it is still too early to determine how successful the movement will be, it is clear that it will be the subject of continued discussion in the near future.

Theologies of the Developing World

I n some parts of the nonwestern world Christianity has been present for some considerable time. An excellent example is provided by India, where a significant Christian presence seems to have come into being in the fourth century. The issue of the relation of Christianity to Hinduism has always been of particular importance to the theological agenda in this region.

In other parts of the nonwestern world Christianity is a more recent arrival. As the global expansion of Christianity continued in the modern period, Christianity became established in parts of the world in which it had previously been unknown. The spectacular growth of Christianity during the twentieth century in sub-Saharan Africa and Korea illustrates this trend, which runs counter to the western European experience of Christianity. Christianity continues to expand within southeast Asia, including mainland China, although communication difficulties and the hostile attitude of the authorities toward Christianity make it difficult to establish exactly what is happening in some situations. In such situations, a major item on the theological agenda is the relation of Christianity to the local culture, including other religions in the region.

In what follows, we shall offer some brief comments on theology in India, in which there has been a Christian theological tradition for some time, and southern Africa, in which such a tradition is still in the process of emerging.

India

Christianity became established in the Indian subcontinent at a relatively early stage. Traditionally, it is believed that the apostle Thomas founded the Indian Mar Thoma church in the first century; even allowing for a degree of pious exaggeration here, there are excellent reasons for believing that Christianity was an indigenous element of the Indian religious scene by the fourth century. European travelers reaching India by land prior to the opening of the ocean trading route by the Portuguese navigator Vasco da Gama in May 1498 regularly report the presence of Christians in the region.

The arrival of the Portuguese may be taken to signal the opening of a significant new period in Indian Christianity, in which indigenous Christian traditions were supplemented by imported versions of the gospel, each reflecting aspects of its European context. As time went on, Dutch, English, and French settlers moved into India, bringing their own versions of Christianity with them.

Initially, evangelization was seen as peripheral to the more serious business of trading. While missionary societies and individuals were able to operate in India without any major opposition, they nevertheless received no support from the British authorities. The East India Company, for example, was opposed to their activities, on the grounds that they might create ill-will among native Indians, and thus threaten the trade upon which it depended. However, the Charter Act (passed by the British parliament on July 13, 1813) gave British missionaries protected status, and a limited degree of freedom to carry out evangelistic work on the Indian subcontinent. It was inevitable that religious tensions would develop. In 1830 the Dharma Sabha was formed, apparently as a reaction against intrusive forms of westernization in Bengal. The uprising of 1857 (generally referred to as "the Indian Mutiny" by contemporary English writers) is often regarded as the outcome of this growing resentment at westernization.

It is therefore of considerable importance to explore the development of indigenous Indian approaches to Christianity, rather than note the expansion of theologies of essentially European provenance in the region. In its initial phases, such a theology tended to arise through Hindus assimilating Christianity to their own worldview. An excellent example of this tendency can be seen in the case of Rammohun Roy (1772–1833), who founded the Atmiya Sabha, a movement dedicated to the reform of Hinduism. His growing alienation from orthodox Hinduism (evident in his debate with Subrahmanya Sastri) led to an increasing interest in Christianity, which he came to regard as embodying a moral code which would be acceptable to right-thinking Hindus. In 1829 he founded the Brahmo Samaj, a theistic society which drew upon ideas derived from both Hinduism and Christianity; among the ideas derived from the latter was the practice of regular congregational worship, then unknown in Hinduism. Under his successor Devendranath Tagore, however, the Samaj moved in a more definitely Hindu direction.

Aspects of Rammohun Roy's critique of orthodox Christology were soon to come under criticism from other Hindus who had converted to Christianity: for example, the Bengali writer Krishna Mohan Banerjee argued that there were close affinities between the Vedic idea of Purusha sacrifice and the Christian doctrine of atonement.

Keshub Chunder Sen (1838–84) developed an approach to Christian theology which rested upon the assumption that Christ brought to fulfillment all that was best in Indian religion. Unlike Rammohun Roy, however, Keshub embraced the doctrine of the Trinity with enthusiasm. He argued that although *Brahman* was indivisible and indescribable, it could nevertheless be considered in terms of its inner relations of *Sat* ("being"), *Cit* ("reason"), and *Ananda* ("bliss"). These three relations were to be correlated with the Christian understanding of God the Father as "Being," God the Son as "Logos," and God the Holy Spirit as "comforter" or "bringer of joy and love." A related idea has been developed more recently by Raimundo Panikkar in his *Unknown Christ of Hinduism* (1964), in which he argued for the hidden presence of Christ in Hindu practice, especially in relation to matters of justice and compassion.

A similar approach was developed by Brahmabandhab Upadhyaya (1861–1907), based on an analysis of the relation of the Christian faith and its articulation in terms of non-Christian philosophical systems (as in Thomas Aquinas's use of Aristotelianism as a vehicle for his theological exposition). Why should Indian Christians not be at liberty to draw upon indigenous Indian philosophical systems, in undertaking a similar task? Why should not Vedanta be used in the expression of Christian theology, and the Vedas be regarded as the Indian Old Testament? Increasingly, the issue of an authentically Indian Christian theology came to be seen as linked with that of independence from Britain: theological and political self-determination came to be seen as inextricably linked.

The move toward independence resulted in Christianity finding itself in competition with two rival ideologies: Gandhism and Marxism. A particularly important participant in this debate is Madathiparamil Mammen Thomas (born 1916). From a Mar Thoma Christian background, M. M. Thomas has come to be regarded as a leading representative of an authentically Indian voice in modern theology.

The continuing exploration of the relationship between Christianity and Hinduism is likely to remain a significant feature of Indian Christian theology for some time. For example, the relation between the Christian doctrine of incarnation and the Hindu notion of *avatar* has emerged as a significant debate within Indian theology. At least five ways of approaching this question may be discerned within contemporary Indian Christian thought:

1   The cosmic Christ included all the various pluralities of religious experience, including Hinduism and other religions in the Indian context.
2   Christ is the ultimate goal of the religious quest of Hinduism.
3   Hinduism is related to Christianity as its Old Testament Scriptures, thus playing a role similar to Judaism.
4   Christianity is totally incompatible and discontinuous with Hinduism.
5   The Hindu context gives rise to a specifically Indian form of Christianity.

Africa

Christianity was first brought to sub-Saharan Africa through missionaries, chiefly from England. From the outset there was a strong association between Christianity and western interests, both commercial and political. In a famous speech at Cambridge in 1857, the

British missionary David Livingstone (1818–73) declared his intention to return to Africa to "make an open path for commerce and Christianity." Most European missionaries had little knowledge of African culture, and as a result were often insensitive to the local situation, failing to realize the importance of interacting with local belief systems. As a result, "African theology" was simply European theology carried out in Africa, without any real interaction with the local culture.

As Africa began to emerge from its colonial past in the 1960s and 1970s, there was increasing interest in the reappropriation of African culture and values, which were regarded as having been suppressed by the European colonial powers. One of the most important developments since the 1970s has been the emergence of indigenous African Christian theologians, such as the Kenyan John Mbiti and the Ghanaian Kwame Bediako, who are concerned to develop authentically African theological paradigms rather than capitulate to western theological norms. For example, western theologians have often been dismissive of critical traditional African views, such as the importance attached to ancestors. African Christians refuse to adopt such dismissive attitudes, and argue for the need to take such views seriously, exploiting their apologetic potential and Christianizing them from within. The Tanzanian theologian Charles Nyamiti provides an example of such an approach in his *Christ as Our Ancestor* (1984).

The interaction with traditional African culture and religions is thus of foundational importance in southern Africa. Yet in the recent past the agenda of Christian theology in southern Africa has tended to be dominated by interaction with an ideology – *apartheid* (an Afrikaaner word meaning "separateness") – which enforced racial segregation in South Africa during the period of white domination. For many years the theological agenda of southern Africa was virtually confined to this single issue, arguing for the total unacceptability of the ideology on theological grounds. This trend was encouraged by western theologians, who were able to understand the theological interaction with *apartheid* in terms similar to those of liberation theology – that is, the struggle for freedom and justice. Yet with the ending of *apartheid* in the early 1990s, Christian theology is now obliged to return to engage with the more traditional task of interacting with local culture.

It will be clear from this brief survey of the last few centuries that Christianity has both expanded and undergone considerable development during this period. We must now turn to consider its major themes in greater detail, beginning by considering issues of sources and methods.

KEY NAMES, WORDS, AND PHRASES

By the end of this chapter you will have encountered the following terms, which will recur during the work. Ensure that you are familiar with them!

black theology	neo-orthodoxy
dialectical theology	postliberalism
Enlightenment	postmodernism
evangelicalism	quest of the historical Jesus
feminism	radical orthodoxy
liberalism	*rationalism
liberation theology	*ressourcement*
modernism	Romanticism

Those terms marked with an asterisk (*) will be explored in greater detail later in this work.

QUESTIONS FOR CHAPTER 4

1 What are the main features of the Enlightenment?

2 Which areas of Christian theology were especially affected by the ideas of the Enlightenment? Why?

3 Summarize some of the features of the following movements: liberal Protestantism, neo-orthodoxy, evangelicalism, liberation theology.

4 With which theological movements would you associate the following individuals: Karl Barth, Leonardo Boff, James Cone, Stanley Hauerwas, Yves Congar, Rosemary Radford Ruether, F. D. E. Schleiermacher?

5 On the basis of your reading of the first four chapters of this book, consider the list of theologians which follows. It includes examples of the following schools of thought or groups of writers: the Cappadocian fathers, humanism, liberal Protestantism, medieval scholasticism, Reformed theology. Some categories include more than one theologian. Assign the following theologians to those groups: Anselm of Canterbury, Basil of Caesarea, John Calvin, Erasmus of Rotterdam, Gregory of Nazianzus, Thomas Aquinas, Paul Tillich, William of Ockham.

Part II

Sources and Methods

5

Getting Started: Preliminaries

This chapter will survey some general points which underlie the discipline of Christian theology. Before engaging with the ideas of Christian theology, it is essential to explore the manner in which those ideas are derived. On what are they based? And how do they arise? The second part of this book will consider these and many other related matters, before we move on to deal with the substance of Christian theology in the third part of this work.

Defining Theology

So what exactly is theology? The word is used in slightly different ways within the world of Christian theology, and you will find it being used in a number of senses. It is often used in a rather functional sense, meaning something like "a course of specialized religious study usually at a college or seminary." In what follows, however, we shall try to identify some of the hallmarks of Christian theology.

A working definition of theology

The term "theology" is widely used to mean something like "the systematic study of the ideas of a religion," including the foundations, historical development, mutual relationship, and application to life of these ideas. The phrase "Christian theology" is therefore generally understood to mean the systematic study of the ideas of the Christian faith, including the following issues:

1 *Foundations*. This relates to identifying the sources on which these ideas are based, and how they relate to each other. For most Christian theologians, these sources include the Christian Bible, tradition, reason, and experience. Some of the most important debates within Christian theology have concerned the priority that ought to be given to each of these elements.

2 *Development*. This concerns the ways in which these ideas have emerged over time. Christian theology is often likened to a growing plant. At times, it grows; at others, it needs pruning. This aspect of Christian theology is often referred to as "historical theology."

3 *Relationships*. This considers the way in which Christian ideas relate to each other. The English theologian Charles Gore once spoke of the "wonderful coherence of Christian dogma," which seemed to him to be like an interconnected network

of ideas – an intellectual spider's web, with each element related to and supporting others. To mention only two examples that we shall consider later in this volume, there is a very close relationship between the Christian doctrines of incarnation and the Trinity; between the person of Christ and the work of Christ.

4   *Applications.* This has to do with the difference that the ideas of Christian theology make to the way in which Christians relate to each other, pray, worship, and exist within the world. Christian theology is not just a set of ideas; it is about making possible a new way of seeing ourselves, others, and the world, with implications for the way in which we behave. This aspect of Christian theology is summed up in some famous words of the English lay theologian C. S. Lewis: "I believe in Christianity as I believe that the Sun has risen – not only because I see it, but because by it, I see everything else."

The historical development of the idea of theology

The word "theology" is easily broken down into two Greek words: *theos* (God) and *logos* (word). "Theology" is thus discourse about God, in much the same way as "biology" is discourse about life (Greek: *bios*). If there is only one God, and if that God happens to be the "God of the Christians" (to borrow a phrase from the second-century writer Tertullian), then the nature and scope of theology are relatively well defined: theology is reflection upon the God whom Christians worship and adore.

Yet Christianity came into existence in a polytheistic world, where belief in the existence of many gods was commonplace. Part of the task of the earliest Christian writers appears to have been to distinguish the Christian god from other gods in the religious marketplace. At some point, it had to be asked which god Christians were talking about, and how this god related to the "God of Abraham, Isaac, and Jacob," who figures so prominently in the Old Testament. The doctrine of the Trinity appears to have been, in part, a response to the pressure to *identify* the god that Christian theologians were speaking about (see pp. 264–5).

As time passed, polytheism began to be regarded as outdated and rather primitive. The assumption that there is only one god, and that this god is identical to the Christian god, became so widespread that, by the early Middle Ages in Europe, it seemed self-evident. Thus Thomas Aquinas, in developing arguments for the existence of God, did not think it worth demonstrating that the god whose existence he had proved was the "god of the Christians": after all, what other god was there? To prove the existence of God was, by definition, to prove the existence of the *Christian* god.

Although "theology" was initially understood to mean "the doctrine of God," the term developed a subtly new meaning in the twelfth and thirteenth centuries, as the University of Paris began to develop. A name had to be found for the systematic study of the Christian faith at university level. Under the influence of Parisian writers such as Peter Abelard and Gilbert of Poitiers, the Latin word *theologia* came to mean "the discipline of sacred learning," embracing the totality of Christian doctrine, not merely the doctrine of God.

A further development is more recent. Since the time of the Enlightenment, partly in response to the development of sociology and anthropology, attention has shifted away from anything that lies beyond human investigation, such as God, to the study of the human phenomenon of religion. "Religious studies" or "the study of religions" is concerned with investigating religious matters – for example, the beliefs or religious practices of Christianity and Buddhism.

With this development has come a shift in the meaning of theology. Not all religions profess faith in one god: for example, Theravada Buddhism and Advaitin Hinduism seem to be radically atheist at heart, while other forms of Hinduism are polytheist. So where theology was once thought of as discourse about God, it now becomes analysis of religious beliefs – even if these beliefs make reference to no god at all, or to a cluster of gods, as in the Hindu pantheon. Even Oxford theologian John Macquarrie's helpful definition of theology is slightly vulnerable at this point: "Theology may be defined as the study which, through participation in and reflection upon a religious faith, seeks to express the content of this faith in the clearest and most coherent language available." Atheist writers, particularly during the heyday of the "death of God" movement in the 1960s, coined the term "atheology" to refer to a system of belief which was based on atheist assumptions. Furthermore, the Greek word *theos* is masculine. As a result, the word "theology" seems to imply reference to a male god. This has caused offense to many feminist writers, some of whom have urged that the term "thealogy" (from the Greek word *thea*, "goddess") should be used instead.

Alternative terms certainly exist. One example may be noted here: the older English word "divinity," which designates both "God" and "a system of thought which attempts to take rational trouble to make sense of God." Nevertheless, the term "theology" seems to be here to stay, despite the slight problems of definition which it raises. The phrase "Christian theology" is used throughout this volume in the gender-neutral sense of the systematic study of the fundamental ideas of the Christian faith. "Theology is the *science* of faith. It is the conscious and methodical explanation and explication of the divine revelation received and grasped in faith" (Karl Rahner).

The development of theology as an academic discipline

As this book has stressed, Christian theology is one of the most worthwhile and exciting academic subjects it is possible to study. But how did this subject emerge? How did theology come to find its way onto the academic curriculum? What is the history of the word in the first place?

The word "theology" is not biblical, but came to be used occasionally in the early patristic period to refer to at least some aspects of Christian beliefs. Thus Clement of Alexandria, writing in the late second century, contrasted Christian *theologia* with the *mythologia* of pagan writers, clearly understanding "theology" to refer to "Christian truth claims about God," which could be compared with the spurious stories of pagan mythology. Other writers of the patristic period, such as Eusebius of Caesarea, also use the term to refer to something like "the Christian understanding of God." However, it seems that the word was not used to refer to the entire body of Christian thought, but only to those aspects relating directly to God.

Perhaps the most important moment in the history of theology as an academic discipline was the founding of universities in western Europe during the twelfth century. Medieval universities – such as Paris, Bologna, and Oxford – generally had four faculties: arts, medicine, law, and theology. The faculty of arts was seen as entry level, qualifying students to go on to more advanced studies in the three "higher faculties." The result of this development was that theology became established as a significant component of advanced study at European universities. As more and more universities were established in western Europe, so the academic study of theology became more widespread.

Initially, the study of Christianity in western Europe was focused on schools attached to cathedrals and monasteries. Theology was generally understood to be concerned with practical matters, such as issues of prayer and spirituality, rather than as a theoretical subject. However, with the founding of the universities, the academic study of the Christian faith gradually moved out of monasteries and cathedrals into the public arena. The word "theology" came to be used extensively at the University of Paris during the thirteenth century to refer to the systematic discussion of Christian beliefs in general, and not simply beliefs about God. The use of the word in this sense can be seen to a limited extent in earlier works, such as the writings of Peter Abelard. However, the work which is widely regarded as being of decisive importance in establishing the general use of the term appeared in the thirteenth century – Thomas Aquinas's *Summa Theologiae*. Increasingly, theology came to be seen as a theoretical rather than a practical subject, despite reservations about this development.

Many early thirteenth-century theologians, such as Bonaventure and Alexander of Hales, were concerned about the implications of neglecting the practical side of theology. However, Thomas Aquinas's argument that theology was a speculative and theoretical discipline gained increasing favor among theologians. This alarmed many medieval spiritual writers, such as Thomas à Kempis, who felt that this encouraged speculation about God rather than obedience to God. At the time of the Reformation, writers such as Martin Luther attempted to rediscover the practical aspects of theology. The Genevan Academy, founded by Calvin in 1559, was initially concerned with the theological education of

pastors, orientated toward the practical needs of ministry in the church. This tradition of treating theology as concerned with the practical concerns of Christian ministry would continue in many Protestant seminaries and colleges. However, later Protestant writers operating in a university context generally returned to the medieval understanding of theology as a theoretical subject, even if they made it clear that it had certain definite practical implications in the areas of spirituality and ethics.

The rise of the Enlightenment during the eighteenth century, particularly in Germany, called the place of theology in the university into question. Enlightenment writers argued that academic inquiry should be free from any kind of external authority. Theology was regarded with suspicion, in that it was seen to be based on "articles of faith," such as those contained in the Christian creeds or in the Bible. Theology came increasingly to be seen as outmoded. Kant argued that university faculties of philosophy were concerned with the pursuit of truth, while other faculties (such as theology, medicine, or law) were concerned with more practical matters, such as ethics and good health. Increasingly, philosophy came to be seen as the discipline which was concerned with issues of truth; the continuing existence of a university faculty of theology would have to be justified on other grounds.

One of the most robust justifications of the need for university faculties of theology was provided in the early nineteenth century by F. D. E. Schleiermacher, who argued that it was essential for the good of both the church and state to have a well-educated clergy. In his *Brief Outline of the Study of Theology* (1811), Schleiermacher argued that theology had three major components: philosophical theology (which identifies the "essence of Christianity"); historical theology (which deals with the history of the church, in order to understand its present situation and needs); and practical theology (which is concerned with "techniques" of church leadership and practice). This approach to theology had the result of linking its academic credentials with public agreement that it was important for society to have a well-educated clergy. This assumption was perfectly acceptable in early nineteenth-century Berlin, where Schleiermacher was based. But with the rise of secularism and pluralism in the west, its validity has come increasingly to be questioned.

In countries in which a strongly secular approach came to be adopted, Christian theology was virtually excluded from the university curriculum. The French Revolution of 1789 led to a series of measures designed to eliminate Christian theology from public education at every level. Most of the older universities in Australia (such as the Universities of Sydney and Melbourne) were founded on the basis of strongly secular assumptions, with theology being excluded as a matter of principle. These strongly secular ideologies are now being relaxed, so that undergraduate degrees in theology, or with significant theological components, are now available in Australia.

However, it is a pluralist rather than a secular approach which is now more widespread in the west, particularly in North America. Here, the distinctive position of Christian theology in public education has been called into question, in that this is held to privilege one religion over others. One result of this trend has been the formation of "faculties of religion" in state universities, in which a variety of religious positions are tolerated. Christian theology can therefore be taught in such a context, but only as one aspect of religious studies as a whole. For this reason, the most important centers of Christian theological education and research now tend to be in seminaries, in which a more committed approach to the issues can be adopted.

We may now turn to explore the architecture of theology, as we consider its various components.

The Architecture of Theology

E tienne Gilson once likened the great systems of scholastic theology to "cathedrals of the mind." It is a powerful image, which suggests permanence, solidity, organization, and structure – qualities which were highly prized by the writers of the period. Perhaps the image of a great medieval cathedral, evoking gasps of admiration from parties of camera-laden tourists, seems out of place today; the most that many university teachers of theology can expect these days, it seems, is a patient tolerance. But the idea of theology possessing a structure remains important. For theology is a complex discipline, bringing together a number of related fields in an uneasy alliance. Some of them are noted below.

Biblical studies

The ultimate source of Christian theology is the Bible, which bears witness to the historical grounding of Christianity in both the history of Israel and the life, death, and resurrection of Jesus Christ. (Note that the word-pairs "Scripture" and "the Bible," and "scriptural" and "biblical," are synonymous for the purposes of theology.) As is often pointed out, Christianity is about belief in a person (Jesus Christ), rather than belief in a text (the Bible). Nevertheless, the two are closely interlocked.

Historically, we know virtually nothing reliable about Jesus Christ, other than the historical material which is embedded in the New Testament itself. Other sources – such as the group of ancient documents discovered near

Nag Hammadi, Upper Egypt, in 1945 – are not regarded as reliable historical sources, partly on account of their late dates. In trying to wrestle with the identity and significance of Jesus Christ, Christian theology is thus obliged to wrestle with the text which transmits knowledge of him. This has the result that Christian theology is intimately linked with the science of biblical criticism and interpretation – in other words, with the attempt to appreciate the distinctive literary and historical nature of the biblical texts, and to make sense of them.

The importance of biblical studies to theology is easily demonstrated. The rise of humanist biblical scholarship in the early 1500s demonstrated a series of translation errors in existing Latin versions of the Bible. As a result, pressure grew for the revision of some existing Christian doctrines, which were grounded in biblical passages that were once held to support them, but which now turned out to say something rather different. The sixteenth-century Reformation may plausibly be argued to represent an attempt to bring theology back into line with Scripture, after a period in which it had departed considerably from it.

Systematic theology is thus dependent upon biblical scholarship, although the extent of that dependence is controversial. The reader must therefore expect to find reference to modern scholarly debates over the historical and theological role of the Bible in the present volume. To give an example, it is impossible to understand the development of modern Christologies without coming to terms with at least some of the developments in biblical scholarship over the last two centuries. Rudolf Bultmann's kerygmatic approach to theology can be argued to bring together contemporary New Testament scholarship, systematic theology, and philosophical theology (specifically, existentialism). This illustrates a vitally important point: systematic theology does not operate in a watertight compartment, isolated from other intellectual developments. It responds to developments in other disciplines (especially New Testament scholarship and philosophy).

Systematic theology

The term "systematic theology" has come to be understood as "the systematic organization of theology." But what does "systematic" mean? Two main understandings of the term have emerged. First, the term is understood to mean "organized on the basis of educational or presentational concerns." In other words, the prime concern is to present a clear and ordered overview of the main themes of the Christian faith, often following the pattern of the Apostles' creed. In the second place it can mean "organized on the basis of presuppositions about method." In other words, philosophical ideas about how knowledge is gained determine the way in which material is arranged. This approach is of particular importance in the modern period, when a concern about theological method has become more pronounced.

In the classic period of theology, the subject matter of theology was generally organized along lines suggested by the Apostles' creed or Nicene creed, beginning with the doctrine of God and ending with eschatology. Classic models for the systematization of theology are provided by a number of writings. The first major theological textbook of western theology is Peter Lombard's *Four Books of the Sentences*, compiled at the University of Paris during the twelfth century, probably during the years 1155–8. In essence, the work is a collection of quotations (or "sentences"), drawn from patristic writers in general, and Augustine in particular. These quotations were arranged topically. The first of the four books deals with the Trinity, the second with creation and sin, the third with incarnation and

Christian life, and the fourth and final book with the sacraments and the last things. Commenting on these sentences became a standard practice for medieval theologians, such as Thomas Aquinas, Bonaventure, and Duns Scotus. Thomas Aquinas's *Summa Theologiae*, dating from a century later, surveyed the totality of Christian theology in three parts, using principles similar to those adopted by Peter Lombard, while placing greater emphasis on philosophical questions (particularly those raised by Aristotle) and the need to reconcile the different opinions of patristic writers.

Two different models were provided at the time of the Reformation. On the Lutheran side, Philip Melanchthon produced the *Loci communes* ("Commonplaces") in 1521. This work provided a survey of the main aspects of Christian theology, arranged topically. John Calvin's *Institutes of the Christian Religion* is widely regarded as the most influential work of Protestant theology. The first edition of this work appeared in 1536, and its definitive edition in 1559. The work is arranged in four books, the first of which deals with the doctrine of God, the second with Christ as mediator between God and humanity, the third with the appropriation of redemption, and the final book with the life of the church. Other more recent major works of systematic theology to follow similar lines include Karl Barth's massive *Church Dogmatics*.

In the modern period, issues of method have become of greater importance, with the result that the issue of "prolegomena" (see p. 111) has become significant. An example of a modern work of systematic theology which is heavily influenced by such concerns is F. D. E. Schleiermacher's *Christian Faith*, the first edition of which appeared in 1821–2. The organization of material within this work is governed by the presupposition that theology concerns the analysis of human experience. Thus Schleiermacher famously places the doctrine

of the Trinity at the *end* of his systematic theology, whereas Aquinas placed it toward the beginning.

Philosophical theology

Theology is an intellectual discipline in its own right, concerned with many of the questions that have intrigued humanity from the dawn of history. Is there a God? What is God like? Why are we here? Questions such as this are asked outside the Christian community, as well as within it. So how do these conversations relate to one another? How do Christian discussions of the nature of God relate to those within the western philosophical tradition? Is there a common ground? Philosophical theology is partly concerned with what might be called "finding the common ground" between Christian faith and other areas of intellectual activity. Thomas Aquinas's Five Ways (that is, five arguments for the existence of God) are often cited as an example of philosophical theology, in which nonreligious arguments or considerations are seen to lead to religious conclusions.

Philosophical theology also serves another major role – that of the clarification of ideas. Many of the great debates in theology concern issues that are philosophically important, and which can be illuminated by rigorous philosophical reflection. Examples of this include God's relationship to time, concepts such as divine immutability and omnipotence, and general issues concerning the foundations and reliability of knowledge. An excellent example, discussed in some detail in this work, is how philosophical reflection on the idea of a "person" – particularly in the writings of Martin Buber – has been of major important to clarifying what Christians mean when speaking of a "personal God." Indeed, the general area of philosophical theology is often regarded as one of the most exciting fields of modern theology, with writers such as Richard Swinburne, Alvin Plantinga, and Nicholas Wolterstorff making landmark contributions to a number of areas of theology.

In the course of this work we shall explore some of the areas in which philosophical considerations have made a considerable impact upon Christian theology. Examples include the patristic analysis of the nature of God, which shows a marked influence from classical Greek philosophy; Thomas Aquinas's arguments for the existence of God, which are influenced by Aristotelian physics; the Christology of nineteenth-century writers such as D. F. Strauss, which draw upon a Hegelian understanding of the historical process; and the existential approach to Christology, developed by Rudolf Bultmann. In each case, a philosophical system is treated as a resource or dialogue partner in the development of a theology.

Some theologians have expressed reservations about the place of philosophical theology. Thus Tertullian raised the question in the second century: "What has Athens to do with Jerusalem? Or the Academy with the church?" More recently, the same critical reaction may be seen in the writings of Karl Barth (see p. 76), who argued that the use of philosophy in this way ultimately made God's self-revelation dependent upon a particular philosophy, and compromised the freedom of God. However, the consensus within Christian theology as a whole is that this process of dialogue and reflection is both helpful and productive, and is integral to the theological task.

Historical theology

Theology has a history. This insight is too easily overlooked, especially by those of a more philosophical inclination. Christian theology can be regarded as an attempt to make sense of the foundational resources of faith in the light of what each day and age regards as first-rate methods. This means that local circumstances have a major impact upon theological formulations. Christian theology regards itself as universal, in that it is concerned with the application of God's saving action to every period in history. Yet it is also characterized by its particularity as an experience of God's saving work in particular cultures, and is shaped by the insights and limitations of persons who were themselves seeking to live the gospel within a particular context. The *universality* of Christianity is thus complemented, rather than contradicted, by its particular application.

Historical theology is the branch of theology which aims to explore the historical situations within which ideas developed or were specifically formulated. It aims to lay bare the connection between context and theology. For example, it demonstrates that it was no accident that the doctrine of justification by faith first became of foundational significance in the late Renaissance. It shows how, for example, the concept of salvation found in Latin American liberation theology is closely linked with the socioeconomic situation of the region. It illustrates how secular cultural trends – such as liberalism or conservatism – find their corresponding expression in theology.

It may seem to be little more than stating a self-evident fact to say that Christianity often unconsciously absorbs ideas and values from its cultural backdrop. Yet that observation is enormously important. It points to the fact that there is a *provisional* or *conditional* element to Christian theology, which is not necessitated by or implied in its foundational resources. In other words, certain ideas which have often been regarded as Christian ideas may turn out to be ideas imported from a secular context. A classic example is the notion of the *impassibility of God* – that is, the idea that God cannot suffer. This idea was well established in Greek philosophical circles. Early

Christian theologians, anxious to gain respect and credibility in such circles, did not challenge this idea. As a result, it became deeply embedded in the Christian theological tradition.

The study of the history of Christianity provides a powerful corrective to static views of theology. It allows us to see:

1 That certain ideas came into being under very definite circumstances; and that these ideas require to be tested and validated over time – a process often referred to as "reception."
2 That theological development is not irreversible; theological formulations of the past which are seen to be inadequate or unhelpful may be corrected.

The study of historical theology is thus both positive and subversive, as it indicates how easily theologians are led astray by the "self-images of the age" (Alasdair MacIntyre). Nor is this something that is restricted to the past! Too often, modern trends in theology are little more than knee-jerk reactions to short-term cultural trends. The study of history makes us alert both to the mistakes of the past, and to the alarming way in which they are repeated in the present. "History repeats itself. It has to. Nobody listens the first time round" (Woody Allen).

It is for such reasons that the present volume aims to provide its readers with the maximum amount of historical background to contemporary issues. All too often, theological issues are conducted as if the debate began yesterday. An understanding of how we got to be where we are is essential to an informed debate of such issues.

Pastoral theology

It cannot be emphasized too strongly that Christianity does not occupy its present position as a global faith on account of university faculties of theology or departments of religion. There is a strongly pastoral dimension to Christianity, which is generally inadequately reflected in the academic discussion of theology. Indeed, many scholars have argued that Latin American liberation theology represents an overdue correction of the excessively academic bias of western theology, with a healthy adjustment in the direction of social applicability. Theology is here seen as offering models for transformative action, rather than purely theoretical reflection.

This academic bias is, however, a recent development. Puritanism is an excellent instance of a movement which placed theological integrity alongside pastoral applicability, believing that each was incomplete without the other. The writings of individuals such as Richard Baxter and Jonathan Edwards are saturated with the belief that theology finds its true expression in pastoral care and the nurture of souls. In more recent years, this concern to ensure that theology finds its expression in pastoral care has led to a resurgence of interest in *pastoral theology*. This development is reflected in the present volume, which is written on the basis of the assumption that many of its readers, like its writer, are concerned to bring the full critical resources of Christian theology to the sphere of pastoral ministry.

Spirituality, or mystical theology

The term "spirituality" has gained wide acceptance in the recent past as the preferred way of referring to aspects of the devotional practices of a religion, and especially the interior individual experiences of believers. Older terms which are still encountered in the scholarly literature to refer to this aspect of theology include "spiritual theology" and "mystical theology." The use of the word "mystical" to refer to the spiritual (as opposed to purely academic) dimension of theology can be traced back to the treatise *On mystical theology*, written in the early sixth century by Dionysius the Areopagite. The modern terms "spirituality" and "mysticism" both trace their origins back to seventeenth-century France, and specifically to the rather elitist circles of salon society associated with Madame de Guyon. The French terms *spiritualité* and *mysticisme* were both used to refer to direct interior knowledge of the divine or supernatural, and were apparently treated as more or less synonymous at the time. Since then, both terms have been brought back into circulation, although changes in their associations have led to some degree of confusion over their precise meaning, with some writers suggesting that the two are just different ways of speaking about an authentic personal relationship with God, while others suggest that mysticism is to be seen as a special type of spirituality which places particular emphasis on a direct and unmediated personal experience of God. Many recent writers have avoided the use of the term "mysticism," believing that it has become unhelpful and confusing. The term "spirituality" has thus come to be used in preference to many terms which are encountered in older writings, including "mystical theology," "spiritual theology," and "mysticism.".

Spirituality is often contrasted with a purely academic, objective, or detached approach to a religion, which is seen as merely identifying and listing the key beliefs and practices of a religion, rather than dealing with the manner in which individual adherents of the religion experience and practice their faith. The term is resistant to precise definition, partly due to the variety of senses in which it is used, and partly due to controversy within the community of scholars specializing in the field over the manner in which the term ought to be used. However, it is clear that spirituality is generally understood to mean the experiencing of God and the transformation of lives as outcomes of that experience. Spirituality thus refers to a lived experience of God, and the life of prayer and action which results from this; however, at the same time it cannot be conceived apart from the theological beliefs which undergird that life.

This point is made clearly by Thomas Merton (1915–68), a Trappist monk who had a major influence on modern western spirituality during the late twentieth century. Merton affirms that there is a close link between theology and spirituality, which must be affirmed and recognized for the mutual good of each.

Contemplation, far from being opposed to theology, is in fact the normal perfection of theology. We must not separate intellectual study of divinely revealed truth and contemplative experience of that truth as if they could never have anything to do with one another. On the contrary, they are simply two aspects of the same thing. Dogmatic and mystical theology, or theology and "spirituality," are not to be set in mutually exclusive categories, as if mysticism were for saintly women and theological study were for practical but, alas, unsaintly men. This fallacious division perhaps explains much that is actually lacking in both theology and spirituality. But the two belong together. Unless they are united there is no fervour, no life and no spiritual value in theology; no substance, no meaning and no sure orientation in the contemplative life.

Merton thus forges a link between the two disciplines, and indicates that their artificial separation is to their mutual impoverishment.

While there is agreement that spirituality is an important aspect of Christian theology, and that growing attention is being paid to teaching and research in this field within Christian seminaries, the question of exactly how theology and spirituality interact has been the subject of intense discussion in recent decades. While this debate lies beyond this introduction, it may easily be studied from any good introduction to the field of Christian spirituality.

The Question of Prolegomena

Anyone beginning the study of an unfamiliar subject faces the same problem: where should you begin? There seem to be so many ways of approaching subjects such as philosophy, the natural sciences, and theology that some kind of confusion over this question is inevitable. In theology, the debate over where theology should start has become known as the "question of prolegomena." The Greek term *prolegomena* could be translated as "forewords" – in other words, things that need to be said before beginning the study of theology itself.

The question of what starting point should be adopted is of importance not merely to theology, but also to a number of related subjects. An obvious example is apologetics, the discipline which aims to make Christianity credible to those outside the faith. For example, the second-century Apologists (writers such as Justin Martyr, whose concern was to gain a serious hearing for Christianity among its educated opponents) took considerable trouble to find experiences and beliefs which Christians shared with their pagan counterparts. By beginning from this point they believed that they could show how Christianity built upon and complemented these shared experiences and ideas.

Since the time of the Enlightenment the question of prolegomena has become of especial importance. Before theology can explore the content of the Christian faith, it has to be shown how anyone can know anything about God in the first place. Talking about *how* we can know anything about God comes to be at least as important as discussing *what* we know about God. Increasing secularization in Europe and North America meant that theologians could no longer assume that their audiences would have any sympathy with the Christian faith. Accordingly, many theologians regarded it as vitally important to find some common starting point which would allow those outside the faith to have access to its insights.

Among these approaches, which seek to anchor Christian theology in the basic experiences of human existence, the following are especially important.

1 F. D. E. Schleiermacher argued that a common feature of human experience was "the feeling of absolute dependence." Christian theology expressed and interpreted this basic human emotion as "a feeling of dependence *upon God*," and related it to the Christian doctrines of sin and redemption.
2 Paul Tillich developed a "method of correlation" (see p. 76), based on his belief that human beings asked certain "ultimate questions" about their existence. "In using the method of correlation, systematic theology proceeds in the following way: It makes an analysis of the human situation out of which the existential questions arise, and it demonstrates that the symbols used in the Christian message are the answers to these questions."
3 Karl Rahner drew attention to the importance of the basic human urge to transcend the limitations of human nature. Human beings are aware of a sense of being made for more than they now are, or more than they can ever hope to achieve by their own abilities. The Christian revelation supplies this "more," to which human experience points.

Nevertheless, such approaches (especially as developed by Schleiermacher and his immediate followers) have provoked hostile reactions. The most significant of these is to be found in the neo-orthodox school (see pp. 85–7), which protested against what it believed to be a reduction of theology to human needs, or an imprisonment of theology within the confines of some philosophy of human existence.

Barth declared that Christian theology was not in any sense dependent upon human philosophy, but was autonomous and self-supporting. God was perfectly capable of revealing himself without any human assistance. The word "prolegomena" was not to be understood as "things which need to be said before theology is possible." Rather, it was to be understood as "the things that must be said first in theology" – in other words, the doctrine of the Word of God.

There has thus been little agreement within Christian theology on this point. There has been a temptation to assume that philosophy is somehow capable of establishing a secure foundation upon which theology can build – particular favorites being Kant, Hegel, and Alfred North Whitehead. Inevitably, this means that the credibility of such theologies is linked with the intellectual fortunes of the philosophies to which they are hitched.

Questions of method have dominated modern theology, not least on account of the challenge of the Enlightenment to establish reliable foundations for knowledge. However, as Jeffrey Stout of Princeton University observed: "Preoccupation with method is like clearing your throat: it can go on for only so long before you lose your audience." There has thus been a reaction against the contemporary preoccupation with method, especially within postliberalism (see pp. 92–4). Writers such as Hans Frei, George Lindbeck, and Ronald Thiemann have argued that Christian faith is like a language: either you speak it, or you don't. Christianity is viewed as one option in a pluralist context, with no need to appeal to universal criteria or principles of argument. To its opponents, this represents little more than a degeneration into fideism – that is, a system which is justified by its own internal standards, which need not be shared or approved by anyone else.

Commitment and Neutrality in Theology

To what extent should theologians be "committed?" To put this question in an especially pointed way: can Christian theology be taught by someone who is not a Christian? Is commitment to the Christian faith an essential qualification for anyone who wants to teach or study Christian theology?

This question has been debated at length within the Christian tradition. The debate is usually regarded as having got fully under way in the twelfth century, with the founding of the University of Paris. Public confrontations developed between thinkers who believed that theology was about a committed defense of the Christian faith (Bernard of Clairvaux), and those who insisted that theology was an academic discipline, demanding detachment on the part of its practitioners (Peter Abelard). Significantly, the former tended to be based in monasteries, and the latter in universities. The debate is unresolved, in that each view has a number of significant arguments in its favor. The following are the main points put forward by each side. First, let us consider two arguments for detachment and neutrality.

1 A total detachment on the part of a scholar is necessary in the quest for truth. If a scholar is already committed to a theory (such as the truth of Christianity), this will prejudice his or her evaluation of the material to be studied. With the Enlightenment came the idea that "commitment" and "truth" were mutually incompatible. The only person who is intellectually

112

qualified to pass judgment on the Christian faith is someone who is neutral toward it.

2   Theology must be prepared to ask hard questions about its intellectual credibility, its methods, and its ideas. The critical environment of a modern university forces theologians to ask the hard questions which otherwise might not get asked. "If theology were now forced to disappear from the universities on the grounds maintained by many people (that it is essentially tied to authority and therefore unscientific), this would be a severe setback for the Christian understanding of truth" (Wolfhart Pannenberg). David Tracy's emphasis upon the need for Christianity to ground Christian truth claims in public, universal norms of intelligibility and justification also points firmly in this direction.

Having considered two of the arguments advocated for neutrality, we may now note three in support of commitment.

1   Latin American liberation theologians have been scathing of the notion of "academic detachment," regarding this as a severe hindrance to the cause of social justice and political transformation. If something is true, ought one not to be committed to it? Basing their arguments partly on Marxist principles, and partly on some fairly traditional Christian ideas, liberation theologians have argued that there is no tension between truth and commitment: indeed, the former demands the latter.

2   Scholarship is in reality precommitted to certain ideas and values, whether these are explicitly identified or not. For example, the sophisticated analysis of the nature of theories in physics or psychology offered by Roy A. Clouser in *The Myth of Religious Neutrality* (1991) suggests that precommitments exercise a major, if hidden, role

in these areas. Far from being "neutral," such disciplines turn out to have hidden commitments. Might not the same be true of theology? In other words, even those who claim to be "detached" are, in reality, servants of hidden precommitments and presuppositions.

3   Christian theology arises in response to the faith of a community. It is, to use the celebrated phrase of Anselm of Canterbury, *fides quaerens intellectum,* "faith seeking understanding" (see p. 34). Faith thus implies commitment. To study Christian theology as a purely academic subject, from a disinterested standpoint, is to lose sight of the fact that Christianity is about proclamation, prayer, and worship. It is these activities which give rise to theology – and if a theologian does not proclaim the faith, pray to God, and worship the risen Christ, he or she cannot really be said to have understood what theology is all about.

Each of these arguments for and against neutrality has its strengths and weaknesses. For example, consider the suggestion that only someone outside the Christian faith can provide a reliable account of its ideas, that is, that the person best qualified to write about Christian theology is someone who is not a Christian. This suggestion has its strengths. An outside observer is more likely to ask hard questions, to make critical judgments, and to notice the strangeness of things which those inside the Christian faith take as self-evident. Yet, because the outside observer does not share the inner dynamics of the Christian faith – such as its life of prayer or worship – he or she will not be able to understand the motivation for theological development. A critical perspective is achieved at the cost of a lack of understanding.

For reasons such as these, the debate about commitment in theology has found itself at something of a stalemate. In recent decades, however, a social development has taken place which is tending to lead to Christian theology being studied in seminaries, rather than universities – and hence in a committed context. With the rise of multiculturalism in Europe, North America, and Australia, there has been increasing disquiet within secular circles over the privileged status of Christian theology in the universities. Why should Christian – and not Jewish or Islamic – thought be given this special status?

The result of this development in the United States has been the birth of "faculties of religion" or "faculties of religious studies," which aim to study a variety of specific religions, or religion in general, rather than Christianity. As most individuals studying Christian theology do so with a view to ordination, the result of this has tended to be an exodus of students to the seminaries, where *Christian* theology is taught. Thus a significant number of major theologians – including major European Roman Catholic theologians such as Hans Urs von Balthasar and Yves Congar – have never held university appointments. Equally, many modern American evangelical theologians prefer to remain in seminary contexts, rather than work within the "religious studies" faculties of secular universities.

Orthodoxy and Heresy

The terms "orthodoxy" and "heresy" have now largely lost their original theological meanings. The rise of antiauthoritarian attitudes in modern times has led to "orthodoxy" (that is, literally, "right opinion") being seen as little more than "a dogma imposed upon people by coercive authority," with "heresy" often being viewed as the victim of suppression by intolerant church or state authorities. As we shall see, Walter Bauer (1877–1960) advanced the thesis that forms of Christianity which later generations regarded as "heretical" were actually earlier and more influential than "orthodox" views; the Roman church deliberately suppressed these ideas, declaring them to be heretical, and enforced its own less popular ideas as "orthodoxy." Recent scholarship has cast considerable doubt on this thesis, although it remains popular in more liberal circles today.

It should be noted that heresy has often been associated with marginalized social groupings: for example, the Donatists (a group of heretics in late fourth-century north Africa, see pp. 394–6) drew their support mainly from the indigenous Berber people of the region, whereas their Catholic opponents were mainly Roman settlers. While the Christian church has frequently fallen into the temptation of suppressing its opponents, inside and outside its ranks, the notion of "heresy" is and remains of genuine theological importance, and needs to be examined more closely. In what follows, we shall consider both historical and theological aspects of the ideas of heresy and orthodoxy.

Historical aspects

The ideas of "orthodoxy" and "heresy" are especially associated with the early church. So how did they develop? Are we to think of heresy as a degeneration from orthodoxy? In his study *Orthodoxy and Heresy in Earliest Christianity* (1934), Walter Bauer argued that the basic unity within the early Christian churches did not seem to be located at the level of doctrines, but at the level of relationship with the same Lord. Christian unity lay in the worship of the same Lord, rather than in the formal statement of doctrine (which is how "orthodoxy" tends to be defined).

Bauer went on to argue that a variety of views which were tolerated in the early church gradually began to be regarded with suspicion by the later church. An orthodox consensus began to emerge, in which opinions that had once been tolerated were discarded as inadequate. But how was this distinction between heresy and orthodoxy drawn? Bauer argued that "orthodoxy" was the result of the growing power of Rome, which increasingly came to impose its own views upon others, using the term "heresy" to refer to views it rejected. Bauer's argument is that, to him, the difference between orthodoxy and heresy often seems arbitrary. Bauer's hostility to the idea of doctrinal norms reflects his conviction that these were a late development within Christianity.

A more nuanced approach to the same question is taken by the Oxford patristic scholar Henry Chadwick. In his important essay "The Circle and the Ellipse" (1959), Chadwick contrasted a patristic view of orthodoxy, which regarded only Rome as normative, and the rival view, which recognized that all Christian communities were linked by the foundational events which took place at Jerusalem and continued to be of defining importance in the process of the forging of doctrinal orthodoxy. Where Bauer focused on the single center of Rome, Chadwick suggested that the image of an ellipse, with its two foci at Rome and Jerusalem, was more appropriate. Historically, Chadwick's account appears to be much the more plausible.

Theological aspects

The debate over the historical origins of the notions of heresy and orthodoxy might suggest that the ideas are of purely antiquarian interest. In fact, there is a continuing theological significance associated with the ideas. Heresy is important theologically. This point is perhaps best seen from one of the most important discussions of heresy, found in F. D. E. Schleiermacher's *Christian Faith* (1821–2). Schleiermacher argued that heresy was that which preserved the *appearance* of Christianity, yet contradicted its *essence*:

> If the distinctive essence of Christianity consists in the fact that in it all religious emotions are related to the redemption wrought by Jesus Christ, there will be two ways in which heresy can arise. That is to say: This fundamental formula will be retained in general [...] but *either* human nature will be so defined that a redemption in the strict case cannot be accomplished, *or* the Redeemer will be defined in such a way that he cannot accomplish redemption.

Schleiermacher's discussion of heresy is of such interest that we shall consider it in detail, partly because it illuminates the distinction between heresy and unbelief, and partly because it shows the continuing need for the notion of "heresy" in theology, even if the word itself risks becoming discredited through overuse.

Schleiermacher argues that the central and distinctive idea of Christianity is that God has redeemed us through Jesus Christ, and through no one else and in no other way. It must therefore follow that the Christian understandings of God, Jesus Christ, and human nature should be consistent with this doctrine of redemption. To give some obvious applications of this point:

1 The Christian understanding of the nature of *God* must be such that God can effect the redemption of humanity through Christ;

2 The Christian understanding of the identity of *Christ* must be such that God can bring about our redemption through him, and him alone;

3 The Christian understanding of *humanity* must be such that redemption is both possible and genuine.

In other words, it is essential that the Christian understanding of God, Christ, and humanity is *consistent with* the principle of redemption through Christ alone.

According to Schleiermacher, to deny that God has redeemed us through Jesus Christ is to deny the most fundamental truth claim of the Christian faith. The distinction between what is *Christian* and what is not lies in whether this principle is accepted. The distinction between what is *orthodox* and what is *heretical*, however, lies in how this principle, once conceded and accepted, is understood. In other words, heresy is not a form of unbelief; it is a faulty or inadequate understanding of core Christian beliefs that arises within the context of faith itself. For Schleiermacher, heresy is fundamentally an *inadequate or inauthentic form of Christian faith*.

On the basis of his analysis of the theme of redemption in Christ, Schleiermacher identifies four heresies that arise from an inadequate grasp of the doctrine of redemption, as follows:

1 Ebionitism, which interprets the person of Christ in such a way that he does not possess the essential superiority to humanity which makes Christ, and Christ alone, our redeemer.
2 Docetism, which interprets the person of Christ in such a way that he only has the appearance of being human, and thus lacks the capacity to relate to us that is essential to redemption.
3 Pelagianism, which sees humanity as capable of securing its own redemption, and hence not needing Christ.
4 Manichaeism, which sees humanity as incapable of responding to the salvation made possible in Christ.

The four heresies described above may, according to Schleiermacher, be regarded as the four "natural heresies" of the Christian faith, each of which arises through an inadequate interpretation of the doctrine of redemption in Christ. It is no accident that these were by far the most important heresies to be debated in the early church.

The Theology of the Relation of Christianity and Secular Culture

Theology is undertaken in a context – that of culture at large. The word "culture" is not especially easy to define. In his work *Christianity and Civilization* (1948), the Swiss twentieth-century theologian Emil Brunner defined culture as "the materialization of meaning." A study of church history strongly suggests that the Christian church is engaged in a perennial struggle to clarify its relationship with culture. Where should Christians see themselves as located? Inside the culture? Or outside it? Should they ignore it? Or isolate themselves from it? Or should they try to transform it? And, more importantly, what is the theological basis for these attitudes? How does what people believe about the essence of the Christian gospel affect their attitudes towards culture?

While these debates have taken place throughout Christian history, it proved to be of especial importance in the patristic period. One of the most important debates in the early church concerned the extent to which Christians could appropriate the immense cultural legacy of the classical world – poetry, philosophy, and literature. In what way could the *ars poetica* ("the poetic art") be adopted and adapted by Christian writers, anxious to use such classical modes of writing to expound and communicate their faith? Or was the very use of such a literary medium tantamount to compromising the essentials of the Christian faith? It was a debate of immense significance, as it raised the question of whether Christianity would turn its back on the classical heritage, or appropriate it, even if in a modified form. In view of its importance and interest, we shall cite extensively from some of the most important writings offered as contributions to this debate.

Justin Martyr

One early answer to this important question was given by Justin Martyr, a second-century writer with a particular concern to exploit the parallels between Christianity and Platonism as a means of communicating the gospel. For Justin, the seeds of divine wisdom had been sown throughout the world, which meant that Christians could and should expect to find aspects of the gospel reflected outside the church. For Justin, Christians were therefore at liberty to draw upon classical culture, in the knowledge that whatever "has been said well" ultimately draws upon divine wisdom and insight.

Important though Justin's argument may have been, it received a somewhat frosty reception in most sections of the Christian church. The main difficulty was that it was seen to virtually equate Christianity with classical culture by failing to articulate adequate grounds for distinguishing them, apparently suggesting that Christian theology and Platonism were simply different ways of viewing the same divine realities. Justin's pupil Tatian (born c.120) was skeptical concerning the merits of classic rhetoric and poetry, both of which he regarded as encouraging deception and a disregard for matters of truth.

Tertullian

The most severe criticism of this kind of approach was to be found in the writings of Tertullian, a third-century Roman lawyer who converted to Christianity. What, he asked, has Athens to do with Jerusalem? What relevance has the Platonic Academy for the church? The manner in which the question is posed makes Tertullian's answer clear: Christianity must maintain its distinctive identity by avoiding such secular influences. This wholesale rejection of every aspect of pagan culture had the advantage of being simple to understand. Christianity, according to Tertullian, was basically a countercultural movement, which refused to allow itself to be contaminated in any way by the mental or moral environment in which it took root. Yet there were difficulties with this consistently negative approach. It seemed to deny Christians access to or use of any of the intellectual and cultural heritage for a thoroughly laudable purpose – namely, the preaching of the gospel. Many early Christian writers studied classic rhetoric as a means of improving their preaching and writing, and thus facilitate the communication of the faith to those outside the church. Was Tertullian excluding this?

Alongside this pragmatic approach could be found a more theological issue. Does not all true wisdom have its origins in God? And if so, should not Christians honor that truth where it is to be found? To his critics, Tertullian seemed to offer little in the way of response to these questions.

The matter became of greater significance with the conversion of the Roman emperor Constantine, which opened the way to a much more positive evaluation of the relation of every aspect of Christian life and thought to classical culture. In view of the importance of this development, we need to explore the background to it in a little detail. Since it first established a significant presence at Rome in the fifth century AD, Christianity had had a decidedly ambiguous legal status. On the one hand, it was not legally recognized, and so did not enjoy any special rights; on the other, it was not forbidden. However, its growing numerical strength led to periodic attempts to suppress it by force. Sometimes these persecutions were local, restricted to regions such as north Africa; sometimes, they were sanctioned throughout the Roman Empire as a whole.

Under such conditions it is hardly surprising that many Christians felt negatively toward classic Roman culture. This was the culture of an oppressor, determined to eliminate Christianity. It was easy to see the force of Tertullian's arguments under these circumstances. To adopt Roman cultural norms was tantamount to betrayal of the Christian faith. Yet if the relation of classical culture to Christianity were to change, the force of Tertullian's arguments might be weakened significantly.

With the conversion of Constantine, the issue of the interaction of Christianity and classical culture assumed a new significance. Rome was now the servant of the gospel; might not the same be true of its culture? If the Roman state could be viewed positively by Christians, why not also its cultural heritage? It seemed as if a door had opened upon some very interesting possibilities. Prior to 313, this situation could only have been dreamt of. After 313, its exploration became a matter of urgency for leading Christian thinkers – supreme among whom was Augustine of Hippo.

Augustine of Hippo

It is no surprise that the answer which would finally gain acceptance was set out by Augustine of Hippo, and can perhaps be best described as the "critical appropriation of classical culture." For Augustine, the situation is comparable to Israel fleeing from captivity in Egypt at the time of the Exodus. Although they left the idols of Egypt behind them, they carried the gold and silver of Egypt with them, in order to make better and proper use of such riches, which were

thus liberated in order to serve a higher purpose than before. In much the same way, the philosophy and culture of the ancient world could be appropriated by Christians, where this seemed right, and thus allowed to serve the cause of the Christian faith. Augustine clinched his argument by pointing out how several recent distinguished Christians had made use of classical wisdom in advancing the gospel.

If those who are called philosophers, particularly the Platonists, have said anything which is true and consistent with our faith, we must not reject it, but claim it for our own use, in the knowledge that they possess it unlawfully. The Egyptians possessed idols and heavy burdens, which the children of Israel hated and from which they fled; however, they also possessed vessels of gold and silver and clothes which our forebears, in leaving Egypt, took for themselves in secret, intending to use them in a better manner (Exodus 3: 21–2; 12: 35–6). [...] In the same way, pagan learning is not entirely made up of false teachings and superstitions. [...] It contains also some excellent teachings, well suited to be used by truth, and excellent moral values. Indeed, some truths are even found among them which relate to the worship of the one God. Now these are, so to speak, their gold and their silver, which they did not invent themselves, but which they dug out of the mines of the providence of God, which are scattered throughout the world, yet which are improperly and unlawfully prostituted to the worship of demons. The Christian, therefore, can separate these truths from their unfortunate associations, take them away, and put them to their proper use for the proclamation of the gospel. [...] What else have many good and faithful people from amongst us done? Look at the wealth of gold and silver and clothes which Cyprian – that eloquent teacher and blessed martyr – brought with him when he left Egypt! And think of all that Lactantius brought with him, not to mention Marius Victorinus, Optatus, and Hilary of Poitiers, and others who are still living! And look at how much the Greeks have borrowed! And before all of these, we find that Moses, that most faithful servant of God, had done the same thing: after all, it is written of him that "he was learned in all the wisdom of the Egyptians" (Acts 7: 22).

The fundamental theme is that of taking a way of thinking – or writing, or speaking – which had hitherto been put to pagan use, and liberating it so that it might be put to the service of the gospel. Augustine argues that what are essential, neutral, yet valuable ways of thinking or self-expression have been quarried in "the mines of the providence of God"; the difficulty is the use to which they were put within pagan culture, in that they had been "improperly and unlawfully prostituted to the worship of demons."

Augustine's approach thus laid the foundation for the assertion that whatever was good, true, or beautiful could be used in the service of the gospel. It was this approach which would prove dominant in the western church, providing a theological foundation for the critical appropriation by Christian writers of literary genres whose origins lay outside the church. In addition to literary forms already known within the church, and widely recognized as entirely appropriate in Christian usage – such as the sermon and the biblical commentary – might be added others, whose cultural pedigree was thoroughly secular. Examples would include drama and – to anticipate a later development – the novel.

The scene was thus set for the creative interaction of Christian theology, liturgy, and spirituality with the cultural tradition of the ancient world – unquestionably one of the most interesting and fertile examples of cultural cross-fertilization in human intellectual history.

The twentieth century: H. Richard Niebuhr

As noted earlier, theologians have debated the relationship of Christianity and culture for the last two thousand years. In recent years, a theological framework developed by the American writer H. Richard Niebuhr (1919–62) has found wide acceptance as a useful tool for reflection on this issue. In his highly influential *Christ and Culture* (1951), Niebuhr set out five theological paradigms or frameworks. This book was originally based on lectures gives at Austin Theological Seminary, Texas, in January and February 1949.

For Niebuhr, the importance of clarifying the theological relationship of faith and culture had been given new importance by World War II, which had only recently come to an end. Western culture has changed considerably since then, leading many theologians to wonder whether Niebuhr's five categories have now outlived their usefulness. Yet they are still widely cited in theological literature, and are helpful in outlining the main approaches to culture found within Christian theology.

The five approaches identified by Niebuhr are the following:

1 "Christ against Culture." This view encourages opposition, total separation, and hostility toward culture. The values of the Kingdom of God, on this view, stand in contrast to those of the world. As we have seen, Tertullian could be included in this category. Niebuhr also includes the world-renouncing Russian writer Leo Tolstoy, and Anabaptist writers, such as Menno Simons, in this category. Anabaptist writers stressed the need to form alternative Christian communities, often in rural areas. They refused to have anything to do with secular power or authority, rejecting the use of force. A tension can be discerned

at this point between radical writers and the mainline reformers (such as Luther and Calvin), who encouraged a more positive and interactive approach to society and culture. Similar attitudes can be found within North American fundamentalist circles today

2   "Christ of Culture." This approach is more or less the direct opposite of the "Christ against Culture" view, in that it attempts to bring culture and Christianity together, regardless of their differences. A world-affirming approach can be found in nineteenth-century German liberal Protestantism, which tended to amalgamate German culture with Christian ideals. Liberal Protestantism was inspired by the vision of a humanity which was ascending upwards into new realms of progress and prosperity. The doctrine of evolution gave new vitality to this belief, which was nurtured by strong evidence of cultural stability in western Europe in the late nineteenth century. Liberation, process, and feminist theologies are current examples of a similar trend.

3   "Christ above Culture." This position attempts to correlate the fundamental questions of the culture with the answer of Christian revelation. The famous maxim of St Thomas Aquinas (c.1225–74) can be seen as underlying this approach: "Grace does not abolish nature, but perfects it".

4   "Christ and Culture in Paradox." This model rests on what could be described as a "dualist" approach, which holds that the Christian belongs to "two realms (the spiritual and temporal)," and must therefore live in the tension of fulfilling responsibilities to both. Niebuhr saw the sixteenth-century German reformer Martin Luther (1483–1546) as an excellent representative of this understanding of the relation of Christianity and culture. According to this model, the Christian community must ex-

pect to live in a degree of tension with the world. Luther set out this tension in terms of his doctrine of the "two kingdoms" – the "kingdom of the world" and the "kingdom of God." These two very different realms of authority coexist and overlap, with the result that Christians experience the tension of living in one kingdom, yet trying to obey the authority of another.

5   "Christ the Transformer of Culture." This model includes "conversionists" who attempt to convert the values and goals of secular culture into the service of the kingdom of God. We have already seen that Augustine of Hippo belongs to this category. John Calvin, John Wesley, and Jonathan Edwards take similar positions.

In this chapter, we have explored a number of issues which are preparatory to engaging with the study of theology. The aim has been, in effect, to clear the ground a little, before we move on to deal with specific issues of substance relating to theology. Much the same remarks must apply to the next chapter, which aims to explore the sources upon which theology must draw.

QUESTIONS FOR CHAPTER 5

1   Critique the following definition of theology: "Theology is talk about God."

2   What difficulties with the idea of theology as an academic discipline lie behind the growing interest in spirituality within the churches and seminaries?

3   Explain the role played by the following in the development of theology: Peter Lombard's *Sentences*, John Calvin's *Institutes*, F. D. E. Schleiermacher's *Christian Faith*.

4   Do you have to be a Christian to be a Christian theologian?

5   Is the notion of "heresy" now an outdated irrelevance for Christian theology?

6

The Sources of Theology

Christian theology, like most disciplines, draws upon a number of sources. There has been considerable discussion within the Christian tradition concerning the identity of these sources, and their relative importance for theological analysis. The present chapter aims to explore the identity of these sources, and provide an assessment of their potential for constructive theology.

Broadly speaking, four main sources have been acknowledged within the Christian tradition:

1 Scripture
2 Tradition
3 Reason
4 Experience

Though not regarded as being of equal importance, each of these sources has a distinct contribution to make within the discipline of theology, and will be considered in detail in what follows.

Scripture

The terms "Bible" and "Scripture," along with the derived adjectives "biblical" and "scriptural," are virtually interchangeable. Both designate a body of texts which are recognized as authoritative for Christian thinking (although the nature and extent of that authority is a matter of debate). It must be stressed that the Bible is not merely the object of formal academic study within Christianity; it is also read and expounded within the context of public worship, and is the subject of meditation and devotion on the part of individual Christians.

The Old Testament

The term "Old Testament" is used by Christian writers to refer to those books of the Christian Bible which were (and still are) regarded as sacred by Judaism. For Christians, the Old Testament is seen as setting the scene for the coming of Jesus, who brings its leading themes and institutions to fulfillment. Early Christians – including Jesus himself and many of the writers of the New Testament – simply used the word "scripture" or "writing" (Greek: *graphē*) to refer to what is now known as the Old Testament. It is not clear when this specific way of referring to these books became established.

The same texts, of course, continue to be held as sacred by Jews to this day. This means that the same collection of texts is referred to in different ways by different groups. This has led to some proposals for renaming this collection of texts, none of which has gained general acceptance. Three may be noted.

1 The Hebrew Bible. This way of referring to the Old Testament stresses the fact that it was written in Hebrew, and is sacred to the Hebrew people. However, it fails to do justice to the way in which Christianity sees an essential continuity between the Old and New Testaments. A minor difficulty is also caused by the fact that parts of the Old Testament are written in Aramaic, rather than Hebrew.

2 The First Testament. This way of referring to the collection of texts avoids using the word "old," which is held by some to be pejorative. "Old," it is argued, means "outdated" or "invalid." Referring to the Old Testament as the "First Testament" and the New as the "Second Testament" stresses the continuity between the two collections of texts.

3 Tanakh – an acronym of the Hebrew words for "law, prophets, and writings (torah, nevi'im, ketuvim)," which is the standard Jewish description of the works that Christians call the "Old Testament." This is perfectly acceptable for Jewish use, but does not reflect the specifically Christian understanding of continuity between Israel and the church.

There is presently no generally accepted alternative to the traditional term "Old Testament," which will therefore be used throughout this study. Nevertheless, readers should be aware of the alternatives, and the issues which led to their being proposed.

The New Testament

The New Testament, which consists of 27 books, is considerably shorter than the Old Testament. It is entirely written in Greek. The New Testament opens with the four *Gospels*: Matthew, Mark, Luke, and John. The word "gospel" basically means "good news." Each of the four Gospel writers – or "evangelists," as they are sometimes known – sets out the basic events lying behind the good news. These four books describe the life of Jesus Christ, which reaches its climax in his resurrection, as well as presenting his teachings.

This is followed by an account of the expansion of Christianity. How were events described in the Gospels received at the time? How did the gospel spread from Palestine to Europe? These questions are addressed in the fifth work to be found in the New Testament, the full title of which is "the Acts of the Apostles," but which is more usually referred to simply as "Acts." The Gospel of Luke and Acts are widely agreed to have been written by the same person – Luke.

The next major section of material in the New Testament are the *letters*, sometimes still referred to by the older English word *epistles*. These letters provide teaching concerning both Christian beliefs and behavior, as important today as they were when they were first written. Some of the false teachings which arose in the early period of the church's history are in circulation once more, and these letters provide important resources for defending the integrity of the Christian faith today.

Most of the letters were written by Paul, whose conversion to the Christian faith led him to undertake a major program of evangelism and church planting. Many of his letters were written to churches he had planted, giving them advice. Other letters are attributed to the apostles Peter and John. Often, the letters describe the hardship being faced for the gospel, or the joy which it brings to the writer and those he is writing to. This reminds us that Christianity is not just about beliefs; it is about changed lives. The letters should not be thought of primarily as doctrinal textbooks, but living testimonies to every aspect of the Christian faith, which include doctrinal teaching along with moral guidance and spiritual encouragement. The term *pastoral letters* is sometimes used to refer to the two letters Paul addressed to Timothy and his letter to Titus, which deal particularly with issues of pastoral importance.

The New Testament then ends with the book of Revelation, which stands in a class of its own. It represents a vision of the end of history, in which the writer is allowed to see into heaven, and gain a glimpse of the new Jerusalem which is prepared for believers.

Other works: deutero-canonical and apocryphal writings

The adjective "canonical" is often used to refer to Scripture. This term, deriving from the Greek word *kanōn* (meaning "rule," "norm," or "yardstick"), is used to indicate that limits have been set by the consensus of the Christian community to the texts which may be regarded as "scriptural," and hence as authoritative for Christian theology. A longstanding debate between Roman Catholic and Protestant theologians concerns the status of a further group of texts which are often referred to as "apocryphal" or " deutero-canonical."

A comparison of the contents of the Old Testament in the Hebrew Bible on the one hand, and the Greek and Latin versions (such as the Septuagint or Vulgate) on the other, shows that the latter contain a number of works not found in the former. Following the lead of Jerome, the sixteenth-century reformers argued that the only Old Testament writings which could be regarded as belonging to the canon of Scripture were those originally included in the Hebrew Bible.

A distinction was thus drawn between the "Old Testament" and the "Apocrypha": the former consisted of works found in the Hebrew Bible, while the latter consisted of works found in the Greek and Latin Bibles but *not* in the Hebrew Bible. While some reformers allowed that the apocryphal works were edifying reading, there was general agreement that these works could not be used as the basis of Christian theology. In 1546 the Council of Trent defined the Old Testament as "those Old Testament works contained in the Greek and Latin Bibles," thus eliminating any distinction between "Old Testament" and "Apocrypha."

In practice this distinction is not as significant as might at first seem to be the case. An examination of the sixteenth-century debates over the matter suggests that the only theological issue of any real importance which was linked to this question was whether it was proper to pray for the dead. The (apocryphal) Books of the Maccabees encourage this practice, which Protestant theologians were not inclined to accept.

The issue which remains of real theological significance today concerns the canon of Scripture. Does the fact that the church drew up the canon imply that the church has authority over Scripture? Or did the church merely recognize and give formal assent to an authority which the canonical Scriptures already possessed? Does the process of shaping the canon of Scripture reflect the *imposition* of the external authority of the church upon the Bible, or the *recognition* by the church of the intrinsic authority of the Bible? The former position is particularly attractive to Catholic, and the latter to Protestant scholars.

In practice there has been increased recognition of late that the community of faith and Scripture, the people and the book, coexist with one another, and that attempts to draw sharp lines of distinction between them are somewhat arbitrary. The canon of Scripture may be regarded as emerging organically from a community of faith already committed to using and respecting it.

Box 1 Abbreviations of the books of the Bible

Old Testament

Genesis	Gen/Ge	Zephaniah	Zeph/Zep
Exodus	Ex	Haggai	Hag
Leviticus	Lev	Zechariah	Zech/Zec
Numbers	Num/Nu	Malachi	Mal
Deuteronomy	Deut/Dt		
Joshua	Josh/Jos	*New Testament*	
Judges	Judg/Jdg		
Ruth	Ru/Ruth	Matthew	Mt/Matt
1 Samuel	1 Sam/Sa	Mark	Mk/Mark
2 Samuel	2 Sam/Sa	Luke	Lk/Luke
1 Kings	1 Kgs/Ki	John	Jn/John
2 Kings	2 Kgs/Ki	Acts	Ac/Acts
1 Chronicles	1 Chron/Ch	Romans	Rom/Ro
2 Chronicles	2 Chron/Ch	1 Corinthians	1 Cor/Co
Ezra	Ezr/Ezra	2 Corinthians	2 Cor/Co
Nehemiah	Neh/Ne	Galatians	Gal
Esther	Est/Esth	Ephesians	Eph
Job	Job	Philippians	Phil/Php
Psalms	Ps	Colossians	Col
Proverbs	Prov/Pr	1 Thessalonians	1 Thess/Th
Ecclesiastes	Eccles/Ecc	2 Thessalonians	2 Thess/Th
Song of Songs	SS/Song	1 Timothy	1 Tim/Ti
Isaiah	Isa/Is	2 Timothy	2 Tim/Ti
Jeremiah	Jer	Titus	Tit
Lamentations	Lam/La	Philemon	Philem/Phm
Ezekiel	Exek/Eze	Hebrews	Heb
Daniel	Dan/Da	James	Jas
Hosea	Hos	1 Peter	1 Pet/Pe
Joel	Joel	2 Peter	2 Pet/Pe
Amos	Am/Amos	1 John	1 Jn/John
Obadiah	Obad/Ob	2 John	2 Jn/John
Jonah	Jon/Jnh	3 John	3 Jn/John
Micah	Mic	Jude	Jude
Nahum	Nah/Na	Revelation (or "The Apocalypse")	Rev
Habakkuk	Hab		

Box 2   Referring to books of the Bible

The standard method of referring to the Bible involves *three* elements. First, the *book* in question is identified (note that the term "book" is invariably used, even when the "book" in question is actually a letter). This is followed by the *chapter* of the book, followed by the *verse(s)* within that chapter.

The book may be identified in a full or abbreviated form. The chapter may be given in roman or arabic numerals. The chapter and verse numbers are usually separated by a colon or period. However, occasionally the verse numbers are printed in superscript.

The following are all commonly encountered ways of referring to one of the most familiar sayings from St Paul, which has become widely known as "the grace."

2 Corinthians 13.14; II Corinthians xiii, 14; 2 Cor. 13[14]; 2 Co 13:14

Note the following points:

1   It is not necessary to distinguish between the Old and New Testaments in referring to biblical works.

2   It is not necessary to identify the author of a biblical book when referring to it.

Box 3   Common terms used in relation to the Bible

Pentateuch (Five books of the Law)   The first five books of the Old Testament (Genesis, Exodus, Leviticus, Numbers, and Deuteronomy)

Major prophets   The first four prophetic writings of the Old Testament (Isaiah, Jeremiah, Ezekiel, and Daniel)

Minor prophets   The 12 remaining prophetic writings of the Old Testament (Hosea, Joel, Amos, Obadiah, Jonah, Micah, Nahum, Habakkuk, Zephaniah, Haggai, Zechariah, and Malachi)

Synoptic Gospels   The first three Gospels (Matthew, Mark, and Luke)

Pastoral epistles (or letters)   A way of referring collectively to 1 Timothy, 2 Timothy, and Titus, which takes note of their particular concern for pastoral matters and church order

Catholic epistles (or letters)   Those New Testament letters which are not explicitly addressed to individuals (James, 1 Peter, 2 Peter, 1 John, 2 John, 3 John, Jude). In older works, sometimes referred to as "epistles general."

The relation of the Old and New Testaments

The Christian terms "Old Testament" and "New Testament" are strongly theological in nature. These Christian terms rest upon the belief that the contents of the Old Testament belong to a period of God's dealings with the world which has in some way been superseded or relativized by the coming of Christ in the New Testament. Roughly the same collection of texts is referred to by Jewish writers as "the law, prophets, and writings" and by Christian writers as the "Old Testament." There is thus no particular reason why someone who is not a Christian should feel obliged to refer to this collection of books as the Old Testament, apart from custom of use.

The Christian theological framework which leads to this distinction is that of "covenants" or "dispensations." The basic Christian belief that the coming of Christ inaugurates something *new* expresses itself in a distinctive attitude toward the Old Testament, which could basically be summarized thus: religious *principles and ideas* (such as the notion of a sovereign God who is active in human history) are appropriated; religious *practices* (such as dietary laws and sacrificial routines) are not.

How, then, are the Old and New Testaments related to one another, according to Christian theology? One option was especially associated with the second-century writer Marcion, who was excommunicated in the year 144. This was to treat the Old Testament as the writings of a religion which had nothing to do with Christianity. According to Marcion, Christianity was a religion of love, which had no place whatsoever for the legalistic God of the Old Testament. The Old Testament relates to a different God from the New; the Old Testament God, who merely created the world, was obsessed with the idea of law. The New Testament God, however, redeemed the world and was concerned with love. According to Marcion, the purpose of Christ was to depose the Old Testament God (who bears a considerable resemblance to the Gnostic "demiurge," a semidivine figure responsible for fashioning the world), and usher in the worship of the true God of grace.

There are faint echoes of this idea in the writings of Luther. Although Luther insists that both Old and New Testaments relate to the actions of the same God, he nevertheless insists upon the total opposition of law and grace. Judaism, according to Luther, was to-

tally preoccupied with the idea of justification by works, believing that it was possible to merit favor in the sight of God by one's achievements. The gospel, in contrast, emphasized that justification was completely gratuitous, resting only on the grace of God. Although grace could be detected in the Old Testament (e.g., Isaiah 40–55), and law in the New (e.g., the Sermon on the Mount, Matthew 5–7), Luther often seemed to suggest that the Old Testament was primarily a religion of law, contrasted with the New Testament emphasis on grace.

The majority position within Christian theology has on the one hand emphasized the *continuity* between the two testaments, while on the other noting the *distinction* between them. Calvin provides a lucid and typical discussion of their relation. He argues that there exists a fundamental similarity and continuity between Old and New Testaments on the basis of three considerations. First, Calvin stresses the immutability of the divine will. God cannot do one thing in the Old Testament, and follow it by doing something totally different in the New. There must be a fundamental continuity of action and intention between the two. Second, both celebrate and proclaim the grace of God manifested in Jesus Christ. The Old Testament may only be able to witness to Jesus Christ "from a distance and darkly"; nevertheless, its witness to the coming of Christ is real. In the third place, both testaments possess the "same signs and sacraments," bearing witness to the same grace of God.

Calvin thus argues that the two testaments are basically identical. They differ in *administratio* but not in *substantia*. In terms of their substance and content there is no radical discontinuity between them. The Old Testament happens to occupy a different chronological position in the divine plan of salvation from the New; its content (rightly understood), however, is the same.

Throughout this discussion of the distinction between the Old and New Testaments, and the superiority of the latter over the former, Calvin is careful to allow that certain individuals within the old covenant – for example, the patriarchs – were able to discern hints of the new covenant. At no point do the divine purposes or nature alter; they are merely made clearer, in accordance with the limitations imposed upon human understanding. Thus, to give but one example, it was not as if God had originally determined to restrict grace to the nation of Israel alone, and then decided to make it available to everyone else as well; rather, the evolutionary thrust of the divine plan was only made clear with the coming of Jesus Christ. Calvin summarizes this general principle with the assertion that "where the entire law is concerned, the gospel differs from it only in clarity of presentation." Christ is shown forth and the grace of the Holy Spirit is offered in both Old and New Testaments – but more clearly and more fully in the latter.

This viewpoint has been characteristic of mainline Christianity. It can be found, for example, in the declarations of the Second Vatican Council, which affirms the importance of the Old Testament for Christians:

> The Church of Christ acknowledges that in God's plan of salvation the beginning of her faith and election is to be found in the patriarchs, Moses and the prophets. She professes that all Christ's faithful, who as men of faith are sons of Abraham (cf. Galatians 3:7), are included in the same patriarch's call and that the salvation of the Church is mystically prefigured in the exodus of God's chosen people from the land of bondage. On this account the Church cannot forget that she received the revelation of the Old Testament by way of that people with whom God in his inexpressible mercy established the ancient covenant.

The Word of God

The phrases "the Word of God" and "the Word of the Lord" are at least as deeply rooted in Christian worship as they are in Christian theology. "Word" implies action and communication. Just as a person's character and will are expressed through the words he or she uses, so Scripture (especially the Old Testament) understands God to address the people, who are thus made aware of God's intentions and will for them.

The term "Word of God" is complex and highly nuanced, bringing together a cluster of ideas. Three broad, and clearly related, senses of the term may be discerned, both within the Christian tradition and within Scripture itself.

1 The phrase is used to refer to Jesus Christ as the Word of God made flesh (John 1: 14). This is the most highly developed use of the term in the New Testament. In speaking of Christ as the "Word of God incarnate," Christian theology has attempted to express the idea that the will, purposes, and nature of God are made known in history through the person of Jesus Christ. It is the deeds, character, and theological identity of Jesus Christ, and not merely the words that he uttered, which make known the nature and purpose of God.

2 The term is also used to refer to "the gospel of Christ" or the "message or proclamation about Jesus." In this sense, the term refers to what God achieved and made known through the life, death, and resurrection of Christ.

3 The term is used in a general sense to refer to the whole Bible, which can be regarded as setting the scene for the advent of Christ, telling the story of his coming, and exploring the implications of his life, death, and resurrection for believers.

Considerations of this kind lie behind Karl Barth's use of the phrase "the Word of God." Barth's doctrine of "the threefold form of the Word of God" distinguishes a threefold movement from the Word of God in Christ to the witness to this Word in Scripture, and finally to the proclamation of this Word in the preaching of the community of faith. There is thus a direct and organic connection between the preaching of the church and the person of Jesus Christ.

Narrative theology

The literary form which dominates Scripture is that of narrative. The Bible tells stories – a series of stories which disclose the nature and character of God, and the shape of the redemption achieved through Christ. The story of the calling of Abraham, the exodus from Egypt, the exile in Babylon, and the coming of Jesus Christ are all individual parts of the greater narrative that discloses God's nature and purposes. So what implications does this observation have for relating Scripture to theology? The recently developed concept of "narrative theology" has much to say on this theme.

Narrative theology is based on the observation that the Bible tells stories about God, just as much as it makes doctrinal or theological statements. For example, the Old Testament could be said to be dominated by the telling and retelling of the story of how God led Israel out of Egypt into the promised land, and all that this implies for the people of God. In a similar way, the New Testament is also dominated by a story of God's redeeming action in history, this time centering on the life, death, and resurrection of Jesus Christ. What does this story mean for Christians? How does it affect the way in which they think and act? It is helpful to think of Paul's letters, for example, as systematic attempts to spell out the relevance of the story of Jesus Christ for Christians

– how it affects the way they think, and the way they behave.

It is insights like these which lie behind the emergence of one of the most important theological movements to develop in the last few decades – *narrative theology*. It has developed largely in North America, with many observers detecting especially close links with Yale Divinity School and writers based there, such as Hans Frei, George Lindbeck, and Ronald Thiemann. Among other writers to have contributed to this development, we may note James Gustafson and Stanley Hauerwas, George Lindbeck, and Ronald Thiemann. It must, however, be stressed that narrative theology is by no means a well-defined movement.

What, then, are the advantages and drawbacks of such an approach? Why has it gained such a following in academic theology? The following points are important in understanding the appeal of this new approach, especially among writers concerned to reclaim the centrality of scripture in modern theology.

1 Narrative is the main literary type found in Scripture. Indeed, some recent writers have even suggested that it is the *only* literary form in Scripture – an obvious, though perhaps understandable, exaggeration. It can occur in various forms: the Old Testament histories, the gospel accounts of the history of Jesus, and the parables which Jesus himself told – all are examples of narratives. To approach theology from a narrative point of view is, potentially, to be much more faithful to Scripture itself than to take a more theoretical approach.

2 The approach avoids the dulling sense of *abstraction* which is often claimed to be a feature of much academic theological writing. The abstract, generalizing approach of theology is set to one side. Instead, narrative theology invites us to reflect

upon a story – a vivid, memorable account of something that actually happened (such as the story of Jesus), or that may be treated as if it really happened (such as the parables of Jesus). There is an appeal to the imagination (a point especially stressed by writers such as C. S. Lewis), a sense of realism, of personal involvement, which is often conspicuously absent from more conceptual approaches to theology.

3   Narrative theology affirms that God meets us in history, and speaks to us as one who has been involved in history. The doctrine of the incarnation affirms that the story of Jesus Christ is also the story of God. Narrative theology declares that God really became involved in our world of space and time, that God really entered into history, that God really came to meet us where we are. Often, systematic theology creates the impression that God has presented us with a set of ideas, as if revelation were some kind of data bank (see pp. 153–9). Narrative theology enables us to recover the central insight that God became involved in our history. God's story intersects with our story. We can understand our story by relating it to the story of God, as we read it in Scripture.

This aspect of narrative theology has had a considerable impact, most strikingly in the field of ethics. Stanley Hauerwas is perhaps the most distinguished of a group of ethical writers who have argued that the Gospel narratives set out a pattern of behavior which is appropriate for Christian believers. The story of Jesus Christ, for example, is seen as establishing a pattern which is characteristic of the story of Christian believers. Ethics, approached from a narrative standpoint, becomes thoroughly grounded in real life. The gospel is not primarily about a set of ethical principles; it is about the effect of an encounter with God upon the lives of individuals and the histories of nations. By relating such stories, the biblical writers are able to declare: "This is the result of being transformed by the grace of God. That is an appropriate model for Christian behavior."

4   Recognition of the narrative character of Scripture allows us to appreciate how Scripture effectively conveys the tension between the limited knowledge on the part of the human characters in the story, and the omniscience of God. In his *Art of Biblical Narrative* (1985), Robert Alter makes this point as follows: "The biblical tale might usefully be regarded as a narrative experiment in the possibilities of moral, spiritual, and historical knowledge, undertaken through a process of studied contrasts between the variously limited knowledge of the human characters and the divine omniscience quietly but firmly represented by the narrator." Perhaps Job illustrates this point with especial clarity in the Old Testament. The narrative structure of Scripture allows the reader to see the story from God's point of view, and appreciate the interplay between the human ignorance or misunderstanding of the situation and its reality, seen from God's point of view.

Methods of interpretation of Scripture

Every text demands to be interpreted; Scripture is no exception. There is a sense in which the history of Christian theology can be regarded as the history of biblical interpretation. In what follows, we shall explore some of the approaches to biblical interpretation likely to be of interest to students of theology. It will, however, be clear that the vastness of the subject makes it impossible to do more than give a representative selection of approaches to the matter.

We open our discussion by dealing with the patristic period. The *Alexandrian* school of biblical interpretation drew on the methods devised by the Jewish writer Philo of Alexandria (c.30 BC–c.AD 45) and earlier Jewish traditions, which allowed the literal interpretation of Scripture to be supplemented by an appeal to allegory. But what is an allegory? The Greek philosopher Heracleitus had defined it as "saying one thing, and meaning something other than what is said." Philo argued that it was necessary to look beneath the surface meaning of Scripture to discern a deeper meaning which lay beneath the surface of the text. These ideas were taken up by a group of theologians based in Alexandria, of which the most important are generally agreed to be Clement, Origen, and Didymus the Blind. (Indeed, Jerome playfully referred to the last-mentioned as "Didymus the Sighted," on account of the spiritual insights which resulted from his application of the allegorical method of biblical interpretation.)

It might at first sight seem that this represents a degeneration into *eisegesis*, in which the interpreter simply reads any meaning he or she likes into the text of Scripture. However, as the writings of Didymus (which were rediscovered, incidentally, in an ammunition dump in Egypt during World War II) make clear, this need not be the case. It seems that a consensus developed about the images and texts of the Old Testament which were to be interpreted allegorically. For example, Jerusalem regularly came to be seen as an allegory of the church.

In contrast, the *Antiochene* school placed an emphasis upon the interpretation of Scripture in the light of its historical context. This school, especially associated with writers such as Diodore of Tarsus, John Chrysostom, and Theodore of Mopsuestia, gave an emphasis to the historical location of Old Testament prophecies, which is quite absent from the writings of Origen and other representatives of the Alexandrian tradition. Thus Theodore, in dealing with Old Testament prophecy, stresses that the prophetic message was relevant to those to whom it was directly addressed, as well as having a developed meaning for a Christian readership. Every prophetic oracle is to be interpreted as having a single consistent historical or literal meaning. In consequence, Theodore tended to interpret relatively few Old Testament passages as referring directly to Christ, whereas the Alexandrian school regarded Christ as the hidden content of many Old Testament passages, both prophetic and historical.

In the western church a slightly different approach can be seen to develop. In many of his writings, Ambrose of Milan developed a threefold understanding of the senses of Scripture: in addition to the *natural* sense, the interpreter may discern a *moral* sense and a *rational* or *theological* sense. Augustine chose to follow this approach, but instead argued for a twofold sense – a *literal-fleshly-historical* sense and an *allegorical-mystical-spiritual* sense, although he allowed that some passages could possess both senses. "The sayings of the prophets are found to have a threefold meaning, in that some have in mind the earthly Jerusalem, others the heavenly city, and others refer to both." To understand the Old Testament at a purely historical level is unacceptable; the key to its understanding lies in its correct interpretation.

We see here the basic concept of *typology* (Greek: *typos* – "a figure"). Here, an historical event is seen as an anticipation of some aspect of the coming of Christ. Whereas allegory refers primarily to biblical images, typology refers primarily to historical events or historical individuals. The classic example of this is the Old Testament story of Abraham and Isaac (Genesis 22: 1–14). This story tells of how Abraham believed God was calling him to offer his son Isaac as a "burnt offering." As they travel into the wilderness, Isaac asks his father why they had not brought a lamb to sacrifice. Abraham replies that "God himself will provide the lamb for a burnt offering." When Abraham is about to kill Isaac, the angel of the Lord intervenes, providing instead a ram, which is trapped in a nearby thicket of thorns by its horns. Typologically this episode was seen to prefigure God's sacrifice of his only son Jesus Christ, the Lamb of God, who carries his cross on his own back, is sacrificed on that cross, and who like Isaac is raised from his own death.

The essential point is that these types need to be interpreted correctly. For Augustine, the key question is how the language, signs, and symbols of a fallen world can point to God. If all human signs are corrupted and imperfect after the Fall, Augustine argues, the truth of their meaning may only be retrieved with the assistance of what he terms "divine illumination." Human language, on account of the Fall, tends to point only to carnal or earthly things. For this language to point to divine things, our limitations as fallen human beings must be overcome, or at least reduced. Augustine sees this as taking place partly through humanity continuing to bear the image of God as creator, partly because of God's gracious self-revelation, and partly through the incarnation which, Augustine argues, enables the signs and language of the material order to point to its creator. Augustine sets out his approach as follows:

It is not the Old Testament that is abolished in Christ but the concealing veil, so that it may be understood through Christ. That which without Christ is obscure and hidden is, as it were, opened up [. . . Paul] does not say: "The Law or the Old Testament is abolished." It is not the case, therefore, that by the grace of the Lord that which was covered has been abolished as useless; rather, the covering which concealed useful truth has been removed. This is what happens to those who earnestly and piously, not proudly and wickedly, seek the sense of the Scriptures. To them

is carefully demonstrated the order of events, the reasons for deeds and words, and the agreement of the Old Testament with the New, so that not a single point remains where there is not complete harmony. The secret truths are conveyed in figures that are to be brought to light by interpretation.

By the use of such lines of analysis, Augustine is able to stress the unity of the Old and New Testaments. They bear witness to the same faith, even if their modes of expression may be different (an idea developed by John Calvin). Augustine expresses this idea in a text which has become of major importance to biblical interpretation, especially as it bears on the relation between Old and New Testaments: "The New Testament is hidden in the Old; the Old is made accessible by the New" (*In Vetere Novum latet et in Novo Vetus patet*).

This distinction between the *literal* or *historical* sense of Scripture on the one hand, and a deeper *spiritual* or *allegorical* meaning on the other, came to be generally accepted within the church during the early Middle Ages. The standard method of biblical interpretation used during the Middle Ages is usually known as the *Quadriga*, or the "fourfold sense of Scripture." The origins of this method lie specifically in the distinction between the literal and spiritual senses. Scripture possesses four different senses. In addition to the literal sense, three nonliteral senses could be distinguished: the allegorical, defining what Christians are to believe; the tropological or moral, defining what Christians are to do; and the anagogical, defining what Christians were to hope for. The four senses of Scripture were thus the following:

1 The *literal* sense of Scripture, in which the text could be taken at face value.
2 The *allegorical* sense, which interpreted certain passages of Scripture to produce statements of doctrine. Those passages

tended either to be obscure, or to have a literal meaning which was unacceptable, for theological reasons, to their readers.

3   The *tropological* or *moral* sense, which interpreted such passages to produce ethical guidance for Christian conduct.

4   The *anagogical* sense, which interpreted passages to indicate the grounds of Christian hope, pointing toward the future fulfillment of the divine promises in the New Jerusalem.

An excellent example of allegorical interpretation can be found in Bernard of Clairvaux's twelfth-century exposition of the Song of Songs. Bernard here provides an allegorical interpretation of the phrase "the beams of our houses are of cedar, and our panels are of cypress," illustrating the way in which doctrinal or spiritual meaning was "read into" otherwise unpromising passages at this time.

> By "houses" we are to understand the great mass of the Christian people, who are bound together with those who possess power and dignity, rulers of the church and the state, as "beams." These hold them together by wise and firm laws; otherwise, if each of them were to operate in any way that they pleased, the walls would bend and collapse, and the whole house would fall in ruins. By the "panels" which are firmly attached to the beams and which adorn the house in a royal manner, we are to understand the kindly and ordered lives of a properly instructed clergy, and the proper administration of the rites of the church.

A potential weakness was avoided by insisting that nothing should be believed on the basis of a nonliteral sense of Scripture, unless it could first be established on the basis of the literal sense. This insistence on the priority of the literal sense of Scripture may be seen as an implied criticism of the allegorical approach adopted by Origen, which virtually allowed interpreters of Scripture to read into any passage whatever "spiritual" interpretations they liked. As Luther states this principle in 1515: "In the Scriptures no allegory, tropology, or anagogy is valid, unless that same truth is explicitly stated literally somewhere else. Otherwise, Scripture would become a laughing matter."

Luther is fully aware of the distinctions noted above, and has no hesitation in using them to the full in his biblical exposition. In his analysis of the Psalter, he distinguishes eight senses of the Old Testament. This amazing precision (which may strike some readers as typical of scholasticism) results from combining the four senses of Scripture with the insight that each of these senses can be interpreted *historically* or *prophetically*. Luther argues that a distinction had to be made between what he terms "the killing letter" (*litera occidens*) – in other words, a crudely literal or historical reading of the Old Testament – and "the life-giving spirit" (*spiritus vivificans*) – in other words, a reading of the Old Testament which is sensitive to its spiritual nuances and prophetic overtones. As a worked example, we may consider Luther's analysis of an Old Testament image using this eightfold scheme of interpretation.

The image in question is Mount Zion, which can be interpreted either in a woodenly historical and literal sense as a reference to ancient Israel or as a prophetic reference to the New Testament church. Luther explores the possibilities as follows:

1   Historically, according to "the killing letter":
(a) literally: the land of Canaan;
(b) allegorically: the synagogue, or a prominent person within it;
(c) tropologically: the righteousness of the Pharisees and the Law;
(d) anagogically: a future glory on earth.

2 Prophetically, according to "the life-giving spirit":
(a) literally: the people of Zion;
(b) allegorically: the church, or a prominent
person within it;
(c) tropologically: the righteousness of faith;
(d) anagogically: the eternal glory of the
heavens.

The *Quadriga* was a major component of academic study of the Bible within scholastic theological faculties of universities. But it was not
the only option available to biblical interpreters in the first two decades of the sixteenth
century. Indeed, Luther may be argued to be
the only reformer to make significant use of
this scholastic approach to biblical interpretation. By far the most influential approach to
the subject within reforming and humanist
circles in the early Reformation period was
that associated with Erasmus of Rotterdam,
to which we may now turn.

Erasmus's *Handbook of the Christian Soldier*
(see p. 37) made much of the distinction between the "letter" and the "spirit" – that is,
between the words of Scripture and their real
meaning. Especially in the Old Testament, the
words of the text are like a shell, containing –
but not identical with – the kernel of the meaning. The surface meaning of the text often
conceals a deeper hidden meaning, which it is
the task of the enlightened and responsible
exegete to uncover. Biblical interpretation,
according to Erasmus, is concerned with establishing the underlying sense, not the letter, of
Scripture. There are strong affinities here with
the Alexandrian school, noted earlier.

Zwingli's basic concern echoes that of Erasmus. The interpreter of the Bible is required to
establish the "natural sense of Scripture,"
which is not necessarily identical with the literal sense of Scripture. Zwingli's humanist
background allows him to distinguish various
figures of speech, especially alloiosis, catachre-
sis, and synecdoche.

An example will make this difficult point
clear. Take the statement of Christ at the Last
Supper, in which, when breaking the bread, he
spoke the words "this is my body" (Matthew
26: 26). The literal sense of these words would
be "this piece of bread is my body," but the
natural sense is "this piece of bread signifies
my body" (see p. 440).

Zwingli's search for the deeper meaning of
Scripture (to be contrasted with the superficial
meaning) is well illustrated by the story of
Abraham and Isaac (Genesis 22). The historical details of the story are too easily assumed
to be its real meaning. In fact, Zwingli argues,
the real meaning of that story can only be
understood when it is seen as a prophetic anticipation of the story of Christ, in which Abraham represents God and Isaac is a figure (or,
more technically, a "type") of Christ.

With the advent of the modern period, the
science of biblical interpretation has become
considerably more complex, reflecting the increased acceptance within academic circles of
new rational methods of interpretation,
grounded in the assumptions of the Enlightenment. It is impossible to survey these developments adequately in the scope of this work.
However, it will be helpful to note some broad
tendencies in biblical interpretation during the
last two and a half centuries. Under the influence of the Enlightenment, four main approaches can be seen in academic biblical
interpretation.

1 The *rational* approach, found in the writings of H. S. Reimarus. This regards both
Old and New Testaments as resting on a
series of supernatural fictions. By a process
of radical logical criticism, Reimarus argued that the supernatural elements of
the Bible could not be taken seriously.
It was therefore necessary to interpret
Scripture along rational lines, as stating
(although in a somewhat muddled

manner) the universal truths of the religion of reason. With the general collapse in confidence in both the universality and the theological competence of reason in more recent times, the attractions of this approach have dwindled drastically.

2   The *historical* approach, which treats Scripture as an account of Christian origins. F. C. Baur, probably the most distinguished early representative of this tradition, argued that it was no longer permissible to explain the origins of the Christian faith in terms of "the only-begotten Son of God descending from the eternal throne of the Godhead to earth, and becoming a human person in the womb of the virgin." Instead, Baur argued that it was possible to account for the origins of Christianity in rational and nonsupernatural terms. Believing that Hegelianism held the key to explaining how Christianity came into being, Baur made a direct appeal to its philosophy of history as an alternative explanation to the traditional accounts of the origins of Christian faith, and interpreted the New Testament in its light. With the waning of Hegelianism, Baur's impact also diminished.

3   The *sociological* approach. By the 1890s, many liberal Christians had lost interest in matters of Christian doctrine or theology, and begun to explore the wider category of "religion" in general – a trend which undergirds the development of faculties of "religious studies" in many western universities. Yet religion is a social phenomenon; concerned with far more than "ideas" as such, it comes under the category of "social history." The way was thus opened for a sociological approach to biblical interpretation, which treated Christianity as a specific example of a general phenomenon – religion. An example of this approach is provided by Sir James Frazer's *The Golden Bough* (1890–1915), which applied comparative ethnology (the study of peoples and their traditions) to the Bible on an unprecedented scale.

4   The *literary* approach, which is concerned to do justice to the distinctive literary categories of Scripture. One such approach which has had major impact of late is *narrative theology*, discussed earlier in this chapter (see pp. 128–9).

Theories of the inspiration of Scripture

The notion that the special status of Scripture within Christian theology rests upon its divine origins, however vaguely this may be stated, can be discerned both in the New Testament itself, and in subsequent reflection on it. An important element in any discussion of the manner in which Scripture is inspired, and the significance which is to be attached to this, is 2 Timothy 3: 16–17, which speaks of Scripture as "God-breathed" (*theopneustos*). This idea was common in early Christian thought, and was not regarded as controversial. The Greek-speaking Jewish philosopher Philo of Alexandria regarded Scripture as fully inspired, and argued that God used the authors of scriptural books as passive instruments for communicating the divine will.

The issue began to surface as potentially controversial at the time of the Reformation, especially through the writings of John Calvin. Calvin was concerned to defend the authority of Scripture against two groups of people. On the one hand were those on the more Catholic wing of the church, who argued that the authority of Scripture rested in its being recognized as authoritative by the church. On the other were the more radical evangelical writers, such as the Anabaptists, who argued that every individual had the right to ignore

Scripture altogether in favor of some direct personal divine revelation. Calvin declared that the Spirit worked through Scripture (not bypassing it, as the radicals held), and that the Spirit lent direct authority to Scripture by inspiring it, thus doing away with the need for any external support to its authority (such as that of the church).

This point is important, in that it indicates that the reformers did not see the issue of inspiration as linked with the absolute historical reliability or factual inerrancy of the biblical texts. Calvin's doctrine of accommodation implied that God revealed himself in forms tailored to the abilities of the communities which were to receive this revelation; thus in the case of Genesis 1, Calvin suggests that a whole series of ideas – such as the "days of creation" – are simply accommodated ways of speaking, a kind of divine "baby-talk." The development of ideas of "biblical infallibility" or "inerrancy" within Protestantism can be traced to the United States in the middle of the nineteenth century.

The general Christian consensus on the inspiration and authority of Scripture can be studied from a number of major confessional documents, both Protestant and Roman Catholic. For example, the definitive 1994 *Catechism of the Catholic Church* clearly grounds the authority of Scripture in its divine inspiration.

> In order to reveal himself to men, in the condescension of his goodness God speaks to them in human words: indeed, the words of God, expressed in the words of men, are in every way like human language, just as the Word of the eternal Father, when he took on himself the flesh of human weakness, became like men. [...] God is the author of Sacred Scripture. The divine revealed realities, which are contained and presented in the text of Sacred Scripture, have been written down under the inspiration of the Holy Spirit. For Holy Mother Church, relying on the faith of the apostolic age, accepts as sacred and canonical the books of the Old and the New Testaments, whole and entire, with all their parts, on the grounds that, written under the inspiration of the Holy Spirit, they have God as their author and have been handed on as such to the Church herself. God inspired the human authors of the sacred books. To compose the sacred books, God chose certain men who, all the while he employed them in this task, made full use of their own faculties and powers so that, though he acted in them and by them, it was as true authors that they consigned to writing whatever he wanted written, and no more.

With the coming of the Enlightenment, the idea of the Bible having special status was called into question, largely on account of the presuppositions of the rationalism of the period, and increased interest in the critical study of Scripture. A number of approaches to the issue of inspiration which developed around this period are of interest.

1 J. G. Herder (1744–1803), who can be argued to anticipate certain important aspects of Romanticism, argued that the idea of inspiration was to be interpreted in an artistic or aesthetic sense. In his *Spirit of Hebrew Poetry* (1782–3), Herder suggested that the most appropriate model for biblical inspiration was provided by works of art. Just as one might speak of a great novel, poem, or painting as "inspired," so the same idea can be applied to Scripture. Inspiration is thus seen as a human achievement, rather than a gift of God.

2 The Old Princeton School, represented by Charles Hodge (1797–1878) and Benjamin B. Warfield (1851–1921), developed strongly supernatural theories of inspiration, in conscious opposition to the naturalist approach favored by Herder. "Inspiration is that extraordinary, supernatural influence ... exerted by the Holy Ghost on the writers of our Sacred

Books, by which their words were rendered also the words of God, and, therefore, perfectly infallible." Although Warfield is careful to stress that the humanity and individuality of biblical writers are not abolished by inspiration, he nonetheless insists that their humanity "was so dominated that their words became at the same time the words of God, and thus, in every case and all alike, absolutely infallible."

3   Others held that inspiration was also to be regarded as God's guidance of the reader of Scripture, which enabled that reader to recognize the word of God in the biblical text. As we have just seen, Warfield located the inspiration of Scripture in the biblical text itself, thus implying that Scripture was objectively, in itself, the word of God for all who read it. Others argued for a subjective understanding of inspiration, by which the reader's perception of Scripture – rather than Scripture itself – was to be regarded as "inspired." Augustus H. Strong (1836–1921) stressed that the authority of Scripture could not be located simply in the words of Scripture, as if these could have authoritative status apart from their reception by individual believers, or the community of faith. Inspiration thus had to be recognized to have objective and subjective aspects.

Having considered some questions relating to Scripture as a source of Christian theology, we may now turn to a consideration of the role of tradition.

Tradition

If any controversy served to emphasize the importance of tradition, it was the Gnostic debates of the second century. Faced with repeated assertions from his Gnostic critics that he had misrepresented the Bible, Irenaeus argued that they had simply chosen to interpret the Bible according to their own taste. What had been handed down was not merely the biblical texts, but a certain way of reading and understanding those texts.

> Everyone who wishes to perceive the truth should consider the apostolic tradition, which has been made known in every church in the entire world. We are able to number those who are bishops appointed by the apostles, and their successors in the churches to the present day, who taught and knew nothing of such things as these people imagine.

Irenaeus's point is that a continuous stream of Christian teaching, life, and interpretation can be traced from the time of the apostles to his own period. The church is able to point to those who have maintained the teaching of the church, and to certain public standard creeds which set out the main lines of Christian belief. This, he argues, contrasts with the secret and mystical teaching of the Gnostics, which is not available for public inspection, and which cannot be traced back to the apostles themselves. Tradition is thus the guarantor of faithfulness to the original apostolic teaching, a safeguard against the innovations and misrepresentations of biblical texts on the part of the Gnostics.

This point was further developed in the early fifth century by Vincent of Lérins, who was concerned that certain doctrinal innovations were being introduced without adequate reason. Vincent was especially troubled by some of Augustine's views on predestination, which he regarded as unwise and hasty improvisations. There was a need to have public standards by which such doctrines could be judged. So what standard was available, by which the church could be safeguarded from such errors? For Vincent, the answer was clear – tradition:

> On account of the number and variety of errors, there is a need for someone to lay down a rule for the interpretation of the prophets and the apostles in such a way that is directed by the rule of the catholic church. Now in the catholic church itself the greatest care is taken that we hold that which has been believed everywhere, always, and by all people [*quod ubique, quod semper, quod ab omnibus creditum est*]. This is what is truly and properly catholic. This is clear from the force of the word and reason, which understands everything universally. We shall follow "universality" in this way, if we acknowledge this one faith to be true, which the entire church confesses throughout the world. We affirm "antiquity" if we in no way depart from those understandings which it is clear that the greater saints and our fathers proclaimed. And we follow "consensus" if in this antiquity we follow all (or certainly nearly all) the definitions of the bishops and masters.

This threefold criterion – universality, antiquity, and consensus – has come to be known as the "Vincentian Canon," and has been of considerable importance in ecumenical discussions in recent years.

Yet this approach to tradition was vulnerable at certain points. For example, it seemed to suggest that "tradition" was a purely static notion – the views of the past, which the present was bound to repeat. Concern over this view became apparent within some Roman Catholic circles during the nineteenth century. Of particular interest are the views of Johann Adam Möhler (also spelled "Moehler"), the founder of the Catholic Tübingen School. In his much-read *Symbolism*, published in 1832, Möhler set out an understanding of tradition as a living voice within the church, by which the Christian community's interpretation of Scripture is safeguarded from error.

Tradition is the living Word, perpetuated in the hearts of believers. To this sense, as the general sense, the interpretation of Holy Writ is entrusted. The declaration, which it pronounces on any controverted subject, is the judgment of the Church; and, therefore, the Church is judge in matters of faith. Tradition, in the objective sense, is the general faith of the Church through all ages, manifested by outward historical testimonies; in this sense, tradition is usually termed the norm, the standard of Scriptural interpretation – the rule of faith.

It will be clear that Möhler understands tradition to have both subjective and objective aspects. The objective sense corresponds roughly to Vincent's notion of doctrinal consensus – that is, to "the general faith of the Church through all ages, manifested by outward historical testimonies." Yet the subjective element prevents this from becoming a mere process of ecclesiastical fossilization. Tradition is something living and dynamic.

This issue remains important. In the twentieth century, a concerted effort has been made within both the Roman Catholic and Orthodox churches to distinguish "tradition" from "traditionalism." The latter is understood as a slavish and wooden adherence to the doctrinal or moral formulations of the past, whereas the former is understood as the living faithfulness of the church to the faith which it expresses. This approach may also be discerned within the 1994 *Catechism of the Catholic Church*, which draws attention to the close connection between Scripture and tradition.

> In keeping with the Lord's command, the Gospel was handed on in two ways:
> – *orally*, by the apostles who handed on, by the spoken word of their preaching, by the example they gave, by the institutions they established, what they themselves had received – whether from the lips of Christ,

from his way of life and his works, or whether they had learned it at the prompting of the Holy Spirit.

– *in writing*, by those apostles and other men associated with the apostles who, under the inspiration of the same Holy Spirit, committed the message of salvation to writing.

In order that the full and living Gospel might always be preserved in the Church the apostles left bishops as their successors. They gave them their own position of teaching authority. Indeed, the apostolic teaching, which is expressed in a special way in the inspired books, was to be preserved in a continuous line of succession until the end of time. This living transmission, accomplished in the Holy Spirit, is called Tradition, since it is distinct from Sacred Scripture, though closely connected to it. Through Tradition, the Church, in her doctrine, life, and worship perpetuates and transmits to every generation all that she herself is, all that she believes. [. . .] The Father's self-communication made through his Word in the Holy Spirit remains present and active in the Church.

Note the emphasis which is placed here upon the role of the church as a living organism, which passes down the content of the faith, based in Scripture, to each generation. "Tradition" is here understood as a living and active process of passing on the Christian faith, rather than as a static source of revelation, independent of Scripture.

A similar emphasis can be found in the writings of leading Orthodox theologians, such as John Meyendorff. In his influential work *Living Tradition* (1978) Meyendorff stresses that tradition is not to be understood as an accumulated body of propositional truths, which simply repeats the insights of the past:

True tradition is always a *living* tradition. It changes while remaining always the same. It changes because it faces different situations, not because its essential content is modified.

This content is not an abstract proposition; it is the living Christ Himself, who said, "I am the Truth."

It will thus be clear that the word "tradition" implies not merely something that is handed down, but an active process of reflection by which theological or spiritual insights are valued, assessed, and transmitted from one generation to another. Three broad approaches to tradition may be detected within Christian theology, and will be considered in what follows.

A single-source theory of tradition

In response to various controversies within the early church, especially the threat from Gnosticism, a "traditional" method of understanding certain passages of Scripture began to develop. Second-century patristic theologians such as Irenaeus of Lyons began to develop the idea of an authorized way of interpreting certain texts of Scripture, which he argued went back to the time of the apostles themselves. Scripture could not be allowed to be interpreted in any arbitrary or self-serving way: it had to be interpreted within the context of the historical continuity of the Christian church. The parameters of its interpretation were historically fixed and "given." "Tradition" here means simply "a traditional way of interpreting Scripture within the community of faith." This is a *single-source* theory of theology: theology is based upon Scripture, and "tradition" refers to a "traditional way of interpreting Scripture."

The mainstream Reformation adopted this approach, insisting that traditional interpretations of Scripture – such as the doctrine of the Trinity or the practice of infant baptism – could be retained, provided they could be shown to be consistent with Scripture. On the basis of this observation, it will be clear that it is incorrect to suggest that the magisterial reformers elevated private judgment above the corporate judgment of the church, or that they descended into some form of individualism. This is, however, unquestionably true of the radical Reformation (see below).

A dual-source theory of tradition

In the fourteenth and fifteenth centuries there developed a somewhat different understanding of tradition from that noted above. "Tradition" was understood to be a separate and distinct source of revelation, *in addition to Scripture*. Scripture, it was argued, was silent on a number of points, but God had providentially arranged for a second source of revelation to supplement this deficiency: a stream of unwritten tradition, going back to the apostles themselves. This tradition was passed down from one generation to another within the church. This is a *dual-source* theory of theology: theology is based upon two quite distinct sources, Scripture and unwritten tradition.

A belief which is not to be found in Scripture may thus, on the basis of this dual-source theory, be justified by an appeal to an unwritten tradition. This position was defended strongly at the Council of Trent, which was charged with stating and defending the Roman Catholic position against the threat posed by the Reformation. Trent ruled that Scripture could not be regarded as the only source of revelation. The Council therefore argued that Scripture and tradition alike were to be regarded as inspired by the same Holy Spirit, and safeguarded and handed down by the same catholic church:

> This truth and discipline are contained in the written books, and the unwritten traditions which, received by the apostles from the mouth of Christ himself, or from the apostles themselves, the Holy Spirit dictating, have come down to us, transmitted as it were

from hand to hand; following the examples of the orthodox Fathers, [the church] receives and venerates with an equal affection of piety, and reverence, all the books both of the Old and of the New Testament – seeing that the one God is the author of both – as also the said traditions, whether these relate to faith or to morals, as having been dictated, either by Christ's own word of mouth, or by the Holy Spirit, and preserved in the Catholic Church by a continuous succession.

Interestingly, however, the Second Vatican Council (1962–5) seems to move away from this approach, in favor of the "traditional interpretation of Scripture" approach, noted above.

The two approaches just discussed affirm the value of tradition. A third approach, which in effect rejected tradition, came to be influential within the radical wing of the Reformation, often known as "Anabaptism," and subsequently was developed by writers sympathetic to the Enlightenment.

The total rejection of tradition

For certain radical theologians of the sixteenth century, such as Thomas Müntzer and Caspar Schwenkfeld, every individual had the right to interpret Scripture as he or she pleased, subject to the guidance of the Holy Spirit. For the radical Sebastian Franck, the Bible "is a book sealed with seven seals which none can open unless he has the key of David, which is the illumination of the Spirit." The way was thus opened for individualism, with the private judgment of the individual raised above the corporate judgment of the church. Thus the radicals rejected the practice of infant baptism (to which the magisterial Reformation remained committed) as nonscriptural. (There is no explicit reference to the practice in the New Testament.)

Similarly, doctrines such as the Trinity and the divinity of Christ were rejected as resting upon inadequate scriptural foundations. The radicals had no place whatsoever for tradition. As Sebastian Franck wrote in 1530: "Foolish Ambrose, Augustine, Jerome, Gregory, of whom not one even knew the Lord, so help me God, nor was sent by God to teach. Rather, they were all apostles of Antichrist."

This approach was developed further during the Enlightenment, which was anxious to liberate itself from the shackles of tradition. Political emancipation from the oppression of the past (a key theme of the French Revolution) meant a total abandoning of the political, social, and religious ideas of the past. One of the reasons why Enlightenment thinkers placed such a high value upon human reason was that it relieved them of the need to appeal to tradition for ideas; any ideas worth knowing about were accessible to reason alone.

A respect for tradition was thus seen as capitulation to the authority of the past, a self-imposed bondage to outdated social, political, and religious structures. "Modern thought was born in a crisis of authority, took shape in flight from authority, and aspired from the start to autonomy from all traditional influence whatsoever" (Jeffrey Stout). Or, as the philosopher of science Michael Polanyi puts it:

> We were warned that a host of unproven beliefs were instilled in us from earliest childhood. That religious dogma, the authority of the ancients, the teaching of the schools, the maxims of the nursery, all were united to a body of tradition which we tended to accept merely because these beliefs had been previously held by others, who wanted us to embrace them in our turn.

The Enlightenment thus represented a radical rejection of tradition. Reason required no supplementation by voices from the past.

Theology and worship: the importance of liturgical tradition

One of the most important elements of the Christian tradition is fixed forms of worship, usually known as *liturgy*. In recent years there has been a rediscovery of the fact that Christian theologians pray and worship, and that this devotional context shapes their theological reflections. This point has been appreciated since the first centuries of the Christian church. The tag *lex orandi, lex credendi*, which could be translated roughly as "the way you pray determines what you believe," expresses the fact that theology and worship interact with each other. What Christians believe affects the manner in which they pray and worship; the manner in which Christians pray and worship affects what they believe.

Two controversies within the early church, centering on Gnosticism and Arianism, illustrate the importance of this point particularly well. On the basis of their radical dualism between the "physical" and the "spiritual," the Gnostics argued that matter was inherently evil. In refuting this position, Irenaeus pointed to the fact that bread, wine, and water were used in the Christian sacraments. How could they be evil, if they were given so prominent a position in Christian worship?

Arius argued that Christ was supreme among God's creatures. His opponents, such as Athanasius, retorted that this Christology was totally inconsistent with the way in which Christians worshiped. Athanasius stressed the theological importance of the practice of praying to Christ and worshiping him. If Arius was right, Christians were guilty of idolatry, through worshiping a creature, rather than God. Where Arius believed that theology should criticize liturgy, Athanasius believed that worship patterns and practices had to be taken into account by theologians.

In recent times, there has been renewed interest in the relation between liturgy and theology. In his *Doxology* (1980), the Methodist writer Geoffrey Wainwright drew attention to the way in which theological motifs were incorporated into Christian worship from the earliest of times. The liturgy of the church includes intellectual elements, and is not purely emotive in character. As a result, the close relationship between theology and liturgy, noted above, is entirely natural, in that worship and theological reflection are linked together organically.

In his *On Liturgical Theology* (1984), the Roman Catholic theologian Aidan Kavanagh argued that worship was the primary source and stimulus of Christian theology. Kavanagh drew a sharp distinction between *primary theology* (worship) and *secondary theology* (theological reflection). This suggests that worship has the upper hand over theology. But what happens if liturgical development becomes irresponsible? Does theology have a role in *limiting* or *criticizing* liturgy? This question of the relative authority of the *lex orandi* and *lex credendi* remains to be further explored, and is likely to be the subject of lively debate for some time to come.

Reason

T he second major resource to be considered is human reason. Although the importance of reason for Christian theology has always been recognized, it assumed an especial importance at the time of the Enlightenment (see pp. 67–9). We open our discussion by considering the changing emphasis which has come to be placed upon reason within the Christian tradition.

Reason and revelation: three models

In that human beings are rational, it is to be expected that reason should have a major role to play in theology. There has, however, been considerable debate within Christian theology concerning what that role might be. In our discussion of the development of patristic attitudes to secular culture, including philosophy (see pp. 116–19), we noted a variety of attitudes that developed at the time, including a rather uncritical acceptance of Platonism (e.g., Justin Martyr), a vigorous rejection of any role for philosophy in theology (e.g., Tertullian), and a willingness to appropriate at least some ideas from secular philosophy (e.g., Augustine). It will be helpful to survey attitudes since the patristic period, during which three broad categories of positions can be discerned.

Theology is a rational discipline

This position, associated with writers such as Thomas Aquinas, works on the assumption that the Christian faith is fundamentally rational, and can thus be both supported and explored by reason. Aquinas's Five Ways, considered earlier, illustrate his belief that reason is capable of lending support to the ideas of faith.

But Aquinas, and the Christian tradition which he represented, did not believe that Christianity was limited to what could be ascertained by reason. Faith goes beyond reason, having access to truths and insights of revelation, which reason could not hope to fathom or discover unaided. Reason has the role of building upon what is known by revelation, exploring what its implications might be. In this sense, theology is a *scientia* – a rational discipline, using rational methods to build upon and extend what is known by revelation. As we have already noted, Etienne Gilson saw Christianity being like a cathedral which rests upon the bedrock of human reason, but whose superstructure rises beyond the realms accessible to pure reason. It rests upon rational foundations; but the building erected on that foundation went far beyond what reason could uncover. Philosophy was thus the *ancilla theologiae,* "the handmaid of theology" (see the more extended discussion at 174–6).

Theology is the republication of the insights of reason

By the middle of the seventeenth century, especially in England and Germany, a new attitude began to develop. Christianity, it was argued, was reasonable. But where Thomas Aquinas understood this to mean that faith rested securely upon rational foundations, the new school of thought had different ideas. If faith is rational, they argued, it must be capable of being deduced in its entirety by reason. Every aspect of faith, every item of Christian belief, must be shown to derive from human reason.

An excellent example of this approach is to be found in the writings of Lord Herbert of Cherbury, especially *De veritate religionis,* "On the truth of religion" (1624), which argued for a rational Christianity based upon the innate sense of God and human moral obligation. This had two major consequences. First, Christianity was in effect reduced to those ideas which could be proved by reason. If Christianity was rational, then any parts of its system which could not be proved by reason could not be counted as "rational." They would have to be discarded. And second, reason was understood to take priority over revelation. Reason comes first, revelation comes second.

Reason thus came to be regarded as being capable of establishing what is right without needing any assistance from revelation; Christianity has to follow, being accepted where it endorses what reason has to say, and being disregarded where it goes its own way. So why bother with the idea of revelation, when reason could tell us all we could possibly wish to know about God, the world, and ourselves? This absolutely settled conviction in the total competence of human reason underlies the rationalist depreciation of the Christian doctrine of revelation in Jesus Christ and through Scripture.

Theology is redundant; reason reigns supreme

Finally, this potentially rationalist position was pushed to its logical outcome. As a matter of fact, it was argued, Christianity does include a series of major beliefs which are inconsistent with reason. Reason has the right to judge religion, in that it stands above it. This approach is usually termed "Enlightenment rationalism" and is of such importance that it will be considered in more detail. We begin by looking at an English movement which laid the foundations of this form of rationalism in religion: Deism.

Deism

The term "Deism" (from the Latin *deus,* "god") is often used in a general sense to refer to that view of God which maintains God's creatorship, but denies a continuing divine involvement with, or special presence within, that creation. It is often contrasted with "theism" (from the Greek *theos,* "god"), which allows for continuing divine involvement within the world.

In its more specific sense, Deism is used to refer to the views of a group of English thinkers during the "Age of Reason," in the late seventeenth and early eighteenth centuries. In his *Principal Deistic Writers* (1757), Leland grouped together a number of writers – including Lord Herbert of Cherbury, Thomas

Hobbes, and David Hume – under the broad term "deist." Close examination of their religious views shows that they have relatively little in common, apart from a general skepticism of specifically Christian ideas. Yet Leland's grouping of these writers into a single category proved irresistible. "Deism" was thus firmly established as a genuine category of belief.

John Locke's *Essay Concerning Human Understanding* (1690) developed an idea of God which became characteristic of much later Deism. Indeed, Locke's *Essay* can be said to lay much of the intellectual foundations of Deism. Locke argued that "reason leads us to the knowledge of this certain and evident truth, that there is an *eternal, most powerful and most knowing Being.*" The attributes of this being are those which human reason recognizes as appropriate for God. Having considered which moral and rational qualities are suited to the deity, Locke argues that "we enlarge every one of these with our idea of infinity, and so, putting them together, make our complex *idea of God.*" In other words, the idea of God is made up of human rational and moral qualities, projected to infinity.

Matthew Tindal's *Christianity as Old as Creation* (1730) argued that Christianity was nothing other than the "republication of the religion of nature." God is understood as the extension of accepted human ideas of justice, rationality, and wisdom. This universal religion is available at all times and in every place, whereas traditional Christianity rested upon the idea of a divine revelation which was not accessible to those who lived before Christ. Tindal's views were propagated before the modern discipline of the sociology of knowledge created skepticism of the idea of "universal reason," and are an excellent model of the rationalism characteristic of the movement, and which later became influential within the Enlightenment.

The ideas of English Deism percolated through to the continent of Europe (especially to Germany) through translations, and through the writings of individuals familiar with and sympathetic to them, such as Voltaire's *Philosophical Letters*. Enlightenment rationalism, to which we now turn, is often considered to be the final flowering of the bud of English Deism.

Enlightenment rationalism

The basic presupposition of Enlightenment rationalism is that human reason is perfectly capable of telling us everything we need to know about the world, ourselves, and God (if there is one). One of the most graphic portrayals of this enormous confidence in reason is the frontispiece to the eighteenth-century rationalist philosopher Christian Wolff's ambitiously titled book *Reasonable Thoughts about God, the World, the Human Soul, and just about everything else* (1720). The engraving in question portrays a world enveloped in shadows and gloom, representing the old ideas of superstition, tradition, and faith. But on part of the engraving, the sun has broken through, lighting up hills and valleys, and bringing smiles to the faces of what we must assume to have been a hitherto rather gloomy group of peasants. The message is clear: reason enlightens, dispelling the fog and darkness of Christian faith, and ushering in the glorious light of human rationality. Divine revelation is an irrelevance, if it exists at all. The consequences of this approach were noted in more detail earlier, as we surveyed the general impact of the Enlightenment upon Christian theology.

At this point, we need to stress the difference between "reason" and "rationalism," which may appear identical to some readers. *Reason* is the basic human faculty of thinking, based on argument and evidence. It is theologically neutral, and poses no threat to faith – unless it is regarded as the only source of knowledge about God. It then becomes *rationalism*, which is an exclusive reliance upon human reason alone, and a refusal to allow any weight to be given to divine revelation.

Enlightenment rationalism may be said to rest upon the belief that unaided human reason can deliver everything that humanity needs to know. There is no need to listen to other voices, having first consulted reason. By definition, the Christian cannot have anything to say that is at one and the same time distinctive and right. If it is distinctive, it departs from the path of reason – and thus must be untrue. To be different is, quite simply, to be wrong.

An excellent example of this rationalist critique of Christianity can be seen in relation to the doctrine of Christ (how could Jesus be both God and man at one and the same time?) and the doctrine of the Trinity (how can one God be three persons simultaneously, without lapsing into crude logical contradiction?). One of the early American presidents, Thomas Jefferson, who was deeply influenced by eighteenth-century French rationalism, poured reasoned scorn upon such doctrines. Jesus, he argued, was really a very simple rational teacher, who taught a very simple and reasonable gospel about a very simple and rational idea of God. And at every point, Christianity chose to make things more complicated than they need be.

A direct consequence of this was the movement in New Testament studies known as the "quest of the historical Jesus" (see pp. 310–19). This quest, which dates from the late eighteenth century, was based upon the belief that the New Testament got Jesus entirely wrong. The real Jesus – the "Jesus of history" – was a simple Galilean teacher, who taught entirely sensible ideas based upon reason. The New Testament quite erroneously presented him as the risen savior of sinful humanity.

Reason was thus held to be able to judge Christ. In his celebrated work *Religion Within the Limits of Reason Alone* (1793), Immanuel Kant argued powerfully for the priority of reason and conscience over the authority of Jesus Christ. Where Jesus endorses what reason has to say, he is to be respected; where he goes against or goes beyond reason, he is to be rejected. Iris Murdoch writes of this type of approach in *The Sovereignty of Good*:

> How recognizable, how familiar to us, is the man so beautifully portrayed in the *Grundlegung* [i.e., Kant's *Groundwork of the Metaphysics of Morals*] who confronted even with Christ turns away to consider the judgement of his own conscience and to hear the voice of his own reason. Stripped of the exiguous metaphysical background which Kant was prepared to allow him, this man is still with us, free, independent, lonely, powerful, rational, responsible, brave, the hero of so many novels and books of moral philosophy.

Enlightenment rationalism, then, upheld the sovereignty of reason, arguing that human reason was capable of establishing all that it was necessary to know about religion without recourse to the idea of "revelation." Furthermore, reason possessed an ability to judge the truths of religions, such as Christianity, and eliminate vast tracts of its ideas as "irrational." Influential though such ideas were in the late eighteenth and nineteenth centuries, they are now regarded with suspicion. The following section explores why.

Criticisms of Enlightenment rationalism

A series of developments, of which we may here note a few, have destroyed the credibility of the Enlightenment approach. This approach could be said to rest upon the idea of the "immediately given," whether in reason or in experience. Knowledge rests upon a foundation, whether this is self-evident truths, immediately recognized as such by the human mind, or immediate experience, deriving directly from contact with the outside world. But these foundations do not seem to exist.

The idea that human reason was capable of basing itself upon self-evident first principles, and, by following these through logically, deducing a complete system, suffered some serious setbacks in the late eighteenth century and beyond. Most writers sympathetic to the ideas of the Enlightenment made an appeal to Euclid's five principles of geometry. On the basis of his five principles, Euclid was able to construct an entire geometrical system, which had seemed to be an example of a universal and necessarily true system based upon reason alone. Philosophers, such as Spinoza, argued that the same method could be applied in philosophy. A secure edifice of philosophy and ethics could be erected on the basis of a secure and universal rational foundation, as in Euclid's geometry. The discovery of non-Euclidian geometry during the nineteenth century destroyed the appeal of this analogy. It turned out that there were other ways of doing geometry, each just as internally consistent as Euclid's. But which is right? The question cannot be answered. They are all different, each with its own special merits and problems.

Much the same observation is now made concerning rationalism itself. Where once it was argued that there was one single rational principle, it was increasingly conceded that there are – and always have been – many different "rationalities." At the end of his penetrating historical analysis of rationalist approaches to truth and meaning, Alasdair MacIntyre concludes:

> Both the thinkers of the Enlightenment and their successors proved unable to agree as to precisely what those principles were which would be found undeniable by all rational persons. One kind of answer was given by

the authors of the *Encyclopédie*, a second by Rousseau, a third by Bentham, a fourth by Kant, a fifth by the Scottish philosophers of common sense and their French and American disciples. Nor has subsequent history diminished the extent of such disagreement. Consequently, the legacy of the Enlightenment has been the provision of an ideal of rational justification which it has proved impossible to attain.

Reason promises much, yet fails to deliver its benefits. It is for such reasons that Hans-Georg Gadamer wrote scathingly of the "Robinson Crusoe dream of the historical Enlightenment, as artificial as Crusoe himself." The notion of "universal rationality" is today viewed by many as little more than a fiction. Postmodernism has argued that there exist a variety of "rationalities," each of which has to be respected in its own right; there is no privileged vantage point, no universal concept of "reason," which can pass judgment upon them.

Having considered some aspects of reason as a theological resource, we may now turn to consider the place of religious experience in theology.

Religious Experience

"Experience" is an imprecise term. The origins of the word are relatively well understood: it derives from the Latin term *experientia*, which could be interpreted as "that which arises out of traveling through life." In this broad sense, it means "an accumulated body of knowledge, arising through first-hand encounter with life." When one speaks of "an experienced teacher" or "an experienced doctor," the implication is that the teacher or doctor has learned his or her craft through first-hand application.

Yet the term has developed an acquired meaning, which particularly concerns us here. It has come to refer to the inner life of individuals, in which those individuals become aware of their own subjective feelings and emotions. It relates to the inward and subjective world of experience, as opposed to the outward world of everyday life. An emphasis on the importance of religious experience was characteristic of early Methodism, and the term "the Wesleyan Quadrilateral" is sometime used to refer to the grouping of Scripture, tradition, reason, and experience, reflecting John Wesley's insistence that the task of interpreting the Bible was to be illuminated by the collective Christian wisdom of other ages and cultures between the Apostolic Age and our own, as well as being protected from obscurantism by means of the disciplines of critical reason. Most importantly, for Wesley, the message of Scripture must be received in the heart by faith – hence the emphasis on experience.

Wesley is not on his own in stressing the importance of experience. A series of writings, including William James's celebrated study *The Varieties of Religious Experience* (1902), have stressed the importance of the subjective aspects of religion in general, and Christianity in particular. Christianity is not simply about ideas (as our discussion of Scripture, reason, and tradition might suggest); it is about the interpretation and transformation of the inner life of the individual. This concern with human experience is particularly associated with the movement generally known as *existentialism*, which we may consider briefly, before moving on.

Existentialism: a philosophy of human experience

In what way do human beings differ from other forms of life? Humans have always been aware of some basic distinction between themselves on the one hand, and all other forms of life on the other. But what *is* this difference? And what does it *mean* to exist? Perhaps the most important thing which distinguishes human beings from other forms of life is the fact that they are aware of their own existence, and ask questions about it.

The rise of existentialist philosophy is ultimately a response to this crucial insight. We not only exist: we *understand*, we *are aware* that we exist, and we are aware that our existence will one day be terminated by death. The sheer fact of our existence is important to us, and we find it difficult, probably impossible, to adopt a totally detached attitude to it. Existentialism is basically a protest against the view that human beings are "things," and a demand that we take the personal existence of the individual with full seriousness.

The term "existentialism" can bear two meanings. At its most basic level, it means an *attitude* toward human life which places special emphasis upon the immediate, real-life experience of individuals. It is concerned with the way in which individuals encounter others, and gain an understanding of their finitude. In a more developed sense, the term refers to a *movement*, which probably reached its zenith in the period 1938–68, the origins of which lie primarily in the writings of the Danish philosopher Søren Kierkegaard (1813–55). Kierkegaard stressed the importance of individual decision and an awareness of the limits of human existence. In terms of the history of modern theology, the most important contribution to the development of existentialism was made by Martin Heidegger (1888–1976), particularly in his *Being and Time* (1927). This work provided Rudolf Bultmann with the basic ideas and vocabulary he required to develop a Christian existentialist account of human existence, and the manner in which this is illuminated and transformed by the gospel.

Of fundamental importance is Heidegger's distinction between "inauthentic existence" and "authentic existence," which Bultmann creatively reinterprets in the light of the New Testament. According to Bultmann, the New Testament recognizes two types of human existence. First, there is unbelieving, unredeemed existence, which is an inauthentic form of existence. Here, individuals refuse to recognize themselves for what they really are: creatures who are dependent upon God for their well-being and salvation. Such individuals seek to justify themselves by trying to secure existence through moral actions or material prosperity. This attempt at self-sufficiency on the part of humanity is designated by both the Old and New Testaments as "sin."

Against this inauthentic mode of human existence, the New Testament sets the mode of believing, redeemed existence, in which we abandon all security created by ourselves, and trust in God. We recognize the illusion of our self-sufficiency, and trust instead in the sufficiency of God. Instead of denying that we are God's creatures, we recognize and exult in this fact, and base our existence upon it. Instead of clinging to transitory things for security, we learn to abandon faith in this transitory world in order that we may place our trust in God himself. Instead of trying to justify ourselves, we learn to recognize that God offers us our justification as a free gift. Instead of denying the reality of our human finitude and the inevitability of death, we recognize that these have been faced and conquered through the death and resurrection of Jesus Christ, whose victory becomes our victory through faith.

The rise of existentialism is a reflection of the importance attached to the inner world of human experience in the modern period. Nevertheless, it must be appreciated that this concern with human experience is not something new; it can arguably be discerned in both Old and New Testaments, and it permeates the writings of Augustine of Hippo. Martin Luther declared that "experience makes a theologian," and argued that it was impossible to be a proper theologian without an experience of the searing and terrifying judgment of God upon human sin. As we noted earlier, the literary movement known as Romanticism (see pp. 70–1) gave considerable importance to the role of "feeling," and opened the way for a new interest in this aspect of Christian life.

Experience and theology: two models

Two main approaches to the question of the relation of experience to theology may be discerned within Christian theology:

1 Experience provides a foundational resource for Christian theology.
2 Christian theology provides an interpretive framework within which human experience may be interpreted.

The second has been the dominant theme, and will be considered in more detail.

Experience as a foundational resource

The idea that human religious experience can act as a foundational resource for Christian theology has obvious attractions. It suggests that Christian theology is concerned with human experience – something which is common to all humanity, rather than the exclusive preserve of a small group. To those who are embarrassed by the "scandal of particularity" the approach has many merits. It suggests that all the world religions are basically human responses to the same religious experience – often referred to as "a core experience of the transcendent." Theology is thus the Christian attempt to reflect upon this common human experience, in the knowledge that the same experience underlies the other world religions.

We shall return to this point later in dealing with the question of the relation of Christianity to the other religions.

This approach also has considerable attractions for Christian apologetics, as the writings of Paul Tillich and David Tracy make clear. If humans share a common experience, whether they choose to regard it as "religious" or not, Christian theology can address that experience. The problem of agreeing upon a common starting point is thus avoided; the starting point is already provided, in human experience. Apologetics can demonstrate that the Christian gospel makes sense of common human experience. This approach is probably seen at its best in Paul Tillich's volume of sermons *The Courage to Be*, which attracted considerable attention after its publication in 1952. It seemed to many observers that Tillich had succeeded in correlating the Christian proclamation with common human experience.

But there are difficulties here. The most obvious is that there is actually very little empirical evidence for a "common core experience" throughout human history and culture. The idea is easily postulated and virtually impossible to verify. This criticism has found its most mature and sophisticated expression in the "Experiential-Expressive Theory of Doctrine," to use a term employed by the distinguished Yale theologian George Lindbeck. In his volume *The Nature of Doctrine* (1984), Lindbeck provides an important analysis of the nature of Christian doctrine (see pp. 92–3).

Lindbeck suggests that theories of doctrine may be divided into three general types. The *cognitive–propositionalist* theory lays stress upon the cognitive aspects of religion, emphasizing the manner in which doctrines function as truth claims or informative propositions (see p. 156). The *experiential–expressive* theory interprets doctrines as noncognitive symbols of inner human feelings or attitudes. A third

possibility, which Lindbeck himself favors, is the *cultural–linguistic* approach to religion. Lindbeck associates this model with a "rule" or "regulative" theory of doctrine. It is Lindbeck's criticism of the second of these approaches which is of particular interest to us at this point.

The experiential–expressive approach, according to Lindbeck, holds that there is some common universal "religious experience," which Christian theology (as well as other religions) attempts to express in words. The experience comes first; the theology comes in later. As Lindbeck argues, the attraction of this approach to doctrine is grounded in a number of features of late twentieth-century western thought. For example, the contemporary preoccupation with interreligious dialogue is considerably assisted by the suggestion that the various religions are diverse expressions of a common core experience, such as an "isolable core of encounter" or an "unmediated awareness of the transcendent."

The principal objection to this theory, thus stated, is its resistance to verification. As Lindbeck points out, "religious experience" is a hopelessly vague idea. "It is difficult or impossible to specify its distinctive features, and yet unless this is done, the assertion of commonality becomes logically and empirically vacuous." The assertion that "the various religions are diverse symbolizations of one and the same core experience of the Ultimate" is ultimately an unverifiable hypothesis, not least on account of the difficulty of locating and describing the "core experience" concerned. As Lindbeck rightly points out, this would appear to suggest that there is "at least the logical possibility that a Buddhist and a Christian might have basically the same faith, although expressed very differently." The theory can only be credible if it is possible to isolate a common core experience from religious language and behavior, and demonstrate that the latter two are articulations of or responses to the former.

For such reasons, the second approach to the understanding of the relation between experience and theology has regained a hearing.

Experience as something which requires to be interpreted

According to this approach, Christian theology provides a framework within which the ambiguities of experience may be interpreted. Theology aims to interpret experience. It is like a net which we can cast over experience, in order to capture its meaning. Experience is seen as something which is to be interpreted, rather than something which is itself capable of interpreting.

The classic example of this approach is usually thought to be Martin Luther's "theology of the cross," which is of continuing significance as a critique of the role of experience in theology. Luther's position is that experience is of vital importance to theology; without experience, theology is impoverished and deficient, an empty shell waiting to be filled. Yet experience cannot by itself be regarded as a reliable theological resource; it must be interpreted and corrected by theology.

Luther suggests that we attempt to imagine what it was like for the disciples of Jesus on the first Good Friday. They had given up everything to follow Jesus. Their whole reason for living centered on him. He seemed to have the answers to all their questions. Then, in front of their eyes, he was taken from them and publicly executed. God was experienced as being absent. There was no way in which anyone experienced God as being present on that occasion. Even Jesus himself seems to have had a momentary sense of the absence of God – "My God, my God, why have you forsaken me?" (Matthew 27: 46). This way of thinking, according to Luther, demonstrates how unreliable experience and feelings can be as guides to the presence of God.

Luther argues that those around the cross did not experience the presence of God – so they concluded that God was absent from the scene. The resurrection overturns that judgment: God was present in a hidden manner, which experience mistook for absence. Theology interprets our feelings, even to the point of contradicting them when they are misleading. It stresses the faithfulness of God and the reality of the resurrection hope – even where experience seems to suggest otherwise. Theology thus gives us a framework for making sense of the contradictions of experience. God may be experienced as absent from the world – yet theology insists that this experience is provisional and flawed, and cannot be taken at face value.

Yet theology also allows experience to be interpreted in a more positive manner. The dialectic between the Christian doctrines of creation and sin can be deployed to provide an interpretation of a common human experience – an awareness of dissatisfaction, or a curious sense of longing for something undefined. To illustrate the relation between theology and experience, we may consider Augustine's analysis of the implications for experience of the Christian doctrine of creation.

According to Augustine, our feeling of dissatisfaction is a consequence of the Christian doctrine of creation – that we are made in the image of God. There is thus an inbuilt capacity within human nature to relate to God. Yet, on account of the fallenness of human nature, this potential is frustrated. There is now a natural tendency to try to make other things fulfill this need. Created things thus come to be substituted for God. Yet they do not satisfy. Human beings are thus left with a feeling of longing – longing for something indefinable.

This phenomenon has been recognized since the dawn of human civilization. In his dialogue

Gorgias, Plato compares human beings to leaky jars. Somehow, human beings are always unfulfilled. Perhaps the greatest statement of this feeling, and its most famous theological interpretation, may be found in the famous words of Augustine: "You have made us for yourself, and our hearts are restless until they rest in you."

Throughout Augustine's reflections, especially in his autobiographical *Confessions*, the same theme recurs. Humanity is destined to remain incomplete in its present existence. Its hopes and deepest longings will remain nothing but hopes and longings. The themes of creation and redemption are brought together by Augustine, to provide an interpretation of the human experience of "longing." Because humanity is created in the image of God, it desires to relate to God, even if it cannot recognize that desire for what it is. Yet on account of human sin, humanity cannot satisfy that desire unaided. And so a real sense of frustration, of dissatisfaction, develops. And that dissatisfaction – though not its theological interpretation – is part of common human experience. Augustine expresses this feeling when he states that he "is groaning with inexpressible groanings on my wanderer's path, and remembering Jerusalem with my heart lifted up toward it – Jerusalem my home land, Jerusalem my mother."

Augustine finds one of his finest recent apologetic interpreters in the writings of the twentieth-century Oxford literary critic and theologian C. S. Lewis. Perhaps one of the most original aspects of Lewis's writing is his persistent and powerful appeal to the religious imagination, in developing Augustine's maxim *desiderium sinus cordis* ("longing makes the heart deep"). Like Augustine, Lewis was aware of certain deep human emotions which pointed to a dimension of our existence beyond time and space. There is, Lewis suggested, a deep and intense feeling of longing within human beings, which no earthly object or experience can satisfy. Lewis terms this sense "joy," and argues that it points to God as its source and goal (hence the title of his celebrated 1955 autobiography, *Surprised by Joy*). Joy, according to Lewis, is "an unsatisfied desire which is itself more desirable than any other satisfaction [. . .] anyone who has experienced it will want it again."

Lewis addressed this question further in a sermon entitled "The Weight of Glory," preached at the University of Oxford on June 8, 1941. Lewis spoke of "a desire which no natural happiness will satisfy," "a desire, still wandering and uncertain of its object and still largely unable to see that object in the direction where it really lies." There is something self-defeating about human desire, in that what is desired, when achieved, seems to leave the desire unsatisfied. Lewis illustrates this from the age-old quest for beauty, using recognizably Augustinian imagery:

> The books or the music in which we thought the beauty was located will betray us if we trust to them; it was not *in* them, it only came *through* them, and what came through them was longing. These things – the beauty, the memory of our own past – are good images of what we really desire; but if they are mistaken for the thing itself they turn into dumb idols, breaking the hearts of their worshippers. For they are not the thing itself; they are only the scent of a flower we have not found, the echo of a tune we have not heard, news from a country we have not visited.

The basic point being emphasized is thoroughly Augustinian: the creation creates a sense of longing for its creator, which it cannot satisfy by itself. In this way, an essentially Augustinian framework is applied to common human experience, to provide a plausible theological interpretation.

Ludwig Feuerbach's critique of experience-based theologies

As noted above, many theologians regarded experience-based theologies as providing an escape from the impasse of Enlightenment rationalism, or from difficulties relating to the alleged particularity of Christian revelation. F. D. E. Schleiermacher is an excellent instance of a theologian concerned to use human experience as a starting point for Christian theology. In particular, Schleiermacher drew attention to the importance for theology of "a feeling of absolute dependence." By exploring the nature and origins of this feeling, it was possible to trace it back to its origins with God. This approach has enormous attractions. However, as Ludwig Feuerbach demonstrated, it is also enormously problematical.

In the foreword to the first edition of his highly influential *Essence of Christianity* (1841), Ludwig Feuerbach states that the "purpose of this work is to show that the supernatural mysteries of religion are based upon quite simple natural truths." The leading idea of the work is deceptively simple: human beings have created the gods, who embody their own idealized conception of their aspirations, needs, and fears. Human "feeling" has nothing to do with God; it is of purely human origin, misunderstood by an overactive human imagination. "If feeling is the essential instrumentality or organ of religion, then God's nature is nothing other than an expression of the nature of feeling. [. . .] The divine essence, which is comprehended by feeling, is actually nothing other than the essence of feeling, enraptured and delighted with itself – nothing but self-intoxicated, self-contented feeling."

For Schleiermacher, the nature of the religious self-consciousness was such that the existence of the redeemer could be inferred from it; for Feuerbach, this species of self-consciousness was nothing more and nothing less than human beings' awareness of themselves. It is experience of oneself, not of God. "God-consciousness" is merely human self-awareness, not a distinct category of human experience.

Feuerbach's analysis continues to be influential in western liberal Christianity. The existence of God is held to be grounded in human experience. But, as Feuerbach emphasizes, human experience might be nothing other than experience of *ourselves*, rather than of God. We might simply be projecting our own experiences, and calling the result "God," where we ought to realize that they are simply experiences of our own very human natures. Feuerbach's approach represents a devastating critique of humanity-centered ideas of Christianity.

It may be noted that Feuerbach's critique of religion loses much of its force when dealing with nontheistic religions, or theologies (such as that of Karl Barth) which claim to deal with a divine encounter with humanity from outside. However, when it is applied to a theistic construction or interpretation of human emotional or psychological states, it is in its element. Has anyone really spoken about God or Christ? Or have we simply projected our longings and fears onto an imaginary transcendent plane, or onto a distant historical figure about whom we know so little?

The growing conviction that Christology must be objectively grounded in the history of Jesus of Nazareth (especially prominent, for example, in the writings of Wolfhart Pannenberg) is due at least in part to Feuerbach's critique of religion. The very idea of "God" was, according to Feuerbach, an illusion which we could in principle avoid, and, with sufficient progress in self-knowledge, could discard altogether. It is, of course, a small – and perhaps an inevitable – step from this assumption to the Marxist view that religious feeling is itself the product of an alienated social existence.

This chapter has provided a brief exploration of the resources available to Christian theology, and some of the debates concerning their potential and their limitations. In the chapter which follows, we shall consider the notion of revelation, which plays a leading role in much Christian thought.

QUESTIONS FOR CHAPTER 6

1   Why did narrative theology become so attractive to many theologians in the late twentieth century?

2   "The Bible alone is the religion of Protestants" (William Chillingworth). Do you agree with this famous statement?

3   How would you distinguish between a "rational" and a "rationalist" approach to theology?

4   Why has the Enlightenment approach to human reason come under criticism?

5   Why did Irenaeus find tradition such an important resource for his arguments against his Gnostic critics?

6   Outline the teaching of the Council of Trent on the relation of Scripture and tradition.

7   Outline Ludwig Feuerbach's critique of experience-based theologies. How persuasive do you find his argument? What theologies do you think are most vulnerable to his critique?

7

Knowledge of God: Natural and Revealed

How can God be known? For some, God is to be sought out within the complexities and ambiguities of the world. The "human quest for God" involves the careful weighing of evidence drawn from the natural world, including human reason and conscience. For others, human nature is limited in its abilities, and is unable to discern the existence or nature of God in this way. Humanity needs to be told what God is like.

The issue being debated is fundamentally that of *revelation* – the Christian notion that God chooses to be known, and makes this possible through self-disclosure in nature and human history. The great Scottish theologian Hugh Ross Mackintosh (1870–1936) once summarized the questions centering on revelation as follows: "A religious knowledge of God, wherever existing, comes by revelation; otherwise we should be committed to the incredible position that a man can know God without His willing to be known."

The discussion of the nature and necessity of revelation within the Christian tradition has been both interesting and important, and will be addressed in this chapter. One of the most significant aspects of this debate concerns the way in which a "natural" knowledge of God – acquired through reflection on the natural order – relates to a "revealed" knowledge. We shall consider this point in the second part of the chapter; our attention is first claimed by the question of what the term "revelation" might be understood to mean.

The Idea of Revelation

A central theme of Christian theology down the ages has been that the human attempts to discern fully the nature and purposes of God are ultimately unsuccessful. Although a natural knowledge of God is generally held to be possible (the early writings of Karl Barth being a notable exception to this consensus), this is limited both in scope and in depth. The idea of *revelation* expresses the pervasive belief of Christian theology, to the effect that we need to be "told what God is like" (Eberhard Jüngel).

The 1960s saw a major upheaval in Christian theology, with many traditional ideas being challenged and redefined. One such challenge was to the notion of revelation. Two issues emerged, each of which seemed to call into doubt the traditional Christian understanding of revelation. In the first place, F. G. Downing suggested that the modern interest in revelation was due not to the biblical material itself, but to the prominence of epistemological issues in modern philosophy. The prominence of questions concerning "right knowledge" in, for example, the philosophy of science had been improperly transferred to theology. The Bible, it was argued, was concerned with salvation, not knowledge. The dominant question in the New Testament was "What must I *do* to be saved?" not "What must I *know?*"

In response to this, it was pointed out that the biblical conception of salvation is often expressed in terms of "knowledge," and that human salvation was understood to rest upon the knowledge of the possibility of salvation in Christ, and the proper response which was necessary for salvation to take place. "Knowledge of God," understood biblically, does not mean simply "information about God," but a life-giving and salvation-bringing self-disclosure of God in Christ.

In the second place, biblical scholars such as James Barr argued that the issue of revelation appeared to be of marginal importance to both the Old and the New Testaments. They suggested that revelational language was neither fundamental to, nor uniform within, the biblical writings. However, it soon became clear that their analyses rested upon the uncritical acceptance of systematically developed ideas of "revelation," rather than a careful consideration of the revelational vocabulary of Scripture itself. It is certainly true that medieval or modern notions of revelation are not found explicitly stated in either the Old or the New Testament. However, this by no means indicates that revelational language is absent from, or even marginalized within, Scripture.

It is certainly correct to say that the New Testament does not regard "revelation" as meaning "disclosure of a hitherto unknown God." In its everyday use, the term "revelation" might be taken to imply "making something known in all its fullness," or "the total disclosure of what had hitherto been obscure

or unclear." Yet to speak of a "revelation of God" in a theological context is not to imply that the self-revelation of God is *total*.

For example, many writers within the Greek Orthodox tradition stress that the *revelation* of God does not abolish the *mystery* of God. John Henry Newman's doctrine of "reserve" emphasizes the same point. There is always more to God than what we can come to know. Again, Luther suggests that God's self-revelation is only partial, yet that partial revelation is reliable and adequate. He develops the idea of a "hidden revelation of God" – one of the most important aspects of his "theology of the cross" – to make this point.

Yet the idea of revelation implies more than imparting knowledge of God; it carries with it the idea of the *self-disclosure* of God. In speaking about other persons, we might draw a distinction between "knowing about someone" and "knowing someone." The former implies cerebral knowledge, or an accumulation of data about an individual (such as height, weight, and so on). The latter implies a personal relationship.

In its developed sense, "revelation" does not mean merely the transmission of a body of knowledge, but the personal self-disclosure of God within history. God has taken the initiative through a process of self-disclosure, which reaches its climax and fulfillment in the history of Jesus of Nazareth. This point has been stressed in the twentieth century by writers influenced by various types of personalist philosophies, such as Friedrich Gogarten, Dietrich Bonhoeffer, and Emanuel Hirsch. Emil Brunner, who also belongs to this group of thinkers, emphasized the importance of the doctrine of the incarnation to revelation: in Christ may be seen the personal self-disclosure of God. Believers are "God's dialogue partners in history." Revelation takes a personal form. We shall explore this question further in dealing with the idea of a personal God (pp. 205–9).

Models of Revelation

R evelation, in common with most theological notions, is a complex concept. The Greek word usually translated as "revelation" (*apokalypsis*) has the basic meaning of "removing a veil so that something can be seen." In an attempt to unravel and cast light on the various elements of this idea, theologians have developed various models of revelation. In what follows, we shall consider four such models. It must be stressed that these are not mutually exclusive. The affirmation of one does not imply the negation of any one or all three of the remainder. Correctly understood, they represent different emphases within the Christian understandings of revelation.

Revelation as doctrine

This approach has been characteristic of conservative evangelical and Catholic neo-scholastic schools, and, in modified or supplement forms, continues to exercise considerable influence within the Christian tradition. Whereas evangelicals have stressed the role of Scripture in the mediation of revelation, Catholic neoscholastics have generally given considerably more weight to the role of tradition, and especially the teaching office of the church (the *magisterium*). The term "the deposit of revelation" or "the deposit of truth," meaning the accumulated insights of the church over the years, is often employed in such contexts. According to this approach, revelation is to be thought of primarily (although not exclusively) in propositional forms.

For some conservative Protestants, this information is mediated through the Bible, which is treated as a collection of doctrinal statements. These propositions may then be woven together to create the matrix of Christian theology. Such an approach can be found in the six volumes of Carl F. H. Henry's *God, Revelation, and Authority*, which has had some influence within American evangelical circles. Revelation is "referential information about the nature of God," which is provided by the Bible. Other writers within an evangelical tradition have insisted that revelation is to be understood as the intermingling of divine action and divine words. A good example is James I. Packer (born 1926), who writes as follows:

> God has not abandoned His purpose to have us as His friends; instead, He has resolved in His love to rescue us from sin and restore us to Himself. His plan for doing this was to make Himself known to us as our Redeemer and Re-creator, through the incarnation, death, resurrection and reign of His Son. The working out of this plan required a long series of preparatory events, starting with the promise to the woman's seed (Genesis 3: 15) and spanning the whole of Old Testament history. [...] Thus the history of salvation (the acts of God) took place in the context of the history of revelation (the oracles of God).

A related approach has been taken by a number of Roman Catholic theologians, most notably Reginald Garrigou-Lagrange (1877–1964) and Hermann Dieckmann. The foundation of this approach lies in the dogmatic declarations of the First Vatican Council on the nature of faith, which include the following statement:

> Wherefore, by divine and catholic faith all those things are to be believed which are contained in the Word of God as found in Scripture and tradition, and which are proposed by the church as matters to be believed as divinely revealed, whether by her solemn judgment or in her ordinary and universal *magisterium*.

It is clear that this approach regards revelation as taking the form of doctrinal statements which are set forth by the church. Such statements can be found in both Scripture and unwritten tradition (note how the Council here affirms the earlier view on this matter associated with the Council of Trent: see p. 139).

This approach has been severely criticized, most notably by the postliberal theologian George Lindbeck in his *Nature of Doctrine* (1984; see pp. 93, 148–9). Lindbeck designates this view of revelation as "propositionalist" or "cognitive." It views revelation as "informational propositions or truth claims about objective realities." Lindbeck argues that this approach is to be rejected as intellectualist and literalist, as resting on the mistaken assumption that it is possible to state the objective truth about God definitively, exhaustively, and timelessly in a propositional form.

Lindbeck's criticism of "cognitive" theories of revelation or doctrines has considerable force when directed against neo-scholastic understandings of revelation. For example, the view of the neo-scholastic writer Hermann Dieckmann, to the effect that supernatural revelation transmits conceptual knowledge by means of propositions, is clearly open to serious criticism along the lines suggested by Lindbeck.

Nevertheless, not all cognitive theories of doctrine are vulnerable in this respect. It is necessary to make a clear distinction between the view that an exhaustive and unambiguous account of God is transmitted through revelation conceptually by propositions, on the one hand, and the view that there is a genuinely cognitive element to doctrinal statements, on the other. For example, most theologians of the medieval period actually understood revelation as a dynamic concept. It was to be seen as a "perception of divine truth, tending toward this truth" (Alan of Lille). For such theologians, revelation provides a *reliable* yet *incomplete* description of reality.

Nor need a propositional approach to revelation exclude other approaches. Perhaps the greatest weakness within Christian theology is its reluctance to recognize that models are complementary, rather than mutually exclusive. To assert that revelation involves information about God is not to deny that it can also involve the mediation of the presence of God, or the transformation of human experience.

An important variant on this approach to revelation can be found in the writings of Karl Barth. For Barth, the Bible is not itself revelation; it is a witness to revelation. This is linked with Barth's concept of the "threefold form of the Word of God." According to Barth, it is necessary to distinguish a threefold movement from the Word of God in Christ to the witness to this Word in Scripture, and finally to the proclamation of this Word in the preaching of the community of faith. It is thus Jesus Christ who embodies the revealing God, and Scripture which bears witness to this revelation of God in Christ. While Barth continued to give the greatest importance to the theological engagement with Scripture, it is clear that his emphasis falls upon the one to whom Scripture bears witness – Christ – rather than the text of Scripture itself.

Revelation as presence

This model of revelation is especially associated with writers of the dialectical school of theology (see pp. 85–7) influenced by the dialogical personalism of the Jewish philosopher Martin Buber (1878–1965; see pp. 207–9). Perhaps the most important statement of the approach may be found in Emil Brunner's *Truth as Encounter*, which sets out the idea of revelation as a personal communication of God – that is to say, a communication or impartation of the personal presence of God within the believer. "The Lordship and love of God can be

communicated in no other way than by God's self-giving."

Brunner's point is that God does not merely convey information in the process of revelation. Revelation concerns the conveying of God's personal presence, rather than mere information concerning God. Brunner, basing his ideas upon Martin Buber's analysis of "I – Thou" and "I – It" relationships, insists that there is a strongly relational element to revelation. God is experienced as a "Thou" rather than an "It." Revelation is teleological, a process directed toward a goal – and that goal is the establishment of a mutual relationship between the revealing God and responding humanity.

Brunner's concept of "truth as encounter" thus conveys the two elements of what he regards as a correct understanding of revelation: it is *historical* and it is *personal*. By the former, Brunner wishes us to understand that truth is not something permanent within the eternal world of ideas which is disclosed or communicated to us in revelation; rather, it is something which *happens* in space and time. Truth comes into being, as the act of God in time and space. By the latter, Brunner intends to emphasize that the content of this *act* of God is none other than the *person* of God, rather than a complex of ideas or doctrines concerning God. The revelation of God is God's self-impartation to humanity. For Brunner, divine revelation is necessarily Christocentric: he counters the pure objectivism of orthodoxy's doctrine of propositional revelation with Luther's dictum to the effect that the Scriptures are "the manger in which Christ is laid."

On the basis of this approach, Brunner develops a critique of any notion of revelation which represents itself as words or propositions about God. These objectify God, in the sense of reducing God to the status of an *object*, rather than a *person*. "No speech, no word, is adequate to the mystery of God as a Person." Revelation cannot be understood as the impartation of data about God: "It is never the mere communication of knowledge, but a life-giving and life-renewing fellowship." Revelation is thus understood primarily as the communication or establishment of a personal relationship.

Of course, related ideas can be instanced from earlier periods of church history. The recognition that revelation involves a personal presence is stated with particular clarity in John Henry Newman's 1866 hymn "Praise to the Holiest":

> And that a higher gift than grace
> Should flesh and blood refine;
> God's presence and God's very self
> And essence all-divine.

Revelation as experience

A third influential model centers upon human experience. God is understood to be revealed or made known through the experience of the individual. This approach is widely held to be associated with German liberal Protestantism in the nineteenth century, especially F. D. E. Schleiermacher and A. B. Ritschl. In view of the significance of Schleiermacher's approach, we shall consider it in a little detail.

Schleiermacher's background was that of Moravian Pietism, which placed considerable emphasis upon a personal devotion to Christ, and the importance of a personal awareness of conversion. Most forms of eighteenth-century Pietism, including Methodism, placed considerable emphasis upon such notions as "experimental religion" (meaning "a religion grounded in experience") and a "living faith" (as opposed to a wooden theological orthodoxy).

In 1796, Schleiermacher moved to Berlin to take up his new duties as a hospital chaplain.

Within a year of his arrival, he had attached himself to "The Athenaeum," a group of thinkers and writers who were hostile to the spirit of the Enlightenment. He mixed with leading figures of the Romantic movement, such as Novalis and Friedrich Schlegel. The outcome of this interaction was a theology deeply grounded in the outlook of Romanticism (see pp. 70–1), with a new emphasis upon the role of the individual's religious consciousness and feeling.

The first expression of Schleiermacher's theological method can be found in his *On Religion: Speeches to its Cultured Despisers*, published anonymously in 1799. (Although entitled "Speeches" (*Reden*), the book did not actually have its origins in a series of lectures or addresses.) The work develops a defense of Christianity, based partly on the argument that religion is a vivid consciousness of a greater whole, of which the individual is but part and upon which he or she is totally dependent. The essence of religion is declared to lie in a "fundamental, distinct and integrative element of human life and culture." Schleiermacher identifies this as a feeling of being totally and utterly dependent upon something infinite, which is nevertheless made known in and through finite things. Religion in general (rather than Christianity in particular) is commended as the necessary context of science and art, without which human culture is needlessly impoverished.

In *The Christian Faith* (second edition, 1834) Schleiermacher emphasizes that the Christian faith is not primarily conceptual; rather, doctrines are to be seen as second-order expressions of its primary religious truth, which is the experience of redemption. Christian piety (*Frömmigkeit*) may be regarded as the fundamental basis of Christian theology; however, this should not be understood to mean the piety of the individual, but the corporate piety of the church. The essence of this piety is not some rational or moral principle, but "feeling" (*das Gefühl*), the immediate self-consciousness. The general human consciousness of being dependent upon something undefined is, according to Schleiermacher, recognized and interpreted within the context of the Christian faith as a sense of total dependence upon *God*. This "feeling of absolute dependence" constitutes the starting point for Christian theology. As A. E. Biedermann later commented, Schleiermacher's theology may be regarded as a critical exploration of the deep inner feelings of humanity. The human intellect thus reflects upon human feeling, and by doing so, interprets it.

One of the greatest weaknesses of the model can be seen through the criticisms directed against it by Ludwig Feuerbach (1804–72), who argued that such "experience" was little more than "experience of the self." We have already considered this difficulty (pp. 151–2) and noted its importance for experience-based theologies, such as that of Schleiermacher. The approach has also been criticized by postliberal writers such as George Lindbeck, who have argued that any appeal to an unmediated religious experience common to all of humanity is unmerited, in that it is a "false universal."

Revelation as history

A quite distinct approach, especially associated with the German theologian Wolfhart Pannenberg (born 1928), centers on the theme of "revelation as history" (see pp. 323–5). According to Pannenberg, Christian theology is based upon an analysis of universal and publicly accessible history, rather than the inward subjectivity of personal human existence or a special interpretation of that history. History itself is (or has the capacity to become) revelation. For Pannenberg, revelation is essentially a public and universal historical event which is recognized and *interpreted* as an "act of God." Pannenberg's "Dogmatic Theses on the Doctrine of Revelation" (1968) set out this position in seven theses, of which the first five are of especial interest in relation to this model of revelation:

1   The self-revelation of God in Scripture did not take place directly, after the fashion of a theophany, but indirectly, in the acts of God in history. (A "theophany" is an appearance of God in a temporary form, not necessarily material, which is to be contrasted with the incarnation,¹ in which God is understood to have been revealed permanently in the person of Christ.)

2   Revelation is not completely apprehended at the beginning, but only at the end of revelatory history.

3   In contrast to special divine manifestations, the revelation of God in history is publicly and universally accessible, and open to anyone who has eyes to see it.

4   The universal revelation of God is not fully realized in the history of Israel; it was first realized in the destiny of Jesus of Nazareth, insofar as the end of history is anticipated in that destiny.

5   The Christ-event cannot be regarded as revealing God in isolation; it is set in the context of the history of God's dealings with Israel.

On this basis, Pannenberg is able to argue for the resurrection of Christ as a central act of divine revelation in history, a point to which we shall return later in our analysis of the resurrection.

Pannenberg's approach to revelation has aroused excitement and criticism in about equal measure. The idea of establishing the gospel on the basis of universal history seemed a daring and creative gesture, allowing theology to reclaim the intellectual high ground that many had thought had long been forfeited to Marxism. In particular, it seemed to bypass the trap laid by Ludwig Feuerbach (see p. 151), who had argued that Schleiermacher's approach to revelation, beginning from human experience, was little more than a theology constructed through the objectification of human feelings. Pannenberg, by his appeal to history, is able to avoid the line of thought which leads to Feuerbach's impasse by insisting that theology arises out of history, not out of human feelings of redemption or the presence of God.

Natural Theology: Its Scope and Limits

We now turn to consider the important question of the extent to which God may be known through the natural order. This important area of theological debate is traditionally known as "natural theology," and has assumed increased importance in recent years on account of the growing interest in promoting dialogue between Christian theology and the natural sciences. Might the study of the natural world lead to an increased appreciation of its creator?

"The heavens declare the glory of God; the heavens proclaim the work of God's hands" (Psalm 19: 1). This well-known text can be seen as representing a general theme within the Christian Bible – that something of the wisdom of the God who made the world can be known through the world that was created. The exploration of this theme has proved to be one of the most fruitful areas of theology. We begin our discussion by considering what is widely regarded as a landmark in this matter: the contribution of Thomas Aquinas, which has been particularly influential in Catholic theology.

Thomas Aquinas on natural theology

The doctrine of creation is of central importance to a classic approach to the concept of natural theology. This is perhaps best seen from what is widely regarded as one of the greatest texts to address this theme: Thomas Aquinas's *Summa contra Gentiles*, written during the period 1259–61, initially at Paris and subsequently at Naples. One of its most significant discussions concerns the manner in which God may be understood to be related to the creation – a relationship which Aquinas analyzes in terms of causality, as follows.

For Aquinas, there exists a fundamental "likeness [*similitudo*] to God" within the created order as a consequence of God being the cause, in some sense of the word, of all created things. In that no created thing can be said to come into existence spontaneously, the existence of all things can be considered to be a consequence of a relationship of causal dependence between the creation and its creator. Using what are essentially Aristotelian categories of causality, Aquinas sets out a position which we may summarize as follows:

1 Suppose that A causes B.
2 Suppose also that A possesses a quality Q.
3 Then B will also possess that quality Q as a result of its being caused by A.

The full argument set out by Aquinas is complex and not without its difficulties; nevertheless, its conclusion is clear. There is a presence in the effect of characteristics that could serve to identify its cause. There are, so to speak, physical or metaphysical fingerprints within what is caused, which provide the basis for an inductive argument to the existence of that cause, and allow at least some aspects of its nature to be established. If God made the world, God's "signature" (so to speak) may be found within the created order. Aquinas puts this point as follows:

> Meditation on [God's] works enables us, at least to some extent, to admire and reflect on God's wisdom. [...] We are thus able to infer God's wisdom from reflection upon God's works. [...] This consideration of God's works leads to an admiration of God's sublime power, and consequently inspires reverence for God in human hearts. [...] This consideration also incites human souls to the love of God's goodness. [...] If the goodness, beauty, and wonder of creatures are so delightful to the human mind, the fountainhead of God's own goodness (compared with the trickles of goodness found in creatures) will draw excited human minds entirely to itself.

Something of the torrent of God's beauty can thus be known in the rivulets of the beauty of the creation.

For Aquinas, one of the most fundamental qualities which is to be attributed to God is that of "perfection." Although this concept can clearly be understood in moral terms, Aquinas uses it to characterize the distinctiveness of God in respect to the created order. "Perfection" is a quality which is possessed by God, and is possessed by that which God has created:

1 to a lesser extent than this perfection is possessed by God; and
2 as a result of its having been created by God.

In this sense, "perfection" may be thought of as an attribute which is characteristic of God, but is reflected in the created order on account of the metaphysically primary relationship of God to all other things.

Subsequent Catholic approaches to natural theology have built upon, refined, or qualified the position first articulated by Thomas. The First Vatican Council's "Dogmatic Constitution on the Catholic Faith" (1870) laid it down as a matter of faith that God has revealed himself in two ways, naturally and supernaturally.

Holy mother Church holds and teaches that God, the beginning and end of all things, can certainly be known [certo cognosci] by the light of natural human reason from created things: "his eternal power and divine nature, invisible though they are, have been understood and seen through the things he has made" (Romans 1: 20); nevertheless, it has pleased his wisdom and goodness to reveal himself and the eternal decrees of his will to the human race in another and supernatural way.

Two points of particular importance emerge from these later discussions. First, the recognition of a legitimate role for natural theology does not mean that reason has replaced faith. Nor does it mean that philosophical reflection has displaced the grace of God revealed in Christ. Faith and grace remain primary for all believers. Natural theology, however, offers the opportunity to establish certain truths by means common to all persons. It plays an important apologetic role. It is important to remember in this respect that Thomas Aquinas's *Summa contra Gentiles* is thought to have been written partly in order to help Islamic readers gain an understanding of Christian faith through shared beliefs based on reason.

Second, whatever can be known of God through nature is not to be taken as the "grounds" or "foundations" of additional, revealed truths. Catholics are generally inclined to recognize a continuum between natural theology, that which is known of God by the light of natural reason, and revealed theology, that which is known by the light of faith. In contrast, many Protestants tend to accentuate the distinctiveness of natural and revealed knowledge of God at this point.

John Calvin on natural theology

The first book of Calvin's *Institutes* opens with discussion of this fundamental problem of Christian theology: how do we know anything about God? Calvin affirms that a general knowledge of God may be discerned throughout the creation – in humanity, in the natural order, and in the historical process itself. Two main grounds of such knowledge are identified: one subjective, the other objective. The first ground is a "sense of divinity" (*sensus divinitatis*) or a "seed of religion" (*semen religionis*), which has been planted within every human being by God. God has endowed human beings with some inbuilt sense or presentiment of the divine existence. It is as if something about God has been engraved in the heart of every human being.

Calvin identifies three consequences of this inbuilt awareness of divinity: the universality of religion (which, if uninformed by the Christian revelation, degenerates into idolatry), a troubled conscience, and a servile fear of God. All of these, Calvin suggests, may serve as points of contact for the Christian proclamation. The second such ground lies in experience of and reflection upon the ordering of the world. The fact that God is creator, together with an appreciation of the divine wisdom and justice, may be gained from an inspection of the created order, culminating in humanity itself.

It is important to stress that Calvin makes no suggestion whatsoever that this knowledge of God from the created order is peculiar to, or even restricted to, Christian believers. Calvin is arguing that *anyone*, by intelligent and rational reflection upon the created order, should be able to arrive at the idea of God. The created order is a "theater" or a "mirror" for the displaying of the divine presence, nature, and attributes. Although invisible and incomprehensible, God wills to be known under the form of created and visible things, by donning the garment of creation.

> There is within the human mind, and that by natural instinct, a sense of divinity. This we take to be beyond controversy. So that no one might take refuge in the pretext of ignorance, God frequently renews and sometimes increases this awareness, so that all people, recognizing that there is a God and that he is their creator, are condemned by their own testimony because they have failed to worship him and to give their lives to his service. [...] There are innumerable witnesses in heaven and on earth that declare the wonders of his wisdom. Not only those more arcane matters for the closer observation of which astronomy, medicine, and all of natural science are intended, but also those which force themselves upon the sight of even the most unlearned and ignorant peoples, so that they cannot even open their eyes without being forced to see them.

A similar theme can be seen clearly in the writings of the French Renaissance thinker Jean Bodin (1539–96), especially his *Universae naturae theatrum* ("The Theater of the Universe of Nature"):

> We have come into this theater of the world for no other reason than to understand the admirable power, goodness, and wisdom of the most excellent creator of all things, to the extent that this is possible, by contemplating the appearance of the universe and all his actions and individual works, and thus to be swept away more ardently in praise of him.

Calvin thus commends the natural sciences (such as astronomy and medicine), on account of their ability to illustrate further the wonderful ordering of the creation, and the divine wisdom which this indicates. Significantly, however, Calvin makes no appeal to specifically *Christian* sources of revelation at this point. His argument is based upon empirical observation and reasoning. If Calvin introduces scriptural quotations, it is to consolidate a general natural knowledge of God, rather than to establish that knowledge in the first place. There is, he stresses, a way of discerning God within creation which is common to those inside and outside the Christian community.

Having thus laid the foundations for a general knowledge of God, Calvin stresses its shortcomings; his dialogue partner here is the classical Roman writer Cicero, whose *On the Nature of the Gods* is perhaps one of the most influential classical expositions of a natural knowledge of God. Calvin argues that the epistemic distance between God and humanity, already of enormous magnitude, is increased still further on account of human sin. Our natural knowledge of God is imperfect and confused, even to the point of contradiction on occasion. A natural knowledge of God serves to deprive humanity of any excuse for ignoring the divine will; nevertheless, it is inadequate as the basis of a fully fledged portrayal of the nature, character, and purposes of God.

Having stressed this point, Calvin then introduces the notion of revelation. Scripture reiterates what may be known of God through nature, while simultaneously clarifying this general revelation and enhancing it. "The knowledge of God, which is clearly shown in the ordering of the world and in all creatures, is still more clearly and familiarly explained in the Word." It is only through Scripture that the believer has access to knowledge of the redeeming actions of God in history, culminating in the life, death, and resurrection of Jesus Christ. For Calvin, revelation is focused upon the person of Jesus Christ; our knowledge of God is mediated through him. God may thus be fully known only through Jesus Christ, who may in turn be known only through Scripture; the created order, however, provides important points of contact for and partial resonances of this revelation.

The basic idea here, then, is that a knowledge of God the creator may be had both through nature and through revelation, with the latter clarifying, confirming, and extending what may be known through the former. Knowledge of God the redeemer – which for Calvin is a distinctively *Christian* knowledge of God – may only be had by the Christian revelation, in Christ and through Scripture.

The Reformed tradition on natural theology

This concept of natural theology received a particularly significant development within the confessional element of the Reformed tradition. The *Gallic Confession of Faith* (1559) argues that God reveals himself to humanity in two manners:

> First, in God's works, both in their creation and their preservation and control. Second, and more clearly, in God's Word, which was revealed through oracles in the beginning, and which was subsequently committed to writing in the books which we call the Holy Scriptures.

A related idea was set out in the *Belgic Confession* (1561), which expanded the brief statement on natural theology found in the *Gallic Confession*. Once more, knowledge of God is affirmed to come about by two means:

> First, by the creation, preservation, and government of the universe, which is before our eyes as a most beautiful book, in which all creatures, great and small, are like so many characters leading us to contemplate the invisible things of God, namely, his eternal power and Godhead, as the Apostle Paul de-

clares (Romans 1: 20). All of these things are sufficient to convince humanity, and leave them without excuse. Second, he makes himself known more clearly and fully to us by his holy and divine Word; that is to say, as far as is necessary for us to know in this life, to his glory and our salvation.

The two themes which emerge clearly from these confessional statements can be summarized as follows:

1 There are two modes of knowing God, one through the natural order, and the second through Scripture; and
2 The second mode is clearer and fuller than the first.

God's two books: nature and Scripture

During the seventeenth century, a growing awareness of the ability of the natural science to illuminate the structures of nature catalyzed the emergence of what is known as the "two books" tradition, especially in England. This approach regarded nature and Scripture as two distinct yet complementary sources of our knowledge of God. Francis Bacon commended the study of "the book of God's word" and the "book of God's works" in his *Advancement of Learning* (1605).

This latter work had considerable impact on English thinking on the relation of science and religion. For example, in his 1674 tract *The Excellency of Theology compared with Natural Theology*, Robert Boyle noted that "as the two great books, of nature and of scripture, have the same author, so the study of the latter does not at all hinder an inquisitive man's delight in the study of the former." At times Boyle referred to the world as "God's epistle written to mankind." Similar thoughts can be found expressed in Sir Thomas Browne's 1643 classic *Religio Medici*:

There are two books from whence I collect my divinity. Besides that written one of God, another of his servant, nature, that universal and publick manuscript, that lies expansed unto the eyes of all. Those that never saw him in the one have discovered him in the other.

This metaphor of the two books with the one divine author was of considerable importance in holding together Christian theology and piety and the emerging interest and knowledge of the natural world in the seventeenth and early eighteenth centuries.

Approaches to Discerning God in Nature

T he doctrine of creation gives theological foundation to the notion of a natural knowledge of God. If God created the world, it is to be expected that God's creation should bear the mark of the divine handiwork. Just as the sculptor's distinctive style might be evident in the sculpture, or a painting might be signed with the artist's name, so the presence of God, it is argued, can be discerned within the creation. But what part of creation? Where in creation is God to be found?

Three major answers may be discerned within the rich tradition of reflection upon this issue down the centuries: human reason, the ordering of the world, and the beauty of the world.

Human reason

Augustine of Hippo addresses this question at some length in *De Trinitate* ("On the Trinity"). His line of argument can be summed up as follows. If God is indeed to be discerned within the creation, we ought to expect to find God at the height of the creation. Now the height of God's creation, Augustine argues (based on Genesis 1 and 2), is human nature. And, on the basis of the neo-Platonic presuppositions which he inherited from his cultural milieu, Augustine further argued that the height of human nature is the human capacity to reason. Therefore, he concluded, one should expect to find traces of God (or, more accurately, "vestiges of the Trinity") in human processes of reasoning. On the basis of this belief, Augustine develops what have come to be known as "psychological analogies of the Trinity" (see pp. 258–60).

The ordering of the world

We have already seen how Thomas Aquinas's arguments for the existence of God base themselves on the perception that there is an ordering within nature, which requires to be explained. Equally, the fact that the human mind can discern and investigate this ordering of nature is of considerable significance. There seems to be something about human nature which prompts it to ask questions about the world. And there seems to be something about the world which allows answers to those questions to be given. The noted theoretical physicist and Christian apologist John Polkinghorne comments on this point as follows, in his *Science and Creation*:

> We are so familiar with the fact that we can understand the world that most of the time we take it for granted. It is what makes science possible. Yet it could have been otherwise. The universe might have been a disorderly chaos rather than an orderly cosmos. Or it might have had a rationality which was inaccessible to us. [...] There is a congruence between our minds and the universe, between the rationality experienced within and the rationality observed without.

There is a deep-seated congruence between the rationality present to our minds, and the rationality – the *orderedness* – which we observe as present in the world. Thus the abstract structures of pure mathematics – a free creation of the human mind – provide important clues to understanding the world. All of this, Polkinghorne argues, is a form of natural theology, preparing the way for the full knowledge of the Christian revelation.

The beauty of the world

A number of theologians have developed natural theologies, based on the sense of beauty which arises from contemplating the world. Perhaps the most powerful exploration of this theme is made by the celebrated American theologian Jonathan Edwards.

> The immense magnificence of the visible world in inconceivable vastness, the incomprehensible height of the heavens, etc., is but a type of the infinite magnificence, height and glory of God's world in the spiritual world: the most uncomprehensible expression of His power, wisdom, holiness and love in what is wrought and brought to pass in the world, and the exceeding greatness of the moral and natural good, the light, knowledge, holiness, and happiness which shall be communicated to it, and therefore to that magnificence of the world, height of heaven.

This sense of aesthetic ecstasy pervades Edwards' autobiographical writings, especially his *Miscellanies*. The perception of beauty that we experience "when we are delighted with flowery meadows and gentle breezes" is, for Edwards, an intimation of the holiness of God, which Scripture clarifies and confirms, placing it upon a reliable theological foundation.

Hans Urs von Balthasar is an example of a twentieth-century writer who stresses the theological importance of beauty. However, von Balthasar distances himself from any idea of an "aesthetic theology." His major study

Herrlichkeit (English title: "The Glory of the Lord") is to be seen as a "theological aesthetics" rather than an "aesthetic theology." The category of "beauty" is, according to von Balthasar, to be reclaimed as a description of the revelation of God, rather than some human category which can be applied to God.

These, then, are some of the ways in which Christian theologians have attempted to describe the manner in which God can be known, however fleetingly and inadequately, through nature. But these approaches have not gone unchallenged. In what follows, we shall consider some objections to natural theology within the Christian theological tradition.

Objections to Natural Theology

If this positive approach to a natural knowledge of God represents the majority report within the Christian tradition, it is important to acknowledge that there have been other views. The whole enterprise of natural theology has been subjected to a powerful critique at both the theological and philosophical levels. In what follows, we shall consider both aspects of the matter.

A theological objection: Karl Barth

The Swiss Protestant theologian Karl Barth mounts a theologically informed and responsible critique of certain approaches to natural theology, which he regards as perpetuating the human quest for autonomy, which reached its high-water mark in the culture of the Enlightenment. For Barth, "natural theology" represents a concerted human attempt to subvert revelation, by declaring that what needs to be known about God can be determined without recourse to divine self-disclosure.

For Barth, natural theology is a human attempt to subvert the necessity of divine revelation. It is an attempt to know God in a manner and under conditions which are determined by humanity, not by God. Barth's polemic against natural theology can be seen as a principled attempt to safeguard the integrity of divine revelation against human attempts to construct their own notions of God, or undermine the necessity of revelation.

Although Barth's earlier polemic against human attempts to subvert revelation were framed in terms of a critique of the category of *religion*, from II/2 of the *Church Dogmatics* onwards, this is directed specifically against the category of natural theology. Barth offers an extended and systematic critique of natural theology, arguing that this represents a theology "which comes to humanity from nature," expressing humanity's "self-preservation and self-affirmation" in the face of God. Barth treats natural theology as the supreme expression of the human longing for self-justification and intellectual autonomy.

Barth's hostility towards natural theology thus rests on his fundamental belief that it undermines the necessity and uniqueness of God's self-revelation. If knowledge of God can be achieved independently of God's self-revelation in Christ, then it follows that humanity can dictate the place, time, and means of its knowledge of God. For Barth, there is a close link between natural theology and the theme of human autonomy. As Barth understands the concept, natural theology affirms and expresses the human desire to find God on our own terms. Natural theology thus appears to posit a second source of revelation alongside Jesus Christ. For Barth, revelation is only to be had through God, as a consequence of God's gracious decision that God wishes to be known. There is no manner in which God can be known outside and apart from God's self-revelation.

Three major criticisms have been directed against Barth's critical attitude towards natural theology, as follows:

1 It seems, to his critics, to rest on inadequate biblical foundations. Barth's engagement with the biblical texts have increasingly been seen in terms of the imposition of Barth's views upon those texts, rather than a faithful attempt to expound them. Writers such as James Barr have argued that Barth's rejection of natural theology was never really based on biblical exegesis, but rather reflected trends and developments in modern theology, philosophy, and society.
2 Barth's views on natural theology clearly represent a significant departure from the Reformed tradition which he clearly regards himself as representing. Barth tends to represent Calvin as a critic of natural theology in his *Church Dogmatics*, which is an extremely problematic judgment.
3 Barth's negative attitude to natural theology tends to create at least a disinterest in the natural sciences, thus impoverishing the dialogue between theology and the sciences.

All these points could be met. In what follows, we shall look at a major theologian in the Barthian tradition who adopts a significantly different attitude towards natural theology.

A theological response: Thomas F. Torrance

A related yet distinct approach to natural theology has been developed on other grounds by the noted Scottish theologian Thomas F. Torrance (born 1913). There are clear parallels between Torrance and Barth. Torrance identifies Barth's fundamental objection to natural theology as the radical separation it presupposes between "revealed theology" and a totally autonomous and unconnected "natural theology." For Torrance

> what Barth objects to in traditional natural theology is not any invalidity in its argumentation, nor even its rational structure, as such, but its *independent* character – i.e. the autonomous rational structure that natural theology develops on the ground of "nature alone," in abstraction from the active self-disclosure of the living and Triune God.

Torrance also stresses that Barth's criticism of natural theology does not rest on any form of dualism; for example, some kind of deistic dualism between God and the world which implies that there is no active relation between God and the world; or with some form of Marcionite dualism between redemption and creation implying a depreciation of the creature. It is clear that Torrance himself sympathizes with Barth at these junctures.

Torrance also notes a fundamental philosophical difficulty which seems to him to lie behind the forms of natural theology rejected by Barth. This kind of autonomous natural theology is, he argues, a

> desperate attempt to find a *logical bridge* between concepts and experience in order to cross the fatal separation between God and the world which it had posited in its initial assumptions, but it had to collapse along with the notion that science proceeds by way of abstraction from observational data.

It attempted, by means of establishing a logical bridge between ideas and being, to reach out inferentially toward God, and thus to produce a logical formalization of empirical and theoretical components of the knowledge of God. For Torrance, the "traditional abstractive form" of natural theology rested on a "deistic disjunction between God and the world" – a disjunction to which we shall return presently. The concerns which lay behind the Barthian challenge can thus be argued to have been met, in a manner which Torrance believed had Barth's support.

Other objections, however, have been raised against the idea of a "natural theology" from within Protestantism, particularly those found in the writings of the leading Reformed philosopher of religion, Alvin Plantinga.

A philosophical objection: Alvin Plantinga

In recent years, philosophers of religion working within a Reformed theological perspective have risen to considerable prominence. Alvin Plantinga and Nicholas Wolterstorff are examples of writers belonging to this category of thinkers, who have made highly significant contributions to the philosophy of religion in recent decades. Plantinga understands "natural theology" to be an attempt to prove or demonstrate the existence of God, and vigorously rejects it on the basis of his belief that it depends on a fallacious understanding of the nature of religious belief. The roots of this objection are complex, and can be summarized in terms of two foundational considerations:

1 Natural theology supposes that belief in God must rest upon an evidential basis. Belief in God is thus not, strictly speaking, a basic belief – that is, something which is self-evident, incorrigible, or evident to the senses. It is therefore a belief which requires to be itself grounded in some more basic belief. However, to ground a belief in God upon some other belief is, in effect, to depict that latter belief as endowed with a greater epistemic status than belief in God. For Plantinga, a properly Christian approach is to affirm that belief in God is itself basic, and does not require justification with reference to other beliefs.

2   Natural theology is not justified with reference to the Reformed tradition, including Calvin and his later followers.

The latter point seems to be inaccurate historically and is probably best overlooked. It is possible that Plantinga has been swayed here by Barth's view that Calvin did not support the concept of natural theology. However, his first line of argument against natural theology has met with growing interest.

Plantinga clearly regards Thomas Aquinas as the "natural theologian *par excellence*," and directs considerable attention to his methods. For Plantinga, Aquinas is a foundationalist in matters of theology and philosophy, in that "*scientia*, properly speaking, consists in a body of propositions deduced syllogistically from self-evident first principles." The *Summa contra Gentiles* shows, according to Plantinga, that Aquinas proceeds from evidential foundations to argue for a belief in God, which clearly makes such belief dependent upon appropriate evidential foundations. Many scholars have noted the importance of the growing criticism of classic foundationalism in modern philosophy and theology; our concern here is to note that Plantinga's conception of natural theology involves his belief that it intends to *prove* the existence of God.

It is clearly not necessary that a natural theology should make any such assumption; indeed, there are excellent reasons for suggesting that, as a matter of historical fact, natural theology is to be understood as a demonstration, from the standpoint of faith, of the consonance between that faith and the structures of the world. In other words, natural theology is not intended to prove the existence of God, but presupposes that existence; it then asks "what should we expect the natural world to be like if it has indeed been created by such a God?" The search for order in nature is therefore not intended to demonstrate that God exists, but to reinforce the plausibility of an already existing belief. This kind of approach can be found in the writings of William P. Alston, who can be seen as sharing at least some of Plantinga's commitments to a Reformed epistemology, while tending to take a considerably more positive attitude to natural theology.

A philosophical response: William Alston

In his major study *Perceiving God* (1991), Alston sets out what he regards as a responsible and realistic approach. He defines natural theology as "the enterprise of providing support for religious beliefs by starting from premises that neither are nor presuppose any religious beliefs." Conceding that it is impossible to construct a demonstrative proof of the existence of God from extrareligious premises, Alston argues that this is not, in any case, a proper approach to natural theology.

Properly speaking, natural theology begins from a starting point such as the existence of God or the ordering of the world, and shows that this starting point leads us to recognize the existence of a being which would be accepted as God. There is thus, in Alston's view, a strong degree of convergence between natural theology and traditional arguments for the existence of God, particularly those deriving from Thomas Aquinas. Yet his conception of natural theology goes beyond such narrow proofs, and encourages the engagement with other areas of human life and concern, among which he explicitly includes science. Natural theology thus offers "metaphysical reasons for the truth of theism as a general worldview," and allows us to build bridges to other disciplines.

It will be clear from the above discussion that both Plantinga and Barth have raised significant concerns about the nature and scope of natural theology, which will remain important in future discussions of this issue. We now turn to consider some issues that follow on immediately from this point – namely, the question of the place of philosophical analysis in theology. What role should philosophy play in theology? Are issues such as those raised by Alvin Plantinga of importance to theology? Or should they be disregarded, as having no bearing on Christian discourse about God? We shall give thought to these matters in the following chapter.

A debate: Karl Barth versus Emil Brunner (1934)

Every now and then, a theological debate takes place which is seen by both sides as representing a landmark. A good example is the debate of 1524–5 between Martin Luther and Erasmus of Rotterdam over the freedom of the human will, which is still seen by many as setting the benchmarks for future discussion. For many, the landmark debate over natural theology is still the exchange between Karl Barth and Emil Brunner, dating from 1934 (although the origins of their differences go back at least to 1929).

In 1934 Brunner published a work entitled *Nature and Grace*. In this work he argued that "the task of our theological generation is to find a way back to a legitimate natural theology." Brunner located this approach in the doctrine of creation, specifically the idea that human beings are created in the *imago Dei*, the "image of God." Human nature is constituted in such a way that there is an analog with the being of God. Despite the sinfulness of human nature, the ability to discern God in nature remains. Sinful human beings remain able to recognize God in nature and in the events of history, and to be aware of their guilt before God. There is thus a "point of contact" (*Anknüpfungspunkt*) for divine revelation within human nature.

Brunner had used this idea of the "point of contact" back in 1927, and it is integral to his understanding of human nature. For Brunner, human nature is constituted in such a way that there is a ready-made point of contact for divine revelation. Revelation thus addresses itself to a human nature which already has some idea of what that revelation is about. For example, take the gospel demand to "repent of sin." Brunner argues that this makes little sense, unless human beings already have some idea of what "sin" is. The gospel demand to repent is thus addressed to an audience which already has at least something of an idea of what "sin" and "repentance" might mean. Revelation brings with it a fuller understanding of what sin means – but in doing so, it builds upon an existing human awareness of sin.

Barth believed that Brunner's positive evaluation of natural theology seemed to imply that God needed help to become known, or that human beings somehow cooperated with God in the act of revelation. "The Holy Spirit [. . .] needs no point of contact other than that which that same Spirit establishes." For Barth there was no "point of contact" inherent within human nature. Any such "point of contact" was itself the result of divine revelation. It is something that is evoked by the Word of God, rather than something which is a permanent feature of human nature. Barth had begun to have misgivings about Brunner's more "dialogical" approach to revelation in the late 1920s, and had already come close to severing their relationship in 1929.

While Barth's response to Brunner can be read in a number of ways, the most helpful is to see it as a rejection of the notion of continuity between the creation and its creator. For Barth, this idea was expressed by the concept of *analogia entis* – a correspondence between God and the creation resulting from the creation itself. Barth began to focus his attack on the idea of *analogia entis* from 1929 onwards, and it is clear that he saw this notion underlying Brunner's approach to natural theology. Because of Barth's rejection of the *analogia entis*, human and divine language are not naturally convergent. As Barth later put it in the *Church Dogmatics*, although humans are "permitted and commanded" to speak of God, their language "consists only in 'approximations' [. . . and] stands in need of correction at every point." Even these "approximations" or "pictures" with which humans speak of God are in themselves unsuited to this object and thus inappropriate to express and affirm the knowledge of Him. For God – the living God who encounters us in Jesus Christ – cannot be appropriated by us in our own capacity. Natural theology thus rests upon a theologically flawed understanding of human nature, with important implications for how we use language about God, and construct our concepts of God.

The debate over natural theology has not been settled by this landmark confrontation, and it continues to this day – supplemented by a not unwelcome subsidiary debate over what Barth and Brunner actually thought they were doing in their works of 1934.

The Natural Sciences and Christian Theology: Models of Interaction

It is impossible to talk about "natural theology" without considering the importance of the increasingly influential dialogue now taking place between Christian theology and the natural sciences. During the nineteenth century the Darwinian controversy broke out. The publication of Charles Darwin's *On the Origin of Species* (1859) and *The Descent of Man* (1871) offered purely naturalistic theories of the origin and development of humanity. In the eyes of many observers, Darwinism did not merely make Christian approaches to creation redundant; they were now untenable. Darwin's evolutionary approach to human origins and development provoked a major theological reaction from Protestant and Roman Catholic theologians alike. The full details of the resulting controversy, which was particularly heated in Darwin's native England, need not concern us here. However, the debates raised a fundamental question which continues to be of importance today: what is the relation between Christian theology and the natural sciences? Four main approaches have developed, and will be explored in what follows.

The continuity between science and theology

The dominant force within Protestant theology in the nineteenth century was liberal Protestantism. Even in its earliest forms, as seen in the writings of F. D. E. Schleiermacher, liberal Protestantism showed itself to be committed to the reinterpretation of the Christian faith in terms which were consistent with the accepted wisdom of the age. Although Schleiermacher died nearly a quarter of a century before the publication of *On the Origin of Species*, his general approach was applied to the issue by his successors, such as Albrecht Ritschl. Liberal Protestantism thus argued that evolutionary theories allowed theology to appreciate the specific way in which God was present and active within the creation. Evolution was not inconsistent with divine providence; rather, it cast light on the way in which this providence operated.

Process theology is a particularly good example of a form of theology which has attempted to adapt the Christian tradition to the insights of modern science. Drawing on the insights of writers such as Alfred North Whitehead and Charles Hartshorne, process theology conceives God as the source of novelty and order. However, the traditional Christian idea of God as creator *ex nihilo* is treated with skepticism. Thus John B. Cobb Jr. and David R. Griffin prefer to speak in terms of God creating order out of chaos, and think of God as a source of novelty who produces order in the universe through persuasive love.

Although there are similarities between process theology and the ideas developed in the writings of Pierre Teilhard de Chardin, there are also important differences. Teilhard de Chardin, a Jesuit paleontologist with an interest in the theory of evolution, argued that the universe is in a state of evolution towards more complex structures. In writings such as *The Phenomenon of Man* (1955), Teilhard de Chardin declares that God is immanent within this process of evolution, guiding it towards its final convergence at "Omega Point" (see pp. 222–3). This idea of evolution towards a final goal is not generally typical of process theology.

The distinctiveness of science and theology

Partly in reaction against the tendency of various forms of liberal theology to accommodate to secular ideas and methods, neo-orthodoxy affirmed the distinctiveness of theology. This tendency can probably be seen at its clearest in Karl Barth's discussion of the doctrine of creation in his *Church Dogmatics*. For Barth, creation is a theological event, which cannot be illuminated or interpreted in the light of the natural sciences. Barth's refusal to allow philosophy to have any foundational role in theology is thus extended to the natural sciences. They have their proper spheres of competence; these do not, however, include the justification or explanation of the Christian faith.

A similar approach is found in the writings of American theologians influenced by neo-orthodoxy. A good example is provided by Langdon Gilkey's 1959 account of the doctrine of creation, *Maker of Heaven and Earth*. Gilkey here argues that theology and the natural sciences are independent and different ways of approaching reality. The natural sciences ask "how" questions; theology asks "why" questions. The former deal with secondary causes (that is, with interactions within nature); the latter deals with primary causes (that is, the ultimate origin and purpose of nature in the first place).

The distinctiveness of the disciplines is also affirmed by Karl Rahner. Using a framework similar to that adopted by Gilkey, Rahner argues that the sciences are concerned with "*a posteriori* experiences," whereas theology deals with "*a priori* questions." Rahner argues that things begin to go wrong when scientists start playing at being theologians, and vice versa, in that they refuse to respect the distinctive characteristics and limitations of their respective disciplines.

The convergence of science and theology

Where neo-orthodoxy regarded theology and the natural sciences as having independent agendas and methodologies, some more recent Protestant writers have argued for the need for a dialogue between the two disciplines. Thus Wolfhart Pannenberg has argued that the insights of the natural sciences can illuminate the Christian understanding of the doctrine of creation. Although Pannenberg insists that the two disciplines are distinct, he maintains that they can mutually interact, to the benefit of both. Related ideas can be found in the writings of the leading Scottish theologian, Thomas F. Torrance.

Torrance argues that both theology and the natural sciences are committed to some form of realism, in that they deal with a reality whose existence is prior to their attempts to comprehend it. Both require openness to the way things are, and that their modes of inquiry are conformed to the nature of the reality which they encounter. Torrance's approach is grounded in an approach which stresses the priority of God's self-revelation. This is seen as an objective reality, independent of human rational activity. Although Torrance is no uncritical supporter of Barth, this would unquestionably be one area in which he identifies with Barth's agenda.

A similar approach is developed by Alister E. McGrath in the three volumes of his *Scientific Theology* (2001–3). McGrath argues that both the natural sciences and Christian theology represent an engagement with an external reality, which is open to being represented theoretically. "A scientific theology conceives the theological enterprise as a principled attempt to give an account of the reality of God, which it understands to be embedded at different levels in the world." McGrath develops a form of critical realism which acknowledges the active involvement of the knower in the process of knowing, while using Roy Bhaskar's notion of the "stratification of reality" to explore the various levels of theological analysis.

The opposition of science and theology

According to this approach, the Genesis creation accounts represent a legitimate and valid understanding of the origins of the world, which remain valid in the face of the rival theories offered by the natural sciences. This view does not regard biblical and scientific approaches as complementary. Rather, it regards the biblical material as presenting a valid and objective account of the origins and development of humanity, which is in tension with theories of evolution – and, for this reason, says that theories of evolution are incorrect. This approach is particularly associated with conservative American evangelicalism. It is increasingly referred to as "scientific creationism" and can be studied from writings such as Henry M. Morris, *Scientific Creationism* (1974).

QUESTIONS FOR CHAPTER 7

1 What do you understand by the term "revelation"?

2 Many theologians argue that theology is fundamentally an exposition of the revealed truths found in the Bible. What are the strengths and weaknesses of this position?

3 Why does Emil Brunner place such an emphasis upon truth as a personal notion? What points does he aim to make in this way? What criticisms might be directed against this position?

4 What impact does the idea of the "two books" of divine revelation have for the relation of Christian theology and the natural sciences?

5 Give a critical assessment of Karl Barth's critique of natural theology.

6 How would you assess the four approaches to the relation of science and theology set out in this chapter?

8

Philosophy and Theology: Introducing a Dialogue

"What," asked Tertullian in the third century, "has Athens to do with Jerusalem? Or the Academy with the church?" Tertullian's basic question concerned the relation of Christian theology with secular philosophy, especially Platonism. The Greek city of Athens was the home of the Academy, an institution of secular learning founded by Plato in 387 BC. For Tertullian, Christian theologians inhabited a completely different mental world to their pagan counterparts. How could there be a dialogue between them?

This question has resonated throughout Christian history. For example, in 797 the English writer Alcuin rebuked the monks of Lindisfarne Abbey for reading too many Nordic sagas, including a number dealing with the exploits of the pagan hero Ingeld. "What," he asked, "has Ingeld to do with Christ?" – thus posing exactly the same question raised by Tertullian centuries earlier. Alcuin's remedy for the situation was direct and to the point: "Let the words of God be read aloud at table in your refectory. It is the reader who should be heard there, not someone playing the flute. It is the fathers of the church, and not the songs of the heathen, who should be heard."

Yet others were not so sure about this attitude, and encouraged a friendly dialogue and constructive engagement with the world of secular philosophy. Was not all truth God's truth? And did not this insight mandate an interaction between Christian theology and secular philosophy? Justin Martyr adopted a particularly warm attitude to Platonism during the second century, prompting his critics to suggest he had merely baptized Platonist ideas, without interacting with them sufficiently critically. Augustine commended a critical appropriation of secular philosophy, likening this process to plundering Egypt of its riches at the time of the Exodus under Moses. Was not Moses "learned in all the wisdom of the Egyptians" (Acts 7: 22)?

From this brief introduction, it will be clear that it is important that we examine the debate over the interaction of Christian theology and philosophy. How do we obtain secure knowledge? What is the status of religious language? Can God's existence be said to be "proved"? It is a huge subject, demanding several volumes in its own right to survey it adequately. In what follows, we offer what can only be a very brief introduction to the general themes of the discussion, in the hope that readers will want to take the subject further.

Philosophy and Theology: The Notion of the "Handmaid"

One of the most interesting aspects of Christian theology is the manner in which it has interacted with various schools of philosophy throughout the two thousand years of its existence. These schools of thought have at times been seen as allies, and at times enemies of the Christian faith, as we noted when considering the interaction of Christianity with classical culture (pp. 116–19). Philosophical systems which have had the greatest impact on Christianity include the following:

1 Platonism, which, in various forms, was highly influential in shaping eastern and western Christian theology during the patristic period.
2 Aristotelianism, which exercised considerable influence during the Middle Ages, especially in the case of Thomas Aquinas.
3 Ramism, the system developed by Pierre de la Ramée (1515–72), which was seen by various Puritan writers as offering a philosophical system especially suited for the defense and communication of Reformed theology.
4 Cartesianism, the system associated with René Descartes (1596–1650), which sought to ground both philosophy and theology on absolutely secure first principles of knowledge.
5 Kantianism, which exercised considerable influence over late eighteenth- and early nineteenth-century German theology.
6 Hegelianism, based on the writings of G. W. F. Hegel (1770–1831), which is reflected in different ways in the writings of Ludwig Feuerbach and Karl Marx, and which was taken up and developed by Idealist philosophers and theologians in the nineteenth century and early twentieth-century theologians.
7 Existentialism, a general category of philosophies which emerged partly from the legacy of the Danish philosopher and theologian Søren Kierkegaard (1813–55), which have influenced twentieth-century theologians such as Rudolf Bultmann, Paul Tillich, and John Macquarrie. We considered this approach in more detail earlier, and examined its importance for theology (pp. 146–7).

We now turn to consider one of the most interesting aspects of the relation of faith and reason – the use of "helpmates" or "dialogue partners" in theology, often referred to using the Latin term *ancilla theologiae*, a Latin phrase which literally means "a handmaid of theology."

The "handmaid": the dialogue between theology and philosophy

There is a long tradition within Christian theology of drawing on intellectual resources outside the Christian tradition as a means of developing a theological vision. This approach, usually referred to using the Latin phrase *ancilla theologiae*, is grounded in the basic idea that philosophical systems can be a very helpful way of stimulating theological development, and enabling a dialogue to be opened up between Christian thinkers and their cultural environment. The two most important historical examples of this approach to theology are the dialogues with Platonism and Aristotelianism.

The dialogue with Platonism was of immense importance during the first five centuries of the Christian church, especially in the Greek-speaking world of the eastern Mediterranean. As Christianity expanded in that region, it encountered rival worldviews, of which Platonism was the most important. Such worldviews could be seen positively or negatively: they were both an opportunity for dialogue and intellectual development, and also a threat to the existence of Christianity. The task faced by writers such as Justin Martyr or Clement of Alexandria was how to make use of the obvious intellectual merits of Platonism in constructing a Christian worldview, without compromising the integrity of Christianity itself. After all, despite their occasional similarities, Christianity is not Platonism.

A new debate opened up in the thirteenth century, during the golden age of scholastic theology. The rediscovery of Aristotle by medieval writers seemed to offer new resources to help in every aspect of intellectual life, including physics, philosophy, and ethics. It was inevitable that theologians should also want to see what use they could make of Aristotelian ideas and methods in constructing a systematic theology – such as Thomas Aquinas's massive *Summa Theologiae*, widely regarded as one of the greatest works of theology ever written.

In both these cases, using another intellectual discipline as the *ancilla theologiae* offers opportunities and risks in about equal measure. It is clearly important to appreciate what these opportunities and risks are. The two major opportunities offered to theology by the critical appropriation of another discipline can be summarized as follows.

1   It allows for a much more rigorous exploration of ideas than would otherwise be possible. Problems that Christian theology encounters in trying to develop its ideas often have their parallels in other disciplines. Thomas Aquinas, for example, found Aristotle's notion of an "'unmoved mover" helpful in setting out some reasons for defending the existence of God.
2   It allows Christian theology to engage in a dialogue with another worldview – a major element of the church's witness to its secular context. In the second century, Justin Martyr clearly believed that many Platonists would be so impressed by the parallels between Platonism and Christianity that they might consider conversion. Similarly, in his "Areopagus address" (Acts 17: 22–31), Paul draws on some themes from Stoic philosophy in attempting to communicate the Christian message to Athenian culture.

Yet alongside these positive aspects of such an engagement, an obvious risk must also be noted – that ideas which are not distinctively Christian come to play a significant (perhaps even normative) role in Christian theology. For example, Aristotelian ideas about the proper manner of logical reasoning, or Cartesian ideas about the proper starting point for any intellectual discipline, might find their way into Christian theology. On some occasions, this might turn out to be a neutral development; on others, it may eventually be recognized to have negative implications, undermining the integrity of Christian theology, and ultimately causing it to be distorted. Martin Luther, the great German reformer, argued that medieval theology had allowed a number of such distortions to arise through an excessive, and partially uncritical, use of Aristotelian ideas in the Middle Ages.

Despite these concerns, the approach continues to be widely used. Many German theologians of the nineteenth century found G. W. F. Hegel and Immanuel Kant to be helpful dialogue partners. In the twentieth century, Rudolf Bultmann and Paul Tillich both found a dialogue with existentialism to be theologically productive. More recently, Alister McGrath has argued that the working methods and assumptions of the natural sciences can be theologically significant (see his three-volumed work *A Scientific Theology*).

In what follows, we shall explore how two major classic schools of philosophy have helped shape the development of Christian theology, not least by forcing discussion of some of the issues which it has raised. This analysis is not exhaustive, and is intended simply to indicate the general ways in which philosophy has related to theology.

Platonism

Plato (427–347 BC) is widely regarded as one of the greatest philosophers of the ancient world. He was born into an aristocratic family in Athens at the time of Pericles, perhaps its greatest statesman. At some point during his youth, Plato came to know Socrates, for whom he formed a great personal admiration. Following the condemnation and execution of Socrates in 399 BC, Plato left Athens and began to write the dialogues for which he is remembered. These are generally held to fall into three groups.

1 The early dialogues, which are often regarded as memorials or tributes to Socrates. These include *Euthyphro*, *Crito*, and *Apology*.
2 The middle dialogues, begun after the founding of the Academy at Athens in 387BC, which includes the famous dialogue *The Republic*. This reflects Plato's belief that philosophers should be kings, and kings philosophers, and can be seen as reflecting Plato's hopes for the education of Dionysius the Younger at Syracuse in 367BC.
3 The late dialogues, dating from after Plato's return to Athens from Syracuse in 360BC. In these dialogues, the figure of Socrates has receded into the background, and does not play a prominent role.

Perhaps the most important aspect of Plato's thought is the "theory of Forms." The "Forms" can be understood as the principles of being within the world. The world of appearances can be understood and accounted for in terms of being particular images of the Forms. Plato ascribed particular importance to the Form of the good, and to the notion of the *logos* (Greek: "word") through which the rationality of the world is communicated and conceptualized.

Platonism underwent a significant development after Plato's death. Many scholars distinguish various stages in its later development, including the period of "Middle Platonism" and "Neo-Platonism." Christian theologians of the patristic period found the Platonic notion of the *logos* immensely important, especially in dealing with the doctrines of divine revelation and Christology. The Platonic notion of the *logos spermatikos* ("seed-bearing word") was widely invoked as a means of explaining how the wisdom of the Christian God could be discerned in non-Christian contexts, such as Greek philosophy. Similarly, the role of Christ in mediating God to the world was seen as paralleling the role of the *logos* in Middle Platonism.

The idea of Christ as the one who makes the order of the creation visible to humanity can clearly be seen in the writings of many Christian Platonists. Clement of Alexandria, presumably with a Platonic audience in mind, stresses that it is Christ who, as *logos*, is able to reveal what would otherwise be inaccessible to humanity. The truth is something that can be made known – that can be *seen*:

The Word of God himself says "I am the Truth." Now it is by the Spirit that God can be contemplated. But, Plato says, who are the true philosophers? Those who wish to see the truth. And in the *Phaedrus*, he speaks of Truth as an idea. But this "idea" is none other than the thought of God, which the pagans called his *logos*. Now the *logos* proceeds from God as the cause of the creation. Then the *logos* is himself begotten, when he becomes incarnate, in order that he may become visible.

Clement thus simultaneously builds his thinking on Platonic ideas, while at the same time stressing the inadequacy of the philosophical system in comparison with Christianity. How can Truth be *seen*? Plato has no answer to give; having stressed the importance of "seeing" the truth, he cannot make this happen. Christianity, however, speaks and knows of the *logos* incarnate – and hence available and displayed to human sight.

Aristotelianism

Aristotle (384–322BC) was born in the northern Greek region of Stagira, and began to develop his considerable talents of observation in response to his father's interest in the natural world. Aristotle's influence was such that he can be said, perhaps more than any other thinker, to have determined the orientation and the content of much of western intellectual history, especially as a result of the Aristotelian Renaissance of the thirteenth century.

Aristotle was the author of a philosophical and scientific system that through the centuries became the support and vehicle for both medieval Christian and Islamic scholastic thought. Indeed, it can be argued that until the end of the seventeenth century, western culture was Aristotelian. Even after the intellectual revolutions of the centuries that followed, Aristotelian concepts and ideas remained embedded in western thinking. It will be clear that the potential impact of Aristotelianism upon Christian theology was therefore considerable.

Aristotle began to attend the Platonic Academy in 387BC, at the age of 17. However, it became clear that he had a concern for the observation of the natural order that had no direct parallel in Plato. His studies on animals laid the foundations for the biological sciences, and were not superseded until more than two thousand years after his death. The enquiries upon which those great works were based were probably carried out largely in Assos and Lesbos. Aristotle also disagreed with Plato on issues of politics, holding that it was not merely unnecessary for a king to be a philosopher; this was a positive liability. Kings ought to take the advice of true philosophers, rather than try to become philosophers themselves.

The differences between Plato and Aristotle could hardly be overlooked, and led to a certain coolness towards Aristotle within the Academy. Having failed to secure the position of head of the Academy, Aristotle responded by founding his own school – the Lyceum – in Athens in 335BC. The Platonic Academy had tended to be rather narrow in its teaching interests; Aristotle ensured that the Lyceum pursued a broader range of subjects. Prominence was given by Aristotle to the detailed study of nature. Aristotle wrote some 30 works, none of which appears to have been intended for publication. They were provided with their current titles in 60BC by Andronicus of Rhodes, the last head of the Lyceum. The writings include important works on both the observation of nature – such as the *Physics* – and logic, including the important *Analytics*, which deals with the structure and progression of logical reasoning.

Aristotle's influence on Christian theology has been considerable. An excellent example is provided by one of Thomas Aquinas's Five Ways – that is, arguments for the existence of God, which we shall consider presently. Aquinas bases his argument from motion on the following principle: everything that is moved is moved by something else. This principle is taken directly from Aristotelian physics.

It could therefore be suggested that some of Aquinas's arguments in defense of the

Christian faith actually rest on Aristotelian ideas. In his *Summa contra Gentiles* Aquinas makes extensive use of Aristotelian arguments, apparently believing that the Islamic scholars who he hoped would read this book would find this an acceptable way into the Christian faith. Aristotle was taken with great seriousness by many Islamic scholars of the early Middle Ages, and Aquinas appears to have seen him as the basis of an apologetic for an Islamic audience. Indeed, Thomas's argument from motion – the first of his "Five Ways" – rests heavily on the assumptions of Aristotelian physics.

Having considered two classic philosophical influences on Christian theology, we may now turn to consider two modern debates, which continue to this day. First, we ask whether the ideas of Christian theology are capable of being verified.

Verification and falsification: can Christian ideas be proved?

One of the most significant philosophical movements to arise in the twentieth century, logical positivism, had its origins in the University of Vienna. The "Vienna Circle" is generally regarded as the group of philosophers, physicists, mathematicians, sociologists, and economists who gathered around Moritz Schlick during the period 1924–36. One of their most fundamental and distinctive arguments was that *beliefs must be justified on the basis of experience.* This belief can be seen to be grounded in the writings of David Hume, and is clearly empirical in tone. For this reason, the members of the group tended to place a particularly high estimation on the methods and norms of the natural sciences (which were seen as the most empirical of human disciplines) and a correspondingly low estimation of metaphysics (which was seen as an attempt to disengage with experience).

These views were popularized in the English-language world through the publication of A. J. Ayer's book *Language, Truth and Logic* in 1936. Although World War II interfered with the process of its reception and evaluation, this single work is widely regarded as setting the philosophical agenda for at least the two decades which followed that war. Its vigorous and radical application of the verification principle eliminated as "meaningless" virtually everything which had tended to be thought of as metaphysical or religious.

As might be expected from the above analysis, logical positivism has little time for religious statements, which are dismissed as meaningless due to an inability to verify them. Carnap asserted that religious statements were unscientific:

> Systematic theology claims to represent knowledge concerning alleged beings of a supernatural order. A claim of this kind must be examined according to the same rigorous standards as any other claim of knowledge. Now in my considered opinion this examination has clearly shown that traditional theology is a remnant of earlier times, entirely out of line with the scientific way of thinking in the present century.

Sentences which make statements about "God," "the transcendent," or "the Absolute" are meaningless, in that there is nothing in experience which can verify them. Ayer allowed that religious statements might provide indirect information concerning the state of mind of the person making such a statement. They could not, however, be considered as making meaningful statements concerning the external world.

But not all were persuaded by this approach. The Austrian philosopher Karl Popper thought that the verification principle associated with the Vienna Circle was far too rigid, and ended up excluding many valid scientific statements.

My criticism of the verifiability criterion has always been this: against the intention of its defenders, it did not exclude obvious metaphysical statements; but it did exclude the most important and interesting of all scientific statements, that is to say, the scientific theories, the universal laws of nature.

But he was also convinced that the emphasis on verification was misplaced for another reason. It ended up by allowing a number of "pseudosciences" such as Freudianism and Marxism to pass themselves off as being "scientific" when they were, in reality, nothing of the sort.

So what criterion could be used to judge a theory? Popper insists that a theory must be capable of being tested against observation of the world. But where logical positivism stressed the need for stating the conditions under which a theoretical statement could be verified, Popper held that the emphasis must fall upon being able to state the conditions under which the system could be falsified.

Popper's approach had considerable influence within the philosophy of religion during the 1950s and 1960s, and is especially linked with what has come to be known as the "falsification" debate. In his 1950 study "Theology and Falsification," Anthony Flew argues that religious statements cannot be regarded as meaningful, in that nothing drawn from experience can be regarded as falsifying them. In effect, Flew is following Popper's criticisms of Marxism and Freudianism, which he held to be capable of interpreting observational or experiential evidence in whatever manner they pleased.

Flew sets out his concerns by way of what he calls a parable. Two explorers come across a clearing in the jungle. One of the explorers states his belief that there is an invisible gardener who looks after the clearing. The second explorer denies this, and suggests that they try to confirm this by means of various sensory tests – such as watching for the gardener to visit the clearing, and using bloodhounds and electric fences to detect his presence. None of the tests detects the gardener. The second explorer argues that this demonstrates that there is no gardener. The first, however, meets all these objections with qualifications. "There is a gardener," he argues, "who has no scent and makes no sound." In the end, Flew argues that the idea of the gardener meets the "death of a thousand qualifications." The gardener cannot be seen, heard, smelled, or touched. So might one not be forgiven for concluding that there really is no gardener? That, certainly, was Flew's conclusion. It rested upon the fact that religious statements cannot be formulated in a manner in which they can be falsified.

However, the demand for falsification – like the earlier demand for verification – proves to be much more complex than might at first have been thought. For example, Flew's absolute demands cannot be met by the natural sciences, which introduce precisely the modifications or "qualifications" to which Flew objects so strongly in the process of theory development. Anomalous data is generally accommodated within theories by a subtle and complex process of adjustment, modification, and qualification. The absolute demand for something which incontestably falsifies a theory – often stated in terms of a "crucial experiment" – is actually unrealistic in the natural sciences – a point famously demonstrated by the French philosopher and physicist Pierre Duhem (1861–1916).

Having considered this important philosophical debate, we may now turn to look at another. This time, we shall look at whether Christian theological statements can be said to refer to an ultimate reality, opening up the question of the place of realism in theology.

The debate over realism: to what do theological statements refer?

Do theological statements actually refer to something – such as God? Or are they products of the human imagination? Such questions open up the question of realism in theology. Traditionally, most theologians have been realists, arguing that theological statements ultimately refer to divine realities. It is also encountered in more recent writers, such as Thomas F. Torrance (born 1913) and Alister E. McGrath (born 1953), who have made an appeal to the assumptions and methods of the natural sciences in defending a form of theological realism, in which every level of reality is investigated using methods appropriate to its distinctive nature.

Most natural scientists would argue that, despite difficulties in representing or detecting them, "theoretical" or "unobservable entities" may be held to genuinely exist. The fact that they cannot be observed cannot be taken to imply that they do not exist. There are excellent reasons for supposing that electrons, quarks, and neutrons exist, even though they cannot be "perceived" or observed directly. As John Polkinghorne – himself a distinguished explorer of the interface between physics and theology – has further pointed out, difficulties in depiction cannot be taken as an indication that something does not exist:

> It is our ability to understand the physical world which convinces us of its reality, even when, in the elusive world of quantum theory, that reality is not picturable. This gives physics a good deal in common with theology as the latter pursues its search for an understanding of the Unpicturable.

One form of realism which is of particular significance to theology is what is usually referred to as "critical realism." What is often referred to as a "naive realism" holds that there is a direct relationship between the external world and human perception, so that "reality" can be perceived directly. Critical realism holds that this perception, although real, is indirect, and is mediated through models or analogies. For example, we will never know exactly what an electron looks like, and can never expect to see one. But that does not stop us from believing that electrons really exist, nor from developing models of electrons which help us understand their behavior.

The relevance of this debate to religion will be obvious. One of the most significant questions to be debated, particularly within the discipline of the philosophy of religion, is whether God is simply a construct of the human mind, or exists independently of human thought. In many areas of religious thinking, there is growing interest in "critical realism," which can be summarized in terms of two propositions.

1 God exists independently of human thought.
2 Humans are obliged to use models or analogies to depict God, who cannot be known directly.

For this reason, the use of models and analogies in both science and religion is a subject of considerable interest.

Yet not all agree with such realist approaches to theology. A good example of a nonrealist is the British philosopher of religion Don Cupitt (born 1934). Cupitt argues for a form of antirealism which allows us to create our concepts of God as we please. There is no "objectively real" God to which we are under some kind of obligation to respect. The world, he argues, has been completely cut adrift from the moorings of realism. Instead of responding to reality, we create whatever we choose to regard as real. Reality is thus something which we construct, not something to which we respond. "We constructed all the world-views, we made all the theories [. . .] They depend on us, not we on them."

Over the years, Cupitt has gradually shifted from an early commitment to a form of critical realism (which recognizes that what we say about God never fully represents the reality of God) to a robust antirealism, which insists that there is no objective reality "out there" at all. Everything that we say about "reality" – including God – is really about ourselves. We see here an argument very similar to that developed by Ludwig Feuerbach: humanity creates metaphysical entities to suit its own needs.

This brief survey of some philosophical issues in contemporary theological debate is intended simply to demonstrate how important philosophical issues are to theology. We have looked at two areas of philosophical importance; many others could easily be added, if space permitted.

The Nature of Faith

Since the time of the Enlightenment, the word "faith" has come to mean something like "a lower form of knowledge." Faith is understood to mean "partial knowledge," characterized by a degree of uncertainty, and based upon either a lack of evidence, or evidence which is inadequate to convince fully. Kant argued that faith (*Glaube*) is basically a belief which is held on grounds that are subjectively adequate, but objectively inadequate. Faith is thus seen as a firm commitment to a belief which is not adequately justified on the basis of the evidence available.

Although this understanding of faith may be adequate for some limited purposes, it is seriously inadequate for the purposes of Christian theology. Faith, as understood within the Christian tradition, has both epistemological and soteriological aspects; that is, it concerns how things (especially things about God) may be known, and also how salvation may be grasped. For example, Luther's doctrine of justification by faith alone cannot be understood if faith is understood to mean "a belief which goes beyond the evidence available."

To explore this point further, we may consider these two aspects of faith in more detail. The cognitive or epistemological aspects of faith can easily be appreciated by looking at Thomas Aquinas's discussion of the issue, while the soteriological aspects of faith are probably best studied from the early writings of Martin Luther.

Faith and knowledge

Aquinas adopts a strongly intellectualist approach to faith, treating it as something which is midway between knowledge (*scientia*) and opinion. For Aquinas, *scientia* has the sense of "something which is self-evidently true," or "something which can be demonstrated to be derived from something which is self-evidently true." In the case of *scientia*, truth compels assent on the part of the human intellect either because it is self-evidently correct, or because it is supported by such powerfully persuasive logical arguments that no rational mind could fail to be convinced. In the case of faith, however, the evidence is not sufficient to compel the human intellect to accept it.

Faith accepts as true the articles of the Christian faith, as they are summarized, for example, in the creeds. The object of faith is propositions about God, or about the Christian faith in general. To "have faith" is to accept these articles of faith as true, even though they cannot be demonstrated to be so beyond doubt, on the basis of the evidence available.

Aquinas insists upon the rationality of the Christian faith. In other words, he stresses that the contents of the Christian faith can be shown to be consistent with human reason. His arguments for the existence of God (the Five Ways) are basically an attempt to show that the Christian belief in God is consistent with rational reflection on the world of human experience. Nevertheless, Aquinas is also concerned to insist that Christian faith and theology are ultimately a response to something which lies beyond human reason – divine revelation. We consider this point further elsewhere (see pp. 187–9).

The commonsense understanding of faith, as a lower form of knowledge, thus seems to be well grounded in the writings of Thomas Aquinas. It has had a profound impact upon the philosophy of religion, as well as upon popular understandings of the nature of Christian faith. For example, the popular understanding of the first statement of the creed, "I believe in God," is little more than "I believe that there is a god." Yet with the sixteenth-century Reformation, there came a sustained attempt to rediscover aspects of the biblical understanding of the nature of faith, which had become obscured by the scholastic concern for right knowledge of God. We can explore this by considering Luther's emphasis upon the soteriological aspects of faith.

Faith and salvation

The most significant contribution to the classic evangelical understanding of faith was unquestionably made by Martin Luther. Luther's doctrine of justification by faith alone made faith, rightly understood, the cornerstone of his spirituality and theology. Luther's fundamental point is that "the Fall" (Genesis 1–3) is first and foremost a fall from faith. Faith is the right relationship with God (cf. Genesis 15: 6). To have faith is to live as God intends us to live.

Luther's notion of faith has three basic elements.

1 Faith has a personal, rather than a purely historical, reference.
2 Faith concerns trust in the promises of God.
3 Faith unites the believer to Christ.

We shall consider each of these points individually.

Faith is not simply historical knowledge

Luther argues that a faith which is content to believe in the historical reliability of the Gospels is not a saving faith. Sinners are perfectly capable of trusting in the historical details of the Gospels; but these facts of themselves are not adequate for true Christian faith. Saving faith concerns believing and trusting that Christ was born for us personally, and has accomplished for us the work of salvation.

Faith includes an element of trust (fiducia)

The notion of trust is prominent in the Reformation conception of faith, as a nautical analogy used by Luther indicates: "Everything depends upon faith. The person who does not have faith is like someone who has to cross the sea, but is so frightened that he does not trust the ship. And so he stays where he is, and is never saved, because he will not get on board and cross over." Faith is not merely believing that something is true; it is being prepared to act upon that belief, and relying upon it. To use Luther's analogy: faith is not simply about believing that a ship exists – it is about stepping into that ship, putting to sea, and entrusting ourselves to it.

But what are we being asked to trust? Are we being asked simply to have faith in faith? For Luther, the question could perhaps be phrased more accurately as follows: who are we being asked to trust? For Luther, the answer was unequivocal: faith is about being prepared to put one's trust in the promises of God, and the integrity and faithfulness of the God who made those promises. Faith is only as strong as the one in whom we believe and trust. The efficacy of faith does not rest upon the intensity with which we believe, but in the reliability of the one in whom we believe. The content of faith matters at least as much as, and probably far more than, its intensity. It is pointless to trust passionately in someone who is not worthy of trust; even a modicum of faith in someone who is totally reliable is vastly to be preferred. Trust is not, however, an occasional attitude. For Luther, it is an undeviating trusting outlook upon life, a constant stance of conviction of the trustworthiness of the promises of God.

Faith unites the believer to Christ

Luther states this principle clearly in his 1520 work, *The Liberty of a Christian*.

> Faith does not merely mean that the soul realizes that the divine word is full of all grace, free and holy; it also unites the soul with Christ, as a bride is united with her bridegroom. From such a marriage, as St Paul says (Ephesians 5: 31–2), it follows that Christ and the soul become one body, so that they hold all things in common, whether for better or worse. This means that what Christ possesses belongs to the believing soul; and what the soul possesses, belongs to Christ. Thus Christ possesses all good things and holiness; these now belong to the soul. The soul possesses lots of vices and sin; these now belong to Christ.

Faith, then, is not assent to an abstract set of doctrines. Rather, it is a "wedding ring," pointing to mutual commitment and union between Christ and the believer. It is the response of the whole person of the believer to God, which leads in turn to the real and personal presence of Christ in the believer. Faith makes both Christ and his benefits – such as forgiveness, justification, and hope – available to the believer.

On the basis of this brief discussion, it will be clear that Aquinas and Luther adopt very different understandings of faith. The main points of difference may be summarized as follows:

1 Aquinas tends to adopt a philosophical approach to faith, where Luther's approach is more explicitly religious.
2 Aquinas tends to regard faith as relating to propositions about God; Luther understands it to relate to the promises of God.
3 Aquinas relates faith to evidence; Luther relates it to the personal trustworthiness of God.
4 Aquinas's notion of faith is theological, in that it relates to God himself; Luther's is more Christological, for two reasons. First, because the object of faith is to unite the believer to Christ; second, because Christ is the historical manifestation or demonstration of the faithfulness of God to the divine promises.

Having explored some of the issues relating to the nature of faith itself, we may now turn to one of the most interesting questions debated in philosophical theology.

Can God's Existence be Proved?

The relation of faith and reason is often discussed in terms of whether God's existence can be proved, and whether such proof would be adequate to bring a nonbeliever to faith. Although some writers have suggested that this is the case, the general consensus within Christian theology seems to be that, although reason does not bring individuals to faith in God, believers are nonetheless able to give rational reasons for their faith in God.

Thomas Aquinas's contribution to this discussion is of major importance. Although some philosophers suggest that Aquinas was out to prove the existence of God, this is clearly not the case. In front of me, I have a copy of one of the standard editions of Aquinas's *Summa Theologiae* (see p. 35). It is more than four thousand pages long. His discussion of "whether God exists" occupies just over two pages. The phrase "proofs of God's existence" is not found in Aquinas's own discussion. Later writers have imposed it upon his thought. Yet it is perfectly clear that Aquinas does not believe in God on account of any of the considerations he mentions so briefly; his primary reason for believing in the existence of God is God's self-revelation. Aquinas expects his readers to share his faith in God, not that he should have to prove it to them first. The Austrian philosopher Ludwig Wittgenstein made this point clearly in his *Culture and Value*:

> A proof of God's existence ought really to be something by means of which one could convince oneself that God exists. But I think that what believers who have furnished such proofs have wanted to do is to give their "belief" an intellectual analysis and foundation, although they themselves would never have come to believe as a result of such proofs.

The classic statement of such questions, to which all modern discussion makes reference, is to be found in the writings of Anselm of Canterbury and Thomas Aquinas. The former developed what has come to be known as "the ontological argument" for the existence of God. The latter developed the "Five Ways," arguing from the effects of nature to their cause in God its creator. We shall consider these two categories of arguments individually, before moving on to consider some more recent discussions of the theme.

Anselm of Canterbury's ontological argument

Anselm of Canterbury (c.1033–1109) was born in Italy. He migrated to Normandy in 1059, entering the famous monastery of Bec, becoming its prior in 1063, and abbot in 1078. In 1093 he was appointed Archbishop of Canterbury. He is chiefly noted for his strong defense of the intellectual foundations of Christianity, and is especially associated with the "ontological argument" for the existence of God. This ontological argument is first set out in his *Proslogion,* a work which dates from 1079. (The term "ontological" refers to the branch of philosophy which deals with the notion of "being.") Anselm himself does not refer to his discussion as an "ontological" argument. The *Proslogion* is really a work of meditation, not of logical argument. In the course of this work, Anselm reflects on how self-evident the idea of God has become to him, and what the implications of this might be.

In his *Proslogion,* Anselm offers a definition of God as "that than which no greater thing can be conceived" (*aliquid quo maius cogitari non potest*). (Note that the Latin verb *cogitare* is sometimes translated as "think," leading to the definition of God as "that than which no greater thing can be thought." Both translations are acceptable.) So what are the implications of this? Anselm argues that, if someone agrees that God is indeed "that than which no greater thing can be conceived," and then argues that there is no God, there is a contradiction. Why? Because we can conceive of something still greater than a nonexistent God – namely, a God who exists.

God is thus defined as "that than which nothing greater can be conceived." Now the idea of such a being is one thing; the reality is another. Thinking of a hundred dollar bill is quite different from having a hundred dollar bill in your hands – and much less satisfying, as well! Anselm's point is this: the idea of something is inferior to the reality. So the idea of God as "that than which nothing greater can be conceived" contains a contradiction – because the reality of God would be superior to this idea. In other words, if this definition of God is correct, and exists in the human mind, then the corresponding reality must also exist.

It may be helpful to set out Anselm's argument in a series of numbered steps.

1   God is the greatest possible being.
2   God exists in the human mind or understanding.
3   A being who exists only as a mental notion is not so great as a being who exists in reality, and not merely as a mental idea.
4   If God exists only in the human mind, then God is not the greatest possible being.
5   It therefore follows that God must exist in reality, as well as an idea in the mind.

Anselm expresses these points as follows, in a passage which has been studied intently (and, it must be said, also inconclusively) down the centuries.

This [definition of God] is indeed so true that it cannot be thought of as not being true. For it is quite possible to think of something whose nonexistence cannot be thought of. This must be greater than something whose nonexistence can be thought of. So if this thing (than which no greater thing can be thought) can be thought of as not existing, then, that very thing than which a greater thing cannot be thought is not that than which a greater cannot be thought. This is a contradiction. So it is true that there exists something than which nothing greater can be thought, that it cannot be thought of as not existing. And you are this thing, O Lord our God!

This is an important argument, but it did not persuade one of his earliest critics, an eleventh-century Benedictine monk of the Abbey of Marmoutier named Gaunilo, who made a response known as "A Reply on Behalf of the Fool" (the reference being to Psalm 14: 1, cited by Anselm, "The fool says in his heart that there is no God"). There is, according to Gaunilo, an obvious logical weakness in Anselm's "argument" (although it must be stressed that Anselm does not really regard it as an argument in the first place). Imagine, Gaunilo suggests, an island, so lovely that a more perfect island cannot be conceived. By the same argument, Gaunilo suggested, that island must exist, in that the reality of the island is necessarily more perfect than the mere idea. In much the same way, we might argue that the idea of a hundred dollar bill seems, according to Anselm, to imply that we have such a bill in our hands. The mere idea of something – whether a perfect island or God – thus does not guarantee its existence. Gaunilo sets out his objections as follows:

People say that somewhere in the ocean there is an island which, because of the difficulty (or rather the impossibility) of finding that which does not exist, some have called the "Lost Island." And we are told that it is blessed with all manner of priceless riches and delights in abundance, far more than the Happy Isles, and, having no owner or inhabitant, it is superior in every respect in the abundance of its riches to all those other lands that are inhabited by people. Now, if someone were to tell me about this, I shall easily understand what is said, since there is nothing difficult about it. But if I am then told, as though it were a direct consequence of this: "You cannot any more doubt that this island that is more excellent than all other lands truly exists somewhere in reality than you can doubt that it is in your mind; and since it is more excellent to exist not just in your mind but in reality as well, therefore it must exist. For if it did not exist, any other land existing in reality would be more excellent than it, and so this island, already conceived by you to be more excellent than others, will not be more excellent." I say that if anyone wanted to persuade me in this way that this island really exists beyond all doubt, I should either think that they were joking, or I should find it hard to decide which of us I ought to think of as the bigger fool: I myself, if I agreed with them, or they, if they thought that they had proved the existence of this island with any certainty, unless they had first persuaded me that its very excellence exists in my mind precisely as a thing existing truly and indubitably and not just as something unreal or doubtfully real.

The response offered by Gaunilo is widely regarded as exposing a serious weakness in Anselm's argument. The text itself is so clear that no comment is needed. It may, however, be pointed out that Anselm is not so easily dismissed. Part of his argument is that it is an essential part of the definition of God that he is "that than which nothing greater can be conceived." God therefore belongs to a totally different category than islands or dollar bills. It is part of the nature of God to transcend everything else. Once the believer has come to understand what the word "God" means, then God really does exist for him or her. This is the intention of Anselm's meditation in the *Proslogion*: to reflect on how the Christian understanding of the nature of God reinforces belief in his reality. The "argument" does not really have force outside this context of faith, and Anselm never intended it to be used in this general philosophical manner.

Furthermore, Anselm argued that Gaunilo had not entirely understood him. The argument which he set out in the *Proslogion* did not involve the idea that there is a being that is, as a matter of fact, greater than any other being; rather, Anselm had argued for a being so great that a greater one could not even be conceived. The argument continues, and it remains a disputed question to this day as to whether Anselm's argument has a genuine basis.

A good example of this is found in the writings of Immanuel Kant (1724–1804), widely agreed to be the founder of modern critical philosophy. Kant was born in the German town of Königsberg (now Kaliningrad) and was educated at the local university, where he became Professor of Logic and Metaphysics. His major writings include *The Critique of Pure Reason* (1781), *Critique of Practical Reason* (1788), and *Religion within the Bounds of Reason Alone* (1793). Kant offered a major critique of the ontological argument for the existence of God, the central thesis of which takes the following form.

Kant insists that "existence is not a predicate." As a result, conceiving the idea of God cannot in any way be thought to necessarily lead to conceiving the further idea "God exists." Kant's analogy of the "hundred dollars" makes more or less the same point made earlier by Gaunilo with his image of the "ideal island": conceiving an idea does not imply that its object necessarily exists. Kant makes this point as follows:

> Now "Being" is clearly not a genuine predicate; that is, it is not a concept of something which could be added to the concept of a thing. It is merely the positing of a thing, or of certain determinations, as existing in themselves. Logically, it is merely the copula of a judgment. The proposition "God is omnipotent" contains two concepts, each of which has its object – God and omnipotence. The little word "is" adds no new predicate, but only serves to posit the predicate *in its relation* to the subject. Now if we take the subject (God) with all its predicates (among which is omnipotence), and say "God exists,"

or "There is a God," we do not attach any new predicate to the concept of God; we merely posit the subject in itself with all its predicates.

This line of argument had considerable influence within Christian theology, especially in the field of apologetics.

Thomas Aquinas's Five Ways

Thomas Aquinas (c.1225–74) is probably the most famous and influential theologian of the Middle Ages. Born in Italy, he achieved his fame through his teaching and writing at the University of Paris and other northern universities. His fame rests chiefly on his *Summa Theologiae*, composed towards the end of his life and not totally finished at the time of his death. However, he also wrote many other significant works, particularly the *Summa contra Gentiles*, which represents a major statement of the rationality of the Christian faith, and especially the existence of God. Aquinas believed that it was entirely proper to identify pointers towards the existence of God, drawn from general human experience of the world. His Five Ways represent five lines of argument in support of the existence of God, each of which draws on some aspect of the world which "points" to the existence of its creator.

So what kind of pointers does Aquinas identify? The basic line of thought guiding Aquinas is that the world mirrors God, as its creator – an idea which is given more formal expression in his doctrine of the "analogy of being." Just as an artist might sign a painting to identify it as his or her handiwork, so God has stamped a divine "signature" upon the creation. What we observe in the world – for example, its signs of ordering – can be explained on the basis of the existence of God as its creator. God is both its first cause and its designer. God both brought the world into existence, and impressed the divine image and likeness upon it.

So where might we look in creation to find evidence for the existence of God? Aquinas argues that the ordering of the world is the most convincing evidence of God's existence and wisdom. This basic assumption underlies each of the Five Ways, although it is of particular importance in the case of the argument often referred to as the "argument from design" or the "teleological argument." We shall consider each of these "ways" individually, before focusing on two in a subsequent part of this chapter.

The first way begins from the observation that things in the world are in motion or change. The world is not static, but dynamic. Examples of this are easy to list. Rain falls from the sky. Stones roll down valleys. The earth revolves around the sun (a fact, incidentally, unknown to Aquinas). This, the first of Aquinas's arguments, is normally referred to as the "argument from motion"; however, it is clear that the "movement" in question is actually understood in more general terms, so that the term "change" is more appropriate as a translation at points.

So how did nature come to be in motion? Why is it changing? Why is it not static? Aquinas argues that everything which moves is moved by something else. For every motion, there is a cause. Things don't just move – they are moved by something else. Now each cause of motion must itself have a cause. And that cause must have a cause as well. And so Aquinas argues that there is a whole series of causes of motion lying behind the world as we know it. Now since there cannot be an infinite number of these causes, Aquinas argues, there must be a single cause right at the origin of the series. From this original cause of motion, all other motion is ultimately derived. This is the origin of the great chain of causality which we see reflected in the way the world behaves.

From the fact that things are in motion, Aquinas thus argues for the existence of a single original cause of all this motion – and this, he concludes, is none other than God.

> The existence of God can be proved in five ways. The first and most obvious proof is the argument from change [*ex parte motus*]. It is clearly the case that some things in this world are in the process of changing. Now everything that is in the process of being changed is changed by something else . [. . .] If, then, whatever is changing it is itself changed, this also must be changed by something else, and this in turn by something else again. But this cannot go on forever, since there would then be no first cause to this process of change, and consequently no other agent of change, because secondary things which change cannot change unless they are changed by a first cause, in the same way as a stick cannot move unless it is moved by the hand. We are therefore bound to arrive at a first cause of change which is not changed by anything, and everyone understands that this is God.

Once more, it may be helpful to summarize this as a series of brief statements, so that the direction of the argument is clearer.

1 There is motion in the universe – e.g., a stick moves.
2 Things do not move themselves; they are moved by something else. Something moves the stick.
3 There cannot be an infinite regression of things being moved by other things.
4 Therefore there must be a "prime mover," who is not moved by anything else.
5 This unmoved prime mover is God.

The second way begins from the idea of causation. In other words, Aquinas notes the existence of causes and effects in the world. One event (the effect) is explained by the influence of another (the cause). The idea of motion, which we looked at briefly above, is a good example of this cause-and-effect sequence. Using a line of reasoning similar to that used above, Aquinas thus argues that all effects may be traced back to a single original cause – which is God.

The third way concerns the existence of contingent beings. In other words, the world contains beings (such as human beings) which are not there as a matter of necessity. Aquinas contrasts this type of being with a necessary being (one who is there as a matter of necessity). While God is a necessary being, Aquinas argues that humans are contingent beings. The fact that we *are* here needs explanation. Why are we here? What happened to bring us into existence? Aquinas argues that a being comes into existence because something which already exists brought it into being. In other words, our existence is caused by another being. We are the effects of a series of causation. Tracing this series back to its origin, Aquinas declares that this original cause of being can only be someone whose existence is necessary – in other words, God.

The fourth way begins from human values, such as truth, goodness, and nobility. Where do these values come from? What causes them? Aquinas argues that there must be something which is in itself true, good, and noble, and that this brings into being our ideas of truth, goodness, and nobility. The origin of these ideas, Aquinas suggests, is God, who is their original cause.

The fifth and final way is often referred to as "the teleological argument" or the "argument from design." Aquinas notes that the world shows obvious traces of intelligent design. Natural processes and objects seem to be adapted with certain definite objectives in mind. They seem to have a purpose. They seem to have been designed. But things don't design themselves:

they are caused and designed by someone or something else. Arguing from this observation, Aquinas concludes that the source of this natural ordering must be conceded to be God.

It will be obvious that most of Aquinas's arguments are rather similar in terms of their structure. Each depends on tracing a causal sequence back to its single origin, and identifying this with God. A number of criticisms of the Five Ways were made by Aquinas's critics during the Middle Ages, such as Duns Scotus and William of Ockham. The following are especially important.

1 Why is the idea of an infinite regression of causes impossible? For example, the argument from motion only really works if it can be shown that the sequence of cause and effect stops somewhere. There has to be, according to Aquinas, a prime unmoved mover. But he fails to demonstrate this point.

2 Why do these arguments lead to belief in only *one* God? The argument from motion, for example, could lead to belief in a number of prime unmoved movers. There seems to be no especially pressing reason for insisting that there can only be one such cause, except for the fundamental Christian insistence that, as a matter of fact, there is only one such God.

3 These arguments do not demonstrate that God continues to exist. Having caused things to happen, God might cease to exist. The continuing existence of events does not necessarily imply the continuing existence of their originator. Aquinas's arguments, Ockham suggests, might lead to a belief that God existed once upon a time – but not necessarily now. Ockham developed a somewhat complex argument, based on the idea of God continuing to sustain the universe, which attempts to get round this difficulty.

These, then, are some of the classic arguments which have been used and developed within the philosophy of religion. So how have these medieval arguments been developed in more recent times? In what follows, we shall look briefly at some modern restatements.

The *kalam* argument

The argument which we shall refer to as the "kalam" argument derives its name from an Arabic school of philosophy which flourished in the early Middle Ages. A. E. Sabra has defined *kalam* as "an inquiry into God, and into the world as God's creation, and into man as the special creature placed by God in the world under obligation to his creator." The *mutakallimun* (as the practitioners of the *kalam* approach were known) developed an argument for the existence of God which stressed the importance of causality. Some scholars regard this as a variant of the cosmological argument, already set out above. However, others regard it as having distinct features, meriting its treatment in its own right. The basic structure of the argument can be set out as four propositions:

1 Everything which has a beginning must have a cause.
2 The universe began to exist.
3 Therefore the beginning of the existence of the universe must have been caused by something.
4 The only such cause can be God.

It will be clear that the basic contours of this argument can be discerned within Aquinas's Five Ways, discussed earlier.

The structure of the argument is clear, and its implications need little in the way of further development. If the existence of something can be said to have begun, it follows – so it is argued – that it must have a cause. If this type of argument is linked with the idea of a Big Bang, its relevance for our discussion will be clear. Modern cosmology strongly suggests that the universe had a beginning. If the universe began to exist at a certain time, it must have had a cause. And what cause could there be other than God?

This form of the "kalam" argument has been widely debated in recent years. One of its most significant defenders has been William Lane Craig (born 1949), who sets out its main features as follows:

> Since everything that begins to exist has a cause of its existence, and since the universe began to exist, we conclude, therefore, the universe has a cause of its existence. [. . .] Transcending the entire universe there exists a cause which has brought the universe into being.

Debate over the argument has centered on three questions, as follows:

1 Can something have a beginning without being caused? In one of his dialogues, the noted Scottish philosopher David Hume argues that it is possible to conceive of something that comes into being, without necessarily pointing to some definite cause of that existence. Nevertheless, this suggestion raises considerable difficulties.

2 Can one speak of the universe having a beginning? At one level, this is a profoundly philosophical question. At another, however, it is a scientific question, depending on issues of physics and astronomy, which can be considered on the basis of known observations concerning the rate of expansion of the universe, and the background radiation evidence for the Big Bang.

3 If the universe can be considered to have been "caused," can this cause be directly identified with God? One line of argument of note here takes the following form. A cause must be prior to the event which it causes. To speak of a cause for the beginning of the existence of the universe is thus to speak of something which existed before the universe. And if this is not God, what is it?

It will be clear that the traditional "kalam" argument has been given a new lease of life by the Big Bang theory of the origins of the universe, which became of especial importance in the late twentieth century. However, the philosophical issues which are raised are likely to remain disputed. A similar debate focuses on the question of whether the universe can be said to be "designed," and we shall consider this issue in what follows.

The classic argument from design: William Paley

The "argument from design" – also known as the "teleological argument" – is among the most widely discussed of the philosophical arguments for the existence of God. As we saw earlier, it is stated by Thomas Aquinas as the fifth of his Five Ways. Aquinas argues that there exist clear signs of design within the natural order. Things do not simply exist; they appear to have been designed with some form of purpose in mind. The term "teleological" (meaning "directed towards some goal") is widely used to indicate this apparently goal-directed aspect of nature.

It is this aspect of nature which has often been discussed in relation to the natural sciences. The orderliness of nature – evident, for example, in the laws of nature – seems to be a sign that nature has been "designed" for some purpose. How else, it is argued, can this order be explained? It is for this reason that naturalist approaches to science, especially those which argue that matter possesses an intrinsic capacity to organize itself, are seen as such a threat by some modern Christian apologists.

It is widely agreed that the most significant contribution to the classic "argument from design" is due to the English theologian and natural philosopher William Paley (1743–1805). His *Natural Theology; or Evidences of the Existence and Attributes of the Deity, Collected from the Appearances of Nature* (1802) had a profound influence on popular English religious thought in the first half of the nineteenth century, and is known to have been read by Charles Darwin. Paley was deeply impressed by Newton's discovery of the regularity of nature, especially in relation to the area usually known as "celestial mechanics." It was clear that the entire universe could be thought of as a complex mechanism, operating according to regular and understandable principles. For Paley, the Newtonian image of the world as a mechanism immediately suggested the metaphor of a clock or watch, raising the question of who constructed the intricate mechanism which was so evidently displayed in the functioning of the world.

One of Paley's most significant arguments is that mechanism implies "contrivance." Writing against the backdrop of the emerging Industrial Revolution, Paley sought to exploit the apologetic potential of the growing interest in machinery – such as "watches, telescopes, stocking-mills, steam engines" – within England's literate classes. At the time, England was experiencing the Industrial Revolution, in which machinery was coming to play an increasingly important role in industry. Paley argues that only someone who is mad would suggest that such complex mechanical technology came into being by purposeless chance.

Mechanism presupposes contrivance – that is to say, a sense of purpose and an ability to design and fabricate. Both the human body in particular, and the world in general, are to be seen as mechanisms which have been designed and constructed in such a manner as to achieve harmony of both means and ends. The world, Paley argues, may therefore be compared to a watch – to something that has clearly been constructed, with a specific purpose in mind.

The opening paragraphs of Paley's *Natural Theology* are well known, mainly on account of the image of God as creator that they contain. God is a watchmaker; nature is a watch.

In crossing a heath, suppose I pitched my foot against a *stone*, and were asked how the stone came to be there. I might possibly answer, that for any thing I knew to the contrary it had lain there for ever; nor would it, perhaps, be very easy to show the absurdity of this answer. But suppose I had found a *watch* upon the ground, and it should be inquired how the watch happened to be in that place. I should hardly think of the answer which I had before given, that for any thing I knew the watch might have always been there. Yet why should this answer not serve for the watch as well as for the stone; why is it not admissible in the second case as in the first? For this reason, and for no other, namely, that when we come to inspect the watch, we perceive – what we could not discover in the stone – that its several parts are framed and put together for a purpose, e.g. that they are so formed and adjusted as to produce motion, and that motion so regulated as to point out the hour of the day; that if the different parts had been differently shaped from what they are, or placed after any other manner or in any other order than that in which they are placed, either no motion at all would have been carried on in the machine, or none which would have answered the use that is now served by it.

Paley then offers a detailed description of the watch, noting in particular its container, coiled cylindrical spring, many interlocking wheels, and glass face. Having carried his readers along with this careful analysis, Paley turns to draw his critically important conclusion:

> This mechanism being observed – it requires indeed an examination of the instrument, and perhaps some previous knowledge of the subject, to perceive and understand it; but being once, as we have said, observed and understood, the inference we think is inevitable, that the watch must have had a maker – that there must have existed, at some time and at some place or other, an artificer or artificers who formed it for the purpose which we find it actually to answer, who comprehended its construction and designed its use.

Paley's English prose is a little florid, reflecting the taste of the period. Nevertheless, the points which he is concerned to establish are clear.

The essential point is that nature bears witness to a series of biological structures which are "contrived" – that is, constructed with a clear purpose in mind. "Every indication of contrivance, every manifestation of design, which existed in the watch, exists in the works of nature." Indeed, Paley argues, the difference is that nature shows an even greater degree of contrivance than the watch.

The influence of Paley upon English attitudes to arguments for God's existence based on nature was immense. The celebrated *Bridgewater Treatises* show his influence at many points, even if they develop an independent approach at others. The noted antitheistic evolutionary biologist Richard Dawkins pays him a somewhat backhanded compliment in the title of one of his best-known antiteleological works – *The Blind Watchmaker*. For Dawkins, the "watchmaker" who Paley identified with God was none other than the blind and purposeless process of natural selection.

The "argument from design" was subjected to criticism on a number of grounds by the Scottish philosopher David Hume. The most significant of Hume's criticisms can be summarized as follows.

1   The direct extrapolation from the observation of design in the world to a God who created that world is not possible. It is one thing to suggest that the observation of design leads to the inference that there is a design-producing being; it is quite another to insist that this being is none other than God. There is thus a logical weak link in the chain of argument.

2   To suggest that there is a designer of the universe could lead to an infinite regression. Who designed the designer? We noted that Aquinas explicitly rejected the idea of an infinite regression of causes; however, he fails to offer a rigorous justification of this point, apparently assuming that his readers will regard his rejection of this series as being self-evidently correct. Hume's point is that this is not the case.

3   The argument from design works by analogy with machines. The argument gains its plausibility by a comparison with something that has clearly been designed and constructed – such as a watch. But is this analogy valid? Why could the universe not be compared to a plant, or some other living organism? Plants are not designed; they just grow. The importance of this point in relation to Paley's argument will be obvious.

Having considered something of the classic arguments for God's existence, we must now move on to consider another classic theological debate – the nature of theological language. Can human words refer meaningfully to God?

The Nature of Theological Language

Theology is "talk about God." But how can God ever be described or discussed using human language? The Austrian philosopher Ludwig Wittgenstein made this point forcefully: if human words are incapable of describing the distinctive aroma of coffee, how could they possibly cope with something as subtle as God?

Apophatic and kataphatic approaches to theology

A classic debate in Christian theology concerns what may be said about God. This debate is often framed in terms of apophatic and kataphatic approaches to theology. Each of these needs explanation.

1 The term "apophatic" comes from the Greek word *apophatikos*, meaning "negative," which is derived from the verb *apophēmi*, meaning "to say no," or "to deny." It denotes an approach to theology which stresses that we cannot use human language to refer to God, who ultimately lies beyond such language. It is sometimes also referred to as the *via negativa* ("the negative way").

2 The term "kataphatic" (sometimes spelled "cataphatic") comes from the Greek word *kataphatikos*, meaning "positive," which is derived from the verb *kataphaskō*, meaning "to say yes," or "to affirm." It denotes an approach to theology which holds that positive statements may indeed be made about God. It is sometimes also referred to as the *via positiva* ("the positive way").

While generalizations are dangerous, the apophatic approach tends to be found in eastern Orthodoxy, whereas the western theological tradition has tended to be much more kataphatical.

The point at issue is difficult, but important. The western approach is easier to understand. Writers such as Thomas Aquinas argue that it is possible to make positive, affirmative statements about God, such as the following:

> God exists.
> God is wise.
> God is Father.

God is here described in positive terms. For example, in describing God as Father, Aquinas argues that Christian theology is recognizing that we are able to speak meaningfully about God using human language. While Aquinas is careful to stress the limits of such language, he nevertheless insists that, following the use of the Bible and the Christian tradition, we are justified in making such positive statements in terms of ideas and images that are familiar and accessible to the human mind. Theological reflection is thus based on considering these ideas and images, and extracting as much understanding from them as possible through proper use of the human reason.

Apophatic theology argues that the limitations placed upon human language is such that it can never do justice to God, and runs the risk of reducing God to the level of humanity. The Cappadocian fathers are representative of this tradition. In his Epistle 234 Basil of Caesarea comments, in speaking of God:

> I know that God exists. Yet I consider his essence to be beyond intelligence [...] The object of our worship is not that of which we comprehend the essence, but of which we comprehend that the essence exists.

The point that Basil is making is that while we can indeed say that God exists, human language is totally unable to comprehend God's nature. It does not have the capacity to enfold God. It is impossible for human reason to grasp the nature of God, even though it can handle the somewhat less demanding insight that God exists.

The two approaches have their respective strengths and weaknesses, and we may note a few in bringing this section to a close. The kataphatic approach allows us to say positive things about God – for example, that "God is love." This is helpful in explaining the basics of Christianity to those outside the church. However, it runs the risk of reducing God to the level of human love, in that God is clearly far more than what this human term can convey. The apophatic approach preserves the mystery of God through its emphasis on the limitations of language. However, many find its principled refusal to make positive statements frustrating, in that it implies that we are doomed to remain ignorant of even the most basic knowledge of what God is like. The debate continues today.

In what follows, we shall focus on the kataphatic tradition, and ask how it calibrates its language about God to avoid the potential problems identified by exponents of the apophatic approach.

Analogy

How can we speak meaningfully and positively about God? How can we use human language to speak about God, without reducing God to the human level? Perhaps the most basic idea which underlies the theological reply to such questions is usually referred to as "the principle of analogy." The fact that God created the world points to a fundamental "analogy of being" (*analogia entis*) between God and the world. There is a continuity between God and the world on account of the expression of the being of God in the being of the world.

For this reason, it is argued that it is legitimate to use entities within the created order as analogies for God. In doing this, theology does not reduce God to the level of a created object or being; it merely affirms that there is a likeness or correspondence between God and that being, which allows the latter to act as a signpost to God. A created entity can be *like* God, without being *identical* to God.

Consider the statement "God is our Father." Aquinas argues that this should be understood to mean that God is *like* a human father. In other words, God is analogous to a father. In some ways God is like a human father, and in others not. There are genuine points of similarity. God cares for us, as human fathers care for their children (note Matthew 7: 9–11). God is the ultimate source of our existence, just as our fathers brought us into being. God exercises authority over us, as do human fathers. Equally, there are genuine points of dissimilarity. God is not a human being, for example. Nor does the necessity of a human mother point to the need for a divine mother, that is, *two* gods.

The point that Aquinas is trying to make is clear. Divine self-revelation makes use of images and ideas which tie in with our world of everyday existence, yet which do not reduce God to that everyday world. To say that "God is our father" is not to say that God is just yet another human father. Nor, as we shall later explore, does it mean that God is to be thought of as *male* (see pp. 203–5). Rather, it is to say that thinking about human fathers helps us think about God. They are analogies. Like all analogies, they break down at points. However, they are still extremely useful and vivid ways of thinking about God, which allow us to use the vocabulary and images of our own world to describe something which ultimately lies beyond it.

In saying that "God is love," we are referring to our own capacity to love, in order to try to imagine this love in all its full perfection in

God. We are not reducing the "love of God" to the level of human love. Rather, it is being suggested that human love provides a pointer toward the love of God, which, to some limited extent, it is capable of mirroring.

But, as we all know from experience, analogies break down. There comes a point when they cannot be pressed further. There are two major problems that have to be confronted here. First, and most obviously, we might mistakenly assume that an *analogy* is actually an *identity*. Instead of thinking that "God is *like* a rock" – to pick up on one of the Old Testament's favorite analogies (see Psalms 28: 1, 31: 2–3) – we mistakenly think that God *is* a rock. This fails to take account of the way in which human language struggles to represent the divine.

So how do we know when analogies break down? When we have pressed them too far? To illustrate this problem, we may consider an example from another area of theology, before moving on to consider its solution. The New Testament talks about Jesus giving his life as a "ransom" for sinners (Mark 10: 45, 1 Timothy 2: 6). What does this analogy mean? The everyday use of the word "ransom" suggests three ideas:

1 *Liberation*: A ransom is something which achieves freedom for a person who is held in captivity. When someone is kidnapped, and a ransom demanded, the payment of that ransom leads to liberation.
2 *Payment*: A ransom is a sum of money which is paid in order to achieve an individual's liberation.
3 *Someone to whom the ransom is paid*: A ransom is usually paid to an individual's captor, or an intermediary.

These three ideas thus seem to be implied by speaking of Jesus's death as a "ransom" for sinners. But are they *all* present in Scripture?

There is no doubt whatsoever that the New Testament proclaims that we have been liberated from captivity through the death and resurrection of Jesus. We have been set free from captivity to sin and the fear of death (Romans 8: 21, Hebrews 2: 15). It is also clear that the New Testament understands the death of Jesus as the price which had to be paid to achieve our liberation (1 Corinthians 6: 20, 7: 23). Our liberation is a costly and a precious matter. In these two respects, the scriptural use of "redemption" corresponds to the everyday use of the word. But what of the third aspect?

There is not a hint in the New Testament that Jesus's death was the price paid to some specific person or spiritual force (such as the devil) to achieve our liberation. Some of the writers of the first four centuries, however, assumed that they could press this analogy to its limits, and declared that God had delivered us from the power of the devil by offering Jesus as the price of our liberation (see pp. 334–5). This idea surfaces repeatedly in patristic discussions of the meaning of the death of Christ. Yet it needs to be asked whether it rests upon pressing an analogy beyond its acceptable limits.

So how do we know whether an analogy has been pressed too far? How can the limits of such analogies be tested? Such questions have been debated throughout Christian history. An important twentieth-century discussion of this point may be found in British philosopher of religion Ian T. Ramsey's *Christian Discourse: Some Logical Explorations* (1965), which puts forward the idea that models or analogies are not freestanding, but interact with and qualify each other.

Ramsey argues that Scripture does not give us one single analogy (or "model") for God or for salvation, but uses a range of analogies. Each of these analogies or models illuminates certain aspects of our understanding of God, or the nature of salvation. However, these analogies also interact with each other. They modify each other. They help us understand the limits of other analogies. No analogy or parable is exhaustive in itself; taken together, however, the range of analogies and parables builds up to give a comprehensive and consistent understanding of God and salvation.

An example of how images interact may make this point clearer. Take the analogies of king, father, and shepherd. Each of these three analogies conveys the idea of authority, suggesting that this is of fundamental importance to our understanding of God. Kings, however, often behave in arbitrary ways, and not always in the best interests of their subjects. The analogy of God as a king might thus be misunderstood to suggest that God is some sort of tyrant. However, the tender compassion of a father toward his children commended by Scripture (Psalm 103: 13–18), and the total dedication of a good shepherd to the welfare of his flock (John 10: 11), show that this is not the intended meaning. Authority is to be exercised tenderly and wisely.

Aquinas's doctrine of analogy, then, is of fundamental importance to the way we think about God. It illuminates the manner in which God reveals himself to us through scriptural images and analogies, allowing us to understand how God can be *above* our world, and yet simultaneously be revealed *in and through* that world. God is not an object or a person in space and time; nevertheless, such persons and objects can help us deepen our appreciation of God's character and nature. God, who is infinite, may be revealed in and through human words and finite images.

Metaphor

The precise nature of the differences between analogies and metaphors remains disputed. Aristotle defined a metaphor as involving "the transferred use of a term that properly belongs to something else." So broad is this definition that it embraces just about every figure of speech, including analogy. In modern use, the word "metaphor" would be taken to mean something rather different, with the following being a useful definition. A metaphor is a way of speaking about one thing in terms which are suggestive of another. It is, to use Nelson Goodman's famous phrase, "a matter of teaching an old word new tricks." This definition clearly includes analogy; so what is the difference between them?

Once more, it is necessary to note that there is no general agreement on this matter. Individual writers offer their own definitions, often reflecting their personal agendas. Perhaps a working solution to the problem could be stated as follows: analogies seem to be *appropriate*, where metaphors involve a sense of surprise or initial incredulity. For example, consider these two statements:

1 God is wise.
2 God is a lion.

In the first case, it is being affirmed that there is an analogical connection between the nature of God and the human notion of "wisdom." It is being suggested that, at both the linguistic and the ontological level, there is a direct parallel between human and divine notions of wisdom. Human wisdom serves as an analogy of divine wisdom. The comparison does not cause us any surprise.

In the second case, the comparison can cause a slight degree of consternation. It does not seem to be appropriate to compare God to a lion. However many similarities there may be between God and a lion, there are obviously many differences. For some modern writers, a metaphor mingles similarity and dissimilarity, stressing that there are both parallels and divergences between the two objects being compared.

With these points in mind, we may explore three features of metaphors which have attracted theological attention in recent decades.

1 Metaphors imply both *similarity* and *dissimilarity* between the two things being compared. It is perhaps for this reason that some recent writings – particularly those of Sallie McFague – have stressed the metaphorical, rather than the analogical, nature of theological language. As McFague puts it:

Metaphor always has the character of "is" and "is not": an assertion is made but as a likely account rather than a definition. That is, to say, "God is mother," is not to define God as mother, nor to assert identity between the terms "God" and "mother," but to suggest that we consider what we do not know how to talk about – relating to God – through the metaphor of mother. The assumption here is that all talk of God is indirect: no words or phrases refer directly to God, for God-language can refer only through the detour of a description that properly belongs elsewhere. To speak of God as mother is to invite us to consider some qualities associated with mothering as one partial but perhaps illuminating way of speaking of certain aspects of God's relationship to us.

To speak of "God as father" should be seen as a metaphor, rather than an analogy, implying significant differences between God and a father, rather than (as in the case of an analogy) a direct line of similarities.

2 Metaphors cannot be reduced to definitive statements. Perhaps the most attractive feature of metaphors for Christian theology is their *open-ended character*. Although some literary critics have suggested that metaphors can be reduced to a set of equivalent literal expressions, others have insisted that no limits can be set to the extent of the comparison. Thus the metaphor "God as father" cannot be reduced to a set of precise statements about God, valid for every place and every time. It is meant to be suggestive, allowing future readers and interpreters to find new meanings within it. A metaphor is not simply an elegant description or memorable phrasing of something that we already know. It is an invitation to discover further levels of meaning, which others may have overlooked or forgotten.

3 Metaphors often have strongly emotional overtones. Theological metaphors are able to express the emotional dimensions of Christian faith in a way which makes them appropriate to worship. For example, the metaphor of "God as light" has enormously powerful overtones, including those of illumination, purity, and glorification. Ian G. Barbour summarizes this aspect of metaphorical language as follows:

Where poetic metaphors are used only momentarily, in one context, for the sake of an immediate expression or insight, *religious symbols* become part of the language of a religious community in its scripture and liturgy and in its continuing life and thought. Religious symbols are expressive of human emotions and feelings, and are powerful in calling forth response and commitment.

Accommodation

A third approach declines to speculate on the precise nature of theological language, and instead focuses on the general principles which seem to underlie the nature of theological language. The basic ideas of the approach we propose to consider derive from classical Greek rhetorical theory, taken up with enthusiasm by patristic writers such as

Origen. Origen suggests that God faced much the same problems in addressing sinful humanity as those experienced by a human father in trying to communicate to small children. "God condescends and comes down to us, accommodating to our weakness, like a schoolmaster talking a 'little language' to his children, or like a father caring for his own children and adopting their ways." When you are talking to small children, Origen argues, you have to appreciate that they have limited intellectual resources at their disposal. If you treat them as adults, and use words and ideas that are beyond their understanding and experience, you will fail to communicate with them. You have to adapt yourself to their capacities.

This approach was taken up in the sixteenth century by John Calvin, who developed the theory usually referred to by the term "accommodation." The word "accommodation" here means "adjusting or adapting to meet the needs of the situation and the human ability to comprehend it." In revelation, Calvin argues, God accommodates to the capacities of the human mind and heart. God paints a self-portrait which we are capable of understanding. The analogy which lies behind Calvin's thinking at this point is that of a human orator. Good speakers know the limitations of their audience, and adjust the way they speak accordingly. The gulf between the speaker and the hearer must be bridged if communication is to take place. God has to come down to our level in the process of revelation. Just as a human mother stoops down to reach her child, so God stoops down to come to our level.

An example of this accommodation is provided by the scriptural portraits of God. God is often, Calvin points out, represented as possessing a mouth, eyes, hands, and feet. That might seem to suggest that God is a human being. It might seem to imply that somehow the eternal and spiritual God has been reduced to a physical human being. (The point at issue is often referred to as "anthropomorphism" – in other words, God being portrayed in human form.) Calvin argues that God is obliged to configure the divine self-revelation in this pictorial manner on account of our weak intellects. Images of God which represent God as having a mouth or hands are divine "baby-talk," a way in which God comes down to our level and uses images which we can handle. More sophisticated ways of speaking about God are certainly proper, but we might not be able to understand them.

Calvin's concern was not to generalize concerning the nature of theological language – whether it is analogical or metaphorical, or any of the other figures of speech with which he was familiar. His basic concern was to stress that theological language cannot necessarily be taken at face value. The theologian has to decide on the nature and extent of that accommodation. It is this principle which underlies Calvin's response to a major controversy in which the status of theological language proved to be of decisive importance: the Copernican theory of the solar system. So important is this case study that it deserves to be considered in some detail, to illustrate the application of the ideas we have just been dealing with.

A case study: the Copernican debate

One of the most significant confrontations between theology and the natural sciences took place during the sixteenth century, with the publication of Copernicus's heliocentric theory of the solar system. Up to that point, the generally accepted understanding was geocentric: the sun and every other heavenly body revolved around the earth. This theory seemed to be supported by the Bible, which referred, for example, to the motion of the sun.

In his *De revolutionibus orbium coelestium*, "On the revolutions of the heavenly bodies"

(1543), Copernicus (1473–1543) argued that the earth revolved around the sun. With the publication of Copernicus's theory, a radical challenge was posed to the received view – and also to the accepted way of interpreting the Bible. As the scientific merits of Copernicus's theory became apparent, a new threat seemed to be posed to the authority and reliability of the Bible. How could Copernicus's heliocentric theory be reconciled with the Bible's apparently geocentric outlook? There are excellent reasons for suggesting that Calvin's theological method may have been of decisive importance, both in gaining a sympathetic hearing for Copernicus's theory of the solar system, and in preserving the credibility of the Bible.

Calvin may be regarded as making two major contributions to the appreciation and development of the natural sciences. First, he positively encouraged the scientific study of nature; second, he eliminated a major obstacle to the development of that study. His first contribution is specifically linked with his stress upon the orderliness of creation; both the physical world and the human body testify to the wisdom and character of God. Calvin thus commends the study of both astronomy and medicine. They are able to probe more deeply than theology into the natural world, and thus uncover further evidence of the orderliness of the creation and the wisdom of its creator.

Calvin thus gave a new religious motivation to the scientific investigation of nature, which came to be seen as a means of discerning the wise hand of God in creation. God can thus be discerned through the detailed study of the creation. We have already noted the importance of natural theology within the Reformed tradition (pp. 161–3); there is ample evidence to suggest that an interest in natural theology went hand in hand with an interest in the natural sciences.

Such ideas were taken up with enthusiasm within the Royal Society, the most significant organization devoted to the advancement of scientific research and learning in England. Many of its early members were admirers of Calvin, familiar with his writings and their potential relevance to their fields of study. Thus Richard Bentley (1662–1742) delivered a series of lectures in 1692, based on Newton's *Principia Mathematica* (1687), in which the regularity of the universe, as established by Newton, is interpreted as evidence of design. There are unambiguous hints here of Calvin's reference to the universe as a "theater of the glory of God," in which humans are an appreciative audience. The detailed study of the creation leads to an increased awareness of the wisdom of its creator.

It is Calvin's second major contribution which is of especial interest to us here. Calvin is widely regarded as having eliminated a significant obstacle to the development of the natural sciences: biblical literalism, which remains influential within fundamentalist circles today. Calvin insisted that not all biblical statements concerning God or the world were to be taken literally, for they were accommodated to the abilities of their audiences. Scripture, in apparently speaking of the sun rotating around the earth, was simply accommodating itself to the worldview of its audience, not making scientific statements about the universe. Calvin's discussion of the relationship between scientific findings and the statements of the Bible is generally regarded as one of his most valuable contributions to Christian thought.

The impact of these ideas upon scientific theorizing, especially during the seventeenth century, was considerable. For example, the seventeenth-century English writer Edward Wright defended Copernicus's heliocentric theory of the solar system against biblical literalists by arguing, in the first place, that Scripture was not concerned with physics, and in the second, that its manner of speaking was "accommodated to the understanding and way of speech of the common people, like nurses to little children." Both these arguments derive directly from Calvin, who may be argued to have made a fundamental contribution to the emergence of the natural sciences at these points.

We have now concluded our brief survey of some issues of method in theology. It is now time to engage directly with the leading themes of Christian theology, beginning with the Christian doctrine of God.

QUESTIONS FOR CHAPTER 8

1 Why did Tertullian want theologians to have nothing to do with philosophy? Was he right?

2 Should theology be able to verify or falsify its statements?

3 The cosmological argument has come to be of new importance as a result of the growing interest in the advances in astronomy and physics. How would you evaluate the potential of this argument in modern debates over the existence of God?

4 Give an account of William Paley's analogy of the watch. What points did he hope to make in this way? Why has the analogy been criticized since his time?

5 How would you distinguish between an analogy and a metaphor?

6 What theological issues were at stake in the Copernican debate?

Part III

Christian Theology

9

The Doctrine of God

In preceding chapters, we have been considering the historical development of Christian theology, as well as some issues of sources and methods. Issues relating to history and method will be a recurring feature of the remainder of this work. However, this remaining part of the volume is primarily devoted to questions of theological substance. The most appropriate – and certainly the most traditional – way of beginning such a discussion is by considering the Christian doctrine of God.

The present chapter will explore some general issues relating to the doctrine of God, concentrating upon a series of questions of particular relevance to the modern period: questions raised by the rise of feminism, a new concern for the suffering of the world, and increased anxiety concerning the environment. The chapter which follows will deal with the distinctively Christian doctrine of the Trinity, perhaps one of the most difficult aspects of Christian theology – yet also one of the most rewarding.

We begin our discussion of the Christian doctrine of God by turning to deal with a question of gender that has become increasingly important in western culture since the 1960s. Is God male? Indeed, can one speak of God as having a "gender" in the first place? As this question is so important to so many

people, it seemed a highly appropriate place to start our explorations.

Is God Male?

Both Old and New Testaments use male language about God. The Greek word *theos* is unquestionably masculine, and most of the analogies used for God throughout Scripture – such as father, king, and shepherd – are male. Does this mean that God *is* male? If so, it would raise important, and difficult, questions concerning the relation of male and female believers, as many feminist writers have correctly pointed out.

Earlier, we noted the analogical nature of theological language (pp. 194–6). The use of such analogies means that persons or social roles, largely drawn from the rural world of the ancient Near East, were regarded as suitable models for the divine activity or personality. One such analogy is that of a father. Yet the statement that "a father in ancient Israelite society is a suitable model for God" is not equivalent to saying that "God is a male human being," or that "God is confined to the cultural parameters of ancient Israel." Neither male nor female sexuality is to be attributed to

God, in that this sexuality is an attribute of the created order. There is no reason to suppose that such a polarity exists within the creator God.

Indeed, the Old Testament avoids attributing sexual functions to God, on account of the strongly pagan overtones of such associations. The Canaanite fertility cults emphasized the sexual functions of both gods and goddesses; the Old Testament refuses to endorse the idea that the gender or the sexuality of God is a significant matter. As Mary Hayter puts it in her work *The New Eve in Christ* (1987):

> Today a growing number of feminists teach that the God/ess combines male and female characteristics. They, like those who assume that God is exclusively male, should remember that *any* attribution of sexuality to God is a reversion to paganism.

There is no need to revert to pagan ideas of gods and goddesses to recover the idea that God is neither masculine nor feminine; those ideas are already potentially present, if neglected, in Christian theology. Wolfhart Pannenberg develops this point further in his *Systematic Theology* (1990):

> The aspect of fatherly care in particular is taken over in what the Old Testament has to say about God's fatherly care for Israel. The sexual definition of the father's role plays no part. [...] To bring sexual differentiation into the understanding of God would mean polytheism; it was thus ruled out for the God of Israel. [...] The fact that God's care for Israel can also be expressed in terms of a mother's love shows clearly enough how little there is any sense of sexual distinction in the understanding of God as Father.

In an attempt to bring out the fact that God is not male, a number of recent writers have explored the idea of God as "mother" (which brings out the female aspects of God), or as "friend" (which brings out the more gender-neutral aspects of God). An excellent example of this is provided by Sallie McFague in her *Models of God*. Recognizing that speaking of "God as father" does not mean that God is male, she writes:

> God as mother does not mean that God is mother (or father). We imagine God as both mother and father, but we realize how inadequate these and any other metaphors are to express the creative love of God. [...] Nevertheless, we speak of this love in language that is familiar and dear to us, the language of mothers and fathers who give us life, from whose bodies we come, and upon whose care we depend.

A similar point is made by the 1994 *Catechism of the Catholic Church*, which stresses the way in which parental imagery, particularly that of fatherhood, brings out central themes of the gospel.

> By calling God "Father," the language of faith indicates two main things: that God is the first origin of everything and transcendent authority; and that he is at the same time goodness and loving care for all his children. God's parental tenderness can also be expressed by the image of motherhood, which emphasizes God's immanence, the intimacy between Creator and creature. The language of faith thus draws on the human experience of parents, who are in a way the first representatives of God for man. But this experience also tells us that human parents are fallible and can disfigure the face of fatherhood and motherhood. We ought therefore to recall that God transcends the human distinction between the sexes. He is neither man nor woman; he is God. He also transcends human fatherhood and motherhood, although he is their origin and standard; no one is father as God is Father.

The new interest in the issues raised by the maleness of most of the biblical images of God has led to a careful reading of the spiritual literature of early periods in Christian history, resulting in an increased appreciation of the use of female imagery during these earlier periods. An excellent example of this is provided by the *Revelations of Divine Love*, an account of 16 visions which appeared to the English writer Julian of Norwich in May 1373. The visions are notable for their distinctive tendency to refer to both God and Jesus Christ in strongly maternal terms.

> I saw that God rejoices to be our Father, and also that he rejoices to be our Mother; and yet again, that he rejoices to be our true Husband, with our soul as his beloved bride. [...] He is the foundation, substance and the thing itself, what it is by nature. He is the true Father and Mother of what things are by nature.

A Personal God

Down the ages, theologians and ordinary Christian believers alike have had no hesitation in speaking about God in personal terms. For example, Christianity has ascribed to God a whole series of attributes such as love, trustworthiness, and purpose which seemed to have strongly personal associations. Many writers have pointed out that the Christian practice of prayer seems to be modeled on the relationship between a child and a parent. Prayer expresses a gracious relationship which "is simply trust in a person whose whole dealing with us proves him worthy of trust" (John Oman).

One of Paul's leading soteriological images, "reconciliation," is clearly modeled on human personal relationships. It implies that the transformation through faith of the relationship between God and sinful human beings is like the reconciliation of two persons – perhaps an alienated husband and wife.

There are thus powerful reasons for suggesting that the idea of a "personal God" is integral to the Christian outlook. But such a suggestion raises a number of difficulties, which require careful consideration. The following problems are particularly important.

1 It might be taken to imply that God is a human being. To speak of God as "a person" is to reduce God to our level. Paul Tillich points to "difficulties of location" in speaking of God in personal terms. To refer to God as a person is to imply that God, in common with human beings, is located at some definite place. Given the modern understanding of the universe, this assumption seems very out of place.

2 The doctrine of the Trinity speaks of God as "three persons." To speak of God as "a person" thus amounts to a denial of the Trinity. Historically, this objection is well justified. In the sixteenth century, those writers who spoke of God as "*a* person" were generally denying that God was *three* persons. Thus, in his *Philosophical Commentaries*, the famous English empiricist philosopher Bishop Berkeley (1685–1753) made a note not to speak of God as "a person" for this very reason.

These difficulties can, however, be mitigated. In response to the first, it may be pointed out that talking of God as "a person" is analogical. To say that God is like a person is to affirm the divine ability and willingness to relate to others. This does not imply that God is human, or located at a specific point in the universe. All analogies break down at some point. These aspects of the analogy are not intended to be taken up.

In response to the trinitarian difficulty, it will be noticed that the word "person" has changed its meaning significantly over the centuries. The word "person" does not have the same meaning in the two sentences which follow:

1 God is three persons.
2 God is a person.

We shall explore this point further in dealing with the doctrine of the Trinity itself (see pp. 249–56). Our attention now turns to further exploration of the term "person."

Defining "person"

In everyday English the word "person" has come to mean little more than "an individual human being." This makes it somewhat problematic to speak of a "personal God." However, as might be expected, there are hidden depths to the idea of personhood, which are too easily overlooked. The English word "person" derives from the Latin *persona*, which originally had the sense of a "mask."

The development of the meaning of *persona* is a fascinating subject in its own right. There may be an etymological connection between this Latin word and the Etruscan word for the goddess Persephone. (Etruscan was the language of a region of ancient Italy, near Rome.) Masks were worn by those participating in her festivals, which tended, by all reports, to degenerate into orgies. By the time of Cicero, the word had acquired a range of meanings. Although the sense of "mask" still predominated, important overtones had developed. Masks were used much in Roman theaters, being worn by actors to indicate the parts they were playing in dramas. *Persona* thus came to mean both "a theatrical mask" and "a theatrical character" or "a role in a play."

The early development of this idea in Christian theology is due to Tertullian, who was active in the third century. For Tertullian, a person is a being who speaks and acts. (The theatrical origins of the word can be seen clearly.) The final development of this definition is due to Boethius. Writing at the beginning of the sixth century, he offered the following definition: *persona est naturae rationabilis individua substantia*, "a person is the individual substance of a rational nature."

For early Christian writers, the word "person" is an expression of the individuality of a human being, as seen in his or her words and actions. Above all, there is an emphasis upon the idea of social relationships. A person is someone who plays a role in a social drama, who relates to others. A person has a part to play within a network of social relationships. "Individuality" does not imply social relationships, whereas "personality" relates to the part played by an individual in a web of relationships, by which that person is perceived to be distinctive by others. The basic idea expressed by the idea of "a personal God" is thus a God with whom we can stand in a relationship which is analogous to that which we could have with another human person.

It is helpful to consider what overtones the phrase "an impersonal God" would convey. The phrase suggests a God who is distant or aloof, who deals with humanity (if God deals with us at all) in general terms which take no account of human individuality. The idea of a personal relationship, such as love, suggests a reciprocal character to God's dealings with us. This idea is incorporated into the notion of a personal God, but not into impersonal conceptions of the nature of God. There are strongly negative overtones to the idea of "impersonal," which have passed into Christian thinking about the nature of God.

This point can be more fully appreciated by considering the impersonal concepts of God associated with Aristotle and Spinoza. As C. C. J. Webb points out:

Aristotle does not and could not speak of a love of God for us in any sense. God, according to the principles of Aristotle's theology, can know and love nothing less than himself. [...] He is utterly transcendent, and beyond the reach of personal communion. It is very instructive to study the modifications which Aristotle's faithful follower, St Thomas Aquinas, has to introduce into his master's notion of God, in order to make room for the providence of God for man, and the communion of man with God which his religious faith and religious experience demanded.

Spinoza experienced the same difficulty. He allowed that we, as human beings, should love God; yet he could not allow that this love is in any way reciprocated by God. It is a one-way street. Spinoza did not permit the two-way relationship implied by a personal God who loves, and is loved by, individual human beings. For Spinoza, any passion on the part of God involves a change in his being. Either he moves to a greater perfection, or to a lesser. In either case, the perfection of God is compromised, in that God either becomes more perfect (in which case God was not perfect to start with), or less perfect (in which case, suffering leads to God ceasing to be perfect). As a result, Spinoza argues, it is not possible to speak of God loving anyone, as this proves to be inconsistent with the idea of a perfect God. This point is made clearly in his *Ethics* (1677):

Proposition 17. God is without passions, nor is God affected with any experience of joy or sadness. *Demonstration.* All ideas, in so far as they have reference to God, are true, that is, they are adequate: and therefore God is without passions. Again, God cannot pass to a higher or a lower perfection: and therefore God is affected with no emotion of joy or sadness. Q.E.D. *Corollary:* God, strictly speaking, loves no one nor hates anyone. For God is affected with no emotion of joy or sadness, and consequently loves no one nor hates anyone.

So how can we begin to explore the idea of what it means to be a "person" in more detail? In a moment, we shall consider a significant twentieth-century contribution to this discussion, in the form of dialogical personalism. But we should first return to the question of why Christians speak of God both as "a person" and as "three persons."

When Christians now speak of God as a person, they are referring to the fact that it is possible to enter into a personal relationship with God. Human personal relationships are declared to be appropriate analogies or models for our relationship with God. Paul's use of the image of reconciliation is important here, as it implies an analogy between the reconciliation of two estranged people on the one hand, and of sinful human beings to God on the other.

To speak of God as three persons is to recognize the complexity of this relationship with God, and the manner in which it is established. It is to appreciate the complexity of the divine activity which lies behind God's ability to relate to us as persons. It is to understand that a network of relationships exists within the Godhead itself, and that this network undergirds our relationship with God. These points will be explored further in our discussion of the Trinity itself. Our attention now turns to a modern philosophical analysis of the idea of a "person" which is of considerable interest to Christian theology.

Dialogical personalism: Martin Buber

In his major work *I and You* (1927; the German original is *Ich und Du*, which is often translated as "I and Thou," to bring out the fact that the "you" is the singular, familiar form), the Jewish writer Martin Buber drew a fundamental distinction between two categories of relations: *I–You* relations, which are "personal," and *I–It* relations, which are impersonal. We shall explore these basic distinctions further, before considering their theological importance.

1 *I–It relations*: Buber uses this category to refer to the relation between subjects and objects; for example, between a human being and a pencil. The human being is active, whereas the pencil is passive. This distinction is often referred to in more philosophical language as a *subject–object relation*, in which an active subject (in this case, the human being) relates to an inactive object (in this case, the pencil). According to Buber, the subject acts as an *I*, and the object as an *It*. The relation between the human being and pencil could thus be described as an *I–It* relation.

2 *I–You relations*: At this point, we come to the heart of Buber's philosophy. An I–You relation exists between two active subjects, between two *persons*. It is something which is *mutual* and *reciprocal*. "The I of the primary word I–You makes its appearance as a person, and becomes conscious of itself." In other words, Buber is suggesting that human personal relationships exemplify the essential features of an I–You relation. It is the relationship itself, that intangible and invisible bond which links two persons, which is the heart of Buber's idea of an I–You relation.

I–It knowledge is indirect, mediated through an object, and has a specific content. In contrast, I–You knowledge is direct, immediate, and lacks a specific content. An "It" is known by measurable parameters – its height, weight, color, and so on. We can give a good physical description of it. But a "You" is known directly. The English language allows us to make a vital distinction between "knowing *about* something" and "*knowing* someone." Roughly the same distinction lies behind Buber's categories of "I–It" and "I–You" relations. We know *about* an "It" – but we know, *and are known by*, a "You." To "know about" something is to be able to express the content of that knowledge. Yet strictly speaking, there is no content to "knowing someone." The "knowledge" in question cannot really be expressed.

For Buber, an "I–You" relation is thus *mutual*, *reciprocal*, *symmetrical*, and *contentless*. Both partners retain their own subjectivity in the encounter, in which they become aware of the other person as a subject, rather than an object. Whereas an I–It relation can be thought of as the active subject pursuing and investigating the passive object, an I–You relation involves the encounter of two mutually active subjects. It is the relationship – something which has no real content, but which really exists nonetheless – which is the real focus of personal interaction. It is, to use Buber's terms, "not a specific *content*, but a *Presence*, a Presence as power."

Buber sets out these ideas at various points in *I and You*. The following statements are helpful in illuminating his meaning. The basic distinction between I–It and I–Thou relations is explained as follows "The world as experience belongs to the basic word I–It. The basic word I–You establishes the world of relation." Buber stresses that the importance of reciprocity as an element in an I–You relationship is identified, and insists that this relationship is direct and unmediated:

> The You encounters me by grace – it cannot be found by seeking. But that I speak the basic word to it is a deed of my whole being, is my essential deed. The You encounters me. But I enter into a direct relationship to it. Thus the relationship is election and electing, passive

and active at once. [. . .] The relation to the You is unmediated. Nothing conceptual intervenes between I and You.

What, then, are the theological implications of this approach to personhood? How does Buber's philosophy help us to understand and explore the idea of God as a person? A number of key ideas emerge, all of which have important and helpful theological applications. Furthermore, Buber anticipated some of these himself. In the final sections of *I and You* he explores the implications of his approach to thinking and speaking about God – or, to use his preferred term, "the Absolute You."

1   Buber's approach affirms that God cannot be reduced to a concept, or to some neat conceptual formulation. According to Buber, only an "It" can be treated in this way. For Buber, God is the "Thou who can, by its nature, never become an It. That is, God is a being who escapes all attempts at objectification and transcends all description." Theology must learn to acknowledge and wrestle with the presence of God, realizing that this presence cannot be reduced to a neat package of contents.

2   The approach allows valuable insights into the idea of revelation (see pp. 156–7). For Christian theology, God's revelation is not simply a making known of facts about God, but a self-revelation of God. Revelation of ideas about God is to be supplemented by revelation of God as a person, a presence as much as a content. We could make sense of this by saying that revelation includes knowledge of God as an "It" and as a "You." We come to know things about God; yet we also come to know God. Similarly, "knowledge of God" includes knowledge of God as both It and You. "Knowing God" is not simply a collection of data about God, but a personal relationship.

3   Buber's "dialogical personalism" also avoids the idea of God as an object, perhaps the weakest and most heavily criticized aspect of some nineteenth-century liberal theology. The characteristic noninclusive nineteenth-century phrase "man's quest for God" summed up the basic premise of this approach: God is an "It," a passive object, waiting to be discovered by (male) theologians, who are viewed as active subjects. Writers within the dialectical school, especially Emil Brunner in his *Truth as Encounter*, argued that God had to be viewed as a You, an active subject. As such, God could take the initiative away from humans, through self-revelation and a willingness to be known in a historical and personal form, namely Jesus Christ. Theology would thus become the human response to God's self-disclosure, rather than the human quest for God.

This emphasis upon a "personal God" raises a number of questions, one of which concerns the extent to which human experiences can be said to be shared by God. If God is personal, one can speak of God "loving" people. But how far can this be taken? Can, for example, one speak of God "suffering"?

Can God Suffer?

Christian theology throws up many fascinating questions. Some of them are interesting in themselves. Others are interesting because they open up wider issues. A question which belongs to both of these categories is this: can God be said to suffer? If God can be said to suffer, a point of contact is immediately established between God and the pain of the human world. God cannot then be thought of as being immune from the suffering of the creation. The implications of this for reflecting upon the problem of evil and suffering would be considerable.

But the question is also of interest in another respect. It invites us to consider why so many writers have an inbuilt aversion to thinking and speaking about "a suffering God." To explore this point, we may consider the historical background to early Christian theology. Although Christianity had its origins in Palestine, it rapidly expanded into other areas of the eastern Mediterranean world, such as modern-day Turkey and Egypt, establishing strongholds in cities such as Antioch and Alexandria. In the course of doing so, it came into contact with Hellenistic culture and Greek ways of thinking.

One of the major questions that arise from this observation is the following. Did Christian theologians, operating in a Hellenistic environment, inadvertently incorporate some Greek ideas into their thought? In other words, did a basically Palestinian gospel become distorted by being refracted through a Hellenistic prism? Particular attention was focused on the introduction of metaphysical terms into theology. Some scholars regarded this as the imposition of a static Greek way of thinking upon a dynamic semitic worldview. The result, they argued, was a distortion of the gospel.

Since the time of the Enlightenment, this question has been taken with considerable seriousness. A movement of major importance in this respect is known as the "history of dogma" movement (a working translation of the somewhat formidable German term *Dogmengeschichte*). Writers such as Adolf von Harnack (1851–1930) studied the historical development of Christian doctrine with a view to establishing whether this kind of deformation could be identified and eliminated. In his substantial *History of Dogma* (1886–9), which takes up seven volumes in English translation, Harnack argued that metaphysics should never have been allowed to find its way into Christian theology. For Harnack, the classic example of a doctrine which rested on metaphysical, rather than evangelical, foundations was the incarnation.

Many writers who felt that Harnack was wrong to single out the doctrine of the incarnation for criticism in this way nevertheless believed that classical Greek ideas had found their way into Christian theology. The search for these unwelcome intruders continued. It is now generally agreed that the idea of a God who lies beyond suffering may represent exactly the sort of Hellenistic invasion that Harnack was worried about. In what follows, we shall explore the classic pagan idea of the *apatheia* or "impassibility" of God – the view according to which God lies beyond all human emotions and pain.

The classic view: the impassibility of God

The notion of perfection dominates the classical understanding of God, as it is expressed in the Platonic dialogues such as *The Republic*. To be perfect is to be unchanging and self-sufficient. It is therefore impossible for such a perfect being to be affected or changed by anything outside itself. Furthermore, perfection was understood in very static terms, as we noted when considering Spinoza's approach to divine perfection (see p. 207). If God is perfect, change in any direction is an impossibility. If God changes, it is either a move *away from* perfection (in which case God is no longer perfect), or *toward* perfection (in which case, God was not perfect in the past). Aristotle, echoing such ideas, declared that "change would be change for the worse," and thus excluded his divine being from change and suffering.

This understanding passed into Christian theology at an early stage. Philo, a Hellenistic Jew whose writings were much admired by early Christian writers, wrote a treatise entitled *Quod Deus immutabilis sit* ("That God is unchangeable"), which vigorously defended the impassibility of God. Biblical passages that seemed to speak of God suffering were, he argued, to be treated as metaphors, and not to be allowed their full literal weight. To allow that God changes was to deny the divine perfection. "What greater impiety could there be than to suppose that the Unchangeable changes?" asked Philo. It seemed to be an unanswerable question.

For Philo, God could not be allowed to suffer, or undergo anything which could be spoken of as "passion." Anselm of Canterbury, influenced by this idea, argued that God was compassionate in terms of our experience, but not in terms of the divine being itself. The language of love and compassion is treated as purely figurative when used in relation to God. We may *experience* God as compassionate; this does not mean that God *is* compassionate. Anselm meditates along these lines in his *Proslogion*:

> You are truly compassionate in terms of our experience. Yet you are not so in terms of your own. For when you see us in our misery, we experience the effect of compassion; you, however, do not experience this feeling. Therefore you are compassionate, in that you save the miserable and spare those who sin against you; and you are not compassionate, in that you are not affected by any sympathy for misery.

Thomas Aquinas develops a similar approach when reflecting on the love of God for sinners. Love implies vulnerability and, potentially, that God could be affected by our sorrows, or moved by our misery. Yet Aquinas regarded this as an impossibility: "Mercy is especially to be attributed to God, provided that it is considered as an effect, not as a feeling of suffering. [. . .] It does not belong to God to grieve over the misery of others."

An obvious difficulty arises here. Jesus Christ suffered and died on the cross. Traditional Christian theology declared that Jesus Christ was God incarnate. It therefore seems to follow that God suffered in Christ. (The issue in question is the "communication of attributes," to be discussed at pp. 289–90). Not so, declared most of the patristic writers, deeply influenced by the pagan idea of the impassibility of God. Christ suffered in his human nature, not his divine nature. God thus did not experience human suffering, and remained unaffected by this aspect of the world.

A suffering God: Jürgen Moltmann

We have seen how the idea of an impassible God achieved considerable influence during the patristic and medieval periods. Yet there were protests against these developments. Perhaps the most celebrated of these is Martin Luther's "theology of the cross," which emerged during the period 1518–19. In the *Heidelberg Disputation* (1518), Luther contrasted two rival ways of thinking about God. A *theologia gloriae* ("theology of glory") perceives God's glory, power, and wisdom in creation. A *theologia crucis* ("theology of the cross") discerns God hidden in the suffering and humiliation of the cross of Christ. Luther deliberately uses the provocative and perhaps puzzling phrase *Deus crucifixus*, "a crucified God," as he speaks of the manner in which God shares in the sufferings of the crucified Christ.

In the late twentieth century, it has become "the new orthodoxy" to speak of a suffering God. Jürgen Moltmann's *The Crucified God* (1972) is widely regarded as the most significant and influential work to have expounded this idea, and has been the subject of intense discussion. What pressures led to the rediscovery of the idea of a suffering God? Three can be identified, all focusing on the period immediately after World War I. These three factors, taken together, gave rise to widespread skepticism concerning traditional ideas about the impassibility of God.

1   *The rise of protest atheism*: The sheer horror of World War I made a deep impact upon western theological reflection. The suffering of the period led to a widespread perception that liberal Protestantism was fatally compromised by its optimistic views of human nature. It is no accident that dialectical theology arose in the aftermath of this trauma. Another significant response was the movement known as "protest atheism," which raised a serious moral protest against belief in God. How could anyone believe in a God who was above such suffering and pain in the world?

Traces of such ideas can be found in Fyodor Dostoyevsky's nineteenth-century novel *The Brothers Karamazov*. The ideas were developed more fully in the twentieth century, often using Dostoyevsky's character Ivan Karamazov as a model. Karamazov's rebellion against God (or, perhaps more accurately, against the *idea* of God) has its origins in his refusal to accept that the suffering of an innocent child could ever be justified. Albert Camus developed such ideas in *L'Homme révolté* ("The Rebel"), which expressed Karamazov's protest in terms of a "metaphysical rebellion." Writers such as Jürgen Moltmann saw in this protest against an invulnerable God "the only serious atheism." This intensely moral form of atheism demanded a credible theological response – a theology of a suffering God.

2   *The rediscovery of Luther*: In 1883 – the celebration of the 400th anniversary of Luther's birth – the Weimar edition of Luther's works was launched. The resulting availability of Luther's works (many of which were hitherto unpublished) led to a resurgence in Luther scholarship, especially in German theological circles. Scholars such as Karl Holl opened the way for a new interest in the reformer during the 1920s. The result was a perceptible quickening in interest in many of Luther's ideas, especially the "theology of the cross." Luther's ideas about the "God who is hidden in suffering" became available at almost exactly the moment when they were needed.

3   *The growing impact of the "history of dogma" movement*: Although this movement reached its climax in the closing days of the nineteenth century, it took some while for the implications of its program to percolate into Christian theology as a whole. By the time World War I had ended, there was a general awareness that numerous Greek ideas (such as the impassibility of God) had found their way into Christian theology. Sustained attention was given to eliminating these ideas. Protest atheism created a climate in which it was apologetically necessary to speak of a suffering God. The "history of dogma" movement declared that Christian thinking had taken a wrong turn in the patristic period, and that this could be successfully reversed. Christian declarations that God was above suffering, or invulnerable, were now realized to be inauthentic. It was time to recover the authentically Christian idea of the suffering of God in Christ.

Three additional considerations may also be noted. First, the rise of process thought (see pp. 221–2) gave new impetus to speaking of God as "a fellow sufferer who understands" (A. N. Whitehead). Yet many who welcomed this insight were hesitant over the theological framework that engendered it. Process thought's emphasis upon the primacy of creativity seemed inconsistent with much traditional Christian thinking concerning the transcendence of God. An acceptable alternative was to ground the notion of God as a fellow-sufferer in the self-limitation of God, especially in the cross of Christ.

Second, fresh studies of the Old Testament – such as Abraham Heschel's *God of the Prophets* (1930) and T. E. Fretheim's *Suffering of God* (1984) – drew attention to the manner in which the Old Testament often portrayed God as sharing in the *pathos* of Israel. God is hurt and moved by the suffering of God's people. If classical theism could not accommodate that insight, it was argued, then so much the worse for it.

Third, the notion of "love" itself has been the subject of considerable discussion in the twentieth century. Theologians rooted in the classical tradition – such as Anselm and Aquinas – defined love in terms of expressions and demonstrations of care and goodwill toward others. It is thus perfectly possible to speak of God "loving impassibly" – that is, loving someone without being emotionally affected by that person's situation. Yet the new interest in the problem has raised questions over this notion of love. Can one really speak of "love," unless there is some mutual sharing of suffering and feelings? Surely "love" implies the lover's intense awareness of the suffering of the beloved, and thus some form of sharing in the beloved's distress? Such considerations have undermined the intuitive plausibility (yet not, interestingly, the intellectual credibility) of an impassible God.

Among major contributions to the discussion of the theological implications of a suffering God, two should be singled out as being of special importance.

1 In *The Crucified God* (1974) Jürgen Moltmann argued that the cross is both the foundation and the criterion of true Christian theology. The passion of Christ, and especially his cry of Godforsakenness – "My God! My God! Why have you forsaken me?" (Mark 15: 34) – stands at the center of Christian thinking. The cross must be seen as an event between the Father and the Son, in which the Father suffers the death of his Son in order to redeem sinful humanity.

Moltmann argues that a God who cannot suffer is a *deficient*, not a perfect, God. Stressing that God cannot be *forced* to change or undergo suffering, Moltmann declares that God willed to undergo suffering. The suffering of God is the direct consequence of the divine *decision* to suffer, and the divine *willingness* to suffer:

> A God who cannot suffer is poorer than any human. For a God who is incapable of suffering is a being who cannot be involved. Suffering and injustice do not affect him. And because he is so completely insensitive, he cannot be affected or shaken by anything. He cannot weep, for he has no tears. But the one who cannot suffer cannot love either. So he is also a loveless being.

Moltmann here brings together a number of the considerations we noted earlier, including the idea that love involves the lover participating in the sufferings of the beloved.

2 In *A Theology of the Pain of God* (1946) the Japanese writer Kazoh Kitamori argued that true love was rooted in pain. "God is the wounded Lord, having pain in himself." God is able to give meaning and dignity to human suffering on account of the fact that he also is in pain, and suffers. Like Moltmann, Kitamori draws heavily upon Luther's theology of the cross.

The idea of a suffering God might at first sight seem to be heretical in the eyes of Christian orthodoxy. The patristic period identified two unacceptable views relating to the suffering of God: *patripassianism* and *theopaschitism*. The former was regarded as a heresy, and the latter as a potentially misleading doctrine. They merit brief discussion before proceeding further.

Patripassianism arose during the third century and was associated with writers such as Noetus, Praxeas, and Sabellius. It centered on the belief that the Father suffered as the Son. In other words, the suffering of Christ on the cross is to be regarded as the suffering of the Father. According to these writers, the only distinction within the Godhead was a succession of modes or operations. In other words, Father, Son, and Spirit were just different modes of being, or expressions, of the same basic divine entity. This form of modalism, often known as Sabellianism, will be explored further in relation to the doctrine of the Trinity (see pp. 254–5).

Theopaschitism arose during the sixth century and was linked with writers such as John Maxentius. The basic slogan associated with the movement was "one of the Trinity was crucified." The formula can be interpreted in a perfectly orthodox sense (it reappears as Martin Luther's celebrated formula "the crucified God") and was defended as such by Leontius of Byzantium. However, it was regarded as potentially misleading and confusing by more cautious writers, including Pope Hormisdas (d. 523), and the formula gradually fell into disuse.

The doctrine of a suffering God rehabilitates theopaschitism, and interprets the relation of the suffering of God and of Christ in such a way that it avoids the patripassian difficulty. For example, Kitamori distinguishes the ways in which Father and Son suffer. "God the Father who hid himself in the death of God the Son is God in pain. Therefore the pain of God is neither merely the pain of God the Son, nor merely the pain of God the Father, but the pain of two persons who are essentially one."

Perhaps the most sophisticated statement of this doctrine is to be found in Moltmann's *Crucified God*, which develops the following position.

The Father and the Son suffer – but they experience that suffering in different manners. The Son suffers the pain and death of the cross; the Father gives up and suffers the loss of the Son. Although both Father and Son are involved in the cross, their involvement is not *identical* (the patripassian position), but *distinct*. "In the passion of the Son, the Father himself suffers the pains of abandonment. In the death of the Son, death comes upon God himself, and the Father suffers the death of his Son in his love for forsaken man."

Moltmann's confident assertion that "death comes upon God" naturally leads us to consider whether God can be thought of as having died – or, even more radically, as being dead.

The death of God?

If God can suffer, can God also die? Or is God now dead? These questions demand consideration as part of any discussion of the suffering of God in Christ. Hymns, as much as theology textbooks, bear witness to the beliefs of Christianity. A number of significant hymns of the Christian church make reference to the death of God, exulting in the paradox that the immortal God should die on the cross. Perhaps the most celebrated example is Charles Wesley's eighteenth-century hymn "And can it be?," which includes the following lines:

> Amazing love! how can it be
> That thou, my God, shouldst die for me?

These lines express the idea of the immortal God being given up to death as an expression of love and commitment. This thought is also expressed elsewhere in that same hymn, as here:

'Tis mystery all! th'immortal dies!
Who can explore his strange design?

But how, one wonders, can one speak of God "dying?" For a few weeks in 1965, theology hit the national headlines in the United States. *Time* magazine ran an edition declaring that God was dead. Slogans such as "God is dead" and "the death of God" became of national interest. In its issue of February 16, 1966, the *Christian Century* provided a satirical application form for its readers to join the "God-Is-Dead-Club." Puzzling new terms began to appear in the learned journals: "theothanasia," "theothanatology," and "theothanatopsis" became buzz-words, before happily lapsing into fully merited obscurity.

Two quite distinct lines of interpretation may be discerned lying behind the slogan "the death of God."

1 The belief, especially linked with the nineteenth-century German philosopher Nietzsche, that human civilization has reached the stage at which it may dispense with the notion of God. The crisis of faith in the west, especially western Europe, which developed during the nineteenth century, finally matured. Nietzsche's declaration (in *The Happy Science*, 1882) that "God is dead! God remains dead! And we have killed him!" expresses the general cultural atmosphere which finds no place for God. This secular outlook is well explored in Gabriel Vahanian's *Death of God: The Culture of Our Post-Christian Era* (1961). William Hamilton expressed this feeling as follows:

We are not talking about the absence of the experience of God, but about the experience of the absence of God. [...] The death of God must be affirmed; the confidence with which we thought we could speak of God is gone. [...] There remains a sense of not having, of not believing, of having lost, not just the idols or the gods of religion but God himself. And this is an experience that is not peculiar to a neurotic few, nor is it private or inward. Death of God is a public event in our history.

Although subsequent predictions of the total secularization of western society remain conspicuously unfulfilled, the "death of God" motif seems to capture the atmosphere of an important moment in western cultural history.

This development had important implications for those Christian theologians who took their lead from cultural developments. In his *Secular Meaning of the Gospel* (1963), Paul van Buren, arguing that the word "God" had ceased to have any meaning, sought to ascertain how the gospel might be stated in purely atheological terms. Belief in a transcendent God was replaced by commitment to a "Jesus-ethic," centered on respect for the lifestyle of Jesus. Thomas J. J. Altizer's *Gospel of Christian Atheism* (1966) refocused the question by suggesting that, while it was no longer acceptable to talk about Jesus being God, one could still talk about God being Jesus – thus giving a moral authority to Jesus's words and deeds, even if belief in a God was no longer to be retained.

2 The totally distinct belief that Jesus Christ has such a high profile of identification with God that one can speak of God "dying" in Christ. Just as God suffers in Christ, so one can speak of God experiencing death or "perishability" (Eberhard Jüngel) in the same manner. This approach is considerably less interesting culturally, although it is probably much more significant theologically. Partly in reaction to developments in the United States, especially the widespread circulation given to

the slogan "God is dead," Jüngel wrote a paper entitled "The Death of the Living God" (1968), in which he argued that, through the death of Christ, God becomes involved in *Vergänglichkeit* – a German word which is often translated as "perishability," but is perhaps better rendered as "transience" or "transitoriness." Jüngel, who developed these ideas at greater length in *God as the Mystery of the World* (1983), thus sees the theme of "the death of God" as an important affirmation of God's self-identification with the transitory world of suffering.

Developing related ideas in his *Crucified God*, Jürgen Moltmann speaks (a little cryptically, one feels) of "death in God." God identifies with all who suffer and die, and thus shares in human suffering and death. These aspects of human history are thereby taken up into the history of God. "To recognize God in the cross of Christ [. . .] means to recognize the cross, inextricable suffering, death and hopeless rejection in God." Moltmann makes this point using a poignant episode from a famous passage in Elie Wiesel's novel *Night*, describing an execution at Auschwitz. As a crowd watched three people die by hanging, someone asked "Where is God?" Moltmann uses this episode to make the point that, through the cross of Christ, God tastes and is affected by death. God knows what death is like.

The Omnipotence of God

The Nicene creed opens with the confident words "I believe in God, the Father almighty." Belief in an "almighty" or omnipotent God is thus an essential element of traditional Christian faith. But what does it mean to speak of God being "omnipotent?"

The commonsense approach to the matter defines omnipotence like this: if God is omnipotent then God can do anything. Of course, God cannot make a square circle, or a round triangle; this is a logical self-contradiction. But the idea of divine omnipotence seems to imply that God must be able to do anything which does not involve obvious contradiction.

A more subtle problem is raised by the following question: can God create a stone which is too heavy for God to lift? If God cannot create such a stone, the idea of total divine omnipotence would seem to be denied. Yet if God could create such a stone, then there is something else which God *cannot* do – namely, lift that stone. And so, at least on the face of it, God turns out not to be omnipotent.

Such logical explorations are unquestionably valuable, in that they cast light on the difficulties of speaking about God. One of the most important rules of Christian theology is to ask closely concerning the meaning of words. Words with one meaning in a secular context often have more developed, subtle, or nuanced meanings in a theological setting. "Omnipotence" is an excellent example, as we shall see.

Defining omnipotence

We may explore the definition of omnipotence by considering some arguments developed by C. S. Lewis in his celebrated book *The Problem of Pain* (1940). Lewis begins by stating the problem as follows: "If God were good, he would wish to make his creatures perfectly happy, and if God were almighty he would be able to do what he wished. But the creatures are not happy. Therefore God lacks either the goodness, or power, or both." This is the problem of pain, in its simplest form. But what does it mean to say that God is omnipotent? Lewis argues that it does *not* mean that God can do anything. Once God has opted to do certain things, or to behave in a certain manner, then other possibilities are excluded.

> If you choose to say "God can give a creature free will and at the same time withhold free will from it", you have not succeeded in saying *anything* about God: meaningless combinations of words do not suddenly acquire a meaning because we prefix to them the two other words: "God can". It remains true that all *things* are possible with God: the intrinsic impossibilities are not things but non-entities.

God, then, cannot do anything that is *logically* impossible. But Lewis takes the case further: God cannot do anything that is inconsistent with the divine nature. It is not merely logic, he argues, but the very nature of God, which prevents God from doing certain things.

The point at issue here was made firmly by Anselm of Canterbury in his *Proslogion*, as he meditated upon the nature of God. Anselm made the point that omnipotence – understood as the ability to do all things – was not necessarily a good thing. If God is omnipotent, God could do things such as tell lies or pervert justice. Yet this is clearly inconsistent with the Christian understanding of the nature of God. The concept of divine omnipotence must therefore be modified by the Christian understanding of the divine nature and character. This point is brought out particularly clearly by Thomas Aquinas, as he discusses the issue of whether God can sin.

> It is commonly said that God is almighty. Yet it seems difficult to understand the reason for this, on account of the doubt about what is meant when it is said that "God can do 'everything'." [...] If it is said that God is omnipotent because he can do everything possible to his power, the understanding of omnipotence is circular, doing nothing more than saying that God is omnipotent because

he can do everything that he can do. [...] To sin is to fall short of a perfect action. Hence to be able to sin is to be able to be deficient in relation to an action, which cannot be reconciled with omnipotence. It is because God is omnipotent that he cannot sin.

Aquinas's discussion makes it clear that further clarification is needed concerning the idea of divine omnipotence. An important advance in this matter was the distinction between "the two powers of God," especially associated with the fourteenth-century writer William of Ockham. We may turn to this discussion now.

The two powers of God

How can God act absolutely reliably, without being subject to some external agency which compels God to act in this reliable way? This question was debated with some heat at the University of Paris in the thirteenth century, in response to a form of determinism linked with the writer Averroes. For Averroes, the reliability of God ultimately rested upon external pressures. God was compelled to act in certain ways – and thus acted reliably. This approach was, however, regarded with intense suspicion by most theologians, who saw it as a crude denial of the freedom of God. But how could God be said to act reliably, unless it was through external compulsion?

The answer given by Christian writers such as Duns Scotus and William of Ockham can be stated as follows: the reliability of God is ultimately grounded in the divine nature itself. God does not act reliably because someone or something makes God act in this way, but because of a deliberate and free divine *decision* to act like this.

In his discussion of the opening line of the Apostles' creed – "I believe in God the Father almighty" – Ockham asks precisely what is meant by the word "almighty" (*omnipotens*). It cannot, he argues, mean that God is *presently* able to do everything; rather, it means that God was *once* free to act in this way. God has now established an order of things which reflects a loving and righteous divine will and that order, once established, will remain until the end of time.

Ockham uses two important terms to refer to these different options. The "absolute power of God" (*potentia absoluta*) refers to the options which existed before God had committed himself to any course of action or world ordering. The "ordained power of God" (*potentia ordinata*) refers to the way things now are, which reflects the order established by God their creator. These do not represent two different sets of options now open to God. They represent two different moments in the great history of salvation. And our concern is with the ordained power of God, the way in which God orders the creation at present.

The distinction is important, yet difficult. In view of this, we shall explore it in a little more detail. Ockham is inviting us to consider two very different situations in which we might speak of the "omnipotence of God." The first is this: God is confronted with a whole array of possibilities – such as creating the world, or not creating the world. God can choose to actualize any of these possibilities. This is the *absolute* power of God.

But then God selects some options, and brings them into being. We are now in the realm of the ordained power of God – a realm in which God's power is restricted, by virtue of God's own decision. Ockham's point is this: by choosing to actualize some options, God has to choose not to actualize others. Choosing to do something means choosing to reject something else. Once God has chosen to create the world, the option of *not* creating the world is set to one side. This means that there are certain things which God could do *once* which can

no longer be done. Although God could have decided not to create the world, God has now deliberately rejected that possibility. And that rejection means that this possibility is no longer open.

This leads to what seems, at first sight, to be a paradoxical situation. On account of the divine omnipotence, God is not now able to do everything. By exercising the divine power, God has limited options. For Ockham, God *cannot* now do everything. God has deliberately limited the possibilities. God chose to limit the options which are now open. Is that a contradiction? No. If God is really capable of doing anything, then God must be able to become committed to a course of action – and stay committed to it. God, in exercising omnipotence, chose to restrict the range of options available. This notion of divine self-limitation, explored by Ockham, is important in modern theology, and merits further exploration.

The notion of divine self-limitation

The idea of God's self-limitation began to be explored with new interest in the nineteenth century, specifically within a Christological context. The favored framework for the discussion of the idea of divine self-limitation was usually that suggested by Philippians 2: 6–7, which speak of Christ "emptying himself." The term "kenoticism" (from the Greek *kenosis*, "an emptying") came to be widely used to refer to this approach.

Writers in the German tradition such as Gottfried Thomasius (1802–75), F. H. R. von Frank (1827–94), and W. F. Gess (1819–91) argued that God chose a course of self-limitation in becoming incarnate in Christ. Thomasius adopted the position that God (or, more accurately, the divine Logos) set aside (or became emptied of) the divine *metaphysical* attributes (such as omnipotence, omniscience, and omnipresence) in Christ while retaining the *moral* attributes (such as the divine love, right- eousness, and holiness). Gess, however, insisted that God set aside all the attributes of divinity in the incarnation, thus making it virtually impossible to speak of Christ being "divine" in any sense of the term.

In England, the idea of kenoticism was later in developing, and took a somewhat different form. Convinced that traditional Christologies did not do justice to the humanity of Christ (tending to portray him in terms which approached Docetism), writers such as Charles Gore (1853–1932) and P. T. Forsyth (1848–1921) argued that those attributes of divinity which tended to be seen as obliterating Christ's humanity had been set to one side. Thus Gore's *Incarnation of the Son of God* (1891) developed the idea that Christ's full earthly humanity involved a voluntary self-emptying of his divine knowledge, with a resulting human ignorance. There was thus no difficulty raised by the observation that the Gospel records seemed to suggest that Jesus was possessed of a limited knowledge at points.

Perhaps the most dramatic statement of this notion of divine self-limitation can be found in Dietrich Bonhoeffer's *Letters and Papers from Prison*, dating from the closing years of World War II:

> God lets himself be pushed out of the world on to the cross. He is weak and powerless in the world, and that is precisely the way, the only way, in which he is with us and helps us. [. . .] The Bible directs us to God's powerlessness and suffering; only the suffering God can help.

In an age which has become increasingly suspicious of the idea of "power," it is perhaps refreshing to be reminded that talk about "God almighty" does not necessarily imply that God is a tyrant, but that God chooses to stand alongside people in their powerlessness – a major theme in interpretations of the cross of Christ, to which we shall return shortly.

God's Action in the World

I n what sense can God be said to be present and active within the world? A number of models have been developed to articulate the richness of the Christian understanding of this matter, and are probably best regarded as complementary rather than competitive. In what follows, we shall explore a representative selection of approaches.

Deism: God acts through the laws of nature

In an earlier chapter (pp. 142–3) we noted the rise of the movement known as "Deism." The Deist position could be summarized very succinctly as follows. God created the world in a rational and ordered manner, which reflected God's own rational nature. The ordering of the world is open to human investigation. On being discovered, this ordering demonstrates the wisdom of God. The laws of nature have been set in place by God; it merely remained for a brilliant human being to discover them. Alexander Pope's celebrated epitaph for Newton brings out the popular understanding of the scientist's importance.

> Nature and Nature's Law lay hid in Night
> God said, let Newton be, and all was light.

Deism defended the idea that God created the world, and endowed it with the ability to develop and function without the need for his continuing presence or interference. This viewpoint, which became especially influential in the eighteenth century, regarded the world as a watch, and God as the watchmaker. God endowed the world with a certain self-sustaining design, such that it could subsequently function without the need for continual intervention. It is thus no accident that William Paley chose to use the image of a watch and watchmaker as part of his celebrated defense of the existence of a creator God (see pp. 190–2).

So how does God act in the world, according to Deism? The simple answer to this question is that God does *not* act in the world. Like a watchmaker, God endowed the universe with its regularity (seen in the "laws of nature") and set its mechanism in motion. Having provided the impetus to set the system in motion, and establishing the principles which govern that motion, there is nothing left for God to do. The world is to be seen as a large-scale watch, which is completely autonomous and self-sufficient. No action by God is necessary.

Inevitably, this led to the question of whether God could be eliminated completely from the Newtonian worldview. If there was nothing left for God to do, what conceivable need was there for any kind of divine being? If it can be shown that there are self-sustaining principles within the world, there is no need for the traditional idea of "providence" – that is, for the sustaining and regulating hand of God to be present and active throughout the entire existence of the world. The Newtonian worldview thus encouraged the view that, although God may well have created the world, there was no further need for divine involvement. The discovery of the laws of conservation (for example, the laws of conservation of momentum) seemed to imply that God had endowed the creation with all the mechanisms which it required in order to continue. It is this point which is encapsulated in the mathematician and astronomer Pierre-Simon Laplace's famous comment, made in relation to the idea of God as a sustainer of planetary motion: "I have no need of that hypothesis."

A more activist understanding of the manner in which God acts in the world is due to Thomas Aquinas and modern writers influenced by him, which focuses on the use of secondary causes.

Thomism: God acts through secondary causes

A somewhat different approach to the issue of God's action in the world can be based on the writings of the leading medieval theologian Thomas Aquinas. Aquinas's conception of divine action focuses on the distinction between primary and secondary causes. According to Aquinas, God does not work directly in the world, but through secondary causes.

The idea is best explained in terms of an analogy. Suppose we imagine a pianist, who is remarkably gifted. She possesses the ability to play the piano beautifully. Yet the quality of her playing is dependent upon the quality of the piano with which she is provided. An out-of-tune piano will prove disastrous, no matter how expert the player. In our analogy the pianist is the primary cause, and the piano the secondary cause, for a performance of, for example, a Chopin nocturne. Both are required; each has a significantly different role to play. The ability of the primary cause to achieve the desired effect is dependent upon the secondary cause which has to be used.

Aquinas uses this appeal to secondary causes to deal with some of the issues relating to the presence of evil in the world. Suffering and pain are not to be ascribed to the direct action of God, but to the fragility and frailty of the secondary causes through which God works. God, in other words, is to be seen as the primary cause, and various agencies within the world as the associated secondary causes.

For Aristotle (from whom Aquinas draws many of his ideas), secondary causes are able to act in their own right. Natural objects are able to act as secondary causes by virtue of their own nature. This view was unacceptable to theistic philosophers of the Middle Ages, whether Christian or Islamic. For example, the noted Islamic writer al-Ghazali (1058–1111) held that nature is completely subject to God, and it is therefore improper to speak of secondary causes having any independence. God is to be seen as the primary cause who alone is able to move other causes. A similar idea is found in Aquinas, who argues that God is the "unmoved mover," the prime cause of every action, without whom nothing could happen at all. (Earlier, we noted the importance of this point in relation to the argument from motion: see pp. 187–8.)

The theistic interpretation of secondary causes thus offers the following account of God's action in the world. God acts indirectly in the world through secondary causes. A great chain of causality can be discerned, leading back to God as the originator and prime mover of all that happens in the world. Yet God does not act *directly* in the world, but through the chain of events which God initiates and guides.

It will thus be clear that Aquinas's approach leads to the idea of God initiating a process which develops under divine guidance. God, so to speak, *delegates* divine action to secondary causes within the natural order. For example, God might move a human will from within so that someone who is ill receives assistance. Here an action which is God's will is carried out *indirectly* by God – yet, according to Aquinas, we can still speak of this action being "caused" by God in some meaningful way.

An approach which is clearly related to this, but differing radically at points of significance, can be found in the movement known as "process thought," to which we now turn.

Process theology: God acts through persuasion

The origins of process thought lie in the writings of the Anglo-American philosopher Alfred North Whitehead (1861–1947), especially his important work *Process and Reality* (1929). Reacting against the rather static view of the world associated with traditional metaphysics (expressed in ideas such as "substance" and "essence"), Whitehead conceived reality as a process. The world, as an organic whole, is something dynamic, not static; something which *happens*. Reality is made up of building blocks of "actual entities" or "actual occasions," and is thus characterized by becoming, change, and event.

All these "entities" or "occasions" (to use Whitehead's original terms) possess a degree of freedom to develop and be influenced by their surroundings. It is perhaps at this point that the influence of biological evolutionary theories can be discerned: like the later writer Pierre Teilhard de Chardin (whom we shall consider below), Whitehead is concerned to allow for development within creation, subject to some overall direction and guidance. This process of development is thus set against a permanent background of order, which is seen as an organizing principle essential to growth. Whitehead argues that God may be identified with this background of order within the process. Whitehead treats God as an "entity," but distinguishes God from other entities on the grounds of imperishability. Other entities exist for a finite period; God exists permanently. Each entity thus receives influence from two main sources: previous entities and God.

Causation is thus not a matter of an entity being coerced to act in a given manner: it is a matter of *influence* and *persuasion*. Entities influence each other in a "dipolar" manner – mentally and physically. Precisely the same is true of God, as for other entities. God can only act in a persuasive manner, within the limits of the process itself. God "keeps the rules" of the process. Just as God influences other entities, so God is also influenced by them. God, to use Whitehead's famous phrase, is "a fellow-sufferer who understands." God is thus affected and influenced by the world.

Process thought thus redefines God's omnipotence in terms of persuasion or influence within the overall world-process. This is an important development, as it explains the attraction of this way of understanding God's relation to the world in relation to the problem of evil. Where the traditional free-will defense of moral evil argues that human beings are free to disobey or ignore God, process theology argues that the individual components of the world are likewise free to ignore divine attempts to influence or persuade them. They are not bound to respond to God. God is thus absolved of responsibility for both moral and natural evil.

The traditional free-will defense of God in the face of evil is persuasive (although the extent of that persuasion is contested) in the case of moral evil – in other words, evil resulting from human decisions and actions. But what of natural evil? What of earthquakes, famines, and other natural disasters? Process thought argues that God cannot force nature to obey the divine will or purpose for it. God can only attempt to influence the process from within, by persuasion and attraction. Each entity enjoys a degree of freedom and creativity, which God cannot override.

While this understanding of the persuasive nature of God's activity has obvious merits, not least in the way in which it offers a response to the problem of evil (as God is not in control, God cannot be blamed for the way things have turned out), critics of process thought have suggested that too high a price is paid. The traditional idea of the transcendence of God appears to have been abandoned, or radically reinterpreted in terms of the primacy and permanency of God as an entity within the process. In other words, the divine transcendence is understood to mean little more than that God outlives and surpasses other entities. Whitehead's basic ideas have been developed by a number of writers, most notably Charles Hartshorne (1897–2000), Schubert Ogden (born 1928), and John B. Cobb (born 1925).

It will be clear that process theology has no difficulty in speaking of "God's action within the world," and that it offers a framework within which this action can be described in terms of "influence within the process." Nevertheless, the specific approach adopted causes anxiety to traditional theism, which is critical of the notion of God associated with process theology. For traditional theists, the God of process thought seems to bear little relation to the God described in the Old or New Testaments.

Pierre Teilhard de Chardin: Point Omega

One of the most remarkable contributions to the twentieth-century debate over the relation of science and religion was made by the distinguished French paleontologist Pierre Teilhard de Chardin (1881–1955). Although he wrote extensively on the way in which God was involved in the world, these writings were never published during his lifetime, presumably because they were considered somewhat unorthodox by his superiors in the Society of Jesus. Shortly after Teilhard de Chardin's death in 1955, his first major work appeared. *Le Phénomène humaine* ("The human phenomenon") was written during the years 1938–40. It finally appeared in French in 1955, and in English translation in 1959. This was followed by *Le Milieu divin*, which was originally written in 1927 and appeared in French in 1957. The title is notoriously difficult to translate into English, on account of the rich connotations of the French word *milieu*.

Teilhard de Chardin viewed the universe as an evolutionary process which was constantly moving towards a state of greater complexity and higher levels of consciousness. Within this process of evolution, a number of critically important transitions (generally referred to as "critical points") can be discerned. For Teilhard, the origination of life on earth and the emergence of human consciousness are two particularly important thresholds in this process. These "critical points" are like rungs on a ladder, leading to new stages in a continuous process of development. The world is to be seen as a single continuous process – a "universal interweaving" of various levels of organization. Each of these levels has its roots in earlier levels, and its emergence is to be seen as the actualization of what was potentially present in earlier levels. Teilhard de Chardin thus does not consider that there is a radical dividing line between consciousness and matter, or between humanity and other animals. The world is a single evolving entity, linked together as a web of mutually interconnected events, in which there is a natural progression from matter to life to human existence to human society.

This clearly raises the question of how God is involved in the process of the evolution of the world. It is clear that Teilhard de Chardin places considerable emphasis on the theme of the consummation of the world in Jesus Christ, an idea which is clearly stated in the New Testament (especially the letters to the Colossians and Ephesians: see Colossians 1: 15–20; Ephesians 1: 9–10, 22–3), and which was developed with particular enthusiasm by some Greek patristic writers, including Origen. Teilhard de Chardin develops this theme with particular reference to a concept which he calls "Omega" (after the final letter of the Greek alphabet). In his earlier writings he tends to think of Omega primarily as the point towards which the evolutionary process is heading. The process clearly represents an upward ascent; Omega defines, so to speak, its final destination. It will be clear that Teilhard de Chardin regards evolution as a teleological and directional process. As his thinking developed, however, he began to integrate his Christian understanding of God into his thinking about Omega, with the result that both the directionality of evolution and its final goal are explained in terms of a final union with God.

The overall vision that Teilhard de Chardin sets out is thus that of a universe in the process of evolution – a massive organism which is slowly progressing towards its fulfillment through a forward and upward movement. God is at work within this process, directing it from inside – yet also at work *ahead* of the process, drawing it toward its divine goal and its final fulfillment.

For many commentators, the real strengths of both process theology and the approach adopted by Teilhard de Chardin lie in their insights into the origin and nature of suffering within the world. Those strengths are best appreciated through an analysis of the various alternatives on offer within the Christian tradition concerning suffering – an area of theology which has come to be known as "theodicy," to which we shall presently turn. But first, we must explore the doctrine of creation, which sets the backdrop to these important discussions.

God as Creator

The doctrine of God as creator has its foundations firmly laid in the Old Testament (e.g., Genesis 1, 2). In the history of theology, the doctrine of God the creator has often been linked with the authority of the Old Testament. The continuing importance of the Old Testament for Christianity is often held to be grounded in the fact that the God of which it speaks is the same God to be revealed in the New Testament. The creator God and the redeemer God are one and the same. In the case of Gnosticism, a vigorous attack was mounted on both the authority of the Old Testament and the idea that God was creator of the world.

Development of the doctrine of creation

The theme of "God as creator" is of major importance within the Old Testament. Attention has often focused on the creation narratives found in the first two chapters of the Book of Genesis, with which the Old Testament canon opens. However, it must be appreciated that the theme is deeply embedded in the wisdom and prophetic literature in the Old Testament. For example, Job 38: 1–42: 6 sets out what is unquestionably the most comprehensive understanding of God as creator to be found in the Old Testament, stressing the role of God as creator and sustainer of the world.

It is possible to discern two distinct, though related, contexts in which the notion of "God as creator" is encountered: first, in contexts which reflect the praise of God within Israel's worship, both individual and corporate; and second, in contexts which stress that the God who created the world is also the God who liberated Israel from bondage, and continues to sustain Israel in the present.

The doctrine of creation plays a different role within the three main bodies of writings within the Old Testament – the historical, prophetic, and wisdom writings. In the historical books, the doctrine of creation is often used to combat the nature religion of Canaan, which held that various nature divinities (such as the Canaanite "El") needed to be propitiated in order to secure a good harvest. Within the prophetic writings, particularly those of the exilic age, the doctrine is used to affirm the universal sovereignty of the God of Israel. The god who made the whole world is ruler of that world – including nations such as Babylonia, who were presently oppressing Israel. The gods of Babylon were merely local creations, lacking the power and authority of the God of Israel. The doctrine of creation thus became the foundation of the hope of liberation. Within the wisdom writings, particularly Job and Proverbs, the doctrine of creation is linked to the acquisition of wisdom. The wise are able to find and discern wisdom within the created world, and order their lives in accord with its precepts.

Of particular interest for our purposes is the Old Testament theme of "creation as ordering" and the manner in which the critically important theme of "order" is established on and justified with reference to cosmological foundations. It has often been pointed out how the Old Testament portrays creation in terms of an engagement with and victory over forces of chaos. This "establishment of order" is generally represented in two different ways:

1   Creation is an imposition of order on a formless chaos. This model is especially associated with the image of a potter working clay into a recognizably ordered structure (e.g., Genesis 2: 7; Isaiah 29: 16, 64: 8; Jeremiah 18: 1–6).
2   Creation concerns conflict with a series of chaotic forces, often depicted as a dragon or another monster (variously named Behemoth, Leviathan, Nahar, Rahab, Tannim, or Yam) who must be subdued (Job 3: 8, 7: 12, 9: 13, 40: 15–41: 11; Psalm 74: 13–15; Isaiah 27: 1.

It is clear that there are parallels between the Old Testament account of God engaging with the forces of chaos and Ugaritic and Canaanite mythology. Nevertheless, there are significant differences at points of importance, not least in the Old Testament's insistence that the forces of chaos are not to be seen as divine. Creation is not to be understood in terms of different gods warring against each other for mastery of a (future) universe, but in terms of God's mastery of chaos and ordering of the world.

Perhaps one of the most significant affirmations which the Old Testament makes is that *nature is not divine*. The Genesis creation account stresses that God created the moon, sun, and stars. The significance of this point is too easily overlooked. Each of these celestial entities was worshiped as divine in the ancient world. By asserting that they were created by God, the Old Testament is insisting that they are subordinate to God, and have no intrinsic divine nature.

Having briefly introduced some aspects of the concept of creation, particularly within a Jewish or Christian context, we may now pass on to consider some of its aspects in a more theological manner.

Creation and the rejection of dualism

The central issue relating to the doctrine of creation which had to be debated in the first period of Christian theology was thus that of *dualism*. The classic example of this is found in some of the forms of Gnosticism, so forcefully opposed by Irenaeus, which argued for the existence of two gods: a supreme god, who was the source of the invisible spiritual world, and a lesser deity who created the world of visible, material things. A similar outlook is associated with Manichaeism, a Gnostic worldview which Augustine found attractive as a young man. This approach is strongly dualist, in that it sets up a fundamental tension between the spiritual realm (which is seen as

being good) and the material realm (which is seen as being evil).

For Gnosticism, in most of its significant forms, a sharp distinction was to be drawn between the God who redeemed humanity from the world, and a somewhat inferior deity (often termed "the demiurge") who created that world in the first place. The Old Testament was regarded by the Gnostics as dealing with this lesser deity, whereas the New Testament was concerned with the redeemer God. As such, belief in God as creator and in the authority of the Old Testament came to be interlinked at an early stage. The doctrine of creation affirmed that the material world was created good by God, despite its subsequent contamination by sin.

The dualist notion of a good realm of the invisible and spiritual, and an evil realm of the visible and material is excluded by the Council of Nicea (325), whose creed opened with an affirmation of faith in "God the Father almighty, creator of all that is, visible and invisible." This was reinforced by the Synod of Toledo (400), which was explicit in its rejection of dualism:

> If anyone says and believes that this world and all its instruments have not been created by the almighty God, let him be anathema [...] If anyone says or believes that the world has been made by a god other than the one of whom it is written, "In the beginning, God created heaven and earth" (Genesis 1: 1), let him be anathema.

This view was further reinforced by Leo I in a letter of 447, in which he defined "true faith" as consisting of the belief that "the substance of all spiritual and physical creatures is good, and that there is no nature of evil. For God, the creator of all things, has not made anything that is not good."

It was, however, Augustine of Hippo who provided the definitive statement of a nondualist theology, which had such a major impact on western thought. The fundamental principles underlying this unitary vision of reality can be summarized as follows:

1 Everything that exists owes that existence to God. There is no alternative source or origin of existence.
2 Everything that exists was created good by a good God.
3 The evil that exists within the world is not to be thought of as something positive and real, possessing its own distinct substance. Rather, it is to be thought of as a "lack of goodness" (*privation boni*).
4 Evil does not derive its origin from God, but from humanity's use of its God-given freedom.

The doctrine of creation *ex nihilo*

A distinct debate centered on the question of creation *ex nihilo* ("out of nothing"). It must be remembered that Christianity initially took root and then expanded in the eastern Mediterranean world of the first and second centuries, which was dominated by various Greek philosophies. The general Greek understanding of the origins of the world could be summarized as follows. God is not to be thought of as having *created* the world. Rather, God is to be thought of as an architect, who ordered pre-existent matter. Matter was already present within the universe, and did not require to be created; it needed to be given a definite shape and structure. God was therefore thought of as the one who fashioned the world from this already existing matter. Thus in one of his dialogues (*Timaeus*), Plato developed the idea that the world was made out of pre-existent matter, which was fashioned into the present form of the world.

This idea was taken up by most Gnostic writers, who were here followed by individual Christian theologians such as Theophilus of Antioch and Justin Martyr. They professed a belief in pre-existent matter, which was shaped into the world in the act of creation. In other words, creation was not *ex nihilo*; rather, it was to be seen as an act of construction, on the basis of material which was already to hand, as one might construct an igloo out of snow, or a house from stone. The existence of evil in the world was thus to be explained on the basis of the intractability of this pre-existent matter. God's options in creating the world were limited by the poor quality of the material available. The presence of evil or defects within the world are thus not to be ascribed to God, but to deficiencies in the material from which the world was constructed.

However, the conflict with Gnosticism forced reconsideration of this issue. In part, the idea of creation from pre-existent matter was discredited by its Gnostic associations; in part, it was called into question by an increasingly sophisticated reading of the Old Testament creation narratives. Reacting against this Platonist worldview, several major Christian writers of the second and third centuries argued that *everything* had to be created by God. There was no pre-existent matter; everything required to be created out of nothing. Irenaeus argued that the Christian doctrine of creation affirmed the inherent goodness of creation, which contrasted sharply with the Gnostic idea that the material world was evil.

Tertullian emphasized the divine decision to create the world. The existence of the world is itself due to God's freedom and goodness, not to any inherent necessity arising from the nature of matter. The world depends on God for its existence. This contrasted sharply with the Aristotelian view that the world depended on nothing for its existence, and that the particular structure of the world was intrinsically necessary. Yet not all Christian theologians adopted this position at this early stage in the emergence of the Christian tradition. Origen, perhaps one of the most Platonist of early Christian writers, clearly regarded the doctrine of creation from pre-existent matter to have some merit.

By the end of the fourth century, most Christian theologians had rejected the Platonist approach, even in the form associated with Origen, and argued for God being the creator of both the spiritual and material worlds. The Nicene creed opens with a declaration of faith in God as "maker of heaven and earth," thus affirming the divine creation of both the spiritual and material realms. During the Middle Ages, forms of dualism once more made their appearance, particularly in the views of the Cathari and Albigenses, who taught that matter is evil, and was created *ex nihilo* by the devil. Against such views, the Fourth Lateran Council (1215) and the Council of Florence (1442) taught explicitly that God created a good creation out of nothing.

Implications of the doctrine of creation

The doctrine of God as creator has several major implications, of which several may be noted here.

1 A distinction must be drawn between God and the creation. A major theme of Christian theology from the earliest of times has been to resist the temptation to merge the creator and the creation. The theme is clearly stated in Paul's letter to the Romans, the opening chapter of which criticizes the tendency to reduce God to the level of the world. According to Paul, there is a natural human tendency, as a result of sin, to serve "created things rather than the creator" (Romans 1: 25). A central task of a Christian theology of creation is

to distinguish God from the creation, while at the same time to affirm that it is *God's* creation.

This process may be seen at work in the writings of Augustine; it is of considerable importance in the writings of reformers such as Calvin, who were concerned to forge a world-affirming spirituality in response to the general monastic tendency to renounce the world, evident in writings such as Thomas à Kempis's *Imitation of Christ*, with its characteristic emphasis upon the "contempt of the world." There is a dialectic in Calvin's thought between the world as the creation of God himself, and the world as the fallen creation. In that it is God's creation, it is to be honored, respected, and affirmed; in that it is a fallen creation, it is to be criticized with the object of redeeming it. These two insights could be described as the twin foci of the ellipse of Calvin's world-affirming spirituality. A similar pattern can be discerned in Calvin's doctrine of human nature, where – despite his stress upon the sinful nature of fallen humanity – he never loses sight of the fact that it remains God's creation. Though stained by sin, it remains the creation and possession of God, and is to be valued for that reason. The doctrine of creation thus leads to a critical world-affirming spirituality, in which the world is affirmed, without falling into the snare of treating it as if it were God.

2 Creation implies God's authority over the world. A characteristic biblical emphasis is that the creator has authority over the creation. Humans are thus regarded as part of that creation, with special functions within it. The doctrine of creation leads to the idea of *human stewardship of the creation*, which is to be contrasted with a secular notion of *human ownership of the world*. The creation is not ours; we hold it

in trust for God. We are meant to be the stewards of God's creation, and are responsible for the manner in which we exercise that stewardship. This insight is of major importance in relation to ecological and environmental concerns, in that it provides a theoretical foundation for the exercise of human responsibility toward the planet.

3   The doctrine of God as creator implies the goodness of creation. Throughout the first biblical account of creation, we encounter the affirmation: "And God saw that it was good" (Genesis 1: 10, 18, 21, 25, 31). (The only thing that is "not good" is that Adam is alone. Humanity is created as a social being, and is meant to exist in relation with others.) There is no place in Christian theology for the Gnostic or dualist idea of the world as an inherently evil place. As we noted earlier in this chapter, even though the world is fallen through sin, it remains God's good creation and is capable of being redeemed.

This is not to say that the creation is presently perfect. An essential component of the Christian doctrine of sin is the recognition that the world has departed from the trajectory upon which God placed it in the work of creation. It has become deflected from its intended course. It has fallen from the glory in which it was created. The world as we see it is not the world as it was intended to be. The existence of human sin, evil, and death are themselves tokens of the extent of the departure of the created order from its intended pattern. For this reason, most Christian reflections on redemption include the idea of some kind of restoration of creation to its original integrity, in order that God's intentions for his creation might find fulfillment. Affirming the goodness of creation also avoids the suggestion, unacceptable to most theologians, that God is responsible for evil. The constant biblical emphasis upon the goodness of creation is a reminder that the destructive force of sin is not present in the world by God's design or permission.

4   Creation as recounted in the Book of Genesis implies that human beings are created in the image of God. This insight, central to any Christian doctrine of human nature, will be discussed at greater length later (pp. 360–2); it is, however, of major importance as an aspect of the doctrine of creation itself. "You made us for yourself, and our hearts are restless until they find their rest in you" (Augustine of Hippo). With these words, the importance of the doctrine of creation for a proper understanding of human experience (pp. 149–50), nature, and destiny is established.

Models of God as creator

The manner in which God acts as creator has been the subject of intense discussion within the Christian tradition. A number of models of, or ways of picturing, the manner in which God is to be thought of as creating the world have been developed, each of which casts some light on the complex and rich Christian understanding of the notion of "creation."

Emanation

This term was widely used by early Christian writers to clarify the relation between God and the world. Although the term is not used by either Plato or Plotinus, many patristic writers sympathetic to the various forms of Platonism saw it as a convenient and appropriate way of articulating Platonic insights. The image that dominates this approach is that of light or heat radiating from the sun, or a human source such as a fire. This image of creation (hinted at in the Nicene creed's phrase "light from light") suggests that the creation of the world can be regarded as an overflowing of the creative energy of God. Just as light derives from the sun and reflects its nature, so the created order derives from God, and expresses the divine nature. There is, on the basis of this model, a *natural* or *organic* connection between God and the creation.

However, the model has weaknesses, of which two may be noted. First, the image of a sun radiating light, or a fire radiating heat, implies an involuntary emanation, rather than a conscious decision to create. The Christian tradition has consistently emphasized that the act of creation rests upon a prior decision on the part of God to create, which this model cannot adequately express.

This naturally leads on to the second weakness, which relates to the impersonal nature of the model in question. The idea of a personal God, expressing a personality both in the very act of creation and the subsequent creation itself, is difficult to convey by this image. Nevertheless, the model clearly articulates a close connection between creator and creation, leading us to expect that something of the identity and nature of the creator is to be found in the creation. Thus the beauty of God – a theme which was of particular importance in early medieval theology, and has emerged as significant again in the later writings of Hans Urs von Balthasar – would be expected to be reflected in the nature of the creation.

Construction

Many biblical passages portray God as a master builder, deliberately constructing the world (for example, Psalm 127: 1). The imagery is powerful, conveying the ideas of purpose, planning, and a deliberate intention to create. The image is important, in that it draws attention to both the creator and the creation. In addition to bringing out the skill of the creator, it also allows the beauty and ordering of the resulting creation to be appreciated, both for what it is in itself, and for its testimony to the creativity and care of its creator.

However, the image has a deficiency, which relates to a point made in connection with Plato's dialogue, *Timaeus*. This portrays creation as involving pre-existent matter. Here, creation is understood as giving shape and form to something which is already there – an idea which, we have seen, causes at least a degree of tension with the doctrine of creation *ex nihilo*. The image of God as a builder would seem to imply the assembly of the world from material which is already to hand, which is clearly at odds with the notion of creation out of nothing.

Nevertheless, despite this difficulty, it can be seen that the model expresses the insight that the character of the creator is, in some manner, expressed in the natural world, just as that of artists is communicated or embodied in their work. In particular, the notion of "ordering" – that is, the imparting or imposing of a coherence or structure to the material in question – is clearly affirmed by this model. Whatever else the complex notion of "creation" may mean within a Christian context, it certainly includes the fundamental theme of ordering – a notion which is especially significant in the creation narratives of the Old Testament.

Artistic expression

Many Christian writers, from various periods in the history of the church, speak of creation as the "handiwork of God," comparing it to a work of art which is both beautiful in itself, as well as expressing the personality of its creator. This model of creation as the "artistic expression" of God as creator is particularly well expressed in the writings of the eighteenth-century North American theologian Jonathan Edwards, as we shall see presently.

Same scripture / man's interpretation

The image is profoundly helpful, in that it supplements a deficiency of both the two models noted above – namely, their impersonal character. The image of God as artist conveys the idea of personal expression in the creation of something beautiful. Once more, the potential weaknesses need to be noted; for example, the model could easily lead to the idea of creation from pre-existent matter, as in the case of a sculptor with a statue carved from an already existing block of stone. However, the model offers us at least the possibility of thinking about creation from nothing, as with the author who writes a novel, or the composer who creates a melody and harmony. It also encourages us to seek for the self-expression of God in the creation, and gives added theological credibility to a natural theology (see pp. 164–70). There is also a natural link between the concept of creation as "artistic expression" and the highly significant concept of "beauty."

Creation and Christian approaches to ecology

In the closing decades of the twentieth century there was growing interest in the way in which the world is valued by human beings. Some writers have argued that the exploitative attitude to nature, typical of the twentieth century, is a direct result of the Christian doctrine of creation. An excellent example of this is provided by an influential 1967 essay by historian Lynn White Jr., who argued that the Judeo-Christian idea of humanity having dominion or authority over creation has led to the view that nature exists to serve human needs, thus legitimating a highly exploitative attitude. Christianity, he argued, thus bears a substantial burden of guilt for the modern ecological crisis.

In particular, White argued that Christianity was to blame for the emerging ecological crisis on account of its using the concept of the "image of God," found in the Genesis creation account (Genesis 1: 26–7), as a pretext for justifying human exploitation of the world's resources. The Book of Genesis, he argued, legitimated the notion of human domination over the creation, hence leading to its exploitation. Despite its historical and theological superficiality, the paper had a profound impact on the shaping of popular scientific attitudes towards Christianity in particular, and religion in general.

With the passage of time, a more informed evaluation of White's paper has gained the ascendancy. The argument is now recognized to be seriously flawed. A closer reading of the Genesis text indicated that such themes as "humanity as the steward of creation" and "humanity as the partner of God" are indicated by the text, rather than that of "humanity as the lord of creation." Far from being the enemy of ecology, the doctrine of creation affirms the importance of human responsibility towards the environment.

In a widely read study, *Imaging God, Dominion as Stewardship* (1986), the noted Canadian theologian Douglas John Hall stressed that the biblical concept of "domination" was to be understood specifically in terms of "stewardship," no matter what kind of interpretation might be placed on the word in a secular context. To put it simply: the Old Testament sees creation as the possession of humanity; it is something which is to be seen as entrusted to humanity, who are responsible for its safekeeping and tending. Similar lines of thought can be found in other religions, with discernible differences of emphasis and grounding; the Assisi Declaration (1986) on the ecological importance of religion may be seen as marking the recognition of this significant point.

A doctrine of creation can thus act as the basis for an ecologically sensitive ethic. In an important study dating from the final decade of the twentieth century ("Ecology and Ethics:

Relation of Religious Belief to Ecological Practice in the Biblical Tradition," 1995), Calvin B. DeWitt has argued that four fundamental ecological principles can readily be discerned within the biblical narratives, reflecting the Christian doctrine of creation.

1   The "earthkeeping principle": just as the creator keeps and sustains humanity, so humanity must keep and sustain the creator's creation.
2   The "sabbath principle": the creation must be allowed to recover from human use of its resources.
3   The "fruitfulness principle": the fecundity of the creation is to be enjoyed, not destroyed.
4   The "fulfillment and limits principle": there are limits set to humanity's role within creation, with boundaries set in place which must be respected.

A further contribution has been made by Jürgen Moltmann, noted for his concern to ensure the theologically rigorous application of Christian theology to social, political, and environmental issues. In his 1985 work *God in Creation*, Moltmann argues that the exploitation of the world reflects the rise of technology, and seems to have little to do with specifically Christian teachings. Furthermore, he stresses the manner in which God can be said to indwell the creation through the Holy Spirit, so that the pillage of creation becomes an assault on God. On the basis of this analysis, Moltmann is able to offer a rigorously trinitarian defense of a distinctively Christian ecological ethic.

Theodicies: The Problem of Evil

A major problem which concerns the doctrine of God centers on the existence of evil in the world. How can the presence of evil or suffering be reconciled with the Christian affirmation of the goodness of the God who created the world? In what follows, we shall explore some of the options available within the Christian tradition.

Irenaeus of Lyons

Irenaeus represents a major element within Greek patristic thought, which regards human nature as a potentiality. Humans are created with certain capacities for growth toward maturity. That capacity for Godward growth requires contact with and experience of good and evil if truly informed decisions are to be made. This tradition tends to view the world as a "vale of soul-making" (to use a term taken from the English poet John Keats), in which encounter with evil is seen as a necessary prerequisite for spiritual growth and development.

> God made humanity to be master of the earth and of all which was there. [...] Yet this could only take place when humanity had attained its adult stage. [...] Yet humanity was little, being but a child. It had to grow and reach full maturity. [...] God prepared a place for humanity which was better than this world [...] a paradise of such beauty and goodness that the Word of God constantly walked in it, and talked with humanity; prefiguring that future time when he would live with human beings and talk with them, associating with human beings and teaching them righteousness. But humanity was a child; and its mind was not yet fully mature; and thus humanity was easily led astray by the deceiver.

This view is not developed fully in the writings of Irenaeus. In the modern period, it has found an able exponent in John Hick, who is widely regarded as the most influential and persuasive exponent of such an approach. In his *Evil and the God of Love* (1966) Hick emphasizes that human beings are created incomplete. In order for them to become what God intends them to be, they must participate in the world. God did not create human beings as automatons, but as individuals who are capable of responding freely to God. Unless a real choice is available between good and evil, the biblical injunctions to "choose good" are meaningless. Good and evil are thus necessary presences within the world, in order that informed and meaningful human development may take place.

The argument is obviously attractive, not least on account of its emphasis upon human freedom. It also resonates with the experience of many Christians, who have found that God's grace and love are experienced most profoundly in situations of distress or suffering. However, criticism has been directed against one aspect of this approach in particular. The objection is often raised that it appears to lend dignity to evil, by allocating it a positive role within the purposes of God. If suffering is seen simply as a means of advancing the spiritual development of humanity, what are we to make of those events – such as Hiroshima or Auschwitz – which destroy those who encounter them? This approach, to its critics, seems merely to encourage acquiescence in the presence of evil in the world, without giving any moral direction or stimulus to resist and overcome it.

Augustine of Hippo

The distinctive approach adopted by Augustine has had a major impact upon the western theological tradition. By the fourth century, the problems raised by the existence of evil and suffering had begun to become something of a theological embarrassment. Gnosticism – including its variant form, Manichaeism, with which Augustine became fascinated as a young man – had no difficulty in accounting for the existence of evil. It arose on account of the fundamentally evil nature of matter. The entire purpose of salvation was to redeem humanity from the evil material world, and transfer it to a spiritual realm which was uncontaminated by matter.

As noted earlier, a central aspect of many Gnostic systems was the idea of a demiurge – that is, a demigod who was responsible for forging the world, in its present form, out of pre-existent matter. The sorry state of the world was put down to the inadequacies of this demigod. The redeemer god was thus regarded as being quite distinct from the creator demigod.

Augustine, however, could not accept this approach. It might offer a neat solution to the problem of evil, yet the intellectual price paid was far too high. For Augustine, creation and redemption were the work of one and the same God. It was therefore impossible to ascribe the existence of evil to creation, for this merely transferred blame to God. For Augustine, God created the world good, meaning that it was free from the contamination of evil. So where does evil come from? Augustine's fundamental insight here is that evil is a direct consequence of the misuse of human freedom. God created humanity with the freedom to choose good or evil. Sadly, humanity chose evil; as a result, the world is contaminated by evil.

This, however, did not really resolve the problem, as Augustine himself appreciated. How could humans choose evil, if there was no evil to choose? Evil had to be an option within the world, if it were to be accessible to human choice. Augustine therefore located the origin of evil in satanic temptation, by which Satan lured Adam and Eve away from obedience to their creator. In this way, he argued, God could not be regarded as being responsible for evil.

Still the problem was not resolved. For where did Satan come from, if God created the world good? Augustine traces the origin of evil back by another step. Satan is a fallen angel, who was originally created good, like all the other angels. However, this particular angel was tempted to become like God, and assume supreme authority. As a result, he rebelled against God, and thus spread that rebellion to the world. But how, Augustine's critics asked, could a good angel turn out to be so bad? How are we to account for the original fall of that angel? And there, Augustine appears to have been reduced to silence.

Karl Barth

Thoroughly dissatisfied with existing approaches to evil, Karl Barth called for a complete rethinking of the entire issue. Barth, who was particularly concerned with the Reformed approach to the issue of providence, believed that a central theological flaw had developed in relation to the notion of the omnipotence of God. He argued that the Reformed doctrine of providence had become virtually indistinguishable from that of Stoicism. (In passing, we may note that many scholars of the Reformation make precisely this point in relation to Zwingli's doctrine of providence, which appears to be based upon the Stoic writer Seneca to a far greater extent than upon the New Testament!) For Barth, the notion of the omnipotence of God must always be understood in the light of God's self-revelation in Christ.

On the basis of this principle, Barth argued that there was a need for a "radical rethinking of the whole issue." He suggested that the Reformed doctrine of omnipotence rested largely upon logical deduction from a set of premises about God's power and goodness. Barth, whose theological program is distinguished by its "Christological concentration," argued for a more Christological approach.

Barth thus rejected *a priori* notions of omnipotence, in favor of a belief in the triumph of God's grace over unbelief, evil, and suffering. A confidence in the ultimate triumph of the grace of God enables believers to maintain their morale and hope in the face of a world which is seemingly dominated by evil. Barth himself had Nazi Germany in mind as he developed this notion; his ideas have proved useful elsewhere, and may be argued to be reflected in the theodicies which have been characteristic of liberation theology in more recent years.

Nevertheless, one aspect of Barth's theodicy has caused considerable discussion. Barth describes evil as *das Nichtige* – a mysterious power of "nothingness," which has its grounds in what God did *not* will in the act of creation. "Nothingness" is that which contradicts the will of God. It is not "nothing," but that which threatens to *reduce* to nothing, and thus poses a threat to the purposes of God in the world. For Barth, the ultimate triumph of grace ensures that "nothingness" need not be feared. However, his critics have found the idea of "nothingness" problematic, and have charged him with lapsing into arbitrary metaphysical speculation at a point at which fidelity to the biblical narrative is of central importance.

Alvin Plantinga

The Reformed philosopher Alvin Plantinga often addressed the questions arising from the existence of evil in the world. The "free will defense" offered by Plantinga is deeply rooted in the Christian tradition, and can be summarized in terms of the following points:

1 Free will is morally important. That means that a world in which human beings possess free will is superior to a hypothetical world in which they do not.

2   If human beings were forced to do nothing but good, that would represent a denial of human free will.

3   God must bring into being the best possible world that he is able to do.

4.   It must therefore follow that God must create a world with free will.

5   This means that God is not responsible if human beings choose to do evil, since God is operating under self-imposed constraints that mean God will not compel human beings to do good.

In reviewing this argument, it is important to note how Plantinga insists that we are cautious and responsible about terms such as "omnipotent." To say that God is omnipotent is not, as we saw earlier, to say that "God can do anything." God operates under self-imposed limitations, reflecting God's nature and character. Plantinga brings this point out frequently. For example, in his essay "God, Evil, and the Metaphysics of Freedom," Plantinga argues convincingly that it is possible that God cannot create every logically possible world. If Plantinga's argument has a weak point, it is not to be found in his discussion of God's omnipotence, but in his assertion that a world with freedom is to be preferred to one that is without freedom.

Other recent contributions

The question of suffering remains high on the agenda of modern theology, and has been given a new sense of urgency and importance through the impact of the horrors of World War II, and the continued struggle of oppressed people against those who oppress them. A number of approaches may be noted, each of which can be set against a different backdrop.

1   Liberation theology develops a distinctive approach to suffering, based on its emphasis upon the poor and the oppressed (see pp. 90–1). The suffering of the poor is not viewed as passive acquiescence in suffering; rather, it is seen as participation in the struggle of God against suffering in the world – a struggle which involves direct confrontation with suffering itself. This idea, in various forms, can be discerned in the writings of Latin American liberation theologians.

However, it is generally thought to find its most powerful expression in the writings of Black theology, especially those of James Cone. The sequence of the cross and resurrection is interpreted in terms of a present struggle against evil, conducted in the knowledge of God's final victory over all suffering and that which causes it. Similar themes can be noted in the writings of Martin Luther King, especially his "Death of Evil upon the Seashore."

2   Process theology locates the origins of suffering and evil within the world in a radical limitation upon the power of God (pp. 221–21). God has set aside the ability to coerce, retaining only the ability to persuade. Persuasion is seen as a means of exercising power in such a manner that the rights and freedoms of others are respected. God is obliged to persuade every aspect of the process to act in the best possible manner. There is, however, no guarantee that God's benevolent persuasion will lead to a favorable outcome. The process is under no obligation to obey God.

God intends good for the creation, and acts in its best interests. However, the option of coercing everything to do the divine will cannot be exercised. As a result, God is unable to prevent certain things happening. Wars, famines, and holocausts are not things which God desires; they are, however, not things which

God can prevent, on account of the radical limitations placed upon the divine power. God is thus not responsible for evil; nor can it be said, in any way, that God *desires* or *tacitly accepts* its existence. The metaphysical limits placed upon God are such as to prevent any interference in the natural order of things.

3   A third strand in recent thinking on suffering has drawn upon Old Testament themes. Jewish writers such as Elie Wiesel, retaining at least the vestiges of a belief in the fundamental goodness of God, point to the numerous passages in the Old Testament which *protest* against the presence of evil and suffering in the world. This approach has been picked up by a number of Christian writers, including John Roth, who has named the approach "protest theodicy." The protest in question is seen as part of the faithful and trusting response of a faithful people to their God, in the face of uncertainties and anxieties concerning God's presence and purposes in the world.

The Holy Spirit

The doctrine of the Holy Spirit really deserves a full chapter in its own right. The Holy Spirit has long been the Cinderella of the Trinity. The other two sisters may have gone to the theological ball; the Holy Spirit got left behind every time. But not now. The rise of the charismatic movement (see pp. 81–2) within virtually every mainstream church has ensured that the Holy Spirit figures prominently on the theological agenda. A new experience of the reality and power of the Spirit has had a major impact upon the theological discussion of the person and work of the Holy Spirit.

Models of the Holy Spirit

"God is spirit" (John 4: 24). But what does this tell us about God? The English language uses at least three words – "wind," "breath," and "spirit" – to translate a single Hebrew term, *ruach*. This important Hebrew word has a depth of meaning which is virtually impossible to reproduce in English. *Ruach*, traditionally translated simply as "spirit," is associated with a range of meanings, each of which casts some light on the complex associations of the Christian notion of the Holy Spirit.

Spirit as wind

The Old Testament writers are careful not to identify God with the wind, and thus reduce God to the level of a natural force. Nevertheless, a parallel is drawn between the power of the wind and that of God. To speak of God as spirit is to call to mind the surging energy of the "Lord of Hosts," and remind Israel of the power and dynamism of the God who had called Israel out of Egypt. This image of the spirit as redemptive power is perhaps stated in its most significant form in the account of the exodus from Egypt in which a powerful wind divides the Red Sea (Exodus 14: 21). Here, the idea of *ruach* conveys both the power and the redemptive purpose of God.

The image of the wind also allowed the pluriformity of human experience of God to be accounted for, and visualized in a genuinely helpful manner. The Old Testament writers were conscious of experiencing the presence and activity of God in two quite distinct manners. Sometimes God was experienced as a judge, one who condemned Israel for its waywardness; yet at other times, God is experienced as one who refreshes the chosen people, like water in a dry land. The image of the wind conveyed both these ideas in a powerful manner.

It must be remembered that Israel bordered the Mediterranean Sea to the west and the great deserts to the east. When the wind blew from the east, it was experienced as a mist of fine sand which scorched vegetation and parched the land. Travelers' accounts of these winds speak of their remarkable force and power. Even the light of the sun is obliterated by the sandstorm thrown up by the wind. This wind was seen by the biblical writers as a model for the way in which God demonstrated the finitude and transitoriness of the creation. "The grass withers and the flowers fall, when the breath of the Lord blows on them" (Isaiah 40: 7). Just as the scorching east wind, like the Arabian sirocco, destroyed plants and grass, so God was understood to destroy human pride (see Psalm 103: 15–18; Jeremiah 4: 11). Just as a plant springs up, fresh and green, only to be withered before the blast of the hot desert wind, so human empires rise only to fall before the face of God.

At the time when the prophet Isaiah was writing, Israel was held captive in Babylon. To many, it seemed that the great Babylonian empire was a permanent historical feature, which nothing could change. Yet the transitoriness of human achievements when the "breath of the Lord" blows upon them is asserted by the prophet, as he proclaims the pending destruction of that empire. God alone is permanent, and all else is in a state of flux and change. The grass withers and the flowers fall, but the word of our God stands for ever.

The western winds, however, were totally different. In the winter, the west and southwest winds brought rain to the dry land as they blew in from the sea. In the summer, the western winds did not bring rain, but coolness. The intensity of the desert heat was mitigated through these gentle cooling breezes. And just as this wind brought refreshment, by moistening the dry ground in winter and cooling the heat of the day in summer, so God was understood to refresh human spiritual needs. In a series of powerful images, God is compared by the Old Testament writers to the rain brought by the western wind (Hosea 6: 3), refreshing the land.

Spirit as breath

The idea of spirit is associated with life. When God created Adam, God breathed into him the breath of life, as a result of which he became a living being (Genesis 2: 7). The basic difference between a living and a dead human being is that the former breathes and the latter does not. This led to the idea that life was dependent upon breath. God is the one who breathes the breath of life into empty shells and brings them to life. God brought Adam to life by breathing into him. The famous vision of the valley of the dry bones (Ezekiel 37: 1–14) also illustrates this point: can these dry bones live? The bones only come to life when breath enters into them (Ezekiel 37: 9–10).

The model of God as spirit thus conveys the fundamental insight that God is the one who gives life, even the one who is able to bring the dead back to life. It is thus important to note that *ruach* is often linked with God's work of creation (e.g., Genesis 1: 2; Job 26: 12–13, 33: 4; Psalm 104: 27–31), even if the precise role of the Spirit is left unspecified. There is clearly an association between "spirit" and the giving of life through creation.

Spirit as charism

The technical term "charism" refers to the "filling of an individual with the Spirit of God," by which the person in question is enabled to perform tasks which would otherwise be impossible. The gift of wisdom is often portrayed as a consequence of the endowment of the Spirit (Genesis 41: 38–9; Exodus 28: 3, 35: 31; Deuteronomy 34: 9). At times, the Old Testament attributes gifts of leadership or military prowess to the influence of the Spirit (Judges 14: 6, 19, 15: 14, 19). However, the most pervasive aspect of this feature of the Spirit relates to the question of prophecy.

The Old Testament does not offer much in the way of clarification concerning the manner in which the prophets were inspired, guided, or motivated by the Holy Spirit. In the pre-exilic era, prophecy is often associated with ecstatic experiences of God, linked with wild behavior (1 Samuel 10: 6, 19: 23–4). Nevertheless, the activity of prophecy gradually became associated with the *message* rather than the *behavior* of the prophet. The prophet's credentials rest upon an endowment with the Spirit (Isaiah 61: 1, Ezekiel 2: 1–2; Micah 3: 8; Zechariah 7: 12), which authenticates the prophet's message – a message which is usually described as "the word [*dabhar*] of the Lord."

The debate over the divinity of the Holy Spirit

The early church found itself puzzled by the Spirit and unable to make much in the way of theological sense of this area of doctrine. This is not to say that the Holy Spirit did not play a prominent role in the early church. The second-century writer Montanus, who is known to have been active during the period 135–75, is an example of a theologian operating in the early period of the church who focused on the activity of the Spirit. The leading ideas of Montanus are known chiefly through the writings of his critics, with the result that our understanding of Montanism may be somewhat distorted. However, it is clear that Montanus placed considerable emphasis on the activity of the Holy Spirit in the present, and particularly on the role of the Spirit in relation to

dreams, visions, and prophetic revelations. It is even possible that Montanus may have identified himself with the Holy Spirit, seeing himself as the source of a divine revelation which was not otherwise available. However, the evidence for this assertion is ambiguous.

The relative absence of extensive discussion of the role of the Holy Spirit in the first three centuries reflects the fact that theological debate centered elsewhere. The Greek patristic writers had, in their view, more important things to do than worry about the Spirit, when vital political and Christological debates were raging all around them. This point was made by the fourth-century writer Amphilochius of Iconium, who pointed out that the Arian controversy had first to be resolved before any serious discussion over the status of the Holy Spirit could get under way. The theological development of the early church was generally a response to public debates; once a serious debate got under way, doctrinal clarification was the inevitable outcome.

The debate in question initially centered upon a group of writers known as the *pneumatomachoi* or "opponents of the spirit," led by Eustathius of Sebaste. These writers argued that neither the person nor the works of the Spirit were to be regarded as having the status or nature of a divine person. In response to this, writers such as Athanasius and Basil of Caesarea made an appeal to the formula which had by then become universally accepted for baptism. Since the time of the New Testament (see Matthew 28: 18–20), Christians were baptized in the name of "the Father, Son and Holy Spirit."

Athanasius argued that this had momentous implications for an understanding of the status of the person of the Holy Spirit. In his *Letter to Serapion* Athanasius declared that the baptismal formula clearly pointed to the Spirit sharing the same divinity as the Father and the Son. This argument eventually prevailed.

However, patristic writers were hesitant to speak openly of the Spirit as "God," in that this practice was not sanctioned by Scripture – a point discussed at some length by Basil of Caesarea in his treatise on the Holy Spirit (374–5). Even as late as 380, Gregory of Nazianzus conceded that many Orthodox Christian theologians were uncertain as to whether to treat the Holy Spirit "as an activity, as a creator, or as God."

This caution can be seen in the final statement of the doctrine of the Holy Spirit formulated by a Council meeting at Constantinople in 381. The Spirit was here described, not as "God," but as "the Lord and giver of life, who proceeds from the Father, and is worshiped and glorified with the Father and Son." The language is unequivocal; the Spirit is to be treated as having the same dignity and rank as the Father and Son, even if the term "God" is not to be used explicitly. The precise relation of the Spirit to Father and Son would subsequently become an item of debate in its own right, as the *filioque* controversy indicates (see pp. 268–71).

The following considerations seem to have been of decisive importance in establishing the divinity of the Holy Spirit during the later fourth century. First, as Gregory of Nazianzus stressed, Scripture applied all the titles of God to the Spirit, with the exception of "unbegotten." Gregory drew particular attention to the use of the word "holy" to refer to the Spirit, arguing that this holiness did not result from any external source, but was the direct consequence of the nature of the Spirit. The Spirit was to be considered as the one who sanctifies, rather than the one who requires to be sanctified.

Second, the functions which are specific to the Holy Spirit establish the divinity of the Spirit. Didymus the Blind (died 398) was one of many writers to point out that the Spirit was responsible for the creating, renewing, and sanctification of God's creatures. Yet how could one creature renew or sanctify another creature? Only if the Spirit was divine could sense be made of these functions. If the Holy Spirit performed functions which were specific to God, it must follow that the Holy Spirit shares in the divine nature. This point is stated with particular clarity by Basil of Caesarea:

> All who are in need of sanctification turn to the Spirit; all those seek him who live by virtue, for his breath refreshes them and comes to their aid in the pursuit of their natural and proper end. Capable of perfecting others, the Spirit himself lacks nothing. He is not a being who needs to restore his strength, but himself supplies life. [. . .] Souls in which the Spirit dwells, illuminated by the Spirit, themselves become spiritual and send forth their grace to others. From here comes foreknowledge of the future, understanding of mysteries, apprehension of what is hidden, the sharing of the gifts of grace, heavenly citizenship, a place in the chorus of angels, joy without end, abiding in God, being made like God and – the greatest of them all – being made God.

For Basil, the Spirit makes creatures both to be like God and to be God – and only one who is divine can bring this about.

Third, the reference to the Spirit in the baptismal formula of the church was interpreted as supporting the divinity of the Spirit. Baptism took place in the name of the "Father, Son, and Holy Spirit" (Matthew 28: 18–20). Athanasius and others argued that this formula established the closest of connections between the three members of the Trinity, making it impossible to suggest that the Father and Son shared in the substance of the Godhead, while the Spirit was nothing other than a creature. In a similar way, Basil of Caesarea argued that the baptismal formula clearly implied the inseparability of Father, Son, and Spirit. This verbal association, according to Basil, clearly had considerable theological implications.

The recognition of the full divinity of the Spirit thus took place at a relatively late stage in the development of patristic theology. In terms of the logical advance of doctrines, the following historical sequence can be discerned.

Stage 1   The recognition of the full divinity of Jesus Christ.
Stage 2   The recognition of the full divinity of the Spirit.
Stage 3   The definitive formulation of the doctrine of the Trinity, embedding and clarifying these central insights, and determining their mutual relationship.

This sequential development is acknowledged by Gregory of Nazianzus, who pointed to a gradual progress in clarification and understanding of the mystery of God's revelation in the course of time. It was, he argued, impossible to deal with the question of the divinity of the Spirit until the issue of the divinity of Christ had been settled.

> The Old Testament preached the Father openly and the Son more obscurely. The New Testament revealed the Son, and hinted at the divinity of the Holy Spirit. Now the Spirit dwells in us, and is revealed more clearly to us. It was not proper to preach the Son openly, while the divinity of the Father had not yet been admitted. Nor was it proper to accept the Holy Spirit before [the divinity of] the Son had been acknowledged. [...] Instead, by gradual advances and partial ascents, we should move forward and increase in clarity, so that the light of the Trinity should shine.

Augustine of Hippo: the Spirit as bond of love

One of the most significant contributions to the development of the theology of the Holy Spirit (an area of theology occasionally referred to as *pneumatology*) is due to Augustine. Augustine had become a Christian partly through the influence of Marius Victorinus, who had himself converted to Christianity from a pagan background. Victorinus had a distinct approach to the role of the Spirit, as can be seen from a hymn which he had penned:

> Help us, Holy Spirit, the bond [*copula*] of Father and Son,
> When you rest, you are the Father; when you proceed, the Son;
> In binding all in one, you are the Holy Spirit.

Although the theology of these lines seems modalist (to anticipate a trinitarian heresy we shall explore presently: see pp. 254–5), an idea of considerable importance is nevertheless expressed: that the Spirit is the "bond of the Father and the Son" (*patris et filii copula*).

It is this idea which Augustine would take up and develop with considerable skill in his treatise *On the Trinity*. Augustine insists upon the distinctiveness of the Spirit; nevertheless, despite this distinctive identity, the Spirit is what is common to the Father and Son. The Father is only the Father of the Son, and the Son only the Son of the Father; the Spirit, however, is the Spirit of both Father and Son, binding them together in a bond of love. In his discussion of this point, Augustine concedes that Scripture does not explicitly state that the Holy Spirit is love; however, in that God is love, and the Spirit is God, it seems to follow naturally that the Holy Spirit is love.

> Scripture teaches us that he is the Spirit neither of the Father alone nor of the Son alone, but of both; and this suggests to us the mutual love by which the Father and the Son love one another. [...] Yet Scripture has not said: "the Holy Spirit is love." If it had, much of our inquiry would have been rendered unnecessary. Scripture does indeed say: "God is love"

(1 John 4: 8, 16); and so leaves us to ask whether it is God the Father, or God the Son, or God the Holy Spirit, or God the Trinity itself, who is love.

Augustine's defense of the identification of the Holy Spirit and love is based on a complex argument, which can be set out as follows. We can find authority for calling the Holy Spirit "love" by a careful examination of the apostle John's language (1 John 4: 7, 19). In what follows, we offer a paraphrase of Augustine's argument, keeping many of his original phrases.

> After saying "Beloved, let us love one another, for love is of God," he goes on to add, "and everyone who loves is born of God; he who does not love has not known God, for God is love." This makes it plain that the love which he calls "God" is the same love which he has said to be "*of God.*" Love, then, is God of (or from) God [*Deus ergo ex deo est dilectio*]. But since the Son is begotten from God the Father and the Spirit proceeds from God the Father, we must ask to which of them we should apply this saying that God is love. Only the Father is God without being "of God"; so that the love which is God and "of God" must be either the Son or the Holy Spirit. Now in what follows the writer refers to the love of God – not that by which we love him, but that by which "he loved us, and sent his Son as expiator for our sins" (1 John 4: 10); and on this he bases his exhortation to us to love one another, that so God may dwell in us, since God (as he has said) is love. And there follows at once, designed to express the matter more plainly, the saying: "hereby we know that we dwell in him, and he in us, because he has given us of his Spirit." Thus it is the Holy Spirit, of whom he has given us, who makes us dwell in God, and God in us. But that is the effect of love. The Holy Spirit himself therefore is the God who is love.

This idea of the Spirit as "bond of love" has important implications for Augustine's doctrine of the Trinity and his doctrine of the church. We shall explore the former in the following chapter; the latter merits discussion at this earlier stage.

Augustine regards the Spirit as the bond of unity between Father and Son on the one hand, and between God and believers on the other. The Spirit is a gift, given by God, which unites believers both to God and to other believers. The Holy Spirit forges bonds of unity between believers, upon which the unity of the church ultimately depends. The church is the "temple of the Holy Spirit," within which the Holy Spirit dwells. The same Spirit which binds together the Father and Son in the unity of the Godhead also binds together believers in the unity of the church.

The functions of the Spirit

What does the Holy Spirit do? The Christian tradition has generally understood the work of the Holy Spirit to focus on three broad areas: revelation, salvation, and the Christian life. In what follows, we shall provide a brief indication of the richness of the Christian understanding of the role of the Spirit in each of these three areas.

The illumination of revelation

There has been a widespread recognition of the pivotal role of the Spirit in relation to the making of God known to humanity. Irenaeus wrote of the "Holy Spirit, through whom the prophets prophesied, and our forebears learned of God and the righteous were led in the paths of justice." Similarly, in his 1536 commentary on the gospels, Martin Bucer argues that revelation cannot occur without the assistance of God's Spirit:

Before we believe in God and are inspired by the Holy Spirit, we are unspiritual and for that reason we are completely unable to apprehend anything relating to God. So all the wisdom and righteousness which we possess in the absence of the Holy Spirit are the darkness and shadow of death.

The task of the Holy Spirit is to lead into God's truth; without that Spirit, truth remains elusive.

The role of the Spirit in relation to the most important theological source of the Christian tradition is of particular importance. The doctrine of the "inspiration of Scripture" affirms that the Bible has a God-given authority by virtue of its origins. This doctrine, in various forms, is the common tradition of Christianity, and has its origins in the Bible itself, most notably the affirmation that "every Scripture is God-breathed" (*theopneustos*) (2 Timothy 3: 16).

In Protestant theology, however, the doctrine of the inspiration of Scripture serves an additional purpose – that of insisting on the primacy of Scripture over the church. Whereas more Catholic writers point to the formation of the canon of Scripture as indicating the authority of the church over that of Scripture, Protestant writers argue that the church merely recognized an authority which was already present within Scripture itself. The Gallic Confession (1559) illustrates this point well.

We know these books to be canonical, and the sure rule of our faith, not so much by the common accord and consent of the Church, as by the testimony and inward persuasion of the Holy Spirit, which enables us to distinguish them from other ecclesiastical books which, however useful, can never become the basis for any articles of faith.

Yet it is not simply God's revelation which is linked with the work of the Spirit; the Spirit is also widely regarded as being involved in the human response to that revelation. Most Christian theologians have regarded faith itself as the result of the work of the Holy Spirit. John Calvin is one writer who draws attention to the pivotal role of the Spirit in revealing God's truth and applying or "sealing" this truth to humanity.

Now we shall have a right definition of faith if we say that it is a steady and certain knowledge of the divine benevolence towards us, which is founded upon the truth of the gracious promise of God in Christ, and is both revealed to our minds and sealed in our hearts by the Holy Spirit.

The appropriation of salvation

We have already noted how patristic writers justified the divinity of the Spirit with reference to the functions of the Spirit. Many of those functions relate directly to the doctrine of salvation; for example, the role of the Spirit in sanctification, making humanity like God, and divinization. This point is particularly important within the eastern Christian churches, with their traditional emphasis on deification; the western concept of salvation, which tends to be relational rather than ontological, nevertheless finds room for a role for the Spirit. Thus in Calvin's doctrine of the application of salvation, the Holy Spirit plays a major role in relation to the establishment of a living relationship between Christ and believer.

The energization of the Christian life

For many writers, the Holy Spirit plays an especially important role in relation to the Christian life, both the individual and the corporate life. The fifth-century writer Cyril of Alexandria is one of many to stress the role of the Spirit in bringing unity within the church.

All of us who have received the one and the same Spirit, that is, the Holy Spirit, are in a sense merged together with one another and with God. [. . .] Just as the power of the holy flesh of Christ united those in whom it dwells into one body, I think that, in much the same way, the one and undivided Spirit of God, who dwells in us all, leads us all into spiritual unity.

However, any properly Christian understanding of the role of the Spirit will go far beyond this, and will include reference to at least two other areas. First, the "making real" of God in personal and corporate worship and devotion. The importance of the role of the Spirit in relation to Christian prayer, spirituality, and worship has been stressed by many writers, classic and modern. Second, the enabling of believers to lead a Christian life, particularly in relation to morality. In his 1536 gospels commentary, Martin Bucer draws attention to the necessity of the Spirit, if believers are to keep the law.

So those who believe are not under the law, because they have the Spirit within them, teaching them everything more perfectly than the law ever could, and motivating them much more powerfully to obey it. In other words, the Holy Spirit moves the heart, so that believers wish to live by those things which the law commands, but which the law could not achieve by itself.

Having discussed the doctrine of God in general, our attention now turns to the more complex area of the doctrine of the Trinity, which seeks to give expression to a sequence of distinctively Christian insights concerning God.

QUESTIONS FOR CHAPTER 9

1 "God reveals himself as Lord" (Karl Barth). What difficulties does this statement raise by its use of masculine language in relation to God?

2 Many Christians talk about having a "personal relationship" with God. What might they mean by this? What theological insights does this way of speaking offer?

3 "God can do anything." How would you respond to this definition of divine omnipotence?

4 Why do so many Christians believe that God suffers? What difference does it make?

5 Summarize and evaluate the main ways of thinking of God as the creator of the world.

6 What is distinctive about the Holy Spirit?

10

The Doctrine of the Trinity

The doctrine of the Trinity is one of the most difficult aspects of Christian theology. Many who are new to the study of theology find the doctrine perplexing. Some hold back from studying it seriously, believing that such study will persuade them that it is a piece of logical nonsense. Others are apprehensive about the Islamic critique of the doctrine, which treats it as tantamount to tritheism. For a monotheistic religion to believe in three gods is both blasphemous and nonsensical, according to some Islamic critics of Christianity.

This chapter sets out to introduce this difficult yet immensely important doctrine, explaining carefully why it is such a fundamental aspect of the Christian vision of God. Because of the difficulty of the idea, we will spend more time examining its foundations and origins than normal. By the end of this discussion, you will hopefully feel much more confident about this doctrine, both in terms of why Christians believe it, and the various ways they have developed for explaining it.

The Origins of the Christian Doctrine of the Trinity

How, many wonder, did the Christian church come to regard such a counter-intuitive notion as the Trinity as fundamental to its vision of God? We may begin by considering some expressions of anxiety about the doctrine, and then move on to consider how these can be met.

The apparent illogicality of the doctrine

Thomas Jefferson (1743–1826), the third president of the United States, was one of the leading critics of orthodox Christian theology in the early nineteenth century. He reserved his most ferocious criticisms for the doctrine of the Trinity. These "metaphysical insanities" hindered the religious growth of humanity and represented "relapses into polytheism, differing from paganism only by being more

243

unintelligible." Many will smile at the criticism, while sharing the concern. Is there not a serious cause for concern here? How can we talk about "a triune God" or the "three-in-one" without talking mathematical and metaphysical nonsense?

The fundamental problem here is the inability of human language to do justice to the transcendent. Human language finds itself pressed to its limits when trying to depict and describe the divine. Words and images are borrowed from everyday life, and put to new uses in an attempt to capture and preserve precious insights into the nature of God. The Christian understanding of both the divine and human natures is such that – if it is right – we are unable to grasp the full reality of God. Can the human mind ever hope to comprehend something which must ultimately lie beyond its ability to enfold?

When I began to study theology at Oxford back in the 1970s, I was taught early medieval theology by a Jesuit scholar at Campion Hall. As we walked to his room together, we passed a large painting, depicting an old man in conversation with a young boy by the seashore. What was it, I asked? And so I was told the famous story about Augustine of Hippo (354–430), who is particularly noted for his massive treatise *de Trinitate*, dealing with the mystery of the Trinity. Perhaps in the midst of composing this treatise, I was told, Augustine found himself pacing the Mediterranean shoreline of his native North Africa, not far from the great city of Carthage. Not for the first time, a theologian found his language and imagery challenged to the utmost, and his intellectual resources exhausted, in his attempt to put into words the greater reality of God. While wandering across the sand, he noticed a small boy scooping seawater into his hands, and pouring as much as his small hands could hold into a hole he had earlier hollowed in the sand. Puzzled,

Augustine watched as the lad repeated his action again and again.

Eventually, his curiosity got the better of him. What, he asked the boy, did he think he was doing? The reply probably perplexed him still further. The youth was in the process of emptying the ocean into the small cavity he had scooped out in the hot sand. Augustine was dismissive: how could such a vast body of water be contained in such a small hole? The boy was equally dismissive in return: how could Augustine expect to contain the vast mystery of God in the mere words of a book?

The story illuminates one of the central themes of Christian theology and spirituality alike – that there are limits placed upon the human ability to grasp the things of God. Our knowledge of God is accommodated to our capacity. As writers from Augustine to Calvin argued, God is perfectly aware of the limitations placed upon human nature – which, after all, is itself a divine creation. Knowing our limits, such writers argued, God both discloses divine truths and enters into our world in forms that are tempered to our limited abilities and competencies.

For Augustine, the point was simple: if you can get your mind around it, it cannot be God. *Si comprehendis non est Deum.* Our thoughts about God are bound to seem illogical and muddled, precisely because what they refer to lies beyond our full knowledge and understanding. Traditionally, Christian theology has been well aware of its limits, and has sought to avoid excessively confident affirmations in the face of mystery. Yet at the same time, Christian theology has never seen itself as totally reduced to silence in the face of divine mysteries. Nor has it prohibited intellectual wrestling with "mysteries" as destructive or detrimental to faith. As the nineteenth-century Anglican theologian Charles Gore rightly insisted:

Human language never can express adequately divine realities. A constant tendency to apologize for human speech, a great element of agnosticism, an awful sense of unfathomed depths beyond the little that is made known, is always present to the mind of theologians who know what they are about, in conceiving or expressing God. "We see", says St Paul, "in a mirror, in terms of a riddle"; "we know in part". "We are compelled", complains St Hilary, "to attempt what is unattainable, to climb where we cannot reach, to speak what we cannot utter; instead of the mere adoration of faith, we are compelled to entrust the deep things of religion to the perils of human expression".

A perfectly good definition of Christian theology is "taking rational trouble over a mystery" – recognizing that there may be limits to what can be achieved, but believing that this intellectual grappling is both worthwhile and necessary. It just means being confronted with something so great that we cannot fully comprehend it, and so must do the best that we can with the analytical and descriptive tools at our disposal.

The Trinity as a statement about Jesus Christ

The distinctively Christian doctrine of God took shape in response to a question about the identity of Jesus Christ. The development of the doctrine of the Trinity is best seen as organically related to the evolution of Christology (see pp. 16–17, 273–90). As we noted earlier, a patristic consensus emerged that Jesus was "of the same substance" (*homoousios*) as God, rather than just being "of similar substance" (*homoiousios*). But if Jesus was God, in any meaningful sense of the word, what did this imply about existing notions of God? If Jesus was God, were there now two Gods? Or was a radical reconsideration of the nature of God

appropriate? Historically, it is possible to argue that the doctrine of the Trinity is closely linked with the development of the doctrine of the divinity of Christ. The more emphatic the church became that Christ was God, the more it came under pressure to clarify how Christ related to God. "If the Word had not been made flesh, there would have been no stumbling block for Jewish monotheism" (A. W. Wainwright).

This point was explored in some detail in an important work of English theology, dating from the final decade of the nineteenth century. In his 1894 Bampton Lectures at Oxford University – traditionally a showcase for English theology – John Richardson Illingworth (1848–1915) dealt with the theme of divine "personality." Illingworth made two fundamental points, which may serve us well as we begin to consider the pressures leading to the formulation of the doctrine of the Trinity. First, Illingworth stresses that the doctrine of the Trinity can be seen to have sprung from reflection on the identity of Jesus Christ, especially the doctrine of the incarnation:

> Belief in the Incarnation, while it intensified and emphasized the notion of divine personality, necessitated a further intellectual analysis of what that notion meant, and issued in the doctrine of the Trinity in Unity – a doctrine which, plainly implied, as we believe it to be, in the New Testament and earlier Fathers of the church, did not attain its finally explicit formulation till the fourth century.

The Trinity as a statement about the Christian God

In the previous section, we noted how the English theologian J. R. Illingworth pointed out how the doctrine of the Trinity arose from the distinctively Christian understanding of the identity of Jesus Christ. The incarnation – a concept we shall examine in much greater depth in chapter 11 – is not simply about the identity of Jesus of Nazareth. It is about the distinctive nature and character of the God who became incarnate in Jesus of Nazareth. For this reason, the doctrine of the Trinity can be seen as an attempt to represent a God who, while remaining transcendent, yet became incarnate in Christ – and, more than that, now indwells believers in the Holy Spirit.

So who is this God? The second major point that Illingworth makes is that the doctrine of the Trinity arises from the Christian insight that God is *personal* - an idea we explored earlier (pp. 205–8). Illingworth argues that the doctrine of the Trinity results from an exploration of the implications of belief in a personal concept of God, For Illingworth, the Christian understanding of a personal God is radically different from the impersonal conceptions of God which are found in many philosophical systems – such as those of Aristotle and Spinoza:

> The doctrine of the Trinity, as dogmatically elaborated, is, in fact, the most philosophical attempt to conceive of God as Personal. Not that it arose from any mere process of thinking. [. . .] It was suggested by the Incarnation, considered as a new revelation about God, and thought out upon the lines indicated in the New Testament. Upon this the evidence of the Fathers is plain. They felt that they were in the presence of a fact which, so far from being the creation of any theory of the day, was a mystery – a thing which could be apprehended when revealed, but which could neither be comprehended nor discovered.

Or, to put this another way, the proper subject matter of the doctrine of the Trinity is the encounter between divine and human persons in the economy of salvation. The basic Christian assertion that God is personal, which is deeply grounded both in the biblical witness to

God and the Christian experience of God in prayer and worship, is thus implicitly trinitarian.

The starting point for Christian reflections on the Trinity is, as we have seen, the New Testament witness to the presence and activity of God in Christ and through the Spirit. For Irenaeus, the whole process of salvation, from its beginning to its end, bore witness to the action of Father, Son, and Holy Spirit. Irenaeus made use of a term which featured prominently in future discussion of the Trinity: "the economy of salvation." The term "economy" needs clarification. The Greek word *oikonomia* basically means "the way in which one's affairs are ordered" (the relation to the modern sense of the word will thus be clear). For Irenaeus, "the economy of salvation" meant "the way in which God has ordered the salvation of humanity in history."

At the time, Irenaeus was under considerable pressure from Gnostic critics, who argued that the creator God was quite distinct from (and inferior to) the redeemer God (see pp. 224–7). In the version favored by Marcion, this idea took the following form: the Old Testament God is a creator God, and totally different from the redeemer God of the New Testament. As a result, the Old Testament should be shunned by Christians, who should concentrate their attention upon the New Testament. Irenaeus vigorously rejected this idea. He insisted that the entire process of salvation, from the first moment of creation to the last moment of history, was the work of the one and the same God. There was a single economy of salvation, in which the one God – who was both creator and redeemer – was at work to redeem the creation.

In his *Demonstration of the Apostolic Preaching*, Irenaeus insisted upon the distinct yet related roles of Father, Son, and Spirit within the economy of salvation. He affirmed his faith in

God the Father uncreated, who is uncontained, invisible, one God, creator of the universe; this is the first article of our faith. [. . .] And the Word *of God*, the Son of God, our Lord Jesus Christ, [. . .] who, in the fullness of time, in order to gather all things to himself, he became a human being amongst human beings, capable of being seen and touched, to destroy death, bring life, and restore fellowship between God and humanity. And the Holy *Spirit* [. . .] who, in the fullness of time, was poured out in a new way on our human nature in order to renew humanity throughout the entire world in the sight of God.

This passage brings out clearly the idea of an economic Trinity – that is to say, an understanding of the nature of the Godhead in which each person is responsible for an aspect of the economy of salvation. Far from being a rather pointless piece of theological speculation, the doctrine of the Trinity is grounded directly in the complex human experience of redemption in Christ, and is concerned with the explanation of this experience.

Islamic critiques of the doctrine of the Trinity

The three great monotheistic faiths of the world – Christianity, Judaism and Islam – share a belief that there is only one supreme being, the Lord and creator of the universe. This is often summarized in an Old Testament verse, known as the *Shema*: "Hear, O Israel, the Lord your God is one Lord" (Deuteronomy 6: 4). Islamic critics of Christianity regularly criticize Christians for apparently deviating from this emphasis upon the unity of God (often referred to by the Arabic word *tawhid*) through the doctrine of the Trinity. This doctrine is argued to be a late invention, which distorts the idea of the unity of God, and ends up teaching that there are three gods.

The witness of the Qu'ran to what Mohammed thought that Christians believe is not

quite as clear as might be hoped for, and has led some interpreters of Islam to suggest that it believes that Christians worship a trinity consisting of God, Jesus, and Mary (*The Qu'ran*, 5: 116). Although there are reasons for suspecting that Mohammed may have encountered heterodox forms of Christian belief in Arabia, including unorthodox statements of the trinity, it seems more likely that the doctrine has simply been misunderstood as implying that Christians either worship three gods, or that they worship a single God with three component parts.

From what has been said thus far, it can be seen that this concern rests on a misunderstanding. Christians believe in one God, and one God only – but a God whose revelation discloses this God to have a certain specific character and nature, which Christian theology has believed must be faithfully reflected and represented, even if this seems counterintuitive. Far from teaching that there are three gods – whether God, Jesus, and Mary, or any others – Christianity proclaims that there is only one God, who became incarnate in Christ. Historically, the starting point for Christian reflection on the doctrine of God has been the divinity of Christ – something that Islam decisively rejects.

For Christians, God is known fully and directly through Christ. Where Islam holds that one may know the will of God but not the face of God, Christianity holds that both have been fully and definitively revealed in Jesus Christ. Mohammed is seen as one who wrote down the revelation entrusted to him by the angel Gabriel; Jesus is one who was himself the definitive revelation of God. Classic Christian theology holds that, as God incarnate, Jesus reveals God and makes restoration to him possible through his saving death and resurrection. Underlying the Islamic criticism of the doctrine of the Trinity is a more fundamental concern about the identity of Jesus Christ himself. For Islam, Jesus is a prophet – and not God incarnate.

Having established the divinity of Christ, Christian theology then asks: what sort of God is made known and available in this way? How are we to think about God, to do justice to the self-revelation of God as the one who created humanity and the world, who redeemed us in Jesus Christ, and is present now in the world through the Holy Spirit? The doctrine of the Trinity has never been seen as compromising or contradicting the unity of God. The Trinity, to put it as simply as possible, is ultimately the distillation and correlation of the Christian tradition's immensely rich teaching about the nature of God.

In view of the importance of this aspect of the doctrine of the Trinity, we shall move on immediately to consider its foundations in the Bible, before exploring its development within the long tradition of Christian reflection on the biblical witness to the identity and actions of God.

The Biblical Foundations of the Doctrine of the Trinity

The casual reader of Scripture will discern a mere two verses in the entire Bible which seem, at first glance, to be capable of a trinitarian interpretation: Matthew 28: 19 ("Go therefore and make disciples of all nations, baptizing them in the name of the Father and of the Son and of the Holy Spirit") and 2 Corinthians 13: 13 ("The grace of the Lord Jesus Christ, the love of God, and the communion of the Holy Spirit be with all of you"). Both these verses have become deeply rooted in the Christian consciousness, the former on account of its baptismal associations, and the latter through the common use of the formula in Christian prayer and devotion. Yet these two verses,

taken together or in isolation, can hardly be thought of as constituting a doctrine of the Trinity.

Happily, the ultimate grounds of the doctrine are not to be sought exclusively in these two verses. Rather, the foundations of the doctrine of the Trinity are to be found in the pervasive pattern of divine activity to which the New Testament bears witness. The Father is revealed in Christ through the Spirit. There is the closest of connections between the Father, Son, and Spirit in the New Testament writings. Time after time, New Testament passages link together these three elements as part of a greater whole. The totality of God's saving presence and power can only, it would seem, be expressed by involving all three elements (for example, see 1 Corinthians 12: 4–6; 2 Corinthians 1: 21–2; Galatians 4: 6; Ephesians 2: 20–2; 2 Thessalonians 2: 13–14; Titus 3: 4–6; 1 Peter 1: 2).

The same trinitarian structure can be seen in the Old Testament. Three major "personifications" of God can be discerned within its pages, which naturally lead on to the Christian doctrine of the Trinity. These are:

1 *Wisdom*: This personification of God is especially evident in the Wisdom literature, such as Proverbs, Job, and Ecclesiastes. The attribute of divine wisdom is here treated as if it were a person (hence the idea of "personification"), with an existence apart from, yet dependent upon, God. Wisdom (who is always treated as female, incidentally) is portrayed as active in creation, fashioning the world in her imprint (see Proverbs 1: 20–3, 9: 1–6; Job 28; Ecclesiastes 2: 12–17).

2 *The Word of God*: Here, the idea of God's speech or discourse is treated as an entity with an existence independent of God, yet originating with God. The Word of God is portrayed as going forth into the world to

confront men and women with the will and purpose of God, bringing guidance, judgment, and salvation (see Psalm 119: 89, 147: 15–20; Isaiah 55: 10–11).

3 *The Spirit of God*: The Old Testament uses the phrase "the spirit of God" to refer to God's presence and power within the creation. The spirit is portrayed as being present in the expected Messiah (Isaiah 42: 1–3), and as being the agent of a new creation which will arise when the old order has finally passed away (Ezekiel 36: 26, 37: 1–14).

These three "hypostatizations" of God (to use a Greek word in place of the English "personification") do not amount to a doctrine of the Trinity in the strict sense of the term. Rather, they point to a pattern of divine activity and presence in and through creation, in which God is both immanent and transcendent. A purely unitarian conception of God proved inadequate to contain this dynamic understanding of God. And it is this pattern of divine activity which is expressed in the doctrine of the Trinity.

The doctrine of the Trinity can be regarded as the outcome of a process of sustained and critical reflection on the pattern of divine activity revealed in Scripture, and continued in Christian experience. This is not to say that Scripture contains a doctrine of the Trinity; rather, Scripture bears witness to a God who demands to be understood in a trinitarian manner. We shall explore the evolution of the doctrine and its distinctive vocabulary in what follows.

The Historical Development of the Doctrine

It is important to appreciate that neither the developed trinitarian vocabulary or the specific concepts developed by Christian theo-

logians to express the Christian vision of God are explicitly stated in the New Testament. Some radical Christian writers of the sixteenth century argued that, since the doctrine was not explicitly set out in the Bible, it was not a biblical idea. Michael Servetus's *On the Errors of the Trinity* (1531) takes this line. It is therefore important to trace the development of the doctrine as the early church realized the implications of its vision of God, and sought to make explicit some of its implicit ideas. We may begin by considering the emergence of the vocabulary of the Trinity.

The emergence of the trinitarian vocabulary

The vocabulary associated with the doctrine of the Trinity is unquestionably one of the biggest difficulties to students. The phrase "three persons, one substance" is not exactly illuminating, to say the least. However, understanding how the terms came to emerge is perhaps the most effective way of appreciating their meaning and importance.

The theologian who may be argued to be responsible for the development of the distinctive trinitarian terminology is Tertullian. According to one analysis, Tertullian was responsible for coining 509 new nouns, 284 new adjectives, and 161 new verbs in the Latin language. Happily, not all seem to have caught on. It is thus hardly surprising that a shower of new words resulted when he turned his attention to the doctrine of the Trinity. Three of these are of particular importance.

Trinitas

Tertullian invented the word "Trinity" (Latin: *Trinitas*), which has become so characteristic a feature of Christian theology since his time. Although other possibilities had been explored, Tertullian's influence was such that this term became normative within the western church.

Persona

Tertullian introduced this Latin term to translate the Greek word *hypostasis*, which had begun to gain acceptance in the Greek-speaking church. Scholars have debated at length over what Tertullian meant by this Latin term, which is invariably translated into English as "person" (on which see pp. 206–7). The following explanation commands a wide degree of assent, and casts some light on the complexities of the Trinity.

The term *persona* literally means "a mask," such as that worn by an actor in a Roman drama. At this time, actors wore masks to allow the audiences to understand which of the different characters in the drama they were playing. The term *persona* thus came to have a developed meaning, along the lines of "the role that someone is playing." It is quite possible that Tertullian wanted his readers to understand the idea of "one substance, three persons" to mean that the one God played three distinct yet related roles in the great drama of human redemption.

Behind the plurality of roles lay a single actor. The complexity of the process of creation and redemption did not imply that there were many gods; simply that there was one God, who acted in a multiplicity of manners within the "economy of salvation" (a term which will be explained in more detail in the following section).

Substantia

Tertullian introduced this term to express the idea of a fundamental unity within the Godhead, despite the inherent complexity of the revelation of God within history. "Substance" is what the three persons of the Trinity have in common. It must not be thought of as something which exists independently of the three persons; rather, it expresses their common foundational unity, despite their outward appearance of diversity.

The emergence of trinitarian concepts

Tertullian did more than give the theology of the Trinity its distinctive vocabulary (see above); he also made significant contributions to shaping its distinctive form. God is one; nevertheless, God cannot be regarded as something or someone totally isolated from the created order. The economy of salvation demonstrates that God is active in creation. This activity is complex; on analysis, this divine action reveals both a *unity* and a *distinctiveness*. Tertullian argues that *substance* is what unites the three aspects of the economy of salvation; *person* is what distinguishes them. The three persons of the Trinity are distinct, yet not divided (*distincti non divisi*), different yet not separate or independent of each other (*discreti non separati*). The complexity of the human experience of redemption is thus the result of the three persons of the Godhead acting in distinct yet coordinated manners in human history, without any loss of the total unity of the Godhead.

By the second half of the fourth century, the debate concerning the relation of the Father and the Son gave every indication of having been settled. The recognition that Father and Son were "of one being" settled the Arian controversy, and established a consensus within the church over the divinity of the Son. But further theological construction was necessary. What was the relation of the Spirit to the Father? And to the Son? There was a growing consensus that the Spirit could not be omitted from the Godhead. The Cappadocian fathers, especially Basil of Caesarea, defended the divinity of the Spirit in such persuasive terms that the foundation was laid for the final element of trinitarian theology to be put in its place. The divinity and coequality of

Father, Son, and Spirit had been agreed; it now remained to develop trinitarian models to allow this understanding of the Godhead to be visualized.

In general, eastern theology tended to emphasize the distinct individuality of the three persons or *hypostases*, and to safeguard their unity by stressing the fact that both the Son and the Spirit derived from the Father. The relation between the persons or *hypostases* is ontological, grounded in what those persons are. Thus the relation of the Son to the Father is defined in terms of "being begotten" and "sonship." As we shall see, Augustine moves away from this approach, preferring to treat the persons in relational terms. We shall return to these points shortly, in discussing the *filioque* controversy (see pp. 268–71).

The western approach, however, was more marked by its tendency to begin from the unity of God, especially in the work of revelation and redemption, and to interpret the relation of the three persons in terms of their mutual fellowship. It is this position which is characteristic of Augustine, and which we shall explore later (see pp. 258–60).

The eastern approach might seem to suggest that the Trinity consists of three independent agents, doing quite different things. This possibility was excluded by two later developments, which are usually referred to by the terms "mutual interpenetration" (*perichoresis*) and "appropriation." Although these ideas find their full development at a later stage in the development of the doctrine, they are unquestionably hinted at by both Irenaeus and Tertullian, and find more substantial expression in the writings of Gregory of Nyssa. We may usefully consider both these ideas at this stage.

Perichoresis

This Greek term, which is often found in either its Latin (*circumincessio*) or English ("mutual

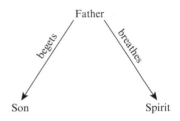

Figure 1 The eastern apporach to the Trinity

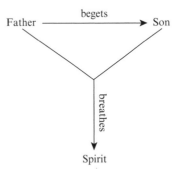

Figure 2 The western approach to the Trinity

interpenetration") translations, came into general use in the sixth century. It refers to the manner in which the three persons of the Trinity relate to one another. The concept of *perichoresis* allows the individuality of the persons to be maintained, while insisting that each person shares in the life of the other two. An image often used to express this idea is that of "a community of being," in which each person, while maintaining its distinctive identity, penetrates the others and is penetrated by them.

This notion has important implications for Christian political thought, as Leonardo Boff (see pp. 90–1) and other theologians concerned with political theology have made clear. The mutual relationships among three coequal persons within the Godhead have been argued to provide a model both for human relationships within communities and for Christian political and social theorizing. Our attention now turns to a related idea of importance in this connection.

Appropriation

This second idea is related to *perichoresis* and follows on from it. The modalist heresy (see pp. 254–5) argued that God could be considered as existing in different "modes of being" at different points in the economy of salvation, so that, at one point, God existed as Father and created the world; at another, God existed as Son and redeemed it. The doctrine of appropriation insists that the works of the Trinity are a unity; every person of the Trinity is involved in every outward action of the Godhead. Thus Father, Son, and Spirit are all involved in the work of creation, which is not to be viewed as the work of the Father alone. For example, Augustine of Hippo pointed out that the Genesis creation account speaks of God, the Word, and the Spirit (Genesis 1: 1–3), thus indicating that all three persons of the Trinity were present and active at this decisive moment in salvation history.

Yet it is *appropriate* to think of creation as the work of the Father. Despite the fact that all three persons of the Trinity are implicated in creation, it is properly seen as the distinctive action of the Father. Similarly, the entire Trinity is involved in the work of redemption (although, as we shall see later, a number of theories of salvation, or *soteriologies*, ignore this trinitarian dimension of the cross, and are impoverished as a result). It is, however, *appropriate* to speak of redemption as being the distinctive work of the Son.

Taken together, the doctrines of *perichoresis* and appropriation allow us to think of the Godhead as a "community of being," in which all is shared, united, and mutually exchanged. But how could these difficult ideas be expressed? And, more importantly, how could they be communicated to ordinary Christians?

One of the most influential answers was given by the great Methodist writer Charles Wesley (1707–88): through hymns. For Wesley, hymns were not merely a means of praising God; they were an instrument of theological education. In 1746, Wesley published a collection of 24 short hymns concerning the Trinity. Individually and collectively, they manage to communicate and explain the two trinitarian notions we have just been considering without technical language or theological fuss. Here, for example, is the concept of appropriation, applied to redemption:

Father of Mankind be ever adorn'd:
Thy Mercy we find, In sending our Lord,
To ransom and bless us; Thy Goodness we praise,
For sending in Jesus, Salvation by Grace.

O Son of His Love, Who deignest to die,
Our Curse to remove, Our Pardon to buy;
Accept our Thanksgiving, Almighty to save,
Who openest Heaven, To all that believe.

O Spirit of Love, of Health, and of Power,
Thy working we prove; Thy Grace we adore,
Whose inward Revealing applies our Lord's Blood,
Attesting and sealing us Children of God.

The problem of visualization: analogies of the Trinity

As noted earlier, the doctrine of the Trinity is not without its difficulties. The real difficulty for most people lies in the *visualization* of the Trinity. How can we make sense of such a complex and abstract idea? St Patrick, the patron saint of Ireland, is rumored to have used the leaf of a shamrock to illustrate how a single leaf could have three different elements. Gregory of Nyssa uses a series of analogies in his letters to help his readers grasp the reality of the Trinity, including:

1   The analogy of a spring, fount and stream of water. The one flows from the other and they share the same substance – water. Although different aspects of the stream of water may be *distinguished*, they cannot be *separated*.

2   The analogy of a chain. There are many links in a chain; yet to be connected to one is to be connected to all of them. In the same way, Gregory argues, someone who encounters the Holy Spirit also encounters the Father and the Son.

3   The analogy of a rainbow. Drawing on the Nicene statement that Christ is "light from light," Gregory argues that the rainbow allows us to distinguish and appreciate the different colors of a sunbeam. There is only one beam of light, yet the colors blend seamlessly into one another.

Useful though these patristic analogies may be, they do not really solve the problem

"Economic" and "essential" approaches to the Trinity

Father, Son, and Spirit are not three isolated and diverging compartments of a Godhead, like three subsidiary components of an international corporation. Rather, they are differentiations within the Godhead, which become evident within the economy of salvation and the human experience of redemption and grace. The doctrine of the Trinity affirms that, beneath the surface of the complexities of the history of salvation and our experience of God, lies one God and one God only.

One of the most sophisticated statements of these points was made by Karl Rahner, in his treatise *The Trinity* (1970). Rahner's discussion of the doctrine of the Trinity is one of the most interesting aspects of his thought. Sadly, however, it is also one of the most difficult aspects of the thought of a writer not noted for his clarity of expression. (The story is told of the American theologian who expressed his delight to a German colleague over the way in which Rahner's German writings were becoming available in English. "It's just great the way Rahner's being translated into English." His colleague laughed bitterly, and replied: "We're still waiting for someone to translate him into German.")

One of the central features of Rahner's discussion concerns the relation of the "economic" and "essential" (or "immanent") Trinities. These do not constitute two different Godheads; rather, they are two different manners of approaching the same Godhead. The "essential" or "immanent" Trinity can be regarded as an attempt to formulate the Godhead outside the limiting conditions of time and space; the "economic Trinity" is the manner in which the Trinity is made known within the "economy of salvation," that is to say, in the historical process itself. Rahner lays down the following axiom (p. 262): "The economic Trinity is the immanent Trinity, and vice versa." In other words:

1   The God who is known in the economy of salvation corresponds to the way in which God actually is. They are the same God. God's self-communication takes on a threefold form because God is essentially threefold. God's self-revelation corresponds to God's essential nature.

2   Human experience of God's action in the economy of salvation is also experience of God's inner history and immanent life. There is only one network of divine relationships; that network exists in two distinct forms, one eternal, and the other historical. One is above history; the other is shaped and conditioned by the limiting factors of history.

It will be clear that this approach (which summarized a broad consensus within Christian theology) ties up some loose ends left by the notion of "appropriation," and allows a rigorous correlation between God's self-disclosure in history, and God's eternal being.

Two Trinitarian Heresies

In an earlier section we introduced the idea of heresy, making the point that the term is best understood as *an inadequate version of Christianity*. In an area of theology as complex as that of the doctrine of the Trinity, it is hardly surprising that a variety of ways of approaching the subject should have developed. Nor should it be cause for surprise that some of them turned out, on closer inspection, to be seriously inadequate. The two heresies which are to be discussed in what follows are the most important for the student of theology.

Modalism: chronological and functional

The term "modalism" was introduced by the German historian of dogma, Adolf von Harnack, to describe the common element of a group of trinitarian heresies, associated with Noetus and Praxeas in the late second century, and Sabellius in the third. Each of these writers was concerned to safeguard the unity of the Godhead, fearing a lapse into some form of tritheism as a result of the doctrine of the Trinity. (As will become clear, this fear was often amply justified.)

This vigorous defense of the absolute unity of God (often referred to as "monarchianism," from the Greek word *monarchia*, meaning "a single principle of authority") led these writers to insist that the self-revelation of the one and only God took place in different ways at different times. The divinity of Christ and the Holy Spirit is to be explained in terms of three different ways or "modes" of divine self-revelation (hence the term "modalism").

Although there are various forms of "modalism," they generally work with much the same understandings of the dynamics of the Trinity:

1   The one God is revealed in the manner of creator and lawgiver. This aspect of God is referred to as "the Father."
2   The same God is also revealed in the manner of savior, in the person of Jesus Christ. This aspect of God is referred to as "the Son."
3   The same God is also revealed in the manner of the one who sanctifies and gives eternal life. This aspect of God is referred to as "the Spirit."

There is thus no difference, save that of appearance and chronological location, between the three entities in question. There are three terms for the same God. This led directly to the doctrine of patripassianism, as noted earlier (p. 214): the Father suffers as the Son, in that there is no fundamental or essential difference between the Father and the Son.

The key difference is that some forms of modalism are *chronological* and some are *functional*. It is important to appreciate this distinction.

1   *Chronological modalism* holds that God was Father at one point in history; that God was then Son at another point; and finally, that God was Spirit. God thus appears in different modes at different times. The classic example of this form of modalism is Sabellianism, which we will discuss in more detail below.
2   *Functional modalism* holds that God operates in different ways at the present moment, and that the three persons refer to these different modes of action.

The main features of Sabellianism were set out by Epiphanius of Constantia in the late fourth century, as follows:

> A certain Sabellius arose not long ago (in fact, quite recently); it is from him that the Sabellians take their name. His opinions, with a few unimportant exceptions, are the same as those of the Noetians. Most of his followers are to be found in Mesopotamia and the region of Rome. [...] Their doctrine is that Father, Son, and Holy Spirit are one and the same being, in the sense that three names are attached to one substance [*hypostasis*]. It is just like the body, soul and spirit in a human being. The body is as it were the Father; the soul is the Son; while the Spirit is to the Godhead as his spirit is to a human being. Or it is like the sun, being one substance [*hypostasis*], but having three manifestations [*energia*]: light, heat, and the orb itself. The heat [...] is analogous to the Spirit; the light to the Son; while the Father himself is represented by the essence of each substance. The Son was at one time emitted, like a ray of light; he accomplished in the world all that related to the dispensation of the gospel and the salvation of humanity, and was then taken back into heaven, as a ray is emitted by the sun and then withdrawn again into the sun. The Holy Spirit is still being sent forth into the world and into those individuals who are worthy to receive it.

From this, it will be clear that Sabellianism is chronological modalism. Its basic feature is the belief that the one supreme God acts in different ways at different points in history.

In contrast, *functional modalism* designates the general belief that the same God acts in three different manners at any given point in history. The three persons of the Trinity thus designate different aspects of the activity of the one God. A simple form of functional modalism could be set out as follows:

God the Father is the creator;
God the Son is the redeemer;
God the Holy Spirit is the sanctifier.

Here, the three persons of the Trinity are held to designate three actions of the one supreme God. God acts as creator (and we call this "Father"); God acts as redeemer (and we call this "Son"); God acts as sanctifier (and we call this the "Holy Spirit." The persons of the Trinity thus refer to different divine functions. The approach to the doctrine of the Trinity set out by John Macquarrie (pp. 264–5) could be interpreted as a variant of this form of modalism, and is worth studying closely from this perspective. Some scholars also argue that Karl Barth's doctrine of the Trinity is modalist, as it can be understood to mean that God operates in different ways in the present. Many Barth scholars, however, dispute this.

Tritheism

If modalism represented one apparently simple (yet ultimately inadequate) solution to the dilemma posed by the Trinity, tritheism offered an equally neat way out. Tritheism invites us to imagine the Trinity as consisting of three equal, independent, and autonomous beings, each of whom is divine. Many students will regard this as an absurd idea. However, the same idea can be stated in more subtle forms, as can be seen from the understated form of tritheism which is often regarded as undergirding the understanding of the Trinity found in the writings of the Cappadocian fathers – Basil of Caesarea, Gregory of Nazianzus, and Gregory of Nyssa – writing in the late fourth century.

To explore this point further, we shall consider the most important of these writings – Gregory of Nyssa's treatise to his colleague Ablabius, subtitled "that there are not three gods." Ablabius had earlier written to Gregory, expressing concern that the formula "three persons, one substance" seemed to lead to tritheism. After all, it was easy to envisage three human persons, each sharing a common human nature. But they were still three different people, weren't they? So how could he avoid falling into tritheism when using this formula?

In replying, Gregory insists that "that the word 'Godhead' does not signify a specific nature but an operation." He illustrates his point by considering how the generic term "orator" affirms both shared generalities and specific particularities:

> For instance, orators share the same occupation, and thus have the same name in each case – yet each of them works by himself as an orator, this one arguing in his own distinctive way, and another in his own way. Thus, since at the human level, the action of each individual sharing the same occupation can be distinguished, they are properly called "many," since each of them is separated from the others within his own environment, according to the special character of his operation.

Gregory then applies this point to God, arguing that it is essential to appreciate the distinctive identity of each person of the Trinity in terms of their operations.

> We say that we who have shared in grace received our life from the one who is the chief source of gifts. When we ask where this good gift came from, we find by the guidance of the Scriptures that it came from the Father, Son, and Holy Spirit. Yet although we set forth Three Persons and three names, we do not consider that we have had bestowed upon us three lives, one from each person separately. Rather, the same life is wrought within us by the Father and prepared by the Son, and depends on the will of the Holy Spirit. Since then the Holy Trinity fulfills

> every operation in a manner similar to that of which I have spoken, not by separate action according to the number of the persons, but so that there is one motion and disposition of the good will which is communicated from the Father through the Son to the Spirit [. . .] so neither can we call those who exercise this divine governing power and operation towards ourselves and all creation, conjointly and inseparably, by their mutual action, three Gods.

It is not an easy argument to follow. The real issue is actually the incapacity of any human model to do justice to the nature of God.

Perhaps the clearest statement of the doctrine of the Trinity to be found in the patristic period is that set out by the Eleventh Council of Toledo (675). This Council, which met in the Spanish city of Toledo and was attended by a mere 11 bishops, is widely credited with setting out the western view of the Trinity with an enviable clarity, and is regularly cited in later medieval discussions of this doctrine. In what follows, the Council explains the relation of the words "Trinity" and "God," and stresses the importance of the relationalities within the godhead.

> This is the way of speaking about the Holy Trinity as it has been handed down: it must not be spoken of or believed to be "threefold" [*triplex*], but to be "Trinity." Nor can it properly be said that in the one God there is the Trinity; rather, the one God is the Trinity. In the relative names of the persons, the Father is related to the Son, the Son to the Father, and the Holy Spirit to both. While they are called three persons in view of their relations, we believe in one nature or substance. Although we profess three persons, we do not profess three substances, but one substance and three persons. For the Father is Father not with respect to Himself but to the Son, and the Son is Son not to Himself but in relation to the Father; and likewise the Holy

Spirit is not referred to Himself but is related to the Father and the Son, inasmuch as He is called the Spirit of the Father and the Son. So when we use the word "God," this does not express a relationship to another, as of the Father to the Son or of the Son to the Father or of the Holy Spirit to the Father and the Son, but "God" refers to Himself only.

The Trinity: Six Classic and Contemporary Approaches

The doctrine of the Trinity, as we have already noted, is a remarkably difficult area of Christian theology. In what follows, we shall survey six approaches, classic and modern, to this doctrine. Each of these approaches casts light on aspects of the doctrine, and allows insights to be gained concerning its foundations and implications. Perhaps the most important of these classic expositions is that of Augustine, whereas in the modern period, that of Karl Barth is of outstanding importance. However, the approach adopted by the Cappadocians continues to be of importance, particularly within modern Greek and Russian Orthodox theology. It is therefore appropriate to begin our discussion by considering this classic approach to the Trinity, which continues to be highly influential in modern Christian thought.

The Cappadocians

As we noted earlier, the Cappadocians played a pivotal role in establishing the full divinity of the Holy Spirit (pp. 237–9). This was formally endorsed by the Council of Constantinople in 381. Once this decisive theological step had been taken, the way was open to a full statement of the doctrine of the Trinity. With the recognition of the identity of substance of Father, Son and Holy Spirit, the door was opened to exploring their mutual relationship within the Trinity. Once more, the Cappadocians played a decisive role in this major theological development.

The Cappadocian approach to the Trinity is best understood as a defense of the divine unity, coupled with a recognition that the one Godhead exists in three different "modes of being." The formula which expresses this approach best is "one substance [ousia] in three persons [hypostaseis]." The one indivisible Godhead is common to all three persons of the Trinity. This one Godhead exists simultaneously in three different "modes of being" – Father, Son, and Holy Spirit.

One of the most distinctive features of this approach to the Trinity is the priority assigned to the Father. Although the Cappadocian writers stress that they do not accept that either the Son or Spirit is subordinate to the Father, they nevertheless explicitly state that the Father is to be regarded as the source or fountainhead of the Trinity. The being of the Father is imparted to both the Son and the Spirit, although in different ways: the Son is "begotten" of the Father, and the Spirit "proceeds" from the Father. Gregory of Nyssa thus writes of "the one person of the Father, from whom the Son is begotten and the Spirit proceeds." Similarly, Gregory of Nyssa argues that the ultimate ground of unity within the Trinity is the Father: "the three have one nature (that is, God), the ground of their unity being the Father."

So how can the one substance be present in three persons? The Cappadocians answered this question by appealing to the relation between a universal and its particulars – for example, humanity and individual human beings. Thus Basil of Caesarea argues that the one substance within the Trinity can be conceived as analogous to a universal, and the three persons to particulars. A common human nature, shared by all people, does not mean that all human beings are identical; it means that they retain their individuality, even though they share this common nature. Thus each of the three persons within the Trinity has a distinctive characteristic.

According to Basil of Caesarea, the distinctives of each of the persons are as follows: the Father is distinguished by fatherhood, the Son by sonship, and the Spirit by the ability to sanctify. For Gregory of Nazianzus, the Father is distinguished by "being ingenerate" (*agennesia*, a difficult word which conveys the idea of "not being begotten" or "not deriving from any other source"), the Son by "being generate" (*gennesis*, which could also be translated as "being begotten" or "deriving one's origins from someone else"), and the Spirit by "being sent" or "proceeding." The difficulty with this analogy, noted earlier (pp. 255–6), is that it does seem to hint at tritheism, even though a more rigorous analysis shows that this is not the case.

Augustine of Hippo

Augustine takes up many elements of the emerging consensus on the Trinity. This can be seen in his vigorous rejection of any form of subordinationism (that is, treating the Son and Spirit as inferior to the Father within the Godhead). Augustine insists that the action of the entire Trinity is to be discerned behind the actions of each of its persons. Thus humanity is not merely created in the image of God; it is created in the image of the Trinity. An important distinction is drawn between the eternal Godhead of the Son and the Spirit, and their place in the economy of salvation. Although the Son and Spirit may appear to be posterior to the Father, this judgment only applies to their role within the process of salvation. Although the Son and Spirit may appear to be subordinate to the Father in history, in eternity

all are coequal. This is an important anticipation of the later distinction between the *essential Trinity*, grounded in God's eternal nature, and the *economic Trinity*, grounded in God's self-revelation within history.

Perhaps the most distinctive element of Augustine's approach to the Trinity concerns his understanding of the person and place of the Holy Spirit; we shall consider specific aspects of this in a later section, as part of our discussion of the *filioque* controversy (see pp. 268–71). However, Augustine's conception of the Spirit as the love which unites the Father and Son demands attention at this early stage.

Having identified the Son with "wisdom" (*sapientia*), Augustine proceeds to identify the Spirit with "love" (*caritas*). He concedes that he has no explicit biblical grounds for this identification; nevertheless, he regards it as a reasonable inference from the biblical material. The Spirit "makes us dwell in God, and God in us." This explicit identification of the Spirit as the basis of union between God and believers is important, as it points to Augustine's idea of the Spirit as the giver of community. The Spirit is the divine gift which binds us to God.

There is therefore, Augustine argues, a corresponding relation within the Trinity itself. The gift must reflect the nature of the giver. God already exists in the kind of relation to which he wishes to bring us. And just as the Spirit is the bond of union between God and the believer, so the Spirit exercises a comparable role within the Trinity, binding the persons together. "The Holy Spirit [...] makes us dwell in God, and God in us. But that is the effect of love. So the Holy Spirit is God who is love."

This argument is supplemented by a general analysis of the importance of love (*caritas*) within the Christian life. Augustine, basing his ideas loosely on 1 Corinthians 13: 13 ("These three remain: faith, hope and love.

But the greatest of these is love"), argues along the following lines:

1   God's greatest gift is love.
2   God's greatest gift is the Holy Spirit.
3   Therefore the Holy Spirit is love.

This style of analysis has been criticized for its obvious weaknesses, not least in leading to a curiously depersonalized notion of the Spirit. The Spirit appears as a sort of glue, binding Father and Son together, and binding both to believers. The idea of "being bound to God" is a central feature of Augustine's spirituality, and it is perhaps inevitable that this concern will appear prominently in his discussion of the Trinity.

One of the most distinctive features of Augustine's approach to the Trinity is his development of "psychological analogies." The reasoning which lies behind the appeal to the human mind in this respect can be summarized as follows. It is not unreasonable to expect that, in creating the world, God has left a characteristic imprint upon that creation. But where is that imprint (*vestigium*) to be found? It is reasonable to expect that God would plant this distinctive imprint upon the height of his creation. Now the Genesis creation accounts allow us to conclude that humanity is the height of God's creation. Therefore, Augustine argues, we should look to humanity in our search for the image of God.

However, Augustine then takes a step which many observers feel to have been unfortunate. On the basis of his neo-Platonic worldview, Augustine argues that the human mind is to be regarded as the apex of humanity. It is therefore to the individual human mind that the theologian should turn, in looking for "traces of the Trinity" (*vestigia Trinitatis*) in creation. The radical individualism of this approach, coupled with its obvious intellectualism, means that he chooses to find the Trinity in the inner mental world of individuals, rather than – for example – in personal relationships (an approach favored by medieval writers, such as Richard of St Victor). Furthermore, a first reading of *On the Trinity* suggests that Augustine seems to regard the inner workings of the human mind as telling us as much about God as about the economy of salvation. Although Augustine stresses the limited value of such analogies, he himself appears to make more use of them than this critical appraisal would warrant.

Augustine discerns a triadic structure to human thought and argues that this structure of thought is grounded in the being of God. He himself argues that the most important such triad is that of mind, knowledge, and love (*mens*, *notitia*, and *amor*), although the related triad of memory, understanding, and will (*memoria*, *intelligentia*, and *voluntas*) is also given considerable prominence. The human mind is an image – inadequate, to be sure, but still an image – of God himself. So just as there are three such faculties in the human mind, which are not ultimately totally separate and independent entities, so there can be three "persons" in God.

There are some obvious difficulties here, possibly even some fatal weaknesses. As has often been pointed out, the human mind cannot be reduced to three entities in quite this neat and simplistic manner. In the end, however, it must be pointed out that Augustine's appeal to such "psychological analogies" is actually illustrative, rather than constitutive. They are intended to be visual aids (although visual aids that are grounded in the doctrine of creation) to insights that may be obtained from Scripture and from reflection on the economy of salvation. Augustine's doctrine of the Trinity is not ultimately grounded in his analysis of the human mind, but in his reading of Scripture, especially of the fourth Gospel.

Augustine's presentation of the Trinity exercised a major influence over later generations, especially during the Middle Ages. Thomas Aquinas's *Treatise on the Trinity* largely represents an elegant restatement of Augustine's ideas, rather than a subtle modification and correction of their deficiencies. Similarly, in the *Institutes* Calvin is content to offer an interpretation of Scripture which is largely a direct repetition of Augustine's approach to the Trinity, indicating a settled consensus within the western tradition at this point. If Calvin distances himself from Augustine at any point, it is in relation to the "psychological analogies." "I doubt if analogies drawn from human things are much use here," he remarked dryly, when considering the intratrinitarian distinctions.

The most significant restatements of the doctrine of the Trinity within the western tradition date from the twentieth century. We shall consider a variety of approaches, beginning with the most significant: that of Karl Barth.

Karl Barth

Barth sets the doctrine of the Trinity at the opening of his *Church Dogmatics*. This simple observation is important, for he totally inverts the position in which it was placed by his rival, Schleiermacher. For Schleiermacher, the Trinity is perhaps the last word which can be said about God; for Barth, it is the word which must be spoken before revelation is even a possibility. It is thus placed at the opening of the *Church Dogmatics*, because its subject matter makes that dogmatics possible in the first place. The doctrine of the Trinity undergirds and guarantees the actuality of divine revelation to sinful humanity. It is an "explanatory confirmation," as Barth puts it, of revelation. It is an exegesis of the fact of revelation.

"*God* reveals himself. He reveals himself *through himself*. He reveals *himself*." With these words (which I have found to be impossible to translate into inclusive language), Barth sets up the revelational framework which leads to the formulation of the doctrine of the Trinity. *Deus dixit!* "God has spoken" – in revelation, and it is the task of theology to inquire concerning what this revelation presupposes and implies. For Barth, theology is *Nach-Denken*, a process of "thinking afterwards" about what is contained in God's self-revelation. We have to "inquire carefully into the relation between our knowing of God, and God himself in his being and nature."

With such statements, Barth sets up the context of the doctrine of the Trinity: given that God's self-revelation has taken place, what must be true of God if this can have happened? What does the actuality of revelation have to tell us about the being of God? Barth's starting point for his discussion of the Trinity is not a doctrine or an idea, but the actuality of God's speaking and God's being heard. For how can God be heard, when sinful humanity is incapable of hearing the Word of God?

The above paragraph is simply a paraphrase of sections of the first half-volume of Barth's *Church Dogmatics*, entitled "The Doctrine of the Word of God." There is an enormous amount being said in this, and it requires unpacking. Two themes need to be carefully noted:

1 Sinful humanity is fundamentally incapable of hearing the Word of God.
2 Nevertheless, sinful humanity has heard the Word of God, in that this Word makes its sinfulness known to it.

The very fact that revelation takes place thus requires explanation. For Barth, this implies that humanity is passive in the process of reception; the process of revelation is, from its beginning to its end, subject to the sovereignty of God as Lord. For revelation to *be* revelation,

God must be capable of effecting self-revelation to sinful humanity, despite their sinfulness.

Once this paradox has been appreciated, the general structure of Barth's doctrine of the Trinity can be followed. In revelation, Barth argues, God must be as shown in the divine self-revelation. There must be a direct correspondence between the revealer and the revelation. If "God reveals himself as Lord" (a characteristically Barthian assertion), then God must be Lord "antecedently in himself." Revelation is the reiteration in time of what God actually is in eternity. There is thus a direct correspondence between:

1   the revealing God;
2   the self-revelation of God.

To put this in the language of trinitarian theology, the Father is revealed in the Son.

So what about the Spirit? Here we come to what is perhaps the most difficult aspect of Barth's doctrine of the Trinity: the idea of "revealedness" (*Offenbarsein*). To explore this, we will have to use an illustration not used by Barth himself. Imagine two individuals, walking outside Jerusalem on a spring day around the year AD 30.

They see three men being crucified, and pause to watch. The first points to the central figure, and says "There is a common criminal being executed." The second, pointing to the same man, replies, "There is the Son of God dying for me." To say that Jesus is the self-revelation of God will not do in itself; there must be some means by which Jesus is *recognized* as the self-revelation of God. It is this recognition of revelation as revelation that constitutes the idea of *Offenbarsein*.

So how is this critical insight achieved? Barth is quite clear: sinful humanity is not capable of reaching this insight unaided. Barth is not prepared to allow humanity any positive role in the interpretation of revelation,

believing that this is to subject divine revelation to human theories of knowledge. (As we have seen, he has been heavily criticized for this, even by those, such as Emil Brunner, who might otherwise be sympathetic to his aims.) The interpretation of revelation as revelation must itself be the work of God – more accurately, the work of the Spirit. Humanity does not become capable of hearing the word of the Lord (*capax verbi domini*), and then hear the word; hearing and capacity to hear are given in the one act by the Spirit.

All this might seem to suggest that Barth is really some kind of modalist, treating the different moments of revelation as different "modes of being" of the same God. It must be conceded immediately that there are those who charge him with precisely this deficiency. Nevertheless, more considered reflection perhaps moves us away from this judgment, although other criticisms can certainly be made. For example, the Spirit fares rather badly in Barth's exposition, which in this respect can be argued to mirror weaknesses in the western tradition as a whole. However, whatever its weaknesses may be, Barth's discussion of the Trinity is generally regarded as having reinstated the importance of the doctrine after a period of sustained neglect within dogmatic theology. That process of reinstatement has been further consolidated through the work of the Jesuit theologian Karl Rahner, to which we now turn.

Karl Rahner

Like Barth, Karl Rahner is widely seen as playing a decisive role in the renewal of trinitarian theology in the twentieth century. Rahner's particular contribution to the development of modern trinitarian theology is generally agreed to be his analysis of the relation between the "economic" and the "immanent" Trinity. The basic distinction here is between the manner in which God is known through revelation in history, and the manner in which God exists internally. The "economic Trinity" can be thought of as the way in which we experience the diversity and unity of God's self-disclosure in history, and the "immanent Trinity" as God's diversity and unity as it is in God, as Rahner's axiom concerning their relationship, which is widely quoted in modern theology, takes the following form: "The 'economic' Trinity is the 'immanent' Trinity, and the 'immanent' Trinity is the 'economic' Trinity." In other words, the way God is revealed and experienced in history corresponds to the way in which God actually is.

Rahner's approach to the Trinity is a powerful corrective to certain tendencies in older Roman Catholic trinitarian theology, especially the tendency to focus on the "immanent Trinity" in such a way as to marginalize both human experience of God and the biblical witness to salvation. For Rahner, the "economic" Trinity relates to the "biblical statements concerning the economy of salvation and its threefold structure." Rahner's axiom allows him to affirm that the entire work of salvation is the work of one divine person. Despite the complexity of the mystery of salvation, a single divine person can be discerned as its source, origin, and goal. Behind the diversity of the process of salvation there is to be discerned only one God.

This fundamental principle of the unity of the economy of salvation can be traced back to Irenaeus, especially in his polemic against the Gnostics (see pp. 246–7), who argued that two divine beings could be distinguished within the economy of salvation. Rahner therefore insists that the proper starting point of trinitarian discussion is our experience of salvation history, and its biblical expression. The "mystery of salvation" happens first; then we move on to formulate doctrines concerning it. This "previous knowledge of the economic Trinity, derived from salvation history and the Bible," is the starting point for the process of systematic reflection. The "immanent Trinity" can therefore be thought of as a "systematic conception of the economic Trinity."

Rahner therefore argues that the process of theological reflection which leads to the doctrine of the immanent Trinity has its starting point in our experience and knowledge of salvation in history. The complexity of that salvation history is ultimately grounded in the divine nature itself. In other words, although we experience diversity and unity within the economy of salvation, that diversity and unity correspond to the way God actually is. Rahner expresses this point as follows:

> The differentiation of the self-communication of God in history (of truth) and spirit (of love) must belong to God "in himself," or otherwise this difference, which undoubtedly exists, would do away with God's self-communication. For these modalities and their differentiation either are in God himself (although we first experience them from our point of view) or they exist only in us.

In other words, "Father," "Son," and "Holy Spirit" are not simply human ways of making sense of the diversity of our experience of the mystery of salvation. Nor are they roles which God somehow temporarily assumes for the purpose of entering into our history. Rather, they correspond to the way God actually is. The same God who *appears* as a Trinity *is* a Trinity. The way in which God is known in self-revelation corresponds to the way God is internally.

Robert Jenson

Writing from a Lutheran perspective, but deeply versed in the Reformed tradition, the contemporary American theologian Robert Jenson has provided a fresh and creative restatement of the traditional doctrine of the Trinity. In many ways, it is appropriate to regard Jenson as providing a development of Barth's position, with its characteristic emphasis upon the need to remain faithful to God's self-revelation. *The Triune Identity: God According to the Gospel* (1982) provides a fundamental reference point for discussion of the doctrine in a period which has seen fresh interest develop in this hitherto neglected matter.

Jenson argues that "Father, Son, and Holy Spirit" is the proper name for the God whom Christians know in and through Jesus Christ. It is imperative, he argues, that God should have a proper name. "Trinitarian discourse is Christianity's effort to identify the God who has claimed us. The doctrine of the Trinity comprises both a proper name, 'Father, Son and Holy Spirit' [...] and an elaborate development and analysis of corresponding identifying descriptions." Jenson points out that ancient Israel was set in a polytheistic context, in which the term "god" conveyed relatively little information. It was necessary to name the god in question. A similar situation was confronted by the writers of the New Testament, who were obliged to identify the god at the heart of their faith, and distinguish this god from the many other gods worshiped and acknowledged in the region, especially in Asia Minor.

The doctrine of the Trinity thus *identifies* and *names* the Christian God – but identifies and names this God in a manner consistent with the biblical witness. It is not a name which we have chosen; it is a name which has been chosen for us, and which we are authorized to use. In this way, Jensen defends the priority of God's self-revelation against human constructions of concepts of divinity. "The gospel identifies its God thus: God is the one who raised Israel's Jesus from the dead. The whole task of theology can be described as the unpacking of this sentence in various ways. One of these produces the church's trinitarian

language and thought." We noted in an earlier section the manner in which the early church tended to accidentally confuse distinctively Christian ideas about God with those deriving from the Hellenistic context into which it expanded. The doctrine of the Trinity, Jenson affirms, is and was a necessary defense mechanism against such developments. It allows the church to discover the distinctiveness of its creed, and avoid becoming absorbed by rival conceptions of God.

However, the church could not ignore its intellectual context. If, on the one hand, its task was to defend the Christian notion of God against rival conceptions of divinity, another of its tasks was to provide "a metaphysical analysis of the gospel's triune identification of God." In other words, it was obliged to use the philosophical categories of its day to explain precisely what Christians believed about their God, and how this distinguished them from alternatives. Paradoxically, the attempt to distinguish Christianity from Hellenism led to the introduction of Hellenistic categories into trinitarian discourse.

The doctrine of the Trinity thus centers on the recognition that God is named by Scripture, and within the witness of the church. Within the Hebraic tradition, God is identified by historical events. Jenson notes how many Old Testament texts identify God with reference to divine acts in history – such as the liberation of Israel from its captivity in Egypt. The same pattern is evident in the New Testament: God is recognized to be identified with reference to historical events, supremely the resurrection of Jesus Christ. God comes to be identified in relation to Jesus Christ. Who is God? Which god are we talking about? The God who raised Christ from the dead. As Jenson puts it, "the emergence of a semantic pattern in which the uses of 'God' and 'Jesus Christ' are mutually determining" is of fundamental importance within the New Testament.

Jenson thus recovers a personal conception of God from metaphysical speculation. "Father, Son, and Holy Spirit" is a *proper name*, which we are asked to use in naming and addressing God. "Linguistic means of identification – proper names, identifying descriptions, or both – are a necessity of religion. Prayers, like other requests and praises, must be addressed." The Trinity is thus an instrument of theological precision, which forces us to be precise about the God under discussion.

John Macquarrie

John Macquarrie, a Scottish theologian with roots in a Presbyterian tradition, approaches the doctrine of the Trinity from an existentialist perspective (see pp. 146–7) in his *Principles of Christian Theology* (1966). Macquarrie here argues that the doctrine of the Trinity "safeguards a dynamic as opposed to a static understanding of God." But how can a dynamic God simultaneously be stable? Macquarrie's reflections on this tension lead him to conclude that "if God had not revealed himself as triune, we should have been compelled to think of him in some such way." He explores the dynamic conception of God within the Christian tradition in the following manner.

1   The Father is to be understood as *primordial Being*. By this, we are meant to understand "the ultimate act or energy of letting-be, the condition that there should be anything whatsoever, the source not only of whatever is but of all possibilities of being."
2   The Son is to be conceived as *expressive Being*. "Primordial Being" needs to express itself in the world of beings, which it does by "flowing out through expressive Being." In adopting this approach, Macquarrie picks up the idea of the Son being the Word or Logos, the agent of the Father in the creation of the world. He explicitly

relates this form of Being to Jesus Christ: "Christians believe that the Father's Being finds expression above all in the finite being of Jesus."
3   The Holy Spirit is to be understood as *unitive Being*, in that it "is the function of the Spirit to maintain, strengthen and, where need be, restore the unity of Being with the beings." The task of the Spirit is to promote new and higher levels of unity between God and the world (between "Being" and "beings," to use Macquarrie's terms); it leads the beings back up into a new and richer unity with Being which let them be in the first place.

It will be clear that Macquarrie's approach is genuinely helpful, in that it links the doctrine of the Trinity with the existential situation of humanity. Yet its weakness also becomes evident, in that there appears to be a certain artificiality involved in the assignment of existential functions to the persons of the Trinity. One wonders what would have happened if the Trinity had happened to have four members; perhaps Macquarrie would have devised a fourth category of Being to deal with this situation? But this is a weakness of existential approaches in general, rather than this specific approach in particular.

It is also interesting to consider whether Macquarrie's approach can be considered to be a form of modalism – specifically, the *functional modalism* which we noted earlier (pp. 254–5). Macquarrie appears to argue that the doctrine of the Trinity is to be viewed as the revelation of three modes of Being within God.

Macquarrie's approach illuminates both the strengths and weaknesses of the existentialist approach to theology. Broadly speaking, these may be stated as follows:

1   The strength of the approach is that it gives a powerful additional dimension to Christian

theology, by indicating the ways in which this theology may be correlated with the structures of human existence.

2 The weakness of the approach is that, although capable of *existential enhancement* of existing Christian doctrines, it is less valuable in *establishing* those doctrines in the first place.

Some Discussions of the Trinity in Recent Theology

The second half of the twentieth century witnessed some remarkable explorations of the doctrine of the Trinity. To give readers an idea of the fertility and creativity of this outburst of reflection, based on a new confidence in the doctrine after the collapse of Enlightenment rationalism and a growing awareness of its implications, we shall report briefly on three recent discussions. We open, however, by considering a classic question: where should the doctrine of the Trinity be located in a systematic theology?

F. D. E. Schleiermacher on the dogmatic location of the Trinity

The doctrine of the Trinity has traditionally been placed toward the beginning of works of Christian theology, not least on account of the influence of the creeds of Christendom upon such works. The creeds open with a declaration of faith in God; it therefore seemed natural to most theologians to follow this pattern, placing any discussion about the doctrine of God at the opening of their works. Thus Thomas Aquinas, perhaps the finest representative of this classical tradition of doing theology, considered it only natural to begin his *Summa Theologiae* with a discussion of the doctrine of God in general, immediately followed by his

account of the doctrine of the Trinity in particular. However, it must be stressed that this pattern is not the only one which could be adopted. To illustrate this point, we shall consider the location of the discussion of the doctrine of God in F. D. E. Schleiermacher's *Christian Faith*.

As we noted earlier, Schleiermacher's approach to theology is to begin with the common human experience of a "feeling of absolute dependence," which is then interpreted in a Christian sense as "a feeling of absolute dependence *upon God.*" As a result of a long process of inference from this feeling of dependence, Schleiermacher finally reaches the doctrine of the Trinity. This doctrine is placed right at the end of the work, as an appendix. For some, such as Karl Barth, this demonstrates that Schleiermacher regarded the Trinity as an appendix to his theology; for others, it suggests that it was the last word that the theologian could utter concerning God – in other words, the climax of the entire theological enterprise.

Jürgen Moltmann on the social Trinity

In *The Trinity and the Kingdom of God* (1980), Jürgen Moltmann attempts to liberate the Christian doctrine of God from the confines both of the ancient Greek metaphysics of substance and of the modern metaphysics of transcendental subjectivity. As we shall see presently, a similar task had been undertaken a few years earlier by Eberhard Jüngel. However, Moltmann's *Trinity and the Kingdom of God* is of particular importance on account of its fully social doctrine of the Trinity. Moltmann's social doctrine of the Trinity emphasizes the relative independence of the person and work of the Holy Spirit in its community with the Father and the Son. Developing this in a way that might cause anxiety to some, Moltmann emphasizes that there is no fixed order in the Trinity. The unity of God is the unity of persons in relationship, as expressed in the Cappadocian doctrine of *perichoresis*. On this reading of this concept, Moltmann argues that "the trinitarian persons form their own unity by themselves in the circulation of the divine life." This conception of God is radically opposed, Moltmann insists, to any "monotheistic" or "monarchical" doctrine of God which would reduce the real subjectivity of the three persons. Of particular interest is how Moltmann uses this notion to develop a fundamentally *theological* understanding of human society.

"The trinity is our social program." For Jürgen Moltmann, the doctrine of the Trinity is to be understood to provide a vision of God as a union of three divine persons or distinct, but related subjects. This specific understanding of God as a mutually loving, interacting, and sustaining society allows Christian theology to develop a theory of society. "The social doctrine of the Trinity is in a position to overcome both monotheism in the concept of God and individualism in the doctrine of man, and to develop a social personalism and personalist socialism." For Moltmann, the Christian concept of the Trinity provides "the exemplar of true human community, first in the church and also in society." Excessively authoritarian and centralized notions of government rests upon a conception of God which stresses God's "monarchy," rather than a trinitarian doctrine of God, which stresses the divine unity and community. Moltmann therefore sees the social view of the Trinity as having both a theological and a social function: theologically, it offers a penetrating critique of a false idea of God; socially, it articulates a notion of God as a social being, capable of functioning as a proper paradigm for society as a whole.

> The triune God is reflected only in a united and uniting community of Christians without

domination and subjection and a united and uniting humanity without class rule and without dictatorial oppression. That is the world in which people are defined by their social relationships and not by their power or their property. That is the world in which human beings have all things in common and share everything with one another except their personal qualities.

Eberhard Jüngel on the Trinity and metaphysics

In his difficult book *God as the Mystery of the World* (1976) Eberhard Jüngel set out to explore how it is possible to speak of God in a responsible manner in a world in which people live *etsi Deus non daretur* ("as if God were not given"). For Jüngel, the problem is clear, as is its solution. The problem is that much western theology has allowed its thinking about God to be shaped, not by the specifics of the Christian revelation, but by ideas of God which derive from secular metaphysics.

Jüngel's concern is that a specific type of metaphysics – which he traces back to Descartes – makes certain imperialistic claims which, if conceded, leads to the erosion of an authentically Christian conception of God. Thus Jüngel notes how J. G. Fichte, Ludwig Feuerbach, and Friedrich Nietzsche derive their understanding of God from the metaphysical tradition, not from the Christian tradition. Jüngel then correctly points out that the major forms of atheism which arose in western culture during the nineteenth and twentieth centuries are not rejections of the Christian God, but are rather reactions against inadequate metaphysical notions of God. Making much the same point, Alasdair MacIntyre remarks that "the God in whom the nineteenth and twentieth centuries came to disbelieve had been invented only in the seventeenth century."

Jüngel's solution is to urge Christianity to rediscover its own distinctive vision of God, which is fundamentally trinitarian in nature. He stresses that God identifies himself with the crucified Christ, so that faith recognizes the crucified human being Jesus of Nazareth as identical to God. Like Moltmann, Jüngel makes the cross the center of the trinitarian history of God. A proper interpretation of the crucifixion of Christ leads decisively away from the philosophical monotheism of classical theism, towards the distinctively and authentically *Christian* doctrine of the Trinity.

Jüngel moves on from here to develop a trinitarian "theology of the cross." The cross reveals a differentiation between Father and Son. (A similar point had made earlier by Jürgen Moltmann, who disentangles the different manners in which Father and Son experience suffering, and draws out their trinitarian implications.) The resurrection, however, affirms the unity of Father and Son, God and Jesus. How is this to be interpreted? Jüngel maps out a road which leads to the doctrine of the Trinity with his declaration that "the knowledge of the identification of God with Jesus necessitates the distinction of God from God." The New Testament itself makes such a distinction, when it distinguishes God the Son (the crucified Jesus) from God the Father (who raised him from the dead). The Father and Son are held together by the bond of unity, the Holy Spirit.

This "self-differentiation" within God, recognized on the basis of the relation between the resurrection and crucifixion of Christ, constitutes the basis of the doctrine of the Trinity. It also forms the basis of the Christian critique of both monotheism and metaphysical theism, as well as the types of atheism which correspond to these forms of theism. From this, it is clear that Jüngel sees the church's task of engaging with the world as depending on a recovery of its own distinctive understanding of God, and breaking free from its recent imprisonment to secular metaphysics. The doctrine of the Trinity, he argues, is central to this development.

Catherine Mowry LaCugna on the Trinity and salvation

One of the most impressive studies of the theological foundations and application of the doctrine of the Trinity to appear in recent years is Catherine Mowry LaCugna's *God for Us: The Trinity and Christian Life* (1991). This richly textured work examines why the doctrine of the Trinity has been so problematic for the western church, and proposes some solutions. In this work, LaCugna – professor of theology at the University of Notre Dame – develops the central insight that western trinitarianism has tended to ignore God's revelation in the economy of salvation, preferring to engage in speculative reflection on the divine nature itself.

LaCugna traces this development back to the tension – which was highly significant at the time of the Council of Nicea – between *theologia* and *oikonomia*, between the so-called immanent or essential Trinity and the economic Trinity. The term *oikonomia*, which we identify with the economic Trinity, refers to the self-communication of God in Jesus Christ and in the Holy Spirit's activity in the history of salvation. All that we know about God is a result of this activity. *Theologia*, or our knowledge of the eternal being of God, should in principle be coextensive with what we have learned from revelation in the divine economy of salvation. We have no access to the immanent life of God that goes beyond what has been revealed. Yet a refusal to accept this, LaCugna argues, has led to the Christian tradition adopting concepts of God which are shaped by Greek philosophy, rather than by the biblical revelation, to define our understanding of the Trinity. As we noted earlier, a similar line of criticism can be found in Eberhard

Jüngel's *God as the Mystery of the World*. LaCugna seeks to correct this problem by returning to the economy of salvation as definitive for our understanding of the nature of God.

This involves her in a creative yet critical engagement with Karl Rahner. LaCugna reworks Rahner's statements concerning the economic and essential Trinity as follows: "Theology is inseparable from soteriology, and vice versa." By arguing for a recovery of the identification of *theologia* with *oikonomia*, LaCugna's believes that theology is liberated from the pointless, and potentially misleading distinction between God's inner and outer aspects. This "return to the biblical and pre-Nicene pattern of thought" reaffirms that there is only one trinitarian life of God, which embraces and enfolds the entire scope of salvation history. Far from being a speculative doctrine, it stands revealed as the expression of the heart of the Christian faith.

> The doctrine of the Trinity, properly understood, is the affirmation of God's intimate communion with us through Jesus Christ and the Holy Spirit. As such, it is an eminently practical doctrine with far-reaching consequences for Christian life. By presenting the doctrine of the Trinity in a way that is more at home with the concrete language and images of the Bible, creeds, and the liturgy, the Christian doctrine of God can be reconnected with other areas of theology, as well as to ethics, spirituality, and the life of the church.

Having considered various approaches to, and applications of, the doctrine of the Trinity, we now turn to consider a debate which has been of considerable importance historically and theologically; namely, the manner in which the Holy Spirit is related to the Son. This controversy has come to be known as the *filioque* debate, and is considered in what follows.

The *Filioque* Controversy

One of the most significant events in the early history of the church was agreement throughout the Roman Empire, both east and west, on the Nicene creed. This document was intended to bring doctrinal stability to the church in a period of considerable importance in its history. Part of that agreed text referred to the Holy Spirit "proceeding from the Father." By the ninth century, however, the western church routinely altered this phrase, speaking of the Holy Spirit "proceeding from the Father and the Son." The Latin term *filioque*, which literally means "and from the Son," has since come to refer to this addition, now normative within the western church, and the theology which it expresses. This idea of a "double procession" of the Holy Spirit was a source of intense irritation to Greek writers: not only did it raise serious theological difficulties for them, it also involved tampering with the supposedly inviolable text of the creeds. Many scholars see this bad feeling as contributing to the split between the eastern and western churches, which took place around 1054 (see p. 23).

The *filioque* debate is of importance, both as a theological issue in itself, and also as a matter of some importance in the contemporary relations between the eastern and western churches. We therefore propose to explore the issues in some detail. The basic issue at stake is whether the Spirit may be said to proceed *from the Father alone*, or *from the Father and the Son*. The former position is associated with the eastern church, and is given its most weighty exposition in the writings of the Cappadocian fathers; the latter is associated with the western church, and is developed in Augustine's treatise *On the Trinity*.

The Greek patristic writers insisted that there was only one source of being within the Trinity. The Father alone was the sole and supreme cause of all things, including the Son and the Spirit within the Trinity. The Son and the Spirit derive from the Father, but in different manners. In searching for suitable terms to express this relationship, theologians eventually fixed on two quite distinct images: the Son is *begotten* of the Father, while the Spirit *proceeds* from the Father. These two terms are intended to express the idea that both Son and Spirit derive from the Father, but in different ways. The vocabulary is clumsy, reflecting the fact that the Greek words involved (*gennesis* and *ekporeusis*) are difficult to translate into modern English.

To assist in understanding this complex process, the Greek fathers used two images. The Father pronounces his word; at the same time as he utters this word, he breathes out in order to make this word capable of being heard and received. The imagery used here, which is strongly grounded in the biblical tradition, is that of the Son as the Word of God, and the Spirit as the breath of God. An obvious question arises here: why should the Cappadocian fathers, and other Greek writers, spend so much time and effort on distinguishing Son and Spirit in this way? The answer is important. A failure to distinguish the ways in which Son and Spirit derive from the one and the same Father would lead to God having two sons, which would have raised insurmountable problems.

Within this context, it is unthinkable that the Holy Spirit should proceed from the Father and the Son. Why? Because it would totally compromise the principle of the Father as the sole origin and source of all divinity. It would amount to affirming that there were *two* sources of divinity within the one Godhead, with all the internal contradictions and tensions that this would generate. If the Son were

to share in the exclusive ability of the Father to be the source of all divinity, this ability would no longer be exclusive. For this reason, the Greek church regarded the western idea of a "double procession" of the Spirit with something approaching stark disbelief.

The Greek tradition, however, was not entirely unanimous on this point. Cyril of Alexandria had no hesitation in speaking of the Spirit as "belonging to the Son," and related ideas were not slow to develop within the western church. Early western Christian writers were deliberately vague about the precise role of the Spirit within the Godhead. In his treatise *On the Trinity*, Hilary of Poitiers contented himself with a declaration that he would "say nothing about [God's] Holy Spirit except that he is [God's] Spirit." This vagueness led some of his readers to suspect that he was really a binitarian, believing in the full divinity only of Father and Son. However, in other passages from the same treatise, it becomes clear that Hilary regards the New Testament as pointing to the Spirit proceeding from both Father and Son, rather than from the Father alone.

This understanding of the procession of the Spirit from Father and Son was developed and given its classic statement by Augustine. Possibly building upon the position hinted at by Hilary, Augustine argued that the Spirit had to be thought of as proceeding from the Son. One of his main proof texts was John 20: 22, in which the risen Christ is reported as having breathed upon his disciples, and said: "Receive the Holy Spirit." Augustine explains this as follows in *On the Trinity*:

> Nor can we say that the Holy Spirit does not also proceed from the Son. After all, the Spirit is said to be the Spirit of both the Father and the Son. [John 20: 22 is then cited] The Holy Spirit proceeds not only from the Father, but also from the Son.

In making this statement, Augustine thought that he was summarizing a general consensus within both the eastern and western churches. Unfortunately, his knowledge of Greek does not appear to have been good enough to allow him to appreciate that the Greek-speaking Cappadocian writers adopted a rather different position. Nevertheless, there are points at which Augustine is obviously concerned to defend the distinctive role of the Father within the Godhead:

> There is good reason why in this Trinity we speak of the Son alone as Word of God, of the Holy Spirit alone as Gift of God, and of God the Father alone as the one of whom the Word is begotten and from whom the Holy Spirit principally proceeds. I add the word "principally," because we learn that the Holy Spirit proceeds also from the Son. But this is again something given by the Father to the Son – not that he ever existed without it, for all that the Father gives to his only-begotten Word he gives in the act of begetting him. He is begotten in such a manner that the common gift proceeds from him as well, and the Holy Spirit is Spirit of both.

So what did Augustine think he was doing, in understanding the role of the Spirit in this way? The answer lies in his distinctive understanding of the Spirit as the "bond of love" between Father and Son. Augustine developed the idea of relation within the Godhead, arguing that the persons of the Trinity are defined by their relations to one another. The Spirit is thus to be seen as the relation of love and fellowship between the Father and Son, a relation which Augustine believed to be foundational to the fourth Gospel's presentation of the unity of will and purpose of Father and Son.

We can summarize the root differences between the two approaches as follows.

1 The *Greek* intention was to safeguard the unique position of the Father as the sole source of divinity. In that both the Son and Spirit derive from him, although in different but equally valid manners, their divinity is in turn safeguarded. To the Greeks, the Latin approach seemed to introduce two separate sources of divinity into the Godhead, and to weaken the vital distinction between Son and Spirit. The Son and Spirit are understood to have distinct, yet complementary roles; whereas the western tradition sees the Spirit as the *Spirit of Christ*. Indeed, a number of modern writers from this tradition, such as the Russian writer Vladimir Lossky, have criticized the western approach. In his essay "The Procession of the Holy Spirit," Lossky argues that the western approach inevitably depersonalizes the Spirit, leads to a misplaced emphasis upon the person and work of Christ, and reduces the Godhead to an impersonal principle.

2 The *Latin* intention was to ensure that the Son and Spirit were adequately distinguished from one another, yet shown to be mutually related to one another. The strongly relational approach to the idea of "person" adopted made it inevitable that the Spirit would be treated in this way. Sensitive to the Greek position, later Latin writers stressed that they did not regard their approach as presupposing two sources of divinity in the Godhead. This is made especially clear by the Eleventh Council of Toledo, to which we have already made reference in this chapter.

> We believe that the Holy Spirit, the third person in the Trinity, is God, one and equal with God the Father and God the Son, of one substance and of one nature; not, however, begotten or created, but proceeding from both, and that He is the Spirit of both. We also believe that the Holy Spirit is neither unbegotten nor begotten, for if we called Him "unbegotten" we would assert two Fathers, or if we called him "begotten" we

would appear to preach two Sons. Yet He is called the Spirit not of the Father alone, nor of the Son alone, but of both Father and Son. For He does not proceed from the Father to the Son, nor from the Son to sanctify creatures, but He is shown to have proceeded from both at once, because He is known as the love or the holiness of both. Hence we believe that the Holy Spirit is sent by both, as the Son is sent by the Father. But He is not less than the Father and the Son.

Similar ideas were stated by later councils. Thus the Council of Lyons (1274) stated that "the Holy Spirit proceeds from the Father and the Son, *yet not as from two origins but as from one origin.*" However, despite such clarifications, the doctrine remains a source of contention between eastern and western Christians, which is unlikely to be removed in the foreseeable future.

Having now considered the Christian doctrine of God, we may turn to the second major theme of Christian theology: the identity and significance of Jesus Christ. We have already noted how the Christian doctrine of the Trinity emerges from Christological considerations. It is now appropriate to explore the development of Christology as a subject in its own right.

QUESTIONS FOR CHAPTER 10

1   Many theologians prefer to speak of "Creator, Redeemer, and Sustainer," rather than the traditional "Father, Son, and Holy Spirit." What is gained by this approach? And what difficulties does it raise?
2   Why did the twentieth century witness a renewal of interest in the doctrine of the Trinity?
3   How could you reconcile these two statements: "God is a person"; "God is three persons"?
4   Is the Trinity a doctrine about God, or about Jesus Christ?
5   Summarize the doctrine of the Trinity found in the writings of either Augustine of Hippo or Karl Barth.
6   Does it matter whether the Spirit proceeds from the Father alone, or from both the Father and the Son?

11

The Doctrine of the Person of Christ

Who is Jesus Christ? And why is he so important for the Christian faith? The Christian doctrine of the person of Christ sets out to explore why the church believes that the little piece of human history called "Jesus of Nazareth" holds the key to the nature of God and of human destiny. This area of theology, often referred to as "Christology," sets out to locate Jesus of Nazareth on a conceptual map. It attempts to place him along the coordinates of time and eternity, humanity and divinity, particularity and universality, and answer the question of how an event which took place at a specific time and place can be relevant for all people and all times.

The classic Christian account of the significance of Jesus of Nazareth is framed in terms of the concept of the "incarnation," and the doctrine of the "two natures" of Christ – divine and human. As these ideas seem strange to those new to the study of theology, some introductory comments are appropriate.

Why, many wonder, do Christians not simply see Jesus of Nazareth as a good religious teacher, and avoid the apparently complicated and puzzling ideas that are traditionally associated with the doctrine of the incarnation? The answer lies in the long tradition of Christian wrestling with the foundational events of their faith, as they are set out and analyzed in the New Testament. Even in the Gospels, we find Jesus provoking amazement, admiration, bewilderment, even outrage on the part of those who see and hear him. Human minds and tongues have never really been fully up to the task of making sense of him. It has proved much easier to identify inadequate ways of speaking and thinking about Jesus than to do justice to his words and ways.

So theology is forced to ask this question: what way of conceiving Jesus is most faithful to the New Testament? What way of picturing him seems best adapted to enfold the complex witness of the New Testament to his impact on people? As the church wrestled with the question of the identity and significance of Jesus of Nazareth, it realized that it had to experiment with a variety of models of understanding Jesus. Slowly and painfully, it would have to focus down on what seemed to be the best way of visualizing his significance, or placing him on the complex map charting the relationship of humanity and divinity. We thus find the first four centuries exploring just about every possibility, trying to establish its strengths and weaknesses.

The church was confronted with a virtually impossible task: it needed to "freeze" the significance of Jesus, in the full knowledge that it could not really be done. How could the dynamic, charismatic person of Jesus be petrified, like a fossil of a once-living organism? How could he be frozen into words, however insightful they might be? Karl Barth, widely recognized as one of the most important Christian theologians of the twentieth century, shrewdly pointed out this paradox in one of this earliest writings – his commentary on Paul's letter to the Romans. God's revelation, he argued, cannot be frozen or pinned down, any more than a bird can be stopped in mid-flight. We can never fully seize the glory of divine revelation.

There was no doubt in the minds of any Gospel writer, or any of the first Christian witnesses to Jesus, that he was a human being. But they were compelled to draw the conclusion that he was more than that – much more than that. Jesus offered access to God, both by making God known and making God available. As part of their discipleship of the mind, Christians had to learn to "think about Jesus as we do about God" (to quote the second letter of Clement, a late first-century Christian writing which was greatly valued by the early church.) But how was this to be expressed? How could the biblical witness to the identity and impact of Jesus be crystallized into verbal formulae?

By the end of the fourth century, the church had made up its collective mind, and decided that the only acceptable way of describing Jesus of Nazareth was using what has come to be known as the "two natures" formula – namely, that Jesus is "truly divine and truly human." This is often referred to as the "Chalcedonian definition," as it was fully set out by the Council of Chalcedon in 451. The doctrine of the incarnation speaks of God entering into the messy, fallen world that we inhabit. In invites us to think of God opening a window into his being, and a door into his presence, through Jesus Christ.

Even to those who have become used to the idea though the preaching and liturgy of the church, the idea of the incarnation is still startling, possibly even baffling. How can such a statement be made about any historical figure? And how on earth are we to make sense of the seemingly nonsensical statement that we are to think of Jesus as truly divine and truly human. This chapter sets out to explain the origins and development of this way of thinking about Jesus Christ, and how it has been understood in the long history of Christian theology.

The area of Christian theology traditionally known as "Christology" deals with the person of Jesus Christ. As will become clear, the issues to be discussed in this chapter can be described as "classic," in the sense that they dominated the Christological agenda of the Christian tradition before the rise of the Enlightenment. The Enlightenment raised a new series of questions concerning the relation of faith and history, opening up a network of debates without any real parallel in the period before 1700. These issues will be discussed at length in the chapter which follows. Our concern in the present chapter is the documentation of classic approaches to Christology, including their discussion in the modern period.

The Place of Jesus Christ in Christian Theology

The person of Jesus Christ is of central importance to Christian theology. Whereas "theology" could be defined as "talk about God" in general, "Christian theology" accords a central role to Jesus Christ. The nature of that role is complex and is best understood by considering its various components. The first such component is historical, whereas the three others are more explicitly theological in character.

Jesus Christ is the historical point of departure for Christianity

This observation is relatively uncontroversial. It is a simple matter of historical fact that the coming of Jesus brought the Christian community into being. However, the interpretation of this matter is actually rather more complex. Consider, for example, the question of whether Jesus of Nazareth introduced anything *new* into the world. For the writers of the Enlightenment, Jesus of Nazareth did little more than republish a religion of nature, which was promptly corrupted by his followers, including Paul. There was nothing new about his words and deeds. The insights of Jesus, where they were valid, could all be obtained through the use of an omnicompetent human reason. Rationalism thus argued that Jesus had nothing that was both *right* and *new* to say; where he was right he merely agreed with what sound human reason always knew to be the case; if he said anything that was new (that is, hitherto unknown to reason), this would, by definition, be irrational and hence of no value.

A very different approach is associated with German liberal Protestantism (see pp. 82–4), especially as this is developed in the writings of Albrecht Benjamin Ritschl. Ritschl argues that Jesus of Nazareth brought something *new* to the human situation, something which reason had hitherto neglected. "Jesus was conscious of a *new and hitherto unknown relation to God.*" Where rationalists believed in a universal rational religion, of which individual world religions were at best shadows, Ritschl argued that this was little more than a dream of reason, an abstraction without any historical embodiment. Christianity possesses certain definite theological and cultural characteristics as a historical religion, partly due to Jesus of Nazareth.

Important though this historical consideration might be, Christian theology has generally located the significance of Jesus Christ in three specifically *theological* areas, which we shall consider in what follows. Nevertheless, it must be stressed that this historical dimension to the significance of Jesus Christ is of continuing importance. Christianity is not a set of self-contained and freestanding ideas; it represents a sustained response to the questions raised by the life, death, and resurrection of Jesus Christ. Christianity is an historical religion, which came into being in response to a specific set of events, which center upon Jesus Christ, and to which Christian theology is obliged to return in the course of its speculation and reflection.

This point is of importance in understanding the continuing importance of Scripture within the Christian tradition. Christology and scriptural authority are inextricably linked, in that it is Scripture which brings us to a knowledge of Jesus Christ. The New Testament is the only document we possess which the Christian church has recognized as authentically embodying and recollecting its understanding of Jesus, and the impact he had upon people's lives and thought. The reports we have concerning Jesus from extracanonical sources are of questionable reliability, and strictly limited value. The authority of Scripture thus rests partly upon historical considerations. However, those historical considerations are to be supplemented with theological reflections – for example, that it is through Jesus Christ that the distinctively Christian knowledge of God comes about, and this knowledge of Jesus is given only in Scripture. We shall now move on to consider such explicitly theological considerations.

Jesus Christ reveals God

A central element of Christian theology centers upon the idea of a *revelatory presence of God* in Christ (see pp. 281, 297–8). Jesus Christ is regarded as making God known in a particular and specific manner, distinctive to Christianity. Perhaps the most radical statement of this conviction may be found in Karl Barth's *Church Dogmatics*:

> When Holy Scripture speaks of God, it does not permit us to let our attention or thoughts wander at random. [...] When Holy Scripture speaks of God, it concentrates our attention and thoughts upon one single point and what is to be known at that point. [...] If we ask further concerning the one point upon which, according to Scripture, our attention and thoughts should and must be concentrated, then from first to last the Bible directs us to the name of Jesus Christ.

This conviction has been central to mainstream Christianity down the ages. Thus the writer of the Second Letter of Clement, probably to be dated from the middle of the second century, opens his letter with the affirmation that "we must think of Jesus Christ as of God." The noted English theological writer Arthur Michael Ramsey (1904–88) makes the same theological point as Barth: "The importance of the confession 'Jesus is Lord' is not only that Jesus is divine, but that God is Christlike."

This "Christological concentration" has been the subject of considerable debate among those concerned for dialogue between Christianity and other religions, and we shall return to consider its implications at a later stage in this work. Our concern at this stage is simply to note that, as a matter of historical fact, Christian theology has recognized that it is impossible to speak of "God" within the parameters of the Christian tradition without relating such statements to the person and work of Jesus Christ.

Jesus Christ is the bearer of salvation

A central theme of mainstream Christian thought is that salvation, in the Christian sense of the term, is manifested in and through, and constituted on the basis of, the life, death, and resurrection of Jesus Christ (see pp. 318–25). It must be noted that the term "salvation" is complex. To assert that "Jesus Christ makes salvation possible" is not to deny that other modes of salvation are accessible by other means; it is simply to insist that, within the Christian tradition, the distinctively Christian understanding of what salvation is can only be realized on the basis of Jesus Christ. We shall explore something of how Christian theology has understood the nature of salvation in the present chapter (pp. 294–304), and how Jesus Christ is understood to be the basis of that salvation in a later chapter (pp. 326–59).

Once more, this central core of Christian belief has been the subject of some concern on the part of revisionists, alarmed at its potential implications for dialogue between Christianity and other religions, and we shall return to explore it at the appropriate point in this work. John Hick, for example, finds his pluralist approach to other religions challenged by certain highly distinctive elements of the Christian faith – including the resurrection of Christ, the divinity of Christ, and the Trinity. His proposals to eliminate these in order to facilitate his agenda of demonstrating that all faiths share the same basic features has not been well received. We shall return to this theme in chapter 17.

Jesus Christ defines the shape of the redeemed life

A central issue in Christian spirituality and ethics concerns the nature of Christian existence, in relation to both its spiritual and its ethical dimensions. The New Testament itself is strongly *Christomorphic* in its view of the redeemed life – that is to say, it affirms that Jesus Christ not only makes that life possible; he also determines its shape. The New

Testament imagery of "being conformed to Christ" expresses this notion well. The issues involved are of some importance, especially in relation to the question of the manner in which Jesus Christ can be an ethical or spiritual example for believers.

This point is made by the Scottish theologian James Denney (1856–1917), who was Principal of the United Free Church College, Glasgow, from 1897 until his death 20 years later. In a major work entitled *The Christian Doctrine of Reconciliation*, published in the year of his death, Denney contrasted two deficient understandings of the place of Christ in the Christian life. The first – which he styles the "Socinian" – treats Christ simply as a moral example; the second – which Denney refers to as an "evangelical" view – regards Christ as the basis of salvation, in that he provided atonement for humanity. Denney declares both, individually, to be deficient; they both require to be affirmed to achieve a fully orbed Christian understanding of the place of Christ in the Christian faith:

> It was a commonplace of Christian teaching a generation ago to contrast Christ as our atonement and reconciliation with Christ as a "mere" example; the latter was the Socinian, the former the evangelical view. But Christ, as the evangelical view sometimes led its adherents to forget, after all *is* an example; and it is at least possible that to be insensible to the inspiration of his example is to lie outside of his reconciling power. [...] Whatever reconciliation may be, it is something which brings into fresh prominence aspects of that character and virtue what have been somewhat overlooked.

The rise of "narrative theology" has given especial importance to this point. It has been emphasized that it is the narrative of Jesus Christ which exercises controlling influence over the Christian community. Christian belief, and especially Christian ethics, are shaped by the narrative of Jesus Christ, which gives flesh and substance to otherwise abstract ideas of values and virtues. The story of Jesus thus exercises a controlling influence over Christian thinking about ethics, in that the manner in which Jesus acted is seen as having continuing importance for the church today.

New Testament Christological Titles

The New Testament is the primary source for Christology. In this section, we shall explore the main Christological titles found in the New Testament, and their implications for our understanding of the identity of Christ. Why are these titles so important? For biblical writers, names convey insights about identity. The terms used to designate Jesus are the outcome of reflection on what he said, what he did, and what was done to him. Each title can be seen as adding a strand of insight to the tapestry of Christology. In what follows, we shall consider six of the main Christological titles of the New Testament, and reflect briefly on their importance.

Messiah

The New Testament's reflections on the significance of Christ are to be set against an Old Testament context. The term "Christ" – so easily treated as a surname – is actually a *title*, with a range of meanings which can only be fully appreciated in the light of the Old Testament expectation concerning the coming of God's "messiah" (Greek: *Christos*). The Greek word *Christos* translates the Hebrew term *mashiah*, most familiar in its anglicized form of "Messiah," with the root meaning of "one who has been anointed." Although ancient Israel anointed both prophets and priests, the term is primarily reserved for the anointing of a king. Within the context of ancient Israel's strongly theocentric worldview, the king was regarded as someone who was appointed by God. Anointing – that is, the rubbing or covering of someone with olive oil – was thus a public sign of having been chosen by God for the task of kingship.

The term became linked to a set of expectations concerning the future of Israel, which focused on the anticipated coming of a new king who, like David, would rule over a renewed people of God. There is evidence that such expectations reached new heights during the period of Roman occupation, with nationalist feelings becoming closely linked to messianic expectations. The discovery of the Dead Sea Scrolls has cast much light on such expectations at this time. To designate any first-century Palestinian as "the anointed one" would be to make a powerful and deeply evocative affirmation of the importance of such a person.

The New Testament evidence for the use of this title for Jesus is complex, and its interpretation is open to dispute. For example, some have suggested that the Messiah was a divine figure; others have argued that this is not the case, in that the Messiah was merely one favored and acknowledged by God. However, it seems that a good case can be made for suggesting that the following four statements are plausible:

1 Jesus was regarded by some of those who were attracted to him as a potential political liberator, who would rally his people to throw off the Roman domination.
2 Jesus himself never permitted his followers to describe him as "Messiah" – something which has subsequently come to be known as the "messianic secret" (William Wrede).
3 If Jesus regarded himself as the Messiah, it was not in the politicized form that was

associated with Zealot or other strongly nationalist circles.
4 The contemporary expectation was that of a victorious Messiah. The fact that Jesus suffered was seriously at odds with this expectation. If Jesus was a Messiah, he was not the kind of Messiah that people were expecting.

What, then, is the significance of the term for an understanding of the importance of Jesus? For the purpose of establishing Jesus's relation to Israel, the term is enormously important. It suggests that Jesus is to be regarded as the fulfillment of classic Jewish expectations, and lays the foundations for an understanding of the continuities between Judaism and Christianity. This issue was certainly important in first-century Palestine, and continues to be of importance in connection with Jewish–Christian relations today.

However, the issue became increasingly irrelevant to Christian writers as time progressed, and the issue of the relation of the church and Israel became increasingly irrelevant in a Hellenistic culture. The church's theologians were now primarily concerned with accurately placing Jesus on the map of humanity and divinity, rather than a somewhat different map relating the church and Israel, or Christianity and Judaism. The early church soon found itself focusing on other New Testament Christological titles, as it sought to clarify the relation of Jesus's humanity and divinity. One of the most important terms to be discussed was "Son of God," to which we now turn.

Son of God

The Old Testament used the term "Son of God" in a broad sense, perhaps best translated as "belonging to God." It was applied across a wide spectrum of categories, including the people of Israel in general (Exodus 4: 22), and especially the Davidic king and his successors who were to rule over that people (2 Samuel 7: 14). In this minimalist sense, the term could be applied equally to Jesus and to Christians. Jesus himself does not appear to have explicitly used the term of himself. It is found used in this way elsewhere in the New Testament, especially by Paul and in the letter to the Hebrews. Paul, for example, stated that Jesus had "been declared Son of God" on account of the resurrection (Romans 1: 4).

Paul uses the term "Son of God" in relation to both Jesus and believers. However, a distinction is drawn between the sonship of believers, which arises through adoption, and that of Jesus, which originates from his being "God's own son" (Romans 8: 32). In the fourth Gospel and the Johannine letters, the term "son" (*huios*) is reserved for Jesus, while the more general term "children" (*tekna*) tends to be applied to believers. The basic notion appears to be that believers are enabled, through faith, to enter into the same kind of relationship as that which Jesus enjoys with the Father; nevertheless, the relationship between Jesus and the Father is either prior to, or foundational for, that between believers and God.

These observations raise an important issue, which must be noted here. Some readers will find references to "Son of God" problematical, on account of the use of exclusive language. The simple solution is to replace the masculine "son" with the more inclusive term "child." Although this substitution is understandable, it blurs a series of crucial distinctions in the New Testament. For Paul, all believers – whether male or female – are "sons of God" by adoption. The point being made is that all believers enjoy inheritance rights – rights which, under the cultural conditions of the period, were enjoyed only by male children. In view of this major cultural problem, the present work will use the traditional exclusive

language forms "Son of God" and "Son of Man" to deal with New Testament Christological titles, in much the same way as the traditional terms "Father" and "Son" are retained in the earlier analysis of the Trinity (see pp. 243–71).

Son of Man

For many Christians, the term "Son of Man" stands as a natural counterpart to "Son of God." It is an affirmation of the humanity of Christ, just as the latter term is a complementary affirmation of his divinity. However, it is not quite as simple as this. The term "Son of Man" (Hebrew *ben adam* or Aramaic *bar nasha*) is used in three main contexts in the Old Testament:

1 as a form of address to the prophet Ezekiel;
2 to refer to a future eschatological figure (Daniel 7: 13–14), whose coming signals the end of history and the coming of divine judgment;
3 to emphasize the contrast between the lowliness and frailty of human nature and the elevated status or permanence of God and the angels (Numbers 23: 19; Psalm 8: 4).

The third such meaning relates naturally to the humanity of Jesus, and may underlie at least some of its references in the Synoptic Gospels. It is, however, the second use of the term which has attracted most scholarly attention.

The German New Testament scholar Rudolf Bultmann argued that Daniel 7: 13–14 pointed to the expectation of the coming of a "Son of Man" at the end of history, and argued that Jesus shared this expectation. References by Jesus to "the Son of Man coming in clouds with great power and glory" (Mark 13: 26) are thus, according to Bultmann, to be understood to refer to a figure *other than* Jesus. Bultmann suggested that the early church subsequently merged "Jesus" and "Son of Man," understanding them to be the one and the same. The early church thus invented the application of the term to Jesus.

This view has not, however, commanded universal assent. Other scholars have argued that the term "Son of Man" carries a range of associations, including suffering, vindication, and judgment, thus making it natural and proper to apply it to Jesus. George Caird is one New Testament scholar to develop such an approach, arguing that Jesus used the term "to indicate his essential unity with mankind, and above all with the weak and humble, and also his special function as predestined representative of the new Israel and bearer of God's judgement and kingdom."

Lord

The acknowledgment that "Jesus Christ is Lord" (Romans 10: 9) appears to have become one of the earliest Christian confessions of faith, serving to distinguish those who believed in Jesus from those who did not. The term "Lord" (Greek *kyrios* and Aramaic *mar*) appears to have had powerful theological associations, partly on account of its use to translate the "Tetragrammaton" – the four Hebrew characters used to represent the sacred name of God in the Hebrew version of the Old Testament, often represented in English as YHWH or "Yahweh." It was regarded as improper within Judaism to pronounce the name of God; an alternative word (*adonai*) was therefore used. In the Septuagint Greek translation of the Old Testament, the term *kyrios* is used to translate the name of God.

The Greek word *kyrios* thus came to be regarded as reserved for God. The important Jewish historian Josephus records an important incident in which Jews refused to take part in the emperor-cult which was a central part of the civil religion of the Roman Empire. They refused to address the emperor as "lord" (*kyrios*), clearly on account of their belief that this term was appropriate to God alone. The use of the term to refer to Jesus in the New Testament thus draws on this rich tradition of association, implying a high degree of identity between Jesus and God.

This trend is illustrated by a number of passages within the New Testament, which take Old Testament passages referring to God, and apply them to Christ. Perhaps the most significant such occurrence is to be found at Philippians 2: 10–11, a passage which is clearly pre-Pauline. Here, a very early Christian writer, whose identity will probably remain forever unknown, takes the great Old Testament declaration (Isaiah 45: 23) that every knee will bow to the Lord God, and transfers it to the Lord Jesus Christ.

Savior

For New Testament writers, Jesus is the "Savior, who is Christ the Lord" (Luke 2:11). This theme is found throughout the New Testament: Jesus saves his people from their sins (Matthew 1: 21); in his name alone is there salvation (Acts 4: 12); he is the "captain of salvation" (Hebrews 2: 10). The basic idea is, at least on the face of it, quite simple: Jesus is the one who saves.

Yet this seemingly simple statement turns out to be rather more complex than might at first seem. It must be recalled that the New Testament affirmations about Jesus Christ are to be set against a Jewish background. And for the Old Testament, there was only one who could save – the Lord God of Israel. The prophets regularly reminded Israel that she could not save herself, nor can she be saved by other nations round about her. It is the Lord, and the Lord alone, who will save, or forgive Israel's sins. This point is made with special force in some of the prophetic writings, such as Isaiah 45: 21–2:

Who declared it of old? Was it not I, the Lord?
And there is no other god apart from me, a righteous God and a Savior.
There is none apart from me.
Turn to me and be saved, all the ends of the earth!

The New Testament use of the word "savior" to refer to Jesus thus turns out to be considerably more significant than a cursory reading might suggest. The title suggests that Jesus of Nazareth is being credited with doing something that, strictly speaking, only God can do.

This theme is also reflected in the Gospel accounts of how Jesus healed a paralytic (Mark 2:1–12). Jesus tells the paralytic that his sins are forgiven, to the outrage and astonishment of the Jewish teachers of the law watching him. Their reaction was one of disbelief: 'He is blaspheming! Who can forgive sins but God alone!' (Mark 2:7). Underlying this objection was a fundamental belief of the Old Testament: only God can forgive sin. Unless Jesus was God, he had no authority whatsoever to speak those words. He was deluded, or blaspheming. Yet Jesus declares that he does have such authority to forgive, and proceeds to heal the man (Mark 2: 10–11). The resurrection of Jesus demonstrated that Jesus had the right to act in this way, retrospectively validating his claims to authority on earth.

God alone forgives sins; yet Jesus forgives sin. God alone saves; yet Jesus also saves. So what does this say about the identity of Jesus? In the full knowledge that it was the Lord God alone who was savior, and that none other God than could save, the first Christians affirmed that Jesus was savior – that *Jesus* could save. This was no misunderstanding on the part of people ignorant of the Old Testament tradition. It was a confident statement of who Jesus had to be, in the light of what he achieved through his saving death and resurrection.

The New Testament's use of the title "savior" to refer to Jesus thus has important implications for an understanding of Jesus's function and identity. In terms of Jesus's function, the title affirms that he is able to bring the salvation that God promised to his people. Salvation is something that Jesus both proclaims and effects. He makes possible what he promises. In terms of Jesus's identity, the title points to the need to think of Jesus in terms that make clear his unique status. If Jesus is able to achieve something that God alone is able to achieve, our understanding of his identity must be brought into line with this insight. Traditionally, Christian theology sees Jesus's role as savior as an important indication of his entitlement to be spoken and thought of as both divine and human.

God

The New Testament was written against a background of the strict monotheism of Israel. The idea that anyone could be described as "God" would have been blasphemous within this context. Nevertheless, New Testament scholar Raymond Brown has argued that there are three clear instances of Jesus being called "God" in the New Testament with the momentous implications that this involves. These are:

1   The opening section of the fourth Gospel which includes the affirmation "the Word was God" (John 1: 1).
2   The confession of Thomas, in which he addresses the risen Christ as "my Lord and my God" (John 20: 28).

3 The opening of the letter to the Hebrews, in which a psalm is addressed to Jesus as God (Hebrews 1: 8).

Given the strong reluctance of New Testament writers to speak of Jesus as "God," because of their background in the strict monotheism of Israel, these three affirmations are of considerable significance. Many other texts have, of course, been argued to make similar affirmations; these three have been chosen to illustrate the point at issue, partly because there is widespread assent within the community of New Testament scholars concerning their importance in this respect.

To these verses which make statements concerning the *identity* of Jesus, there may be added a series of important New Testament passages which speak of the significance of Jesus in *functional* terms – that is to say, in terms which identify him as performing certain functions or tasks associated with God. Several of these prove to be of considerable significance.

Jesus is the savior of humanity

The Old Testament affirmed that there was only one savior of humanity: God. In the full knowledge that it was God alone who was Savior, that it was God alone who could save, the first Christians nevertheless affirmed that Jesus was Savior, that Jesus could save. A fish came to be a symbol of faith to the early Christians, as the five Greek letters spelling out "fish" in Greek (I-CH-TH-U-S) came to represent the slogan "Jesus Christ, Son of God, Savior." For the New Testament, Jesus saves his people from their sins (Matthew 1: 21); in his name alone is there salvation (Acts 4: 12); he is the "captain of salvation" (Hebrews 2: 10); he is the "Savior, who is Christ the Lord" (Luke

2: 11). And in these affirmations, Jesus is understood to function as God, doing something which, properly speaking, only God can do.

Jesus is worshiped

Within the Jewish context in which the first Christians operated, it was God and God alone who was to be worshiped. Paul warned the Christians at Rome that there was a constant danger that humans would worship creatures, when they ought to be worshiping their creator (Romans 1: 23). Yet the early Christian church worshiped Christ as God – a practice which is clearly reflected even in the New Testament. Thus 1 Corinthians 1: 2 speaks of Christians as those who "call upon the name of our Lord Jesus Christ," using language which reflects the Old Testament formulas for worshiping or adoring God (such as Genesis 4: 26, 13: 4; Psalm 105: 1; Jeremiah 10: 25; Joel 2: 32). Jesus is thus clearly understood to function as God, in that he is an object of worship.

Jesus reveals God

"Anyone who has seen me, has seen the Father" (John 14: 9). These remarkable words, so characteristic of the fourth Gospel, emphasize the belief that the Father speaks and acts in the Son – in other words, that God is revealed in and by Jesus. To have seen Jesus is to have seen the Father – in other words, Jesus is understood, once more, to function as God.

The Patristic Debate over the Person of Christ

The patristic period saw considerable attention being paid to the doctrine of the person of Christ. The debate was conducted primarily within the eastern church; interestingly, Augustine of Hippo never wrote anything of consequence on Christology, presumably finding his time to be more than adequately occupied by debates over grace, the church, and the Trinity. The period proved to be definitive, laying down guidelines for the discussion of the person of Christ which remained normative until the dawn of the Enlightenment debates on the relation of faith and history, to be considered in the next chapter.

The task confronting the patristic writers was basically the development of a unified Christological scheme, which would bring together and integrate the various Christological hints and statements, images and models, found within the New Testament, some of which have been considered briefly above. That task proved complex. In view of its enormous importance for Christian theology, we shall consider its main stages of development in what follows.

Early contributions: from Justin Martyr to Origen

The first period of the development of Christology centered on the question of the divinity of Christ. That Jesus Christ was human appeared to be something of a truism to most early patristic writers. What required explanation – indeed, what appeared *exciting* – about Christ concerned the manner in which he differed from, rather than approximated to, other human beings.

Two early viewpoints were quickly rejected as heretical. *Ebionitism*, a primarily Jewish sect which flourished in the early centuries of the Christian era, regarded Jesus as an ordinary human being, the human son of Mary and Joseph. This approach assimilated Jesus to existing Jewish categories, above all, that of

the prophet. This reduced Christology was regarded as totally inadequate by its opponents, and soon passed into oblivion.

More significant was the diametrically opposed view, which came to be known as *Docetism*, from the Greek verb *dokeō*, "to seem or appear." This approach – which is probably best regarded as a tendency within theology rather than a definite theological position – argued that Christ was totally divine, and that his humanity was merely an appearance. The sufferings of Christ are thus treated as apparent rather than real. Docetism held a particular attraction for the Gnostic writers of the second century, during which period it reached its zenith. By this time, however, other viewpoints were in the process of emerging, which would eventually eclipse this tendency. Justin Martyr represents one such viewpoint.

Justin Martyr, among the most important of the second-century Apologists, was especially concerned to demonstrate that the Christian faith brought to fruition the insights of both classical Greek philosophy and Judaism. Adolf von Harnack summarized the manner in which Justin achieved this objective: he argued that "Christ is the Logos and Nomos." Of particular interest is the Logos-Christology which Justin develops, in which he exploits the apologetic potential of the idea of the Logos, current in both Stoicism and the Middle Platonism of the period.

The Logos (a Greek term which is usually translated as "word," e.g., as it occurs at John 1: 14) is to be thought of as the ultimate source of all human knowledge. The one and the same Logos is known by both Christian believers and pagan philosophers; the latter, however, have only partial access to it, whereas Christians have full access to it, on account of its manifestation in Christ. Justin allows that pre-Christian secular philosophers, such as Heraclitus or Socrates, thus had partial access to the truth, because of the manner in which the Logos is present in the world.

An idea of especial importance in this context is that of the *logos spermatikos*, which appears to derive from Middle Platonism. The divine Logos sowed seeds throughout human history; it is therefore to be expected that this "seed-bearing Logos" will be known, even if only in part, by non-Christians. Justin is therefore able to argue that Christianity builds upon and fulfills the hints and anticipations of God's revelation which are to be had through pagan philosophy. The Logos was known temporarily through the theophanies (that is, appearances or manifestations of God) in the Old Testament; Christ brings the Logos to its fullest revelation. Justin states this point clearly in his *Second Apology*:

> Our religion is clearly more sublime than any human teaching in this respect: the Christ who has appeared for us human beings represents the Logos principle in all its fullness. [...] Whatever either lawyers or philosophers have said well, was articulated by finding and reflecting upon some aspect of the Logos. However, since they did not know the Logos – which is Christ – in its entirety, they often contradicted themselves.

The world of Greek philosophy is thus set firmly in the context of Christianity: it is a prelude to the coming of Christ, who brings to fulfillment what it had hitherto known only in part.

It is in the writings of Origen that the Logos-Christology appears to find its fullest development. It must be made clear that Origen's Christology is complex, and that its interpretation at points is highly problematical. What follows is a simplification of his approach. In the incarnation, the human soul of Christ is united with the Logos. On account of the closeness of this union, Christ's human soul comes to share in the properties of the Logos. Nevertheless, Origen insists that, although both the

Logos and Father are coeternal, the Logos is subordinate to the Father.

We noted above that Justin Martyr argued that the Logos was accessible to all, even if only in a fragmentary manner, but that its full disclosure only came in Christ. Related ideas can be found in other writers to adopt the Logos-Christology, including Origen. Origen adopts an illuminationist approach to revelation, in which God's act of revelation is compared to being enlightened by the "rays of God," which are caused by "the light which is the divine Logos." For Origen, both truth and salvation are to be had outside the Christian faith.

The Arian controversy

The Arian controversy remains a landmark in the development of classical Christology, and therefore demands more extensive discussion than was afforded to earlier themes of the patristic period. Certain aspects of the history of the controversy remain obscure, and are likely to remain so, despite the best efforts of historians to clarify them. What concerns us here is the theological aspects of the debate, which are comparatively well understood. However, it must be stressed that we know Arius's views mainly in the form in which they have been mediated to us *by his opponents*, which raises questions about the potential bias of their presentation. What follows is an attempt to present Arius's distinctive Christological ideas as fairly as possible, on the basis of the few reliable sources now available to us.

Arius emphasizes the self-subsistence of God. God is the one and only source of all created things; nothing exists which does not ultimately derive from God. This view of God, which many commentators have suggested is due more to Hellenistic philosophy than to Christian theology, clearly raises the question of the relation of the Father to the Son. In his *Against the Arians*, Arius's critic Athanasius represents him as making the following statements on this point.

> God was not always a father. There was a time when God was all alone, and was not yet a father; only later did he become a father. The Son did not always exist. Everything created is out of nothing [...] so the Logos of God came into existence out of nothing. There was a time when he was not. Before he was brought into being, he did not exist. He also had a beginning to his created existence.

These statements are of considerable importance, and bring us to the heart of Arianism. The following points are of especial significance.

1 The Father is regarded as existing before the Son. "There was a time when he was not." This decisive affirmation places Father and Son on different levels, and is consistent with Arius's rigorous insistence that the Son is a creature. Only the Father is "unbegotten"; the Son, like all other creatures, derives from this one source of being. However, Arius is careful to emphasize that the Son is not like every other creature. There is a distinction of rank between the Son and other creatures, including human beings. Arius has some difficulty in identifying the precise nature of this distinction. The Son, he argued, is "a perfect creature, yet not as one among other creatures; a begotten being, yet not as one among other begotten beings." The implication seems to be that the Son outranks other creatures, while sharing their essentially created and begotten nature.

2 An important aspect of Arius's distinction between Father and Son concerns the unknowability of God. Arius emphasizes the utter transcendence and inaccessibility of God. God cannot be known by any other creature. Yet, as we noted above, the Son is to be regarded as a creature, however elevated above all other creatures. Arius presses home his logic, arguing that the Son cannot know the Father. "The one who has a beginning is in no position to comprehend or lay hold of the one who has no beginning." This important affirmation rests upon the radical distinction between Father and Son. Such is the gulf fixed between them, that the latter cannot know the former unaided. In common with all other creatures, the Son is dependent upon the grace of God if he (the Son) is to perform whatever function has been ascribed to him. It is considerations such as these which have led Arius's critics to argue that, at the levels of revelation and salvation, the Son is in precisely the same position as other creatures.

But what about the many biblical passages which seem to suggest that the Son is far more than a mere creature? Arius's opponents were easily able to bring forward a series of biblical passages, pointing to the fundamental unity between Father and Son. On the basis of the controversial literature of the period, it is clear that the fourth Gospel was of major importance to this debate, with John 3: 35, 10: 30, 14: 10, 17: 3, and 17: 11 being discussed frequently. Arius's response to such texts is significant: the language of "sonship" is variegated in character and metaphorical in nature. To refer to the "Son" is, according to Arius, an honorific, rather than a theologically precise way of speaking. Although Jesus Christ is referred to as "Son" in Scripture, this metaphorical way of speaking is subject to the controlling principle of a God who is totally different in essence from all created beings – including the Son. Arius's position can be summarized in the following manner.

1 The Son is a creature, who, like all other creatures, derives from the will of God.

2 The term "Son" is thus a metaphor, an honorific term intended to underscore the rank of the Son among other creatures. It does not imply that Father and Son share the same being or status.

3 The status of the Son is itself a consequence not of the *nature of the Son*, but of the *will of the Father*.

Athanasius had little time for Arius's subtle distinctions. If the Son is a creature, then the Son is a creature like any other creature, including human beings. After all, what other kind of creaturehood is there? For Athanasius, the affirmation of the creaturehood of the Son had two decisive consequences, each of which had uniformly negative implications for Arianism.

First, Athanasius makes the point that it is only God who can save. God, and God alone, can break the power of sin and bring us to eternal life. An essential feature of being a creature is that one requires to be redeemed. No creature can save another creature. Only the creator can redeem the creation. Having emphasized that it is God alone who can save, Athanasius then makes the logical move which the Arians found difficult to counter. The New Testament and the Christian liturgical tradition alike regard Jesus Christ as Savior. Yet, as Athanasius emphasized, only God can save. So how are we to make sense of this?

The only possible solution, Athanasius argues, is to accept that Jesus is God incarnate. The logic of his argument at times goes something like this:

1 No creature can redeem another creature.
2 According to Arius, Jesus Christ is a creature.
3 Therefore, according to Arius, Jesus Christ cannot redeem humanity.

At times, a slightly different style of argument can be discerned, resting upon the statements of Scripture and the Christian liturgical tradition:

1 Only God can save.
2 Jesus Christ saves.
3 Therefore Jesus Christ is God.

Salvation, for Athanasius, involves divine intervention. Athanasius thus draws out the meaning of John 1: 14 by arguing that the "Word became flesh": in other words, God entered into our human situation, in order to change it.

The second point that Athanasius makes is that Christians worship and pray to Jesus Christ. This represents an excellent case study of the importance of Christian practices of worship and prayer for Christian theology. By the fourth century, prayer to and adoration of Christ were standard features of the way in which public worship took place. Athanasius argues that if Jesus Christ were a creature, then Christians were guilty of worshiping a creature instead of God – in other words, they had lapsed into idolatry. Christians, Athanasius stresses, are totally forbidden to worship anyone or anything except God alone. Athanasius thus argued that Arius seemed to be guilty of making nonsense of the way in which Christians prayed and worshiped. Athanasius argued that Christians were right to worship and adore Jesus Christ, because by doing so, they were recognizing him for what he was: God incarnate.

The Arian controversy had to be settled somehow, if peace was to be established within the church. Debate came to center upon two terms as possible descriptions of the relation of the Father to the Son. The term *homoiousios*, "of like substance" or "of like being," was seen by many as representing a judicious compromise, allowing the proximity between Father and Son to be asserted without requiring any further speculation on the precise nature of their relation. However, the rival term *homoousios*, "of the same substance" or "of the same being," eventually gained the upper hand. Though differing by only one letter from the alternative term, it embodied a very different understanding of the relationship between Father and Son. The fury of the debate prompted Gibbon to comment in his *Decline and Fall of the Roman Empire* that never had there been so much energy spent over a single vowel. The Nicene creed – or, more accurately, the Niceno-Constantinopolitan creed – of 381 declared that Christ was "of the same substance" with the Father. This affirmation has since come to be widely regarded as a benchmark of Christological orthodoxy within all the mainstream Christian churches, whether Protestant, Catholic, or Orthodox.

In turning to deal with Athanasius's response to Arius, we have begun to touch upon some of the features of the Alexandrian school of Christology. It is therefore appropriate now to explore these in more detail, and compare them with the views of the rival school of Antioch.

The Alexandrian school

The outlook of the Alexandrian school, to which Athanasius is to be assigned, is strongly soteriological in character. Jesus Christ is the redeemer of humanity, where "redemption" means "being taken up into the life of God" or "being made divine," a notion traditionally expressed in terms of *deification*. Christology gives expression to what this soteriological insight implies. We could summarize the trajectory of Alexandrian Christology along the following lines: if human nature is to be deified, it must be united with the divine nature. God must become united with human nature in such a manner that the latter is enabled to share in the life of God. This, the Alexandrians argued, was precisely what had happened in and through the incarnation of the Son of God in Jesus Christ. The Second Person of the Trinity assumed human nature, and by doing so, ensured its divinization. God became human, in order that humanity might become divine.

Alexandrian writers thus placed considerable emphasis upon the idea of the Logos assuming human nature. The term "assuming" is important; a distinction is drawn between the Logos "dwelling within humanity" (as in the case of the Old Testament prophets), and the Logos taking human nature upon itself (as in the incarnation of the Son of God). Particular emphasis came to be placed upon John 1: 14 ("the Word became flesh"), which came to embody the fundamental insights of the school, and the liturgical celebration of Christmas. To celebrate the birth of Christ was to celebrate the coming of the Logos to the world, and its taking human nature upon itself in order to redeem it.

This clearly raised the question of the relation of the divinity and humanity of Christ. Cyril of Alexandria is one of many writers within the school to emphasize the reality of their union in the incarnation. The Logos existed "without flesh" before its union with human nature; after that union, there is only one nature, in that the Logos united human nature to itself. This emphasis upon the one nature of Christ distinguishes the Alexandrian from the Antiochene school, which was more receptive to the idea of two natures within Christ. Cyril states this point as follows:

In declaring that the Word was made to "be incarnate" and "made human," we do not assert that there was any change in the nature of the Word when it became flesh, or that it was transformed into an entire human being, consisting of soul and body; but we say that the Word, in an indescribable and inconceivable manner, united personally to himself flesh endowed with a rational soul, and thus became a human being and was called the Son of man. And this was not by a mere act of will or favor, nor simply adopting a role or taking to himself a person.

This raised the question of what kind of human nature had been assumed. Apollinarius of Laodicea had anxieties about the increasingly widespread belief that the Logos assumed human nature in its entirety. It seemed to him that this implied that the Logos was contaminated by the weaknesses of human nature. How could the Son of God be allowed to be tainted by purely human directive principles? The sinlessness of Christ would be compromised, in Apollinarius's view, if he were to possess a purely human mind; was not the human mind the source of sin and rebellion against God? Only if the human mind were to be replaced by a purely divine motivating and directing force could the sinlessness of Christ be maintained. For this reason, Apollinarius argued that, in Christ, a purely human mind and soul were replaced by a divine mind and soul. "The divine energy fulfills the role of the animating soul and of the human mind" in Christ. The human nature of Christ is thus incomplete.

This idea appalled many of Apollinarius's colleagues. The Apollinarian view of Christ may have had its attractions for some; others, however, were shocked by its soteriological implications. It was pointed out above (p. 286) that soteriological considerations are of central importance to the Alexandrian approach. How could human nature be redeemed, it was asked, if only part of human nature had been assumed by the Logos? Perhaps the most famous statement of this position was made by Gregory of Nazianzus, who stressed the redemptive importance of the assumption of human nature in its totality at the incarnation:

If anyone has put their trust in him as a human being lacking a human mind, they are themselves mindless and not worthy of salvation. For what has not been assumed has not been healed; it is what is united to his divinity that is saved. [. . .] Let them not grudge us our total salvation, or endue the Savior only with the bones and nerves and mere appearance of humanity.

The Antiochene school

The school of Christology which arose in Asia Minor (modern-day Turkey) differed considerably from its Egyptian rival at Alexandria. One of the most significant points of difference relates to the context in which Christological speculation was set. The Alexandrian writers were motivated primarily by soteriological considerations. Concerned that deficient understandings of the person of Christ were linked with inadequate conceptions of salvation, they used ideas derived from secular Greek philosophy to ensure a picture of Christ which was consistent with the full redemption of humanity. As we have seen, the idea of the Logos was of particular importance, especially when linked with the notion of incarnation.

The Antiochene writers differed here. Their concerns were moral, rather than purely soteriological, and they drew much less significantly on the ideas of Greek philosophy. The basic trajectory of much Antiochene thinking on the identity of Christ can be traced along the following lines. On account of their disobedience, human beings exist in a state of corruption, from which they are unable to extricate themselves. If redemption is to take place, it must be on the basis of a new obedience on the part of humanity. In that humanity is unable to break free from the bonds of sin, God is obliged to intervene. This leads to the coming of the redeemer as one who unites humanity and divinity, and thus to the re-establishment of an obedient people of God.

The two natures of Christ are vigorously defended. Christ is at one and the same time both God and a real individual human being.

Against the Alexandrian criticism that this was to deny the unity of Christ, the Antiochenes responded that they upheld that unity, while simultaneously recognizing that the one redeemer possessed both a perfect human and a perfect divine nature. There is a "perfect conjunction" between the human and divine natures in Christ. The complete unity of Christ is thus not inconsistent with his possessing two natures, divine and human. Theodore of Mopsuestia stressed this, in asserting that the glory of Jesus Christ "comes from God the Logos, who assumed him and united him to himself. [. . .] And because of this exact conjunction which this human being has with God the Son, the whole creation honors and worships him." The Alexandrians remained suspicious; this seemed to amount to a doctrine of "two sons" – that is, that Jesus Christ was not a single person, but two, one human and one divine. Yet this option is explicitly excluded by the leading writers of the school, such as Nestorius. Christ is, according to Nestorius, "the common name of the two natures":

> Christ is indivisible in that he is Christ, but he is twofold in that he is both God and a human being. He is one in his sonship, but is twofold in that which takes and that which is taken. [. . .] For we do not acknowledge two Christs or two sons or "only-begottens" or Lords; not one son and another son, not a first "only-begotten" and a new "only-begotten," not a first and second Christ, but one and the same.

So how did the Antiochene theologians envisage the mode of union of divine and human natures in Christ? We have already seen the "assumption" model which had gained the ascendancy at Alexandria, by which the Logos assumed human flesh. What model was employed at Antioch? The answer could be summarized as follows:

> Alexandria: Logos assumes a general human nature.
> Antioch: Logos assumes a specific human being.

Theodore of Mopsuestia is a good example of an Antiochene theologian who held that the Logos did not assume "human nature" in general but a specific human being. Theodore appears to suggest that instead of assuming a general or abstract human nature, the Logos assumed a specific concrete human individual. This seems to be the case in his work *On the Incarnation*: "In coming to indwell, the Logos united the assumed [human being] as a whole to itself and made him to share with it in all the dignity in which the one who indwells, being the Son of God by nature, possesses."

So how are the human and divine natures related? Antiochene writers were convinced that the Alexandrian position led to the "mingling" or "confusion" of the divine and human natures of Christ. To avoid this error, they devised a manner of conceptualizing the relationship between the two natures which maintained their distinct identities. This "union according to good pleasure" involves the human and divine natures of Christ being understood to be rather like watertight compartments within Christ. They never interact or mingle with one another. They remain distinct, being held together by the good pleasure of God. The "hypostatic union" – that is, the union of the divine and human natures in Christ – rests in the will of God.

This might seem to suggest that Theodore of Mopsuestia regarded the union of the divine and human natures as being a purely moral union, like that of a husband and wife. It also leads to a suspicion that the Logos merely puts on human nature, as one would put on a coat: the action involved is temporary and reversible, and involves no fundamental change to anyone involved. However, the Antiochene writers do not seem to have intended these conclusions to be drawn. Perhaps the most reliable way of approaching their position is to suggest that their desire to avoid confusing the divine and human natures within Christ led them to stress their distinctiveness – yet in so doing, to inadvertently weaken their link in the hypostatic union.

The problems this raised are best seen from Theodore of Mopsuestia's discussion of the nature of the "union of good pleasure" in his eighth *Catechetical Oration*:

> The distinction between the natures does not annul the exact confunction, nor does the exact conjunction destroy the distinction between the natures, but the natures remain in their respective existence while separated, and the conjunction remains intact because the one who was assumed is united in honor and glory with the one who assumed, according to the will of the one who assumed him [. . .] The fact that a husband and wife are "one flesh" does not impede them from being two. Indeed, they will remain two because they are two, but they are one because they are also one and not two. In this same way here [i.e., in the incarnation] they are two by nature and one by conjunction; two by nature, because there is a great difference between the natures, and one by conjunction because the adoration offered to the one who has been assumed is not divided from that offered to the one who assumed him, since he [i.e., the one that is assumed] is the temple, from which it is not possible for the one who dwells in it to depart.

Here, Theodore seems to regard the hypostatic union as a conjunction according to the will of the parties involved – more of a contractual arrangement, comparable to a human marriage, than a genuine union of natures. This point becomes especially clear through Theodore's use of the marriage analogy to stress the common honor and dignity shared by the couple, rather than their physical union.

The "communication of attributes"

An issue of major concern to many patristic writers centered on the question of the "communication of attributes," a notion often discussed in terms of the Latin phrase *communicatio idiomatum*. The issue involved can be explored as follows. By the end of the fourth century, the following propositions had gained widespread acceptance within the church:

1 Jesus is fully human.
2 Jesus is fully divine.

If both these statements are simultaneously true, it was argued, then what was true of the humanity of Jesus must also be true of his divinity, and vice versa. An example might be the following:

> Jesus Christ is God.
> Mary gave birth to Jesus.
> Therefore Mary is the Mother of God.

This kind of argument became increasingly commonplace within the late fourth-century church; indeed, it often served as a means of testing the orthodoxy of a theologian. A failure to agree that Mary was the "mother of God" became seen as tantamount to a refusal to accept the divinity of Christ.

But how far can this principle be pressed? For example, consider the following line of argument:

> Jesus suffered on the cross.
> Jesus is God.
> Therefore God suffered on the cross.

The first two statements are orthodox, and commanded widespread assent within the church. But the conclusion drawn from them was widely regarded as unacceptable, as we noted in our earlier discussion of the idea of "a suffering God" (pp. 210–11).

It was axiomatic to most patristic writers that God could not suffer. The patristic period witnessed much agonizing over the limits that could be set to this approach. Thus Gregory of Nazianzus insisted that God must be considered to suffer; otherwise the reality of the incarnation of the Son of God was called into question. However, it was the Nestorian controversy which highlighted the importance of the issues.

By the time of Nestorius, the title *theotokos* (literally, "bearer of God") had become widely accepted within both popular piety and academic theology. Nestorius was, however, alarmed at its implications. It seemed to deny the humanity of Christ. Why not call Mary *anthropotokos* ("bearer of humanity") or even *Christotokos* ("bearer of the Christ")? His suggestions were met with outrage and indignation, on account of the enormous theological investment which had come to be associated with the term *theotokos*. Nevertheless, Nestorius may be regarded as making an entirely legitimate point.

In more recent theology, the most interesting radical application of the "communication of attributes" is generally thought to be that of Martin Luther. Luther had no hesitation in arguing along the following lines:

Jesus Christ was crucified.
Jesus Christ is God.
Therefore God was crucified.

As we noted earlier, the phrase "the crucified God" is one of Luther's most famous bequests to modern theology. Or, again:

Jesus Christ suffered and died.
Jesus Christ is God.
Therefore God suffered and died.

Luther's distinctive "theology of the cross" may be regarded as a radical application of the "communication of attributes."

Adolf von Harnack on the evolution of patristic Christology

On the basis of his historical studies of the development of Christian doctrine, the German liberal Protestant scholar Adolf von Harnack argued forcefully that the transition of the gospel from its original Palestinian milieu, dominated by Hebraic modes of thought and rationality, to a Hellenistic milieu, characterized by radically different modes of thinking, represented a decisive turning point in the history of Christian thought. The notion of dogma, Harnack argues, owes nothing to the teaching of Jesus Christ, or to primitive Christianity in its original Palestinian context. Rather, it is due to the specific historical location, characterized by Hellenistic modes of thought and patterns of discourse, within which the dogmatic statements of the early church were formulated.

For Harnack, the gospel is nothing other than Jesus Christ himself. "Jesus does not belong to the gospel as one of its elements, but was the personal realization and power of the gospel, and we still perceive him as such." Jesus himself *is* Christianity. In making this assertion, however, Harnack implies no *doctrine* of Jesus; the basis of the assertion is partly historical (based on an analysis of the genesis of Christianity), and partly a consequence of Harnack's personalist religious assumptions (Jesus's significance resides primarily in the impact he has upon individuals). Nevertheless, the transmission of the gospel within a Hellenistic milieu, with its distinct patterns of rationality and modes of discourse, led to the attempt to conceptualize and give metaphysical substance to the significance of Jesus.

In the first edition of his *History of Dogma* Harnack illustrates this trend with reference to

Gnosticism, the Apologists, and particularly the Logos-Christology of Origen. To a certain extent, the development of doctrine may be likened, in Harnack's view, to a chronic degenerative illness. In the specific case of Christology, Harnack detects in the shift from soteriology (an analysis of the personal impact of Jesus) to speculative metaphysics a classical instance of the Greek tendency to retreat into the abstract.

Harnack makes three historical observations in support of this thesis.

1   A Christology (that is, a doctrine of the *person* of Christ) is not part of the proclamation of Jesus of Nazareth. Jesus's own message is not a Christology; it includes no self-referring affirmations. It is this point which underlies Harnack's famous – and often totally misunderstood – statement that "the gospel, as Jesus proclaimed it, has to do with the Father only and not the Son."

2   In the history of Christian thought, a concern with Christology was both chronologically and conceptually posterior to a concern with soteriology.

3   The concern with Christology arose within a Hellenistic culture, which echoed a characteristic Greek concern for abstract speculation.

Harnack's observations prompted a new interest in the study of the patristic period, which led to growing criticism of his position. Perhaps the most significant criticism concerns his oversimplification of the nature of "Hellenism."

Nevertheless, Harnack's critique of the patristic period is of importance; we have already seen how the patristic notion of an "impassible God" appears to rest on the uncritical absorption of secular ideas into Christianity. Harnack may not be correct in his suggestion that patristic Christology, and above all the idea

of incarnation, is erroneous; nevertheless, he warns us of the dangers of regarding the patristic writers as having an authoritative status in matters of doctrine. They are as open to criticism as any others in the long history of Christian thought.

The Relation of the Incarnation and the Fall in Medieval Christology

The medieval period was noted for its systematic exploration of the logical and philosophical aspects of most areas of theology, and Christology was no exception. To illustrate the kinds of debates that took place at this time, we shall consider a theological question concerning the incarnation that intrigued this era. Was the incarnation dependent on Adam's fall – or would it have happened anyway?

The classic understanding of the grounds of the incarnation could be summarized like this: Humanity fell from grace, and required restoration. This restoration required the incarnation of the Son of God, and his saving work on the cross. Therefore, if humanity had not sinned, there would have been no need for the incarnation. In fact, most Christian writers thought it pointless to speculate about what might have happened if Adam had never sinned. But not all.

Honorius of Autun, who was active as a theologian over the period 1106–35, argued that the incarnation was not ordained as a remedy for human sin, but in order to secure the divinization of humanity. And humanity needed to be made divine, whether it remained innocent or whether it fell. As humanity required to be totally transformed in this way, the incarnation was necessary. "It was necessary, therefore, for [the Son of God] to become incarnate, so that humanity could be deified, and thus it does not follow that sin was the cause of the incarnation." A similar view is found in the writings of the Benedictine theologian Rupert of Deutz (c.1075–1129), who argued that the incarnation was the result of God's wish to dwell among his people. The incarnation can therefore be seen as the climax of the work of creation, rather than a reaction to human sin.

It fell to Thomas Aquinas to adjudicate on this debate. Clearly uneasy about the highly speculative nature of the question, he argued that the coming of Christ was the result of the fall, and declared that there was little to be gained by considering alternatives:

> Some say that the Son of God would have become incarnate, even if humanity had not sinned. Others assert the opposite, and it would seem that our assent ought to be given to this opinion. For those things that originate from God's will, lying beyond what is due to the creature, can only be made known to us through being revealed in Holy Scripture, in which the divine will is made known to us. Therefore, since the sin of the first human being is described as the cause of the incarnation throughout Holy Scripture, it is more in accordance with this to say that the work of the incarnation was ordained as a remedy for sin, so that, if sin had not existed, the incarnation would never have taken place. Yet the power of God is not limited in this way. Even if sin had not existed, God could still have become incarnate.

The Relation Between the Person and Work of Christ

Older works of Christian theology often draw a sharp distinction between "the person of Christ" or "Christology" on the one hand, and "the work of Christ" or "soteriology" on the other. This distinction is maintained in this present work, for purely educational reasons, in that a full discussion of both areas could not be contained within the limits of a single chapter. However, the distinction is increasingly regarded as being unhelpful, save for presentational reasons. Theologically, the close connection between the two areas is now generally recognized. Among the considerations which led to this development, the following are of especial importance.

1 *The Kantian distinction between the* Ding-ansich *("thing in itself") and its perception*: Kant's argument is that we cannot know things directly, but only insofar as we can perceive them or apprehend their impact. Although the ultimate philosophical justification of this assertion lies beyond the scope of this volume, its theological implications are clear: the identity of Jesus is known through his impact upon us. In other words, the person of Christ becomes known through his work. There is thus an organic link between Christology and soteriology. This is the approach adopted by Albrecht Ritschl in his *Christian Doctrine of Justification and Reconciliation* (1874). Ritschl argued that it was improper to separate Christology and soteriology, in that we perceive "the nature and attributes, that is the determination of being, only in the effect of a thing upon us, and we think of the nature and extent of its effect upon us as its essence."

2 *The growing realization of the affinities between functional and ontological Christologies* – that is, between Christologies which make affirmations about the *function or work* of Christ, and those which make affirmations concerning his *identity or being*. Athanasius is one of the earliest Christian writers to make this connection explicit. Only God can save, he asserts. Yet Christ

is savior. What does this statement concerning the *function* of Christ tell us about his *identity*? If Jesus Christ is capable of functioning as savior, who must he be? Christology and soteriology are thus seen as two sides of the same coin, rather than two independent areas of thought.

This point has been stated with particular force by Wolfhart Pannenberg, who stresses the way in which Christology and soteriology have had the closest of connections in Christian thinking.

> The divinity of Jesus and his freeing and redeeming significance for us are related in the closest possible way. To this extent, Melanchthon's famous sentence is appropriate: "Who Jesus Christ is becomes known in his saving action." [...] Since Schleiermacher the close tie between Christology and soteriology has won general acceptance in theology: This is particularly to be seen in one characteristic feature of modern Christology. One no longer separates the divine–human person and the redemptive work of Jesus Christ, as was done in medieval Scholastic theology and, in its wake, in the dogmatics of sixteenth- and seventeenth-century Protestant orthodoxy, but rather, with Schleiermacher, both are conceived as two sides of the same thing.

The importance of this point can be seen by comparing a Nestorian-style Christology (which stresses the humanity of Christ, especially in relation to his moral example: see p. 288) with a Pelagian soteriology (which stresses the total freedom of the human will: see pp. 362–8). For Pelagius, humanity had the ability to do right; it merely needed to be told what to do. The moral example of Christ provided this example. This exemplarist view of Christ is thus linked with a view of human nature which minimizes the extent of human

sin, and the strange and tragic history of humanity in general. As the English theologian Charles Gore pointed out incisively a century ago, in an oft-quoted passage:

> Inadequate conceptions of Christ's person go hand in hand with inadequate conceptions of what human nature wants. The Nestorian conception of Christ [...] qualifies Christ for being an example of what man can do, and into what wonderful union with God he can be assumed if he is holy enough; but Christ remains one man among many, shut in within the limits of a single human personality, and influencing man only from outside. He can be a Redeemer of man if man can be saved from outside by bright example, but not otherwise. The Nestorian Christ is logically associated with the Pelagian man. [...] The Nestorian Christ is the fitting Saviour of the Pelagian man.

Although Gore perhaps overstates his point, an important connection between Christology and soteriology is identified. An exemplarist soteriology, with its associated understanding of the nature and role of the moral example of Jesus Christ, is ultimately the correlative of a Pelagian view of the situation and abilities of humanity. The ontological gap between Christ and ourselves is contracted, in order to minimize the discontinuity between his moral personality and ours. Christ is the supreme human example, who evinces an authentically human lifestyle which we are alleged to be capable of imitating. Our view of who Jesus is ultimately reflects our understanding of the situation of fallen humanity.

Despite this consensus, there is continuing disagreement over the emphasis to be given to soteriological considerations in Christology. For example, as will become clear later, the approach adopted by Rudolf Bultmann appears to reduce Christology to the mere fact "that" an historical figure existed, to whom the *kerygma* (that is, the proclamation of Christ) can be traced and attached (see p. 322). The primary function of the *kerygma* is to transmit the soteriological content of the Christ-event. A related approach, found in the writings of A. E. Biedermann and Paul Tillich, draws a distinction between the "Christ principle" and the historical person of Jesus. This has led some writers, most notably Wolfhart Pannenberg, to express anxiety that a Christology might simply be constructed out of soteriological considerations (and thus be vulnerable to the criticisms of Ludwig Feuerbach), rather than being grounded in the history of Jesus himself (see p. 158–9).

Christological Models – Classic and Contemporary

O ne of the perennial tasks of Christian theology has been the clarification of the relationship between human and divine elements in the person of Jesus Christ. The Council of Chalcedon (451) may be regarded as laying down a controlling principle for classical Christology, which has been accepted as definitive within much Christian theology. The principle in question could be summarized like this: provided that it is recognized that Jesus Christ is both truly divine and truly human, the precise manner in which this is articulated or explored is not of fundamental importance. Oxford patristic scholar Maurice Wiles (1923–2005) summarized Chalcedon's aims as follows:

> On the one hand was the conviction that a saviour must be fully divine; on the other was the conviction that what is not assumed is not healed. Or, to put the matter in other words, the source of salvation must be God; the locus of salvation must be humanity. It is quite clear that these two principles often pulled

in opposite directions. The Council of Chalcedon was the church's attempt to resolve, or perhaps rather to agree to live with, that tension. Indeed, to accept both principles as strongly as did the early church is already to accept the Chalcedonian faith.

In part, Chalcedon's decision to insist upon the two natures of Christ, while accepting a plurality of interpretations regarding their relation, reflects the political situation of the period. At a time in which there was considerable disagreement within the church over the most reliable way of stating the "two natures of Christ," the Council was obliged to adopt a realistic approach, and give its weight to whatever consensus it could find. That consensus concerned the recognition that Christ was both divine and human, but *not* how the divine and human natures related to each other.

An important minority viewpoint must, however, be noted. Chalcedon did not succeed in establishing a consensus throughout the entire Christian world. A dissenting position became established during the sixth century, and is now generally known as *monophysitism* – literally, the view that there is "only one nature" (Greek: *monos*, "only one," and *physis*, "nature") in Christ. The nature in question is understood to be divine, rather than human. The intricacies of this viewpoint lie beyond the scope of this volume; the reader should note that it remains normative within most Christian churches of the eastern Mediterranean world, including the Coptic, Armenian, Syrian, and Abyssinian churches. (The rival Chalcedonian position, which recognized two natures in Christ, one human and the other divine, is occasionally referred to as *dyophysitism*, from the Greek terms for "two natures.")

As Christian theology has expanded into a variety of different cultural contexts, and adopted various philosophical systems as vehicles for theological exploration, it is no cause for surprise that a variety of ways of exploring the relation between the human and divine natures of Christ can be found within the Christian tradition. In what follows, we shall explore some of these approaches.

The substantial presence of God in Christ

The doctrine of the incarnation, especially as developed within the Alexandrian school, affirms the presence of the divine nature or substance within Christ. The divine nature assumes human nature in the incarnation. Patristic writers affirmed the reality of the union of divine and human substances in the incarnation through designating Mary *theotokos* – that is, "bearer of God." The notion of a substantial presence of God within Christ was of vital importance to the Christian church in its controversy with Gnosticism. A central Gnostic notion was that matter was evil and sinful, so that redemption was a purely spiritual affair. Irenaeus links the idea of a substantial presence of God in Christ with the symbolic affirmation of this in the bread and wine of the Eucharist.

If the flesh is not saved, then the Lord did not redeem us with his blood, the cup of the Eucharist is not a sharing in his blood, and the bread which we break is not a sharing in his body. For the blood cannot exist apart from veins and flesh and the rest of the human substance which the divine Logos truly became, in order to redeem us.

This Christological approach is closely linked with the image of salvation as *deification*. Simeon the New Theologian (949–1022) stated this with particular clarity, as he reflected on the union of the human soul with God:

But your nature is your essence, and your essence your nature. So uniting with your body, I share in your nature, and I truly take as mine what is yours, uniting with

your divinity. [...] You have made me a god, a mortal by my nature, a god by your grace, by the power of your Spirit, bringing together as god a unity of opposites.

We shall return to this concept later, in the course of our discussion of the nature of salvation (see p. 351).

The idea of a substantial presence of God in Christ became of particular importance within Byzantine theology and formed one of the theological foundations of the practice of portraying God in images – or, to use the more technical term, *icons*. There had always been resistance to this practice within the eastern church, on account of its emphasis upon the ineffability and transcendence of God. The *apophatic* tradition in theology sought to preserve the mystery of God by stressing the divine unknowability. The veneration of icons appeared to be totally inconsistent with this, and seemed to many to be dangerously close to paganism. In any case, did not the Old Testament forbid the worship of images?

Germanus, Patriarch of Constantinople, argued vigorously for the use of icons in public worship and private devotion on the basis of the following incarnational argument. "I represent God, the invisible one, not as invisible, but in so far as God has become visible for us by participation in flesh and blood." A similar approach was taken by John of Damascus, who argued that, in worshiping icons, he was not worshiping any created object as such, but the creator God who had chosen to redeem humanity through the material order:

Previously there was absolutely no way in which God, who has neither a body nor a face, could be represented by any image. But now that he has made himself visible in the flesh and has lived with people, I can make an image of what I have seen of God [...] and contemplate the glory of the Lord, his face having been unveiled.

This position was regarded as untenable by the iconoclastic party (so called because they wanted to break or destroy icons). To portray God in an image was to imply that God could be described or defined – and that was to imply an unthinkable limitation on the part of God. Aspects of this debate can still be discerned within the Greek and Russian Orthodox churches, where the veneration of icons remains an integral element of spirituality.

Christ as mediator between God and humanity

A major strand of Christological reflection concentrates upon the notion of mediation between God and humanity. The New Testament refers to Christ as a mediator at several points (Hebrews 9: 15; 1 Timothy 2: 5), thus lending weight to the notion that the presence of God in Christ is intended to mediate between a transcendent God and fallen humanity. This idea of "presence as mediation" takes two quite distinct, yet ultimately complementary forms: the mediation of revelation on the one hand, and of salvation on the other.

The Logos-Christology of Justin Martyr and others is an excellent instance of the notion of the mediation of revelation through Christ. Here, the Logos is understood to be a mediating principle which bridges the gap between a transcendent God and God's creation. Although present in a transient manner in the Old Testament prophets, the Logos becomes incarnate in Christ, thus providing a fixed point of mediation between God and humanity. A related approach is found in Emil Brunner's *The Mediator* (1927), and in a more developed form in his 1938 work *Truth as Encounter*. In the latter, Brunner argued that faith was primarily a personal encounter with the God who meets us personally in Jesus Christ. Brunner was convinced that the early church had misunderstood revelation as the divine impartation of doctrinal truth about God, rather than the self-revelation of God. For Brunner, "truth" is itself a personal concept. Revelation cannot be conceived propositionally or intellectually, but must be understood as an act of God, and supremely the act of Jesus Christ.

God *is revealed* personally and historically in Jesus Christ (pp. 297–8). The concept of "truth as encounter" thus conveys the two elements of a correct understanding of revelation: It is *historical* and it is *personal*. By the former, Brunner wishes us to understand that truth is not something permanent within the eternal world of ideas which is disclosed or communicated to us, but something which *happens* in space and time. Truth comes into being as the act of God in time and space. By the latter point Brunner intends to emphasize that the content of this act of God is none other than *God*, rather than a complex of ideas or doctrines concerning God. The revelation of God is God's self-impartation to us. In revelation, God communicates *God*, not *ideas* about God – and this communication is concentrated and focused in the person of Jesus Christ as appropriated by the Holy Spirit. Although Brunner's rejection of any cognitive dimension to revelation seems overstated, a significant point is being made, with important Christological implications.

A more strongly soteriological approach to this issue is best seen in Calvin's *Institutes*, in which the person of Christ is interpreted in terms of the mediation of salvation from God to humanity. Christ is in effect seen as a unique channel or focus, through which God's redeeming work is directed toward and made available to humanity. Humanity, as originally created by God, was good in every respect. On account of the Fall, natural human gifts and faculties have been radically impaired. As a consequence, both the human reason and human will are contaminated by sin. Unbelief is thus seen as an act of will as much as of reason; it is not simply a failure to discern the hand of God within the created order, but a deliberate decision *not* to discern it and *not* to obey God.

Calvin develops the consequences of this at two distinct, although related, levels. At the epistemic level, humans lack the necessary rational and volitional resources to discern God fully within the created order. There are obvious parallels here with the Logos-Christology of Justin Martyr. At the soteriological level, humans lack what is required in order to be saved; they do not *want* to be saved (on account of the debilitation of the mind and will through sin), and they are *incapable* of saving themselves (in that salvation presupposes obedience to God, now impossible on account of sin). True knowledge of God and salvation must both therefore come from outside the human situation. In such a manner, Calvin lays the foundations for his doctrine of the mediatorship of Jesus Christ.

Jesus Christ is the mediator between God and humanity. In order to act as such a mediator, Jesus Christ must be both divine and human. In that it was impossible for us to ascend to God, on account of our sin, God chose to descend to us instead. Unless Jesus Christ was himself a human being, other human beings could not benefit from his presence or activity. "The Son of God became the Son of Man, and received what is ours in such a way that he transferred to us what is his, making that which is his by nature to become ours through grace" (Calvin).

The revelational presence of God in Christ

As we noted earlier, the idea of "revelation" is complex, embracing the idea of a final disclosure or "unveiling" of God at the end of time, as well as the more general and restricted idea of "making God known" (see pp. 153–4). Both these ideas have been of significance in more recent theology, as the notion of a Christologically determined concept of God gained influence in twentieth-century German theology. Jürgen Moltmann's *Crucified God* is an excellent example of a work which seeks to build up an understanding of the nature of God, on the basis of the assumption that God is disclosed through the cross of Christ. In what follows, we shall explore the distinct, though related, approaches to "revelational presence" associated with Karl Barth and Wolfhart Pannenberg.

Karl Barth's *Church Dogmatics* may be regarded as probably the most extensive and complex exposition of the idea of the "revelational presence of God in Christ." Barth frequently emphasizes that all theology necessarily possesses an implicit Christological perspective and foundation, which it is the task of theology to make explicit. Barth rejects any deductive Christology based upon a "Christ-principle" in favor of one based upon "Jesus Christ himself as witnessed to in Holy Scripture."

Every theological proposition in the *Church Dogmatics* may be regarded as Christological, in the sense that it has its point of departure in Jesus Christ. It is this feature of Barth's later thought which has led to its being described as "Christological concentration" or "Christomonism." Hans Urs von Balthasar illustrates this "Christological concentration" by comparing it to an hourglass, in which the sand pours from the upper to the lower section through a constriction. Similarly, the divine revelation proceeds from God to the world, from above to below, only through the central event of the revelation of Christ, apart from which there is no link between God and humanity.

It must be made clear that Barth is not suggesting that the doctrine of either the person or the work of Christ (or both, if they are deemed inseparable) should stand at the center of a Christian dogmatics, nor that a Christological idea or principle should constitute the systematic speculative midpoint of a deductive system. Rather, Barth is arguing that the act of God which is Jesus Christ underlies theology in its totality. A "church dogmatics" must be "Christologically determined," in that the very possibility and reality of theology is determined by the actuality of the act of divine revelation, by the speaking of the Word of God, by the revelational presence of God in Jesus Christ.

A more eschatological approach is associated with Wolfhart Pannenberg, especially in the 1968 work *Jesus – God and Man*. For Pannenberg, the resurrection of Christ must be interpreted within the context of the apocalyptic worldview. Within this context, Pannenberg argues, the resurrection of Jesus must be seen as the anticipation of the general resurrection of the dead at the end of time. It thus brings forward into history both that resurrection and other aspects of the apocalyptic expectation of the end-time – including the full and final revelation of God. The resurrection of Jesus is thus organically linked with the self-revelation of God in Christ:

> Only at the end of all events can God be revealed in his divinity, that is, as the one who works all things, who has power over everything. Only because in Jesus' resurrection the end of all things, which for us has not yet happened, has already occurred can it be said of Jesus that the ultimate already is present in him, and so also that God himself, his glory, has made its appearance in Jesus in a way that cannot be surpassed. Only because the end of the world is already present in Jesus' resurrection is God himself revealed in him.

The resurrection thus establishes Jesus's identity with God, and allows this identity with God to be read back into his pre-Easter ministry, in terms of a "revelational presence."

Pannenberg is careful to stress that the "revelation" he has in mind is not simply the "disclosure of facts or statements about God." He insists upon the notion of *self-revelation* – a personal revelation which cannot be detached from the person of God. We can only speak of Christ revealing God if there is a revelational presence of God in Christ:

> The concept of God's self-revelation contains the idea that the revealer and what is revealed are identical. God is both the subject and content of this self-revelation. To speak of a self-revelation of God in Christ means that the Christ-event, that *Jesus*, belongs to the essence of God. If this is not the case, then the human event of the life of Jesus would veil the God who is active in that life, and thus exclude the full revelation of God. Self-revelation in the proper sense of the word only takes place where the medium through which God is made known is something that is not alien to God. [. . .] The concept of self-revelation demands the identity of God with the event that reveals God.

Christ as a symbolic presence of God

A related approach treats the traditional Christological formulas as *symbols of a presence of God* in Christ, which is not to be understood as a *substantial* presence. This *symbolic* presence points to the possibility of the same presence being available and accessible to others. Perhaps the most important representative of this position is Paul Tillich, for whom Jesus of Nazareth symbolizes a universal human possibility, which can be achieved without specific reference to Jesus.

For Tillich, the event upon which Christianity is based has two aspects: the fact which is called "Jesus of Nazareth," and the reception of this fact by those who claimed him as the Christ. The factual or objective–historical Jesus is not the foundation of faith, apart from his reception as the Christ. Tillich has no interest in the historical figure of Jesus of Nazareth: all that he is prepared to affirm about him (insofar as it relates to the foundation of faith) is that it was a "personal life," analogous to the biblical picture, who might well have had a name other than "Jesus." "Whatever his name, the New Being was and is active in this man."

The symbol "Christ" or "Messiah" means "the one who brings the new state of things, the New Being." The significance of Jesus lies in his being the historical manifestation of the New Being. "It is the Christ who brings the New Being, who saves men from the old being, that is from existential estrangement and its destructive consequences." In one personal life, that of Jesus of Nazareth, "essential manhood" has appeared under the conditions of existence without being conquered by them. We are, in effect, presented with a philosophy of existence which attaches itself to the existence of Jesus of Nazareth in the most tenuous of manners, and which would not be significantly disadvantaged if the specific historical individual Jesus of Nazareth did not exist.

Jesus may thus be said to be a symbol which illuminates the mystery of being, although other sources of illumination are available. Tillich here regards Jesus of Nazareth as a symbol of a particular moral or religious principle. Tillich emphasizes that God himself cannot appear under the conditions of existence, in that he is the ground of being. The "New Being" must therefore come from God, but cannot be God. Jesus was a human being who achieved a union with God open to every other human being. Tillich thus represents a degree Christology, which treats Jesus as a symbol of our perception of God.

This approach has particular attractions for those committed to interfaith dialogue, such as Paul Knitter and John Hick. On the basis of this approach, Jesus Christ can be treated as one symbol among many others of a universal human possibility – namely, relating to the transcendent, or achieving salvation. Jesus is one symbol of humanity's relationship to the transcendent; others are to be found elsewhere among the world's religions.

Christ as the bearer of the Holy Spirit

An important way of understanding the presence of God in Christ is by viewing Jesus as the bearer of the Holy Spirit. The roots of this idea lie in the Old Testament, and especially in the notion of charismatic leaders or prophets, endowed and anointed with the gift of the Holy Spirit. Indeed, the term "Messiah," as noted above, has close links with the idea of "being anointed with the Holy Spirit." There are excellent reasons for supposing that such an approach to Christology may have become influential in early Palestinian Christianity.

On the basis of what we know of the messianic expectations of first-century Palestine, it may be argued that there was a strong belief in the imminent coming of a bringer of eschatological salvation, who would be a bearer of the Spirit of the Lord (Joel 2: 28–32 is of especial importance). Even in his earthly ministry, Jesus appears to have been identified as the one upon whom the Spirit of God rested. The anointing of Jesus with the Spirit at the time of his baptism is of particular importance in this respect. An early approach to this question became known as *adoptionism*; this view, especially associated with Ebionitism, regarded Jesus as an ordinary human being, yet endowed with special divine charismatic gifts subsequent to his baptism.

The understanding of Jesus as the bearer of the Spirit has proved attractive to many who have difficulty with the classical approaches to Christology. An excellent example is provided by the British patristic scholar G. W. H. Lampe, in his 1976 Bampton Lectures at Oxford

University, entitled *God as Spirit*. Lampe argued that the particular significance of Jesus of Nazareth resided in his being the bearer of the Spirit of God, and thus an example of a spirit-filled Christian existence, showing "the indwelling presence of God as Spirit in the freely responding spirit of man as this is concretely exhibited in Christ and reproduced in some measure in Christ's followers."

Perhaps a more significant development of this approach may be found in the writings of the German theologian Walter Kasper, especially in his *Jesus the Christ* (1974). Kasper does not have any particular difficulties with classical Christological models. However, he is concerned to ensure that the Holy Spirit is not ignored in a comprehensive account of the identity and theological function of Christ. Kasper therefore argues for a pneumatologically oriented Christology, which does justice to the fact that the New Testament often portrays Christ in terms of the central Old Testament concept of the "Spirit of the Lord." For Kasper, the uniqueness of Jesus within the Synoptic Gospels resides in his spirit-filled existence. Jesus's real identity can only be accounted for in terms of an unprecedented relationship to the Spirit. This Spirit, according to Kasper, is the life-giving power of the creator, who inaugurates the eschatological age of healing and hope.

In Jesus, Kasper sees the Spirit of the Lord at work, effecting a new and unprecedented relationship between God and humanity, a development confirmed and consolidated by the resurrection. In terms of this Spirit Christology, Kasper regards Jesus as the focal point at which the universal saving intention of God becomes a unique historical person. In this way, the Spirit opens up the possibility of others entering into the inner life of God. The same Spirit who permeated the life of Jesus is now made available to others, in order that they might share in the same inner life of God.

An anxiety about this approach has been raised by Wolfhart Pannenberg. In his influential *Jesus – God and Man*, Pannenberg argues that any Christology which begins from the notion of the presence of the Spirit in Jesus will inevitably lapse into some form of adoptionism. The presence of the Spirit in Jesus is neither a necessary nor a sufficient ground for maintaining the divinity of Christ. God would be present in Jesus "only as the power of the Spirit which fills him." Jesus could, according to Pannenberg, be viewed simply as a prophetic or charismatic figure – in other words, as a human being who had been "adopted" by God and endowed with the gift of the Spirit. As we have seen, for Pannenberg it is the resurrection of Jesus, rather than the presence of the Spirit in his ministry, which is of decisive importance in this respect.

Nevertheless, Kasper is perhaps less vulnerable to Pannenberg's critique than at first might seem to be the case. Pannenberg's anxiety is that an approach such as Kasper's might lead to a Christology which places Jesus on a par with an Old Testament prophet or charismatic religious leader. However, Kasper insists that the resurrection of Jesus is of decisive importance. Both Pannenberg and Kasper regard the resurrection as having a retroactive character. Pannenberg locates this in terms of the validation and justification of the religious claims of Jesus during his ministry. Kasper, on the other hand, sees the resurrection as linked with the work of the Spirit, and justifies this with reference to pivotal New Testament texts (especially Romans 8: 11 and 1 Peter 3: 18). The Christian understanding of the role of the Spirit is grounded in the role of the Spirit at the resurrection, which excludes an adoptionist Christology.

Christ as the example of a godly life

The Enlightenment raised a series of challenges to Christology, which will be explored further in the following chapter. One such challenge was to the notion of Jesus Christ differing in kind from other human beings. If Jesus Christ differed from other human beings, it was in relation to the extent to which he possessed certain qualities – qualities which were, in principle, capable of being imitated or acquired by everyone else. The particular significance of Christ resides in his being an *example* of a godly life – that is, a life which resonates with the divine will for humanity.

This view can be shown to be one aspect of the Antiochene Christology, which was especially concerned to bring out the moral aspects of Christ's character. For a number of Antiochene writers, Christ's divinity serves to give authority and weight to his human moral example. It is also an important aspect of the Christology of the medieval writer Peter Abelard, who was concerned to stress the subjective impact of Christ upon believers. However, these writers all retained the classical conception of the "two natures" of Christ. With the Enlightenment, the affirmation of the divinity of Christ became increasingly problematic. Two main approaches came to be developed.

The Enlightenment itself witnessed the development of a *degree Christology*, which located the significance of Jesus Christ in his human moral example. In his life, Christ was an outstanding moral educator, whose teachings were authoritative, not on account of his identity, but on account of their resonance with the moral values of the Enlightenment itself. In his death, he provided an example of self-giving love which the Enlightenment regarded as foundational to its morality. If Jesus Christ can be spoken of as "divine," it is in the sense of embodying or exemplifying the lifestyle which ought to typify the person who stands in a correct moral relationship to God, to other human beings, and to the world in general.

Liberal Protestantism came to focus upon the inner life of Jesus Christ, or his "religious personality," as being of decisive importance. In Jesus Christ, the appropriate inner or spiritual relationship of the believer to God may be discerned. It is the "inner life of Jesus" which is regarded as being of decisive importance to faith. The "religious personality of Jesus" is seen as something that is compelling, capable of being assimilated by believers, and hitherto without parallel in the religious and cultural history of humanity. An excellent representative of this approach may be found in Wilhelm Herrmann, who understands Jesus to have made *known* and made *available* something that is new, and that this is thence made known in the inner life of the Christian.

It is the "impression of Jesus" which the believer gains from the gospels which is of decisive importance. This gives rise to a personal certainty of faith, which is grounded in an inner experience. "There arises in our hearts the certainty that God himself is turning toward us in this experience." Perhaps the most significant statement of such views is found in Herrmann's 1892 essay, "The Historical Christ as the Ground of our Faith." In this essay, which is basically a study of the manner in which the historical figure of Jesus can function as the basis of faith, Herrmann drew a sharp distinction between the "historical fact of the person of Jesus" and the "fact of the personal life of Jesus," understanding by the latter the psychological impact of the figure of Jesus upon the reader of the Gospels.

Christ as a hero

One of the most interesting developments in the history of Christology took place in England during the Anglo-Saxon era. How could the significance of Christ be portrayed in terms that Anglo-Saxon culture would recognize and appreciate? Heroic ideals were deeply embedded in this culture, both in Germany and subsequently in England. The great stories of heroes such as Beowulf and Ingelt were related with enthusiasm, and served to keep alive the heroic ideas of that culture. So great was the influence of these writings that in 797 Alcuin wrote to Bishop Higbald, asking that Scripture and the works of the Christian fathers – not pagan myths! – should be read aloud at meals in the monastic refectories. So what better way to counter the influence of pagan heroes than to portray Christ himself as the hero above all heroes?

This literary transformation of Christ to conform to the heroic ideals of the age is best seen in the famous Old English poem *The Dream of the Rood*, thought to have been written about the year 750. (The term "rood" means a "cross.") This dramatic and highly original work offers an account and interpretation of Christ's death and resurrection which represents a significant change of emphasis from the original biblical accounts of these events. In order to emphasize the momentous triumph of the crucifixion, the author depicts Christ as a bold and confident warrior who confronts and defeats sin in a heroic battle. This way of representing Christ made a direct appeal to the virtues of honor and courage, which were greatly revered in Anglo-Saxon culture at this time.

The Dream of the Rood is a remarkable piece of poetry, establishing a firm link between the heroic ideals of Anglo-Saxon culture and the achievement of Christ on the cross. The most distinctive feature of the poem is its deliberate and systematic portrayal of Christ as a hero, who mounts the cross in order to achieve a magnificent victory. The poet depicts Christ as enthusiastically preparing for combat, longing to engage with his enemies, rather than endorsing the more traditional imagery of Christ being led passively to the cross.

This active role on the part of Christ the hero is echoed by language used by the cross itself in the poem. The poet hears the cross tell its own story, particularly how it saw "the Lord of all mankind hasten with much fortitude, for he meant to mount upon me." These words tend to suggest a much more active and purposeful image of Christ than the more passive language of certain biblical passages, such as those which speak of the "Passover lamb which has been sacrificed," implying activity on the part of those who killed Christ and passivity on his part as a victim.

The poet regularly styles Christ as "the young hero" or "the warrior," avoiding the traditional language of Christian theology. Christ is portrayed as a heroic, fair, young knight in terms which echoes the description of Beowulf, a much-admired mythical hero of the same era. In Beowulf, the central figure of the narrative is acclaimed as a "king," "hero," and "valiant warrior," possessed of "strength and vigor," "daring," and a "determined resolve." When Beowulf prepares to go to battle against Grendel's mother, he shows no concern for his own life or safety, but is eager to plunge into battle.

Kenotic approaches to Christology

During the early seventeenth century a controversy developed between Lutheran theologians based at the universities of Giessen and Tübingen. The question at issue can be stated as follows. The Gospels make no reference to Christ making use of all his divine attributes (such as omniscience) during his period on earth. How is this to be explained? Two options seemed to present themselves to these Lutheran writers as appropriately orthodox solutions: either Christ used his divine powers in secret, or he abstained from using them altogether. The first option, which came to be known as *krypsis*, was vigorously defended by Tübingen; the second, which came to be known as *kenosis*, was defended with equal vigor by Giessen.

Yet it must be noted that both parties were in agreement that Christ possessed the central attributes of divinity – such as omnipotence and omnipresence – during the period of the incarnation. The debate was over the question of their use: were they used in secret, or not at all? A much more radical approach came to be developed during the nineteenth century, which saw a developing appreciation of the humanity of Jesus, especially his religious personality. Thus A. E. Biedermann stated that "the religious principle of Christianity is to be more precisely defined as the religious personality of Jesus, that is, that relation between God and humanity which, in the religious self-consciousness of Jesus, has entered into the history of humanity as a new religious fact with the power to inspire faith."

The roots of this idea can be argued to lie in German Pietism, especially in the form this takes in the writings of Nikolaus von Zinzendorf (1700–60), whose "religion of the heart" laid particular emphasis upon an intimate personal relationship between the believer and Christ. It was developed and redirected by F. D. E. Schleiermacher, who regarded himself as a "Herrnhuter" (that is, a follower of Zinzendorf) "of a higher order." Schleiermacher's understanding of the manner in which Christ is able to assimilate believers into his fellowship has strong parallels with Zinzendorf's analysis of the role of religious feelings in the spiritual life, and their grounding in the believer's fellowship with Christ.

Nevertheless, the importance attached to the human personality of Jesus left a number of theological loose ends. What about the divinity of Christ? Where did this come into things? Was not the emphasis upon Christ's humanity equivalent to a neglect of his divinity? Such questions and suspicions were voiced within more orthodox circles during the 1840s and early 1850s. However, during the later 1850s an approach to Christology

was mapped out which seemed to have considerable potential in this respect. At one and the same time, it defended the divinity of Christ, yet justified an emphasis upon his humanity. The approach in question is known as "kenoticism," and is especially associated with the German Lutheran writer Gottfried Thomasius.

In his *Person and Work of Christ* (1852–61) Thomasius argues that the incarnation involves *kenosis*, the deliberate setting aside of all divine attributes, so that, in the state of humiliation, Christ has voluntarily abandoned all privileges of divinity. It is therefore entirely proper to stress his humanity, especially the importance of his suffering as a human being. Thomasius's approach to Christology was much more radical than that of the early kenoticists. The incarnation involves Christ's *abandoning* of the attributes of divinity. They are set to one side during the entire period from the birth of Christ to his resurrection. Basing his ideas on Philippians 2: 6–8, Thomasius argued that in the incarnation, the second person of the Trinity reduced himself totally to the level of humanity. A theological and spiritual emphasis upon the humanity of Christ was thus entirely justified.

This approach to Christology was criticized by Isaak August Dorner (1809–84), on the grounds that it introduced change into God himself. The doctrine of the immutability of God was thus, he argued, compromised by Thomasius's approach. Interestingly, this insight contains much truth, and can be seen as an anticipation of the twentieth-century debate over the question of the "suffering of God," noted earlier.

The approach was also taken up with some enthusiasm in England. In his 1889 Bampton Lectures at Oxford University, Charles Gore argued that Christ had emptied himself of the divine attributes, especially omniscience, in the incarnation. This prompted leading traditionalist Darwell Stone to charge that Gore's view "contradicted the practically unanimous teaching of the fathers, and is inconsistent with the immutability of the divine nature." Once more, such comments point to the close connection between Christology and theology, and indicate the importance of Christological considerations for the development of the doctrine of "a suffering God."

In the present chapter, we have surveyed some classical themes of Christology. The issues involved will probably continue to be subjects for perennial debate within Christian theology, and it is essential that the student becomes familiar with at least some of the questions discussed here. However, these issues were largely overshadowed during the period of the Enlightenment, as questions of a more historical nature came to the fore – questions which will be considered in the following chapter.

QUESTIONS FOR CHAPTER 11

1 Can Christian theology do without Jesus Christ?

2 Explore the use of one of the major New Testament titles for Jesus. What are the implications of speaking of Jesus in this way?

3 Summarize the main points of difference between the Alexandrian and Antiochene approaches to Christology.

4 What theological insights are linked with the belief that Jesus Christ is "God incarnate"?

5 What is meant by speaking of Jesus as "the mediator"?

12

Faith and History: The Christological Agenda of Modernity

The modern period has seen a series of developments of fundamental importance to Christology, which have no real parallel in previous Christian history. In view of the importance of these developments, they are considered here in some detail. The previous chapter explored the development of classical Christology, which continues to be a major aspect of theological reflection within the church. However, the rise of the Enlightenment worldview led to the credibility of classical Christology being challenged on a number of fronts. The present chapter documents these developments, and assesses their impact upon Christology.

Faith and History: A Modernist Agenda

The dawn of modernity in the eighteenth century raised some very specific issues for the Christian understanding of the identity of Jesus Christ. In chapter 4 we explored the basic features of Enlightenment rationalism, noting especially its emphasis upon the ability of human reason to uncover the ordering of the world and the place and purpose of human beings within it. It will thus be clear that the rational religion of the Enlightenment found itself in conflict with a number of major areas of traditional Christian theology with a direct bearing upon Christology. For this reason, the development of Christology from about 1750 to 2000 included focused discussion of a series of issues which had not been considered in any detail prior to that point.

The Enlightenment and Christology

The Enlightenment emphasis upon the competence of reason raised questions concerning the necessity of divine revelation. If reason was capable of discovering the nature and purposes of God, what continuing role was there for a historical revelation of God in the person of Jesus Christ? Reason seemed to make revelation – and thus any idea of a "revelational presence" in Christ – superfluous. The significance of Jesus Christ was thus stated in terms of his moral teaching and example. Far from being a supernatural redeemer of humanity, it was argued, Christ was actually the "moral educator of humanity," offering the world a religious teaching which was consistent (although to what extent was a matter of debate) with the highest ideals of human reason. In his life, Jesus was an educator; in his death, he was an example of self-giving love for humanity.

The Enlightenment also insisted that history was homogeneous. This had two major consequences. In the first place, it led to a contraction of the ontological gap between Christ and other human beings. Christ was to be regarded as a human being like other human beings. If he differed from others, it was in the extent to which he possessed certain qualities. The difference between Christ and others was one of *degree*, rather than *kind*. In the second place, it led to growing historical skepticism concerning the resurrection. If history was continuous and homogeneous, the absence of resurrections in present-day human experience must, it was argued, cast serious doubt upon the New Testament reports of the resurrection. The Enlightenment thus tended to treat the resurrection as a nonevent, at best a simple misunderstanding of a spiritual experience, and at worst a deliberate cover-up to hide the shameful end of Jesus's ministry on the cross. We shall explore this point further below.

In view of its emphasis upon the resurrection, the New Testament must therefore be regarded as having misrepresented the significance of Christ. Whereas Jesus of Nazareth was actually little more than a thoroughly human itinerant rabbi, the New Testament writers presented him as a savior and risen Lord. These beliefs were, it was argued, often little more than fanciful additions to or misunderstandings of the history of Jesus. By appropriate use of the latest historical methods, some writers of the Enlightenment period believed that it was possible to reconstruct Jesus "as he actually was." The origins of the "quest of the historical Jesus" (as opposed to the allegedly "mythical Christ of faith") lie in this period, based on such considerations.

Three specific aspects of the Enlightenment critique of classical Christology are of such importance that they require to be noted in more detail.

The philosophical uselessness of history

For the writers of the Enlightenment, history was incapable of disclosing truth. Reason, and reason alone, was the means by which secure, reliable knowledge could be gained. The truths of reason were clear, distinct, necessary, and universal. And they could only be gained by rational reflection. History was all about contingencies, things that happened unpredictably. So how could it be of any value in establishing reliable insights? One of the most fundamental reasons why modernism turned its back on the classical Christian idea that Jesus Christ disclosed the truth about God was its core belief that history was not capable of such disclosure. If anything could be known reliably about God, it had to be known through pure reason. We shall explore this point further presently, particularly in relation to G. E. Lessing's critique of traditional Christologies.

The critique of miracles

Much traditional Christian apologetics concerning the identity and significance of Jesus Christ was based upon the "miraculous evidences" of the New Testament, culminating in the resurrection. The new emphasis upon the mechanical regularity and orderliness of the universe, perhaps the most significant intellectual legacy of Newtonianism, raised doubts concerning the New Testament accounts of miraculous happenings. Hume's *Essay on Miracles* (1748) was widely regarded as demonstrating the evidential impossibility of miracles. Hume emphasized that there were no contemporary analogs of New Testament miracles, such as the resurrection, thus forcing the

New Testament reader to rely totally upon human testimony to such miracles. For Hume, it was a matter of principle that no human testimony was adequate to establish the occurrence of a miracle, in the absence of a present-day analog.

In the 1760s and 1770s, H. S. Reimarus and G. E. Lessing denied that human testimony to a past event (such as the resurrection) was sufficient to make it credible if it appeared to be contradicted by present-day direct experience, no matter how well documented the original event may have been. Similarly, the leading French rationalist Denis Diderot declared that if the entire population of Paris were to assure him that a corpse had just been raised from the dead, he would not believe a word of it. This growing skepticism concerning the "miraculous evidences" of the New Testament forced traditional Christianity to defend the doctrine of the divinity of Christ on grounds other than miracles – which, at the time, it proved singularly incapable of doing. Of course, it must be noted that other religions claiming miraculous evidences were subjected to equally great skeptical criticism by the Enlightenment: Christianity happened to be singled out for particular comment on account of its religious domination of the cultural milieu in which the Enlightenment developed.

The development of doctrinal criticism

The Enlightenment witnessed the origin of the discipline of doctrinal criticism, in which the received teachings of the Christian church were subjected to a penetrating analysis concerning their historical origins and foundations. The origins of the "history of dogma" (to use the traditional English rendering of the German term *Dogmengeschichte*) date from the period of the Enlightenment; the consolidation of the discipline dates from later, more specifically from the period of liberal Protestantism,

especially during the second half of the nineteenth century.

The discipline is generally regarded as having been initiated in the eighteenth century by Johann Friedrich Wilhelm Jerusalem, who argued that dogmas such as the doctrine of the two natures and the Trinity were not to be found in the New Testament. If anything, these arose through confusion of the Platonic *logos-concept* with that found in the fourth Gospel, and the mistaken apprehension that Jesus personified, rather than exemplified, this *logos*. The history of dogma was thus a history of mistakes – mistakes, however, which were in principle reversible, were it not for the immovable hostility of the institutional churches to any such reconstruction.

The "history of dogma" movement clearly had implications for Christology, not least in the assertions, evident from the late eighteenth century, that some of the Christological beliefs of the early church were conditioned or excessively influenced by the Hellenistic environment in which Christianity developed. The influence of the movement reached its peak under Adolf von Harnack, who argued that a series of specific Christological developments were due to the influence of Greek ideas during the patristic period. Harnack argued that the doctrine of the incarnation was not part of the gospel at all; it was a Hellenistic addition to an essentially simple Palestinian gospel (see pp. 290–1).

It will thus be clear that the dawn of the Enlightenment represented a major new challenge to traditional Christology, obliging it to engage with questions which hitherto had not featured prominently, if at all, on its agenda. The Enlightenment set the parameters for future Christian discussion, not just of the *nature* but also of the *plausibility* of its theological heritage. Although the credibility of the Enlightenment worldview, especially its emphasis upon the total adequacy of human reason, has been severely challenged through the recognition of the nonuniversal character of human rationality and the social mediation of traditions of discourse and reasoning, the Enlightenment continues to remain a fundamental reference point for modern Christian thought.

It is now appropriate to begin to explore the Christologies of the Enlightenment in more detail.

The Problem of Faith and History

The problems which confront the Christian appeal to the history of Jesus of Nazareth as the climax of God's self-revelation in history can be summarized under three broad headings. How can we be sure about what really happened in Palestine at the time of Jesus? And, assuming that we can rest assured concerning the reliability of that knowledge, how can a series of events in history give us access to universal truth? And surely the vast difference between modern western culture and that of first-century Palestine makes it impossible to do anything with the history of Jesus? We could state these points more formally as a set of three difficulties, as follows.

1 A *chronological* difficulty, on account of the distance of the past from the present. How can we be certain of what happened nearly two thousand years ago?
2 A *metaphysical* difficulty, posed by the nature of history itself. How can the history of Jesus of Nazareth give access to truth? At first sight, accidental historical truths seem to be rather different from universal and necessary rational truths.
3 An *existential* problem, which arises from the cultural distance between first-century Palestine and modern western society.

How can modern human existence relate to a religious message of the distant past?

It will be clear that these three elements are not absolutely distinct. There is a significant degree of interaction between them. However, together they build up to form the overall problem of "faith and history" which has been of such importance in relation to modern Christology. We shall consider each of these elements in turn, basing our discussion on the writings of Gotthold Ephraim Lessing (1729–81), a leading German rationalist writer and critic of traditional Christianity. Lessing's discussion of these three difficulties is widely regarded as having set the agenda for modern discussion of these questions. From 1780 onward, Christology was obliged to address and answer each of these difficulties. In what follows, we shall consider the difficulties and indicate the responses.

The chronological difficulty

The gospel accounts of Jesus Christ place him firmly in the past. We are unable to verify those accounts, but are obliged to rely upon the eyewitness reports which underlie the Gospels for our knowledge of Jesus. But, Lessing asked, how reliable are those accounts? Why should we trust reports from the past, when they cannot be verified in the present? As we shall see later, Lessing considers this difficulty to be felt with particular force in relation to the resurrection of Christ, which he regards as resting upon distinctly shaky historical foundations.

There is thus uncertainty about what happened in the past. However, Lessing argues that the problem goes deeper than this. Even if we could be certain about the past, a new difficulty would arise: what conceivable value has historical knowledge? How can an historical event give rise to ideas? We shall explore this difficulty in what follows.

The metaphysical difficulty

If one pole of the Enlightenment critique of traditional Christianity was a belief in the omnicompetence of reason, a second pole was a growing skepticism concerning the value of history as a source of knowledge. There was a growing belief that history – including historical figures or events – could not give access to the kind of knowledge that was necessary for a rational religious or philosophical system. How can the move from history (which is a collection of accidental and contingent truths) to reason (which is concerned with necessary and universal truths) take place? Lessing argued there was a gap between *historical* and *rational* truth which could not be bridged.

> If no historical truth can be demonstrated, then nothing can be demonstrated by means of historical truths. That is: Accidental truths of history can never become the proof of necessary truths of reason. [. . .] That, then, is the ugly great ditch which I cannot get across, however often and however earnestly I have tried to make the leap.

Lessing's "ugly great ditch" between faith and history has been seen as summing up the gulf fixed between historical and rational approaches to Christian theology.

"If on historical grounds I have no objection to the statement that this Christ himself rose from the dead, must I therefore accept that this risen Christ was the Son of God?" In answering this question in the negative, Lessing draws a distinction between two different classes of truth. If the chronological ditch concerned a dispute about historical facts – what actually happened in the past – the second ditch concerned the interpretation of those events. How can the transition from the "accidental truths of history" to the "necessary truths of reason" be made? Lessing argued that these are two radically different and totally incommensurable classes of truth.

Rational truth was regarded as possessing the qualities of necessity, eternity, and universality. It was the same at all times and all places. Human reason was capable of penetrating to this universal static realm of truth, which could act as the foundation of all human knowledge. This notion of truth can be found in a definitive form in the writings of Benedict Spinoza, who argued that human reason is capable of basing itself upon self-evident first principles, and, by following these through logically, deducing a complete moral system. Just about everyone who favors this approach makes some sort of appeal to Euclid's five principles of geometry. On the basis of his five principles, he was able to construct his entire geometrical system. Many of the more rationalist philosophers, such as Leibniz and Spinoza, were deeply attracted to this, believing that they could use the same method in philosophy. From a set of certain assumptions, a great secure edifice of philosophy and ethics could be erected. Of course, the dream later turned sour. The discovery of non-Euclidean geometry during the nineteenth century destroyed the appeal of this analogy. It turned out that there were other ways of doing geometry, each just as internally consistent as Euclid's (see pp. 144–5). But this development was not known to writers such as Spinoza or Lessing, who believed that reason was capable of erecting a self-sufficient and universally valid system on the basis of the necessary truths of reason.

Part of Lessing's case against orthodoxy here concerns the "scandal of particularity." Why should one specific historical event have such momentous significance? Why should the history of Jesus of Nazareth – even assuming that it could be known with a degree of certainty that Lessing personally believed to be impossible – be elevated to such epistemological heights?

Lessing argued that the universal human faculty of reason, available at all times and in all places to all people, avoided this scandal. Rationalism thus possessed both a moral and an intellectual superiority to the particularist Christology associated with traditional Christianity.

Lessing's assumption about the existence of a universal rationality has, however, been subject to considerable criticism in modern times. The sociology of knowledge has demonstrated that, for example, "Enlightenment rationalism" is far from being universal, but is merely one of a number of intellectual options. The suggestion that historicity limits intellectual options raises a number of difficulties for Enlightenment rationalism. For our purposes, it is particularly important to stress that individuals (whether theologians, philosophers, or natural scientists) do not begin their quest for knowledge *de novo*, as if they were isolated from society and history. The Enlightenment emphasis upon knowledge gained through individual critical reflection, deriving from Descartes, has been the subject of considerable criticism in recent years on account of its uncritical rejection of the corporate foundations of knowledge.

The existential difficulty

Finally, Lessing poses a series of questions which are existential in their orientation. What, he asks, can the *relevance* of such an outdated and archaic message be for the modern world? The original Christian message is implausible for the modern reader. There is an insuperable credibility gap between a first-century and an eighteenth-century worldview. How can learned and culturally sensitive Europeans enter into the backward world of the New Testament and appropriate its outdated religious message?

It is difficult to analyze this aspect of Lessing's discussion of the problem of faith and history, simply because he himself appears to have some difficulty in conceptualizing the point at issue. Nevertheless, the point is important, and will be a recurring feature of our study of modern Christology. Perhaps it could be said that it is only with the rise of existentially oriented Christologies in the twentieth century that Lessing's point has been fully addressed, and answered.

The Quest of the Historical Jesus

Both English Deism and the German Enlightenment developed the thesis that there was a serious discrepancy between the real Jesus of history and the New Testament interpretation of his significance. Underlying the New Testament portrait of the supernatural redeemer of humanity lurked a simple human figure, a glorified teacher of common sense. While the idea of a supernatural redeemer was unacceptable to Enlightenment rationalism, that of an enlightened moral teacher was not. This view, developed with particular rigor by Reimarus, suggested that it was possible to go behind the New Testament accounts of Jesus, and uncover a simpler, more human Jesus, who would be acceptable to the new spirit of the age. And so the quest for the real and more credible "Jesus of history" began.

Although this quest would ultimately end in failure, the later Enlightenment regarded it as holding the key to the credibility of Jesus within the context of a rational natural religion. Jesus's moral authority resided in the quality of his teaching and religious personality, rather than in the unacceptable orthodox suggestion that he was God incarnate. And it is this suggestion which underlies the celebrated "quest of the historical Jesus."

The original quest of the historical Jesus

The original quest of the historical Jesus was based upon the presupposition that there was a radical gulf between the historical figure of Jesus, and the interpretation which the Christian church had placed upon him. The "historical Jesus" who lies behind the New Testament, was a simple religious teacher; the "Christ of faith" was a misrepresentation of this simple figure by early church writers. By going back to the historical Jesus, a more credible version of Christianity would result, stripped of all unnecessary and inappropriate dogmatic additions (such as the idea of the resurrection or the divinity of Christ).

Such ideas, although frequently expressed by English Deists of the seventeenth century, received their classic statements in Germany in the late eighteenth century, especially through the posthumously published writings of Hermann Samuel Reimarus (1694–1768). Reimarus became increasingly convinced that both Judaism and Christianity rested upon fraudulent foundations, and conceived the idea of writing a major work which would bring this fact to public attention. The resulting work labored under the title of *An Apology for the Rational Worshipper of God*. The volume subjected the entire biblical canon to the standards of rationalist criticism. However, reluctant to cause any controversy, Reimarus did not publish the work. It remained in manuscript form until his death.

At some point the manuscript fell into the hands of Lessing, who decided to publish a selection of extracts from the work. These "fragments of an unknown writer," published in 1774, caused a sensation. The volume contained five fragments, now generally known as the "Wolfenbüttel Fragments," and included a sustained attack on the historicity of the resurrection.

The final fragment, entitled "On the Aims of Jesus and His Disciples," concerned the nature of our knowledge of Jesus Christ, and raised the questions of whether the Gospel accounts of Jesus had been tampered with by the early Christians. Reimarus argued that there was a radical difference between the beliefs and intentions of Jesus himself, and those of the apostolic church. Jesus's language and images of God were, according to Reimarus, those of a Jewish apocalyptic visionary, with a radically limited chronological and political reference and relevance. Jesus accepted the late Jewish expectation of a Messiah who would deliver his people from Roman occupation, and believed that God would assist him in this task. His cry of dereliction on the cross represented his final realization that he had been deluded and mistaken.

However, Reimarus argued, the disciples were not prepared to leave things like this. They invented the idea of a "spiritual redemption" in the place of Jesus's concrete political vision of an Israel liberated from foreign occupation. They invented the idea of the resurrection of Jesus, in order to cover up the embarrassment caused by his death. As a result, the disciples invented doctrines quite unknown to Jesus, such as his death being an atonement for human sin, adding such ideas to the biblical text to make it harmonize with their beliefs. As a result, the New Testament as we now have it is riddled with fraudulent interpolations. The real Jesus of history is concealed from us by the apostolic church, which has substituted a fictitious Christ of faith, the redeemer of humanity from sin.

In his masterly survey *The Quest of the Historical Jesus*, Albert Schweitzer summarizes the importance of Reimarus's radical suggestions as follows. According to Reimarus, if we

> . . . desire to gain an historical understanding of Jesus' teaching, we must leave behind what

311

we learned in the catechism regarding the metaphysical divine sonship, the Trinity, and similar dogmatic conceptions, and go out into a wholly Jewish world of thought. Only those who carry the teachings of the catechism back into the preaching of the Jewish Messiah will arrive at the idea that he was the founder of a new religion. To all unprejudiced persons it is manifest that "Jesus has not the slightest intention of doing away with the Jewish religion and putting another in its place." Jesus was simply a Jewish political figure, who confidently expected to cause a decisive and victorious popular rising against Rome, and was shattered by his failure.

Although Reimarus found few, if any, followers at the time, he raised questions which would become of fundamental importance in subsequent years. In particular, his explicit distinction between the legitimate historical Jesus and the fictitious Christ of faith proved to be of enormous significance. The resulting "quest of the historical Jesus" arose as a direct result of the growing rationalist suspicion that the New Testament portrayal of Christ was a dogmatic invention. It was possible to reconstruct the real historical figure of Jesus, and disentangle him from the dogmatic ideas in which the apostles had clothed him.

The quest for the religious personality of Jesus

A more subtle version of this approach is linked with the rise of liberal Protestantism in the nineteenth century (see pp. 82–3). The emergence of movements such as Romanticism led to rationalism increasingly being regarded as outmoded (see pp. 70–1). A new interest developed in "the human spirit" and in the more specifically religious aspects of human life. This led to a new interest in the religious personality of Jesus. Ideas such as the "divinity" of Christ were regarded as outmoded; the idea of a "religious personality" of Jesus, which could be imitated by anyone, seemed a much more acceptable way of restating Christological issues in the modern period. As a result, renewed attention was paid to the nature of the New Testament sources upon which the life of the historical Jesus could be constructed. It was widely believed that the new literary approach to the New Testament in general, and the Synoptic Gospels in particular, would permit scholars to establish a firmly drawn and lifelike portrait which would bring out clearly the personality of Jesus.

The assumption underlying this "life of Jesus" movement in the later nineteenth century was that the remarkable religious personality of Jesus, whose shape could be determined by conscientious historical inquiry, would provide a solid historical foundation for faith. The firm ground of historical truth upon which Christian faith depended was thus not supernatural or antirational (a perceived weakness of traditional Christology), but merely the religious personality of Jesus, a fact of history open to scientific investigation. The impression which he made upon his contemporaries could be reproduced in his followers of every age.

The remarkable number of "lives of Jesus" produced in the later nineteenth century in England, America, and France, as well as in Germany itself, is an adequate testimony to the popular appeal of the ideas underlying the "life of Jesus" movement. Through it, the religious personality of the "far-off mystic of the Galilean hills" (to use Lord Morley's famous phrase) could be brought into the present, uncluttered by cultural irrelevancies, in order to form the basis of faith for the coming generation.

It was, of course, inevitable that the portrayals of the religious personality of Jesus were radically subjective, so that the rediscovered Jesus of history turned out to be merely the embodiment of an ideal figure by the progressive standards of the nineteenth century.

The relativity of historical research was not immediately obvious to the nineteenth-century "life of Jesus" movement, whose adherents regarded themselves as practitioners of the objective historical method, rather than as an historically conditioned phenomenon in themselves. Earlier writers had labored under misunderstandings; they had access to the most sophisticated historical methods and resources, which allowed them access to the authentic history of Jesus. They certainly saw him as he had never been seen before; sadly, they believed that they saw him as he actually was.

The critique of the quest, 1890–1910

The illusion could not last. The most sustained challenge to the "life of Jesus" movement developed on a number of fronts during the final decade of the nineteenth century. Three main criticisms of the "religious personality" Christology of liberal Protestantism emerged in the two decades before World War I; we shall consider them individually.

The apocalyptic critique

This criticism, primarily associated with Johannes Weiss (1863–1914) and Albert Schweitzer (1875–1965), maintained that the strongly eschatological bias of Jesus's proclamation of the kingdom of God called the essentially Kantian liberal interpretation of the concept into question. In 1892 Johannes Weiss published *Jesus' Proclamation of the Kingdom of God*. In this book he argued that the idea of the "kingdom of God" was understood by the liberal Protestants to mean the exercise of the moral life in society, or a supreme ethical ideal. In other words, it was conceived primarily as something subjective, inward, or spiritual, rather than in spatiotemporal terms. For Weiss himself, Ritschl's concept of the

kingdom of God was essentially continuous with that of the Enlightenment. It was a static moral concept without eschatological overtones. The rediscovery of the eschatology of the preaching of Jesus called into question not merely this understanding of the kingdom of God, but also the liberal portrait of Christ in general. The kingdom of God was thus not to be seen as a settled and static realm of liberal moral values, but as a devastating apocalyptic moment which overturned human values (see pp. 472–3).

For Schweitzer, however, the whole character of Jesus's ministry was conditioned and determined by his apocalyptic outlook. It is this idea which has become familiar to the English-speaking world as "thorough-going eschatology." Where Weiss regarded a substantial part (but not all) of the teaching of Jesus as being conditioned by his radical eschatological expectations, Schweitzer argued for the need to recognize that every aspect of the teaching and attitudes of Jesus was determined by his eschatological outlook. Where Weiss believed that only part of Jesus's preaching was affected by this outlook, Schweitzer argued that the entire content of Jesus's message was consistently and thoroughly conditioned by apocalyptic ideas – ideas which were quite alien to the settled outlook of late nineteenth-century western Europe.

The result of this consistent eschatological interpretation of the person and message of Jesus of Nazareth was a portrait of Christ as a remote and strange figure, an apocalyptic and wholly unworldly person, whose hopes and expectations finally came to nothing. Far from being an incidental and dispensable "husk" which could be discarded in order to reach the true "kernel" of Jesus's teaching concerning the universal fatherhood of God, eschatology was an essential and dominant characteristic of his outlook. Jesus thus appears to us as a strange figure from an alien first-century Jewish apocalyptic milieu, so that, in Schweitzer's famous words, "he comes to us as one unknown."

The skeptical critique

This approach, associated particularly with William Wrede (1859–1906), called into question the historical status of our knowledge of Jesus in the first place. History and theology were closely intermingled in the synoptic narratives, and could not be disentangled. According to Wrede, Mark was painting a theological picture in the guise of history, imposing his theology upon the material which he had at his disposal. The second Gospel was not objectively historical, but was actually a creative theological reinterpretation of history.

It was thus impossible to go behind Mark's narrative and reconstruct the history of Jesus, in that – if Wrede is right – this narrative is itself a theological construction, beyond which one cannot go. The "quest of the historical Jesus" thus comes to an end, in that it proves impossible to establish a historical foundation for the "real" Jesus of history. Wrede identified the following three radical and fatal errors underlying the Christologies of liberal Protestantism.

First, although the liberal theologians appealed to later modifications of an earlier tradition when faced with unpalatable features of the synoptic accounts of Jesus (such as miracles, or obvious contradictions between sources), they failed to apply this principle consistently. In other words, they failed to realize that the later belief of the community had exercised a normative influence over the evangelist at every stage of his work.

Second, the motives of the evangelists were not taken into account. The liberal theologians tended simply to exclude those portions of the narratives they found unacceptable, and content themselves with what remained. By doing so, they failed to take seriously the fact that the evangelist himself had a positive statement to make, and substituted for this something quite distinct. The first priority should be to approach the Gospel narratives on their own terms, and to establish what the evangelist wished to convey to his readers.

Third, the psychological approach to the Gospel narratives tends to confuse what is conceivable with what actually took place, being based upon an inadequate foundation. In effect, liberal theologians tended to find in the Gospels precisely what they were seeking, on the basis of a "sort of psychological guesswork" which appeared to value emotive descriptions more than strict accuracy and certainty of knowledge.

The dogmatic critique

This line of criticism, expressed by Martin Kähler (1835–1912), challenged the theological significance of the reconstruction of the historical Jesus. The "historical Jesus" was an irrelevance to faith, which was based upon the "Christ of faith." Kähler rightly saw that the dispassionate and provisional Jesus of the academic historian cannot become the object of faith. Yet how can Jesus Christ be the authentic basis and content of Christian faith, when historical science can never establish certain knowledge concerning the historical Jesus? How can faith be based upon an historical event without being vulnerable to the charge of historical relativism? It was precisely these questions which Kähler addressed in his *The So-Called Historical Jesus and the Historic Biblical Christ* (1892).

Kähler states his two objectives in this work as follows: first, to criticize and reject the errors of the "life of Jesus" movement; and second, to establish the validity of an alternative approach. For Kähler:

The historical Jesus of modern writers conceals the living Christ from us. The Jesus of the "life of Jesus" movement is merely a modern example of a brainchild of the human imagination, no better than the notorious dogmatic Christ of Byzantine Christology. They are both equally far removed from the real Christ. In this respect, historicism is just as arbitrary, just as humanly arrogant, just as speculative and "faithlessly gnostic," as that dogmatism which was itself considered modern in its own day.

Kähler concedes immediately that the "life of Jesus" movement was completely correct insofar as it contrasted the biblical witness to Christ with an abstract dogmatism.

He nevertheless insists upon its futility, a view summarized in his well-known statement to the effect that the entire "life of Jesus" movement is a blind alley. His reasons for making this assertion are complex. The most fundamental reason is that Christ must be regarded as a "suprahistorical" rather than an "historical" figure, so that the critical–historical method cannot be applied in his case. The critical–historical method could not deal with the suprahistorical (and hence suprahuman) characteristics of Jesus, and hence was obliged to ignore or deny them. In effect, the critical–historical method could only lead to an Arian or Ebionite Christology, on account of its latent dogmatic presuppositions. This point, made frequently throughout the essay, is developed with particular force in relation to the psychological interpretation of the personality of Jesus, and the related question concerning the use of the principle of analogy in the critical–historical method.

Kähler notes that the psychological interpretation of the personality of Jesus is dependent upon the (unrecognized) presupposition that the distinction between ourselves and Jesus is one of degree (Grade) rather than of kind (Art), which Kähler suggests must be criticized on dogmatic grounds. More significantly, Kähler challenged the principle of analogy in the interpretation of the New Testament portrayal of Christ in general, which inevitably led to Jesus being treated as analogous to modern human beings, and hence to a reduced or degree Christology. If it is assumed from the outset that Jesus is an ordinary human being, who differs from other humans only in degree and not in nature, then this assumption will be read back into the biblical texts, and dictate the resulting conclusion that Jesus of Nazareth is a human being who differs from us only in degree.

Second, Kähler argued that "we do not possess any sources for a life of Jesus which an historian could accept as reliable and adequate." This is not to say that the sources are unreliable and inadequate for the purposes of *faith*. Kähler is rather concerned to emphasize that the Gospels are not the accounts of disinterested, impartial observers, but rather accounts of the faith of believers, which cannot be isolated, either in form or content, from that faith: the Gospel accounts "are not the reports of alert impartial observers, but are throughout the testimonies and confessions of believers in Christ." In that "it is only through these accounts that we are able to come into contact with him," it will be clear that the "biblical portrait of Christ" is of decisive importance for faith.

What is important for Kähler is not who Christ was, but what he presently does for believers. The "Jesus of history" lacks the soteriological significance of the "Christ of faith." The thorny problems of Christology may therefore be left behind in order to develop soteriology, "the knowledge of faith concerning the person of the savior." In effect, Kähler argues that the "life of Jesus" movement has done little more than create a fictitious and pseudoscientific Christ, devoid of existential significance. For Kähler, "the real Christ is the preached Christ." Christian faith is not based upon this historical Jesus, but upon the existentially significant and faith-evoking figure of the Christ of faith.

Considerations such as these gradually came to dominate the theological scene, and may be regarded as reaching their climax in the writings of Rudolf Bultmann, to which we may now turn.

The retreat from history: Rudolf Bultmann

Bultmann regarded the entire enterprise of the historical reconstruction of Jesus as a blind alley. History was not of fundamental importance to Christology; it was merely necessary that Jesus existed, and that the Christian proclamation (which Bultmann terms the *kerygma*) is somehow grounded in his person. Bultmann thus famously reduced the entire historical aspect of Christology to a single word – "that." It is necessary only to believe "that" Jesus Christ lies behind the gospel proclamation (or *kerygma*).

For Bultmann, the cross and the resurrection are indeed historical phenomena (in that they took place within human history), but they must be discerned by faith as divine acts. The cross and the resurrection are linked in the *kerygma* as the divine act of judgment and the divine act of salvation. It is this divine act which is of continuing significance, and not the historical phenomenon which acted as its bearer. The *kerygma* is thus concerned not with matters of historical fact but with conveying the necessity of a decision on the part of its hearers, and thus transferring the eschatological moment from the past to the here and now of the proclamation itself:

This means that Jesus Christ encounters us in the *kerygma* and nowhere else, just as he confronted Paul himself and forced him to a

decision. The *kerygma* does not proclaim universal truths or a timeless idea – whether it is an idea of God or of the redeemer – but an historical fact. [. . .] Therefore the *kerygma* is neither a vehicle for timeless ideas nor the mediator of historical information: What is of decisive importance is that the *kerygma* is Christ's "that," his "here and now," a "here and now" which becomes present in the address itself.

One cannot therefore, according to Bultmann, go behind the *kerygma*, using it as a "source" in order to reconstruct an "historical Jesus" with his "messianic consciousness," his "inner life," or his "heroism." That would merely be "Christ according to the flesh," who no longer exists. It is not the historical Jesus, but Jesus Christ the one who is preached, who is the Lord.

This radical move away from history alarmed many. How could anyone rest assured that Christology was properly grounded in the person and work of Jesus Christ? How could anyone begin to check out Christology, if the history of Jesus was an irrelevance? It seemed to an increasing number of writers, within the fields of both New Testament and dogmatic studies, that Bultmann had merely cut a Gordian knot without resolving the serious historical issues at stake.

For Bultmann, all that could be, and could be required to be, known about the historical Jesus was the fact that (*das Dass*) he existed. For the New Testament scholar Gerhard Ebeling (1912–2001), the person of the historical (*historisch*) Jesus is the fundamental basis (*das Grunddatum*) of Christology, and if it could be shown that Christology was a misinterpretation of the significance of the historical Jesus, Christology would be brought to an end. In this, Ebeling may be seen as expressing the concerns which underlie the "new quest of the historical Jesus," to be discussed in the following section.

Ebeling pointed to what he saw as a fundamental deficiency in Bultmann's Christology: its total lack of openness to investigation (perhaps "verification" is too strong a term) in the light of historical scholarship. Might not Christology rest upon a mistake? How can we rest assured that there is a justifiable transition from the preaching *of* Jesus to the preaching *about* Jesus? Ebeling develops criticisms which parallel those of Ernst Käsemann (1906–98), but with a theological, rather than a purely historical, focus.

The new quest of the historical Jesus

A "new quest of the historical Jesus" is generally regarded as having been inaugurated with Ernst Käsemann's lecture of October 1953 on the problem of the historical Jesus. The full importance of this lecture only emerges if it is viewed in the light of the presuppositions and methods of the Bultmannian school up to this point. Käsemann conceded that the Synoptic Gospels are primarily theological documents, and that their theological statements are often expressed in the form of the historical. In this, he endorsed and recapitulated key axioms of the Bultmann school, here based upon insights of Kähler and Wrede.

Nevertheless, Käsemann immediately went on to qualify these assertions in a significant manner. Despite their obviously theological concerns, the evangelists nevertheless believed that they had access to historical information concerning Jesus of Nazareth, and that this historical information was expressed and embodied in the text of the Synoptic Gospels. The Gospels include both the *kerygma* and historical narrative.

Building on this insight, Käsemann points to the need to explore the continuity between the preaching *of* Jesus and the preaching *about* Jesus. There is an obvious discontinuity between the earthly Jesus and the exalted and proclaimed Christ; yet a thread of continuity links them, in that the proclaimed Christ is already present, in some sense, in the historical Jesus. It must be stressed that Käsemann is not suggesting that a new inquiry should be undertaken concerning the historical Jesus in order to provide historical legitimation for the *kerygma*; still less is he suggesting that the discontinuity between the historical Jesus and the proclaimed Christ necessitates the deconstruction of the latter in terms of the former. Rather, Käsemann is pointing to the *theological* assertion of the identity of the earthly Jesus and the exalted Christ being *historically grounded* in the actions and preaching of Jesus of Nazareth.

The theological affirmation is, Käsemann argues, dependent upon the historical demonstration that the *kerygma* concerning Jesus is already contained in a nutshell or embryonic form in the ministry of Jesus. In that the *kerygma* contains historical elements, it is entirely proper and necessary to inquire concerning the relation of the Jesus of history and the Christ of faith.

It will be clear that the "new quest of the historical Jesus" is qualitatively different from the discredited quest of the nineteenth century. Käsemann's argument rests upon the recognition that the discontinuity between the Jesus of history and the Christ of faith does not imply that they are unrelated entities, with the latter having no grounding or foundation in the former. Rather, the *kerygma* may be discerned in the actions and preaching of Jesus of Nazareth, so that there is a continuity between the preaching of Jesus and the preaching about Jesus. Where the older quest had assumed that the discontinuity between the historical Jesus and the Christ of faith implied that the latter was potentially a fiction, who required to be reconstructed in the light of objective historical investigation, Käsemann stressed that such reconstruction is neither necessary nor possible.

The growing realization of the importance of this point led to intensive interest developing in the question of the historical foundations of the *kerygma*. Four positions of interest may be noted.

1   Joachim Jeremias, perhaps representing an extreme element in this debate, seemed to suggest that the basis of the Christian faith lies in what Jesus actually said and did, insofar as this can be established by theological scholarship. The first part of his *New Testament Theology* (1971) was thus devoted in its totality to the "proclamation of Jesus" as a central element of New Testament theology.

2   Käsemann himself identified the continuity between the historical Jesus and the kerygmatic Christ in their common declaration of the dawning of the eschatological kingdom of God. Both in the preaching of Jesus and in the early Christian *kerygma*, the theme of the coming of the kingdom is of major importance.

3   As we saw above, Gerhard Ebeling located the continuity in the notion of the "faith of Jesus," which he understood to be analogous to the "faith of Abraham" (described in Romans 4) – a prototypical faith, historically exemplified and embodied in Jesus of Nazareth, and proclaimed to be a contemporary possibility for believers.

4   Günter Bornkamm (1905–90) laid particular emphasis upon the note of authority evident in the ministry of Jesus. In Jesus, the actuality of God confronts humanity, and calls it to a radical decision. Whereas Bultmann located the essence of Jesus's preaching in the future coming of the kingdom of God, Bornkamm shifted the emphasis from the future to the present confrontation of individuals with God through the person of Jesus. This theme of "confrontation with God" is evident in

both the ministry of Jesus and the proclamation about Jesus, providing a major theological and historical link between the earthly Jesus and the proclaimed Christ.

The "new quest of the historical Jesus" was thus concerned to stress the continuity between the historical Jesus and the Christ of faith. Whereas the "old quest" had the aim of discrediting the New Testament portrayal of Christ, the "new quest" ended up consolidating it, by stressing the continuities between the preaching of Jesus himself, and the church's preaching about Jesus.

Since then, there have been other developments in the field. In the 1970s and 1980s particular attention has been directed toward exploring the relation between Jesus and his environment in first-century Judaism. This development, which is especially associated with English and American writers such as Geza Vermes and E. P. Sanders, has renewed interest in the Jewish background to Jesus, and further emphasized the importance of history in relation to Christology. The Bultmannian approach – which devalues the significance of history in Christology – is widely regarded as discredited, at least for the moment. This can be seen in the new interest in the "historical Jesus" associated with what has come to be known as the "third quest."

The third quest of the historical Jesus

Since the general collapse of the "new quest" during the 1960s, a series of works have appeared offering re-evaluations of the historical Jesus. The term "third quest" has often been applied to this group of works. The designation has been called into question by a number of writers, who point out that the works and scholars who are gathered together under this term do not have enough in common to categorize them in this way. For example, some writers within the group make an appeal to sources outside the New Testament, especially the Coptic Gospel of Thomas, in their analysis; others restrict their analysis to the New Testament materials, especially the Synoptic Gospels. Despite this reservation, the term seems to be gaining acceptance, and it is therefore appropriate to include it in this survey.

The "original quest" approached the stories of Jesus in the light of a series of strongly rationalist presuppositions, inherited from the Enlightenment, and filtered out the miraculous aspects of the Gospel narratives. The "new quest" tended to focus on the words of Jesus, stressing the continuity between and preaching *of* Jesus himself and the New Testament preaching *about* Jesus. The "third quest" seems to involve a focus on the relation of Jesus to his Jewish context as indicative of the distinctive character of his mission, and his understanding of his own goals. Among significant contributions to the "third quest," the following should be noted in particular:

1 John Dominic Crossan argues that Jesus was essentially a poor Jewish peasant with a particular concern to challenge the power structures of contemporary society. In *The Historical Jesus* (1991) and *Jesus: A Revolutionary Biography* (1994), Crossan argues that Jesus broke down prevailing social conventions, especially through his table fellowship with sinners and social outcasts.

2 In books such as *Jesus: A New Vision* (1988) and *Meeting Jesus Again for the First Time* (1994), Marcus L. Borg suggests that Jesus was a subversive sage concerned to renew Judaism in a manner which posed a powerful challenge to the ruling temple elite.

3 In his *Myth of Innocence* (1988) and *The Lost Gospel* (1993), Burton L. Mack argues that Jesus was an individualistic sage along the lines of a Cynic. As a "Hellenistic Cynic Sage" Jesus had little interest in specifically Jewish issues (such as the place of the Temple, or the role of the Law); rather, he was concerned to identify and mock the conventions of contemporary society.

4 E. P. Sanders insists that Jesus is to be seen as a prophetic figure who was concerned with the restoration of the Jewish people. In works such as *Jesus and Judaism* (1985) and *The Historical Figure of Jesus* (1993), Sanders suggests that Jesus envisaged an eschatological restoration of Israel. God would bring the present age to an end and usher in a new order focusing on a new temple, with Jesus himself acting as God's representative.

5 N. T. Wright, in his series *Christian Origins and the Question of God*, offers a critical appropriation of the approach of E. P. Sanders, while retaining the idea that the coming of Jesus Christ introduces something radically new, especially in relation to the identity of the people of God. The first two volumes in this series – *The New Testament and the People of God* (1992) and *Jesus and the Victory of God* (1996) – are widely regarded as among the most significant writings in the field of recent New Testament studies.

On the basis of this brief analysis of a few writers generally regarded as representative of the "third quest," it will be clear that it lacks a coherent theological or historical core. There is significant disagreement concerning whether Jesus is to be seen against a Jewish or Hellenistic background; about his attitude to the Jewish law and its religious institutions; his view of the future of Israel; and the personal significance of Jesus in relation to that future. Nevertheless, the term has found at least a degree of acceptance, despite its clear weaknesses, and it is likely to remain an integral part of scholarly discussion of this important issue.

The Resurrection of Christ: Event and Meaning

The question of the relation of faith and history often comes to focus on the question of the resurrection of Christ. This question – more specifically, whether Christ was indeed raised from the dead, and, if so, what that event might mean – brings together the central components of the Enlightenment critique of traditional Christianity. In what follows, we shall outline some of the main positions to have developed during the modern period, and assess their significance.

The Enlightenment: the resurrection as nonevent

The characteristic Enlightenment emphasis on the omnicompetence of reason and the importance of contemporary analogs to past events led to the development of an intensely skeptical attitude toward the resurrection in the eighteenth century. Gotthold Ephraim Lessing provides an excellent example of this attitude. He confesses that he does not have personal first-hand experience of the resurrection of Jesus Christ; so why, he asks, should he be asked to believe in something which he has not seen? The problem of chronological distance, according to Lessing, is made all the more acute on account of his doubts (which he evidently assumes others will share) concerning the reliability of the eyewitness reports. Our faith eventually rests upon the authority of others, rather than the authority of our own experience and rational reflection upon it.

> That, then, is the ugly great ditch which I cannot cross, however often and however earnestly I have tried to make this leap. If anyone can help me to cross it, I implore them to do so. And so I repeat what I said

earlier. I do not for one moment deny that Christ performed miracles. But since the truths of these miracles has completely ceased to be demonstrable by miracles happening in the present, they are no more than reports of miracles. [...] I deny that they could and should bind me to have even the smallest faith in the other teachings of Jesus.

In other words, as men and women are not raised from the dead now, why should we believe that such a thing happened in the past? At issue here is a central theme of the Enlightenment: human autonomy. Reality is rational, and human beings have the necessary epistemological capacities to uncover this rational ordering of the world. Truth is not something which demands to be accepted on the basis of an external authority; it is to be recognized and accepted by the autonomous thinking person, on the basis of the perception of congruence between what that individual knows to be true, and the alleged "truth" which presents itself for verification. Truth is something which is discerned, not something which is imposed.

For Lessing, being obligated to accept the testimony of others is tantamount to a compromising of human intellectual autonomy. There are no contemporary analogs for the resurrection. Resurrection is not an aspect of modern-day experience. So why trust the New Testament reports? For Lessing, the resurrection is little more than a misunderstood nonevent.

David Friedrich Strauss: the resurrection as myth

In his *Life of Jesus* (1835), Strauss provided a radical new approach to the question of the resurrection of Christ. Strauss himself noted that the resurrection of Christ is of central importance to Christian faith:

The root of faith in Jesus was the conviction of his resurrection. He who had been put to death, however great during his life, could not, it was thought, be the Messiah: his miraculous restoration to life proved so much the more strongly that he *was* the Messiah. Freed by his resurrection from the kingdom of shades, and at the same time elevated above the sphere of earthly humanity, he was now translated to the heavenly regions, and had taken his place at the right hand of God.

Strauss noted that this understanding of what he termed "the Christology of the orthodox system" had come under considerable attack since the Enlightenment, not least on account of its presupposition that miracles (such as a resurrection) are impossible.

On the basis of this *a priori* assumption, which corresponds neatly to the key ideas of the Enlightenment worldview, Strauss declared his intention to explain "the origin of faith in the resurrection of Jesus without any corresponding miraculous fact." In other words, Strauss was concerned to explain how Christians came to believe in the resurrection, when there was no objective historical basis for this belief. Having excluded the resurrection as a "miraculous objective occurrence," Strauss located the origin of the belief at the purely subjective level. Belief in the resurrection is not to be explained as a response to "a life objectively restored," but is "a subjective conception in the mind": faith in the resurrection of Jesus is the outcome of an exaggerated "recollection of the personality of Jesus himself" by which a memory has been projected into the idea of a living presence. A dead Jesus is thus transfigured into an imaginary risen Christ – a *mythical* risen Christ, to use the appropriate term.

Strauss's distinctive contribution to the debate was to introduce the category of "myth" – a reflection of the Gospel writers' social conditioning and cultural outlook. To suggest that their writings were partly "mythical" was thus not so much a challenge to their integrity, but simply an acknowledgment of the premodern outlook of the period in which they were written. The Gospel writers must be regarded as sharing the mythical worldview of their cultural situation. Strauss distances himself from Reimarus's suggestion that the evangelists distorted their accounts of Jesus of Nazareth, whether unconsciously or deliberately. He argues that mythical language is the natural mode of expression of a primitive group culture which had yet to rise to the level of abstract conceptualization.

For Reimarus, the Gospel writers were confused or liars – more likely the latter. Strauss moved the discussion away from this judgment by his introduction of the category of "myth." The resurrection was to be viewed not as a deliberate fabrication, but as an interpretation of events (especially the memory and "subjective vision" of Jesus) in terms which made sense in the culture of first-century Palestine, dominated by a mythical worldview. Belief in the resurrection as an objective event must be regarded as becoming impossible with the passing of that worldview.

Strauss's *Life of Jesus*, along with other rationalizing works of the same period, such as Ernest Renan's work of the same name (1863), attracted enormous attention. The resurrection, traditionally seen as the basis of Christian faith, was now viewed as its product. Christianity was seen as relating to the memory of a dead Jesus, rather than the celebration of a risen Christ. However, the debate was far from over. In what follows, we shall consider later developments in this intriguing chapter of modern theology. Perhaps Strauss's most acute reinterpreter in the twentieth century has been Rudolf Bultmann, to whose distinctive views on the resurrection we may now turn.

Rudolf Bultmann: the resurrection as an event in the experience of the disciples

Bultmann shared Strauss's basic conviction that, in this scientific age, it is impossible to believe in miracles. As a result, belief in an objective resurrection of Jesus is no longer possible; however, it may well prove to be possible to make sense of it in another manner. History, Bultmann argued, is "a closed continuum of effects in which individual events are connected by the succession of cause and effect." The resurrection, in common with other miracles, would thus disrupt the closed system of nature. Similar points had been made by other thinkers sympathetic to the Enlightenment.

Belief in an objective resurrection of Jesus, although perfectly legitimate and intelligible in the first century, cannot be taken seriously today. "It is impossible to use electric light and radio equipment and, when ill, to claim the assistance of modern medical and clinical discoveries, and at the same time believe in the New Testament world of spirits and miracles." The human understanding of the world and of human existence has changed radically since the first century, with the result that modern humanity finds the mythological worldview of the New Testament unintelligible and unacceptable. A worldview is given to someone with the age in which they live, and they are in no position to alter it. The modern scientific and existential worldview means that that of the New Testament is now discarded and unintelligible.

For this reason, the resurrection is to be regarded as "a mythical event, pure and simple." The resurrection is something which happened in the subjective experience of the disciples, not something which took place in the public arena of history. For Bultmann, Jesus has indeed been raised – he has been raised up into the *kerygma*. The preaching of

Jesus himself has been transformed into the Christian proclamation of Christ. Jesus has become an element of Christian preaching; he has been raised up and taken up into the proclamation of the gospel:

> The real Easter faith is faith in the word of preaching which brings illumination. If the event of Easter Day is in any sense an historical event additional to the event of the cross, it is nothing else than the rise of faith in the risen Lord, since it was this faith which led to the apostolic preaching. The resurrection itself is not an event of past history. All that historical criticism can establish is that the first disciples came to believe in the resurrection.

Consistent with his antihistorical approach in general, Bultmann directs attention away from the historical Jesus toward the proclamation of Christ. "Faith in the church as the bearer of the *kerygma* is the Easter faith which consists in the belief that Jesus Christ is present in the *kerygma*."

Karl Barth: the resurrection as an historical event beyond critical inquiry

Barth wrote a small work entitled *The Resurrection of the Dead* in 1924. However, his mature views on the relation of the resurrection to history date from considerably later, and have clearly been influenced by Bultmann. Barth's essay "Rudolf Bultmann – An Attempt to Understand Him" (1952) set out his misgivings concerning Bultmann's approach. This was followed up by a sustained engagement with the issues at stake in volume 4, part 1, of *Church Dogmatics* (1953). In what follows, we shall attempt to set out Barth's position and compare it with that of Bultmann.

In his early writings Barth argued that the empty tomb was of minimal importance in relation to the resurrection. However, he became increasingly alarmed at Bultmann's existential approach to the resurrection, which seemed to imply that it had no objective historical foundation. For this reason, Barth came to place considerable emphasis upon the Gospel accounts of the empty tomb. The empty tomb is "an indispensable sign" which "obviates all possible misunderstanding." It demonstrates that the resurrection of Christ was not a purely inward, interior, or subjective event, but something which left a mark upon history.

This would seem to suggest that Barth regarded the resurrection as being open to historical investigation, to clarify its nature and confirm its place in the public history of the world, rather than in the private interior experience of the first believers. Yet this is not so. He consistently refuses to allow the Gospel narratives to be subjected to critical historical scrutiny. It is not entirely clear why. The following factor appears to have weighed heavily in his thinking at this point.

Barth emphasizes that Paul and the other apostles are not calling for the "acceptance of a well-attested historical report," but for "a decision of faith." Historical investigation cannot legitimate or provide security for such faith; nor can faith become dependent upon the provisional results of historical inquiry. In any case, faith is a response to the risen Christ, not to the empty tomb. Barth was quite clear that the empty tomb, taken by itself, was of little value in laying the foundation for faith in the risen Christ. The absence of Christ from his tomb does not necessarily imply his resurrection: "He might in fact have been stolen, he might have only appeared to be dead."

As a result Barth is left in what initially seems to be a highly vulnerable position. Concerned to defend the resurrection as an act in public history against Bultmann's subjectivist approach, he is not prepared to allow that history to be critically studied. In part, this rests upon his passionate belief that historical scholarship cannot lay the basis for faith; in part, it reflects his assumption that the resurrection of Christ is part of a much larger network of ideas and events, which cannot be disclosed or verified by historical inquiry. However much one may sympathize with Barth's theological concerns at this point, it is difficult to avoid the conclusion that he lacks credibility. It is perhaps for this reason that the approach of Wolfhart Pannenberg has been the subject of considerable attention.

Wolfhart Pannenberg: the resurrection as an historical event open to critical inquiry

The most distinctive feature of Pannenberg's theological program, as it emerged during the 1960s, is the appeal to universal history. Such views are developed and justified in the 1961 essay "Redemptive Event and History", in which these ideas are explored at some length. The essay opens with a powerful appeal to universal history:

> History is the most comprehensive horizon of Christian theology. All theological questions and answers have meaning only within the framework of the history which God has with humanity, and through humanity with the whole creation, directed towards a future which is hidden to the world, but which has already been revealed in Jesus Christ.

These crucially important opening sentences sum up the distinctive features of Pannenberg's theological program at this stage in his career. They immediately distinguish him from the ahistorical theology of Bultmann and his school on the one hand, and the suprahistorical approach of Martin Kähler on the other. Christian theology is based upon an analysis of universal and publicly accessible history. For Pannenberg, revelation is essentially a public and universal historical event which is recognized and *interpreted* as an "act of God." To his critics, this seemed to reduce faith to insight, and deny any role to the Holy Spirit in the event of revelation.

Pannenberg's argument takes the following form. History, in all its totality, can only be understood when it is viewed from its end-point. This point alone provides the perspective from which the historical process can be seen completely, and thus be properly understood. However, where Marx argued that the social sciences, by predicting the goal of history to be the hegemony of socialism, provided the key to the interpretation of history, Pannenberg declared that this was provided only in Jesus Christ. The end of history is disclosed proleptically in the history of Jesus Christ. In other words, the end of history, which has yet to take place, has been disclosed in advance of the event in the person and work of Christ.

like Irenaeus

This idea of a "proleptic disclosure of the end of history" is grounded in the apocalyptic worldview which, Pannenberg argues, provides the key to understanding the New Testament interpretation of the significance and function of Jesus. Whereas Bultmann chose to demythologize the apocalyptic elements of the New Testament, Pannenberg treats them as a hermeneutical grid or framework by which the life, death, and resurrection of Christ may be interpreted.

Perhaps the most distinctive, and certainly the most commented upon, aspect of this work is Pannenberg's insistence that the resurrection of Jesus is an objective historical event, witnessed by all who had access to the evidence. Whereas Bultmann treated the resurrection as an event within the experiential world of the disciples, Pannenberg declared that it belonged to the world of universal public history.

This immediately raised the question of the historicity of the resurrection. As noted earlier, a group of Enlightenment writers had argued that our only knowledge of the alleged resurrection of Jesus was contained in the New Testament. In that there were no contemporary analogs for such a resurrection, the credibility of those reports had to be seriously questioned. In a similar vein, Ernst Troeltsch had argued for the homogeneity of history: in that the resurrection of Jesus appeared to radically disrupt that homogeneity, it was to be regarded as of dubious historicity. Pannenberg initially responded to these difficulties in an essay on "Redemptive Event and History," and subsequently in *Jesus – God and Man*. His basic argument against this position can be set out as follows.

Troeltsch, in Pannenberg's view, has a pedantically narrow view of history, which rules out certain events in advance, on the basis of a set of provisional judgments which have improperly come to have the status of absolute laws. Troeltsch's unwarranted "constriction of historico-critical inquiry" was "biased" and "anthropocentric." It presupposed that the human viewpoint is the only acceptable and normative standpoint within history. Analogies, Pannenberg stresses, are always analogies *viewed from the standpoint of the human observer*; that standpoint is radically restricted in its scope, and cannot be allowed to function as the absolutely certain basis of critical inquiry. Pannenberg is too good a historian to suggest that the principle of analogy should be abandoned; it is, after all, a proven and useful tool of historical research. Yet, Pannenberg insists, that is all that it is: it is a working tool, and cannot be allowed to define a fixed view of reality.

If the historian sets out to investigate the New Testament already precommitted to the belief "dead people do not rise again," that conclusion will merely be read back into the New Testament material. The judgment "Jesus did not rise from the dead" will be the presupposition, not the conclusion, of such an investigation. Pannenberg's discussion of this question represents an impassioned and impressive plea for a neutral approach to the resurrection. The *has Pannenberg presupposed JC = God?*

historical evidence pointing to the resurrection of Jesus must be investigated without the prior dogmatic presupposition that such a resurrection could not have happened.

Having argued for the historicity of the resurrection, Pannenberg turns to deal with its interpretation within the context of the apocalyptic framework of meaning. The end of history has proleptically taken place in the resurrection of Jesus from the dead. This maxim dominates Pannenberg's interpretation of the event. The resurrection of Jesus anticipates the general resurrection at the end of time, and brings forward into history both that resurrection and the full and final revelation of God. The resurrection of Jesus is thus organically linked with the self-revelation of God in Christ; it establishes Jesus's identity with God, and allows this identity with God to be read back into his pre-Easter ministry. It thus functions as the foundation of a series of central Christological affirmations, including the divinity of Christ (however this is expressed) and the incarnation.

Resurrection and the Christian hope

The resurrection of Jesus Christ assumes a number of functions within Christian theology. As we have seen, one foundational role of the resurrection relates to the Christological affirmation of the divinity of Christ. Even in the New Testament, the exalted status of Jesus of Nazareth – however this is conceptualized – is seen as being linked to his resurrection. However, it must be appreciated that the resurrection of Jesus serves an additional function within Christian theology. It establishes and undergirds the Christian hope. This has both *soteriological* and *eschatological* implications. At the soteriological level, it enables the death of Christ upon the cross to be interpreted in terms of God's victory over death and a coalition of allied forces and powers (pp. 334–7). At the eschato-

logical level, it gives both foundation and substance to the Christian hope of eternal life (pp. 464–85). We shall explore these elements in full detail in the final chapter of the present volume; our concern at this stage is merely to alert the reader to the multifaceted theological significance of the resurrection of Christ.

Our primary concern in the present chapter has been to address the issue of faith and history raised by the Enlightenment. It will be clear that the Enlightenment and post-Enlightenment Christological debate has been of major interest, raising a cluster of issues which seem set to continue to be the subject of debate for some time to come. The general collapse of confidence in the Enlightenment worldview has led to a related retreat from its Christological agenda, and a return to a significant part of the concerns of classical Christology. The rise of postmodernity has significantly altered the contours of the debate, much of which is now recognized to have been shaped by the distinctive contours of modernism's notions of history and rationality. Much the same may be said of the doctrine of the work of Christ, to which we may now turn.

QUESTIONS FOR CHAPTER 12

1 What did Lessing mean when he spoke of an "ugly great ditch" between faith and history?

2 Suppose, for the sake of argument, that the New Testament gets the facts about Jesus wrong. How could we correct it?

3 In what ways does the "quest of the historical Jesus" reflect the agenda of the Enlightenment?

4 Assess the contribution of either Martin Kähler or Albert Schweitzer to the failure of the "quest of the historical Jesus."

5 If the bones of Jesus Christ were to be discovered in Palestine, what would remain of Christianity?

13

The Doctrine of Salvation in Christ

Christianity holds that the life, death, and resurrection of Jesus Christ have changed things. The created order, and above all humanity, has fallen into disorder. Things are not what they are meant to be. And something has to be done about this. The same God who made the created order therefore acts to renew and reorder it. The Christian doctrine of sin tries to give an account of what went wrong; the doctrine of salvation deals with the restoration of the created order, and above all humanity, to its proper relationship to God.

The Christian doctrine of salvation focuses on Jesus Christ, as the redeemer and savior of the world. For Christianity, Christ changed things so dramatically, so comprehensively, that both the acts that changed things, and the difference that they make, needed to be explained. Earlier, we noted that one of the distinctive themes of Christian understandings of the significance of Jesus of Nazareth is that he is the ground of salvation (p. 275). In this chapter, we are going to explore Christian understandings of salvation, looking at both the way in which Jesus of Nazareth is understood to be the foundation of this salvation, and what shape that salvation itself takes.

The doctrine of salvation is one of the most fascinating and challenging areas of theology, which displays the great variety of intellectual approaches within the Christian tradition. On the one hand, we find writers who, fired with a wonderful exuberance of the imagination, envisage Christ's death and resurrection as transforming humanity and the entire cosmos, reshaping them and allowing them to share in the divine life. On the other, we find writers who sense the need for caution, and want to remain firmly within the realms of the reasonable. Here, Christ is often depicted as offering humanity a superb religious and moral example, which will guide and inspire them as they seek to find and lead the good life.

The two previous chapters considered a network of issues concerning the identity of Jesus Christ. As we noticed during that discussion, a central question concerning the identity of Jesus Christ relates to his function. What did Jesus do? Or, even more significantly: what *does* Jesus do? There is an organic relationship between the two central questions:

Who is Jesus Christ?
What did Jesus Christ achieve?

The identity and function of Jesus Christ can be thought of as two sides of the same coin. The close connection between *functional* and *ontological* Christologies (pp. 292–4) should be noted in this respect.

Christian Approaches to Salvation

"Salvation" is a complex notion. It does not necessarily have any specifically *Christian* reference. The term can be used in a thoroughly secular manner. For example, it was common for Soviet writers, especially during the late 1920s, to speak of Lenin as the "savior" of the Soviet peoples. Military coups in African states during the 1980s frequently resulted in the setting up of "councils of salvation," concerned to restore political and economic stability. Salvation can be a purely secular notion, concerned with political emancipation or the general human quest for liberation.

Even at the religious level, salvation is not a specifically Christian idea. Many – but not, it must be stressed, all – of the world's religions have concepts of salvation. They differ enormously, in relation to both their understanding of how that salvation is achieved, and the shape or form which it is understood to take. One of the most difficult tasks facing those in the past who, in the tradition of the Enlightenment, wished to argue that "all religions were basically the same," has been to show that there is an underlying unity among the religions, despite all their obvious differences in relation to these two questions. It is generally thought that this quest has failed, on account of the astonishing variety of the phenomena in question.

If the term "salvation" is understood to mean "some benefit conferred upon or achieved by members of a community, whether individually or corporately," all religions offer "salvation." However, this is such a general statement that it is devoid of significant theological value: all religions – along with political theories such as Marxism and psychotherapeutic schools such as Rogerian therapy – could be styled "salvific,"

in some sense of the term, in that they offer something to those who accept them. Yet it does not follow that all religions can be said to offer the *same* "salvation."

Respect for the integrity of the world's religions demands that the distinctive shape of a religion's understanding of salvation (including its basis, its mode of conveyance and appropriation, and its inherent nature) must be respected. It is therefore important to note the distinctive character of each religion in relation to the "salvation" which is offered. Buddhism offers one style of "salvation" just as Christianity offers another. These differences reflect the simple fact that Christianity is not Buddhism. It is essential to respect and honor differences here, and resist the ever-present temptation to force them all into the same mold.

Christianity is, therefore, not in any sense distinctive or unique in attaching importance to the idea of salvation. The distinctiveness of the Christian approach to salvation lies in two distinct areas. In the first place, salvation is understood to be grounded in the life, death, and resurrection of Jesus Christ; in the second, the specific shape of salvation within the Christian tradition is itself formed by Christ. These ideas are complex and require further exploration before we can proceed.

Salvation is linked with Jesus Christ

First, Christianity holds that salvation – however that is subsequently defined – is linked with the life, death, and resurrection of Jesus Christ. That there is such a link is characteristic of Christian theology down the ages. A significant debate in more recent theological literature has concerned whether the cross can be said to be *constitutive* or *illustrative*. In his *Doctrine of Reconciliation* (1898), the noted German theologian Martin Kähler posed the following question concerning theories of the atonement: "Did Christ just make known some insights concerning an unchangeable situation – or did he establish a new situation?" With this question we come to a central aspect of soteriology: does the cross of Christ illustrate the saving will of God, giving shape to a hitherto vague notion? Or does it make such a salvation possible in the first place? Is it illustrative or constitutive?

The second such approach has been characteristic of much traditional Christian theology. Christ is seen as having achieved something which makes possible a new situation. Redemption is the direct result of Christ's life, death, and resurrection. To put it more forcefully: salvation is grounded in the life, death, and resurrection of Christ. There has, of course, been much debate on precisely how Christ made such a new situation possible. For example, Irenaeus developed the idea of "recapitulation" – the "going over again" of all the events in history at which humanity lost its way. Christ thus "recapitulates" the history of Adam, succeeding where Adam failed, and thereby undoing the fall of humanity.

> When [Christ] was incarnate and became a human being, he recapitulated in himself [*in seipso recapitulavit*] the long history of the human race, obtaining salvation for us, so that we might regain in Jesus Christ what we had lost in Adam, that is, being in the image and likeness of God.

The former approach has, however, been characteristic of much writing inspired by the Enlightenment, which treats the cross as a historical symbol of a timeless truth. Christ does not establish a new situation, but discloses what is in reality true, even if humanity has not been fully aware of it. John Macquarrie firmly defends this approach in his *Principles of Christian Theology* (1966):

It is not that, at a given moment, God adds the activity of reconciliation to his previous activities, or that we can set a time when his reconciling activity began. Rather, it is the case that at a given time there was a new and decisive interpretation of an activity that had always been going on, an activity that is equiprimordial with creation itself.

A similar approach is associated with Oxford theologian Maurice F. Wiles, who argues in his *Remaking of Christian Doctrine* (1974) that the Christ-event is "in some way a demonstration of what is true of God's eternal nature." Christ is here understood to reveal the saving will of God, not to establish that saving will in the first place. The coming of Christ is an expression and public demonstration of God's saving will.

Others have vigorously opposed this approach. In his *Actuality of Atonement* (1988) the English theologian Colin Gunton (1941–2003) suggests that nonconstitutive approaches to the atonement run the risk of falling back into exemplarist and subjective doctrines of salvation. It is, he argues, necessary to say that Christ does not just reveal something of importance to us; he achieves something for us – something without which salvation would not be possible. Raising the question of whether "the real evil of the world is faced and healed *ontologically* in the life, death and resurrection of Jesus," Gunton argues that there must be a sense in which Christ is a "substitute" for us: he does for us something that we ourselves cannot do. To deny this is to revert to some form of purely subjective understanding of salvation.

Gunton's approach may be regarded as characteristic of much of the pre-Enlightenment Christian discussion of the foundations of salvation, which reflects the fundamental conviction that something new happened in Christ which makes possible and available a new way of life. This approach continues to be definitive within modern evangelicalism, and has exercised a deep and continuing influence over the hymns and liturgies of the Christian church.

Salvation is shaped by Jesus Christ

Alongside the characteristic Christian insistence that salvation is linked with Jesus Christ may be found a further Christological assertion: salvation is shaped by Christ. In other words, Jesus Christ provides a model or paradigm for the redeemed life. While the Christian tradition has been thoroughly unsympathetic to the idea that the imitation of Christ in itself *is* or *gives rise to* the Christian life, there is widespread agreement that Christ in some sense gives shape or specification to that life.

The idea that the mere external imitation of Christ gives rise to the Christian life has generally been regarded as Pelagian (see pp. 18–20). The mainstream Christian approach has tended to argue that the Christian life is made possible through Christ, while recognizing two quite distinct manners in which the resulting Christian life is "shaped" by him. We shall set these two positions out as follows:

1 The Christian life takes the form of the believer's sustained attempt to imitate Christ. Having become a Christian, the believer now treats Christ as an example of the ideal relationship to God and other people, and attempts to mimic this relationship. This approach may perhaps be seen at its best in the works of some later medieval spiritual writers, especially within a monastic situation, such as the medieval writer Thomas à Kempis' famous *Imitation of Christ*. It places emphasis upon the human responsibility to bring one's life into line with the example set by Christ.

2 The Christian life is a process of "being conformed to Christ," in which the outward aspects of the believer's life are brought into line with the inward relationship to Christ, established through faith. This approach is characteristic of writers such as Luther and Calvin, and is based on the idea of God conforming the believer to the likeness of Christ through the process of renewal and regeneration brought about by the Holy Spirit.

The eschatological dimension of salvation

A final issue which must be addressed at this early stage concerns the chronology of salvation. Is salvation to be understood as something which has happened to the believer? Or is it something currently happening? Or is there an eschatological dimension to it – in other words, is there something which has yet to happen? The only answer to such questions which can be given on the basis of the New Testament is that salvation includes past, present, and future reference. We may illustrate this by considering Paul's statements on justification and related themes.

In dealing with Paul, it is tempting to adopt a simplistic approach to the chronological question just noted. For example, one could attempt to force justification, sanctification, and salvation into a neat past – present – future framework, as follows:

1 Justification: a past event, with present implications (sanctification).
2 Sanctification: a present event, dependent upon a past event (justification), which has future implications (salvation).
3 Salvation: a future event, already anticipated and partially experienced in the past event of justification and the present event of sanctification, and dependent upon them.

But this is clearly inadequate. Justification has a future, as well as past (Romans 2: 13, 8: 33; Galatians 5: 4–5), and appears to relate to both the beginning of the Christian life and its final consummation. Similarly, sanctification can also refer to a past event (1 Corinthians 6: 11) or a future event (1 Thessalonians 5: 23). And salvation is an exceptionally complex idea, embracing not simply a future event, but something which has happened in the past (Romans 8: 24; 1 Corinthians 15: 2) or which is taking place now (1 Corinthians 1: 18).

Justification language appears in Paul with reference to both the inauguration of the life of faith and also its final consummation. It is a complex and all-embracing notion, which anticipates the verdict of the final judgment (Romans 8: 30–4), declaring in advance the verdict of ultimate acquittal. The believer's present justified Christian existence is thus an anticipation of and advance participation in deliverance from the wrath to come, and an assurance in the present of the final eschatological verdict of acquittal (Romans 5: 9–10).

In dealing with the Christian understanding of salvation, we must therefore appreciate that it has both past, present, and future elements. It is not simply a future hope, nor is it simply a past achievement. It is about a past event which secures the foundation of salvation; the present-day assurance that something has happened which transforms the believer's relationship to God and to others; and that something remains to be achieved, both in terms of personal transformation and the consummation of the believer's hopes in the New Jerusalem. Or, to put this in even more simple terms: the Christian understanding of salvation presupposes that something *has* happened, that something *is now happening*, and that something further *will still happen* to believers.

The Foundations of Salvation: The Cross of Christet

The term "theory of the atonement" has become commonplace in English-language theology as a term for "a way of understanding the work of Christ." The term was used especially extensively in the nineteenth and early twentieth centuries. However, there is increasing evidence that this term is seen as cumbersome and unhelpful by many modern Christian writers, across the entire spectrum of theological viewpoints. In view of this trend, it has been avoided in the present work. The term "soteriology" (from the Greek *soteria*, "salvation") is increasingly used to refer to what were traditionally designated "theories of the atonement" or "the work of Christ." Soteriology embraces two broad areas of theology: the question of how salvation is possible and in particular how it relates to the history of Jesus Christ; and the question of how "salvation" itself is to be understood. These questions have been the subject of intense discussion throughout Christian history, especially during the modern period.

Discussions of the meaning of the cross and resurrection of Christ are best grouped around four central controlling themes or images. It must be stressed that these are not mutually exclusive, and that it is normal to find writers adopting approaches which incorporate elements drawn from more than one such category. Indeed, it can be argued that the views of most writers on this subject cannot be reduced to or confined within a single category, without doing serious violence to their ideas.

The cross as a sacrifice

The New Testament, drawing on Old Testament imagery and expectations, presents Christ's death upon the cross as a sacrifice. This approach, which is especially associated with the Letter to the Hebrews, presents Christ's sacrificial offering as an effective and perfect sacrifice, which was able to accomplish that which the sacrifices of the Old Testament were only able to intimate, rather than achieve. In particular, Paul's use of the Greek term *hilastērion* (Romans 3: 25) points to a sacrificial interpretation of Christ's death.

This idea is developed subsequently within the Christian tradition. In order for humanity to be restored to God, the mediator must sacrifice himself; without this sacrifice, such restoration is an impossibility. Athanasius argues that Christ's sacrifice was superior to those required under the Old Covenant in several respects:

> Christ offers a sacrifice which is trustworthy, of permanent effect, and which is unfailing in its nature. The sacrifices which were offered according to the Law were not trustworthy, since they had to be offered every day, and were again in need of purification. In contrast, the Savior's sacrifice was offered once only, and was accomplished in its entirety, and can thus be relied upon permanently.

This point is developed further in Athanasius's *Epistolae Festales* ("Festal Letters"), written annually in celebration of the feast of Easter. Athanasius uses these letters to set out and explain the Christian understanding of Christ's sacrifice on the cross. In his *Festal Letter VII* (written in 335) Athanasius explored the idea of Christ's sacrifice in terms of the Passover sacrifice of the lamb:

> [Christ], being truly of God the Father, became incarnate for our sakes, so that he might offer himself to the Father in our place, and redeem us through his offering and sacrifice. [. . .] This is he who, in former times, was sacrificed as a lamb, having been

foreshadowed in that lamb. But afterwards, he was slain for us. "For Christ, our passover, is sacrificed" (1 Corinthians 5: 7).

Augustine states that Christ "was made a sacrifice for sin, offering himself as a whole burnt offering on the cross of his passion." Augustine brought new clarity to the whole discussion of the nature of Christ's sacrifice through his crisp and highly influential definition of a sacrifice, set out in *City of God*: "A true sacrifice is offered in every action which is designed to unite us to God in a holy fellowship." On the basis of this definition, Augustine has no difficulties in speaking of Christ's death as a sacrifice: "By his death, which is indeed the one and most true sacrifice offered for us, he purged, abolished, and extinguished whatever guilt there was by which the principalities and powers lawfully detained us to pay the penalty." In this sacrifice, Christ was both victim and priest; he offered himself up as a sacrifice: "He offered sacrifice for our sins. And where did he find that offering, the pure victim that he would offer? He offered himself, in that he could find no other."

This understanding of the sacrifice of Christ would become of decisive importance throughout the Middle Ages, and would shape western understandings of Christ's death. In view of Augustine's importance, we may cite in full the passage which is often singled out as the most succinct expression of his thoughts on this matter:

> Thus the true Mediator, who "took the form of a servant" and was thus made "the mediator between God and humanity, the person Christ Jesus" (1 Timothy 2: 5), receives the sacrifice in the "form of God" (Philippians 2: 6–8), in union with the Father, with whom he is one God. And yet, in the "form of a servant," he determined to be himself that sacrifice, rather than to receive it, in order to prevent anyone from thinking that such a

sacrifice should be offered to any creature. Thus he is both the priest, who made the offering himself, and the oblation.

Hugh of St Victor, writing in the early twelfth century, found the imagery of "sacrifice" helpful in explaining the inner logic of the workings of Christ's death on the cross. Christ was able to be an effective sacrifice for human sin precisely because he was able to bring our fallen sinful nature before God:

> From our nature, he took a victim for our nature, so that the whole burnt offering which was offered up might come from that which is ours. He did this so that the redemption to be offered might have a connection with us, through its being taken from what is ours. We are truly made to be partakers in this redemption if we are united through faith to the redeemer who has entered into fellowship with us through his flesh.

The efficacy of Christ's sacrifice thus rested on his humanity, as well as his divinity.

The sacrificial offering of Christ on the cross came to be linked especially with one aspect of the "threefold office of Christ" (*munus triplex Christi*). According to this typology, which dates from the middle of the sixteenth century, the work of Christ could be summarized under three "offices": prophet (by which Christ declares the will of God); priest (by which he makes sacrifice for sin); and king (by which he rules with authority over his people).

This understanding of the threefold office of Christ was formalized during the seventeenth century, and is given full justification in the writings of Protestant theologians of this period. The noted seventeenth-century Genevan theologian François Turrettini (1623–87), a major exponent of the Reformed tradition, here sets out this understanding more fully, in a text originally published in Latin in 1679.

This mediatorial office of Christ is distributed among three functions, which are individual parts of it: the prophetic, priestly, and kingly. [...] The threefold misery of humanity resulting from sin (that is, ignorance, guilt, and the oppression and bondage of sin) required this threefold office. Ignorance is healed through the prophetic office, guilt through the priestly, and the oppression and bondage of sin through the kingly. The prophetic light scatters the darkness of error; the merit of the priest removes guilt and obtains reconciliation for us; the power of the king takes away the bondage of sin and death. The prophet shows God to us; the priest leads us to God; and the king joins us together with God, and glorifies us with him. The prophet illuminates the mind by the spirit of enlightenment; the priest soothes the heart and conscience by the spirit of consolation; the king subdues rebellious inclinations by the spirit of sanctification.

The general acceptance of this taxonomy within Protestantism in the late sixteenth and seventeenth centuries led to a sacrificial understanding of Christ's death becoming of central importance within Protestant soteriologies. Thus John Pearson's *Exposition of the Creed* (1659) insists upon the necessity of the sacrifice of Christ in redemption, and specifically links this with the priestly office of Christ.

> The redemption or salvation which the Messiah was to bring consisteth in the freeing of a sinner from the state of sin and eternal death into a state of righteousness and eternal life. Now a freedom from sin could not be wrought without a sacrifice propitiatory, and therefore there was a necessity of a priest.

Since the Enlightenment, however, there has been a subtle shift in the meaning of the term. A metaphorical extension of meaning has come to be given priority over the original. Whereas the term originally referred to the ritual offering of slaughtered animals as a specifically religious action, it increasingly came to mean heroic or costly action on the part of individuals, especially the giving up of one's life, with no transcendent reference or expectation.

This trend may be seen developing in John Locke's *Reasonableness of Christianity* (1695). Locke argues that the only article of faith required of Christians is that of belief in Christ's Messiahship; the idea of a sacrifice for sin is studiously set to one side. "The faith required was to believe Jesus to be the Messiah, the anointed, who had been promised by God to the world [. . .] I do not remember that Christ anywhere assumes to himself the title of a priest, or mentions anything relating to his priesthood."

These arguments were taken further by the Deist writer Thomas Chubb (1679–1747), especially in his *True Gospel of Jesus Christ Vindicated* (1739). Arguing that the true religion of reason was that of conformity to the eternal rule of right, Chubb argues that the idea of Christ's death as a sacrifice arises from the apologetic concerns of the early Christian writers, which led them to harmonize this religion of reason with the cult of the Jews: "As the Jews had their temple, their altar, their high priest, their sacrifices and the like, so the apostles, in order to make Christianity bear a resemblance to Judaism, found out something or other in Christianity, which they by a figure of speech called by those names." Chubb, in common with the emerging Enlightenment tradition, dismissed this as spurious. "God's disposition to show mercy [. . .] arises wholly from his own innate goodness or mercifulness, and not from anything external to him, whether it be the sufferings and death of Jesus Christ or otherwise."

Even the noted English critic of Deism Joseph Butler, in attempting to reinstate the notion of sacrifice in his *Analogy of Religion* (1736),

found himself in difficulty, given the strongly rationalist spirit of the age. In upholding the sacrificial nature of Christ's death, he found himself obliged to concede more than he cared to:

> How and in what particular way [the death of Christ] had this efficacy, there are not wanting persons who have endeavoured to explain; but I do not find that Scripture has explained it. We seem to be very much in the dark concerning the manner in which the ancients understood atonements to be made, i.e. pardon to be obtained by sacrifice.

Horace Bushnell's *Vicarious Sacrifice* (1866) illustrates this same trend in the Anglo-American theology of the period, but in a more constructive manner. Through his suffering, Christ awakens our sense of guilt. His vicarious sacrifice demonstrates that God suffers on account of evil. In speaking of the "tender appeals of sacrifice," Bushnell might seem to align himself with purely exemplarist understandings of the death of Christ; however, Bushnell is adamant that there are objective elements to atonement. Christ's death affects God, and expresses God. There are strong anticipations of later theologies of the suffering of God, when Bushnell declares:

> Whatever we may say or hold or believe concerning the vicarious sacrifice of Christ, we are to affirm in the same manner of God. The whole Deity is in it, in it from eternity. [. . .] There is a cross in God before the wood is seen on the hill. [. . .] It is as if there were a cross unseen, standing on its undiscovered hill, far back in the ages.

The use of sacrificial imagery has become noticeably less widespread since 1945, especially in German-language theology. It is highly likely that this relates directly to the rhetorical debasement of the term in secular contexts, especially in situations of national emergency. The secular use of the imagery of sacrifice, often degenerating into little more than slogan-mongering, is widely regarded as having tainted and compromised both the word and the concept. The frequent use of such phrases as "he sacrificed his life for King and country" in Britain during World War I, and Adolf Hitler's extensive use of sacrificial imagery in justifying economic hardship and the loss of civil liberties as the price of German national revival in the late 1930s, served to render the term virtually unusable for many in Christian teaching and preaching, on account of its negative associations. Nevertheless, the idea continues to be of importance in modern Roman Catholic sacramental theology, which continues to regard the Eucharist as a sacrifice, and finds in this notion a rich source of theological imagery.

The cross as a victory

The New Testament and early church laid considerable emphasis upon the victory gained by Christ over sin, death, and Satan through his cross and resurrection (see pp. 465–7). This theme of victory, often linked liturgically with the Easter celebrations, was of major importance within the western Christian theological tradition until the Enlightenment. The motif of "Christ the victor" (*Christus victor*) brought together a series of related themes, centering on the idea of a decisive victory over forces of evil and oppression. In one sense, this is not a "theory of the atonement." It is much more an expression of confidence in the difference that Christ's death and resurrection have made. This may well precede, or be the basis of, a theory of the atonement – but it's not a theory itself.

The image of Christ's death as a ransom came to be of central importance to Greek patristic writers, such as Irenaeus. We noted earlier, in discussing the theological role of analogies, that the New Testament speaks of Jesus giving his life as a "ransom" for sinners (Mark 10: 45; 1 Timothy 2: 6). Origen, perhaps the most speculative of early patristic writers, believed that this analogy could legitimately be pressed to its limits. If Christ's death was a ransom, Origen argued, it must have been paid to someone. But to whom? It could not have been paid to God, in that it was not God who was holding sinners to ransom. Therefore, Origen argued, it had to be paid to the devil.

Gregory the Great developed this idea still further. The devil had acquired rights over fallen humanity, which God was obliged to respect. The only means by which humanity could be released from this satanic domination and oppression was through the devil exceeding the limits of his authority, and thus being obliged to forfeit his rights. So how could this be achieved? Gregory suggests that it could come about if a sinless person were to enter the world, yet in the form of a normal sinful person. The devil would not notice until it was too late: in claiming authority over this sinless person, the devil would have overstepped the limits of his authority, and thus be obliged to forfeit his rights.

Gregory suggests the image of a baited hook: Christ's humanity is the bait, and his divinity the hook. The devil, like a great sea-monster, snaps at the bait – and then discovers, too late, the hook. "The bait tempts in order that the hook may wound. Our Lord therefore, when coming for the redemption of humanity, made a kind of hook of himself for the death of the devil." Other writers explored other images for the same idea – that of trapping the devil. Christ's death was like a net for catching birds, or a trap for catching mice. It was this aspect of this approach to the meaning of the cross that caused the most disquiet subsequently. It seemed that God was guilty of deception.

This theme is probably best seen in the writings of Rufinus of Aquileia, particularly his exposition of the Apostles' creed, which dates from around the year 400:

[The purpose of the Incarnation] was that the divine virtue of the Son of God might be like a kind of hook hidden beneath the form of human flesh [...] to lure on the prince of this world to a contest; that the Son might offer him his human flesh as a bait and that the divinity which lay underneath might catch him and hold him fast with its hook. [...] Then, just as a fish when it seizes a baited hook not only fails to drag off the bait but is itself dragged out of the water to serve as food for others; so he that had the power of death seized the body of Jesus in death, unaware of the hook of divinity which lay hidden inside. Having swallowed it, he was immediately caught. The gates of hell were broken, and he was, as it were, drawn up from the pit, to become food for others.

The imagery of victory over the devil proved to have enormous popular appeal. The medieval idea of "the harrowing of hell" bears witness to its power. According to this, after dying upon the cross, Christ descended to hell, and broke down its gates in order that the imprisoned souls might go free. The idea rested (rather tenuously, it has to be said) upon 1 Peter 3: 18–22, which makes reference to Christ "preaching to the spirits in prison." The hymn "Ye Choirs of New Jerusalem," written by Fulbert of Chartres, expresses this theme in two of its verses, picking up the theme of Christ as the "lion of Judah" (Revelation 5: 5) defeating Satan, the serpent (Genesis 3: 15):

For Judah's lion bursts his chains
Crushing the serpent's head;
And cries aloud through death's domain
To wake the imprisoned dead.

Devouring depths of hell their prey
At his command restore;
His ransomed hosts pursue their way
Where Jesus goes before.

A similar idea is found in William Langland's *Piers the Plowman*, one of the most important English-language poems of the fourteenth century. In this poem, Piers falls asleep and dreams of Christ throwing open the gates of Hell, and speaking the following words to Satan:

Here is my soul as a ransom for all these sinful souls, to redeem those that are worthy. They are mine; they came from me, and therefore I have the better claim on them. [...] You, by falsehood and crime and against all justice, took away what was mine, in my own domain; I, in fairness, recover them by paying the ransom, and by no other means. What you got by guile is won back by grace. [...] And as a tree caused Adam and all mankind to die, so my gallows-tree shall bring them back to life.

Notice, by the way, how the text uses the theme of recapitulation – see the parallel between "tree" and "gallows-tree" – in a manner very similar to Irenaeus of Lyons.

With the advent of the Enlightenment, however, the *Christus victor* approach began to fall out of theological favor, increasingly being regarded as outmoded and unsophisticated. However great the popular appeal of the "harrowing of hell" may have been to medieval peasants, it was regarded as utterly primitive by the more sophisticated standards of the Enlightenment. The following factors appear to have contributed to this development.

1 Rational criticism of belief in the resurrection of Christ (pp. 69, 320–1) raised doubts concerning whether one could even begin to speak of a "victory" over death.

335

2   The imagery traditionally linked with this approach to the cross – such as the existence of a personal devil in the form of Satan, and the domination of human existence by oppressive or satanic forces of sin and evil – was dismissed as premodern superstition.

The rehabilitation of this approach in the modern period is usually dated to 1931, with the appearance of Gustaf Aulén's *Christus victor*. This short book, which originally appeared in German as an article in *Zeitschrift für systematische Theologie* (1930), has exercised a major influence over English-language approaches to the subject. Aulén argued that the classic Christian conception of the work of Christ was summed up in the belief that the risen Christ had brought new possibilities of life to humanity through his victory over the powers of evil. In a brief and very compressed account of the history of theories of the atonement, Aulén argued that this highly dramatic "classic" theory had dominated Christianity until the Middle Ages, when more abstract legal theories began to gain ground. A new concern for the morality of atonement led to a focus on justice-centered theories of the atonement, with a gradual loss of interest in the more morally problematic *Christus victor* approach. The situation was radically reversed in the writings of Martin Luther, who reintroduced the theme, perhaps as a reaction to what he regarded as the spiritual aridity of some later scholastic theories of the atonement. However, Aulén argued, the scholastic concerns of later Protestant orthodoxy led to its being relegated once more to the background. Aulén declared that it was time to reverse this process, and rediscover the theory, which deserved a full and proper hearing in the modern period.

In setting out the merits of this theory, Aulén drew a distinction between what he called the "classic" or *Christus victor* approach,

and the two other approaches which he argued had gained currency in modern theology – a purely "objective" approach, which focused on the atonement as marking a change in God, and a purely "subjective" approach which regarded the atonement as bringing about a change within the subjective human consciousness. Aulén argues that the former is associated with Anselm of Canterbury, and the latter with Peter Abelard. The *Christus victor* model is, in Aulén's view, to be distinguished from both these approaches.

> Its central theme is the idea of the Atonement as a Divine conflict and victory; Christ – *Christus Victor* – fights against and triumphs over the evil powers of the world, the "tyrants" under which mankind is in bondage and suffering, and in Him God reconciles the world to Himself. Two points here require to be pressed with special emphasis: first, that this is a doctrine of Atonement in the full and proper sense, and second, that this idea of the Atonement has a clear and distinct character of its own, quite different from the other two types.

It was not long before the historical foundations of Aulén's approach were called into question. Its claims to be treated as the "classic" theory of the atonement had clearly been overstated. The idea of Christ as the victor over death and Satan was indeed an important component of the general patristic understanding of the nature of salvation; however, it was just one image or approach among many others. Aulén had exaggerated its importance for patristic writers. His critics pointed out that, if any theory could justly lay claim to the title of "the classic theory of the atonement," it would be the notion of redemption through unity with Christ.

Nevertheless, Aulén's views were sympathetically received. In part, this reflects growing disenchantment with the Enlightenment worldview in general; more fundamentally, perhaps, it represents a growing realization of the reality of evil in the world, fostered by the horrors of World War I. The insights of Sigmund Freud, which drew attention to the manner in which adults could be spiritually imprisoned by the hidden forces within their subconscious, raised serious doubts about the Enlightenment view of the total rationality of human nature, and lent new credibility to the idea that humans are held in bondage to unknown and hidden forces. Aulén's approach seemed to resonate with a growing awareness of the darker side of human nature. It had become intellectually respectable to talk about "forces of evil."

Aulén's approach also offered a third possibility, which mediated between the two alternatives then on offer within mainstream liberal Protestantism – both of which were increasingly coming to be regarded as flawed. The classic legal theory was regarded as raising difficult theological questions, not least concerning the morality of atonement; the subjective approach, which regarded Christ's death as doing little more than arousing human religious sentiment, seemed to be seriously inadequate religiously. Aulén offered an approach to the meaning of the death of Christ which bypassed the difficulties of legal approaches, yet vigorously defended the objective nature of the atonement. Nevertheless, Aulén's *Christus victor* approach did raise some serious questions. It offered no rational justification for the manner in which the forces of evil are defeated through the cross of Christ. Why the cross? Why not in some other manner?

Since then, the image of victory has been developed in writings on the cross. Rudolf Bultmann extended his program of demythologization to the New Testament theme of victory, interpreting it as a victory over inauthentic existence and unbelief. Paul Tillich offered a reworking of Aulén's theory, in which the victory of Christ on the cross was interpreted as a victory over existential forces which threaten to deprive us of authentic existence. Bultmann and Tillich, in adopting such existentialist approaches, thus converted a theory of the atonement which was originally radically objective into a subjective victory within the human consciousness.

In his *Past Event and Present Salvation* (1989), Oxford theologian Paul Fiddes emphasized that the notion of "victory" retains a place of significance within Christian thinking about the cross. Christ's death does more than impart some new knowledge to us, or express old ideas in new manners. It makes possible a new mode of existence:

> The victory of Christ actually *creates* victory in us. [. . .] The act of Christ is one of those moments in human history that "opens up new possibilities of existence." Once a new possibility has been disclosed, other people can make it their own, repeating and reliving the experience.

The cross and forgiveness

A third approach centers on the idea of the death of Christ providing the basis by which God is enabled to forgive sin. The notion is traditionally associated with the eleventh-century writer Anselm of Canterbury, who developed an argument for the necessity of the incarnation on this basis. This model became incorporated into classical Protestant dogmatics during the period of orthodoxy, and finds its expression in many hymns of the eighteenth and nineteenth centuries. In part, Anselm's reason for developing this model appears to have been a deep-seated dissatisfaction with the *Christus victor* approach, which seemed to rest upon a series of highly questionable assumptions about the "rights of the devil" (*ius diaboli*), and an implicit suggestion that God acted with less than total honesty in redeeming humanity.

Anselm was unable to understand why the devil can be said to have "rights" of any kind over fallen humanity, let alone why God should be under any obligation to respect them. At best, the devil might be allowed to have a *de facto* power over humanity – a power which exists as a matter of fact, even if it is an illegitimate and unjustified power. Yet this cannot be thought of as a *de jure* authority – that is, an authority firmly grounded in some legal or moral principle. "I do not see what force this has," he comments, in dismissing the idea. Equally, Anselm is dismissive of any notion that God deceives the devil in the process of redemption. The entire trajectory of redemption is grounded in and reflects the righteousness of God. Anselm's emphasis falls totally upon the righteousness of God. God redeems humanity in a manner that is totally consistent with the divine quality of righteousness.

Anselm's *Cur Deus homo* ("Why God Became Man") is a sustained engagement with the question of the possibility of human redemption, cast in the form of a dialogue. In the course of his analysis, he demonstrates – although how successfully is a matter of dispute – both the necessity of the incarnation and the saving potential of the death and resurrection of Jesus Christ. The argument is complex, and can be summarized as follows:

1 God created humanity in a state of original righteousness, with the objective of bringing humanity to a state of eternal blessedness.

2 That state of eternal blessedness is contingent upon human obedience to God. However, through sin, humanity is unable to achieve this necessary obedience, which appears to frustrate God's purpose in creating humanity in the first place.

3 In that it is impossible for God's purposes to be frustrated, there must be some means by which the situation can be remedied. However, the situation can only be remedied if a *satisfaction* is made for sin. In other words, something has to be done, by which the offense caused by human sin can be purged.

4 There is no way in which humanity can provide this necessary satisfaction. It lacks the resources which are needed. On the other hand, God possesses the resources needed to provide the required satisfaction.

5 A "God-man" would possess both the *ability* (as God) and the *obligation* (as a human being) to pay the required satisfaction. Therefore the incarnation takes place, in order that the required satisfaction may be made, and humanity redeemed. Anselm also makes the additional point that Christ's obedience to God during his life and in his death endowed his sacrifice with sufficient merit to redeem human nature at large – a theme that would be developed considerably in later writings on this theme.

A number of points require comment. First, sin is conceived of as an offense against God. The weight of that offense appears to be proportional to the status of the offended party. For many scholars, this suggests that Anselm has been deeply influenced by the feudal assumptions of his time, perhaps regarding God as the equivalent of the "lord of the manor." It is, however, much more likely that Anselm is merely using such ways of thinking as analogies familiar to his age; it is clear that his fundamental line of thought is to be found in the Christian tradition itself.

Second, Anselm tends to conceive of sin as something that can be deleted – like a debt – through Christ's death. Anselm shows little awareness that sin might be an ongoing issue – something that requires both forgiveness and purging or remediation. Sin is treated in almost economic terms – as a certain quantity of "offense" that needs to be counterbalanced by an equally large "merit."

Third, Anselm seems to argue that redemption is a necessity – in other words, that Christ's death was *required* in order to effect human salvation. In taking this view, he is in a minority. We may be able to make sense of Christ's death as the basis of salvation – but that does not mean that it *had* to happen this way. For Augustine, Aquinas, and Scotus, God could have redeemed us by other means. We may be able to understand why God chose to act in this way; we cannot assume, however, that such considerations forced God to redeem humanity in this specific manner. As the Canadian Jesuit writer Bernard Lonergan pointed out, intelligibility is not the same as necessity.

Fourth, there has been considerable debate over the origins of the idea of a "satisfaction." It is possible that the idea may derive from the Germanic laws of the period, which stipulated that an offense had to be purged through an appropriate payment. However, most scholars believe that Anselm was appealing directly to the existing penitential system of the church. A sinner, seeking penance, was required to confess every sin. In pronouncing forgiveness, the priest would require that the penitent should do something (such as go on a pilgrimage or undertake some charitable work) as a "satisfaction" – that is, a means of publicly demonstrating gratitude for forgiveness. It is possible that Anselm derived the idea from this source.

The theological basis of the notion of "satisfaction" was developed further in the thirteenth century by Thomas Aquinas. Aquinas grounds the adequacy of the "satisfaction of Christ" to compensate for human sin in three considerations.

> A proper satisfaction comes about when someone offers to the person offended something which gives him a delight greater than

his hatred of the offense. Now Christ by suffering as a result of love and obedience offered to God something greater than what might be exacted in compensation for the whole offence of humanity; firstly, because of the greatness of the love, as a result of which he suffered; secondly, because of the worth of the life which he laid down for a satisfaction, which was the life of God and of a human being; thirdly, because of the comprehensiveness of his passion and the greatness of the sorrow which he took upon himself.

Two aspects of this argument should be noted. Aquinas's first point (the extent of Christ's love) is clearly intended to incorporate Peter Abelard's emphasis on the significance of the love shown by Christ in dying on the cross (see pp. 343–41). Second, Aquinas follows Anselm in arguing that the inherent worth of Christ's death is grounded in his divinity. Why is Christ's death so significant, and possessed of a capacity to redeem us? Because, Aquinas argues, he – and he alone – is God incarnate. As Aquinas puts it, "the worth of Christ's flesh is to be reckoned, not just according to the nature of flesh but according to the person who assumed it, in that it was the flesh of God, from whom it gained an infinite worth." In response to the question of why the death of one person should have possessed such saving significance, Aquinas points out that Christ's significance in this matter does not rest on his humanity, but on his divinity.

Nevertheless, despite this emphasis on the divinity of Christ, it is clear that Aquinas has taken care to ensure that the importance of the humanity of Christ should not be overlooked. The first and third of his three considerations can each be argued to give a significant place to Christ's humanity in the process of redemption, by stressing the saving importance of Christ's love and suffering. Anselm tended to treat Christ's humanity as little more than the means by which Christ was able to justly bear the penalty due for human sin; Aquinas is thus able to offer a more positive assessment of the soteriological role of the humanity of Christ.

However, despite the obvious difficulties which attend Anselm's approach, an important advance had been made. Anselm's insistence that God is totally and utterly obliged to act according to the principles of justice throughout the redemption of humanity marks a decisive break with the dubious morality of the *Christus victor* view. In taking up Anselm's approach, later writers were able to place it on a more secure foundation by grounding it in the general principles of law. The sixteenth century was particularly appreciative of the importance of human law, and saw it as an appropriate model for God's forgiveness of human sin. Three main models came to be used at this time to understand the manner in which the forgiveness of human sins is related to the death of Christ.

Representation

Christ is here understood to be the covenant representative of humanity. Through faith, believers come to stand within the covenant between God and humanity. All that Christ has achieved through the cross is available on account of the covenant. Just as God entered into a covenant with his people Israel, so he has entered into a covenant with his church. Christ, by his obedience upon the cross, represents his covenant people, winning benefits for them as their representative. By coming to faith, individuals come to stand within the covenant, and thus share in all its benefits, won by Christ through his cross and resurrection – including the full and free forgiveness of our sins.

This idea is particularly associated with Reformed theology during the late sixteenth and seventeenth centuries, which developed a sophisticated covenant theology. Adam was humanity's representative under the old covenant of works; Christ has become our representative under the new covenant of grace. These covenant theologies are seen in their most fully developed form in New England Puritanism during the eighteenth century.

Participation

Through faith, believers participate in the risen Christ. They are "in Christ," to use Paul's famous phrase. They are caught up in him, and share in his risen life. As a result of this, they share in all the benefits won by Christ, through his obedience upon the cross. One of those benefits is the forgiveness of sins, in which they share through faith. New Testament scholar E. P. Sanders states the importance of "participation in Christ" for Paul in the following words:

> The prime significance which the death of Christ has for Paul is not that it provides atonement for past transgressions (although he holds the common Christian view that it does so), but that, by *sharing* in Christ's death, one dies to the *power* of sin or to the old aeon, with the result that one belongs to God. [...] The transfer takes place by *participation* in Christ's death.

Participating in Christ thus entails the forgiveness of sins, and sharing in his righteousness. This idea is central to Luther's soteriology, as his image of the marriage between Christ and the believer makes clear. In some way, faith unites us to Christ, and thus enables us to participate in his attributes.

Substitution

Christ is here understood to be a substitute, the one who goes to the cross in our place. Sinners ought to have been crucified, on account of their sins. Christ is crucified in their place.

God allows Christ to stand in our place, taking our guilt upon himself, so that his righteousness – won by obedience upon the cross – might become ours. This idea is not found to any significant extent in the theological writings of the patristic and medieval periods. It becomes significant in the sixteenth century, particularly in the writings of John Calvin, and continues to be developed by conservative Protestant theologians, such as J. I. Packer (see below).

With the onset of the Enlightenment, this general approach to the atonement was subjected to a radical critique. The following major points of criticism were directed against it.

1   It appeared to rest upon a notion of original guilt, which Enlightenment writers found unacceptable. Each human being was responsible for his or her own moral guilt; the very notion of an inherited guilt, as it was expressed in the traditional doctrine of original sin, was to be rejected.

2   The Enlightenment insisted upon the rationality, and perhaps above all the morality, of every aspect of Christian doctrine. This theory of the atonement appeared to be morally suspect to those committed to the Enlightenment worldview, especially in its notions of transferred guilt or merit. The central idea of "vicarious satisfaction" was also regarded with acute suspicion: in what sense was it moral for one human being to bear the penalties due for another?

These criticisms were given added weight through the development of the discipline of the "history of dogma" (see pp. 307–8). The representatives of this movement, from G. S. Steinbart through to Adolf von Harnack, argued that a series of assumptions, each of central importance to the Anselmian doctrine of penal substitution, had become incorporated into Christian theology by what were little more than historical accidents. For example, in his *System of Pure Philosophy* (1778), Steinbart argued that historical investigation disclosed the intrusion of three "arbitrary assumptions" into Christian reflection on salvation:

1   the Augustinian doctrine of original sin;
2   the concept of satisfaction;
3   the doctrine of the imputation of the righteousness of Christ.

For such reasons, Steinbart felt able to declare the substructure of orthodox Protestant thinking on the atonement to be a relic of a bygone era.

More recently, the idea of guilt – a central aspect of legal approaches to soteriology – has been the subject of much discussion, especially in the light of the influential Austrian psychoanalyst Sigmund Freud's views on the origin of guilt in childhood experiences. For some twentieth-century writers, "guilt" is simply a psychosocial projection, whose origins lie not in the holiness of God but in the muddleheadedness of human nature. These psychosocial structures are then, it is argued, projected onto some imaginary screen of "external" reality, and treated as if they were objectively true. While this represents a considerable overstatement of the arguments, it has the advantage of clarity, and allows us to gain an appreciation of the considerable pressure that this approach to the atonement is currently facing.

Nevertheless, this view of the cross continues to find significant supporters. The collapse of the evolutionary moral optimism of liberal Protestantism in the wake of World War I (see pp. 85–6) did much to raise again the question of human guilt and the need for redemption from outside the human situation. Two significant contributions to this discussion may be regarded as precipitated directly by the credibility crisis faced by liberal Protestantism at this time.

P. T. Forsyth's *Justification of God* (1916), written in England during World War I, represents an impassioned plea to allow the notion of the "justice of God" to be rediscovered. Forsyth is less concerned than Anselm for the legal and juridical aspects of the cross; his interest centers on the manner in which the cross is inextricably linked with "the whole moral fabric and movement of the universe." The doctrine of the atonement is inseparable from "the rightness of things." God acts to restore this "rightness of things," in that he makes available through the cross a means of moral regeneration – something which the war demonstrated that humanity needed, yet was unable to provide itself.

> The cross is not a theological theme, nor a forensic device, but the crisis of the moral universe on a scale far greater than earthly war. It is the theodicy of the whole God dealing with the whole soul of the whole world in holy love, righteous judgement and redeeming grace.

Through the cross, God aims to restore the rightness of the world through rightful means – a central theme of Anselm's doctrine of atonement, creatively restated.

More significant is the extended discussion of the theme of "atonement" or "reconciliation" (the German term *Versöhnung* can bear both meanings) to be found in Karl Barth's *Church Dogmatics*. The central section (volume 4, part 1, section 59, 2) addressing the issue is entitled – significantly – "The Judge Judged in Our Place." The title derives from the *Heidelberg Catechism*, which speaks of Christ as the judge who "has represented me before the judgment of God, and has taken away all condemnation from me." The section in question can be regarded as an extended commentary on this classic text of the Reformed tradition, dealing with the manner in which the judgment of God in the first place is made known and enacted, and in the second, is taken upon God himself (a central Anselmian theme, even if Anselm failed to integrate it within a trinitarian context).

The entire section is steeped in the language and imagery of guilt, judgment, and forgiveness. In the cross, we can see God exercising his rightful judgment of sinful humanity (Barth uses the compound term *Sündermensch* – "person of sin" – to emphasize that "sin" is not a detachable aspect of human nature). The cross exposes human delusions of self-sufficiency and autonomy of judgment, which Barth sees encapsulated in the story of Genesis 3: "Human beings want to be their own judges."

Yet alteration of the situation demands that its inherent wrongness be acknowledged. For Barth, the cross of Christ represents the locus in which the righteous judge makes known his judgment of sinful humanity, and simultaneously takes that judgment upon himself.

> What took place is that the Son of God fulfilled the righteous judgement on us human beings by himself taking our place as a human being, and in our place undergoing the judgement under which we had passed. [...] Because God willed to execute his judgement on us in his Son, it all took place in his person, as *his* accusation and condemnation and destruction. He judged, and it was the judge who was judged, who allowed himself to be judged. [...] Why did God become a human being? So that God as a human being might do and accomplish and achieve and complete all this for us wrongdoers, in order that in this way there might be brought about by him our reconciliation with him, and our conversion to him.

The strongly substitutionary character of this will be evident. God exercises his righteous judgment by exposing our sin, by taking it upon himself, and thus by neutralizing its power.

For Barth, the cross thus both speaks "for us" and "against us." Unless the cross is allowed to reveal the full extent of our sin, it cannot take that sin from us:

> The "for us" of his death on the cross included and encloses this terrible "against us." Without this terrible "against us," it would not be the divine and holy and redemptive and effectively helpful "for us," in which the conversion of humanity and the world to God has become an event.

Legal or penal approaches to the meaning of the death of Christ have continued to be of particular importance within evangelical theology. One of the most notable features of the evangelical renaissance since World War II has been its focus on the contemporary exploration of New Testament understandings of the atonement, with works such as Leon Morris's *The Apostolic Preaching of the Cross* (1955) and John Stott's *The Cross of Christ* (1986) setting out the continuing centrality of penal approaches to the cross within the evangelical understanding of the Christian faith. The general features of this approach were stated with particular clarity in 1974 by James I. Packer:

> Christ's death had its effect first on God, who was hereby *propitiated* (or, better, who hereby propitiated himself), and only because it had this effect did it become an overthrowing of the powers of darkness and a revealing of God's seeking and saving love. The thought here is that by dying Christ offered to God what the West has called *satisfaction* for sins, satisfaction which God's own character dictated as the only means whereby his "no" to

us could become a "yes." [. . .] By undergoing the cross Jesus expiated our sins, propitiated our Maker, turned God's "no" to us into a "yes," and so saved us.

The cross as a demonstration of God's love

A central aspect of the New Testament understanding of the meaning of the cross relates to the demonstration of the love of God for humanity. Augustine of Hippo was but one of many patristic writers to stress that one of the motivations underlying the mission of Christ was the "demonstration of the love of God toward us."

A similar emphasis can be found at an earlier stage in the Christian theological tradition, such as the third-century writings of Clement of Alexandria. Clement points out how the incarnation of Christ, and especially his death, represents a powerful affirmation of the love of God for humanity, and a demand that humanity demonstrate a comparable love for God.

> For [Christ] came down, for this he assumed human nature, for this he willingly endured the sufferings of humanity, that by being reduced to the measure of our weakness, he might raise us to the measure of his power. And just before he poured out his offering, when he gave himself as a ransom, he left us a new testament: "I give you my love" (John 13: 34). What is the nature and extent of this love? For each of us he laid down his life, the life which was worth the whole universe, and he requires in return that we should do the same for each other.

Perhaps the most important medieval statement of this emphasis can be found in the writings of Peter Abelard. It must be stressed that Abelard does not, as some of his interpreters suggest, *reduce* the meaning of the cross to a demonstration of the love of God. This is one among many components of Abelard's soteriology, which includes traditional ideas concerning Christ's death as a sacrifice for human sin. It is Abelard's emphasis upon the subjective impact of the cross that is distinctive.

For Abelard, "the purpose and cause of the incarnation was that Christ might illuminate the world by his wisdom, and excite it to love of himself." In this, Abelard restates the Augustinian idea of Christ's incarnation as a public demonstration of the extent of the love of God, with the intent of evoking a response of love from humanity. "The Son of God took our nature, and in it took upon himself to teach us by both word and example even to the point of death, thus binding us to himself through love." This insight is pressed home with considerable force, as the subjective impact of the love of God in Christ is explored further:

> Love is increased by the faith which we have concerning Christ because, on account of the belief that God in Christ has united our human nature to himself, and by suffering in that same nature has demonstrated to us that supreme love of which Christ himself speaks: "Greater love has no one than this" (John 15: 13). We are thus joined through his grace to him and our neighbor by an unbreakable bond of love. [...] Therefore, our redemption through the suffering of Christ is that deeper love within us which not only frees us from slavery to sin, but also secures for us the true liberty of the children of God, in order that we might do all things out of love rather than out of fear – love for him who has shown us such grace that no greater can be found.

Abelard fails to provide an adequate theological foundation to allow us to understand precisely why Christ's death is to be understood as a demonstration of the love of God. Nevertheless, his approach to the meaning of the death of Christ brought home the powerful subjective impact of that death, which had been totally ignored by some contemporary writers, such as Anselm of Canterbury.

This theme is developed throughout Christian theology, and has clear applications in the sphere of spirituality. We find it in one of the most reflective Spanish spiritual writers of this period – Juana de la Cruz (1481–1534). Juana is noted particularly for her *Libro de Conorte* ("Book of Consolation"), which was widely admired during the Spanish Golden Age. Although Juana de la Cruz never achieved the same status as other women writers of this era – such as Teresa of Avila – she repays careful study, not least because of her use of vivid imagery in describing the relationship of the believer to God. Her discussion of the passion of Christ is notable in several respects, particularly her explicit use of feminine images to unlock its theological significance. The crucifixion of Christ is here compared to a woman giving birth. For Juana, reflecting on the pain and sorrow that Christ suffered in order to give life to the children of God is a powerful affirmation of the love of God for humanity – a love which is here expressed using maternal imagery.

> Christ gave birth to us all with very great pains and torments at the time of his cruel and bitter passion. And since we cost him so dearly and the labor through which he gave birth to us was so grueling that it made him sweat drops of blood, he can do nothing but pray and plead for us before the Father, like a very compassionate mother [*como madre muy piadosa*], desiring that we should be saved and that our souls should be enlightened, so that he might not have suffered his pain and torment in vain.

The text that underlies Juana's reflections at this point is Matthew 23:37 "Jerusalem, Jerusalem, the city that kills the prophets and stones those who are sent to it! How often have I desired to gather your children together as a hen gathers her brood under her wings, and you were not willing!" Juana finds the image of a hen gathering her chicks under her wings to be an agreeably feminine way of conceiving the love of God for humanity, and links this with Christ's death as a birthing process, which gives rise to faith in individuals, as they respond to God's love.

With the rise of the Enlightenment worldview, increasingly critical approaches were adopted to theories of the atonement which incorporated transcendent elements – such as the idea of a sacrifice which had some impact upon God, or Christ dying in order to pay some penalty or satisfaction which was due for sin. The increasingly skeptical attitude to the resurrection associated with the Enlightenment tended to discourage theologians from incorporating this element into their theologies of atonement with anything even approaching the enthusiasm of earlier generations. As a result, the emphasis of theologians sympathetic to the Enlightenment came to focus upon the cross itself.

However, many Enlightenment theologians also had difficulties with the traditional "two natures" doctrine, which affirmed that Christ was at one and the same time both perfectly human and perfectly divine. The form of Christology which perhaps expresses the spirit of the Enlightenment most faithfully is a degree Christology – that is to say, a Christology which recognizes a difference of degree, but not of nature, between Christ and other human beings. On this view, Jesus Christ was recognized as embodying certain qualities which are present, actually or potentially, in all other human beings, the difference lying in the superior extent to which he embodied them.

When such considerations are applied to theories of atonement, a consistent pattern begins to emerge. This can be studied from the eighteenth-century writings of G. S. Steinbart, I. G.

Töllner, G. F. Seiler, and I. G. Bretschneider. Its basic features can be summarized as follows.

1 The cross has no transcendent reference or value; its value resides directly and solely in its impact upon humanity. Thus the cross represents a "sacrifice" only in that it represents Christ giving up his life.
2 The person who died upon the cross was a human being, and the impact of that death is upon human beings. That impact takes the form of inspiration and encouragement to model ourselves upon the moral example set us in Jesus himself.
3 The only theologically valid interpretation of the cross is that it demonstrates the love of God toward us.

This approach became enormously influential in rationalist circles throughout nineteenth-century Europe. The mystery and apparent irrationalism of the cross had been neutralized; what remained was a powerful and dramatic plea for the moral improvement of humanity, on the basis of the example provided in the lifestyle and attitudes of Jesus Christ. The model of a martyr, rather than a savior, describes the attitude increasingly adopted toward Jesus within such circles.

The most significant challenge to this rationalist approach to the cross was expressed by F. D. E. Schleiermacher, who insisted upon the *religious* – as opposed to purely moral – value of the death of Christ. Christ did not die to make or endorse a moral system; he came in order that the supremacy of the consciousness of God could be established in humanity. Schleiermacher argues that redemption consists in the stimulation and elevation of the natural human God-consciousness through the "entrance of the living influence of Christ." He attributes to Christ "an absolutely powerful God-consciousness." This, he argues, possesses an assimilative power of such intensity that it is able to bring about the redemption of humanity.

Schleiermacher seems to have in mind something like the model of a charismatic political leader, who is able to communicate his vision with such clarity and power that it is both understood by his audience, and also captivates them in such a way that they are transformed by it, and come to be caught up in it. Yet it remains his idea; he has assumed others into it, without compromising his personal uniqueness, in that it is and remains *his* vision:

> Let us now suppose that some person for the first time combines a naturally cohesive group into a civil community (legend tells of such cases in plenty); what happens is that the idea of the state first comes to consciousness in him, and takes possession of his personality as its immediate dwelling-place. Then he assumes the rest into the living fellowship of the idea. He does so by making them clearly conscious of the unsatisfactoriness of their present condition by effective speech. The power remains with the founder of forming in them the idea which is the innermost principle of his own life, and of assuming them into the fellowship of that life.

Yet this is not exemplarism, in the strict sense of the word. Two central German terms – *Urbildlichkeit* and *Vorbildlichkeit* – are employed by Schleiermacher in exploring this question, both of which are difficult to translate adequately into English.

1   *Urbildlichkeit* may be rendered as "the quality of being an ideal." For Schleiermacher, Jesus of Nazareth is the ideal of human God-consciousness, and the ultimate in human piety (*Frömmigkeit*). Taken on its own, this notion might seem to come close to the rationalist notion of Jesus as a human moral example. Schleiermacher is able to evade this difficulty in two ways.

First, he stresses that Jesus of Nazareth is not simply a moral example, someone who illustrates permanent moral truths. He is the one ideal example of a perfect human consciousness of God – a *religious*, rather than a purely moral or rational idea. Second, Christ possesses the ability to communicate this God-consciousness to others, as noted above – a quality which Schleiermacher discusses in terms of *Vorbildlichkeit*, to which we now turn.

2   *Vorbildlichkeit* may be translated as "the quality of being able to evoke a given ideal in others." Jesus of Nazareth is not simply the instantiation of an ideal, but one who possesses an ability to evoke or arouse this quality in others.

On the basis of this approach, Schleiermacher criticizes existing manners of conceiving the person of Christ. For Enlightenment writers, Jesus of Nazareth was merely a religious teacher of humanity, or perhaps the exemplar of a religious or moral principle. As noted earlier, this does not mean that Jesus established such principles or teachings; their authority lies in their being recognized to be consonant with rational ideas and values. The authority of Jesus is thus derivative and secondary, while that of reason is immediate and primary. Schleiermacher designates this as an "empirical" understanding of the work of Christ, which "attributes a redemptive activity on the part of Christ, but one which is held to consist only in bringing about an increasing perfection in us, and which cannot take place other than by teaching and example." Nevertheless Schleiermacher was – and is – often represented as teaching a view of the atonement as *Lebenserhöhung*, a kind of moral elevation of life. One of the paradoxes here is that Schleiermacher's distinctive ideas ultimately proved to be capable of being interpreted as a purely exemplarist understanding of the death of Christ, rather than posing a coherent challenge to such a view.

The most significant statement of an exemplarist approach in England is to be found in the 1915 Bampton Lectures of the noted modernist Hastings Rashdall (see p. 85). In these lectures, Rashdall launched a vigorous attack on traditional approaches to the atonement. The only interpretation of the cross which was adequate for the needs of the modern age was that already associated with the medieval writer Peter Abelard:

> The church's early creed, "There is none other name given among men by which we may be saved," may be translated so as to be something of this kind: "There is none other ideal given among men by which we may be saved, except the moral ideal which Christ taught us by his words, and illustrated by his life and death of love."

Although Abelard did not actually hold precisely the opinions which Rashdall attributed to him, Rashdall's argument is independent of this fact. In an age which had discovered both Darwinianism and biblical criticism, there no longer seemed to be any place for any understanding of Christ's death which was based upon an objective notion of sin or divine punishment. Other later English writers who adopted similar or related approaches include G. W. H. Lampe (1912—80) and John Hick (born 1922). In his essay "The Atonement: Law and Love," contributed to the liberal Catholic volume *Soundings*, Lampe launched a fierce attack on legal approaches to his subject, before commending an exemplarist approach based on "the paradox and miracle of love."

The position of John Hick is of especial interest, in that it relates to the place of the work of Christ in interfaith dialogue. The religious pluralist agenda has certain important theological consequences. Traditional Christian theology does not lend itself particularly well to the homogenizing agenda of religious pluralists (see pp. 460–2). The suggestion that all religions are more or less talking about vaguely the same thing finds itself in difficulty in relation to certain essentially Christian ideas – most notably, the doctrines of the incarnation, atonement, and the Trinity. The suggestion that something unique is made possible or available through the death of Christ is held to belittle non-Christian religions.

In response to this pressure, a number of major Christological and theological developments took place within the writings of theologians sympathetic to a pluralist approach to Christianity and other religions. Doctrines such as the incarnation, which imply a high profile of identification between Jesus Christ and God, are discarded in favor of various degree Christologies, which are more amenable to the reductionist program of liberalism. This has important implications for soteriology, as will become clear. A sharp distinction is thus drawn between the *historical person* of Jesus Christ, and the *principles* which he is alleged to represent. Paul Knitter is but one of a small galaxy of pluralist writers concerned to drive a wedge between the "Jesus-event" (which is unique to Christianity) and the "Christ-principle" (accessible to all religious traditions, and expressed in their own distinctive, but equally valid, ways).

Viewed in this pluralist light, the cross of Christ is understood to make known something which is accessible in other manners, and which is a universal religious possibility. Thus Hick argues that the Christ-event is only "one of the points at which God has been and still is creatively at work within human life"; his distinctiveness relates solely to his being a "visible story," and not an "additional truth."

The chief difficulty associated with purely exemplarist approaches to the cross concerns their understanding of human sin. The Enlightenment tended to regard the idea of "sin" as a hangover from a period of superstition, which the modern age could dispense with. If "sin" had any real meaning, it was that of "ignorance concerning the true nature of things." Christ's death was thus treated as the correlative of this notion of sin – the conveying of information concerning God to a confused or ignorant humanity.

However, this idea of sin seemed rather weak and inadequate in the light of the atrocities of World War II, such as the extermination camp of Auschwitz. The Enlightenment belief in the fundamental goodness of human nature received a severe setback through such events. A growing anxiety about the plausibility of the Enlightenment view of sin has brought in its wake a growing disenchantment with the Enlightenment notion of "redemption through knowledge" – including exemplarist approaches to the meaning of the death of Christ.

Violence and the cross: the theory of René Girard

Thus far, we have tended to treat the cross of Christ in somewhat abstract, theoretical terms. Some readers might not unreasonably point out that the cross was actually an act of *violence*, in which suffering and death were inflicted on Christ. How can the sheer violence of the act of crucifixion be incorporated into Christian reflection on the meaning of the cross? And given the tendency of humanity to use violence as a means of resolving its problems, what does the cross have to say about this disturbing human propensity?

In recent years, theologians have begun to reflect on the insights of the French anthropologist René Girard (born 1923), who taught for many years at Stanford University, and many of whose works deal with the theme of violence. René Girard offers an anthropological approach to religion which sees violence as integral to the sacred practices of all cultures

and races. In his influential book *Violence and the Sacred* (1977), Girard defends his thesis that destructive violence is at the heart of the sacred, tracing this development through anthropological studies of sacrifice (both human and animal), through mythology and ritual. Girard finds the roots of violence in what he terms "mimetic desire" and the rivalry that this desire creates. "The rival desires the same object as the subject, and to assert the primacy of the rival can lead to only one conclusion. Rivalry does not arise because of the fortuitous convergence of the two desires on a single object; rather, *the subject desires the object because the rival desires it*." As this desire escalates, it can lead to violence that can overwhelm the community and destroy it. One act of violence leads to another, escalating to the point at which it cannot be controlled. however, in this situation, violence can "be diverted to another object, something it can sink its teeth into."

The "other object" that is turned too, according to Girard, is the sacrificial victim – a victim which Girard significantly terms the "scapegoat," using imagery drawn from the Old Testament. This scapegoat is an innocent third party, who becomes the focus of the community's violence, and the means of its transformation. The victim is not a substitute for just one individual, but "it is a substitute for all the members of the community, offered up by the members themselves. The sacrifice serves to protect the entire community from its own violence; it prompts the entire community to choose victims outside itself." The surrogate victim, the scapegoat, is sacrificed on behalf of the community, so that the violence unleashed is diverted and the community is saved. "The purpose of the sacrifice is to restore harmony to the community, to reinforce the social fabric."

So how does this relate to Christian understandings of the atonement? After all, the New Testament does not use the scapegoat imagery to refer to the death of Christ. Girard has an answer:

> "But never," you will tell me, "does the New Testament resort to the term 'scapegoat' to designate Jesus as the innocent victim of an escalation of mimetic contagion." You are right, no doubt, but it does use an expression equal and even superior to "scapegoat," and this is *lamb of God*. It eliminates the negative attributes and unsympathetic connotations of the goat. Thereby it better corresponds to the idea of an innocent victim sacrificed unjustly.

Girard's analysis is of potential importance, in that it helps us understand how an act of violence leads to a community which is characterized by its emphasis on reconciliation and peace. Christ's atonement is the fundamental perquisite for a nonviolent community – the church. Girard recently remarked that he had set out on a "search for the anthropology of the Cross, which turns out to rehabilitate orthodox theology." While Girard himself does not claim to provide an adequate alternative theological model of the atonement, he can be argued to illuminate both the nature of the human situation, which is characterized by violence (according to Genesis, the fall led immediately to violence and murder), and the nature of divine redemption (by providing a means by which this addictive and self-perpetuating cycle of violence can be ended). Girard does not offer a foundation for a Christian doctrine of atonement; he does, however, offer illumination of some of its core themes.

Models of Salvation in Christ – Classic and Contemporary

As noted earlier, the idea of "salvation" is exceptionally complex. One of the tasks of theology is to provide a critical analysis of the constituent elements of this idea. However, even this project is considerably more complex than it might seem. Different aspects of the Christian understanding of salvation have proved to have especial attraction for different periods of church history, or specific situations, reflecting the manner in which one aspect of this understanding interlocks with the specifics of the situation it addresses.

Recent studies of the theory of Christian mission have laid considerable emphasis upon the importance of *contextualization* and the notion of the *receptor-orientation* of the Christian proclamation. In other words, the Christian gospel is recognized to address specific situations and to *contextualize* the notion of salvation in those situations. To those who are oppressed, whether spiritually or politically, the gospel message is that of liberation. To those who are burdened by the weight of personal guilt, the "good news" is that of forgiveness and pardon.

The gospel is thus related to the specific situation of its audience – in other words, it is *receptor-oriented*. If any of the following models of salvation were to be regarded as totally constitutive of the Christian understanding of salvation, a severely truncated and reduced gospel would result. However, it is widely agreed that a difference of *emphasis* within the range of understandings of the nature of salvation is acceptable.

In what follows, we shall explore a selection of components of this understanding, and indicate the situations in which they have particular appeal and relevance. However, it must be appreciated that others – such as salvation as moral perfection or deliverance from the transience of this world – could easily be instanced.

We may begin our consideration of the way in which "salvation" is to be understood by exploring some of the central soteriological terms used in Paul's letters in the New Testament, which have had a significant impact on subsequent theological reflection.

Some Pauline images of salvation

The Pauline letters set out to explain some aspects of the Christian faith to their readers – often in controversial circumstances – and to encourage their application to the life of believers. It should therefore be no cause for surprise that Paul often deals with the issue of precisely what it is that has been achieved for believers through the death of Christ. Among the images that Paul uses in this respect, we may here consider four, as follows.

1   *Adoption*: At several points, Paul speaks of Christians as having been "adopted" into the family of God (Romans 8: 15, 23; Galatians 4: 5). It is widely thought that Paul is here drawing on a legal practice, common in Greco-Roman culture (yet, interestingly, not recognized within traditional Jewish law). According to many interpreters of Paul at this point – such as F. F. Bruce – to speak of "believers" having been adopted into the family of God is to make the point that believers share the same inheritance rights as Jesus Christ, and will hence receive the glory which Christ achieved (although only after first sharing in his sufferings).

2   *Justification*: Especially in those letters dealing with the relation of Christianity to Judaism (such as Galatians and Romans), Paul affirms that believers have been "justified through faith" (e.g., Romans 5: 1–2). This is widely held to entail a change in a believer's legal status in the sight of God, and their ultimate assurance of acquittal before God, despite their sinfulness. The term "justification" and the verb "to justify" thus came to signify "entering into a right relationship with God," or perhaps "being made righteous in the sight of God." The Reformation witnessed an important debate over the meaning of the term justification, which we shall consider presently.

3   *Redemption*: This term primarily bears the sense of "secure someone's release through payment." In the ancient world which acted as the backdrop to Paul's thought, the term could be used to refer to the liberation of prisoners of war, or to the securing of liberty of those who had sold themselves into slavery, often to pay off a family debt. Paul's basic idea appears to be that the death of Christ secures the freedom of believers from slavery to the law or to death, in order that they might become slaves of God instead (1 Corinthians 6: 20, 7: 23).

4   *Salvation*: It is important to appreciate that Paul uses a rich range of images to illuminate and clarify what benefits Christ secures for believers. One such term is "salvation." For understandable reasons, this term has often been seen as of primary importance, overshadowing the others. In fact, the term has a series of specific associations, which need to be appreciated. The basic notion is that of deliverance from danger or captivity, including the idea of being delivered from some form of fatal illness. Notions such as "healing" and "liberation" can be seen as embraced by this important Pauline term. As pointed out earlier, Paul sees salvation as having past (e.g., Romans 8: 24), present (e.g., 1 Corinthians 1: 18), and future (e.g., Romans 13: 11) dimensions. This has important implications for the eschatological understanding of salvation.

Having examined some of Paul's language about salvation, we may now turn to consider how this has been explored and developed within the Christian theological tradition.

Deification: being made divine

"God became human, in order that humans might become God." This theological refrain may be discerned as underlying much of the soteriological reflection of the eastern Christian tradition, both during the patristic period and in the modern Greek and Russian Orthodox theological traditions. As the citation suggests, there is an especially strong link between the doctrine of the incarnation and this understanding of salvation. For Athanasius, salvation consists in the human participation in the being of God. The divine Logos is imparted to humanity through the incarnation.

On the basis of the assumption of a universal human nature, Athanasius concluded that the Logos did not merely assume the specific human existence of Jesus Christ, but that of human nature in general. As a consequence, all human beings are able to share in the deification which results from the incarnation. Human nature was created with the object of sharing in the being of God; through the descent of the Logos, this capacity is finally realized.

A modern Orthodox writer who places considerable emphasis on the notion of deification is the Russian writer Vladimir Lossky. In a 1953 essay on the theme of "redemption and deification," Lossky sets out the distinctive Orthodox understanding of the relation of the descent of God to humanity and the subsequent ascent of humanity to God:

> The descent (*katabasis*) of the divine person of Christ makes human persons capable of an ascent (*anabasis*) in the Holy Spirit. It was necessary that the voluntary humiliation, the redemptive self-emptying (*kenosis*) of the Son of God should take place, so that fallen men might accomplish their vocation of *theo-*

sis, the deification of created beings by uncreated grace. Thus the redeeming work of Christ – or rather, more generally speaking, the Incarnation of the Word – is seen as directly related to the ultimate goal of creatures: to know union with God. If this union has been accomplished in the divine person of the Son, who is God become man, it is necessary that each human person should in turn become god by grace, or become "a partaker in the divine nature," according to St Peter's expression (2 Peter 1: 4).

A distinction must be drawn between the idea of deification as "becoming God" (*theosis*) and as "becoming like God" (*homoiosis theoi*). The first, associated with the Alexandrian school, conceives of deification as a union with the substance of God; the second, associated with the Antiochene school, interprets the believer's relationship with God more in terms of a participation in that which is divine, often conceived in terms of ethical perfection. The distinction between these approaches is subtle, and reflects significantly different Christologies.

Righteousness in the sight of God

"How do I find a gracious God?" Martin Luther's question has resonated down the centuries for those who shared his heartfelt conviction that sinners could not hope to find acceptance in the sight of a righteous God. For Luther, the question of salvation came to be linked with the issue of how guilt-ridden humans could ever possess a righteousness which would enable them to stand in God's presence. This concern is by no means outdated, as can be seen from C. S. Lewis's words in *Mere Christianity*: "In my most clearsighted moments not only do I not think myself a nice man, but I know that I am a very nasty one. I can look at some of the things I have done with horror and loathing." Such concerns naturally led to the use of legal or forensic categories in relation to the question of justification. For Luther, the gospel offered a justifying righteousness to believers – a righteousness which would shield them from condemnation, and permit them to enter into the presence of God (see pp. 372–6).

Such insights were developed within later Protestant orthodoxy, and achieved a wide circulation in popular Protestant devotional writings and hymns. In a period in which the threat of divine punishment was taken with considerable seriousness (witness Jonathan Edwards's passionate sermons on this theme), the idea of deliverance from condemnation on account of sin was regarded as of central importance to the gospel. One of the hymns to express this concern for righteousness in the sight of God with particular force is Charles Wesley's "And Can it Be?", the last verse of which includes the following lines:

> No condemnation now I dread;
> Jesus, and all in him, is mine!
> Alive in him, my living head!
> And clothed in righteousness divine.

Personal holiness

One of the most important movements in western Christianity has placed considerable emphasis on the cross as the basis of personal holiness. The Wesleyan or Holiness traditions, which includes the Church of the Nazarene, stress the importance of the personal demonstration of holiness. The holiness of the believer is grounded in the work of Christ, and effected through the work of the Holy Spirit. The origins of this approach are to be traced back to John Wesley. While Wesley asserted the primacy of justification, and the assurance the believer could have based upon the righteousness of Christ, he insisted upon the need for development in holiness.

Wesley's notion of perfection was not that of sinlessness, but of an ever deepening process of comprehensive moral change. In developing this point, Wesley drew upon the works of those whom he termed the "mystic writers" (a category including Anglicans such as William Law, Roman Catholics such as François Fenélon, Francis de Sales, and Madame Guyon, and the Lutheran Pietist Augustus H. Francke. From them, Wesley learned that the heart of true godliness is a motivating spirit of love to God and humanity, without which religion is hollow and empty.

These ideas were developed further within American Methodism. Francis Asbury held that believers should be encouraged to expect "entire sanctification" at some point in their lives. The growing emphasis on revivalism within nineteenth-century American Protestantism emphasized the importance of definable turning points in a Christian's life. This form of "holiness preaching" tended to center around Wesley's teaching of "entire sanctification" as a second crisis experience, subsequent to and dependent upon justification. In part, this emphasis on the need for holiness represents a response to the moral devastation of the American nation resulting from the Civil War. In 1870, Methodist bishops in the southern states began to re-emphasize sanctification, arguing that "nothing is so much needed at the present time throughout all these lands, as a general and powerful revival of scriptural holiness."

A key figure in the later development of this holiness teaching was Phoebe Worrall Palmer (1807–74), undoubtedly the most influential Methodist woman of her generation. Palmer developed Wesley's doctrine of entire sanctification, modifying it in some significant ways. Like Wesley, she taught that entire sanctification is a second distinct work of grace in which God cleanses the believer's heart of sin, and fills it wholly with divine love. Such holiness of the heart is a requirement for entry into heaven. Because God commands this holiness, Palmer argues, God must also supply the ability to attain it, and God gives that ability in response to the Christian's faith.

Where Wesley had seen holiness as a gift, Palmer now tended to see it as an obligation. The focus of sanctification tended to be wholly upon a single point of wholehearted commitment, and divorced from any gradual process. And where Wesley had tended to conceive holiness as something that is gradually attained, Palmer tended to emphasize its instantaneous elements. This point is significant, as it points to links between Palmer's holiness teaching and that later associated with Pentecostalism. In this context, it is important to note Palmer's identification of entire sanctification with the baptism of the Holy Spirit, and the related link that she identified between holiness and power.

Authentic human existence

The rise of existentialism brought with it a new concern for authentic human existence (pp. 146–7). Existentialism, protesting against the dehumanizing tendency to treat humans as objects devoid of any subjective existence, demanded that attention be paid to the inner lives of individuals. Martin Heidegger's distinction between "authentic existence" and "inauthentic existence" represented an important statement of the bipolar structure of human existence. Two options were open. Rudolf Bultmann, developing such an approach, argued that the New Testament spoke of two possible modes of human existence: an authentic or redeemed existence, characterized by faith in God, and an inauthentic existence, characterized by being fettered to the transient material order. For Bultmann, Christ made possible and available, through the *kerygma*, authentic existence.

Bultmann does not entirely reduce salvation to the notion of "authentic existence," as if Christianity related solely to the experiential world of individuals. However, the emphasis which he placed upon this notion tended to create the impression that this was the sum total of the "salvation" offered through the gospel.

A related approach was developed by Paul Tillich, using a slightly different set of terms. Within the context of Tillich's system, "salvation" does indeed seem to be reduced to little more than a general human philosophy of existence, offering insights to those who are aware of tensions within their personal existence. This outlook has been criticized by many concerned with the transcendent elements of salvation, as well as those wishing to draw attention to the political and social aspects of the Christian gospel, such as liberation theology.

Political liberation

Latin American liberation theology places considerable emphasis upon the idea of salvation as liberation (see pp. 90–1). The title of Leonardo Boff's *Jesus Christ Liberator* makes this point forcefully. Salvation is here contextualized in the political world of Latin America, including its radical and pervasive poverty, and the struggle for social and political justice. God is seen to side with the exploited peoples of the world, as in the deliverance of Israel from captivity and oppression under Pharaoh. Similarly, Jesus appears to have expressed and exercised a preferential option for the poor in his teaching and ministry. Jesus Christ brings liberation, through both his teaching and his lifestyle.

Liberation theology has been criticized for viewing both the figure of Jesus and the concept of salvation in the light of a predetermined interpretive grid derived from the Latin American context. However, all Christologies and soteriologies are vulnerable to this charge. For example, the writers of the Enlightenment interpreted both the person and the work of Jesus Christ in terms of a predetermined framework, derived in part from the middle-class European context in which most of them existed, and partly from the severely rationalist outlook characteristic of the movement. Equally, it can be argued that the Greek patristic writers tended to view Christ through a Hellenistic prism, which had significant consequences for their Christologies and soteriologies. However, the criticism just noted has validity, if the understanding of either the person or the work of Christ is *reduced* to a purely political or social conception of liberation.

Spiritual freedom

The *Christus victor* approach to the death and resurrection of Christ lays considerable emphasis upon the notion of Christ's victory over forces which enslave humanity – such as satanic oppression, evil spirits, fear of death, or the power of sin. The early patristic writers had little difficulty in regarding these forces as real oppressive and hostile presences in the everyday world. In consequence, the proclamation of liberty from their oppression through the cross and resurrection of Christ came to be of central importance, as can be seen from the Easter homilies of writers such as John Chrysostom. Similar ideas can be shown to be prominent in the popular devotional and spiritual writings of the Middle Ages. Martin Luther continued this tradition, placing considerable emphasis upon the objective power of Satan in the world, and the liberation resulting from the gospel.

With the rise of the Enlightenment worldview, belief in objective evil spirits or a personal devil became increasingly problematic. Writers sympathetic to the Enlightenment generally dismissed such beliefs as outmoded superstitions which had no place in the modern world. If the idea of "salvation as victory" was to remain current, it would have to be reinterpreted. Such a process can be seen taking place in the writings of Paul Tillich, where salvation is understood in terms of a victory over *subjective* forces which enslave humanity and trap it in inauthentic modes of existence. What the patristic writers treated as objective forces were thus treated as subjective or existential.

The Appropriation of Salvation in Christ

The Christian hope of salvation rests upon the death and resurrection of Christ. Yet there remains the question of how that salvation is mediated and appropriated. In what follows, we shall consider two very different models of the appropriation of salvation. One emphasizes the role of the church, the other the personal commitment of the believer.

The institutionalization of salvation: the church

In the third century of the Christian era, Cyprian of Carthage penned a slogan which would have a decisive impact on Christian understandings of the role of the church as the mediator and guarantor of redemption: "Outside the church, there is no salvation." This pithy maxim was open to a number of interpretations. That which predominated throughout the Middle Ages can be argued to result directly from the growth in institutional authority of the church after the collapse of the Roman Empire. Salvation was only to be had through membership of the church. Christ may have made the hope of heaven possible; only the church could make it available. There was an ecclesiastical monopoly on the dispensation of redemption.

The insight that the institution of the church was the guarantor of the hope of heaven was rapidly assimilated into church architecture. The great portals of Romanesque churches were often adorned with elaborate sculptures depicting the glory of heaven as a tactile affirmation that it was only by entering the church that this reality could be experienced. Inscriptions were often placed over the great west door of churches, declaring that it was only through entering the church that heaven could be attained. The portal was allowed to be identified with Christ for this purpose, speaking words directed to those passing by, or pausing to admire its magnificent ornamentation. An excellent example is provided by the Benedictine priory church of St-Marcel-lès-Sauzet in southern France, which was founded in 985 and extensively developed during the twelfth century. The portal to the church depicts Christ addressing these words to all who draw near:

> Vos qui transitis, qui crimina flerae venitis,
> Per me transite quoniam sum ianua vitae.

("You who are passing through, you who are coming to weep for your sins, pass through me, since I am the gate of life.") Although the words are clearly to be attributed to Christ (picking up on the image of Christ as the "gate of the sheepfold" from John 10), a tactile link has been forged with the building of the church itself. This was often reinforced visually through the physical location of the baptismal font close to the door of the church, thereby affirming that entrance to heaven is linked with the sacrament of baptism.

While not all were persuaded by this theology of the church, which placed such emphasis upon the role of the church – considered both as institution and physical structure – as

guarantor and visualization of the hope of salvation, there is no doubting its massive impact upon the culture of the Middle Ages and beyond. It should be a cause for no surprise that many Protestant writers reacted against what they regarded as an improper emphasis upon the institution of the church, and sought to regain a genuine theological role for the individual soul in the process of salvation. This is best seen in Pietism, to which we now turn.

The privatization of salvation: personal faith

The Pietist movement (see pp. 53–4) is usually regarded as having been inaugurated with the publication of Philip Jakob Spener's *Pia desideria* ("Pious Wishes," 1675). In this work, Spener lamented the state of the German Lutheran church in the aftermath of the Thirty Years' War (1618–48), and set out proposals for the revitalization of the church of his day. Chief among these was a new emphasis upon personal Bible study. The proposals were treated with derision by academic theologians; nevertheless, they were to prove influential in German church circles, reflecting growing disillusionment and impatience with the sterility of orthodoxy in the face of the shocking social conditions endured during the war. For Pietism, a reformation of doctrine must always be accompanied by reformation of life.

Pietism developed in a number of different directions, especially in England and Germany. Nikolaus Ludwig Graf von Zinzendorf (1700–60) founded the Pietist community generally known as the "Herrnhuter," named after the German village of Herrnhut. Alienated from what he regarded as the arid rationalism and barren religious orthodoxy of his time, Zinzendorf stressed the importance of a "religion of the heart," based on an intimate personal relationship between Christ and the believer.

Similar ideas were developed in England by John Wesley and his brother Charles. Charles underwent a similar conversion experience a day before John, and published a hymn in which he set out his experience. This is widely believed to be the hymn now known as "Where Shall My Wondering Soul Begin?", the final verse of which reads as follows:

> For you the purple current flowed
> In pardons from His wounded side,
> Languished for you the eternal God,
> For you the Prince of glory died:
> Believe, and all your sin's forgiven;
> Only believe, and yours is heaven!

The hymn sets out with great clarity the basic conviction which underlies the Pietist worldview – that it is the individual's free decision to repent and admit Christ into the soul which secures the hope of heaven. Wesley thus sees the human heart as the ultimate "gateway to heaven," in that the individual has the final decision as to whether he or she enters into the heavenly realms. The institution of the church plays no critical role in this process whatsoever, however valuable it may subsequently be as a means of pastoral support and spiritual nourishment.

For those who stand in this tradition, the door through which people enter heaven is not the institution of the church and its attending sacramental system, but personal conversion – a deliberate decision on the part of individuals to throw open the doors of their lives, and admit Christ as a living presence within them – a presence which may be experienced and felt. The experience of Christ in the believer's soul serves both as a reassurance of faith now, and an anticipation of finally being with Christ in heaven.

A similar theme echoes in the poetry of the great American Pietist writer Fanny J. Crosby (1820–1915). In her poem "The Valley of Silence" she set out her experience of receiving a "second blessing" which gave her a new assurance of salvation. A similar theme is found in her popular revivalist hymn, "Blessed Assurance":

> Blessed assurance, Jesus is mine!
> Oh what a foretaste of glory divine!
> Heir of salvation, purchase of God,
> Born of His Spirit, washed in His blood.

The institution of the church is marginalized; her faith was a matter between her and God alone.

The Scope of Salvation in Christ

The Christian tradition has witnessed intense debate over the extent of the salvation which is made available and possible through Christ. Two central affirmations, both of which are deeply grounded in the New Testament, may be discerned as exercising a controlling influence over this discussion:

1 God wishes all people to be saved.
2 Salvation is possible only in and through Christ.

The various approaches to the question of the scope of salvation rest upon different manners of resolving the dialectic between these assumptions. An important parallel should be noted here between the discussion of the scope of salvation and the relation of Christianity to other religions, to be discussed at greater length in chapter 17.

Universalism: all will be saved

The view that all people will be saved, irrespective of whether they have heard or responded to the Christian proclamation of redemption in Christ, has exerted a powerful influence within the Christian tradition. It represents a powerful affirmation of the universal saving will of God, and its ultimate actualization in the universal redemption of all people. Its most significant early exponent was Origen, who defended the idea at length in his *De principiis* ("First principles"). Origen was deeply suspicious of any form of dualism – that is, any belief system which acknowledged the existence of two supreme powers, one good and one evil. This belief was characteristic of many forms of Gnosticism, and was very influential in the eastern Mediterranean world in the late second century.

Arguing that dualism was fatally flawed, Origen pointed out that this had important implications for the Christian doctrine of salvation. To reject dualism is to reject the idea that God and Satan rule over their respective kingdoms for eternity. In the end, God will overcome evil and restore creation to its original form. In its original form, creation was subject to the will of God. It therefore follows, on the basis of this "restorationist" soteriology, that the final redeemed version of creation cannot include anything along the lines of "a hell" or "a kingdom of Satan." All "will be restored to their condition of happiness [. . .] in order that the human race [. . .] may be restored to that unity promised by the Lord Jesus Christ."

Related ideas have been developed in the twentieth century, most notably by Karl Barth. We shall explore his approach elsewhere in the context of his doctrine of predestination, to allow the relation of his doctrines of salvation and grace to be appreciated more fully (pp. 384–5). A different approach may be found in the writings of John A. T. Robinson, a radical English theologian active in the 1960s, especially in his *In the End God* (1968). In this book, Robinson considers the nature of the love of God. "May we not imagine a love so strong that ultim-ately no one will be able to restrain himself from free and grateful surrender?" This notion of omnipotent love functions as the central idea of Robinson's universalism. In the end, love will conquer all, making the existence of hell an impossibility. "In a universe of love there can be no heaven which tolerates a chamber of horrors."

Only believers will be saved

The position to be discussed in this section is one of the most influential positions in relation to the scope of salvation. Its most vigorous defender in the early church was Augustine, who consciously distanced himself from the universalism associated with Origen by stressing the need for faith as a precondition for salvation. In doing so, Augustine cited a large number of New Testament passages which emphasize the conditionality of salvation or eternal life upon faith. A classic example of such a text is John 6: 51, in which Christ refers to himself as a bread which, if eaten, will bring eternal life. "I am the living bread that came down from heaven. If anyone eats of this bread, they will live for ever. This bread is my flesh, which I will give for the life of the world."

This position was maintained by most writers of the Middle Ages. Thomas Aquinas argued that an act of faith was a necessary condition of salvation. This view is echoed in many popular devotional writings of the period, including the highly sophisticated *Divine Comedy* of Dante Alighieri.

One of the most vigorous defenders of this position at the time of the Reformation was John Calvin, who dismissed the views of his fellow reformer Huldrych Zwingli to the effect that pious pagans could attain salvation. "All the more vile is the stupidity of those people who open heaven to all the impious and unbelieving, without the grace of him whom Scripture teaches to be the only door by which we enter into salvation."

So what do such writers make of the biblical assertions that God wishes all to be saved, and all to come to a knowledge of the truth? Augustine and Calvin argue that such texts are to be interpreted sociologically: God wishes *all kinds of people* – but not *all people* – to be saved. Redemption embraces all nationalities, cultures, languages, geographical regions, and walks of life. This is the soteriological equivalent of the doctrine of the catholicity of the church, to be considered later.

However, a number of modified versions of this approach should be noted. For example, is it necessary to have a fully *Christian* faith in God in order to be saved? This question is of major importance in relation to an understanding of mission and evangelism, and also of the relation of Christianity to other religions. In his sermon "On Faith," John Wesley argued for the need for faith in God in order to be saved – but affirmed that this faith need not be explicitly Christian in character. The requirement for salvation is "such a divine conviction of God, and the things of God, as, even in its infant state, enables every one that possesses it to fear God and work righteousness. And whosoever, in every nation, believes thus far, the Apostle declares is accepted." What, then, is the advantage of a specifically Christian belief, as opposed to this more general theistic belief? According to Wesley, two differences may be noted. First, such people have yet to attain the full benefits of the redeemed life. They are "servants of God" but not "sons of God." Second, they do not have full assurance of salvation, which is only possible on the basis of Christ.

A similar position is associated with the twentieth-century literary critic and apologist C. S. Lewis (1898–1963). In his *Mere Christianity* Lewis argues that those who commit themselves to the pursuit of goodness and truth will be saved, even if they have no formal knowledge of Christ. Although Lewis has philosophers in mind, he extends his approach to include other religions. "There are people in other religions who are being led by God's secret influence to concentrate on those parts of their religion which are in agreement with Christianity, and who thus belong to Christ without knowing it." There are clear parallels here with the writings of the Jesuit theologian Karl Rahner, to be discussed later (pp. 458–60).

Particular redemption: only the elect will be saved

A final approach which should be noted is variously termed "limited atonement" or "particular redemption." This has Reformed associations, and is particularly influential in such circles in the United States. The basis of the doctrine lies in the Reformed doctrine of predestination, to be discussed in the next chapter. However, its historical origins can be discerned in the ninth century, in the writings of Godescalc of Orbais (also known as Gottschalk). Godescalc argued along the following lines. Let us suppose that Christ died for all people. But not all people will be saved. Therefore it follows that Christ died to no effect for those who are not saved. This raises the gravest of questions concerning the efficacy of his death. But if Christ died only for those who are to be saved, he will have succeeded in his mission in every case. Therefore Christ died only for those who are to be saved.

Related lines of argument can be discerned in the later sixteenth century, and especially during the seventeenth century. The doctrine which emerged at this time, especially within Puritan circles, can be summarized as follows: Christ died only for the elect. Although his death is *sufficient* to achieve the redemption of all people, it is *effective* only for the elect. As a result, Christ's work was not in vain. All those for whom he died are saved. Although this approach clearly possesses a certain logical coherence, its critics tend to regard it as compromising the New Testament's affirmation of the universality of God's love and redemption.

The present chapter has explored central aspects of the Christian doctrine of salvation, demonstrating both the richness and the variety of Christian thinking on the subject. It is clear that there is a close connection between the doctrine of salvation and that of grace, especially in relation to predestination. For this reason, we shall now move on to consider these, and related, matters in more detail.

QUESTIONS FOR CHAPTER 13

1 How are Christian understandings of the person of Christ related to understandings of the work of Christ?
2 Assess the importance of one of the following approaches to the meaning of the cross: a victory over sin and death; forgiveness of sin; a demonstration of the love of God toward humanity.
3 From what are we saved?
4 Is a human response to salvation necessary?
5 How are the cross and resurrection related in Christian understandings of salvation?

14

The Doctrines of Human Nature,
Sin, and Grace

The previous chapter considered the foundations of the Christian doctrine of salvation, paying particular attention to the basis and nature of salvation. A series of issues relating to salvation remain to be addressed: what must human beings do in order to share in the salvation which is made known and made available through Christ's death upon the cross? The issues which this question raises are traditionally discussed under the general heading of "the doctrine of grace," which embraces an understanding of human nature and sin, as well as the role of God in salvation. There is the closest of connections within the Christian tradition between the doctrine of salvation on the one hand, and that of grace on the other. We have already explored some aspects of these doctrines in earlier discussions; it is now time to explore them at greater length individually.

The Place of Humanity Within Creation: Early Reflections

The Christian tradition, basing itself largely upon the accounts of creation found in the Book of Genesis, has insisted that humanity is the height of God's creation, set over and above the animal kingdom. The theological justification of this rests largely upon the doctrine of creation in the image of God, to which we now turn.

The image of God

A text of central importance to a Christian understanding of human nature is Genesis 1: 27, which speaks of humanity being made in God's image and likeness – an idea which is often expressed with reference to the Latin phrase *imago Dei*. What does this affirmation mean? Especially during the early patristic period, a distinction was drawn between the two phrases "image of God" and "likeness of God." For Tertullian, humanity retained the image of God after sinning; it could only be restored to the likeness of God through the renewing activity of the Holy Spirit:

> [In Baptism] death is abolished by the washing away of sins: for the removal of guilt also removes the penalty. Thus humanity is restored to God into "his likeness," for he had originally been "in his image." The state of being "in the image of God" relates to his form; "in the likeness" refers to his eternity:

for humanity receives back that Spirit of God which at the beginning was received from God's inbreathing, but which was afterwards lost through falling away.

Origen adopted a related approach, arguing that the term "image of God" referred to humanity after the Fall, whereas the term "likeness of God" referred to human nature after its perfection at the final consummation.

> And God said, "Let us make man in our image and likeness" (Genesis 1: 26). He then adds: "In the image of God he made him" (Genesis 1: 27), and is silent about the likeness. This indicates that in his first creation man received the dignity of the image of God, but the fulfillment of the likeness is reserved for the final consummation. [. . .] The possibility of perfection given to him at the beginning by the dignity of the image, and then in the end, through the fulfillment of his works, should bring to perfect consummation the likeness of God.

A second approach found during the patristic period interpreted "the image of God" in terms of human reason. The "image of God" is understood to be the human rational faculty, which here mirrors the wisdom of God. Augustine argues that it is this faculty which distinguishes humanity from the animal kingdom: "We ought therefore to cultivate in ourselves the faculty through which we are superior to the beasts, and to reshape it in some way. [. . .] So let us therefore use our intelligence [. . .] to judge our behavior." It should be emphasized that Augustine does not use this theological premise to justify the human exploitation of animals, as has sometimes been suggested. Augustine's point is that the central distinctive element of human nature is its God-given ability to relate to God. Although human reason has been corrupted by the Fall, it may be renewed by grace: "For after original sin,

humanity is renewed in the knowledge of God according to the image of its creator."

The fact that humanity is created in the image of God is widely regarded as establishing the original uprightness and dignity of human nature. This idea was developed in a political direction by Lactantius. In his *Divine Institutions* (c.304–11) Lactantius argued that being created in the image of God established the common identity and dignity of all human beings, leading directly to a series of political doctrines concerning human rights and responsibilities.

> I have spoken about what is due to God; now I shall speak about what is due to other people, although what is due to people still equally relates to God, since humanity is the image of God. [. . .] The strongest bond which unites us is humanity. Anyone who breaks it is a criminal and a parricide. Now it was from the one human being that God created us all, so that we are all of the same blood, with the result that the greatest crime is to hate humanity or do them harm. That is why we are forbidden to develop or to encourage hatred. So if we are the work of the same God, what else are we but brothers and sisters? The bond which unites our souls is therefore stronger than that which unites our bodies.

The doctrine of creation in the image of God was also seen as being directly related to the doctrine of redemption. Redemption involved bringing the image of God to its fulfillment, in a perfect relation with God, culminating in immortality. Earlier, we noted how both Tertullian and Origen saw an important link in this respect. Other Greek patristic writers emphasized the state of blessedness enjoyed by Adam and Eve in the garden of Eden. Athanasius taught that God created human beings in the "image of God," thus endowing humanity with a capacity which was granted to no other creature – that of being able to relate to and partake in the life of God. This fellowship with the Logos is seen at its most perfect in Eden, when Adam enjoyed a perfect relation with God. However, things went wrong. Athanasius stresses that Adam and Eve could enjoy a perfect relationship with God as long as they were not distracted by the material world.

The concept of sin

For the Cappadocians, the fact that Adam was created in the image of God meant that he was free from all normal weaknesses and disabilities which subsequently afflicted human nature – such as death. Cyril of Jerusalem emphasizes that there was no need for Adam or Eve to fall from this state of grace. It took place as a result of their decision to turn away from God to the material world. As a result, the image of God in human nature has been defaced and disfigured. In that all of humanity traces its origins to Adam and Eve, he argued, it follows that all humanity shares in this defacement of the image of God.

It should, however, be noted that Greek patristic writers do not express this fall in terms of a doctrine of original sin, such as that which would later be associated with Augustine. Most Greek writers insisted that sin arises from an abuse of the human free will. Gregory of Nazianzus and Gregory of Nyssa both taught that infants are born without sin, an idea which stands in contrast with Augustine's doctrine of the universal sinfulness of fallen humanity. Chrysostom, commenting on Paul's assertion that the many were made sinners through the disobedience of Adam (Romans 5: 19), interprets the passage to mean that all are made *liable* to punishment and death. The idea of transmitted *guilt*, a central feature of Augustine's later doctrine of original sin, is totally absent from the Greek patristic tradition.

Nevertheless, aspects of Augustine's notion of original sin can be discerned in the writings of the period. The Oxford patristic scholar J. N. D. Kelly identifies three areas in which a notion of "original sin" can be discerned in the Greek patristic tradition.

1 All humanity is understood to be involved, in some manner, in the disobedience of Adam. A strong sense of the mystical unity of all humanity with Adam can be discerned within the writings of this period. All of humanity is somehow wounded by Adam's disobedience.
2 The fall of Adam is understood to affect the human moral nature. All human moral weaknesses, including lust and greed, can be put down to Adam's sin.
3 Adam's sin is often represented as being transmitted, in some undefined manner, to his posterity. Gregory of Nyssa speaks of a predisposition to sin within human nature, which can be put down, at least in part, to the sin of Adam.

It is, however, during the Pelagian debate, to which we will now turn, that the issues of this chapter were first discussed at length during the patristic period.

Augustine of Hippo and the Pelagian Controversy

The Pelagian controversy, which erupted in the early fifth century, brought a cluster of questions concerning human nature, sin, and grace into sharp focus. Up to this point, there had been relatively little controversy within the church over human nature. The Pelagian controversy changed that, and ensured that the issues associated with human nature were placed firmly on the agenda of the western church.

The controversy centered upon two individuals: Augustine of Hippo and Pelagius. The controversy is complex, at both the historical and the theological level, and, given its impact upon western Christian theology, needs to be discussed at some length. We shall summarize the main points of the controversy under four heads:

1 The understanding of the "freedom of the will."
2 The understanding of sin.
3 The understanding of grace.
4 The understanding of the basis of salvation.

The "freedom of the will"

For Augustine, the total sovereignty of God and genuine human responsibility and freedom must be upheld at one and the same time, if justice is to be done to the richness and complexity of the biblical statements on the matter. In Augustine's own lifetime, he was obliged to deal with two heresies which simplified and compromised the gospel in this way. Manichaeism was a form of fatalism (to which Augustine himself was initially attracted) which upheld the total sovereignty of God but denied human freedom, while Pelagianism upheld the total freedom of the human will while denying the sovereignty of God. Before developing these points, it is necessary to make some observations concerning the term "free will."

The term "free will" (translating the Latin term *liberum arbitrium*) is not biblical, but derives from Stoicism. It was introduced into western Christianity by the second-century theologian Tertullian. (We noted earlier Tertullian's gift for coining new theological terms: see p. 249.) Augustine retained the term, but attempted to restore a more Pauline meaning to it by emphasizing the limitations placed upon the human free will by sin. Augustine's basic ideas can be summarized as follows. First, natural human freedom is affirmed: we do not do things as a matter of necessity, but as a matter of freedom. Second, human free will has been weakened and incapacitated – but not eliminated or destroyed – through sin. In order for that free will to be restored and healed, it requires the operation of divine grace. Free will really does exist; it is, however, distorted by sin.

In order to explain this point, Augustine deploys a significant analogy. Consider a pair of scales, with two balance pans. One balance pan represents good, and the other evil. If the pans were properly balanced, the arguments in favor of doing good or doing evil could be weighed, and a proper conclusion drawn. The parallel with the human free will is obvious: we weigh up the arguments in favor of doing good and evil, and act accordingly.

But what, asks Augustine, if the balance pans are loaded? What happens if someone puts several heavy weights in the balance pan on the side of evil? The scales will still work, but they are seriously biased toward making an evil decision. Augustine argues that this is exactly what has happened to humanity through sin. The human free will is biased toward evil. It really exists, and really can make decisions – just as the loaded scales still work. But instead of giving a balanced judgment, a serious bias exists toward evil. Using this and related analogies Augustine argues that the human free will really exists in sinners, but that it is compromised by sin.

For Pelagius and his followers (such as Julian of Eclanum), however, humanity possessed total freedom of the will, and was totally responsible for its own sins. Human nature was essentially free and well created, and was not compromised or incapacitated by some mysterious weakness. According to Pelagius, *consensor*

any imperfection in humanity would reflect negatively upon the goodness of God. For God to intervene in any direct way to influence human decisions was equivalent to compromising human integrity. Going back to the analogy of the scales, the Pelagians argued that the human free will was like a pair of balance pans in perfect equilibrium, and not subject to any bias whatsoever. There was no need for divine grace in the sense understood by Augustine (although Pelagius did have a quite distinct concept of grace, as we shall see later).

In 413, Pelagius wrote a lengthy letter to Demetrias, who had recently decided to turn her back on wealth in order to become a nun. In this letter, Pelagius spelled out with remorseless logic the consequences of his views on human free will. God has made humanity, and knows precisely what it is capable of doing. Hence all the commands given to us are capable of being obeyed, and are meant to be obeyed. It is no excuse to argue that human frailty prevents these commands from being fulfilled. God has made human nature, and only demands of it what it can endure.

[Instead of regarding God's commands as a privilege ...] we cry out at God and say, "This is too hard! This is too difficult! We cannot do it! We are only human, and hindered by the weakness of the flesh!" What blind madness! What blatant presumption! By doing this, we accuse the God of knowledge of a twofold ignorance – ignorance of God's own creation and of God's own commands. It would be as if, forgetting the weakness of humanity – which, after all, is God's own creation! – God had laid upon us commands which we were unable to bear. And at the same time (may God forgive us!) we ascribe to the righteous One unrighteousness, and cruelty to the Holy One; first, by complaining that God has commanded the impossible, second, by imagining that some

will be condemned by God for what they could not help; so that – the blasphemy of it! – God is thought of as seeking our punishment rather than our salvation.

Pelagius thus makes the uncompromising assertion that "since perfection is possible for humanity, it is obligatory." The moral rigor of this position, and its unrealistic view of human nature, served only to strengthen Augustine's hand as he developed the rival understanding of a tender and kindly God attempting to heal and restore wounded human nature.

The nature of sin

For Augustine, humanity is universally affected by sin as a consequence of the Fall. The human mind has become darkened and weakened by sin. Sin makes it impossible for the sinner to think clearly, and especially to understand higher spiritual truths and ideas. Similarly, as we have seen, the human will has been weakened (but not eliminated) by sin. For Augustine, the simple fact that we are sinners means that we are in the position of being seriously ill, and unable to diagnose our own illness adequately, let alone cure it. It is through the grace of God alone that our illness is diagnosed (sin), and a cure made available (grace).

The essential point which Augustine makes is that we have no control over our sinfulness. It is something which contaminates our lives from birth, and dominates our lives thereafter. It is a state over which we have no decisive control. We could say that Augustine understands humanity to be born with a sinful disposition as part of human nature, with an inherent bias toward acts of sinning. In other words, sin causes sins: the state of sinfulness causes individual acts of sin. Augustine develops this point with reference to three important analogies: original sin as a "disease," as a "power," and as "guilt."

1   The first analogy treats sin as a hereditary disease, which is passed down from one generation to another. As we saw above, this disease weakens humanity and cannot be cured by human agency. Christ is thus the divine physician, by whose "wounds we are healed" (Isaiah 53: 5), and salvation is understood in essentially sanative or medical terms. We are healed by the grace of God, so that our minds may recognize God and our wills may respond to the divine offer of grace.

2   The second analogy treats sin as a power which holds us captive, and from whose grip we are unable to break free by ourselves. The human free will is captivated by the power of sin, and may only be liberated by grace. Christ is thus seen as our liberator, the source of the grace which breaks the power of sin.

3   The third analogy treats sin as an essentially judicial or forensic concept – guilt – which is passed down from one generation to another. In a society which placed a high value on law, such as the later Roman Empire in which Augustine lived and worked, this was regarded as a particularly helpful way of understanding sin. Christ thus comes to bring forgiveness and pardon.

For Pelagius, however, sin is to be understood in a very different light. The idea of a human disposition toward sin has no place in Pelagius's thought. For Pelagius, the human power of self-improvement could not be thought of as being compromised. It was always possible for humans to discharge their obligations toward God and their neighbors. Failure to do so could not be excused on any grounds. Sin was to be understood as an act committed willfully against God.

Pelagianism thus seems at times to be a rather rigid form of moral authoritarianism – an insistence that humanity is under obligation to be sinless, and an absolute rejection of any excuse for failure. Humanity is born sinless, and sins only through deliberate actions. Pelagius insisted that many Old Testament figures actually remained sinless. Only those who were morally upright could be allowed to enter the church – whereas Augustine, with his concept of fallen human nature, was happy to regard the church as a hospital where fallen humanity could recover and grow gradually in holiness through grace (see pp. 394–6).

The nature of grace

One of Augustine's favorite biblical texts is John 15: 5: "apart from me you can do nothing." In Augustine's view, we are totally dependent upon God for our salvation, from the beginning to the end of our lives. Augustine draws a careful distinction between the natural human faculties – given to humanity as its natural endowment – and additional and special gifts of grace. God does not leave us where we are naturally, incapacitated by sin and unable to redeem ourselves, but gives us grace in order that we may be healed, forgiven, and restored.

Augustine's view of human nature is that it is frail, weak, and lost, and needs divine assistance and care if it is to be restored and renewed. Grace, according to Augustine, is God's generous and quite unmerited attention to humanity, by which this process of healing may begin. Human nature requires transformation through the grace of God, so generously given. The general features of Augustine's position can be seen in the following passage taken from the important anti-Pelagian writing *de natura et gratia* ("on nature and grace"), dating from 415:

Human nature was certainly originally created blameless and without any fault [*vitium*]; but the human nature by which each one of us is now born of Adam requires a physician, because it is not healthy. All the good things, which it has by its conception, life, senses, and mind, it has from God, its creator and maker. But the weakness which darkens and disables these good natural qualities, as a result of which that nature needs enlightenment and healing, did not come from the blameless maker but from original sin, which was committed by free will [*liberum arbitrium*]. For this reason our guilty nature is liable to a just penalty. For if we are now a new creature in Christ, we were still children of wrath by nature, like everyone else. But God, who is rich in mercy, on account of the great love with which He loved us, even when we were dead through our sins, raised us up to life with Christ, by whose grace we are saved. But this grace of Christ, without which neither infants nor grown persons can be saved, is not bestowed as a reward for merits, but is given freely [*gratis*], which is why it is called grace [*gratia*].

Note in particular the link Augustine establishes between the Latin terms *gratis* ("freely" or "without cost") and *gratia* ("grace").

Pelagius used the term "grace" but interpreted it in a very different way. First, grace is to be understood as the natural human faculties. For Pelagius, these are not corrupted or incapacitated or compromised in any way. They have been given to humanity by God, and they are meant to be used. When Pelagius asserted that humanity could, through grace, choose to be sinless, what he meant was that the natural human faculties of reason and will should enable humanity to choose to avoid sin. As Augustine was quick to point out, this is not what the New Testament understands by the term.

Second, Pelagius understood grace to be external enlightenment provided for humanity by God. Pelagius gave several examples of

such enlightenment – for example, the Ten Commandments, and the moral example of Jesus Christ. Grace informs us what our moral duties are (otherwise, we would not know what they were); it does not, however, assist us to perform them. We are enabled to avoid sin through the teaching and example of Christ. God does not just demand that human beings should be perfect; God provides certain specific guidance as to what form of perfection is required – such as keeping the Ten Commandments, and becoming like Christ.

Augustine argued that this was "to locate the grace of God in the law and in teaching." The New Testament, according to Augustine, envisaged grace as divine assistance to humanity, rather than just moral guidance. For Pelagius, grace was something external and passive, something outside us. Augustine understood grace as the real and redeeming presence of God in Christ within us, transforming us; something that was internal and active.

For Pelagius, then, God created humanity, and provided information concerning what is right and what is wrong – and then ceased to take any interest in humanity, apart from the final day of judgment. On that day, individuals will be judged according to whether they have fulfilled all their moral obligations in their totality. Failure to have done so will lead to eternal punishment. Pelagius's exhortations to moral perfection are characterized by their emphasis upon the dreadful fate of those who fail in this matter.

For Augustine, however, humanity was created good by God, and then fell away from him – and God, in an act of grace, came to rescue fallen humanity from its predicament. God assists us by healing us, enlightening us, strengthening us, and continually working within us in order to restore us. For Pelagius, humanity merely needed to be shown what to do, and could then be left to achieve it unaided; for Augustine, humanity needed to be shown what to do, and then gently aided at every point, if this objective was even to be approached, let alone fulfilled.

The basis of salvation

For Augustine, humanity is justified as an act of grace: even human good works are the result of God working within fallen human nature. Everything leading up to salvation is the free and unmerited gift of God, given out of love for sinners. Through the death and resurrection of Jesus Christ, God is enabled to deal with fallen humanity in this remarkable and generous manner, giving us that which we do not deserve (salvation), and withholding from us that which we do deserve (condemnation).

Augustine's exposition of the parable of the laborers in the vineyard (Matthew 20: 1–16) is of considerable importance in this respect. As we shall see, Pelagius argued that God rewarded each individual strictly on the basis of merit. Augustine, however, pointed out that this parable indicates that the basis of the reward given to the individual is the promise made to that individual. Augustine emphasized that the laborers did not work for equal periods in the vineyard, yet the same wage (a denarius) was given to each. The owner of the vineyard had promised to pay each individual a denarius, providing he worked from the time when he was employed to sundown – even though this meant that some worked all day, and others only for an hour.

Augustine thus drew the important conclusion that the basis of our justification is the divine promise of grace made to us. God is faithful to that promise, and thus justifies sinners. Just as the laborers who began work in the vineyard so late in the day had no claim to a full day's wages, except through the generous promise of the owner, so sinners have no claim to justification and eternal life, except through the gracious promises of God, received through faith.

For Pelagius, however, humanity is justified on the basis of its merits: human good works are the result of the exercise of the totally autonomous human free will, in fulfillment of an obligation laid down by God. A failure to meet this obligation opens the individual to the threat of eternal punishment. Jesus Christ is involved in salvation only to the extent that he reveals, by his actions and teaching, exactly what God requires of the individual. If Pelagius can speak of "salvation in Christ," it is only in the sense of "salvation through imitating the example of Christ."

It will thus be clear that Pelagianism and Augustinianism represent two radically different outlooks, with sharply divergent understandings of the manner in which God and humanity relate to one another. Augustinianism would eventually gain the upper hand within the western theological tradition; nevertheless, Pelagianism continued to exercise influence over many Christian writers down the ages, not least those who felt that an emphasis upon the doctrine of grace could too easily lead to a devaluation of human freedom and moral responsibility.

The Synod of Arles – a city in southern France – is an important witness to the early reaction to the Pelagian controversy. Although the date of this synod is unclear, it appears to have taken place around 470. The synod condemned a series of propositions which are clearly Pelagian in nature, while affirming others of a more generally Augustinian nature. Among those condemned were the following.

1. That after the fall of Adam, human free choice [*arbitrium voluntatis*] was extinguished;
2. That Christ, our Lord and Savior, did not die for the salvation of all people;
3. That the foreknowledge of God forces people violently towards death, or that those who perish, perish on account of the will of God.

In contrast, the following statements were affirmed:

1 Human effort and endeavor is to be united with the grace of God.
2 Human freedom of will [*libertas voluntatis*] is not extinct but attenuated and weakened [*non extinctam sed adtenuatam et infirmatam esse*].
3 Those who are saved could still be lost, and those that have perished could have been saved.

The Pelagian controversy clearly raised the issue of the relation of grace and merit, which was discussed at some length in the Augustinian revival of the Middle Ages. In what follows, we shall examine some of the issues which arose.

The Medieval Synthesis of the Doctrine of Grace

The repercussions of the Pelagian controversy were considerable. It forced discussion of a number of issues upon the church, especially during the medieval period, in which Augustine's legacy was subjected to a process of evaluation and development. While the modern discussion of the meaning of both terms may be said to have been initiated by Augustine, in the course of the Pelagian controversy, the medieval period saw his ideas being developed and modified.

The Augustinian legacy

At its heart, the term "grace" (*gratia*) has a connection with the idea of "a gift." This idea is taken up by Augustine, who stresses that salvation is a gift from God, rather than a reward. This immediately suggests a tension between the ideas of "grace" and "merit," the former referring to a gift and the latter to a reward. In fact, the question is considerably more complex than this, and merits – if the pun may be excused – careful discussion. In what follows, we shall consider the medieval debate over the meaning of the terms, to illustrate some of the issues at stake, and also as background material to the Reformation debates on the issues.

Augustine explored the nature of grace using several images, as noted earlier (pp. 365–7). Two may be noted once more in the present context.

First, grace is understood as a liberating force, which sets human nature free from its self-incurred bondage to sin. Augustine used the term "the captive free will" (*liberum arbitrium captivatum*) to describe the free will which is so heavily influenced by sin, and argued that grace is able to liberate the human free will from this bias, to give the "liberated free will" (*liberum arbitrium liberatum*). To go back to the scales analogy, grace removes the weights loading the scales toward evil and allows us to recognize the full weight of the case for choosing God. Thus Augustine was able to argue that grace, far from abolishing or compromising the human free will, actually establishes it.

Second, grace is understood as the healer of human nature. One of Augustine's favorite analogies for the church is that of a hospital, full of sick people. Christians are those who recognize that they are ill, and seek the assistance of a physician, in order that they may be healed. Thus Augustine appeals to the parable of the good Samaritan (Luke 10: 30–4), in suggesting that human nature is like the man who was left for dead by the roadside, until he was rescued and healed by the Samaritan (representing Christ as redeemer, according to Augustine). On the basis of illustrations such as these, Augustine argues that the human free will is unhealthy, and needs healing.

In exploring the functions of grace, Augustine developed three main notions, which have had a major impact upon western theology. The three categories are as follows:

1 *Prevenient grace*: The Latin term *preveniens* literally means "going ahead." In speaking of "prevenient grace," Augustine is defending his characteristic position, that God's grace is active in human lives before conversion. Grace "goes ahead" of humanity, preparing the human will for conversion. Augustine stresses that grace does not become operational in a person's life only after conversion; the process leading up to that conversion is one of preparation, in which the prevenient grace of God is operative.

2 *Operative grace*: Augustine stresses that God effects the conversion of sinners without any assistance on their part. Conversion is a purely divine process, in which God operates upon the sinner. The term "operative grace" is used to refer to the manner in which prevenient grace does not rely upon human cooperation for its effects, in contrast with cooperative grace.

3 *Cooperative grace*: Having achieved the conversion of the sinner, God now collaborates with the renewed human will in achieving regeneration and growth in holiness. Having liberated the human will from its bondage to sin, God is now able to cooperate with that liberated will. Augustine uses the term "cooperative grace" to refer to the manner in which grace operates within human nature after conversion.

The medieval distinction between actual and habitual grace

The theologians of the early Middle Ages were generally content to regard "grace" as a short-hand term for the graciousness or liberality of God. However, increasing pressure for systematization led to the development of an increasingly precise and meticulous vocabulary of grace. The most important statement of the medieval understanding of the nature and purpose of grace is that of Thomas Aquinas. Although Aquinas treats Augustine's analysis of grace with considerable respect, it is clear that he also has considerable misgivings concerning its viability. A fundamental distinction is drawn between two different types of grace, as follows.

1 *Actual grace* (often referred to by the Latin slogan *gratia gratis data*, or "grace which is freely given"). Aquinas understands this to mean a series of divine actions or influences upon human nature.

2 *Habitual grace* (often referred to by the Latin slogan *gratia gratis faciens*, or "grace which makes pleasing"). Aquinas understands this to mean a created habit of grace within the human soul. This notion is difficult and requires further explanation.

Aquinas argues that there is an enormous gulf between humanity and God. God cannot establish a direct presence within human nature. Instead, an intermediate stage is established, in which the human soul is made ready for the habitation of God. This permanent alteration to the human soul is termed "a habit of grace," where the term "habit" means "something which is permanent." Habitual grace is thus a substance, "something supernatural in the soul." This change in human nature is regarded by Aquinas as the basis of human justification. Something has happened to human nature which allows it to be acceptable to God. Whereas the reformers would locate the basis of justification in God's gracious favor, by which sinners are accepted in the sight of God, Aquinas argues for the need for an intermediary in the process of being accepted by God – the habit of grace, or "habitual grace."

Aquinas's discussion of the nature of grace in the *Summa Theologiae* involves the exploration of the three senses in which the word grace is used in everyday life.

> As used in everyday language, "grace" is commonly understood to mean three things. First, it can mean someone's love, as when it is said that a soldier has the king's favor – that is, that the king holds him in favor. Secondly, it can mean a gift which is freely given, as when it is said: "I do you this favor." Thirdly, it can mean the response to a gift which is freely given, as when we are said to give thanks for benefits which we have received. Now the second of these depends upon the first, as someone freely bestows a gift on someone else on account of their love for them. And the third depends upon the second, since thankfulness is appropriate to gifts which are freely given. Now if "grace" is understood in either the second or third sense of the word, it will be clear that it leaves something in the one who receives it – whether it is the gift which is freely given, or the acknowledgement of that gift. [...] To say that someone has the grace of God is to say that there is something supernatural in the soul, coming forth from God.

Aquinas's argument here is based on the recognition that every sense of the word "grace" is ultimately subordinate to the notion that anyone who is "favored" in this way is changed as a result. In other words, to "have the grace of God" is to possess the favor of God in such a manner that a supernatural change comes about, within the soul of the one who has thus found favor. This "change" is described using the imagery of a supernatural habit of grace – that is, a permanent change in the recipient, rather than a series of transient gracious actions.

The late medieval critique of habitual grace

The idea of "habitual grace" became the subject of considerable criticism in the later Middle Ages. William of Ockham used his famous "razor" to eliminate unnecessary hypotheses from every area of theology. It seemed to him that a habit of grace was totally unnecessary. God was perfectly capable of accepting a sinner directly, without the need for any intermediate stage or intermediate entity. The principle "God can do directly what could otherwise be done through intermediate causes" led Ockham to question the need for habitual grace.

So persuasive was his argument that, by the end of the fifteenth century, the notion was widely regarded as discredited. Grace increasingly came to be understood as divine graciousness – that is, a divine attitude towards humanity, rather than a divine or quasi-divine substance within humanity. In many ways, this can be seen as laying the foundations for the Protestant Reformation's insistence that grace was, at heart, nothing more and nothing less than the "gracious favor of God" (*favor Dei*).

The medieval debate over the nature and grounds of merit

The Pelagian controversy drew attention to the question of whether salvation was a reward for good behavior, or a free gift of God (see pp. 365–8). The debate indicated the importance of clarifying what the term "merit" actually meant. Once more, it was the medieval period which saw clarification of the term. By the time of Thomas Aquinas, the following points had been generally agreed.

1   There is no way in which human beings can claim salvation as a "reward," on the basis of strict justice. Salvation is an act of God's grace, in which sinners are enabled to gain something which would otherwise lie completely beyond them. Left to their own devices, human beings would be unable to achieve their own salvation. The view that humans could earn their salvation through their own achievements was rejected as Pelagianism.

2   Sinners cannot earn salvation, in that there is nothing which they can achieve or perform which obliges God to reward them with faith or justification. The beginning of the Christian life is a matter of grace alone. However, although the grace of God *operates* on sinners to achieve their conversion, it subsequently *cooperates* with them to bring about their growth in holiness. And this cooperation leads to merit, by which God rewards the moral actions of believers.

3   A distinction is drawn between two kinds of merit: *congruous* and *condign* merit. Condign merit is a merit which is justified on the basis of the moral actions of the individual in question; congruous merit is based upon the liberality of God.

Within the context of this general consensus over the nature of merit, a debate developed during the later Middle Ages over the ultimate ground of merit, with two rival positions being distinguishable. The debate illustrates the growing influence of voluntarism in the later Middle Ages. The older position, which can be described as intellectualist, is represented by writers such as Thomas Aquinas. Aquinas argued for a direct proportional representation between the moral and the meritorious value of an action on the part of a believer. The divine intellect recognizes the inherent value of an action, and rewards it accordingly.

In contrast, the voluntarist approach, represented by William of Ockham, placed the emphasis upon the divine will. God determines the meritorious value of an action, by an act of divine will. For Ockham, the intellectualist approach compromised the freedom of God, in that God was placed under an obligation to reward a moral action with a meritorious response. In defending the divine freedom, Ockham argued that God had to be free to reward a human action in any way that seemed fit. There was thus no direct link between the moral and the meritorious value of a human action. To his critics, Ockham seemed to have snapped the connection between human and divine notions of justice and fairness – an issue to which we shall return when we consider the issue of predestination, which brings the role of the will of God into full focus.

Our attention now turns to the great controversy which engulfed the church at the time of the Reformation during the sixteenth century, centering upon the doctrine of justification by faith.

The Reformation Debates over the Doctrine of Grace

As we have seen, the idea that Christ's work on the cross opens up a new way of existence for human beings is articulated in a number of metaphors or images, such as "salvation" and "redemption," initially in the writings of the New Testament (especially the Pauline letters: see p. 350) and subsequently in Christian theological reflection, based upon these texts. We now turn to consider a major new direction in Christian discussion of the doctrine of grace, which is associated with the Reformation.

From "salvation by grace" to "justification by faith"

During the Protestant Reformation of the six-teenth century, a fundamental shift in the vo-cabulary of salvation began to take place. Earlier Christian theologians – such as Augus-tine – had given priority to those New Testa-ment texts which used the language of "salvation by grace" (e.g., Ephesians 2: 5). However, Martin Luther's wrestling with the issue of how God was able to accept sinners led him to focus on those passages in which Paul spoke primarily of "justification by faith" (e.g., Romans 5: 1–2).

Although it can be argued that the same fundamental point is being made in both con-texts, the *language* used to express that point is different. One of the most important influences of the Reformation was the displacement of the language of "salvation by grace" by that of "justification by faith." It is not clear why this transition took place. The most likely ex-planation is through the personal influence of Martin Luther, for whom the idea of "justifica-tion by faith" took on an especially significant role during his formative years.

The doctrine of justification came to be seen as dealing with the question of what an indi-vidual had to do in order to be saved. As con-temporary sources indicate, this question came to be asked with increasing frequency as the sixteenth century dawned. The rise of humanism brought with it a new emphasis upon individual consciousness, and a new awareness of human individuality. In the wake of this dawn of the individual conscious-ness came a new interest in the doctrine of justification – the question of how human be-ings, *as individuals*, could enter into a relation-ship with God. How could a sinner hope to do this? This question lay at the heart of the theo-logical concerns of Martin Luther, and came to dominate the early phase of the Reformation. In view of the importance of the doctrine to this period, we shall consider it in some detail, beginning with Luther's discussion of the doctrine.

Martin Luther's theological breakthrough

In 1545, the year before he died, Luther con-tributed a preface to the first volume of the complete edition of his Latin writings, in which he described how he came to break with the church of his day. The preface was clearly written with the aim of introducing Luther to a readership which might not know how he came to hold the radical reforming views linked with his name. In this "autobio-graphical fragment" (as it is usually known) Luther aimed to provide those readers with background information about the develop-ment of his vocation as a reformer. After deal-ing with some historical preliminaries, taking his narrative up to the year 1519, he turned to describe his personal difficulties with the prob-lem of the "righteousness of God":

> I had certainly wanted to understand Paul in his letter to the Romans. But what prevented me from doing so was not so much cold blood in my heart as that one phrase in the first chapter: "the righteousness of God is revealed in it" (Romans 1: 17). For I hated that phrase, "the righteousness of God," which I had been taught to understand as the righteousness by which God is righteous, and punishes un-righteous sinners. Although I lived a blame-less life as a monk, I felt that I was a sinner with an uneasy conscience before God. I also could not believe that I had pleased him with my works. Far from loving that righteous God who punished sinners, I actually hated him. [...] I was in desperation to know what Paul meant in this passage. At last, as I meditated day and night on the relation of the words "the righteousness of God is revealed in it, as

it is written, the righteous person shall live by faith," I began to understand that "righteousness of God" as that by which the righteous person lives by the gift of God (faith); and this sentence, "the righteousness of God is revealed," to refer to a passive righteousness, by which the merciful God justifies us by faith, as it is written, "the righteous person lives by faith." This immediately made me feel as though I had been born again, and as though I had entered through open gates into paradise itself. From that moment, I saw the whole face of Scripture in a new light. [...] And now, where I had once hated the phrase, "the righteousness of God," I began to love and extol it as the sweetest of phrases, so that this passage in Paul became the very gate of paradise to me.

What is Luther talking about in this famous passage, which vibrates with the excitement of discovery? It is obvious that his understanding of the phrase "the righteousness of God" has changed radically. But what is the nature of this change?

The basic change is fundamental. Originally, Luther regarded the precondition for justification as a human work, something which the sinner had to perform, before he or she could be justified. Increasingly convinced, through his reading of Augustine, that this was an impossibility, Luther could only interpret the "righteousness of God" as a *punishing* righteousness. But in this passage, he narrates how he discovered a "new" meaning of the phrase – a righteousness which God *gives* to the sinner. In other words, God himself meets the precondition, graciously giving sinners what they require if they are to be justified. An analogy (not used by Luther) may help bring out the difference between these two approaches.

Let us suppose that you are in prison, and are offered your freedom on condition that you pay a heavy fine. The promise is real – so long as you can meet the precondition, the promise will be fulfilled. As we noted earlier, Pelagius works on the presupposition, initially shared, at least in part, by Luther, that you have the necessary money stacked away somewhere. As your freedom is worth far more, you are being offered a bargain. So you pay the fine. This presents no difficulties, so long as you have the necessary resources.

Luther, however, increasingly came to share the view of Augustine – that sinful humanity simply does not possess the resources needed to meet this precondition. To go back to our analogy, Augustine and Luther work on the assumption that, as you don't have the necessary money, the promise of freedom has little relevance to your situation. For both Augustine and Luther, therefore, the good news of the gospel is that you have been *given* the necessary money with which to buy your freedom. In other words, the precondition has been met for you by someone else.

Luther's insight, which he describes in this autobiographical passage, is that the God of the Christian gospel is not a harsh judge who rewards individuals according to their merits, but a merciful and gracious God who bestows righteousness upon sinners as a gift. The general consensus among Luther scholars is that his theology of justification underwent a decisive alteration at some point in 1515.

Luther on justifying faith

Central to Luther's insights was the doctrine of "justification by faith alone." The idea of "justification" is already familiar. But what about the phrase "by faith alone"? What is the nature of justifying faith?

"The reason why some people do not understand why faith alone justifies is that they do not know what faith is." In writing these words, Luther draws our attention to the need to inquire more closely concerning that deceptively simple word "faith." Three points relating to Luther's idea of faith may be singled out as having special importance to his doctrine of justification. Each of these points was taken up and developed by later writers, such as Calvin, indicating that Luther made a fundamental contribution to the development of Reformation thought at this point. These three points are:

1 Faith has a personal, rather than a purely historical, reference.
2 Faith concerns trust in the promises of God.
3 Faith unites the believer to Christ.

We shall consider each of these points individually.

1 First, faith is not simply historical knowledge. Luther argues that a faith which is content to believe in the historical reliability of the Gospels is not a faith which justifies. Sinners are perfectly capable of trusting in the historical details of the Gospels; but these facts of themselves are not adequate for true Christian faith. Saving faith involves believing and trusting that Christ was born *pro nobis* ("for us"), born for us personally, and has accomplished for us the work of salvation.

2 Second, faith is to be understood as "trust" (*fiducia*). The notion of trust is prominent in the Reformation conception of faith, as a nautical analogy used by Luther indicates. "Everything depends upon faith. The person who does not have faith is like someone who has to cross the sea, but is so frightened that he does not trust the ship. And so he stays where he is, and is never saved, because he will not get on board and cross over." Faith is not merely believing that something is true; it is being prepared to act upon that belief, and relying upon it. To use Luther's analogy: faith is not simply about believing that a ship exists – it is about stepping into it, and entrusting ourselves to it.

3 In the third place, faith unites the believer with Christ. Luther stated this principle clearly in his 1520 work, *The Liberty of a Christian*, cited earlier in this connection (see p. 183). Faith is not assent to an abstract set of doctrines, but is a union between Christ and the believer. It is the response of the whole person of the believer to God, which leads in turn to the real and personal presence of Christ in the believer. "To know Christ is to know his benefits," wrote Philip Melanchthon, Luther's colleague at Wittenberg. Faith makes both Christ and his benefits – such as forgiveness, justification, and hope – available to the believer.

The doctrine of "justification by faith" thus does not mean that the sinner is justified because he or she believes, on account of that faith. This would be to treat faith as a human action or work. Luther insists that God provides everything necessary for justification, so that all that the sinner needs to do is to receive it. God is active, and humans are passive, in justification. The phrase "justification *by* grace *through* faith" brings out the meaning of the doctrine more clearly: The justification of the sinner is based upon the grace of God, and is received through faith.

The doctrine of justification by faith alone is thus an affirmation that God does everything necessary for salvation. Even faith itself is a gift of God, rather than a human action. God himself meets the precondition for justification. Thus, as we saw, the "righteousness of God" is not a righteousness which judges whether or not we have met the precondition for justification, but the righteousness which is given to us so that we may meet that precondition.

The concept of forensic justification

One of the central insights of Luther's doctrine of justification by faith alone is that the individual sinner is incapable of self-justification. It is God who takes the initiative in justification, providing all the resources necessary to justify that sinner. One of those resources is the "righteousness of God." In other words, the righteousness on the basis of which sinners are justified is not their own righteousness, but a righteousness which is given to them by God. Augustine had made this point earlier: Luther, however, gives it a subtle new twist which leads to the development of the concept of "forensic justification."

The point at issue is difficult to explain, and centers on the question of the location of justifying righteousness. Both Augustine and Luther are agreed that God graciously gives sinful humans a righteousness which justifies them. But where is that righteousness located? Augustine argued that it was to be found within believers; Luther insisted that it remained outside believers. For Augustine, the righteousness in question is internal; for Luther, it is external.

For Augustine, God bestows justifying righteousness upon the sinner, in such a way that it becomes part of his or her person. As a result this righteousness, although originating from *outside* the sinner, becomes part of his or her person. For Luther, the righteousness in question remains outside the sinner: it is an "alien righteousness" (*iustitia aliena*). God treats, or "reckons," this righteousness *as if* it were part of the sinner's person. In his Romans lectures of 1515–16, Luther developed the idea of the "alien righteousness of Christ" imputed – not imparted – to us by faith, as the grounds of justification. His comments on Romans 4: 7 are especially important:

Since the saints are always conscious of their sin, and seek righteousness from God in accordance with his mercy, they are always reckoned as righteous by God. Thus in their own eyes, and as a matter of fact, they are unrighteous. But God reckons them as righteous on account of their confession of their sin. In fact, they are sinners; however, they are righteous by the reckoning of a merciful God. Without knowing it they are righteous; knowing it they are unrighteous. They are sinners in fact but righteous in hope.

Believers are righteous on account of the alien righteousness of Christ which is imputed to them – that is, treated as if it were theirs through faith. Earlier, we noted that an essential element of Luther's concept of faith is that it unites the believer to Christ. Justifying faith thus allows the believer to link up with the righteousness of Christ and be justified on its basis. Christians are thus "righteous by the imputation of a merciful God."

Through faith, the believer is clothed with the righteousness of Christ in much the same way, Luther suggests, as Ezekiel 16: 8 speaks of God covering our nakedness with his garment. For Luther, faith is the right (or righteous) relationship to God. Sin and righteousness thus coexist; we remain sinners inwardly, but are righteous extrinsically, in the sight of God. By confessing our sins in faith, we stand in a right and righteous relationship with God. From our own perspective we are sinners; but in the perspective of God, we are righteous.

Luther does not necessarily imply that this coexistence of sin and righteousness is a permanent condition. The Christian life is not static, as if – to use a very loose way of speaking – the relative amounts of sin and righteousness remained constant throughout. Luther is perfectly aware that the Christian life is dynamic, in that the believer grows in righteousness. Rather, his point is that the existence of sin does not negate our status as Christians. God shields our sin through his righteousness. This righteousness is like a protective covering, under which we may battle with our sin.

This approach accounts, in Luther's view, for the persistence of sin in believers, while at the same time accounting for the gradual transformation of the believer and the future elimination of that sin. But it is not necessary to be perfectly righteous to be a Christian. Sin does not point to unbelief, or a failure on the part of God; rather, it points to the continued need to entrust one's person to the gentle care of God. Luther thus declares, in a famous phrase, that a believer is "at one and the same time righteous and a sinner" (*simul iustus et peccator*); righteous in hope, but a sinner in fact; righteous in the sight and through the promise of God, yet a sinner in reality.

These ideas were subsequently developed by Luther's follower Philip Melanchthon to give the doctrine now generally known as "forensic justification." Where Augustine taught that the sinner is *made righteous* in justification, Melanchthon taught that the sinner is *counted as righteous* or *pronounced to be righteous*. For Augustine, "justifying righteousness" is *imparted*; for Melanchthon, it is *imputed*. Melanchthon drew a sharp distinction between the event of being *declared* righteous and the process of being *made* righteous, designating the former "justification" and the latter "sanctification" or "regeneration."

For Augustine, both were simply different aspects of the same thing. According to Melanchthon, God pronounces the divine judgment – that the sinner is righteous – in the heavenly court (*in foro divino*). This legal approach to justification gives rise to the term "forensic justification," from the Latin word *forum* ("marketplace" or "courtyard") – the place traditionally associated with the dispensing of justice in classical Rome.

The importance of this development lies in the fact that it marks a complete break with the teaching of the church up to that point. From the time of Augustine onward, justification had always been understood to refer to both the event of being declared righteous and the process of being made righteous. Melanchthon's concept of forensic justification diverged radically from this. As it was taken up by virtually all the major reformers subsequently, it came to represent a standard difference between the Protestant and Roman Catholic churches from that point onward.

In addition to their differences on how the sinner was justified, there was now an additional disagreement on what the word "justification" designated in the first place. As we shall see, the Council of Trent, the Roman Catholic Church's definitive response to the Protestant challenge, reaffirmed the views of Augustine on the nature of justification, and censured the views of Melanchthon as woefully inadequate.

John Calvin on justification

The model of justification which would eventually gain the ascendancy in the later Reformation was formulated by Calvin in the 1540s and 1550s. Calvin defines justification as follows:

> To be justified in God's sight is to be reckoned as righteous in God's judgment, and to be accepted on account of that righteousness. [...] The person who is justified by faith is someone who, apart from the righteousness of works, has taken hold of the righteousness of Christ through faith, and having been clothed with it, appears in the sight of God not as a sinner, but as a righteous person. Therefore justification is to be understood simply as the acceptance by which God receives us into his favor as righteous people. We say that it consists of the remission of sins and the imputation of the righteousness of Christ. [...] believers are not righteous in

themselves, but on account of the communication of the righteousness of Christ through imputation, something to be noted carefully. [...] Our righteousness is not in us, but in Christ. We possess it only because we participate in Christ; in fact, with him, we possess all his riches.

The basic elements of Calvin's approach can be summarized as follows. Faith unites the believer to Christ in a "mystic union." (Here, Calvin reclaims Luther's emphasis upon the real and personal presence of Christ within believers, established through faith.) This union with Christ has a twofold effect, which Calvin refers to as "a double grace." First, the believer's union with Christ leads directly to his or her *justification*. Through Christ, the believer is declared to be righteous in the sight of God. Second, on account of the believer's union with Christ – and *not* on account of his or her justification – the believer begins the process of being made like Christ through regeneration. Calvin asserts that both justification and regeneration are the results of the believer's union with Christ through faith.

The Council of Trent on justification

By 1540, Luther had become something of a household name throughout Europe. His writings were being read and digested, with various degrees of enthusiasm, even in the highest ecclesiastical circles in Italy. Something had to be done if the Catholic Church was to re-establish its credibility in relation to this matter. The Council of Trent, summoned in 1545, began the long process of formulating a comprehensive response to Luther. High on its agenda was the doctrine of justification.

The sixth session of the Council of Trent was brought to its close on January 13, 1547. The Tridentine Decree on Justification sets out the Roman Catholic teaching on justification with a considerable degree of clarity. ("Tridentine" is the adjective derived from "Trent.") Trent's critique of Luther's doctrine of justification can be broken down into four main sections:

1 The nature of justification.
2 The nature of justifying righteousness.
3 The nature of justifying faith.
4 The assurance of salvation.

We shall consider each of these four matters individually.

The nature of justification

In his earlier phase, around the years 1515–19, Luther tended to understand justification as a process of becoming, in which the sinner was gradually conformed to the likeness of Jesus Christ through a process of internal renewal (see pp. 372–3). In his later writings, however, dating from the mid-1530s and beyond, perhaps under the influence of Melanchthon's more forensic approach to justification (see p. 376), Luther tended to treat justification as a matter of being declared to be righteous, rather than a process of becoming righteous. Increasingly, he came to see justification as an event, which was complemented by the distinct process of regeneration and interior renewal through the action of the Holy Spirit. Justification alters the outer status of the sinner "in the sight of God" (*coram Deo*), while regeneration alters the sinner's inner nature.

Trent strongly opposed this view, and vigorously defended the idea, originally associated with Augustine, that justification is the process of regeneration and renewal within human nature, which brings about a change in both the outer status and the inner nature of the sinner. The fourth chapter of the Decree provides the following precise definition of justification:

The justification of the sinner may be briefly defined as a translation from that state in which a human being is born a child of the first Adam, to the state of grace and of the adoption of the sons of God through the second Adam, Jesus Christ our Savior. According to the Gospel, this translation cannot come about except through the cleansing of regeneration, or a desire for this, as it is written, "Unless someone is born again of water and the Holy Spirit, he or she cannot enter into the Kingdom of God" (John 3: 5).

Justification thus includes the idea of regeneration. This brief statement is amplified in the seventh chapter, which stresses that justification "is not only a remission of sins but also the sanctification and renewal of the inner person through the voluntary reception of the grace and gifts by which an unrighteous person becomes a righteous person." This point was given further emphasis through canon 11, which condemned anyone who taught that justification takes place "either by the sole imputation of the righteousness of Christ or by the sole remission of sins, to the exclusion of grace and charity [. . .] or that the grace by which we are justified is only the good will of God."

In brief, then, Trent maintained the medieval tradition, stretching back to Augustine, which saw justification as comprising both an event and a process – the event of being declared to be righteous through the work of Christ, and the process of being made righteous through the internal work of the Holy Spirit. Reformers such as Melanchthon and Calvin distinguished these two matters, treating the word "justification" as referring only to the process of being declared to be righteous; the accompanying process of internal renewal, which they termed "sanctification" or "regeneration," they regarded as theologically distinct.

Serious confusion thus resulted: Roman Catholics and Protestants used the same word "justification" to mean very different things. Trent used the term "justification" to mean what, to Protestants, was *both* justification *and* sanctification.

The nature of justifying righteousness

Luther placed emphasis upon the fact that sinners possessed no righteousness in themselves. They had nothing within them which could ever be regarded as the basis of God's gracious decision to justify them. Luther's doctrine of the "alien righteousness of Christ" (*iustitia Christi aliena*) made it clear that the righteousness which justified sinners was outside them. It was imputed, not imparted; external, not internal.

Early critics of the Reformation argued, following Augustine, that sinners were justified on the basis of an internal righteousness, graciously infused or implanted within their persons by God. This righteousness was itself given as an act of grace; it was not something merited. But, they argued, there had to be something within individuals which could allow God to justify them. Luther dismissed this idea. God can justify individuals directly, rather than through an intermediate gift of righteousness.

Trent strongly defended the Augustinian idea of justification on the basis of an internal righteousness. The seventh chapter makes this point perfectly clear:

> The single formal cause [of justification] is the righteousness of God – not the righteousness by which he himself is righteous, but the righteousness by which he makes us righteous, so that, when we are endowed with it, we are "renewed in the spirit of our mind," and are not only counted as righteous, but are called, and are in reality, righteous. [. . .] Nobody can be righteous except God communicates the merits of the passion of our Lord Jesus Christ to him or her, and this takes place in the justification of the sinner.

The phrase "single formal cause" needs explanation. A "formal" cause is the *direct*, or most immediate, cause of something. Trent is thus stating that the direct cause of justification is the righteousness which God graciously imparts to us – as opposed to more distant causes of justification, such as the "efficient cause" (God), or the "meritorious cause" (Jesus Christ).

But the use of the word "single" should also be noted. One proposal for reaching agreement between Roman Catholic and Protestant, which gained especial prominence at the Colloquy of Ratisbon in 1541, was that *two* causes of justification should be recognized – an external righteousness (the Protestant position) and an internal righteousness (the Roman Catholic position). This compromise seemed to hold some potential. Trent, however, had no time for it. The use of the word "single" was deliberate, intended to eliminate the idea that there could be more than one such cause. The *only* direct cause of justification was the interior gift of righteousness.

The nature of justifying faith

Luther's doctrine of justification by faith alone came in for severe criticism. Canon 12 condemns a central aspect of Luther's notion of justifying faith, when it rejects the idea that "justifying faith is nothing other than confidence in the mercy of God, which remits sin for the sake of Christ." In part, this rejection of Luther's doctrine of justification reflects the ambiguity, noted above (pp. 377–8), concerning the meaning of the term "justification." Trent was alarmed that anyone should believe that they could be justified – in the Tridentine sense of the term – by faith, without any need for obedience or spiritual renewal. Trent, interpreting "justification" to mean *both* the beginning of the Christian life *and* its continuation and growth, believed that Luther was suggest-

ing that simply trusting in God (without any requirement that the sinner be changed and renewed by God) was the basis of the entire Christian life.

Luther, however, did not actually hold this position, although his occasionally rather strident manner of expressing himself could have allowed this misunderstanding to arise. Rather, he was affirming that the Christian life was begun through faith, and faith alone; good works followed justification, and did not cause that justification in the first place. Trent itself was perfectly prepared to concede that the Christian life was begun through faith, thus coming very close indeed to Luther's position. As chapter 8 of the Decree on Justification declares, "we are said to be justified by faith, because faith is the beginning of human salvation, the foundation and root of all justification, without which it is impossible to please God." This is perhaps a classic case of a theological misunderstanding, resting upon the disputed meaning of a major theological term.

The assurance of salvation

For Luther, as for the reformers in general, one could rest assured of one's salvation. Salvation was grounded upon the faithfulness of God to his promises of mercy; to fail to have confidence in salvation was, in effect, to doubt the reliability and trustworthiness of God. Yet this must not be seen as a supreme confidence in God, untroubled by doubt. Faith is not the same as certainty; although the theological foundation of Christian faith may be secure, the human perception of and commitment to this foundation may waver.

The Council of Trent regarded the reformers' doctrine of assurance with considerable skepticism. Chapter 9 of the Decree on Justification, entitled "Against the Vain Confidence of Heretics," criticized the "ungodly confidence" of the reformers. While no one should doubt God's goodness and generosity, the reformers erred seriously when they taught that "nobody is absolved from sins and justified, unless they believe with certainty that they are absolved and justified, and that absolution and justification are effected by this faith alone." Trent insisted that "nobody can know with a certainty of faith which is not subject to error, whether they have obtained the grace of God."

Trent's point seems to be that the reformers were seen to be making human confidence or boldness the grounds of justification, so that justification rested upon a fallible human conviction, rather than upon the grace of God. The reformers, however, saw themselves as stressing that justification rested upon the promises of God; a failure to believe boldly in such promises was tantamount to calling the reliability of God into question.

The Doctrine of Predestination

I n discussing the nature of grace earlier in this chapter, we noted the close relationship between "grace" and "graciousness." God is under no obligation to bestow grace upon anyone, as if it were a commodity which functioned as a reward for meritorious actions. Grace is a gift, as Augustine never tired of emphasizing. Yet this emphasis upon the gift-character of grace, as will become clear, leads directly to the doctrine of predestination, often regarded as one of the most enigmatic and puzzling aspects of Christian theology. To explore how this connection developed, we shall consider some aspects of the theology of Augustine, before moving on to deal with the definitive exposition of a doctrine of predestination in the Reformed theological tradition.

Augustine of Hippo

Grace is a gift, not a reward. This insight is fundamental to Augustine (see pp. 365–6). If grace were a reward, humans could purchase their salvation through good works. They could earn their redemption. Yet this, according to Augustine, was totally contrary to the New Testament proclamation of the doctrine of grace. Affirming the gift-character of grace was a bulwark against inadequate theories of salvation. We have already spent much time dealing with Augustine's understanding of grace, and need not develop this point further here.

Augustine's insight had much to commend it. However, on further inspection it proved to have its darker side. As the Pelagian controversy became increasingly hardened and bitter, the more negative implications of Augustine's doctrine of grace became clearer. In what follows, we shall explore those implications.

If grace is a gift, God must be free to offer it, or not to offer it, without any external consideration. If it is offered on the basis of any such consideration, it is no longer a gift – it is a reward for a specific action or attitude. Grace, according to Augustine, only remains gracious if it is nothing more and nothing less than a gift, reflecting the liberality of the one who gives. But the gift is not given to all. It is particular. Grace is only given to some. Augustine's defense of "the graciousness of God," which rests on his belief that God must be free to give or withhold grace, thus entails the recognition of the *particularity*, rather than the *universality*, of grace.

If this insight is linked with Augustine's doctrine of sin, its full implications become clear. All of humanity is contaminated by sin, and unable to break free from its grasp. Only grace can set humanity free. Yet grace is not bestowed universally; it is only granted to some individuals. As a result, only some will be saved – those to whom grace is given. Predestination, for Augustine, involves the recognition that God withholds the means of salvation from those who are not elected.

> This is the predestination of the saints, and nothing else: the foreknowledge and preparation of the benefits of God, whereby whoever are set free are most certainly set free. And where are the rest left by the just judgment of God, except in that mass of perdition, in which the inhabitants of Tyre and Sidon were left? Now they would have believed, if they had seen the wonderful signs of Christ. However, because it was not given to them to believe, they were not given the means to believe. From this, it seems that certain people have naturally in their minds a divine gift of understanding, by which they may be moved to faith, if they hear the words or see the signs which are adapted to their minds. But if, by virtue of a divine judgment which lies beyond us, these people have not been predestined by grace and separated from the mass of perdition, then they are without contact with either these divine words or deeds which, if heard or seen by them, would have allowed them to believe.

It is important to note that Augustine emphasized that this did not mean that some were predestined to damnation. It meant that God had selected some from the mass of fallen humanity. The chosen few were indeed predestined for salvation. The remainder were not, according to Augustine, actively condemned to damnation; they were merely not elected to salvation.

Augustine tends (although he is not entirely consistent in this respect) to treat predestination as something which is *active* and *positive* – a deliberate decision to redeem on God's part. However, as his critics pointed out, this decision to redeem some was equally a decision *not* to redeem others.

This question surfaced with new force during the great predestinarian controversy of the ninth century, in which the Benedictine monk Godescalc of Orbais (c.804–c.869, also known as Gottschalk) developed a doctrine of double predestination similar to that later to be associated with Calvin and his followers. Pursuing with relentless logic the implications of his assertion that God has predestined some to eternal damnation, Godescalc pointed out that it was thus quite improper to speak of Christ dying for such individuals; if he had, he would have died in vain, for their fate would be unaffected.

Hesitant over the implications of this assertion, Godescalc proposed that Christ died *only for the elect*. The scope of his redeeming work was restricted, limited only to those who were predestined to benefit from his death. Most ninth-century writers reacted to this assertion critically. It was, however, to resurface in later Calvinism.

John Calvin

Calvin is often regarded as making the doctrine of predestination the center of his theological system. A close reading of his *Institutes* does not, however, bear out this often-repeated judgment. Calvin adopts a distinctly low-key approach to the doctrine, devoting a mere four chapters to its exposition (book III, chapters 21–4). Predestination is defined as "the eternal decree of God, by which he determined what he wished to make of every person. For he does not create everyone in the same condition, but ordains eternal life for some and eternal damnation for others." In writing of predestination at one point, Calvin appears to speak of it as a "horrible decree": "The decree, I admit, is *horribile*." However, the Latin term *horribile* is better translated as "awesome"; Calvin's own

French translation of the passage (1560) reads: "I confess that this decree must frighten us" (*doit nous epouvanter*).

The very location of Calvin's discussion of predestination in the 1559 edition of the *Institutes* is significant in itself. It follows his exposition of the doctrine of grace. It is only after the great themes of this doctrine – such as justification by faith – have been expounded that Calvin turns to consider the mysterious and perplexing subject of predestination. Logically, predestination ought to precede such an analysis; predestination, after all, establishes the grounds of an individual's election, and hence his or her subsequent justification and sanctification. Yet Calvin declines to be subservient to the canons of such logic. Why?

Calvin's analysis of predestination begins from observable facts. Some believe the gospel. Some do not. The primary function of the doctrine of predestination is to explain why some individuals respond to the gospel, and others do not. It is an attempt to explain the variety of human responses to grace. Calvin's predestinarianism is to be regarded as reflection upon the data of human experience, interpreted in the light of Scripture, rather than something which is deduced on the basis of preconceived ideas concerning divine omnipotence. Belief in predestination is not an article of faith in its own right, but is the final outcome of scripturally informed reflection on the effects of grace upon individuals in the light of the enigmas of experience.

Far from being a central premise of Calvin's thought, predestination is an ancillary doctrine, concerned with explaining a puzzling aspect of the consequences of the proclamation of the gospel of grace. Yet as Calvin's followers sought to develop and recast his thinking in the light of new intellectual developments, it was perhaps inevitable (if this lapse into a potentially predestinarian mode of speaking may be excused) that alterations to his structuring of Christian theology might occur. In the section which follows, we shall explore the understandings of predestination which gained influence within Calvinism after Calvin's death.

Reformed orthodoxy

It is not correct to speak of Calvin developing a "system" in the strict sense of the term. Calvin's religious ideas, as presented in the 1559 *Institutes*, are *systematically arranged* on the basis of pedagogical considerations; they are not, however, *systematically derived* on the basis of a leading speculative principle. Calvin regarded biblical exposition and systematic theology as virtually identical, and refused to make the distinction between them which became commonplace after his death. However, as noted earlier, a new interest in the area of method developed after Calvin's death. The question of the proper starting point for theology became increasingly debated (see pp. 50–1).

It is this concern for establishing a logical starting point for theology which allows us to understand the new importance that came to be attached to the doctrine of predestination within Reformed orthodoxy. Calvin focused upon the specific historical event of Jesus Christ and then moved out to explore its implications (that is, to deploy the appropriate technical language, Calvin's approach is analytic and inductive). In contrast, Theodore Beza – a later follower of Calvin (see p. 51) – begins from general principles and proceeds to deduce their consequences for Christian theology (that is, his approach is deductive and synthetic).

So what general principles does Beza use as a logical starting point for his theological systematization? The answer is that he bases his system on the divine decrees of election – that is, the divine decision to elect certain people to salvation, and others to damnation. All the remainder of theology is concerned with the exploration of the consequences of these decisions. The doctrine of predestination thus assumes the status of a controlling principle.

One major consequence of this development may be noted: the doctrine of "limited atonement" or "particular redemption." (The term "atonement" is often used to refer to "the benefits resulting from the death of Christ.") Consider the following question. For whom did Christ die? The traditional answer to this question took the following form: Christ died for everyone; yet although his death has the potential to redeem all, it is only effective for those who choose to allow it to have this effect. This doctrine was regarded with intense distaste by Arminianism, to which we shall presently turn.

Before doing so, the idea of "Five Point Calvinism" needs to be introduced and explained. This term refers to the five central principles of Reformed soteriology (that is, the understanding of redemption associated with Calvinist writers), as they were laid down definitively by the Synod of Dort (1618–19). The "Five Points" are often referred to using the mnemonic TULIP (highly appropriate, one would think, for a synod that took place in Holland, home of that famous bulb):

T	total depravity of sinful human nature;
U	unconditional election, in that humans are not predestined on the basis of any foreseen merit, quality, or achievement;
L	limited atonement, in that Christ died only for the elect;
I	irresistible grace, by which the elect are infallibly called and redeemed;
P	perseverance of the saints, in that those who are truly predestined by God cannot in any way defect from that calling.

An important controversy emerged within Calvinist circles in the early seventeenth century concerning the logical ordering of the "decrees of election." Two classic positions may be discerned within this notoriously pedantic debate, which has often become a symbol of theological obscurantism.

1. The *infralapsarian* position, associated with François Turrettini (1623–87), stated that election presupposes the fall of humanity. The decrees of election are thus oriented toward all of humanity as a "mass of sin" (*massa perditionis*). In other words, God's decision to predestine some to election and others to damnation is in response to the event of the Fall. The object of the decision is fallen human beings.

2. The alternative *supralapsarian* position, associated with Beza, regards election as prior to the Fall. Here, the object of the divine decree of predestination is seen as humanity prior to the Fall. The Fall is thus seen as a means of carrying out the decree of election.

A third position may also be noted, associated especially with Moses Amyraut (1596–1664) and the Calvinist Academy at Saumur, France. This position, often referred to as *hypothetical universalism*, has had relatively little impact within Calvinism.

Arminianism

Arminianism takes its name from Jakob Arminius (1560–1609), who reacted against the Reformed doctrine of particular redemption. For him, Christ had died for all, not merely for the elect. Such views were taken up within Dutch Reformed circles in the aftermath of the Synod of Dort, leading to the publication of the *Remonstrance* of 1610. This statement affirmed the universal character and scope of Christ's work:

God, by an eternal and unchangeable decree in Christ before the existence of the world, determined to elect from the fallen and sinful human race to everlasting life all those who, through God's grace, believe in Jesus Christ and persevere in faith and obedience. [. . .] Christ the Savior of the world died for all and every human being, so that he obtained, through his death on the cross, reconciliation and pardon for all, in such a way, however, that only the faithful actually enjoy the same.

The idea of predestination is thus maintained; however, its frame of reference is radically altered. Whereas the Synod of Dort understood predestination to be an individual matter, the Arminians understood it corporately: God has predestined that a specific group of people will be saved – namely, those who believe in Jesus Christ. By believing, individuals fulfilled the predestined condition of salvation.

Arminianism soon achieved a major presence within eighteenth-century evangelicalism. Despite the more Calvinist views of George Whitefield, Arminian ideas were forcefully stated within Methodism by Charles Wesley (1707–88). For example, his hymn "Would Jesus Have the Sinner Die?" states the doctrine of the universal redemption of humanity with considerable force (my italics):

> O let thy love my heart constrain,
> Thy love for *every* sinner free,
> That *every* fallen soul of man,
> May taste the grace that found out me;
> That all mankind with me may prove
> Thy sovereign, everlasting love.

The position also achieved considerable prominence in North America during the eighteenth century: Jonathan Edwards's writings make frequent reference to what he regarded as the inconsistencies and shortcomings of his Arminian opponents. It was clearly a popular opinion, despite the misgivings regularly expressed by its critics.

Karl Barth

One of the most interesting features of Karl Barth's theology is the manner in which it interacts with the theology of the period of Reformed orthodoxy. It is in part the seriousness with which Barth takes the writings of this period that has given rise to the term "neo-orthodoxy" to refer to Barth's general approach (pp. 85–7). Barth's treatment of the Reformed doctrine of predestination is especially interesting, in that it demonstrates the manner in which he can take traditional terms, and give them a radically new meaning within the context of his theology. Barth's discussion of predestination (*Church Dogmatics*, volume 2, part 2) is based upon two central affirmations:

1 Jesus Christ is the electing God.
2 Jesus Christ is the elected human being.

This strongly Christological orientation of predestination is maintained throughout his analysis of the doctrine. "In its simplest and most comprehensive form, the doctrine of predestination consists of the assertion that the divine predestination is the election of Jesus Christ. But the concept of election has a double reference – to the elector and the elected." So exactly what has God predestined? Barth's answer to this has several components, of which the following are especially important.

1 "God has chosen to be the friend and partner of humanity." God has elected, in a free and sovereign decision, to enter into fellowship with humanity. Barth thus affirms God's commitment to humanity, despite its sin and fallenness.

2　God chose to demonstrate that commitment in giving Christ for the redemption of humanity. "According to the Bible, this was what took place in the incarnation of the Son of God, in his death and passion, and in his resurrection from the dead." The very act of the redemption of humanity is the expression of God's self-election as redeemer of fallen humanity.

3　God elected to bear totally the pain and cost of redemption. God chose to accept the cross of Golgotha as a royal throne. God chose to accept the lot of fallen humanity, especially in suffering and death. God chose the path of self-humiliation and self-abasement in order to redeem humanity.

4　God elected to take from us the negative aspects of his judgment. God rejects Christ in order that we might not be rejected. The negative side of predestination, which ought Barth suggests, properly to have fallen upon sinful humanity, is instead directed toward Christ the electing God and elected human being. God willed to bear the "rejection and condemnation and death" which are the inevitable consequences of sin. Thus "rejection cannot again become the portion or affair of humanity." Christ bore what sinful humanity ought to have borne, in order that they need never bear it again.

In so far as predestination contains a "No," it is not a "No" spoken against humanity. In so far as it involves exclusion and rejection, it is not the exclusion and rejection of humanity. In so far as it is directed to perdition and death, it is not directed to the perdition and death of humanity.

Barth thus eliminates any notion of a "predestination to condemnation" on the part of humanity. The only one who is predestined to condemnation is Jesus Christ who "from all eternity willed to suffer for us."

The consequences of this approach are clear. Despite all appearances to the contrary, humanity cannot be condemned. In the end, grace will triumph, even over unbelief. Barth's doctrine of predestination eliminates the possibility of the rejection of humanity. In that Christ has borne the penalty and pain of rejection by God, this can never again become the portion of humanity. Taken together with his characteristic emphasis upon the "triumph of grace," Barth's doctrine of predestination points to the universal restoration and salvation of humanity – a position which has occasioned a degree of criticism from others who would otherwise be sympathetic to his general position. Emil Brunner is an example of such a critic:

> What does this statement, "that Jesus is the only really rejected person," mean for the situation of humanity? Evidently this: That there is no possibility of condemnation. [...] The decision has already been made in Jesus Christ – for all of humanity. Whether they know it or not, believe it or not, is not so important. They are like people who seem to be perishing in a stormy sea. But in reality they are not in a sea in which one can drown, but in shallow waters, in which it is impossible to drown. Only they do not know it.

Predestination and economics: the Weber thesis

One of the most fascinating consequences of the Calvinist emphasis upon predestination is its impact upon the attitudes of those who held the belief. Of especial importance is the question of *assurance*: how may the believer know that he or she really is among the elect? Although Calvin stressed that works are not the grounds of *salvation*, he nevertheless allowed it to be understood that they are, in some vague way, the grounds of *assurance*. Works may be regarded as "the testimonies of God dwelling and ruling within us." Believers are not saved by works; rather, their salvation is demonstrated by works. "The grace of good works [...] demonstrates that the spirit of adoption has been given to us." This tendency to regard works as evidence of election may be seen as the first stage in the articulation of a work ethic with significant pastoral overtones: it is by worldly activism that believers can assure their troubled conscience that they are among the elect.

Anxiety over this question of election was subsequently a pervasive feature of Calvinist spirituality, and was generally treated at some length by Calvinist preachers and spiritual writers. The basic answer given, however, remained substantially the same: the believer who performs good works has indeed been chosen. This idea was often stated in terms of the "practical syllogism," an argument constructed along the following lines:

> All who are elected exhibit certain signs as a consequence of that election.
> But I exhibit those signs.
> Therefore I am among the elect.

This *syllogismus practicus* thus locates the grounds of certainty of election in the presence of "certain signs" in the life of the believer. There was thus a significant psychological pressure to demonstrate one's election to oneself and the world in general by exhibiting its signs – among which was the wholehearted commitment to serve and glorify God by laboring in the world. It is this pressure which, according to sociologist Max Weber, lies behind the emergence of capitalism within Calvinist societies.

The popular version of the Weber thesis declares that capitalism is a direct result of the

Protestant Reformation. This is historically untenable and, in any case, is not what Weber actually said. Weber stressed that he had

> no intention whatsoever of maintaining such a foolish and doctrinaire thesis as that the spirit of capitalism [...] could only have arisen as a result of certain effects of the Reformation. In itself, the fact that certain important forms of capitalistic business organizations are known to be considerably older than the Reformation is a sufficient refutation of such a claim.

Rather, Weber argued that a new "spirit of capitalism" emerged in the sixteenth century. It is not so much *capitalism* as *a specific form* of capitalism which needs to be explained.

Protestantism, Weber argued, generated the psychological preconditions essential to the development of modern capitalism. Indeed, Weber located the fundamental contribution of Calvinism as lying in its generation of psychological impulses on account of its belief systems. Weber laid especial stress upon the notion of "calling," which he linked with the Calvinist idea of predestination. Calvinists, assured of their personal salvation, were enabled to engage in worldly activity without serious anxiety regarding their salvation as a consequence. The pressure to prove one's election led to the active pursuit of worldly success – a success which, as history indicates, was generally not slow in coming.

It is not our concern here to provide a critique of the Weber thesis. In some circles, it is regarded as utterly discredited; in others, it lives on. Our concern is simply to note that Weber rightly discerned that religious ideas could have a powerful economic and social impact upon early modern Europe. The very fact that Weber suggested that the religious thought of the Reformation was capable of providing the stimulus needed for the development of modern capitalism itself is a powerful testimony to the need to study theology if human history is to be fully understood. It also indicates that apparently abstract ideas – such as predestination – can prove to have a very concrete impact upon history!

The Darwinian Controversy and the Nature of Humanity

One of the most vigorous debates within modern Christian thought concerns the implications of Darwinism for religious belief, above all the theological status of human nature. Traditional Christian theology regarded humanity as the height of God's creation, distinguished from the remainder of the created order by being created in the image of God. On this traditional reading of things, humanity is located within the created order as a whole, yet stands above it on account of its unique relationship to God, articulated in the notion of the *imago Dei*. Yet Darwin's *Origin of Species* posed an implicit, and *The Descent of Man* an explicit, challenge to this view. Humanity had emerged, over a vast period of time, from within the natural order.

If there was one aspect of his own theory of evolution which left Charles Darwin feeling unsettled, it was its implications for the status and identity of the human race. In every edition of the *Origin of Species*, Darwin consistently stated that his proposed mechanism of natural selection did not entail any fixed or universal law of progressive development. It was not an easy conclusion for Darwin, or for his age. The conclusion to the *Descent of Man* speaks of humanity in exalted terms, while insisting upon its "lowly" biological origins:

Man may be excused for feeling some pride at having risen, though not through his own exertions, to the very summit of the organic scale; and the fact of his having thus risen, instead of having been aboriginally placed there, may give him hope for a still higher destiny in the distant future. But we are not here concerned with hopes or fears, only with the truth as far as our reason permits us to discover it; and I have given the evidence to the best of my ability. We must, however, acknowledge, as it seems to me, that man with all his noble qualities [. . .] still bears in his bodily frame the indelible stamp of his lowly origin.

Most Darwinists would insist that it is a corollary of an evolutionary worldview that we must recognize that we are animals, part of the evolutionary process. Darwinism thus critiques the absolutist assumptions concerning the place of humanity within nature that lies behind "speciesism" – a term introduced by Richard Ryder, and given wider currency by Peter Singer, currently of Princeton University. This has raised considerable difficulties beyond the realm of traditional religion, in that many political and ethical theories are predicated on the assumption of the privileged status of humanity within nature, whether this is justified on religious or secular grounds.

So what are the Christian responses to Darwinism? It is now a century and a half since the publication of Darwin's *Origin of Species*. During that time, at least four categories of response have emerged, each of which will be considered briefly below.

Young earth creationism

This position represents the continuation of the "common reading" of Genesis, which was widely encountered in popular and at least some academic writing before 1800. On this view, the earth was created in its basic form between 6,000 and 10,000 years ago. Young earth creationists generally read the first two chapters of the book of Genesis in a way that allows for no living creatures of any kind before Eden, and no death before the Fall. Most young earth creationists hold that all living things were created simultaneously, within the timeframe proposed by the Genesis creation accounts, with the Hebrew word *yom* ("day") meaning a period of 24 hours. The fossil records, which point to a much greater timescale and to the existence of extinct species, are often understood to date from the time of Noah's flood. This viewpoint is often, but not universally, stated in forms of a 144-hour creation and a universal flood. Representative young earth creationists include Henry Madison Morris (1918–2006) and Douglas F. Kelly.

Old earth creationism

This view has a long history, and is probably the majority viewpoint within conservative Protestant circles. It has no particular difficulty with the vast age of the world, and argues that the "young earth" approach requires modification in at least two respects. First, that the Hebrew word *yom* may need to be interpreted as an "indefinite time participle" (not unlike the English word "while"), signifying an indeterminate period of time which is given specificity by its context. In other words, the word "day" in the Genesis creation accounts is to be interpreted as a long period of time, not a specific period of 24 hours. Second, that there may be a large gap between Genesis 1.1 and Genesis 1.2. In other words, the narrative is not understood to be continuous, but to make way for the intervention of a substantial period of time between the primordial act of creation of the universe, and the emergence of life on earth. This viewpoint is advocated by the famous *Schofield Reference Bible*, first published in 1909, although the ideas can be traced back to writers such as the earlier nineteenth-century Scottish divine Thomas Chalmers.

Intelligent design

This movement, which has gained considerable influence in the United States in recent years, argues that the biosphere is possessed of an "irreducible complexity" which makes it impossible to explain its origins and development in any other method other than positing intelligent design. Intelligent design does not deny biological evolution; its most fundamental criticism of Darwinism is teleological – that evolution has no goal. The Intelligent Design movement argues that standard Darwinism runs into significant explanatory difficulties, which can only be adequately resolved through the intentional creation of individual species. Its critics argue that these difficulties are overstated, or that they will in due course be resolved by future theoretical advances. Although the movement avoids direct identification of God with this intelligent designer (presumably for political reasons), it is clear that this assumption is intrinsic to its working methods. The movement is particularly associated with Michael Behe, author of *Darwin's Black Box* (1996), and William Dembski, author of *Intelligent Design: The Bridge Between Science and Theology* (1999). Both Dembski and Behe are fellows of the Discovery Institute, a Seattle research institute.

Evolutionary theism

A final approach argues that evolution is to be understood as God's chosen method of bringing life into existence from inorganic materials, and creating complexity within life. Whereas Darwinism gives a significant place to random events in the evolutionary process, evolutionary theism sees the process as divinely directed. Some evolutionary theists propose that each level of complexity is to be explained on the basis of "God working within the system," perhaps at the quantum level. Others, such as Howard van Till, adopt a "fully-gifted creation" perspective, arguing that God built in the potential for the emergence and complexity of life in the initial act of creation, so that further acts of divine intervention are not required. Van Till argues that the character of divine creative action is not best expressed in terms of "reference to occasional interventions in which a new form is imposed on raw materials that are incapable of attaining that form with their own capabilities," but rather by reference to "God's giving being to a creation fully equipped with the creaturely capabilities to organize and/or transform itself into a diversity of physical structures and life-forms." Variations on such approaches are found elsewhere, as in the writings of Arthur Peacocke (born 1924).

How should we evaluate these positions, and their underlying religious and scientific concerns? Perhaps the most important point to make is simply this: the natural sciences, including the various Darwinian paradigms, are patient of atheist, theist, and agnostic interpretations and accommodations – but demand and necessitate none of them. Darwinism can be "spun" in ways that are seemingly totally consistent and seemingly totally opposed to Christian belief. Both "Darwinism" and "Christianity" designate a spectrum of possibilities, making determining their conceptual overlaps and tensions problematic, and critically dependent on definitional issues. Perhaps one of the more interesting paradoxes of the contemporary religious scene is that, for precisely these reasons, Darwinism has been prematurely and unnecessarily branded as "atheist" on the left by writers such as Richard Dawkins, and on the right by various American creationist individuals and organizations.

As Benjamin B. Warfield uncontroversially pointed out, serious issues of biblical interpretation often underlie such controversies. Perhaps somewhat more controversially, but almost certainly correctly, Warfield also observed that scientific advance offered a means by which the church could "check out" its interpretation of the Bible, avoiding being locked into an arcane or archaic biblical interpretation which, by force of tradition, was assumed to be the self-evident meaning of the Bible itself. It is for this reason that Darwinism has proved to be especially controversial within the conservative American Protestant constituency, whose general approach to biblical interpretation is often based on the seemingly straightforward (but actually nuanced and complex) notion of the "plain sense of Scripture." (Similar issues arise within the Islamic constituency concerning the interpretation of the *Qu'ran*). For precisely the same reason, Darwinism has proved much more acceptable to Roman Catholic writers, on account of the notion of the magisterial interpretation of an occasionally opaque Scripture.

Yet one point must be made in closing. When all is said and done, Darwinism is a scientific theory, provisional in its status and open to modification, correction, development, or even ultimate abandonment as the process of scientific advance continues. It may be the received scientific wisdom of our age; no study of the history of science would be unwise enough to suggest that it is necessarily, and possibly uniquely, immune to the process of radical theory change that has characterized scientific advance in the past. So what will this debate look like in a century? Will we have moved on, scientifically and theologically? I am no prophet, and have no answers on this. It would, however, be extremely unwise to suppose that the present age has settled, or even begun to settle, the question of the relation of religious faith to the scientific exploration of the biological origins of life.

The present chapter has briefly surveyed a vast amount of material relating to the Christian understandings of human nature, sin, and grace. Only a fraction of the debates within the Christian tradition have been explored. Nevertheless, central landmarks have been identified, which remain of decisive importance to the continuing debates within Christianity on such issues.

QUESTIONS FOR CHAPTER 14

1 Give a concise summary of the main issues at stake in the Pelagian controversy.
2 Why did Augustine believe in original sin?
3 Imagine that you are explaining the idea of "grace" to a nontheologian with a limited attention span. What could you say about the idea in 200 words or less?
4 Martin Luther is associated with the doctrine of "justification by faith alone." What did he mean by this? And what were the alternatives he rejected?
5 "If you aren't predestined, then go and get yourself predestined." How does this Calvinist attitude relate to Weber's thesis concerning the origins of capitalism?
6 Why was Darwinism such a powerful challenge to traditional Christian belief? And how has Christian theology responded to this challenge?

15

The Doctrine of the Church

The area of Christian theology which deals with the doctrine of the church is usually referred to as *ecclesiology* (Greek: *ekklēsia*, "church"), and is of major importance to anyone proposing to engage in pastoral ministry of any kind. Ecclesiological questions break into ministry at point after point. What sort of body is the church? How does this understanding of what the church is affect what the church is meant to do? Ecclesiology is that area of theology which seeks to give theoretical justification to an institution which has undergone development and change down the centuries, set against an altering social and political context.

Yet it is important to appreciate that the church existed as an institution, as a historical reality, before Christians began to reflect seriously and systematically about what kind of institution the church was mean to be. Theoretical reflection on the identity and calling of the church follow on from the existence of the church as a community of faith. To study Christian understandings of the church is to gain insights into the way in which institutions adapt in order to develop and to survive. The present chapter aims to explore some of the issues which arise from this remarkable history of development down the ages.

Biblical Models of the Church

Any attempt to study the development of Christian theories of the church must begin with the origins of the community of faith, described in the Bible, as well as the emerging understandings of the nature and identity of that community. The church has always stressed its historical and theological continuity with the people of Israel; for this reason, we must begin our exploration with the Old Testament.

The Old Testament

How did Israel understand its identity, and how were these maintained by its institutions? The noted American Old Testament scholar Walter Brueggemann argues that three distinct phases can be seen in Israel's development of its sense of identity and purpose as a people. In an article titled "Rethinking Church Models Through Scripture," in *Theology Today* 48 (1991), Brueggemann distinguishes three phases in Israel's self-understanding, reflecting the different situations in which it found itself.

The first phase of its existence lasted until the founding of the monarchy under Saul (c.1250–1000 BC). During this period, Israel existed without a temple, priests, sages, or prophets. Its identity as a people was not defined by institutions, but by "a common commitment to Israel's central story."

The second phase pertained from 1000 to 587 BC. During this long period, which ends with the Babylonian captivity of the people of Jerusalem, Israel was governed by a monarchy. Brueggemann points to four features which ensured that Israel was able to maintain and consolidate its identity:

1   The temple and its priests provided legitimate and stable leadership over an extended period.
2   The kings provided essentially secular leadership of the nation, while at the same time being committed to the same religious ideas and values as the temple and its priests.
3   The Book of Proverbs bears witness to a group of "sages," corresponding to the western notion of an "intelligentsia," who provided intellectual legitimacy to the nation.
4   During this period, the prophets represented a means of divine guidance at points of particular difficulty or turbulence.

Brueggemann finds a third model arising after the return of the inhabitants of Jerusalem from their exile in Babylon. In this "postexilic" or "second temple" period, Israel was a much smaller nation, faced with serious problems in maintaining its identity in the face of occupation, initially by the Persians, and subsequently by the Greeks. Faced with the erosion of its distinctive identity in the face of these "universalizing cultures," Israel sought to find its identity through links with the past. Brueggemann emphasizes the importance of texts during this era, as these provided a means by which the "threatened present generation" could connect up with "the horizon of reference points from the past."

The New Testament

The New Testament stresses the continuity between Israel and the Christian church, and offers a series of models for understanding the theological identity of the church. In what follows, we shall note five of these models.

1   *The church as the people of God*: This image emphasizes the continuity of the church with Israel, sharing the covenant promises made to Abraham. It is thus especially important for Paul that Christians are seen to share the same faith as Abraham (Romans 4: 1–16; Galatians 3: 6–18). The church has been chosen or called to be the people of God, just as God called Israel in the past. "You are a chosen race, a royal priesthood, a holy nation, God's own people, in order that you may proclaim the mighty acts of him who called you out of darkness into his marvelous light" (1 Peter 2: 9).
2   *The church as a community of salvation*: This image emphasizes that the church is called into being, both in response to God's work of salvation, and also as a means of proclaiming and extending that work to the world. This theme is evident in the evangelistic imperatives within the New Testament, which speak of the church as the body which is called to bear witness as the "salt of the earth" and the "light of the world" (Matthew 5: 13–16), charged with the responsibility of going out to "make disciples of all nations" (Matthew 28: 19).
3   *The church as the body of Christ*: This imagery is found particularly in the Pauline letters (see especially 1 Corinthians 12: 12–31). The faith of the individual believer and baptism (Romans 6: 3–5) are understood

to secure incorporation into the body of Christ. This corporate understanding of the church is also reinforced by other types of imagery in the New Testament, such as the Johannine image of the believer being attached or connected to Jesus Christ as the "true vine" (John 15: 5).

4   *The church as a servant people*: Once more, this image emphasizes the continuity between the old and new covenants. God chose and called Israel to serve him; in the same way, God chose and called the church for service. This theme is reflected in the terminology of the early church for its leaders. The two main Greek words for church leaders are *doulos* ("servant," or possibly even "slave") and *diakonos* ("someone who waits at a table"). Paul brought this theme to sharp focus when he told the Corinthian Christians that he and his companions "proclaim Jesus Christ as Lord and ourselves as your slaves for Jesus' sake" (2 Corinthians 4: 5).

5   *The church as the community of the Spirit*: The early history of the church, as related in the Acts of the Apostles, stresses the presence and activity of the Holy Spirit within the church. The presence of the Spirit enables the church to witness and to grow. For Paul, the Spirit is not merely a theological resource, useful in ministry. Its presence within the church is a sign of the coming of God's new age, and the distinctive role that the church must play in bringing about the kingdom of God on earth. The Spirit is to be seen as a "seal" of the individual's redemption and the church's mission (Ephesians 4: 30).

These, then, are some of the models of the church found in the New Testament. Yet they are not fully developed. The task of enlarging the Christian vision of the identity of the church was bequeathed to their successors by the New Testament writers. In what follows, we shall explore some of the ways in which they did this.

The Early Development of Ecclesiology

Ecclesiology was not a major issue in the early church. The eastern church showed no awareness of the potential importance of the issue. Most Greek patristic writers of the first five centuries contented themselves with describing the church using recognizably scriptural images, without choosing to probe further. Thus Isidore of Pelusium defined the church as "the assembly of saints joined together by correct faith and an excellent manner of life." The following elements can be discerned as having achieved a wide consensus at the time:

1   The church is a spiritual society, which replaces Israel as the people of God in the world.
2   All Christians are made one in Christ, despite their different origins and backgrounds.
3   The church is the repository of true Christian teaching.
4   The church gathers the faithful throughout the world together, in order to enable them to grow in faith and holiness.

In part, this lack of interest in developing the doctrine of the church reflected the political situation of the time. The church was at best a barely tolerated, and at worst a vigorously persecuted, organization within the sphere of authority of a hostile pagan state – namely, the Roman Empire.

With the conversion of Constantine, the situation changed radically. Increasingly, theologians began to draw parallels between the Roman Empire and the Christian church – whether negatively (as with Hippolytus of Rome, who saw the empire as a satanic imitation of the church), or positively (as with Eusebius, who saw the empire as a divinely ordained institution, charged with the task of preparing the world for the coming of the kingdom of Christ).

One practical issue led to increased reflection on an ecclesiological issue. At an early stage, rivalry developed between the leaders of the churches, especially those at Rome and Constantinople. A number of centers were held in particular esteem during the first four centuries, of which Alexandria, Antioch, Constantinople, Jerusalem, and Rome were of notable importance. However, by the end of the fourth century it was becoming increasingly clear that Rome, as the center of the Roman Empire, had acquired a position of especial prominence. The term "pope," from the Latin *papa*, "father," was initially used of any Christian bishop; gradually, the term came to be used more often of the most important bishop in the church – the Bishop of Rome. From 1073 the title was reserved exclusively for the Bishop of Rome. The question therefore began to arise: what authority does the Bishop of Rome have outside his own diocese?

In practical terms, the answer was quite simple: a lot. The Bishop of Rome (we shall use the term "pope" from now on, despite the slight anachronism this involves) was often called upon to arbitrate in church disputes of various kinds, throughout the entire Mediterranean. When Nestorius and Cyril of Jerusalem became embroiled in endless Christological debates in the fifth century, and it became clear that no resolution was in sight, they each hastened to Rome to gain papal support.

But did this priority rest upon any theological foundation? The eastern churches had no hesitation in declaring that it did not.

Others, however, were not so sure. The pope was the successor to St Peter, who had been martyred at Rome. In view of the apparent "primacy of Peter" in the New Testament (Matthew 16: 18), did this not give the successors of Peter authority over others? It seemed to many, even within the eastern churches, that, in some inscrutable manner, the spiritual authority of Peter had been transmitted to his successors as bishops of Rome. Cyprian of Carthage is an example of a western writer who is a vigorous defender of the primacy of the Roman see throughout the Christian world. This question would become of renewed importance at a number of junctures in church history, of which the Reformation is a particularly obvious instance.

The Donatist Controversy

In the end, it was the western church that forced the pace of theological reflection on the nature and identity of the church. It seems to be a general rule of the development of Christian doctrine that development is occasioned by controversy. A stimulus seems to have been required to provoke sustained theological reflection. In the case of ecclesiology, that stimulus was provided by a controversy centering upon Roman north Africa, which has passed into history as "the Donatist controversy."

Under the Roman emperor Diocletian (284–313) the Christian church was subject to various degrees of persecution. The origins of the persecution date from 303; it finally ended with the conversion of Constantine, and the issuing of the Edict of Milan in 313. Under an edict of February 303, Christian books were ordered to be burned and churches demolished. Those Christian leaders who handed over their books to be burned came to be known as *traditores* – "those who handed over [their books]." The modern word "traitor" derives from the same root. One such *traditor* was Felix of Aptunga, who later consecrated Caecilian as Bishop of Carthage in 311.

Many local Christians were outraged that such a person should have been allowed to be involved in this consecration, and declared that they could not accept the authority of Caecilian as a result. The new bishop's authority was compromised, it was argued, on account of the fact that the bishop who had consecrated him had lapsed under the pressure of persecution. The hierarchy of the Catholic church was thus tainted as a result of this development. The church ought to be pure, and should not be permitted to include such people.

By the time Augustine returned to Africa in 388, a breakaway faction had established itself as the leading Christian body in the region, with especially strong support from the local African population. Sociological issues clouded theological debate; the Donatists (see p. 24), named after the breakaway African church leader Donatus (c.311–c.355), tended to draw their support from the indigenous population, whereas the Catholics drew theirs from Roman colonists.

The theological issues involved are of considerable importance, and relate directly to a serious tension within the theology of a leading figure of the African church in the third century – Cyprian of Carthage. In his *Unity of the Catholic Church* (251), Cyprian had defended two major related beliefs. First, schism is totally and absolutely unjustified. The unity of the church cannot be broken, on any pretext whatsoever. To step outside the bounds of the church is to forfeit any possibility of salvation. Second, it therefore follows that lapsed or schismatic bishops are deprived of all ability to administer the sacraments or act as a minister of the Christian church. By passing outside the sphere of the church, they have lost

their spiritual gifts and authority. They should therefore not be permitted to ordain priests or bishops. Any whom they have ordained must be regarded as invalidly ordained; any whom they have baptized must be regarded as invalidly baptized.

But what happens if a bishop lapses under persecution, and subsequently repents? Cyprian's theory is profoundly ambiguous, and is open to two lines of interpretation.

1 By lapsing, the bishop has committed the sin of apostasy (literally, "falling away"). He has therefore placed himself outside the bounds of the church, and can no longer be regarded as administering the sacraments validly.

2 By his repentance, the bishop has been restored to grace, and is able to continue administering the sacraments validly.

The Donatists adopted the first such position, the Catholics (as their opponents came to be universally known) the second.

The Donatists believed that the entire sacramental system of the Catholic church had become corrupted. How could the sacraments be validly administered by people who were tainted in this way? (We shall return to this point in the following chapter, when we consider the Donatist understanding of sacramental efficacy.) It was therefore necessary to replace *traditores* with people who had remained firm in their faith under persecution. It was also necessary to rebaptize and reordain all those who had been baptized and ordained by *traditores*. Inevitably, this resulted in the formation of a breakaway faction. By the time Augustine returned to Africa, the breakaway faction was larger than the church from which it had originally broken away.

Yet Cyprian had totally forbidden schism of any kind. One of the greatest paradoxes of the Donatist schism is that it resulted from principles which were due to Cyprian – yet contradicted those very same principles. As a result, both Donatists and Catholics appealed to Cyprian as an authority, but to very different aspects of his teaching. The Donatists stressed the outrageous character of apostasy; the Catholics equally emphasized the impossibility of schism. A stalemate resulted, that is, until Augustine arrived and became Bishop of Hippo in the region. Augustine was able to resolve the tensions within the legacy of Cyprian, and put forward an "Augustinian" view of the church, which has remained enormously influential ever since.

First, Augustine emphasizes the *sinfulness of Christians*. The church is not meant to be a society of saints, but a "mixed body" (*corpus permixtum*) of saints and sinners. Augustine finds this image in two biblical parables: the parable of the net which catches many fishes, and the parable of the wheat and the tares. It is this latter parable (Matthew 13: 24–30) which is of especial importance, and requires further discussion.

The parable tells of a farmer who sowed seed, and discovered that the resulting crop included both wheat and tares – grain and weeds. What could be done about it? To attempt to separate the wheat and the weeds while both were still growing would be to court disaster, probably involving damaging the wheat while trying to get rid of the weeds. But at the harvest, all the plants – wheat and tares – are cut down and sorted out without any danger of damaging the wheat. The separation of the good and the evil thus takes place at the end of time, not in history.

For Augustine, this parable refers to the church in the world. It must expect to find itself including both saints and sinners. To attempt a separation in this world is premature and improper. That separation will take place in God's own time, at the end of history. No human can make that judgment or separation in God's place.

So in what sense is the church holy? For Augustine, the holiness in question is not that of its members, but of Christ. The church cannot be a congregation of saints in this world, in that its members are contaminated with original sin. However, the church is sanctified and made holy by Christ – a holiness which will be perfected and finally realized at the last judgment.

In addition to this theological analysis, Augustine makes the practical observation that the Donatists failed to live up to their own high standards of morality. The Donatists, Augustine suggests, were just as capable as Catholics of getting drunk or beating people up.

Second, Augustine argues that schism and *traditio* (the handing over of Christian books, or any form of lapse from faith) are indeed both sinful – but that, for Cyprian, schism is by far the more serious sin. The Donatists are thus guilty of serious misrepresentation of the teaching of the great north African martyrbishop.

On the basis of these considerations Augustine argues that Donatism is fatally flawed. The church is, and is meant to be, a mixed body. Sin is an inevitable aspect of the life of the church in the present age, and is neither the occasion nor the justification for schism. Yet precisely the schism which Augustine feared and detested so much would eventually come about in the sixteenth century, with the formation of breakaway Protestant churches in western Europe as a result of the Reformation. It is to these major developments that we now turn.

Early Protestant Doctrines of the Church

The sixteenth century was a period of crucial importance for reflection on the nature and identity of the Christian church. The reformers were convinced that the church of their day and age had lost sight of the doctrine of grace, which Luther regarded as the center of the Christian gospel. Thus Luther declared that his doctrine of justification by faith alone was the *articulus stantis et cadentis ecclesiae*, "the article by which the church stands or falls." Convinced that the Catholic Church had lost sight of this doctrine, he concluded (with some reluctance, it would seem) that it had lost its claim to be considered the authentic Christian church.

His Catholic opponents responded to this suggestion with derision: Luther was simply creating a breakaway faction which had no connection with the church. In other words, he was a schismatic – and had not Augustine himself condemned schism? Had not he placed enormous emphasis upon the unity of the church, which Luther now threatened to disrupt? Luther, it seemed, could only uphold Augustine's doctrine of grace by rejecting Augustine's doctrine of the church. It is in the context of this tension between two aspects of Augustine's thought, which proved to be incompatible in the sixteenth century, that the Reformation understandings of the nature of the church are to be seen.

In what follows, we shall consider early Protestant doctrines of the church, noting some of the most distinctive developments within both the mainline (or "magisterial") Reformation, and the smaller radical wing of the Reformation. We begin by considering the new lines of development found in the writings of Martin Luther.

Martin Luther

Luther's early views on the nature of the church reflect his emphasis on the Word of God: the Word of God goes forth conquering, and wherever it conquers and gains true obedience to God *is* the church.

Now, anywhere you hear or see [the Word of God] preached, believed, confessed, and acted upon, do not doubt that the true *ecclesia sancta catholica*, a "holy Christian people" must be there, even though there are very few of them. For God's word "shall not return empty" (Isaiah 55: 11), but must possess at least a fourth or a part of the field. And even if there were no other sign than this alone, it would be enough to prove that a holy Christian people must exist there, for God's word cannot be without God's people and conversely, God's people cannot be without God's word. For who would preach the word, or hear it preached, if there were no people of God? And what could or would God's people believe, if there were no word of God?

An episcopally ordained ministry is therefore not necessary to safeguard the existence of the church, whereas the preaching of the gospel is essential to the identity of that church. "Where the word is, there is faith; and where faith is, there is the true church." The visible church is constituted by the preaching of the Word of God: no human assembly may claim to be the "church of God" unless it is founded on this gospel. It is more important to preach the same gospel as the apostles than to be a member of an institution which is historically derived from them. A similar understanding of the church was shared by Philip Melanchthon, Luther's colleague at Wittenberg, who conceived of the church primarily in terms of its function of administering the means of grace.

But if the church was defined not in *institutional* terms, but by the preaching of the gospel, how could Luther distinguish his views from those of the radical reformers? Luther himself had conceded that "the church is holy even where the fanatics [Luther's term for the radicals] are dominant, so long as they do not deny the word and the sacraments." Luther asserted the need for an institutional church, declaring that the historical institution of the church is a divinely ordained means of grace. But in countering the radicals by asserting that the church was indeed visible and institutional, Luther found himself having difficulty in distinguishing his views from those of his Catholic opponents. Luther is thus obliged to assert that "the false church has only the appearance, although it also possesses the Christian offices." In other words, the medieval church may have *looked like* the real thing, but it was really something rather different.

It will thus be clear that there are certain difficulties and shortcomings associated with Luther's approach. In part, this may reflect the general belief within reforming circles during the 1520s that separation from the Catholic church was a temporary matter. What point was there in developing extensive theories of the church, to give legitimation to the breakaway evangelical factions, when reunion with a reformed Catholic church was only a matter of time? It was only in the 1540s, when such reunion was finally realized to be nothing more than a dream, that Protestant theologians began to give sustained attention to formulating distinctively Protestant doctrines of the church. John Calvin is perhaps the most significant such writer.

John Calvin

An event of major importance to the Reformation took place in 1541. The Colloquy of Ratisbon collapsed. This conference, held at Regensburg, represented a last-ditch attempt to reach a compromise between Catholics and Protestants, which would allow the latter to rejoin the church from which they had temporarily withdrawn. It must be stressed that the reformers initially regarded themselves as having removed themselves from the Catholic church only temporarily. There was a full expectation of a return, once the situation had improved. The failure of Regensburg put paid to that hope.

A new situation now developed. Up to 1541, there had been no real need for Protestant writers to develop theories of the church. Luther's early ecclesiology is actually a holding measure, designed to justify a temporary withdrawal from the church. It lacks rigor and conviction, precisely because Luther believed that there was no need to develop a full-blown theory of the church. After all, a return to the Catholic church was just around the corner. The second generation of reformers, among whom Calvin stands out as supreme, was faced with the challenge of developing a coherent and systematic ecclesiology, on the basis of the realization that separation from the main body of the Catholic church would continue indefinitely.

Calvin rose to this challenge, and offered what is widely regarded as the most sophisticated statement of a Protestant ecclesiology of the sixteenth century. For Calvin, the marks of the true church were:

1 that the Word of God should be preached, and
2 that the sacraments should be rightly administered.

Since the Roman Catholic Church did not, in Calvin's view, conform to this definition of the church, the evangelicals were perfectly justified in leaving it. And as the evangelical churches conformed to this definition of a church, there was no justification for further division within them. This point is of particular importance, reflecting Calvin's political judgment that further fragmentation of the evangelical congregations would be disastrous to the cause of the Reformation.

Calvin further argued that there were specific scriptural directions regarding the right order of ministry in the visible church, so that a specific form of ecclesiastical order now became an item of doctrine. In other words, he included a specific form of ecclesiastical administration (and he here borrows the term *administratio* from the field of secular government) in "the gospel purely preached."

Calvin's minimalist definition of the church now took on a new significance. The true church is indeed to be found where the gospel is rightly preached, and the sacraments rightly administered – and understood to be included within this definition is a specific form of ecclesiastical institution and administration. Calvin referred to the "order by which the Lord willed his church to be governed," and developed a detailed theory of church government based upon his exegesis of the New Testament, drawing extensively upon the terminology of the imperial Roman administration. Contrary to what the radicals asserted, Calvin insisted that a specific form of church structure and administration is laid down by Scripture. Thus Calvin held that the ministerial government of the church is divinely ordained, as are the distinctions between "minister," "elder," "deacon," and "people."

Calvin drew an important distinction between the *visible* and the *invisible* church. At one level, the church is the community of Christian believers, a visible group. It is also, however, the fellowship of saints and the company of the elect – an *invisible* entity. In its invisible aspect, the church is the invisible assembly of the elect, known only to God; in its visible aspect, it is the community of believers on earth. The former consists only of the elect; the latter includes both good and evil, elect and reprobate. The former is an object of faith and hope, the latter of present experience. The distinction between them is eschatological: the invisible church is the church which will come into being at the end of time, as God ushers in the final judgment of humanity. Calvin stresses that all believers are obliged to honor and to remain committed to the visible church, despite its weaknesses, on account of the invisible church, the true body of Christ. Despite this, there is only one church, a single entity with Jesus Christ as its head.

The distinction between the visible and invisible churches has two important consequences. In the first place, it is to be expected that the visible church will include both the elect and the reprobate. Augustine of Hippo had made this point against the Donatists, using the parable of the wheat and the tares (Matthew 13: 24–30) as his basis. It lies beyond human competence to discern their difference, correlating human qualities with divine favor (in any case, Calvin's doctrine of predestination precludes such grounds of election).

In the second place, however, it is necessary to ask which of the various visible churches corresponds to the invisible church. Calvin thus recognizes the need to articulate objective criteria by which the authenticity of a given church may be judged. Two such criteria are stipulated: "Wherever we see the Word of God preached purely and listened to, and the sacraments administered according to the institution of Christ, we cannot doubt that a church exists." It is thus not the quality of its members, but the presence of the authorized means of grace, which constitutes a true church. Interestingly, Calvin does not follow the example of Martin Bucer – the Strasbourg reformer from whom he learned so much – in making *discipline* a mark of the true church; although passionately concerned with the need for charitable discipline of church members, Calvin did not regard this as essential to the definition or evaluation of the credentials of a church.

Calvin is also of importance in relation to another aspect of the doctrine of the church. Having defined the nature of the church, Calvin proceeds to explore its importance. Why is there any need for a church – understood, that is, as an institution, rather than a building – in the first place? Just as God redeemed human beings within the historical process through the incarnation, so God sanctifies them within that same process by founding an institution dedicated to that goal. God uses certain definite earthly means to work out the salvation of the elect. The church is thus identified as a divinely founded body, within which God effects the sanctification of the elect. Calvin expresses this idea as follows:

> I shall begin then, with the church, into the bosom of which God is pleased to gather his children, not only so that they may be nourished by her assistance and ministry while they are infants and children, but also so that they may be guided by her motherly care until they mature and reach the goal of faith. "For what God has joined together, no one shall divide" (Mark 10: 9). For those to whom God is Father, the church shall also be their mother.

Calvin confirms this high doctrine of the church by citing the two great ecclesiological maxims of Cyprian of Carthage: "You cannot have God as your father unless you have the church for your mother," and "Outside the church there is no hope of remission of sins nor any salvation" (see pp. 354–5).

Calvin's doctrine of the church reminds us that it is seriously inadequate to portray the reformers as rampant radical individualists, with no place for corporate conceptions of the Christian life. The image of the "church as mother" (which Calvin gladly borrows from Cyprian of Carthage) underscores the corporate dimensions of Christian faith:

> Let us learn from this simple word "mother" how useful (indeed, how necessary) it is to know her. There is no other way to life, unless this mother conceives us in her womb, nourishes us at her breast, and keeps us under her care and guidance.

Powerful theological imagery nestles within this way of speaking, above all that of the Word of God which conceives us within the womb of the church. But it is the practical aspects of this way of thinking about the church which command our attention at this point. The institution of the church is a necessary, helpful, God-given, and God-ordained means of spiritual growth and development. The contrast with the radical Reformation, to which we now turn, will be clear.

The radical Reformation

For the radicals, such as Sebastian Franck and Menno Simons, the apostolic church had been totally compromised through its close links with the state, dating back to the conversion of the Emperor Constantine. As an institution, the church was corrupted by human power struggles and ambition. Franck wrote thus:

> I believe that the outward Church of Christ, including all its gifts and sacraments, because of the breaking in and laying waste by antichrist right after the death of the Apostles, went up into heaven, and lies concealed in the Spirit and in truth. I am thus quite certain that for fourteen hundred years now there has existed no gathered Church nor any sacrament.

The true church was in heaven, and its institutional parodies were on earth. The radical emphasis upon the need for the church to become separated from secular society is especially clear in its attitudes to authority, especially the authority of the magistracy. The radical Reformation conceived of the church as an "alternative society" within the mainstream of sixteenth-century European culture. Just as the pre-Constantinian church existed within the Roman Empire, yet refused to conform to its standards, so the radical Reformation envisaged itself existing parallel to, but not within, its sixteenth-century environment. For Menno Simons, the church was "an assembly of the righteous," at odds with the world, and not a "mixed body":

> In truth, those who merely boast of his name are not the true congregation of Christ. The true congregation of Christ is those who are truly converted, who are born from above of God, who are of a regenerate mind by the operation of the Holy Spirit through the hearing of the Word of God, and have become the children of God.

It will be clear that there are strong parallels with the Donatist view of the church as a holy and pure body (see pp. 394–6), isolated from the corrupting influences of the world, and prepared to maintain its purity and distinctiveness by whatever disciplinary means proved necessary.

This notion of the church as a faithful remnant in conflict with the world harmonized with the Anabaptist experience of persecution by the forces of Antichrist, personified in the magistrates. The radical Reformation was generally hostile to the use of coercion, and advocated a policy of nonresistance. Jakob Hutter gave this apolitical stance a theological justification through an appeal to the example of Christ: "As all can see, we have no physical weapons, such as spears or muskets. We wish to show, by our words and deeds, that we are true followers of Christ." Hans Denck appealed to the meekness of Christ, and his silence before his accusers, in declaring that "force is not an attribute of God."

The clearest statement of the general Anabaptist attitude toward secular authority may be found in the Schleitheim Confession (1527), the sixth and seventh articles of which explain and justify the policy of noninvolvement in secular affairs and nonresistance to secular authorities. Coercion has its place "outside the perfection of Christ" (that is, outside the radical community); inside that community, physical force has no place.

> The sword is ordained of God outside the perfection of Christ. [. . .] It is not appropriate for a Christian to serve as a magistrate, for the following reasons. The government magistracy is according to the flesh, but the Christian's is according to the Spirit. Their houses and dwelling places are in this world, but the Christian's is in heaven; their citizenship is of this world, but the Christian's is in heaven; the weapons of their war and conflict are physical, and against the flesh, whereas the Christian's weapons are spiritual, against the fortification of the devil. The worldlings are armed with steel and iron, but the Christian is armed with the armor of God, with truth, righteousness, peace, faith, salvation, and the word of God.

Anabaptism maintained discipline within its communities through "the ban" – a means by which church members could be excluded from Anabaptist congregations. This means of discipline was regarded as essential to the identity of a true church. Part of the Anabaptist case for radical separation from the mainstream churches (a practice which continues to this day among the Amish of Lancaster County, Pennsylvania) was the failure of those churches to maintain proper discipline within their ranks. The Schleitheim Confession grounded its doctrine of the ban on Christ's words, as they are recorded in Matthew 18: 15–20:

> The ban shall be used in the case of all those who have given themselves to the Lord, to walk in his commandments, and with all those who are baptized into the one body of Christ and are called brothers or sisters, yet who lapse on occasion, and inadvertently fall into error and sin. Such people shall be admonished twice in secret, and on the third

occasion, they shall be disciplined publicly, or banned according to the command of Christ (Matthew 18).

The ban was seen as being both deterrent and remedial in its effects, providing both an incentive for banned individuals to amend their way of life and a disincentive for others to imitate them in their sin. The Polish Racovian Catechism lists five reasons for maintaining rigorous discipline within Anabaptist communities, most of which reflect its policy of radical separation:

1 So that the fallen church member may be healed, and brought back into fellowship with the church.
2 To deter others from committing the same offense.
3 To eliminate scandal and disorder from the church.
4 To prevent the word of the Lord falling into disrepute outside the congregation.
5 To prevent the glory of the Lord being profaned.

Despite its pastoral intentions, the ban often came to be interpreted harshly, with congregation members often avoiding all social contact (known as "shunning") with both the banned individual and his or her family.

Christ and the Church: Some Twentieth-century Themes

The twentieth century has seen renewed interest in the area of ecclesiology, partly on account of the rise of the ecumenical movement (concerned with the promotion of Christian unity), and partly through the enormous stimulus given to this area of theology through the process of renewal and reform initiated by the Second Vatican Council (1962–5), especially the constitution *Lumen Gentium* ("A Light to the Gentiles" – note that authoritative Roman Catholic conciliar and papal statements are generally referred to by their opening words in Latin). We shall consider the teaching of this Council presently.

A convenient means of grouping together some themes in twentieth-century ecclesiology is to consider the maxim of the first-century writer Ignatius of Antioch, who declared that "where Christ is, there is also the catholic church." This memorable aphorism has had a deep impact on ecclesiological reflection – whether Protestant, Catholic, or Orthodox – throughout Christian history. In what follows, we shall explore three different twentieth-century ways of approaching this aphorism.

Christ is present sacramentally

One of the most distinctive contributions of the Second Vatican Council to the development of ecclesiology is its assertion of the sacramental character of the church. As *Lumen Gentium* puts it, "the church, in Christ, is a kind of sacrament – a sign and instrument, that is, of communion with God and of unity among all human beings." The Council did not suggest that the church *is* a sacrament; the traditional sevenfold understanding of the sacraments (see pp. 421–3) is retained. Rather, the church is "like a sacrament [*veluti sacramentum*]." In making this statement, the Council seems to have been attempting to bring together the idea of the church as constituted by the word of God on the one hand, and as being a visible entity on the other. This idea is certainly present in Augustine's concept of sacraments as "visible words."

The idea of the church as sacrament has had a major impact on Catholic ecclesiology in the twentieth century. Even before the Second Vatican Council, such ideas were gaining momentum within the church. In part, this reflects the rise of a "theology of retrieval," which sought to reappropriate a series of seminal themes from earlier periods in Christian history, most notably the patristic period, which adopted understandings of the nature of the church which contrasted sharply with the more institutional conceptions which had gained the ascendancy since the sixteenth century.

This view can be seen clearly in the writings of Henri de Lubac (1896–1991), a pre-Second Vatican Council theologian noted for his magisterial grasp of the patristic heritage. In his important work *Catholicism*, he wrote:

> If Christ is the sacrament of God, the church is for us the sacrament of Christ; she represents him, in the full and ancient sense of the term, she really makes him present. She not only carries on his work, but she is his very continuation, in a sense far more real than in which it can be said that any human institution is its founder's continuation.

Although retaining an institutional understanding of the church, de Lubac gave a new sense of identity and purpose to Catholic conceptions of the church: the church is there to make Jesus Christ present to the world. Ignatius's aphorism is therefore given new significance through this sacramental understanding of the role of the church.

The idea caught on. In 1953, the German Jesuit theologian Otto Semmelroth (1912–79) published a highly influential study entitled *The Church as Primordial Sacrament*, in which he argued for the church as being the "primordial sacrament" (*Ursakrament*), demonstrating God's ability to use the material order to bear witness to the spiritual. The Dominican theologian Edward Schillebeeckx (born 1914) developed related ideas in his *Christ, The Sacrament of the Encounter with God* (1963). The overall effect of this approach is to integrate the fields of Christology, ecclesiology, and sacramentology into a coherent whole. Hans Urs von Balthasar adopts a strongly incarnational approach to his understanding of the church, arguing that the church is the *elongetur Christi* – the prolongation of Christ in time and space. The Jesuit writer Karl Rahner continues this sacramental understanding of the church, declaring that the church is there to make Christ present in the world, in an historical, visible, and embodied form.

Rahner's approach has attracted considerable interest. For Rahner, the church "is the continuance, the contemporary presence of that real, eschatologically triumphant and irrevocably established presence in Christ in the world of God's saving will." The church is thus a "concrete manifestation of God's salvation of humanity," the enduring presence of God in the world (an idea anticipated in the sixteenth century in the writings of the Spanish mystic Teresa of Avila). And, on account of its real historical presence in the world, it follows that it requires structures.

For this reason, Rahner is able to justify a continuing institutional element in any Catholic understanding of the nature of the church, while at the same time insisting that these particular structures are not necessarily of *defining* importance. Furthermore, Rahner is prepared to concede a degree of flexibility in relation to those structures. What may have been appropriate to the definite historical circumstances of the past may not be appropriate today. The church must be free to achieve its sacramental mission in new historical structures.

Schillebeeckx differs from Rahner at some points of importance, most notably in his rejection of Rahner's argument that the church is the "primal sacrament" (an idea, as we noted above, which can be traced back to Otto Semmelroth). For Schillebeeckx, Christ must be regarded as that primal sacrament; whatever sacramental character the church possesses must be understood to arise through its relation with Christ.

Protestant critics of this approach have expressed anxiety about the relative lack of biblical foundation for the approach, and its relative lack of place for a theology of preaching. In view of the importance of this point, we may move on to consider more Protestant interpretations of Ignatius's axiom, which focus on the presence of Christ resulting from the preaching of the word of God.

Christ is present through the word

A central theme of Protestant understanding of the nature of the church focuses on the presence of Christ resulting from the proclamation of his word, in preaching and the sacraments. For example, consider Calvin's statement on the nature of the church:

> Wherever we see the Word of God purely preached and listened to, and the sacraments administered according to Christ's institution, it is in no way to be doubted that a church of God exists. For his promise cannot fail: "Wherever two or three are gathered in my name, there I am in the midst of them" (Matthew 18: 20). [. . .] If the ministry has the Word and honors it, if it has the administration of the sacraments, it deserves without doubt to be held and considered a church.

For Calvin, the preaching of the word and right administration of the sacrament are linked with the presence of Christ – and wherever Christ is, there his church is to be found as well.

This kerygmatic (Greek *kerygma* = "herald") theme has continued to be of major importance in the twentieth century, particularly in the writings of Karl Barth. For Barth, the church is the community which comes into being in response to the proclamation of the word of God. The church is seen as a kerygmatic community which proclaims the good news of what God has done for humanity in Christ, and which comes into being wherever the word of God is faithfully proclaimed and accepted. As Barth put it in his 1948 address to the World Council of Churches, the church consists of "the gathering together [*congregatio*] of those men and women [*fidelium*] whom the living Lord Jesus Christ chooses and calls to be witnesses of the victory he has already won, and heralds of its future manifestation." Barth's ecclesiology is thoroughly trinitarian at this point, involving Father, Son, and Spirit in a dynamic understanding of the nature of the church. For Barth, the church is not an extension of Christ, but is united with Christ, and called and commissioned by him to serve the world. Christ is present within his church, through the Holy Spirit.

The role of the Holy Spirit is particularly important. Although it would not be correct to say that Barth has a "charismatic" understanding of the church, his Christological approach to the identity of the church allocates a definite and distinctive role to the Holy Spirit, which Barth summarized as follows in his *Dogmatics in Outline*:

> *Credo ecclesiam* ["I believe in the church"] means that I believe that here, at this place, in this assembly, the work of the Holy Spirit takes place. By that is not intended a deification of the creature; the church is not the object of faith, we do not believe *in* the church; but we do believe that in this congregation the work of the Holy Spirit becomes an event.

The church is thus seen as an event, not an institution. Barth does not identify the Holy Spirit with the church, nor limit the operation of the Spirit to the bounds of the institution of the church. He argues that the Spirit empowers and renews the church, unites it with Christ's redemptive work on the cross, and is the means by which the risen Christ is made present to the people of God. In this way, the Spirit safeguards the church from lapsing into purely secular ways of understanding its identity and mission.

Rudolf Bultmann also adopts a strongly kerygmatic approach to the nature of the church, linking Barth's emphasis on the foundational role of "proclamation" with the notion of "church as event":

> The word of God and the church are inseparable. The church is constituted by the word of God as the congregation of the elect, and the word of God is not a statement of abstract truths, but a proclamation which is duly authorized and therefore needs bearers with proper credentials (2 Corinthians 5: 18–19). Just as the word of God becomes his word only in event, so the church is really the church only when it too becomes an event.

Christ is present through the Spirit

A third major theme in twentieth-century ecclesiology has focused on the role of the Holy Spirit as constitutive of the church. Here, Ignatius's aphorism is interpreted in such a way as to emphasize the necessity of the Spirit in actualizing the presence of Christ. We have already seen the importance of this point in relation to Barth's ecclesiology; however, it is present in more developed forms in writers such as the liberation theologian Leonardo Boff and the Orthodox theologian John Zizioulas (born 1930). These two writers interpret their pneumatological (Greek: *pneuma* = "spirit") understanding of the church in a different way. Boff remains Christ-centered, despite his emphasis on the Spirit, on account of his strongly western understanding of the Trinity; Zizioulas develops a much more Ortho-

dox approach, based on a Cappadocian understanding of the role of the Spirit within the Godhead.

For the Brazilian Roman Catholic theologian Leonardo Boff (born 1938), one of the leading representatives of liberation theology, the constitutive role of the Holy Spirit in an understanding of the church rests on the fact that it is the Spirit of Jesus Christ. Whereas writers such as Rahner and von Balthasar had defended the view that the church was the physical embodiment or "re-presentation" of Christ in the world, Boff defends the view that the church is primarily the spiritual body of Christ, and is therefore not confined to any specific existing structures. In this respect, Boff can be seen as mounting a criticism of institutionalized understandings of the church, particularly those that flourished before the Second Vatican Council.

In his *Ecclesiogenesis: The Base Communities Reinvent the Church*, Boff provides a definition of the church which shows some parallels with kerygmatic understandings of the church:

> The church comes into being as church when people become aware of the call to salvation in Jesus Christ, come together in community, profess the same faith, celebrate the same eschatological liberation, and seek to live the discipleship of Jesus Christ. We can speak of church *in the proper sense* only when there is question of this ecclesial consciousness.

For Boff, this "ecclesial consciousness" is the result of the work of the Holy Spirit, whose person and work are inseparable from the risen Christ. Boff interprets the credal doctrine of the procession of the Holy Spirit from the Father *and the Son* as an affirmation of this point.

In the case of Zizioulas, however, the Holy Spirit is allocated a quite distinct role. Zizioulas points out how, especially in 1 Corinthians 12,

Paul appears to allocate a constitutive role within the church to the Holy Spirit. Pneumatology is therefore not about "the well-being of the church [...] it is the very essence of the church." Zizioulas's distinctive approach could be summarized as follows: the church may have been *instituted by Jesus Christ*, but it is *constituted by the Holy Spirit.*

The Second Vatican Council on the Church

The Second Vatican Council introduced a new vitality into the discussion of the doctrine of the church, partly through its reappropriation of biblical imagery relating to the church. Prior to the Council, Roman Catholic writers tended to think of the church in terms of a "perfect society." This style of imagery dates from the later part of the sixteenth century, and emphasized the institutional credentials of the church, especially in the light of the increasing power of European nation-states. Part of the church's strategy for asserting its independence from the increasing power of the state was to affirm its own identity as a society.

This approach can be seen particularly clearly in the writings of Roberto Bellarmine, one of the most important writers of the Catholic Reformation, who argued that the church was as visible and tangible a social reality as "the kingdom of France or the republic of Venice." This institutional approach to the church dominated Catholic thinking for much of the late nineteenth and early twentieth century. Thus the standard edition of the theological textbook of Adolphe Tanquerey (1854–1932) spends some 64 pages demonstrating that the church is (1) an infallible society, (2) a perfect society, (3) a hierarchical society, and (4) a monarchic society. Inevitably, this strongly institutional approach to ecclesiology led to the church being defined primarily in terms of its visible aspects, and particularly its visible structures of government and its codes of belief and conduct. The church was, in effect, modeled on social institutions of the late sixteenth century.

Now we need to be clear that there has always been an institutional aspect to Christian doctrines of the church, whether Protestant or Catholic. Thus both Luther and Calvin stressed the importance of proper church government. But neither of these reformers regarded the institutional element as being of *defining* importance. The critical thing was the gospel, not the institution. Similar insights are generally typical of patristic and medieval authors until the fourteenth century. At this point, increasing papal political power and a growing determination to fend off attacks on the institutions of the church (particularly the papacy and hierarchy) led to a growing tendency to defend these institutions by making them integral to a proper understanding of the church.

This tendency is generally thought to have reached its zenith during the nineteenth century. Responding to an increasingly dangerous political situation in Europe, where secularism and anti-Catholicism appeared to be on the increase, the First Vatican Council defined a strongly hierarchical conception of the church, perhaps seen most clearly in the rigid distinction between "the pastors and the flock."

This general approach to ecclesiology dominated Catholic theology prior to the Second Vatican Council. On this view, the church of Christ is not a community of equals in which all the faithful have the same rights. It is a society of unequals, not only because among the faithful some are clergy and some are laity, but because there is in the church the power from God by which it is given to some to sanctify, teach, and govern, and to others it is not. This point was often expressed in terms of the distinction between *ecclesia docens* ("the teaching church," referring to the hierarchy) and *ecclesia discens* ("the learning church," referring to the laity, whose responsibilities were primarily to obey their superiors).

Yet, by the middle of the twentieth century, Catholic scholars and theologians were expressing increasing misgivings concerning this model. In part, this reflects an awareness of the growing evidence which suggested that the early church did not have a coherent monolithic structure, but had at least a degree of flexibility over its institutions and orders. The emergence of a strongly organized and institutional church increasingly came to be seen as dating from after the apostolic period, and being a response partly to political pressures, such as those resulting from the imperial recognition of Christianity under Constantine. Lucien Cerfaux and others paved the way for a recovery of biblical and patristic insights which had been overlooked on account of the trend toward institutionalization. Others, such as Yves Congar, worked for the recovery of a theology of the laity, concerned over their marginalization in institutional models of the church. The result was that the Second Vatican Council was in a position to revitalize Roman Catholic thinking on this vital area of theology, with all its implications for ecumenism and evangelism. The results may be seen in the document *Lumen Gentium* ("A Light to the Gentiles").

We have already considered the Council's teaching on "the church as sacrament" (p. 402), and the manner in which it has been developed by theologians such as Karl Rahner. In what follows, we shall explore three further aspects of the teaching of the Council on the nature of the church.

The church as communion

In 1943 the German Catholic writer Ludwig von Hertling published a study entitled *Com-munio: Church and Papacy in Early Christianity*, which dealt with the importance of the theme of "communion" (often referred to by the Greek term *koinonia*) for a proper understanding of the nature of the church. This work had a deep influence on the Council's reflections, and its distinctive themes can be found in the final statement on the church. On account of the overtones which the term "communion" now possesses, it is perhaps useful to employ the older English word "fellowship" to bring out the point at issue. The basic biblical theme which is expressed by this term is that of sharing in a common life, whether this life is thought of as the life of the Trinity itself, or the common life of believers within the church. The term possesses both vertical and horizontal aspects, the former referring to the relation between the believer and God, and the latter to the relationship between individual believers.

The recovery of this biblical idea proved to be a powerful corrective to the purely institutional conceptions of the church which had gained the ascendancy during the nineteenth century. The regulatory enforcement of fellowship was now seen to be one aspect of the more fundamental idea of the fellowship between the believer and God, established through the death and resurrection of Christ, and lived out in the life of the church.

The church as the people of God

Of the various models of the church set forth by the Second Vatican Council, the most important is that of the church as "the people of God." This is a strongly biblical idea, with deep roots in both Old and New Testaments. The Second Vatican Council is careful to avoid the direct identification of "the people of God" with "the Roman Catholic Church," or the suggestion that the church has somehow displaced Israel as the people of God. Indeed, the second chapter of the Council's text on the inner life of the church describes the church as the "new people of God," continuous with Israel. The election of the church as the people of God does not entail the rejection of Israel, but rather the extension of God's kingdom.

This point is made particularly clearly in the Council's "Declaration on Non-Christian Religions," which recognizes a special continuing place for Jews in God's purposes of salvation.

> The Church of Christ acknowledges that in God's plan of salvation the beginning of her faith and election is to be found in the patriarchs, Moses, and the prophets. She professes that all Christ's faithful, who as men of faith are sons of Abraham (cf. Galatians 3: 7), are included in the same patriarch's call and that the salvation of the Church is mystically prefigured in the exodus of God's chosen people from the land of bondage. On this account the Church cannot forget that she received the revelation of the Old Testament by way of that people with whom God in his inexpressible mercy established the ancient covenant. Nor can she forget that she draws nourishment from that good olive tree onto which the wild olive branches of the Gentiles have been grafted (cf. Romans 11: 17–24). The Church believes that Christ who is our peace has through his cross reconciled Jews and Gentiles and made them one in himself (cf. Ephesians 2: 14–16).

The church as a charismatic community

The Second Vatican Council took place at the time during which there was widespread interest in the charismatic movement (see pp. 81–2). The impact of this development was felt strongly within some quarters of the Catholic church. It led to the Belgian Cardinal Leo-Josef Suenens delivering a powerful appeal to the Council to include reference to this development in its reflections on the nature of the church. *Lumen Gentium* responded by explicitly recognizing the importance of charismatic gifts

within the life of the church. The Council used the term "charism" (Greek: *charisma* = gift) to refer to such gifts or abilities bestowed upon individuals to fulfill some specific service. This term has a long history of use, and does not necessarily imply the kind of "spiritual gifts" (such as speaking in tongues or the gift of healing) specifically associated with the charismatic movement. Nevertheless, the Pauline use of the Greek term *charisma* clearly includes such gifts, suggesting that the Council was allowing a significant degree of openness to this increasingly important aspect of the twentieth-century Christian experience.

The "Notes" of the Church

A central theme of ecclesiology relates to the four "notes" or "marks" of the church – that is to say, the four defining characteristics of the Christian church, as stated in the creeds of Christendom. These creeds affirm belief in "one holy catholic and apostolic church." The four adjectives included in this phrase – "one," "holy," "catholic," and "apostolic" – have come to be known as the "notes" or "marks" of the church, and have been of importance to ecclesiological discussion since the fourth century. In what follows, we shall consider each briefly.

One

The unity of the church has been of central importance to Christian thinking on the subject. The World Council of Churches, one of the more important agencies in the modern period to be concerned with Christian unity, defines itself as "a fellowship of churches, which confess our Lord Jesus Christ as God and Savior." Yet that very definition concedes the existence of a plurality of churches – Anglican, Baptist,

THE DOCTRINE OF THE CHURCH

Lutheran, Methodist, Orthodox, Presbyterian, Roman Catholic, and so on. How can one speak of "one church," when there are so many churches? Or of the "unity" of the church, when it is so clearly disunited at the institutional level?

Two episodes in church history may be noted as being of especial importance in relation to this question. The first relates to north Africa in the third century, when division within the church became a potentially destructive issue. The Decian persecution (250–1) led to many Christians lapsing or abandoning their faith in the face of persecution. Division arose immediately over how these individuals should be treated: did such a lapse mark the end of their faith, or could they be reconciled to the church by penance? Opinions differed sharply, and serious disagreement and tension resulted. (The Donatist controversy, discussed earlier, may be regarded as a development of this unresolved problem, in response to the later Diocletian persecution.)

In his *On the Unity of the Catholic Church* (251), written in direct response to the crisis arising from the Decian persecution, Cyprian of Carthage insisted upon the absolute unity of the church, comparing it to the "seamless robe of Christ" which could not be divided because it had been woven from the top throughout. Destroy its unity, and its identity was simultaneously devastated.

Anyone who cuts themselves off from the Church and is joined to an adulteress is separated from the promises of the Church, and anyone who leaves the Church of Christ behind cannot benefit from the rewards of Christ. Such people are strangers, outcasts, and enemies. You cannot have God as father unless you have the Church as mother. If any had been able to escape outside Noah's Ark, there might have been a way of escape for those who are outside the church.

There is only one church, and outside its bounds salvation is impossible. *Extra ecclesiam nulla salus* – "outside the church there is no salvation." Cyprian was subsequently martyred, with the result that his distinctive ideas on unity within the church achieved considerable status within the region. Cyprian was a local martyr, and the respect and veneration attached to his person were easily transferred to his theological ideas. This forced Augustine to give them considerable emphasis in his own writings on the topic.

The sixteenth-century Reformation also witnessed controversy over this issue. How, asked the critics of the Reformation, could the reformers legitimately break away from the established church, and form breakaway bodies? Surely this was nothing more and nothing less than violation of the unity of the church? (It must be recalled here that the Reformation took place in western Europe, a region in which the only significant ecclesiastical body was the more or less undivided Roman Catholic Church.) As noted earlier, the reformers' response to this important criticism was to argue that the medieval church had become corrupted to the point at which reformation was inevitable. The medieval church remained, in their view, a *Christian* church. Yet it was in danger of losing sight of its distinctive identity and vocation, and required reform and renewal. If this could not be achieved from within, it would have to be achieved by breaking away, and forming a reformed church outside the flux of medieval Christendom.

Once the principle of breaking away from a parent ecclesiastical body for doctrinal reasons had been established, little could be done to check it. This often led to a cascade of fragmentation within such breakaway bodies. The Church of England broke away from the Roman Catholic Church in the sixteenth century; controversy within the Church of

England led to an exodus of some of its clergy and people, leading to the formation of the Methodist church; controversy within the Methodist church in the nineteenth century led to the formation of Wesleyan and Calvinist groups, each claiming to be "Methodist." From the sixteenth century onwards, it became clear that the classic credal idea of "one church" could no longer be understood in institutional terms. But was it meant to be understood in this way in the first place? Earlier Christian writers, especially in the first phase of the patristic era, had known this tension, and been able to make sense of it.

Faced with this apparent tension between a theoretical belief in "one church" and the brute observable reality of a plurality of churches, Christian writers developed approaches to allow the later observation to be incorporated within the framework of the former. Four major approaches to the issue of the unity of the church may be noted, each of which possesses distinctive strengths and weaknesses.

1   An imperialist approach, which declares that there is only one empirical – that is, observable – church which deserves to be known and treated as the true church. All others are fraudulent pretenders to this title, or are at best little more than approximations to the real thing. This position was maintained by the Roman Catholic Church prior to the Second Vatican Council (1962–5), which took the momentous step of recognizing other Christian churches as "separated" Christian brothers and sisters.

2   A Platonic approach, which draws a fundamental distinction between the empirical church (that is, the church as a visible historical reality) and the ideal church. This has found relatively little support in mainstream Christian theology, al-

though some scholars have suggested that some such idea may lie behind Calvin's distinction between the "visible" and "invisible" church. However, as we noted above, this distinction is better interpreted along eschatological lines.

3   An eschatological approach, which suggests that the present disunity of the church will be abolished on the last day. The present situation is temporary and will be resolved at the time of eschatological fulfillment. This understanding lies behind Calvin's distinction between the "visible" and "invisible" churches (pp. 398–400).

4   A biological approach, which likens the historical evolution of the church to the development of the branches of a tree. This image, developed by the eighteenth-century German Pietist writer Nicolas von Zinzendorf, and taken up with enthusiasm by Anglican writers of the following century, allows the different empirical churches (e.g., the Roman Catholic, Orthodox, and Anglican churches) to be seen as possessing an organic unity, despite their institutional differences.

However, in recent years, many theologians concerned with ecumenism (deriving from the Greek word *oecumene*, "the whole world," and now generally understood to mean "the movement concerned with the fostering of Christian unity") argued that the true basis of the "unity of the church" required to be recovered, after centuries of distortion. The maxim *ubi Christus, ibi ecclesia* ("where Christ is, there is also the church"), which derives from Ignatius of Antioch (see p. 402), pointed to the unity of the church lying in Christ, rather than in any historical or cultural factor. Throughout the New Testament, they argued, the diversity of local churches is not regarded as compromising the unity of the church. The church already possesses a unity through its common calling from God, which expresses itself in different communities in different cultures and situations. "Unity" must not be understood *sociologically* or *organizationally*, but *theologically*. Hans Küng stresses this point in his magisterial study *The Church*:

> The unity of the church is a spiritual entity. It is one and the same God who gathers the scattered from all places and all ages and makes them into one people of God. It is one and the same Christ who through his word and Spirit unites all together in the same bond of fellowship of the same body of Christ. […] The Church is one, and therefore *should be* one.

The point that Küng makes is that the unity of the church is grounded in the saving work of God in Christ. This is in no way inconsistent with that one church adapting itself to local cultural conditions, leading to the formation of local churches. As Küng puts it:

> The unity of the church presupposes a multiplicity of churches; the various churches do not need to deny their origins or their specific situations; their language, their history, their customs and traditions, their way of life and thought, their personal structure will differ fundamentally, and no one has the right to take this from them. The same thing is not suitable for everyone, at every time, and in every place.

An illustration of this may be provided from Anglicanism, a family of churches which owes its historical origins to the English Reformation. The Thirty-Nine Articles (1571), which established the identity of the movement at that time, do not commit Anglicanism to anything other than an affirmation of the main points of the Christian faith, allowing a considerable degree of freedom in relation to areas of potential division (evident in the nuanced discussion of the highly contentious issue of pre-

destination at Article XVII). If Anglicanism possesses "essentials," they are "essentials" that are common to the whole church of God, of which Anglicanism is part. Anglicanism's distinctive features may be argued to lie in its application of the gospel to a specific historical situation – England, and subsequently the British colonies. The American Anglican theologian Louis Weil states this point as follows:

> The gospel in Anglicanism is, then, one facet in a vast mosaic. In its essentials, it corresponds to the gospel as it has been proclaimed and believed all over the world. Yet it is also characterized by its particularity as an experience of God's saving work in particular cultures, and is shaped by the insights and limitations of persons who were themselves seeking to live the gospel within a particular context.

This represents an affirmation of the fundamental unity of the Christian church, while noting the need for adaptation to local circumstances.

The rapid growth of evangelicalism in the modern church is of considerable importance in relation to the doctrine of the church. Evangelicalism is a worldwide transdenominational movement, which is able to coexist within every major denomination in the western church, including the Roman Catholic church. Evangelicalism is not inextricably locked into any specific denominational constituency. An evangelical commitment to a corporate conception of the Christian life does not entail the explicit definition of a theology of the church (see pp. 80–1). Precisely because evangelicalism has no defining or limiting ecclesiology, it can accommodate itself to virtually any form of church order.

This is well illustrated by the history of the movement. Evangelical attitudes are now known to have been deeply embedded within the Italian church during the 1520s and

1530s, with prominent Italian church leaders (including several cardinals) meeting regularly in a number of cities to study Scripture and the writings of the Protestant reformers. No tension was seen between an evangelical spirituality and a Catholic ecclesiology; it was only when the situation was radically politicized in the 1540s through the intrusion of imperial politics into theological debate that evangelicalism came to be seen as a destabilizing influence within the Italian church.

Similar developments are now known to be taking place within the Roman Catholic church in the United States, as an increasing number of members find evangelicalism conducive to their spiritual needs, yet do not feel (and are not made to feel) that their espousal of an evangelical spirituality entails abandoning their loyalty to Catholic church structures. The unity of the church is here grounded, not in any specific ecclesiastical organizational system, but in a common commitment to the *evangel* – the good news of Jesus Christ.

Holy

Earlier, we noted that the idea of the unity of the church appeared to be fatally compromised by rampant denominationalism. The theoretical unity of the church appeared to be contradicted by the empirical reality, in which the church appeared as divided and fragmented. Precisely the same tension between theory and experience arises through the assertion that the church is "holy," when both the past history and present experience of that institution point to sinfulness on the part of both the church and its members.

How is the theoretical holiness of the church to be reconciled with the sinfulness of Christian believers? The most significant attempt to bring experience into line with theory can be seen in sectarian movements such as Donatism and Anabaptism. Both these movements laid considerable emphasis upon the empirical holiness of church members, leading to the exclusion from the church of members who were deemed to have lapsed from these public standards of sanctity. This rigorist approach seemed to contradict substantial parts of the New Testament, which affirmed the fallibility and forgivability – if the neologism may be excused – of believers. Others have asserted that a distinction may be made between the holiness of the church, and the sinfulness of its members. This raises the theoretical difficulty of whether a church can exist without members, and seems to suggest a disembodied church without any real connection with human beings.

A different approach draws upon an eschatological perspective. The church is at present as sinful as its members; nevertheless, it will finally be purified on the last day. "Whenever I have described the church as being without spot or wrinkle, I have not intended to imply that it was like this already, but that it should prepare itself to be like this, at the time when it too will appear in glory" (Augustine). "That the church will be [...] without spot or wrinkle [...] will only be true in our eternal home, not on the way there. We would deceive ourselves if we were to say that we have no sin, as 1 John 1: 8 reminds us" (Thomas Aquinas).

Probably the most helpful approach to this mark of the church is to explore the meaning of the term "holy" in greater detail. In ordinary English, the term has acquired associations of "morality," "sanctity," or "purity," which often seem to bear little relation to the behavior of fallen human beings. The Hebrew term *kadad* which underlies the New Testament concept of "holiness," has the sense of "being cut off," or "being separated." There are strong overtones of *dedication*: to be "holy" is to be set apart for and dedicated to the service of God.

A fundamental element – indeed, perhaps *the* fundamental element – of the Old Testament idea of holiness is that of "something or someone whom God has set apart." The New Testament restricts the idea almost entirely to personal holiness. It refers the idea to individuals, declining to pick up the idea of "holy places" or "holy things." People are "holy" in that they are dedicated to God, and distinguished from the world on account of their calling by God. A number of theologians have suggested a correlation between the idea of "the church" (the Greek word for which can bear the meaning of "those who are called out") and "holy" (that is, those who have been separated from the world, on account of their having been called by God).

To speak of the "holiness of the church" is thus primarily to speak of the holiness of the one who called that church and its members. The church has been separated from the world, in order to bear witness to the grace and salvation of God. In this sense, there are obvious connections between the church being "holy" and the church being "apostolic." The term "holy" is theological, not moral, in its connotations, affirming the calling of the church and its members, and the hope that the church will one day share in the life and glory of God.

Catholic

In modern English, the term "catholic" is often confused, especially in nonreligious circles, with "Roman Catholic." Although this confusion is understandable, the distinction must be maintained. It is not only Roman Catholics who are catholic, just as it is by no means only Eastern Orthodox writers who are orthodox in their theology. Indeed, many Protestant churches, more than a little embarrassed by the use of the term "catholic" in the creeds, have replaced it with the less contentious word "universal," arguing that this brings greater intelligibility to belief in "one holy universal and apostolic church."

The term "catholic" derives from the Greek phrase *kath' holou* ("referring to the whole"). The Greek words subsequently found their way into the Latin word *catholicus*, which came to have the meaning "universal or general." This sense of the word is retained in the English phrase "catholic taste," meaning a "wide-ranging taste" rather than a "taste for things that are Roman Catholic." Older versions of the English Bible often refer to some of the New Testament letters (such as those of James and John) as "catholic epistles," meaning that they are directed to all Christians (rather than those of Paul, which are directed to the needs and situations of individual identified churches, such as those at Rome or Corinth).

At no point does the New Testament use the term "catholic" to refer to the church as a whole. The New Testament uses the term *ekklesia* to refer to local churches or worshiping communities, which it nevertheless understands to represent or embody something which transcends that local body. While an individual church is not the church in its totality, it nevertheless shares in that totality. It is this notion of "totality" which is subsequently encapsulated in the term "catholic." The term is introduced in later centuries, in an attempt to bring together central New Testament insights and attach them to a single term. The first known use of the phrase "the catholic church" occurs in the writings of Ignatius of Antioch, who was martyred at Rome around 110: "Where Jesus Christ is, there is the catholic church." Other writings of the second century use the term to refer to the existence of a universal church alongside local congregations.

The meaning of the term changed fundamentally with the conversion of Constantine. By the end of the fourth century, the term *ecclesia catholica* ("the catholic church") had come to mean "the imperial church" – that is, the only legal religion within the Roman Empire. Any other form of belief, including Christian beliefs that diverged from the mainstream, was declared to be illegal.

Further expansion of the church in this period contributed to a developing understanding of the term "catholic." By the beginning of the fifth century, Christianity was firmly established throughout the entire Mediterranean world. In response to this development, the term "catholic" came to be interpreted as "embracing the entire world."

In terms of its early development, the term "catholic" as applied to the church thus went through three stages of meaning:

1 A universal and all-embracing church, which underlies and undergirds individual local churches. In this sense, the term is descriptive and nonpolemical, pointing to the fact that a local church was the representative of the universal church. There is an obvious correlation here between the notions of "unity" and "catholicity."

2 A church which is orthodox in its theology. The term now takes on a strongly prescriptive and polemical tone. "Catholicism" is now contrasted with "schism" and "heresy," by which individuals place themselves outside the boundaries of a doctrinally orthodox church.

3 A church which extends throughout the world. In the first phase of the Christian church, this interpretation of the term would have been implausible, given the localized character of Christianity. However, the strongly missionary character of Christianity (linked, as we shall see, with the idea of "apostolicity") led to the expansion of the church throughout the civilized world of the Mediterranean. The term thus came to possess a geographical reference, originally absent.

The developed sense of the word is perhaps best seen in the fourth-century catechetical writings of Cyril of Jerusalem. In his eighteenth catechetical lecture, Cyril teases out a number of senses of the Greek work *katholikos*:

> The church is thus called "catholic" because it is spread throughout the entire inhabited world [*oikoumene*], from one end to the other, and because it teaches in its totality [*katholikos*] and without leaving anything out every doctrine which people need to know relating to things visible and invisible, whether in heaven and earth. It is also called "catholic" because it brings to obedience every sort of person – whether rulers or their subjects, the educated and the unlearned. It also makes available a universal [*katholikos*] remedy and cure to every kind of sin.

Note the following senses of the term "catholic" in this passage:

1 *"Spread throughout the entire inhabited world"*: Here, Cyril notes the geographical sense of the word. The notion of "wholeness" or "universality" is thus understood to mandate the church to spread into every region of the world.

2 *"Without leaving anything out"*: With this phrase, Cyril stresses that the "catholicity" of the church involves the complete proclamation and explanation of the Christian faith. It is an invitation to ensure that the totality of the gospel is preached and taught.

3 *"Every sort of person"*: Cyril here makes an essentially sociological point. The gospel and the church are for all kinds of human beings, irrespective of their race, gender, or social status. We can see here a clear echo of St Paul's famous declaration that "there is neither Jew nor Greek, there is neither slave nor free, there is neither male nor female; for you are all one in Christ Jesus" (Galatians 3: 28).

4 *"A universal remedy and cure to every kind of sin"*: Here, Cyril makes a soteriological statement: the gospel, and the church which proclaims that gospel, can meet every human need and distress. Whatever sins there may be, the church is able to offer an antidote.

The various senses of the term "catholic" are also brought out clearly by Thomas Aquinas, in his discussion of the section of the Apostles' creed dealing with the doctrine of the church. In this analysis, Aquinas singles out three essential aspects of the idea of "catholicity."

> The church is catholic, i.e., universal, first with respect to place, because it is throughout the entire world [*per totum mundum*], against the Donatists. See Romans 1: 8: "Your faith is proclaimed in all the world"; Mark 16: 15: "Go into all the world and preach the gospel to the whole creation." In ancient times, God was known only in Judea, but now throughout the entire world. This church, moreover, has three parts. One is on earth, another is in heaven, and the third is in purgatory. Secondly, the Church is universal with respect to the condition of people, because no one is rejected, whether master or slave, male or female. See Galatians 3: 28: "There is neither male nor female." Thirdly, it is universal with respect to time. For some have said that the church should last until a certain time, but this is false, because this church began from the time of Abel and will last to the end of the world. See Matthew 28: 20: "And I am with you always, to the close of the age." And after the close of the age it will remain in heaven.

Note how catholicity is here understood in terms of geographical, anthropological, and chronological universality.

As we saw earlier, a fundamental re-examination of the notion of "catholicity" took place at the time of the Reformation. It seemed to many that the catholicity and unity of the church were destroyed simultaneously with the fragmentation of the western European church in the sixteenth century. Protestant writers argued that the essence of catholicity lay, not in church institutions, but in matters of doctrine. The fifth-century writer Vincent of Lérins had defined catholicity in terms of "that which is believed everywhere, at all times, and by all people." The reformers argued that they remained catholic, despite having broken away from the medieval church, in that they retained the central and universally recognized elements of Christian doctrine. Historical or institutional continuity was secondary to doctrinal fidelity. For this reason, the mainstream Protestant churches insisted they were simultaneously *catholic* and *reformed* – that is, maintaining continuity with the apostolic church at the level of teaching, having eliminated spurious nonbiblical practices and beliefs.

The notion of "catholicity" which has come to the fore in recent years, especially in ecumenical discussions subsequent to the Second Vatican Council, is the oldest sense of the term – namely, that of totality. Local churches and particular denominations are to be seen as the manifestations, representations, or embodiments of the one universal church. As Hans Küng states this position:

> The catholicity of the church therefore consists in a notion of entirety, based on identity, and resulting in universality. From this it is clear that unity and catholicity go together; if the church is one, it must be universal; if it is universal, it must be one. Unity and catholicity are two interwoven dimensions of one and the same church.

In the twentieth century, increasing attention has also been paid by western theologians to the notions of "catholicity" which have been dominant in the Orthodox churches. This is often expressed using the Russian word *Sobornost*, which has no exact equivalent in other languages. While the term denotes the general idea of "universality," it also stresses the unity of believers within the fellowship of the church. The idea, which is developed most fully in the writings of Sergei Bulgakov and A. S. Khomyakov, attempts to do justice to both the distinctiveness of individual members of the church, and the overall harmony of its corporate life. This is linked with the notion of "conciliarity" (the Russian word *sobor* means "a council" or "an assembly"), by which the life of the church is governed in such a way that authority is dispersed among all the faithful, rather than centralized and concentrated in any single quasi-papal figure.

Apostolic

The term "apostolic," like "catholic," is not used to refer to the church in the New Testament. Unlike "catholic," it is restricted to Christian use, and is therefore not subject to the kinds of confusion with secular ideas noted in the case of other marks of the church. The fundamental sense of the term is "originating with the apostles" or "having a direct link with the apostles." It is a reminder that the church is founded on the apostolic witness and testimony.

The term "apostle" requires explanation. Its use in the New Testament suggests that it bears two related meanings:

1 Someone who has been commissioned by Christ, and charged with the task of preaching the good news of the kingdom.
2 Someone who was a witness to the risen Christ, or to whom Christ revealed himself as risen.

In declaring the church to be "apostolic," the creeds thus appear to emphasize the historical roots of the gospel, the continuity between the church and Christ through the apostles whom he appointed, and the continuing evangelistic and missionary tasks of the church.

The notion of the "apostolicity" of the church was the subject of considerable discussion within English theological circles from about 1870 to the beginning of World War I in 1914. In a series of lectures given at Cambridge University during the academic year 1913–14, H. B. Swete (1835–1917) set out the contours of a biblically informed ecclesiology, which made extensive use of the early patristic discussion of the matter. Swete – who was Regius Professor of Divinity at Cambridge University from 1890 until 1915 – set out three basic themes which he regarded as enfolded in the concept of the "apostolicity" of the church: "The Catholic Church is Apostolic in three respects: as planted in the world by the Apostles; as adhering to the teaching of the Apostles; as carrying on the succession of Apostolic ministry." The first point, according to Swete, can be seen from the New Testament itself, especially the history of the expansion of the church recorded in the Acts of the Apostles.

Before the Ascension our Lord charged the Apostles with the work of preaching the Gospel in Judaea and Samaria and to the uttermost part of the earth. This evangelization of Judaea and Samaria was carried out by the Twelve and their company, as the Acts relate; the Gentile missions, so far as the West was concerned, fell chiefly into other hands. But the mission of St Paul was undertaken with the full approval of the original Apostolate, and was in fact a fulfilment of a part of their task with which they were themselves not qualified to deal. By agreement and fellowship with St Paul the Twelve "were enabled to feel that they were in effect carrying out through him that extension of their sphere which it is incredible that they should ever have dismissed from their minds" [H. J. A. Hort]. Thus Gentile Christendom was ultimately of Apostolic planting, even if we limit the Apostolic college to the Twelve. The churches founded by St Paul and his associates were Apostolic foundations, not only because St Paul was an Apostle, but because his work was done with the concurrence of the original Apostles.

Having established that the historical origins of the Christian church rest with the apostles, Swete goes on to demonstrate that the teaching of that church was equally apostolic:

> The earliest converts, it is noted in Acts, "continued steadfastly in the Apostles' teaching" (Acts 2: 42). On their teaching and the teaching of St Paul there was built up a tradition, or as the Pastorals put it, a "deposit" was formed, which remained as an abiding treasure of the Church (2 Thessalonians 2: 15; 3: 6). Its substance was known as the "rule of faith," and found expression in the early creeds. This Apostolic tradition was held to be preserved with especial purity in churches which could claim Apostolic founders, and more particularly in the Roman church, which had for its founders both St Peter and St Paul. But, in fact, the whole Catholic Church in all parts of the world possessed one and the same faith of Apostolic origin. The tradition was not simply oral; it was embodied also in the Apostolic writings, which by the end of the second century had been collected into a New Testament or "Instrument." Written or unwritten, the witness of the Apostolic age was the heritage of the Catholic Church; she claimed all Apostolic teaching as her own, and admitted no other body of truth.

Swete's attention now turns to the question of the type of ministry exercised by the Christian church. Again, his point mingles historical and theological reflection: the ministry entrusted to the church was of apostolic origin:

> Besides Apostolic tradition, the Catholic Church possessed also an Apostolic ministry. The orderly devolution of ministerial authority from the Apostolate is a clearly marked principle of the first age. The Seven were chosen by the whole body of the disciples, but on their election they were set before the Apostles, and by them admitted to their office. In the new churches among the Gentiles, elders (presbyters) were appointed by Barnabas and Saul. Later on, at Ephesus and in Crete, in the absence of the Apostle, the ordination of presbyter-bishops and deacons was entrusted by St Paul to his delegates, Timothy and Titus. Timothy himself had received the gift of ministerial grace through the laying on of the Apostle's hands (2 Timothy 1: 6).

Swete's discussion of this issue can be seen as reflecting the general tenor of late Victorian reflection on this issue. The three criteria of apostolicity which he identified are:

1 planted in the world by the apostles;
2 adhering to the teaching of the apostles;
3 carrying on the succession of apostolic ministry.

Such ideas were especially influential within the Church of England (where they were of some relevance to debates over ecclesiology resulting from the aftermath of the Oxford Movement of the early nineteenth century), yet would receive acceptance far beyond the English national church.

Having considered aspects of the Christian understanding of the church, we may now turn to a discussion of a related area of theology: the sacraments.

QUESTIONS FOR CHAPTER 15

1 Give a concise summary of the issues at stake in the Donatist controversy.

2 Augustine of Hippo wrote of the Christian church being like a hospital. Why?

3 The doctrine of the church is often described as "the Achilles' heel of the Reformation." Why?

4 "How can anyone speak of one church, when there are dozens of Christian denominations?" Summarize and assess the answers that could be given to this objection.

5 "How can the church be holy, when it is full of sinners?" What answers could be given to this question?

16

The Doctrine of the Sacraments

In the previous chapter we considered issues relating to the identity of the Christian church. Our attention now turns to a set of related issues centering on the sacraments. As with the doctrine of the church, the issues at stake are of considerable relevance to any who are studying theology with a view to entering pastoral ministry. However, they are also of interest to any studying theology for more academic reasons.

As will soon become clear, the term "sacrament" is notoriously difficult to define, given the controversy within the Christian churches upon the nature and number of the sacraments. In general terms, a sacrament may be thought of as an external rite or sign, which in some way conveys grace to believers. The most sustained debates within the church on the identity and function of the sacraments took place during the sixteenth century. For this reason, the discussion of sacramental theology will include extensive reference to the debates of this era. However, the Donatist controversy (see pp. 394–6) also resulted in several issues of importance being debated. The most convenient way of handling the material under consideration is to deal with the issues raised by the Donatist controversy and the Reformation.

The chief debates within Christian history which relate to the sacraments concern the following issues:

1 What is a sacrament?
2 How many sacraments are there?
3 What is the correct name for the sacrament which Christians have variously termed "the mass," "holy communion," "the Eucharist," "the Lord's Supper," and "the breaking of the bread"?
4 In what sense is Christ present at the Eucharist?

The third question is unanswerable! In practice, it may be noted that the term "mass" tends to have Catholic, and "Lord's Supper" Protestant, connotations. In the present work, the term "Eucharist" has been used as a convenient compromise, simply because it has the advantage of possessing an adjectival form ("eucharistic"). Readers of the work who find this term objectionable or problematic are completely at liberty to substitute their preferred alternatives, wherever these are appropriate. No attempt is being made to prescribe this term as correct or normative.

The Early Development of Sacramental Theology

The New Testament does not make use of the specific term *sacrament*. Instead, we find the Greek word *mysterion* (which is naturally translated as "mystery") used to refer to the saving work of God in general. This Greek word is never used to refer to what would now be regarded as a sacrament (for example, baptism). However, it is clear from what we know of the history of the early church that a connection was made at an early stage between the "mystery" of God's saving work in Christ and the "sacraments" of baptism and the Eucharist.

Perhaps the most significant advances in sacramental theology took place in Roman north Africa during the third and fourth centuries, and can be seen in the writings of Tertullian, Cyprian of Carthage, and Augustine of Hippo. It is interesting to ask why these developments are associated with this specific region of the church. One possible factor is that the church in this region was subjected to particularly difficult circumstances, including persecution. (It must be remembered that Cyprian would die as a martyr at the hands of the Roman authorities.) The church in north Africa was thus characterized by a strong sense of solidarity in the face of these difficult conditions. As a result the African church placed considerable emphasis on the solidarity of the faithful, and the means by which this solidarity could be maintained and enhanced. The sacraments were one vital aspect of this strategy.

Tertullian's contribution to the development of sacramental theology can be summarized in terms of three issues.

1 The use of the Latin term *sacramentum* (now familiar to us in its English form "sacrament") to translate the Greek word *mysterion*. It is quite possible that this translation was already familiar to him through existing Latin translations of the New Testament. However, as we saw earlier (p. 249), Tertullian was noted for his ability to invent new Latin words for Greek theological terms, and it is entirely possible that this development was his own idea.

2 The use of the word "sacrament" in the plural. The New Testament spoke of "a mystery" in the singular. As we have just noted, Tertullian translated this as "sacrament," referring to this mystery – but also used the term *in the plural* to refer to the individual sacraments which were linked with this mystery. Tertullian thus uses the Latin word *sacramentum* in two different, though clearly related, senses: first to refer to the mystery of God's salvation; and second, to refer to the symbols or rites which were associated with this salvation in the life of the church.

3 The exploitation of the theological significance of the parallel between sacraments and military oaths. Tertullian pointed out that, in normal Latin use, the word *sacramentum* meant "a sacred oath," referring to the oath of allegiance and loyalty which was required of Roman soldiers. Tertullian used this parallel as a means of bringing out the importance of sacraments in relation to Christian commitment and loyalty within the church. This theme would become of fundamental importance in the sacramental theology of the Swiss reformer Huldrych Zwingli, as we shall see later (p. 429). For Zwingli, the sacraments emphasize the corporate solidarity of the communion of faith, and the believers' solemn responsibilities towards God and the church.

The theology of the sacraments would be developed further by Augustine during the

Donatist controversy (see pp. 394–6, 424–5). A central theme of his reflections is the relation between a sign and the thing which it signifies. For Augustine, the world contains many signs which point to different realities; for example, smoke as a sign of fire, or words as a sign of that to which they refer. However, there are also "sacred signs" which bridge the gap between God and ourselves, in that they serve as physical doorways or gates to spiritual realities. Augustine uses many definitions of sacraments to express this point; perhaps the most famous of these is the idea of sacraments as "visible forms of invisible grace." Yet Augustine is clear that sacraments do not merely *signify* grace; in some way, they evoke or enable what they signify. In one sense, the subsequent development of sacramental theology may be said to concern the way in which the sign and thing signified relate to each other.

We may begin to explore this question by looking at the question of the definition of a sacrament.

The Definition of a Sacrament

In the previous chapter we noted that the first centuries were characterized by a relative lack of interest in the doctrine of the church. Much the same can be said in relation to the sacraments. During the second century some discussions of a general sacramental nature can be found in such writings as the *Didache*, and the works of Irenaeus. It is only in the writings of Augustine that the issues, including that of the definition of a sacrament, begin to be fully addressed.

Augustine is generally regarded as having laid down the general principles relating to the definition of sacraments. These principles are as follows:

1 A sacrament is a *sign*. "Signs, when applied to divine things, are called sacraments."
2 The sign must bear some relation to the thing which is signified. "If sacraments did not bear some resemblance to the things of which they are the sacraments, they would not be sacraments at all."

These definitions are still imprecise and inadequate. For example, does it follow that every "sign of a sacred thing" is to be regarded as a sacrament? In practice, Augustine understood by "sacraments" a number of things that are no longer regarded as sacramental in character; for example, the creed and the Lord's prayer. As time passed, it became increasingly clear that the definition of a sacrament simply as "a sign of a sacred thing" was inadequate. It was during the earlier Middle Ages – the period of sacramental development *par excellence* – that further clarification took place.

In the first half of the twelfth century, the Paris theologian Hugh of St Victor revised Augustine's somewhat imprecise definition as follows:

Not every sign of a sacred thing can properly be called a sacrament (for the letters in sacred writings, or statues and pictures, are all "signs of sacred things," but cannot be called sacraments for that reason). [. . .] Anyone wanting a fuller and better definition of a sacrament can define it as follows: "a sacrament is a physical or material element set before the external senses, representing by likeness, signifying by its institution, and containing by sanctification, some invisible and spiritual grace."

There are thus four essential components to the definition of a sacrament:

1 A "physical or material" element, such as the water of baptism, the bread and wine of the Eucharist, or the oil of extreme unction.

("Extreme unction" is the practice of anointing those who are terminally ill with consecrated olive oil.)

2 A "likeness" to the thing which is signified, so that it can represent the thing signified. Thus the eucharistic wine can be argued to have a "likeness" to the blood of Christ, allowing it to represent that blood in a sacramental context.

3 Authorization to signify the thing in question. In other words, there must be a good reason for believing that the sign in question is *authorized* to represent the spiritual reality to which it points. An example – indeed, the primary example – of the "authorization" in question is institution at the hands of Jesus Christ himself.

4 An efficacity, by which the sacrament is capable of conferring the benefits which it signifies to those who partake in it.

This fourth point is of especial importance. In medieval theology a careful distinction was drawn between the "sacraments of the Old Covenant" (such as circumcision) and the "sacraments of the New Covenant." The essential distinction which early medieval theologians identified as lying between them is that the sacraments of the Old Covenant merely *signified* spiritual realities, whereas the sacraments of the New Covenant *actualized* what they signified. The thirteenth-century Franciscan writer Bonaventure made this point as follows, using a medicinal analogy.

In the Old Law, there were ointments of a kind, but they were figurative and did not heal. The disease was lethal, but the anointings were superficial. [. . .] Genuinely healing ointments must bring both spiritual anointing and a life-giving power; it was only Christ our Lord who did this, since [. . .] through his death, the sacraments have the power to bring to life.

However, Hugh of St Victor's definition of a sacrament remained unsatisfactory. According to Hugh, the following items were "sacraments": the incarnation, the church, and death. Something was still missing. By this time, there was general agreement that there were seven sacraments: baptism, confirmation, the Eucharist, penance, marriage, ordination, and extreme unction. But by Hugh's definition, penance could not be a sacrament. It contained no material element. Theory and practice were thus seriously out of line. A resolution of this difficulty became a matter of urgency.

The final touches were put to the definition shortly afterwards by Peter Lombard, who – by omitting one vital aspect of Hugh's definition – was able to bring theory into line with practice. Peter's achievement was to omit reference to any "physical or material element" in his definition, which takes the following form:

A sacrament bears a likeness to the thing of which it is a sign. "For if sacraments did not have a likeness of the things whose sacraments they are, they would not properly be called sacraments" (Augustine). [. . .] Something can properly be called a sacrament if it is a sign of the grace of God and a form of invisible grace, so that it bears its image and exists as its cause. Sacraments were therefore instituted for the sake of sanctifying, as well as of signifying. [. . .] Those things which were instituted for the purpose of signifying alone are nothing more than signs, and are not sacraments, as in the case of the physical sacrifices and ceremonial observances of the Old Law, which were never able to make those who offered them righteous.

This definition fits each of the seven sacraments noted above, and excludes such things as the creed and the incarnation. As the definition was included in Peter's widely used and authoritative theological textbook *The Four*

Books of the Sentences, it passed into general use in later medieval theology, and remained virtually unchallenged until the time of the Reformation.

The Protestant Reformation challenged a number of aspects of contemporary Christian thought, particularly in relation to understandings of the church and the sacraments. In his reforming treatise of 1520, *The Babylonian Captivity of the Church*, Luther launched a major attack on the Catholic understanding of the sacraments. Where the Catholic church recognized seven sacraments, Luther initially recognized three (baptism, Eucharist, penance), and shortly afterwards only two (baptism and Eucharist). The transition between these two views can be seen in the *Babylonian Captivity* itself, and we may pause to examine this change and understand its basis.

Luther's treatise opens with a powerful statement of principle, which sets to one side the medieval consensus regarding the sacraments:

> To begin with, I must deny that there are seven sacraments, and for the present maintain that there are but three: baptism, penance, and the bread. All three have been subjected to a miserable captivity by the Roman curia, and the church has been robbed of all her liberty.

By the end of the work, however, Luther has come to place considerable emphasis upon the importance of a visible physical sign. Luther signaled this significant change in his views with the following statement:

> Yet it has seemed right to restrict the name of sacrament to those promises of God which have signs attached to them. The remainder, not being connected to signs, are merely promises. Hence, strictly speaking, there are only two sacraments in the church of God – baptism and the bread. For only in these two

do we find the divinely instituted sign and the promise of the forgiveness of sins.

Penance thus ceased to have sacramental status, according to Luther, because the two essential characteristics of a sacrament were:

1 the Word of God;
2 an outward sacramental sign (such as water in baptism, and bread and wine in the Eucharist).

The only true sacraments of the New Testament church were thus baptism and Eucharist; penance, having no external sign, could no longer be regarded as a sacrament.

Like Luther, the Swiss reformer Huldrych Zwingli had grave misgivings about the word "sacrament" itself. He argued that the term has the basic sense of "oath," and initially treated the sacraments of baptism and Eucharist (the remaining five sacraments of the Catholic system being rejected) as signs of God's faithfulness to the church and the divine gracious promise of forgiveness. Thus in 1523 he wrote that the word "sacrament" could be used to refer to those things which "God has instituted, commanded, and ordained with the Word, which is as firm and sure as if God had sworn an oath to this effect." However, Zwingli later came to see the sacraments as signifying the allegiance of believers to the church, rather than of God to believers, a point we shall consider at pp. 428–30.

The Council of Trent, reacting to the Protestant approaches to the sacraments, responded by reaffirming the position outlined by Peter Lombard.

> If anyone says that the sacraments of the new law were not all instituted by our Lord Jesus Christ, or that there are more or less than seven, namely, baptism, confirmation, Eucharist, penance, extreme unction,

ordination, and marriage, or that any one of these seven is not truly and intrinsically a sacrament, let them be condemned.

This basic position has remained characteristic of Roman Catholic theology since the sixteenth century.

The Donatist Controversy: Sacramental Efficacy

In the previous chapter we noted some of the issues which lay behind the Donatist controversy (pp. 394–6). A central issue, of direct relevance to the material to be considered in the present chapter, concerns the personal worthiness or holiness of the minister who administers the sacraments. The Donatists refused to recognize that a *traditor* – that is to say, a Christian minister whose personal credentials had been compromised or tainted through collaboration with the Roman authorities during the Diocletian persecution – could administer the sacraments. Accordingly, they argued that baptisms, ordinations, and Eucharists administered by such ministers were invalid.

This attitude rested in part upon the authority of Cyprian of Carthage. Cyprian had argued that no true sacraments exist outside the church. Heretical baptism was thus not valid, as heretics did not accept the faith of the church, and were thus outside its bounds. Logically unassailable though Cyprian's views may have been, they failed to allow for the situation which arose during the Donatist controversy – that is, ministers who were of orthodox faith, but whose personal conduct was held to be unworthy of their calling. Were doctrinally orthodox yet morally inferior ministers entitled to administer the sacraments? And were such sacraments invalid?

Pressing Cyprian's views beyond their apparently intended limits, the Donatists argued that ecclesiastical actions could be regarded as invalid on account of subjective imperfections on the part of the person administering them. The Donatists thus held that those who were baptized or ordained by Catholic priests or bishops who had not joined the Donatist movement required to be rebaptized and reordained at the hands of Donatist ministers. The sacraments derive their validity from the personal qualities of the person who administers them.

This attitude can be seen in a letter written in 402 by Petilian, the Donatist Bishop of Cirta, to Augustine, criticizing his views on clerical morality. Shortly beforehand, Petilian had circulated a letter to his priests warning against the moral impurity and doctrinal errors of the Catholic church. Augustine's reply, dated 401, led Petilian to write against Augustine in more detail. In this letter, from which Augustine quotes extracts, Petilian sets out fully the Donatist insistence that the validity of the sacraments is totally dependent upon the moral worthiness of those who administer them. Petilian's words are included within quotation marks within Augustine's text.

"What we look for is the conscience" [Petilian] says, "of the one who gives [the sacraments], giving in holiness, to cleanse the conscience of the one who receives. For anyone who knowingly receives 'faith' from the faithless does not receive faith, but guilt." And he will then go on to say: "So how do you test this? For everything consists of an origin" he says, "and a root; if it does not possess something as its head, it is nothing. Nor can anything truly receive a second birth, unless it is born again from good seed."

Responding to this approach, Augustine argued that Donatism laid excessive emphasis upon the qualities of the human agent, and gave insufficient weight to the grace of Jesus Christ. It is, he argued, impossible for fallen human beings to make distinctions concerning who is pure and impure, worthy or unworthy. This view, which is totally consistent with his understanding of the church as a "mixed body" of saints and sinners, holds that the efficacy of a sacrament rests, not upon the merits of the individual administering it, but upon the merits of the one who instituted them in the first place – Jesus Christ. The validity of sacraments is independent of the merits of those who administer them.

Having said this, Augustine qualifies it in an important context. A distinction must be drawn, he argues, between "baptism" and "the right to baptize." Although baptism is valid, even when administered by those who are heretics or schismatics, this does not mean that the right to baptize is indiscriminately distributed among all peoples. The right to confer baptism exists only within the church, and supremely in those ministers whom it has chosen and authorized to administer the sacraments. The authority to administer the sacraments of Christ was committed by him to the apostles, and through them and their successors the bishops to the ministers of the catholic church.

The theological issue at stake has come to be represented by two Latin slogans, each reflecting a different understanding of the grounds of the efficacy of the sacraments.

1   Sacraments are efficacious *ex opere operantis* – literally, "on account of the work of the one who works." Here, the efficacy of the sacrament is understood to be dependent upon the personal qualities of the minister.

2   Sacraments are efficacious *ex opere operato* – literally, "on account of the work which is done." Here, the efficacy of the sacrament is understood to be dependent upon the grace of Christ, which the sacraments represent and convey.

The Donatist position is consistent with an *ex opere operantis*, and Augustine's with an *ex opere operato* understanding of sacramental causality. The latter view became normative within the western church, and was maintained by the mainstream reformers during the sixteenth century.

The *ex opere operato* approach to the efficacy of the sacraments was vigorously defended by Innocent III in the late twelfth century. For Innocent, the merits or demerits of the priest are of no consequence in relation to the efficacy of the Eucharist. In the end, the sacraments are grounded in the word of God, which is not restricted by human weakness or failing:

Nothing more is accomplished by a good priest and nothing less by a wicked priest, because it is accomplished by the word of the creator and not the merit of the priest. Thus the wickedness of the priest does not nullify the effect of the sacrament, just as the sickness of a doctor does not destroy the power of his medicine. Although the "doing of the thing [*opus operans*]" may be unclean, nevertheless the "thing which is done [*opus operatum*]" is always clean.

A similar approach is adopted by mainline Protestant writers during the sixteenth century. The Thirty-Nine Articles of the Church of England (1563) state this point clearly.

For those who receive the sacraments which are administered to them by faith and in proper fashion, the effect of Christ's ordinances is not taken away by the wickedness of the minister, nor is the grace of God's gifts diminished. These are effective on account of the institution and promise of Christ, even if they are administered by wicked people.

The Multiple Functions of the Sacraments

In the course of the development of Christian theology, a number of understandings of the role of the sacraments have developed. In what follows, we shall consider the four most significant views of the function of the sacraments. It must be stressed that these are not mutually incompatible. The view that sacraments convey grace is not, for example, inconsistent with the related view that sacraments reassure believers of the promises of God. The debate has tended to center on which of the functions are essential to a right understanding of the sacraments.

Sacraments convey grace

We noted earlier the insistence on the part of medieval writers that sacraments *convey* the grace which they signify. Traces of this view may be found in the second century. Ignatius of Antioch declared that the Eucharist was "the medicine of immortality and the antidote that we should not die, but live for ever in Jesus Christ." The idea is clearly that the Eucharist does not merely *signify* eternal life, but is somehow instrumental in *effecting* it. The idea is developed subsequently by many writers, especially Ambrose of Milan. Writing in the fourth century, Ambrose argued that in baptism the Holy Spirit "coming upon the font or upon those who are to be baptized, effects the reality of regeneration."

An important distinction, due to Augustine, relates to this point. Augustine distinguishes the sacrament from the "force [*virtus*] of the sacrament." The former is merely a sign, whereas the latter produces the effect to which the sign points. It is clear that a major function of the sacraments, in the thought of Augustine and his medieval successors, is that of the efficacious bestowal of grace.

Medieval writers sympathetic to Duns Scotus argued that it was not strictly proper to speak of the sacraments *causing* grace. The fourteenth-century writer Peter of Aquila put this point as follows:

> When Peter Lombard states that the sacraments effect what they signify, this must not be understood to mean that the sacraments themselves cause grace, in the strict sense of the word. Rather, God effects grace at the presence of the sacraments.

The sacraments are thus seen as causes in the sense of a *causa sine qua non* – that is, an indispensable precondition – rather than as causes in the stricter sense of the word. The idea that grace is "caused" does not mean that the sacrament effects grace by itself, without reference to God's initiative and action. Catholic theology has always insisted that God is to be seen as the agent, the remote efficient cause, and the final cause of grace (to use the classical categories of causality) in any legitimate theory of sacramental causality.

Such views were rejected by the reformers, who found themselves embarrassed by Augustine's insistence upon the efficacious nature of the sacraments, especially baptism. Peter Martyr Vermigli is an example of a sixteenth-century Protestant writer who is critical of Augustine at this point:

> Augustine grievously erred in this doctrine, in ascribing too much to baptism. He does not acknowledge that it is merely an outward symbol of regeneration, but holds that, by the very act of being baptized, we are regenerated and adopted, and enter into the family of Christ.

The efficacious nature of the sacraments was reaffirmed by the Council of Trent, which criticized the Protestant tendency (as seen, for example, in Vermigli) to treat sacraments as mere signs, but not causes, of grace.

If anyone says that the sacraments of the new law do not contain the grace that they signify, or that they do not confer that grace upon those who do not place obstacles in its path (as though they were only outward signs of grace or righteousness, received through faith, and certain marks of Christian profession by which believers are, at the human level, distinguished from nonbelievers), let them be condemned.

Trent prefers to speak of the sacraments "conferring" grace (rather than "causing" grace), thus allowing the Scotist position, noted above, to be maintained.

Sacraments strengthen faith

This understanding of the role of the sacraments is found throughout Christian history. It became of especial importance during the sixteenth-century Reformation, partly on account of the importance placed by leading Protestant thinkers upon the idea of trust (*fiducia*) as a defining characteristic of justifying faith. For the first generation of reformers, the sacraments were God's response to human weakness. Knowing our difficulty in receiving and responding to divine promises, the word of God has been supplemented with visible and tangible signs of the gracious favor. The sacraments represent the promises of God, mediated through objects of the everyday world. In his *Propositions on the Mass* (1521), Melanchthon stressed that sacraments were primarily a gracious divine accommodation to human weakness. In a series of 65 propositions, Melanchthon put forward what he regarded as a reliable and responsible approach to the place of the sacraments in Christian spirituality. "Signs are the means by which we may be both reminded and reassured of the word of faith."

In an ideal world, Melanchthon suggests, human beings would be prepared to trust God on the basis of the Word alone. However, one of the weaknesses of fallen human nature is its need for signs (Melanchthon appeals to the Old Testament story of Gideon as he makes this point). For Melanchthon, sacraments are signs: "What some call sacraments, we call signs – or, if you prefer, sacramental signs." These sacramental signs enhance our trust in God. "In order to mitigate this distrust in the human heart, God has added signs to the word." Sacraments are thus signs of the grace of God, added to the promises of grace in order to reassure and strengthen the faith of fallen human beings.

Signs do not justify, as the apostle says: "circumcision counts for nothing" (1 Corinthians 7: 19), so that baptism is nothing, and participation in the Lord's Supper [*mensa domini*] is nothing, but they are testimonies and "seals" of the divine will toward you which give assurance to your conscience if it doubts God's grace or benevolence toward you. [. . .] The knowledge of signs is very healthful, and I have no idea whether there is anything else that consoles the conscience and strengthens it more effectively than this use of signs. Those things which others call "sacraments" we call "signs," or, if you prefer, "sacramental signs." [. . .] Those who have compared these signs with symbols or military passwords are to be commended for doing so, because signs were only marks by which those to whom the divine promises pertained could be known.

Luther made a similar point, defining sacraments as "promises with signs attached to them" or "divinely instituted signs and the promise of forgiveness of sins." Interestingly, Luther uses the term "pledge" to emphasize the security-giving character of the Eucharist. The bread and the wine reassure us of the reality of the divine promise of forgiveness, making it easier for us to accept it, and, having accepted it, to hold it firmly.

A related view is associated with the revival of sacramental theology within Roman Catholicism during the twentieth century. The resurgence in Catholic interest in the theology of the sacraments can be traced back to the work of the German Benedictine scholar Odo Casel (1886–1948), who wrote extensively on this matter in the period between the two world wars. This interest was developed and sustained by writers such as Edward Schillebeeckx and Karl Rahner, and found its expression at the Second Vatican Council. One of the most notable features of the Council's teaching relates to the sacramental understanding of the church, a matter which has been dealt with in more detail elsewhere (pp. 402–4).

The Second Vatican Council stressed the importance of sacraments in relation to the growth of faith, in terms of both personal commitment and a proper understanding of Christian faith. Christian theology has always recognized a distinction between the act and content of Christian faith. Traditionally, two Latin phrases are used to express this distinction, as follows:

1 *fides qua creditur* (literally, "the faith by which it is believed") refers to the act of trust and assent which lies at the heart of Christian belief;
2 *fides quae creditur* ("the faith which is believed") refers to the specific content of Christian faith, expressed in various creeds, confessions, doctrines, and other statements of faith.

For the Second Vatican Council, sacraments sustain and nourish faith in the sense of both *fides qua creditur* and *fides quae creditur*:

> Because [sacraments] are signs, they also instruct. They not only presuppose faith, but by words and objects they also nourish, strengthen, and express it. That is why they

are called "sacraments of faith." They do indeed confer grace, but in addition the very act of celebrating them most effectively disposes the faithful to receive this grace to their profit, to worship God duly, and to practice charity.

Sacraments enhance unity and commitment within the church

The unity of the church was a source of major concern during the patristic period, especially as division arose in response to the Decian and Diocletian persecutions. Cyprian of Carthage, as we saw earlier (pp. 395, 409), laid considerable emphasis upon the unity of the church, and urged its members to work toward greater harmony within and commitment to the church. This point is developed by Augustine, with especial reference to the sacraments. For a society to have any degree of cohesion, there must be some act in which all can share, which both demonstrates and enhances that unity. "In no religion, whether true or false, can people be held together in association, unless they are gathered together with some common share in some visible signs or sacraments." Although this point was understood by medieval writers, it found its most forceful expression at the time of the Reformation, especially in the writings of Huldrych Zwingli.

Luther asserted that a central function of the sacraments was to reassure believers that they were truly members of the body of Christ, and heirs of the kingdom of God. He developed this point at some length in his 1519 treatise *The Blessed Sacrament of the Holy and True Body of Christ*, stressing the psychological assurance that it made available to believers:

> To receive this sacrament in bread and wine, then, is nothing else than to receive a sure sign of this fellowship and union with Christ and all the saints. It is as if citizens were given a sign, a document, or some other token, to

assure them that they are indeed citizens of the city, and members of that particular community. [. . .] In this sacrament, therefore, we are given a sure sign from God that we are united with Christ and the saints, and have all things in common with them, and that Christ's suffering and life are our own.

This emphasis upon the sacraments as tokens of belonging to the Christian community is, as will become clear presently, perhaps more characteristic of Zwingli than of Luther; nevertheless, it is a significant element of Luther's thought at this point.

For Zwingli, the purpose of the sacraments is primarily to demonstrate that an individual belongs to the community of faith. Baptism represents the public declaration that a child is a member of the household of God. Zwingli pointed out that in the Old Testament, infant males were circumcised within days of their birth as a sign of their membership of the people of Israel. Circumcision was the rite laid down by the Old Testament covenant to demonstrate that the circumcised child belonged to the covenant community. The child had been born into a community, to which it now belonged – and circumcision was a sign of belonging to this community.

It had been a long-standing tradition within Christian theology to see baptism as the Christian equivalent of circumcision. Developing this idea, Zwingli argued that baptism is the New Testament equivalent of the Old Testament rite of circumcision. It is gentler than circumcision, in that it involves no pain or shedding of blood, and more inclusive, in that it embraces both male and female infants. Further, Zwingli stressed that baptism was the sign of belonging to a community – the church. The fact that the child was not conscious of this belonging was irrelevant: it *was* a member of the Christian community, and baptism was the public demonstration of this

membership. The contrast with Luther on this point will be obvious.

In a similar way, attendance at the Eucharist represents a continuing public declaration of loyalty to the church. Zwingli develops this meaning of the Eucharist with a military analogy drawn from his experience as an army chaplain for the Swiss Confederacy:

> If a man sews on a white cross, he proclaims that he wishes to be a confederate. And if he makes the pilgrimage to Nähenfels and gives God praise and thanksgiving for the victory vouchsafed to our forefathers, he testifies that he is a confederate indeed. Similarly, whoever receives the mark of baptism is the one who is resolved to hear what God says to him, to learn the divine precepts, and to live his life in accordance with them. And whoever in the congregation gives thanks to God in the remembrance or supper testifies to the fact that he rejoices in the death of Christ from the depths of his heart, and thanks him for it.

The reference is to the victory of the Swiss over the Austrians in 1388 near Nähenfels, in the canton of Glarus. This victory is usually regarded as marking the beginning of the Swiss (or Helvetic) Confederation, and it was commemorated by a pilgrimage to the site of the battle on the first Thursday in April.

Zwingli makes two points. First, the Swiss soldier wears a white cross (now incorporated into the Swiss national flag, of course) as a *Pflichtszeichen* (sign of commitment) demonstrating publicly his allegiance to the Confederacy. Similarly, the Christian demonstrates his allegiance to the church publicly, initially by baptism, and subsequently by participating in the Eucharist. Baptism is the "visible entry and sealing into Christ."

Second, the historical event which brought the Confederacy into being is commemorated as a token of allegiance to that same Confederacy. Similarly, the Christian commemorates the historical event which brought the Christian church into being (the death of Jesus Christ) as a token of his commitment to that church. The Eucharist is thus a memorial of the historical event leading to the establishment of the Christian church, and a public demonstration of the believer's allegiance to that church and its members. This is related to Zwingli's memorialist approach to the Eucharist, which we shall explore further later (p. 440).

Sacraments reassure us of God's promises toward us

Once more, this function is especially associated with the reformers, who laid particular emphasis upon faith as the human correlative to the promises of God. The reformers were deeply aware of the weakness of fallen human nature, and knew that it required considerable reassurance concerning God's love and commitment. Luther regarded the death of Christ as a token of both the trustworthiness and the enormous price of the grace of God. Luther developed this point by using the idea of a "testament," understood in the sense of a "last will and testament." This point is taken to its full extent in his 1520 work, *The Babylonian Captivity of the Christian Church*.

> A testament is, without doubt, a promise made by someone who is about to die, in which a bequest is identified and heirs are appointed. A testament, therefore, involves first, the death of the testator; and second, the promise of an inheritance and the identification of the heirs. [...] Christ testifies concerning his death when he says: "This is my body, which is given, this is my blood, which is poured out" (Luke 22: 19–20). He names and designates the bequest when he says "for the forgiveness of sins" (Matthew 26: 28). And he appoints the heirs when he says "For you (Luke 22: 19–20; 1 Corinthians

11: 24), and for many" (Matthew 26: 28; Mark 14: 24), that is, for those who accept and believe the promise of the testator.

Luther's insight here is that a testament involves promises which become operational only after the death of the person who made those promises in the first place. The liturgy of the Eucharist thus makes three vitally important points:

1 It affirms the promises of grace and forgiveness.
2 It identifies those to whom those promises are made.
3 It declares the death of the one who made those promises.

The Eucharist thus dramatically proclaims that the promises of grace and forgiveness are now in effect. It is "a promise of the forgiveness of sins made to us by God, and such a promise as has been confirmed by the death of the son of God." By proclaiming the death of Christ the community of faith affirms that the precious promises of forgiveness and eternal life are now effective for those with faith. As Luther himself puts this point:

> So you see that what we call the mass is a promise of the forgiveness of sins, made to us by God, and such a promise as has been confirmed by the death of the Son of God. For a promise and a testament differ only in that a testament involves the death of the one who makes it. A testator is someone who promises and is about to die, while someone who promises (if I may put it thus) is a testator who is not about to die. This testament of Christ is foreshadowed in all the promises of God from the beginning of the world; indeed, whatever value those ancient promises possessed derived totally from this new promise that was to come in Christ. [...] Now God made a testament; therefore, it was necessary that

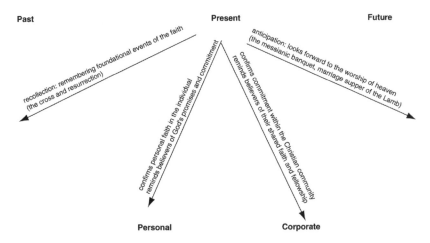

Figure 3   The Theological Functions of the Eucharist

he should die. But God could not die unless he became a human. Thus the incarnation and the death of Christ are both to be understood as being in this one enormously rich word, "testament."

A case study in complexity: the functions of the Eucharist

Our discussion in this section has emphasized the many functions of the sacraments. It will be helpful to end this section by exploring the many functions of the Eucharist in Christian thought, integrating some of the themes developed in our discussion to date. The Eucharist – or Mass, Holy Communion, or Lord's Supper – is an action carried out in the present, with past and future dimensions, as can be seen from Figure 3. In what follows, we shall explore these in more detail.

Recollection: looking backward

First, the Eucharist invites Christians to look backward into the past, and recalls the saving acts of God in general, and above all, the cross and resurrection of Christ. The general prin-

ciple of recalling God's saving acts is firmly established in the Old Testament. For example, many of the Psalms (such as Psalm 136) invite Israel to remember God's past actions in delivering them from Egypt and leading them into the Promised Land. The basic theme is simple: the God who acted faithfully in the past may be relied upon to do the same in the present and the future.

The recollection of the past also emphasizes the continuity between the church and Israel, the New and Old Covenants. It has often been pointed out that the Eucharist can be seen (though the parallel is not exact) as the Christian equivalent of the Passover – the great annual Jewish festival, recalling the events of the Exodus from Egypt. The Passover festival was celebrated with a meal. According to the Synoptic Gospels, the "Last Supper" was a Passover meal, suggesting that Jesus wished his followers to make a connection between the past act of delivering Israel from Egypt, and the greater act of deliverance that was about to take place.

The central items of the Eucharist are bread and wine, which are held to recollect the breaking of Christ's body and the shedding of his blood on the cross. These items played a central role in the last supper. Here is Luke's account of what happened on that occasion (Luke 22: 19–20):

> Then [Jesus] took a loaf of bread, and when he had given thanks, he broke it and gave it to them, saying, "This is my body, which is given for you. Do this in remembrance of me." And he did the same with the cup after supper, saying, "This cup that is poured out for you is the new covenant in my blood."

The Eucharist is thus an invitation to look backwards, recalling all that God has done. It recalls the great acts of divine redemption in the past, such as Israel's deliverance from captivity in Egypt – but above all, the death of Jesus Christ, which is recalled by the liturgy, which incorporates biblical accounts of the Last Supper.

Anticipation – looking forward

Having invited Christians to look backwards in remembrance, the Eucharist then points to the future, inviting Christians to anticipate what has yet to happen. This theme is deeply embedded in the New Testament. For example, Paul's account of the Eucharist makes specific reference to its anticipation of the return of Christ in the future (1 Corinthians 11: 23–6):

> For I received from the Lord what I also handed on to you, that the Lord Jesus on the night when he was betrayed took a loaf of bread, and when he had given thanks, he broke it and said, "This is my body that is for you. Do this in remembrance of me." In the same way he took the cup also, after supper, saying, "This cup is the new covenant in my blood. Do this, as often as you drink it, in remembrance of me." For as often as you eat this bread and drink the cup, you proclaim the Lord's death until he comes.

This theme of anticipation is also focused on another biblical theme – the hope of the New Jerusalem. The vision of the New Jerusalem offered by the Book of Revelation, the last book in the Christian Bible, speaks of "the marriage supper of the Lamb" (Revelation 19: 9). The reference here is to Jesus Christ as the "lamb of God, who takes away the sin of the world" (John 1: 29). It is important to see the Eucharist as a present foretaste of this future event. For this reason, the Second Vatican Council referred to the Eucharist as a "foretaste of the heavenly banquet." This point is made particularly clearly by Theodore of Mopsuestia (c.350–428), a writer standing within the Antiochene school of biblical interpretation. For Theodore, the Eucharist allows us to glimpse the realities of heaven, and anticipate our future presence there.

> Every time that the liturgy of this awesome sacrifice is performed, which is the clear image of the heavenly realities, we should imagine that we are in heaven [...] Faith enables us to picture in our minds those heavenly realities, as we remind ourselves that the same Christ who is now in heaven is [also present] under these symbols. So when faith enables our eyes to contemplate what now takes place, we are brought again to see his death, resurrection, and ascension, which have already taken place for our sakes.

Affirming individual faith

We have already seen (427–8) that sacraments affirm the present faith of individual believers. This process of affirmation takes place through the mind and imagination. The believer, who is located in the present, is able to reflect on what God has done in the past, anticipate what God will do in the future, and deepen his or her faith and trust in God as a consequence.

Affirming corporate belonging

As noted earlier (428–30), sacraments can be regarded as strengthening the mutual commitment and support of members of the Christian community. In a sense, this can be seen as the original meaning of the word *sacramentum* – a solemn oath of obedience and commitment.

The important point to appreciate is that different theologians place their emphases at different points. Some want to emphasize the Eucharist as a memorial of what God has done in the past. Others want to stress its potential to enhance unity and commitment within the church. Yet all these elements are present; the question concerns which is to be accentuated.

In considering these four aspects of the Eucharist, readers will have noticed we have not addressed what is possibly the most interesting, and certainly the most debated, of its aspects – namely, the real presence. In what way, if any, does the Eucharist make Christ present to believers? We shall consider the debates over this question in what follows.

The Eucharist: The Question of the Real Presence

The sacraments have never been of purely theoretical importance for Christianity. From the earliest of times, the sacraments have been of central importance to Christian life and worship. This is especially the case with the Eucharist. Even in the New Testament we find reference to the first Christians obeying Jesus Christ's command to remember him through the bread and wine (1 Corinthians 11: 20–7).

It was therefore inevitable and entirely proper that considerable theological attention should be given to the explanation of the meaning of this practice. What did it achieve? And in what way did the eucharistic bread and wine differ from ordinary bread and wine? The words spoken by Jesus Christ over the bread at the Last Supper, and repeated in the liturgy of the church, were clearly of foundational importance.

But what did those words "this is my body" (Matthew 26: 26) mean? The words certainly suggested that Jesus was really present at the breaking of the eucharistic bread – an idea often referred to as "the real presence." It is this question that we shall consider in the present section of this work. Not only is the question of considerable interest in its own right; it is of importance in relation to the differences which have emerged within Christianity since the time of the Reformation.

A particularly important witness to the early Christian understanding of the fate of the bread and wine is provided by the "catechetical lectures" of Cyril of Jerusalem. This series of 24 lectures of instruction on the beliefs and practices of the Christian church, given at some point around 350 to those preparing for baptism, are an important witness to the ideas which prevailed in the Jerusalem church around this point. It is clear that Cyril regarded the bread and wine as somehow becoming the body and blood of Christ.

[Jesus Christ] by his own will once changed water into wine at Cana in Galilee. So why should we not believe that he can change wine into blood? [. . .] We should therefore have full assurance that we are sharing in the body and blood of Christ. For in the type of bread, his body is given to you, and in the type of wine, his blood is given to you, so that by partaking of the body and blood of Christ you may become of one body and one blood with him.

The question of how this transformation took place was of considerable interest to the patristic writers. Most, like the great Greek theologian John of Damascus, writing in the early eighth century, believed that it was sufficient simply to affirm the mystery:

And now you ask how the bread becomes the body of Christ, and the wine and the water become the blood of Christ. I shall tell you. The Holy Spirit comes upon them, and achieves things which surpass every word and thought. [. . .] Let it be enough for you to understand that this takes place by the Holy Spirit.

Others, however, were inclined to be more speculative, leading to a major controversy over the issue in the western church during the ninth century, to which we now turn.

The ninth-century debates over the real presence

The monastery of Corbie in Picardy was the scene for some theological fireworks during the ninth century, focusing on the doctrine of predestination and the nature of the real presence. The two major combatants were Paschasius Radbertus and Ratramnus, who were both monks at this great French monastery during this period. Each wrote a work with the same title – *De corpore et sanguine Christi* ("Concerning the Body and Blood of Christ") – yet developing very different understandings of the real presence. Radbertus, whose work was completed around 844, developed the idea that the bread and the wine become the body and blood of Christ in reality; Ratramnus, whose work was written shortly afterwards, defended the view that they were merely symbols of the body and blood.

Although Radbertus did not offer an explanation of precisely how ordinary bread was transformed into the body of Christ, he was convinced of the physical reality and spiritual importance of the change:

The same Spirit who created the human being Jesus Christ in the womb of the Virgin without any human seed daily creates the flesh and the blood of Christ by his invisible power through the consecration of this sacrament, even though this cannot be understood outwardly by either sight or taste.

Ratramnus was not convinced, and argued along very different lines. The difference between ordinary and consecrated bread lay in the way in which the believer perceived them. The consecrated bread remained bread; however, the believer was enabled to perceive a deeper spiritual meaning as a result of its consecration. The difference thus lies in the believer, rather than in the bread.

The bread which, through the ministry of the priest, becomes the body of Christ exhibits one thing externally to human senses, and points to something different inwardly to the minds of believers. Externally, the bread has the same shape, color, and flavor as before; inwardly, however, something very different, something much more precious and excellent, is made known, because something heavenly and divine – that is, the body of Christ – is revealed. This is not perceived or received or consumed by the physical senses, but only in the sight of the believer.

A third approach was also developed at this time. Candidus of Fulda, a noted German monastery, argued that the phrase "this is my body" (Matthew 26: 26) refers to the "body of Christ" in the sense of *the Christian church*. The purpose of the sacrament of the body and blood of Christ is to nourish and bring to perfection the church as the body of Christ.

This is the body which was given for you. He took this body from the mass of humanity, broke it in the passion, and, having broken it, raised it again from the dead. [...] What he took from us, he has now given to us. And you are to "eat" it. That is, you are to make perfect the body of the church, so that it might become the entire, perfect one bread, whose head is Christ.

The medieval clarification of the relation of "sign" and "sacrament" in the Eucharist

The development of the doctrine of the sacraments during the Middle Ages gave rise to some technical terms which readers may find it important to understand. Although many find it easiest to think of sacraments in terms of the distinction between the "sign" and "what is signified," medieval theologians used a triple classification, which merits discussion at this point.

During the twelfth-century theological renaissance, the various aspects of sacraments were clarified by means of a threefold distinction, based on the writings of St Augustine. In thinking about the Eucharist, it was argued, three different aspects of the sacrament should be distinguished. The scholastics distinguished between the sacramental sign itself (*sacramentum tantum*), the intermediate effect brought about by the sacrament (*res et sacramentum*), and the ultimate effect or "fruit" of the sacrament (*res tantum*). In what follows, we shall explore these distinctions, using the terminology that you are likely to encounter in more technical discussions.

1   The sign itself (*sacramentum* or *sacramentum tantum*): This refers to the bread and the wine in the Eucharist. This is the easiest of these three ideas to understand. The basic idea is that a physical element (such as bread) has a capacity to signify and cause something beyond itself.

2   Something that is both a reality and a sign (*res et sacramentum*): In the case of the Eucharist, this refers to the consecrated bread and wine, which are understood to become the body and blood of Christ. Both the bread and the wine remain present as signs; however, an additional reality (the *res*, a Latin term meaning "thing") is now present – the body and blood of Christ – which was not there before.

3   The sacramental reality (*res tantum* or *res sacramenti*): This refers to the inward and spiritual grace which results from the sacrament. In the case of the Eucharist, this is understood to be the recipient's participation in the death and resurrection of Christ, and the benefits that this brings. It is important to note that this sacramental reality is to be distinguished from pure signs (bread and wine) on the one hand, and the body and blood of Christ on the other. The question being asked is not "what do the bread and wine become?", but "what benefits do the body and blood of Christ bring to those who receive them?"

To help us understand this difficult distinction, we may consider how a medieval Eucharist would take place, and the changing status of the bread and wine during the event. What follows is a loose paraphrase of Thomas Aquinas's exposition of these concepts in his *Summa Theologiae*.

1   Before consecration, the bread and wine are only signs of the body and blood which they will later become. Each is therefore a *sacramentum tantum* – a mere sign.

2   After the consecration, the "accidents," or outward appearances, of the bread and

wine remain as signs of the reality of the substance of the body and blood of Christ. Yet the body and blood, into which the substance of the bread and wine have now been changed, really are present beneath the outward signs. The bread and wine now fulfill two functions (*res et sacramentum*): first, at the level of their accidents or outward appearances, they act as an outward sign of the body and blood of Christ; and secondly, at the level of "substance" or inward identity, they really are the body and blood of Christ. They therefore act as both sacramental *sign* and sacramental *reality*. But this is not the same as the intended ultimate effect of the sacrament. The purpose of the sacrament is not to make Christ physically present, but to convey a special grace that results from this – and this is the *res tantum*, to which we now turn.

3 To appreciate the concept of the *res tantum* we need to ask what the Eucharist is intended to achieve. What is the goal of the Eucharist? What are its intended outcomes? What is the effect of consuming the bread and wine, both as sacramental sign and sacramental reality? What difference do they make to those who receive them? The *res tantum* of the Eucharist is communion of the believer with Christ, and the pledge of future glory in heaven. Christ is really and truly present in the Eucharist – but his presence is not an end in itself, but is intended to have a transforming effect on the believer. The intended function or final effect of the Eucharist is the union of the members of the church, considered as Christ's Mystical Body, with Christ as their head, and with each other, and reassurance of the hope of glory in heaven.

The debate over the real presence continued in subsequent theological discussion, particularly during the Middle Ages. The issue became particularly controversial at the time of the Reformation, and remains an issue of contention among Christians today. In what follows, we shall outline the three main positions encountered in modern Christianity, and indicate their historical development.

Transubstantiation

We have already noted how Paschasius Radbertus had insisted that the bread and wine became the body and blood of Christ as a result of their consecration, even though he experienced some difficulty in conceptualizing this change. The doctrine of transubstantiation represents a consolidation and development of this position.

The doctrine was formally defined by the Fourth Lateran Council (1215), probably the greatest Council to meet before the Council of Trent in the sixteenth century. Although the Council did not provide a formal, extended discussion of the process of transubstantiation, it offered a definitive statement of its essential features.

> There is one universal church of the faithful, outside of which none can be saved, in which the priest himself is the sacrifice, Jesus Christ, whose body and blood are truly contained under the species of bread and wine, by the bread being changed in substance to the body [*transsubstantis pane in corpus*] and the wine to the blood through the divine power.

Although the Council used Aristotelian language throughout its discussion – notice the references to "substance" and "species" – the doctrine was placed upon more solid Aristotelian foundations – specifically, on Aristotle's distinction between "substance" and "accident" – by Thomas Aquinas. The *substance* of something is its essential nature, whereas its *accidents* are its outward appearances (its color, shape, smell, and so forth). The theory of transubstantiation affirms that the accidents of the bread and wine (their outward appearance, taste, smell, and so forth) remain unchanged at the moment of consecration, while their substance changes from that of bread and wine to that of the body and blood of Jesus Christ. Aquinas is adamant that the substance of the bread and wine does not remain after consecration; their outward appearance may remain unaltered, but their original identity as bread and wine is annihilated.

This approach was heavily criticized by Protestant theologians, especially at the time of the Reformation, for introducing Aristotelian ideas into Christian theology. Luther's own position is somewhat closer to transubstantiation than many realize. His main criticism of the doctrine is that it depends upon the use of pagan philosophical categories (namely, substance and accidents). As we shall consider presently, Luther's own approach – widely referred to (but not by Luther himself) as "consubstantiation" – holds that the body and blood of Christ are indeed given along with, or under, the bread and wine. Other Protestant writers, most notably Huldrych Zwingli, were much more critical of the concept.

It was not until 1551 that the Council of Trent finally set forth the positive position of the Roman Catholic church in the "Decree on the Most Holy Sacrament of the Eucharist." Up to this point, Trent had merely criticized the reformers, without putting forth a coherent alternative position. This deficiency was now remedied. The Decree opens with a strong affirmation of the real substantial presence of Christ: "After the consecration of the bread and wine, our Lord Jesus Christ is truly, really and substantially contained in the venerable sacrament of the holy Eucharist under the appearance of those physical things." The Council vigorously defended both the doctrine and the terminology of transubstantiation. "By the consecration of the bread and wine a change is brought about of the whole substance of the bread into the substance of the body of Christ and of the whole substance of the wine into the blood of Christ. This change the holy catholic church properly and appropriately calls transubstantiation."

Following the Council of Trent, the concept of transubstantiation was regarded as the definitive Catholic position on the matter, and was not subject of serious debate within the Catholic church until the 1960s. The doctrine was not without its difficulties, not least in terms of offering a natural illustration for the strongly counterintuitive ideas lying behind it. One of the most interesting defenses of the doctrine is due to the French Catholic philosopher René Descartes (1596–1650). In a letter of 1645, Descartes suggested that the human digestive system offered a natural analogy for transubstantiation. The human body, he argued, was an organic model for the process. Was not the natural process of digestion about the transformation of bread into a human body? No appeal to the miraculous need be made. If the eucharistic transubstantiation required any kind of miracle, it is in the sense that it implies the assimilation of the bread to the body of Christ without the mediation of the organic functions of the human body. It was an interesting point, but not one that was welcomed by the church authorities of the time.

Transignification and transfinalization

During the 1960s – a time of considerable theological ferment within Catholicism – the idea of transubstantiation came under critical examination by Catholic theologians, such as Edward Schillebeeckx. In response to growing anxiety over the apologetic plausibility of the notion of transubstantiation, two ways of reconceiving the notion were developed.

Each, to its supporters, seemed to retain the essential features of the older dogma, while responding to the metaphysical skepticism of the era.

The notion of *transfinalization* expresses the idea that consecration alters the end or purpose of the bread and wine. The related notion of *transignification* expresses the idea that consecration is primarily concerned with the *change of meaning* of the bread and the wine. Transfinalization thus refers to a fundamental change of the purpose of the bread and wine (for example, the goal of physical nourishment is replaced with that of spiritual nourishment). Transignification refers to a fundamental change in what the bread and wine signifies or points to (for example, from signifying food into signifying Christ). Both these notions rest upon the assumption that the identity of the bread and wine cannot be isolated from their context or use.

The basic ideas involved can be found in the writings of Zwingli during the 1520s. What makes the bread at a communion service different from any other bread? If it is not the body of Christ, what is it? Zwingli answers this question with an analogy. Consider a queen's ring, he suggests. Now consider that ring in two quite different contexts. In the first context, the ring is merely present. Perhaps you can imagine a ring lying on a table. It has no associations. Now imagine that ring transferred to a new context. It is placed on the finger of a queen, as a gift from her king. It now has personal associations, deriving from its connection with him – such as his authority, power, and majesty. Its value is now far greater than that of the gold of which it is made. These associations arise through transfer from the original context to the new context. The ring itself remains completely unchanged.

So it is with the communion bread, Zwingli argues. The bread and the ring are both unchanged in themselves, while their signification alters dramatically. The signification – in other words, the associations of the object – can change, without any difference in the nature of the object itself. Zwingli suggests that exactly the same process can be seen with the bread and the wine. In their ordinary everyday context, they are plain bread and wine, with no especial associations. But when they are moved into a new context, they take on new and important associations. When they are placed at the center of a worshiping community, and when the story of the last night of the life of Christ is retold, they become powerful reminders of the foundational events of the Christian faith. It is their context which gives them this meaning; they remain unchanged in themselves.

However, the terms "transignification" and "transfinalization" began to be used extensively during the 1960s, particularly by a group of Belgian Roman Catholic theologians who found themselves ill at ease with the traditional language of "transubstantiation." In his important study *The Eucharist* (1968), Edward Schillebeeckx argued that the Aristotelian philosophical framework underlying this notion caused difficulties for many modern people. A new approach was needed, he argued, which would retain the essential theological insights of the Council of Trent, without embodying these in an outdated and vulnerable philosophical framework.

Schillebeeckx noted that a growing hostility toward the use of ontological or "physical" interpretations of the Eucharist within Catholic circles after World War II was matched by a "rediscovery of the sacramental symbolic activity" – that is, a realization that "the sacraments are first and foremost symbolic acts or activity as signs." Schillebeeckx suggests that the Italian writer Joseph de Baciocchi gave a new sense of direction to this way of thinking during the 1950s, and introduced the terms "transfunctionalism," "transfinalization" and "transignification" to explain the approach he had in mind. After noting the contribution to this way of thinking by writers such as Piet Schoonenberg and Luchesius Smits, Schillebeeckx sets out his approach to this issue, as follows:

> Christ's gift of himself, however, is not ultimately directed towards bread and wine, but towards the faithful. The real presence is intended for believers, but through the medium of and *in* this gift of bread and wine. In other words, the Lord who gives himself thus is *sacramentally* present. In this commemorative meal, bread and wine become the subject of a new *establishment of meaning*, not by men, but by the living Lord *in* the Church, through which they become the *sign* of the real presence of Christ giving himself to us.

Schillebeeckx's point is that interpretation of the signification of the eucharistic bread and wine is not arbitrary, nor a human imposition upon them; it is an act of discernment by the church, which it has been *authorized* to undertake by Christ.

There is, for Schillebeeckx, no need to invoke the notion of a physical change of substance of the bread and wine. Christ's intention was not to alter the metaphysics of the eucharistic elements, but to ensure that these pointed to his continuing presence within the church, as the community of the faithful.

> Something can be essentially changed without its physical or biological make-up being changed. In relationships between persons, bread acquires a sense quite other than the sense it has for the physicist or the metaphysician, for example. Bread, while remaining physically what it was, can be taken up into an order of significance other than the purely biological. The bread then *is* other than it was, because its determinate relationship to

man plays its part in determining the reality about which we are speaking.

The parallels with Zwingli's position, though not noted by Schillebeeckx himself, can hardly be overlooked.

The official response of the Catholic Church to these developments was to affirm that they were acceptable, provided that they were upheld within the context of the traditional understanding of transubstantiation. If the bread and the wine were indeed changed in the manner that this traditional teaching affirmed, it followed that both the goal and the signification of the bread and wine were changed as well. In his encyclical *Mysterium Fidei* (1965), Pope Paul VI stated the point at issue as follows:

> As a result of transubstantiation, the species of bread and wine undoubtedly take on a new signification and a new finality, for they are no longer ordinary bread and wine but instead a sign of something sacred and a sign of spiritual food. Yet they take on this new signification, this new finality, precisely because they contain a new "reality." [...] For what now lies beneath the aforementioned species [that is, what is now the new substance of the elements] is not what was there before, but something completely different [...] namely, the body and blood of Christ.

Consubstantiation

This view, especially associated with Martin Luther, insists upon the simultaneous presence of both bread and the body of Christ at one and the same time. There is no change in substance; the substance of both bread and the body of Christ are present together. The doctrine of transubstantiation seemed to Luther to be an absurdity, an attempt to rationalize a mystery.

For Luther, the crucial point was that Christ was really present at the Eucharist – not some particular theory as to how he was present. He deploys an image borrowed from Origen to make his point: if iron is placed in a fire and heated, it glows – and in that glowing iron, both the iron and heat are present. For Luther, it was vastly preferable to use some simple everyday analogy such as this to illustrate the mystery of the presence of Christ at the Eucharist, than to rationalize it using some metaphysical subtlety. For Luther, it is not the specific doctrine of transubstantiation which is to be believed, but simply that Christ really is present at the Eucharist. This fact, he argued, was far more important than any theory or explanation invoked subsequent to the actuality of that presence.

A real absence: memorialism

The most metaphysically austere understanding of the "real presence" is especially associated with the Swiss reformer Huldrych Zwingli. For Zwingli, the Eucharist (he preferred to style it "the Remembrance") is "a memorial of the suffering of Christ, and not a sacrifice." For reasons which we shall explore below, Zwingli insists that the words "this is my body" cannot be taken literally, thus eliminating any idea of the "real presence of Christ" at the Eucharist. Just as a man, on setting off on a long journey from home, might give his wife his ring to remember him by until his return, so Christ leaves his church a token to remember him by until the day on which he should return in glory.

But what of the words "this is my body" (Matthew 26: 26), which had been the cornerstone of traditional Catholic views of the real presence, and which Luther had seized upon in his defense of the real presence? Zwingli argued that "there are innumerable passages in Scripture where the word 'is' means 'signi-

fies.'" The question that must therefore be addressed is

> whether Christ's words in Matthew 26, "This is my body" can also be taken metaphorically or figuratively. It has already become clear enough that in this context the word "is" cannot be taken literally. Hence it follows that it must be taken metaphorically or figuratively. In the words "This is my body," the word "this" means the bread, and the word "body" means the body which was put to death for us. Therefore the word "is" cannot be taken literally, for the bread *is* not the body.

Zwingli thus develops a theory of "transignification," in which the bread and the wine change their significance as a result of their location within the eucharistic liturgy. The change is subjective, not objective, lying in the way in which worshipers regard the bread and wine, not in their actual identity. The bread and wine thus become reminders of Christ in his absence, and a central focus for the church's expectation that her Lord will one day return. There is no metaphysical difficulty about the presence of Christ in the Eucharist, precisely because there is no presence to discuss.

The Debate Concerning Infant Baptism

The second major sacrament which is virtually universally recognized throughout Christianity is baptism. Perhaps the most important controversy to center upon this sacrament is whether it is legitimate to baptize infants – and if so, what theological justification may be provided for the practice. It is not clear whether the early church baptized infants. The New Testament includes no specific references to the baptism of infants. However, it does not explicitly forbid the practice, and there are also a number of passages which could be interpreted as condoning it – for example, references to the baptizing of entire households (which would probably have included infants) – at several points (Acts 16: 15, 33; 1 Corinthians 1: 16). Paul treats baptism as a spiritual counterpart to circumcision (Colossians 2: 11–12), suggesting that the parallel may extend to its application to infants.

The practice of baptizing infant members of Christian parents – often referred to as *paedobaptism* – appears to have been a response to a number of pressures. It is possible that the parallel with the Jewish rite of circumcision led Christians to devise an equivalent rite of passage for Christian infants. More generally, there seems to have been a pastoral need for Christian parents to celebrate the birth of a child within a believing household. Infant baptism may well have had its origins partly in response to this concern. However, it must be stressed that there is genuine uncertainty concerning both the historical origins and the social or theological causes of the practice.

What can be said is that the practice had become normal, if not universal, by the second or third century, and would exercise considerable influence over a major theological debate: the Pelagian controversy. In the third century, Origen treated infant baptism as a universal practice, which he justified on the basis of a universal human need for the grace of Christ. A similar argument would later be deployed by Augustine: in that Christ is the savior of all, it follows that all – including infants – require redemption, which baptism confers, at least in part. Opposition to the practice can be seen in the writings of Tertullian, who argued that the baptism of children should be deferred until such time as they "know Christ."

In more recent times, infant baptism has been subjected to intense negative scrutiny in the writings of Karl Barth, who directs three major lines of criticism against the practice, as follows.

1 It is without biblical foundation. All the evidence points to infant baptism having become the norm in the postapostolic period, not the period of the New Testament itself.

2 The practice of infant baptism has led to the disastrous assumption that individuals are Christians as a result of their birth. Barth argues, in terms which remind many of Bonhoeffer's idea of "cheap grace," that infant baptism devalues the grace of God, and reduces Christianity to a purely social phenomenon.

3 The practice of infant baptism weakens the central link between baptism and Christian discipleship. Baptism is a witness to the grace of God, and marks the beginning of the human response to this grace. In that infants cannot meaningfully make this response, the theological meaning of baptism is obscured.

While all of Barth's arguments can be countered, they are an impressive witness to a continuing unease within at least some quarters of the mainstream churches over the potential abuse of the practice of infant baptism.

Three major approaches to the question of infant baptism can be discerned within the Christian tradition. In what follows, we shall consider these individually.

Infant baptism remits the guilt of original sin

This position owes its origins to Cyprian of Carthage, who declared that infant baptism procured remission of both sinful acts and original sin. The final steps in the theological justification of the practice are due to Augustine of Hippo, in responding to the issues surrounding the Pelagian controversy. Had not the creed laid down that there was "one baptism for the forgiveness of sins"? It therefore followed that infant baptism remitted original sin.

This raised a question of potential difficulty. If original sin was remitted by baptism, why did the infants in question behave in a sinful manner in later life? Augustine met this objection by distinguishing between the *guilt* and the *disease* of original sin (see pp. 364–5). Baptism remitted the guilt of original sin, but did nothing to get rid of its effects, which could only be eliminated by the continuing work of grace within the believer.

One major implication of this approach relates to the fate of those who die without being baptized. What happens to those who die without having been baptized, whether in infancy or later in life? If baptism remits the guilt of original sin, people who die without being baptized remain guilty. So what happens to them? Augustine's position demands that such people cannot be saved. Augustine himself certainly held to this belief, and argued forcefully that unbaptized infants were condemned to eternal damnation. However, he conceded that such infants would not have as unpleasant a time in hell as those who lived to adulthood, and committed actual sins. Considerations such as these considerably increased apprehension over the idea of hell, as we shall see later (pp. 477–9).

Nevertheless, Augustine's position was modified in the light of popular pressure, apparently based upon a belief that his doctrine was unjust. Peter Lombard argued that unbaptized infants receive only "the penalty of being condemned" and do not receive the more painful "penalty of the senses." Although they are condemned, that condemnation does not include the experience of the physical pain of hell. This idea is often referred to as "limbo," although this has never become part of the official teaching of any Christian body. It is reflected in Dante's description of hell, which we shall consider later (pp. 470–1).

Infant baptism is grounded in the covenant between God and the church

Earlier, we noted how many theologians interpret sacraments as concerned with the *affirmation of belonging to a community* (see pp. 428–30). A series of Protestant writers have sought to justify the practice of infant baptism by seeing it as a sign of the covenant between God and his people. The baptism of infants inside the church is regarded as a direct counterpart to the Jewish rite of circumcision.

The origins of this approach are to be found with Zwingli. Zwingli regarded the idea of "original guilt" with considerable skepticism. How could an infant be said to be guilty of anything? Guilt implied a degree of moral responsibility which was quite lacking in infants. By rejecting the Augustinian notion of "original guilt" Zwingli found himself temporarily without any justification for the practice of infant baptism – a practice which he regarded as justified, on the basis of the New Testament. So how was this practice to be justified theoretically?

Zwingli found his answer in the Old Testament, which stipulated that male infants born within the bounds of Israel should have an outward sign of their membership of the people of God. The outward sign in question was circumcision – that is, the removal of the foreskin. Infant baptism was thus to be seen as analogous to circumcision – a sign of belonging to a covenant community (see p. 429). Zwingli argued that the more inclusive and gentle character of Christianity was publicly affirmed by infant baptism. The more *inclusive* character of Christianity was affirmed by the baptism of both male and female infants; Judaism, in contrast, recognized only the marking of male infants. The more *gentle* character of the gospel was publicly demonstrated by the absence of pain or the shedding of blood in the sacrament. Christ suffered – in being circumcised himself in addition to his death on the cross – in order that his people need not suffer in this manner.

Infant baptism is unjustified

The rise of the radical Reformation in the sixteenth century, and subsequently of Baptist churches in England during the seventeenth century, witnessed a rejection of the traditional practice of baptizing infants. Baptism was to be administered only when an individual showed signs of grace, repentance, or faith. The silence of the New Testament on the matter is to be taken as indicating that there is no biblical warrant for infant baptism whatsoever.

In part, this position rests upon a particular understanding of the function of sacraments in general, and baptism in particular. A long-standing debate within the Christian tradition centers on whether sacraments are *causative* or *declarative*. In other words, does baptism cause forgiveness of sin? Or does it signify or declare that this forgiveness has already taken place? The practice of "believer's baptism" rests upon the assumption that baptism represents the public declaration of faith upon the part of a converted individual. Conversion has already occurred; baptism represents the public declaration that this has taken place.

There are parallels between this position and that of Zwingli, noted above; the essential difference between Zwingli's view and this Baptist position is that the event which baptism publicly declares is interpreted differently. Zwingli understands the event in question to be *birth into a believing community*; Baptist writers

generally understand it to be *the dawn of a personal faith in the life of an individual*.

This position is set out succinctly by Benajah Harvey Carroll (1843–1914), a leading figure in Southern Baptist life in the state of Texas. For baptism to be valid, Carroll argued, four requirements must be met:

1 The proper *authority* – that is, the church – must administer the sacrament.
2 The proper *subject* – that is, the penitent believer – must receive the sacrament. Carroll insists that conversion precedes baptism.
3 The proper *act* must be performed: baptism is by total immersion in water.
4 The proper *design* must be affirmed: baptism is symbolic, and can in no way be understood to effect the conversion of the individual who is thus baptized.

This represents a slight development of the criteria laid down by James Robinson Graves (1820–93), probably the most significant intellectual force in the early period of the Southern Baptist Convention. Graves had identified three essential characteristics of baptism: the proper subject (a believing Christian); a proper mode, which is total immersion and baptism in the name of the Trinity; and a proper administrator, who must be "an immersed believer, acting under the authority of a gospel church."

We have now considered the major theological aspects of the life of the Christian church, including the question of how the church and its sacraments relate to the gospel. However, a cluster of new questions now awaits us. How does the Christian community relate to other communities outside the Christian faith? This question has become of considerable importance, as western society acknowledges its multicultural nature. How does the Christian church understand its relationship to non-Christian religions? We shall consider such issues in the following chapter.

QUESTIONS FOR CHAPTER 16

1 "A sacrament is a sign of divine things." Why was this early definition eventually realized to be inadequate?
2 Name the seven sacraments recognized by the medieval church.
3 Identify the criteria used by the reformers to reduce the number of the sacraments from seven to two.

4 On what grounds did Zwingli reject the idea of a "real presence" of Christ in the Eucharist?
5 In what way does the concept of "transignification" relate to "transubstantiation"? Can the former be maintained without the latter?
6 Give a brief summary of the main arguments for and against the baptism of infants. Does it make any difference to the infant concerned?

17

Christianity and the World Religions

Christianity is a world religion, having expanded from its origins in Palestine to take root in just about every region of the world. In the course of its expansion, it has encountered other religious traditions, and been forced to consider its relation to them. It is important to remember that Christianity had its origins within the matrix of Judaism, and that significant portions of the New Testament are concerned with the clarification of the relationship of the gospel to its Jewish context.

Christians themselves have always been clear that Christianity is continuous with Judaism. The "God of Abraham, Isaac and Jacob" is the same as the "God and Father of our Lord Jesus Christ." Early Christianity emerged within Judaism, and most of the first converts to the movement were Jews. The New Testament frequently mentions Christians preaching in local synagogues. So similar were the two movements that outside observers, such as the Roman authorities, tended to treat Christianity as a sect within Judaism, rather than as a new movement with a distinct identity.

The emphasis on the continuity between Christianity and Judaism raised a number of serious difficulties for the early Christians. First, there was the question of the role of the Jewish Law in the Christian life. Did the traditional rites and customs of Judaism have any continuing place in the Christian church? There is evidence that this issue was of particular importance during the fifth and sixth decades AD, when non-Jewish converts to Christianity came under pressure from Jewish Christians to maintain such rites and customs. The issue of circumcision was particularly sensitive, with Gentile converts to Christianity often being pressed to become circumcised, in accordance with the Law.

But as Christianity expanded, it encountered other faith systems, with which it had no obvious historical or cultural connection. What about its relationship to the mystery religions? To Gnosticism? And, as its expansion continued, to Islam? To Hinduism? To African indigenous religions? To the various forms of Buddhism? To study the history of Christian theology is to observe the increasing importance of these questions. Indeed, it is fair to suggest that the serious discussion of such issues within the western theological tradition dates from as late as the eighteenth century.

Surprisingly little attention was paid to these issues in the theological literature of the Middle Ages and Reformation periods. There are clear indications that individual writers were aware of the issues. Peter Abelard (1079–1142) wrote of pagan saints such as Job, Noah, and

Enoch. Gregory VII (died 1085) conceded that there was a possibility that Muslims who obey the Qur'an might find salvation in the bosom of Abraham. Thomas Aquinas, who was well aware of the importance of Jewish and Islamic philosophies at the University of Paris in the thirteenth century, developed the notion of "implicit faith" and the "baptism of desire" for those who have not yet heard the gospel, but would have embraced it if they had. Yet the issue did not attract as much serious reflection as we might expect. All that has now changed, as will become clear from what follows.

Western Pluralism and the Question of Other Religions

The Christian proclamation has always taken place in a pluralist world, in competition with rival religious and intellectual convictions. The emergence of the gospel within the matrix of Judaism, the expansion of the gospel in a Hellenistic milieu, the early Christian expansion in pagan Rome, the establishment of the Mar Thoma church in southeastern India – all of these are examples of situations in which Christian apologists and theologians, not to mention ordinary Christian believers, have been aware that there are alternatives to Christianity on offer, and have had to make appropriate responses to this situation.

It is quite possible that most North American and western European Christians of the late nineteenth or early twentieth centuries, unfamiliar with the religious diversity of the world, had little idea of the importance of these issues. For such people, "different religions" would probably have been understood to refer simply to the age-old tension between Protestantism and Roman Catholicism.

Yet things changed radically in the west during the second half of the twentieth century. The western seaboard of the United States and Canada and many cities in Australia experienced an influx of peoples of eastern faiths, especially those originating from a Chinese context. Immigration from the Indian subcontinent has changed things irreversibly within Britain, with Hinduism and Islam becoming foci of identity for ethnic minorities, just as France has been shaken by the new presence of Islam through emigration from its former North African colonies. As a result, western theologians (who still seem to dominate global discussion of such issues) have become increasingly aware of issues which are routine facts of everyday life for Christians in many parts of the world. The result is that providing a theological account of the relation of Christianity to other religions has become of major significance in the modern world.

Two fundamentally different styles of approach to the religions may be adopted, each of which can be readily discerned in modern western academia.

1   The *detached* approach, which seeks to give an account of the religions, Christianity included, from the standpoint of philosophy or the social sciences, or from a loosely "religious" perspective (as in many modern American "faculties of religion"). An excellent example of this approach may be found in Anthony Giddens's highly influential textbook, *Sociology*, which approaches religious matters from a sociological standpoint. His approach is instructive; for example, he gives four illustrations of what religion is *not*, in order to indicate the extent to which western cultural bias can creep into thinking about religions. According to Giddens, who writes from a sociological perspective, religion is *not*:

(a) to be identified with *monotheism*;
(b) to be identified with *moral prescriptions*;
(c) necessarily concerned with explanations of the world;
(d) to be identified with the supernatural.

Giddens's comments in relation to the too-easy identification of religion with monotheism are of considerable interest:

> Religion should not be identified with monotheism (belief in one God). Nietzsche's thesis of the "death of God" was strongly ethnocentric, relating only to western religious ideas. Most religions involve many deities. [...] In certain religions, there are no gods at all.

Giddens's concern as a sociologist is simply to document the phenomenon of religion, without imposing a restrictive interpretive framework upon it.

2 A *committed* approach, which seeks to give an account of the origins and functions of religions from an explicitly Christian perspective. It is this approach which particularly concerns us in this volume, dealing as it does with a specifically *Christian* theology, rather than theories about religion in general.

However, the importance of the question of religions in modern culture is such that it is entirely proper to open this discussion by considering some "detached" approaches to the world religions, before moving on to consider more explicitly Christian approaches.

Approaches to Religions

Addressing the theme of "Christianity and other religions" immediately raises the question of how religion is to be defined. This question is made substantially more problem-atical on account of the fact that no universally accepted definition has emerged. A number of significantly different understandings of the nature of religion, each claiming to be "scientific" or "objective," emerged during the last century. Certain of these attempts (most notably those of Karl Marx, Sigmund Freud, and Emile Durkheim) have been strongly reductionist, generally reflecting the personal or institutional agendas of those who developed them. These reductive approaches have been subjected to severe criticism by writers such as Mircea Eliade, on account of their obvious inadequacies.

Robert Towler has observed that Thomas Luckmann's *The Invisible Religion* (1967) was the last major contribution to the sociology of religion to use the word "religion" in a Durk-heimian manner to denote "beliefs with no super-empirical or supernatural reference"; the term "religion" has now generally been accepted by many writers to refer to "beliefs and practices with a supernatural referent." However, as the comments of Anthony Giddens make clear (see above), this is by no means universally accepted, especially among sociologists with a vested interest in treating religions as a social phenomenon and human construction.

It must be stressed that definitions of religion are rarely neutral, but are often generated to favor beliefs and institutions with which one is in sympathy and penalize those to which one is hostile. Definitions of religions show a marked tendency to depend on the particular purposes and prejudices of individual scholars. Thus a writer who has a particular concern to show that all religions give access to the same divine reality will develop a definition of religion which embodies this belief (for example, F. Max Mueller's famous definition of religion as "a disposition which enables men to apprehend the Infinite under different names and disguises"). A similar agenda underlies more recent writings which are committed to the view that all religions are simply local culturally conditioned responses to the same basic transcendent ultimate. Such attempts often rest on what might be considered an excessive reliance upon a Kantian distinction between "phenomena" and "noumena," with the various religions corresponding to the former and "ultimate reality" to the latter. This distinction has been challenged by the rise of the type of holistic linguistic interpretive approach found in the writings of Donald Davidson and others, raising serious doubts concerning the coherence of the Kantian viewpoint when applied to the case of religions.

Writers specializing in fieldwork anthropology (such as E. E. Evans-Pritchard and Clifford E. Geertz) have offered more complex and reflective models of religion. A major debate within contemporary anthropology and sociology of religion concerns whether religion is to be defined "functionally" (religion has to do with certain social or personal functions of ideas and rituals) or "substantially" (religion has to do with certain beliefs concerning divine or spiritual beings). Despite widespread differences in terminology (many writers disagreeing over how appropriate it is to use key terms such as "supernatural," "spiritual," and "mystical"), there appears to be at least some measure of genuine agreement that religion, however conceived, in some way involves belief and behavior linked with a supernatural realm of divine or spiritual beings.

In what follows, we shall consider a number of major approaches to the religions of the world. Only one such approach – that of Karl Barth and Dietrich Bonhoeffer – can be regarded as explicitly Christian in its orientation. It is included here on account of its impact upon the "death of God" or the "secular meaning of the gospel" movements which emerged in the United States during the 1960s and early 1970s. We begin by considering the views which emerged at the time of the Enlightenment.

The Enlightenment: religions as a corruption of the original religion of nature

The Enlightenment witnessed the birth of the idea that religion was fundamentally a corruption of a primeval rational worldview, engineered by priests as a means of enhancing and preserving their positions within society. This approach is illustrated in the title of Matthew Tindal's highly influential work, *Christianity as Old as Creation, or, The Gospel a Republication of the Religion of Nature* (1730). On the basis of the foundational Enlightenment assumption of the rationality of reality, and the ability of human beings to uncover and apprehend this rationality, it was argued that whatever lay behind the various world religions was ultimately rational in character, and thus capable of being uncovered, described, and analyzed by human reason.

The idea of a universal rational religion was, however, at odds with the diversity of the world religions. As European knowledge of these religions deepened, through the growth of the genre of "voyager literature," and through the increasing availability of Chinese, Indian, Persian, and Vedic religious writings, it became increasingly clear that the notion of a universal religion of reason faced difficulties when confronted with the evidence of the astonishing variety of human religious beliefs and practices. Many Enlightenment writers, perhaps more concerned with championing reason than with wrestling with the empirical evidence, developed a theory of religion which accounted for this diversity, at least in part.

In his *True Intellectual System of the Universe* (1678), Ralph Cudworth argued that all religions were ultimately based upon a common ethical monotheism – a simple religion of nature, basically ethical in character, and devoid of all the arbitrary doctrines and religious rites of Christianity or Judaism. The primordial rational religion of nature had become corrupted through its early interpreters.

The theory that gained an especially wide hearing was that the various world religions were little more than the inventions of cultic leaders or priests, whose main motivation was the preservation of their own interests and status. The Roman historian Tacitus had suggested that Moses invented the Jewish religious rites as a means of ensuring religious cohesion after the expulsion from Egypt; many writers of the early Enlightenment developed this notion, arguing that the variety of human religious rites and practices were simply human inventions in response to specific historical situations, now firmly in the past. The way was open to the recovery of the universal primordial religion of nature, which would put an end to the religious squabbles of humanity.

The idea of "superstition" emerged as significant at this time, often becoming pejoratively synonymous with "religion." In his *Natural History of Superstition* (1709), John Trenchard developed the idea of the inherent credulity of humanity, which permitted natural monotheism to degenerate into the various religious traditions of humanity. The enthusiasm with which this idea was received can be judged from the comments of the *Independent Whig* (December 31, 1720), to the effect that "the peculiar Foible of Mankind is Superstition, or an intrinsick and pannick Fear of invisible and unknown Beings."

For Trenchard, the religions represented the triumph of superstition over reason. By eliminating such superstitious beliefs and rites, a return to the universal and simple religion of nature could be achieved. A similar idea was developed during the French Enlightenment by Paul Henri Thiry, Baron d'Holbach, who argued that religion was little more than a form of pathological disorder. The French Revolution had seemed set to eliminate this disorder; its total failure to do so raised awkward questions for the general Enlightenment approach to religions. For this reason, the approach adopted by Ludwig Feuerbach seemed to offer new possibilities for those disaffected from the European religious situation at the time.

Ludwig Feuerbach: religion as an objectification of human feeling

In the foreword to the first edition of his *Essence of Christianity* (1841), Ludwig Feuerbach (1804–72) states that the purpose of his work is "to show that the supernatural mysteries of religion are based upon quite simple natural truths." The leading idea of the work is deceptively simple: human beings have created their own gods and religions, which embody their own idealized conception of their aspirations, needs, and fears. We have already considered some aspects of Feuerbach's approach (see p. 151); it now demands to be treated in more detail.

It is not correct to suggest that Feuerbach merely reduces the divine to the natural. The permanent significance of Feuerbach's work lies in its detailed analysis of the means by which religious concepts arise within the human consciousness. The thesis that human beings create the gods in their own image is but the conclusion of a radical and penetrating critique of concept-formation in religion, based on the Hegelian concepts of "self-alienation" and "self-objectification."

The Hegelian analysis of consciousness requires that there be a formal relation of subject to object. The concept of "consciousness" cannot be isolated as an abstract idea, in that it is necessarily linked with an object: to be "conscious" is to be conscious *of something*. Human consciousness of feelings, such as fear or love, leads to their objectification and thus to externalization of these feelings. Divine predicates are thus recognized to be human predicates.

Consciousness of God is human self-consciousness; knowledge of God is human self-knowledge. By the God you know the human, and conversely, by the human, you know the God. The two are one. [. . .] What an earlier religion took to be objective, is later recognized to be subjective; what formerly was taken to be God, and worshiped as such, is now recognized to be something human. What was earlier religion is later taken to be idolatry: humans are seen to have adored their own nature. Humans objectified themselves but failed to recognize themselves as this object. The later religion takes this step; every advance in religion is therefore a deepening in self-knowledge.

It is obvious that Feuerbach tends to use the terms "Christianity" and "religion" interchangeably throughout *The Essence of Christianity*, thus glossing over the fact that his theory has some difficulty in accounting for nontheistic religions. Nevertheless, it is clear that his reduction of Christian theology to anthropology is of considerable significance.

The most important epistemological analysis in *The Essence of Christianity* is concerned with the role of feeling in the process of religious concept-formation, and has important consequences for the approach centered on "religious feeling," characteristic of Schleiermacher and the later liberal tradition. For Feuerbach, Christian theology has tended to interpret the externalized image of "feeling" or self-consciousness as a wholly other, absolute essence, whereas in fact it is a "self-feeling feeling": human religious feelings or experience cannot be interpreted as an awareness of God, but only as a misunderstood self-awareness. "If feeling is the essential instrumentality or organ of religion, then God's nature is nothing other than an expression of the nature of feeling. [. . .] The divine essence, which is comprehended by feeling, is actually nothing other than the essence of feeling, en-

raptured and delighted with itself – nothing but self-intoxicated, self-contented feeling."

Important though Feuerbach's analysis may have been, it was overshadowed by that of Karl Marx, to which we may now turn.

Karl Marx: religion as the product of socioeconomic alienation

In his 1844 political and economic manuscripts, the left-wing Hegelian political thinker Karl Marx (1818–83) develops an approach to religion which rests upon ideas that are clearly due to Feuerbach. Religion has no real independent existence. It is a reflection of the material world, and is derived from the social needs and hopes of human beings (see pp. 72–3). "The religious world is but the reflex of the real world." Marx argues that "religion is just the imaginary sun which seems to humans to revolve around themselves until they realize that they themselves are the center of their own revolution." In other words, God is simply a projection of human concerns. Human beings "look for a superhuman being in the fantasy reality of heaven, and find nothing there but their own reflection."

Yet the human nature which generates religious ideas is *alienated*. The notion of alienation is of central importance to Marx's account of the origins of religious belief. "Humans make religion; religion does not make humans. Religion is the self-consciousness and self-esteem of people who either have not found themselves or who have already lost themselves again." Religion is the product of social and economic alienation. It arises from that alienation, and at the same time encourages that alienation by a form of spiritual intoxication which renders the masses incapable of recognizing their situation and doing something about it. Religion is a comfort, which enables people to tolerate their economic alienation. If there were no such alienation, there would be no need for religion. The division of labor and the existence of private property introduce alienation and estrangement into the economic and social orders.

Materialism affirms that events in the material world bring about corresponding changes in the intellectual world. Religion is thus the result of a certain set of social and economic conditions. Change those conditions, so that economic alienation is eliminated, and religion will cease to exist. It will no longer serve any useful function. Unjust social conditions produce religion, and are in turn supported by religion. "The struggle against religion is therefore indirectly a struggle against *the world* of which religion is the spiritual fragrance."

Marx thus argues that religion will continue to exist as long as it meets a need in the life of alienated people. "The religious reflex of the real world can [...] only then vanish when the practical relations of everyday life offer to humanity none but perfectly intelligible and reasonable relations with regard to other human beings and to nature." Feuerbach had argued that religion was the projection of human needs, an expression of the "uttered sorrow of the soul."

Marx agrees with this interpretation. However, his point is more radical. It is not enough to explain how religion arises on account of sorrow and injustice. By changing that world, the causes of religion can be removed. It is important to note that Marx regards Feuerbach as correct in his analysis of the origins of religion, even if having failed to discern how an understanding of those origins might lead to its eventual elimination. It is this insight which underlies his often quoted eleventh thesis on Feuerbach: "The philosophers have only interpreted the world, in various ways; the point, however, is to change it."

Sigmund Freud: religion as wish-fulfillment

Earlier we explored Ludwig Feuerbach's radical idea that the concept of God was fundamentally a human construction, based on the "projection" of fundamental human longings and desires. Feuerbach's basic ideas were taken over, and given a new sense of direction, in the writings of the Austrian psychoanalyst Sigmund Freud (1856–1939). "All I have done – and this is the only thing that is new in my exposition – is to add some psychological foundation to the criticisms of my great predecessors." In fact, it is probably fair to say that Feuerbach's "projection" or "wish-fulfillment" theory is best known today in its Freudian form, rather than in Feuerbach's original version. "Religion," Freud wrote, "is an illusion and it derives its strength from the fact that it falls in with our instinctual desires.'

The most powerful statement of Freud's approach may be found in *The Future of an Illusion* (1927), which develops a strongly reductionist approach to religion. For Freud, religious ideas are "illusions, fulfillments of the oldest, strongest and most urgent wishes of mankind." The parallels with Feuerbach are evident; yet Freud went on to develop a radical and original explanation of religion, grounded in the insights of the newly emerging discipline of psychoanalysis, which took Feuerbach's critique of religion to new heights. Illusions are not deliberate deceptions; they are simply ideas that arise from within the human unconsciousness, as it seeks to fulfill its deepest yearnings and longings. For Marx, those longings were the tragic outcome of social alienation, requiring social transformation for their elimination. For Freud, their origins lie not in society, but in the human unconscious.

The first major statement of Freud's views on the origin of religion – which he increasingly came to refer to as "the psychogenesis of religion" – may be found in *Totem and Taboo* (1913). Developing his earlier observation that religious rites are similar to the obsessive actions of his neurotic patients, Freud declared that religion was basically a distorted form of an obsessional neurosis. The key elements in all religions, he argues, are the veneration of a father figure (such as God or Jesus Christ), faith in the power of spirits, and a concern for proper rituals.

Religion, according to Freud's historical account, arises through inner psychological pressures, which reflect the complex evolutionary history of humanity. In particular, Freud located the origins of belief in God in the human need for a father-figure. In *The Future of an Illusion*, Freud argued that religion represents the perpetuation of a piece of infantile behavior in adult life. Religion is an immature response to the awareness of helplessness, involving regression to childhood experiences of paternal care: "my father will protect me; he is in control." Belief in a personal God is thus little more than an infantile delusion. Religion is wishful thinking, an illusion. The psychological origins of human belief in God are thus to be found in a projection of the intense, unconscious desires of humanity. God is to be seen as a wish-fulfillment, arising from repressed, unconscious infantile longings for protection and security. Therefore, religious beliefs owe their origins to a childlike feeling of helplessness, which arises in response to external dangers, internal impulses, and a fear of death. Just as children look to their parents to protect them from danger, so this infantile pattern is transferred to adulthood, in that adults create gods for themselves precisely because they had similar "gods" in their homes while they were growing up.

The cultural impact of Freud's approach has been immense, especially in North America. It is fair to say that, from about 1920, Freud's account of religion gained the ascendancy within the American intelligentsia, attracting a following exceeding even that of such postmodern writers as Paul de Man and Michel Foucault in more recent times. Freud set the cultural agenda of his day, and for a generation beyond in a way that admirably justifies W. H. Auden's famous description of Freud as "not a person, but a whole climate of opinion." Freud was regarded as having scientifically unlocked the hidden, repressed secrets of the human mind, thus enabling humanity to face its future with confidence and hope – and without religion. Although Freud's theories of the origins of religion are now generally regarded as unscientific speculation, their influence lingers on, and they are still occasionally encountered in some discussions of the nature and origins of religion.

Emile Durkheim: religion and ritual

In his *Elementary Forms of the Religious Life* (1912), the French sociologist Emile Durkheim explored the relation between religion and the institutions of society in general. The case study upon which most of his ideas are grounded is that of totemism in Australian aboriginal societies. For Durkheim, totemism represents the "elementary form of the religious life." The totem was originally an animal or plant which was regarded as having especial symbolic significance for a people. It was thus treated as sacred – that is, as being set apart from the routine aspects of human life.

The reason for this, according to Durkheim, is that the totem comes to represent values which are central to society itself. As a result, it comes to be a symbol of the group. The reverence with which the totem is treated is, in reality, reverence for the group itself and its undergirding values. The true object of worship is thus not the totem, but society itself. The ceremony and ritual which attend this worship are seen as reflections of the need for social cohesion. The special religious ceremonies which are associated with birth, marriage, and death are to be regarded as a reaffirmation of group solidarity at moments of cultural importance. Thus funeral rites demonstrate that the values of a society will outlive the death of any of its individual members.

Despite the development of a scientific worldview, Durkheim believed that religion would continue to play an important role in the future, in view of its providing social cohesion for societies (a point we noted in relation to the sacraments, pp. 428–30). The emergence of "civil religion" in the United States, centering upon the person of the president or the symbol of the Stars and Stripes, could be seen as confirmation of this approach, as could the emergence of an atheist "state religion" in the former Soviet Union under Lenin and Stalin.

Mircea Eliade: religion and myth

The Romanian-born scholar Mircea Eliade (1907–86) was noted for his pioneering work in the systematic study of religions. Although his interests enfolded a wide range of areas, he concentrated on the nature of religious culture, focusing especially on the role of myths and mystical experiences. Eliade's analysis of "rites of passage" – that is, rituals marking key transitional moments in the life cycle, including birth and death), influenced many anthropologists. His often controversial books include scholarly works such as *The Myth of the Eternal Return* (1949) and *The Sacred and the Profane* (1959).

The concept of "the sacred" plays a major role in Eliade's thought. Eliade argues that "the sacred" is to be seen as the source of significance, meaning, power, and being, and its manifestations. "The sacred" has also been the subject of considerable contention. There are some obvious parallels between Eliade's concept and the idea propounded by the German theologian Rudolf Otto (1869–37) that the experience of the holy is "numinous," or "wholly other." There is also a parallel with Emile Durkheim's socially influenced discussion of the "sacred."

While Eliade himself repeatedly identifies the sacred as something that is real, he nevertheless insists that "the sacred is a structure of human consciousness." According to Eliade, any phenomenal entity – for example, a tree – could be apprehended by its perceiver as an hierophany (revelation of the sacred), given appropriate preparation. To some, a tree discloses the sacred; to others, it remains nothing more than a tree. The framework which allows the tree to become a revelation of the sacred is determined by the experience of those. This suggests that, at least to some extent, the "sacred" is a social construction, determined by the history of the perceiver, rather than a universal, objective notion.

One point of particular interest is Eliade's emphasis on the importance of "myth." Myths, he argues, are a particular kind of narrative, characterized by truth and reality, which exceed more scientific accounts of historical reality because of their ability to answer the deeper questions of life. "To tell how things came into existence is to explain them, and at the same time indirectly to answer another question: *Why* did they come into existence?" On account of its truth, a myth is able to become a hierophany – a revelation of the sacred. Myths narrate sacred history. For this reason, Eliade is skeptical of any attempt to eliminate myths from modern culture. It is a universal feature of human nature, which religions continue to develop and embody. Instead of trying to rationalize or eliminate the sacred, Eliade argues, we ought to be trying to understand how it illuminates human nature, and its ultimate aspirations.

Karl Barth and Dietrich Bonhoeffer: religion as a human invention

A final approach of considerable importance has its origins within Christianity, and specifically within the dialectical theology of Karl Barth. This approach develops the idea that "religion" is a purely human construction, often an act of defiance in the face of God. Religion is here seen as an upward search for God on the part of humanity. This contrasts sharply with God's self-revelation, which exposes religion as a human fabrication.

Barth, it will be recalled, received his theological education within German liberal Protestantism. The "culture Protestantism" of the period laid considerable emphasis upon the importance of human religiosity. In a lecture of 1916, entitled "The Righteousness of God," Barth declared that human religiosity was little more than a Tower of Babel: a purely human construction, erected in defiance of God. There is a radical discontinuity between God's self-revelation to humanity, which leads to faith, and humanity's search for God, which leads to religion.

Barth is thus able to endorse criticisms of religion along the lines of Feuerbach and Marx, precisely because he believes these to be directed against the human invention of religion. Religion, for Barth, is an obstacle which must be eliminated if God is to be discerned in Christ. At its worst, it is idolatrous, in that it involves people worshiping a human construction.

Many writers have tried to summarize Barth's view on religion in the phrase "the abolition of religion." It is certainly true that the standard English translation of section 17 of the *Church Dogmatics*, volume 1, part 2, is entitled "The Revelation of God as the Abolition of Religion." This English phrase is, however, profoundly misleading and needs careful explanation. It must be remembered that Barth wrote in German, not English. The German word translated by "abolition" is *Aufhebung*, a term with a long and distinguished history of use within the German philosophical tradition, especially within Hegelianism. It is ambiguous, and possesses two root meanings: "to remove" and "to exalt."

It is certainly true that in his early writings Barth adopts a very negative attitude toward religion, understood as a human invention. Yet Barth is here stressing the natural human tendency to form concepts of God, and to seek justification in relation to them. He is not criticizing other *religions* but *religion* in general. Barth sees the phenomenon of "religion" at work in Christianity as much as anywhere else; cultural values intrude into the gospel, and become merged with it. Barth's intense anxiety about this development was particularly focused upon the German church struggle of the 1930s, in which he believed that Germanic ideals were becoming incorporated into Christian faith. However, Barth's attitude mellowed in his later period. He came increasingly to see the need for religion this side of eternity. "Religion" comes more to mean "human institutions" or "modes of worship," rather than "a human attempt to determine what God is like."

Barth insists that "religion" will continue until the end of time, as a necessary prop or support to faith. Barth's concern here is to emphasize that, by the grace of God, this "religion" is transcended and surpassed by God. It is something neutral, not negative. Barth's references to the *Aufhebung* of religion do not therefore make much sense, if these are translated as referring to the *abolition*. In fact, these comments should be interpreted in terms of the "transformation" or even "sublimation" of religion. Religion, seen as a human construction, and contrasted with divine revelation, certainly needs to be critiqued – yet it serves a useful role.

This is most emphatically *not* what Dietrich Bonhoeffer thought. Bonhoeffer's most significant contribution to modern theology is generally regarded to be his analysis of the cultural situation within which Christ is to be proclaimed in the modern world. On April 5, 1943, Bonhoeffer was arrested by the Gestapo for his alleged involvement in a plot against Adolf Hitler. During the 18 months of his imprisonment at Berlin's Tegel prison, he wrote his celebrated *Letters and Papers from Prison*, in which he reflected on the question of the identity of Jesus Christ in a "world come of age," a time of "no religion at all." He argued passionately for a "religionless Christianity."

This powerful phrase has often been misunderstood, particularly by writers such as John Robinson, in his influential popular work *Honest to God* (1963). Bonhoeffer directed his criticisms against forms of Christianity which were grounded on the assumption that human beings were naturally religious – an assumption that Bonhoeffer regarded as untenable, given the new godless situation. A "religionless Christianity" is a faith which is based not upon the untenable and discredited notion of "natural human religiosity," but upon God's self-revelation in Christ. An appeal to culture, to metaphysics, or to religion was thus to be avoided, in that these were inherently implausible in the new secular world, and inevitably led to distorted understandings of God (there are strong affinities between Barth and Bonhoeffer here).

For Bonhoeffer, the crucified Christ provided us with a model of God appropriate for the modern world – a God who "allows himself to be pushed out of the world and on to the cross." These ideas, especially as they related to the new secularism and the need to ground theology elsewhere than in religion or metaphysics, were to prove seminal to postwar German Christology, and had a deep impact upon many writers in the United States during the 1960s.

There were, however, obvious confusions here. Bonhoeffer's phrase "a religionless Christianity" and Barth's phrase "the abolition of religion" were taken by many more radical writers of the period to mean the end of any corporate Christian life, or an abandoning of traditional Christian ideas. These misunderstandings can be seen in influential popular works of the 1960s, such as John Robinson's *Honest to God* and the "death of God" movement.

Having dealt with one Christian approach to the question of religion in general, we may now move on to examine specifically Christian approaches to other religions.

Christian Approaches to Other Religions

Christianity is but one world religious tradition among a host of others. So how does it relate to other religious traditions? The question is not modern; it has been asked throughout Christian history. Initially the question concerned Christianity's relationship with Judaism, from whose matrix it emerged in the period AD 30–60. And as it expanded, it encountered other religious beliefs and practices, such as classical paganism. As it became established in India in the fifth century, it encountered the diverse native Indian cultural movements which western scholars of religion have misleadingly grouped together and termed "Hinduism." Arab Christianity has long learned to coexist with Islam in the eastern Mediterranean.

In the modern period, the question of the relation of Christianity to other religious traditions has assumed a new importance in western academic theology, partly on account of the rise of multiculturalism in western society. As will become clear, three main approaches have gained currency in the recent past, with a fourth now being given serious consideration. However, it will be helpful to begin by considering the idea of "religion" itself.

A naive view of religion might be that it is an outlook on life which believes in, or worships, a supreme being. This outlook, characteristic of Deism and Enlightenment rationalism, is easily shown to be inadequate. Buddhism is classified as a religion by most people, yet here a belief in a supreme being is conspicuously absent. The same problem persists, no matter what definition of religion is offered. No unambiguously common features can be identified among the religions, in matters of faith or practice. Thus Edward Conze, the great scholar of Buddhism, recalled that he "once read through a collection of the lives of Roman Catholic saints, and there was not one of whom a Buddhist could fully approve. [...] They were bad Buddhists though good Christians." This therefore raises an interesting question: could a Christian be saved within a Buddhist framework? Or a Buddhist within a Christian framework?

There is a growing consensus that it is seriously misleading to regard the various religious traditions of the world as variations on a single theme. "There is no single essence, no one content of enlightenment or revelation, no one way of emancipation or liberation, to be found in all that plurality" (David Tracy). The noted American religious writer John B. Cobb Jr. also notes the enormous difficulties confronting anyone wishing to argue that there is an "essence of religion":

> Arguments about what religion truly is are pointless. There is no such thing as religion. There are only traditions, movements, communities, peoples, beliefs, and practices that have features that are associated by many people with what they mean by religion.

Cobb stresses that the assumption that religion has an essence has bedeviled and seriously misled recent discussion of the relation of the religious traditions of the world. For example, he points out that both Buddhism and Confucianism have "religious" elements, but that does not necessarily mean that they can be categorized as "religions." Many "religions" are better understood as cultural movements with religious components.

The idea of some universal notion of religion, of which individual religions are subsets, appears to have emerged at the time of the Enlightenment. To use a biological analogy, the assumption that there is a genus of religion, of which individual religions are species, is a very western idea, without any real parallel outside western culture – except on the part of those who have been educated in the west and uncritically absorbed its presuppositions.

What, then, of Christian approaches to understanding the relation between Christianity and other religious traditions? In what way can such traditions be understood, within the context of the Christian belief in the universal saving will of God, made known through Jesus Christ? It must be stressed that Christian theology is concerned with evaluating other religious traditions *from the perspective of Christianity itself*. Such reflection is not addressed to, or intended to gain approval from, members of other religious traditions, or their secular observers.

Four broad approaches can be identified:

1 *exclusivism* (also known as *particularism*), which holds that only those who hear and respond to the Christian gospel may be saved;

2 *inclusivism*, which argues that, although Christianity represents the normative revelation of God, salvation is nonetheless possible for those who belong to other religious traditions;

3 *pluralism*, which holds that all the religious traditions of humanity are equally valid paths to the same core of religious reality; and

4 *parallelism*, which recognizes the obvious differences between the religions, and argues that each religion is to be seen as valid, in that it achieves its own specific goals.

We shall consider these four viewpoints individually.

Exclusivism

The viewpoint that is widely known as *exclusivism* can also be described as "particularism," on account of its affirmation of the particular and distinctive features of the Christian faith. Perhaps the most influential statement of this position may be found in the writings of Hendrik Kraemer (1888–1965), especially his *Christian Message in a Non-Christian World* (1938). Kraemer emphasized that "God has revealed *the* Way and *the* Truth and *the* Life in Jesus Christ, and wills this to be known throughout the world." This revelation is *sui generis*; it is in a category of its own, and cannot be set alongside the ideas of revelation found in other religious traditions.

At this point, a certain breadth of opinion can be discerned within this approach. Kraemer himself seems to suggest that there is real knowledge of God outside Christ when he speaks of God shining through "in a broken, troubled way, in reason, in nature and in history." The question is whether such knowledge is only available through Christ, or whether Christ provides the only framework by which such knowledge may be discerned and interpreted elsewhere.

Some exclusivists (or, as some prefer to be styled, particularists), such as Karl Barth, adopt the position that there is no knowledge of God to be had apart from Christ; others (such as Kraemer) allow that God's self-revelation occurs in many ways and places, but insist that this revelation can only be interpreted correctly, and known for what it really is, in the light of the definitive revelation of God in Christ. (There are important parallels here with the debate over natural and revealed knowledge of God.)

What, then, of those who have not heard the gospel of Christ? What happens to them? Are not particularists denying salvation to those who have not heard of Christ or, who having heard the Christian proclamation, choose to reject it? This criticism is frequently leveled against particularism by its critics. Thus John Hick, arguing from a pluralist perspective, suggests that the doctrine that salvation is only possible through Christ is inconsistent with belief in the universal saving will of God. That this is not, in fact, the case is readily demonstrated by considering the view of Karl Barth, easily the most sophisticated of twentieth-century defenders of this position.

Barth declares that salvation is only possible through Christ. He nevertheless insists on the ultimate eschatological victory of grace over unbelief – that is, at the end of history (a point we considered earlier, in connection with his doctrine of election, pp. 384–5). Eventually, God's grace will triumph completely, and all will come to faith in Christ. This is the only way to salvation, but it is a way that, through the grace of God, is effective for all. For Barth, the particularity of God's revelation through Christ is not contradicted by the universality of salvation.

A more recent exposition of the particularist position is associated with Lesslie Newbigin

(1909–98), a British writer who spent a substantial part of his working life as a Christian bishop in India. Newbigin's defense of the particularity of the Christian faith rests on a number of considerations, especially his argument that the pluralist alternative is flawed. He illustrates this by pointing out some of the difficulties associated with the approach of Wilfred Cantwell Smith, which asserts that all religions share a common core experience.

> It is clear that in Smith's view "The Transcendent" is a purely formal category. He, she, or it may be conceived in any way that the worshiper may choose. There can therefore be no such thing as false or misdirected worship, since the reality to which it is directed is unknowable. Smith quotes as "one of the theologically most discerning remarks that I know" the words of the *Yogavasistha*: "Thou art formless. Thy only form is our knowledge of Thee." Any claim for uniqueness made for one concept of the Transcendent, for instance the Christian claim that the Transcendent is present in fullness in Jesus (Colossians 1: 19), is to be regarded as wholly unacceptable. There are no criteria by which different concepts of the Transcendent may be tested. We are shut up to a total subjectivity: the Transcendent is unknowable.

Newbigin therefore reaffirms what he regards as the classic Christian position – that Jesus Christ is the unique and distinctive ground and center of a unique and distinctive faith.

Inclusivism

The most significant advocate of this model is the leading Jesuit writer Karl Rahner (1904–84). In the fifth volume of his *Theological Investigations* Rahner develops four theses, setting out the view, not merely that individual non-Christians may be saved, but that the non-Christian religious traditions in general may have access to the saving grace of God in Christ.

1 Christianity is the absolute religion, founded on the unique event of the self-revelation of God in Christ. But this revelation took place at a specific point in history. Those who lived before this point, or who have yet to hear about this event, would thus seem to be excluded from salvation – which is contrary to the saving will of God.
2 For this reason, despite their errors and shortcomings, non-Christian religious traditions are valid and capable of mediating the saving grace of God, until the gospel is made known to their members. After the gospel has been proclaimed to the adherents of such non-Christian religious traditions, they are no longer legitimate, viewed from the standpoint of Christian theology.
3 The faithful adherent of a non-Christian religious tradition is thus to be regarded as an "anonymous Christian."
4 Other religious traditions will not be displaced by Christianity. Religious pluralism will continue to be a feature of human existence.

We may explore the first three of these theses in a little more detail.

It will be clear that Rahner strongly affirms the principle that salvation may only be had through Christ, as he is interpreted by the Christian tradition. "Christianity understands itself as the absolute religion, intended for all people, which cannot recognize any other religion beside itself as of equal right." Yet Rahner supplements this with an emphasis upon the universal saving will of God: God wishes that all shall be saved, even though not all know Christ. "Somehow all people must be able to be members of the church."

For this reason, Rahner argues that saving grace must be available outside the bounds of the church – and hence in other religious traditions. He vigorously opposes those who adopt too-neat solutions, insisting that *either* a religious tradition comes from God *or* it is an inauthentic and purely human invention. Where Kraemer argued that non-Christian religious traditions were little more than self-justifying human constructions, Rahner argues that such traditions may well include elements of truth.

Rahner justifies this suggestion by considering the relation between the Old and New Testaments. Although the Old Testament, strictly speaking, represents the outlook of a non-Christian religion (Judaism), Christians are able to read it and discern within it elements which continue to be valid. The Old Testament is evaluated in the light of the New, and, as a result, certain practices (such as dietary laws) are discarded as unacceptable, while others (such as the moral law) are retained. The same approach can and should, Rahner argues, be adopted in the case of other religions.

The saving grace of God is thus available through non-Christian religious traditions, despite their shortcomings. Many of their adherents, Rahner argues, have thus accepted that grace, without being fully aware of what it is. It is for this reason that Rahner introduces the term "anonymous Christians," to refer to those who have experienced divine grace without necessarily knowing it.

This term has been heavily criticized. For example, John Hick has suggested that it is paternalist, offering "honorary status granted unilaterally to people who have not expressed any desire for it." Nevertheless, Rahner's intention is to allow for the real effects of divine grace in the lives of those who belong to non-Christian traditions. Full access to truth about God (as it is understood within the Christian tradition) is not a necessary precondition for access to the saving grace of God.

Rahner does not allow that Christianity and other religious traditions may be treated as equal, or that they are particular instances of a common encounter with God. For Rahner, Christianity and Christ have an exclusive status, denied to other religious traditions. The question is can other religious traditions give access to the same saving grace as that offered by Christianity? Rahner's approach allows him to suggest that the beliefs of non-Christian religious traditions are not necessarily true, while allowing that they may, nevertheless, mediate the grace of God by the lifestyles which they evoke – such as a selfless love of one's neighbor.

A somewhat different approach is associated with the Second Vatican Council. In its decree on other faiths (*Nostra Aetate*, October 28, 1965), the Council followed Rahner in affirming that rays of divine truth were indeed to be found in other religions. However, where Rahner allowed other faiths to have soteriological potential, the Council maintained the distinctiveness of the Christian faith at this point.

> The Catholic Church rejects nothing of what is true and holy in these religions. She has a high regard for the manner of life and conduct, the precepts and doctrines which, although differing in many ways from her own teaching, nevertheless often reflect a ray of that truth which enlightens all men. Yet she proclaims and is in duty bound to proclaim without fail, Christ who is the way, the truth and the life (John 14: 6). In him, in whom God reconciled all things to himself (2 Corinthians 5: 18–19), men find the fullness of their religious life.

The distinction between Rahner and Vatican II can be summarized as follows. Rahner is both revelationally and soteriologically inclusive;

Vatican II tends to be revelationally inclusive, yet soteriologically particularist.

The issue of religious pluralism is now being widely discussed within evangelicalism. The general consensus within evangelicalism is strongly particularist. However, a minority opinion should be noted. The Canadian writer Clark H. Pinnock (born 1937) draws on a Logos-Christology similar to that of the Apologists of the second century in building his argument for universal access to salvation, adopting an inclusivist position similar, in respects, to that of Karl Rahner. The following considerations clearly influence his thinking.

> If God really loves the whole world and desires everyone to be saved, it follows logically that everyone must have access to salvation. There would have to be an opportunity for all people to participate in the salvation of God. If Christ died for all, while yet sinners, the opportunity must be given for all to register a decision about what was done for them. They cannot lack the opportunity merely because someone failed to bring the Gospel of Christ to them. God's universal salvific will implies the equally universal accessibility of salvation for all people.

Pinnock clearly believes that the difficulties which he discerns within the "particularist" or "exclusivist" model for understanding the relation of Christianity to other religions can be dealt with using the "inclusivist" approach. Others disagree; while recognizing the force of the difficulties with the "particularist" paradigm, they believe that these are more effectively addressed through a "pluralist" approach, to which we now turn.

Pluralism

The basic feature of the pluralist approach to the relation of Christianity to other faiths is that each religion is understood to represent a distinctive, yet equally valid, grasp of some ultimate spiritual reality, which some religions term "God" and others define in rather more nontheistic or atheistic terms. For these reasons, pluralist writers tend to refer to the spiritual reality which they believe to lie behind all religions in terms such as "ultimate reality" or "the Real," thus avoiding the explicit use of the term "God."

The most significant exponent of a pluralist approach to religious traditions is John Hick (born 1922). In writings such as *God and the Universe of Faiths* (1973) and *The Second Christianity* (1983), Hick argued for a need to move away from a Christ-centered to a God-centered approach. Describing this change as a "Copernican revolution," Hick declared that it was necessary to move away from "the dogma that Christianity is at the centre to the realization that it is *God* who is at the centre, and that all religions [. . .] including our own, serve and revolve around him." As Hick puts this point:

> Now it seems to many of us today that we need a Copernican revolution in our understanding of the religions. The traditional dogma has been that Christianity is the centre of the universe of faiths, with all the other religions seen as revolving at various removes around the revelation in Christ and being graded according to their nearness to or distance from it. But during the last hundred years or so we have been making new observations and have realized that there is deep devotion to God, true sainthood, and deep spiritual life within these other religions; and so we have created our epicycles of theory, such as the notions of anonymous Christianity and of implicit faith. But would it not be more realistic now to make the shift from Christianity at the centre to God at the centre, and to see both our own and the other great world religions as revolving around the same divine reality?

Developing this approach, Hick suggests that the aspect of God's nature of central importance to the question of other faiths was his universal saving will. If God wishes everyone to be saved, it is inconceivable that the divine self-revelation should be effected in such a way that only a small portion of humanity could be saved. In fact as we have seen, this is not a necessary feature of either particularist or inclusivist approaches. However, Hick draws the conclusion that it is necessary to recognize that all religions lead to the same God. Christians have no special access to God, who is universally available through all religious traditions.

Hick uses an essentially Kantian philosophical framework to argue that a distinction must be made between the ultimate spiritual reality which underlies the various religious systems of the world, and the perceptions of this reality which exist within these systems. Kant had insisted that the "thing in itself" could not be known directly; humanity was obliged to limit its reflections to the world of phenomena, which at best offered an indirect knowledge of that reality. "The Real" was thus inaccessible; the religions offered human responses to that "Real," which reflected the historical and social context in which the religions of the world evolved.

> This distinction enables us to acknowledge both the one unlimited transcendent divine Reality and also a plurality of varying human concepts, images, and experiences of and response to that Reality. These different human awarenesses of and response to the Real are formed by and reciprocally inform the religious traditions of the earth. In them are reflected the different ways of thinking, feeling and experiencing which have developed within the worldwide human family.

This suggestion is not without its problems. For example, it is fairly clear that the religious traditions of the world are radically different in their beliefs and practices. Hick deals with this point by suggesting that such differences must be interpreted in terms of "both–and" rather than "either–or." They should be understood as complementary, rather than contradictory, insights into the one divine reality. This reality lies at the heart of all the religions; yet "their differing experiences of that reality, interacting over the centuries with the different thought-forms of different cultures, have led to increasing differentiation and contrasting elaboration." Hick states this point as follows in his *Second Christianity*:

> Thus the concept of deity is concretized as a range of divine *personae* – Yahweh, the Heavenly Father, Allah, Krishna, Shiva, etc. Each of these *personae* has arisen within human experience through the impact of the divine Reality upon some particular stream of human life. Thus Yahweh is the face of God turned towards and perceived by the Jewish people or, in more philosophical language, the concrete form in which the Jews have experienced the infinite divine Reality. As such, Yahweh exists essentially in relation to the Hebrews, the relationship being defined by the idea of covenant. He cannot be extracted from his role in Hebrew historic experience. He is part of the history of the Jews, and they are a part of his history. And as such Yahweh is a quite different divine *persona* from Krishna, who is God's face turned towards and perceived by hundreds of millions of people within the Vaishnavite tradition of India.

It will be clear that this idea is very similar to that propounded by Deist writers, of the "universal rational religion of nature" which became corrupted through time.

These difficulties relate to observed features of religious traditions. In other words, the beliefs of non-Christian religions make it difficult to accept that they are all speaking of the same God. But a more fundamental theological worry remains: is Hick actually talking about the *Christian* God at all? A central Christian conviction – that God is revealed definitively in Jesus Christ – has to be set to one side to allow Hick to proceed. Hick argues that he is merely adopting a *theocentric*, rather than a *Christocentric* approach. Yet the Christian insistence that God is known normatively through Christ implies that authentically Christian knowledge of God is derived through Christ. For a number of critics, Hick's desertion of Christ as a reference point means abandoning any claim to speak from a *Christian* perspective.

The real problem here is that pluralists such as Hick are caught up in a tension that they cannot resolve. The tension is between an implicit need to provide arguments for the superiority of their own pluralist views about human nature and human destiny over and against traditional religious views on the one hand – yet this is coupled with an explicit commitment to principles that exclude the legitimacy of precisely these arguments on the other. Pluralists want to critique and challenge Christian tendencies to be (as they see it) imperialist and condescending in their judgments about non-Christian religions. Yet in doing this, pluralists are themselves engaging in precisely the activity they wish to criticize – namely, critiquing Christians for holding Christian views. Yet why should Christians be blamed for holding Christian ideas? Or Muslims for holding Islamic ideas? No system of thought can sustain such a tension.

For this reason, there has been growing interest in recent years in an alternative, which avoids the intellectual shortcomings of the pluralist position. The new approach is known as "parallelism."

Parallelism

In recent years, growing discontent with the shortcomings of the pluralist approach has led to the emergence of a fourth approach. Irritated at pluralist attempts to shoehorn all the religions into the same basic pattern, writers such as Joseph DiNoia and Mark Heim have insisted that the distinctive features of each religion must be respected. In his *The Diversity of Religions* (1992), DiNoia pleads for religious diversity to be taken seriously, and offers a critique of what he regards as the shortcomings of reductionist approaches. In his *Salvations: Truth and Difference in Religion* (1995), Heim critiques three major pluralistic thinkers in his book: John Hick, Wilfred Cantwell Smith, and Paul Knitter. He argues that all three create paradigms that arise from and are informed by the world of Western liberal thought. The outcome is inevitable: they end up forcing religions into a preconceived mold.

For Heim, it is essential to respect religions for what they are. Instead of arguing that all religions ultimately lead to Christian truth (the inclusivist position) or to some ultimate reality which transcends all religious traditions (the pluralist position), Heim insists that we must take each religion's understanding of its beliefs and goals seriously. Christian beliefs and practices will lead to Christian goals – to the New Jerusalem. Muslims will attain a Muslim paradise on the basis of their beliefs and practices. Buddhist beliefs and practices will lead to Buddhist goals. And so on. Instead of forcing all religions to end up at the same place, Heim insists that we respect their own visions of what they are seeking to achieve.

Heim's position is itself a form of religious particularism. Writing from a Christian perspective, Heim insists that everyone must recognize both the *actuality* and the possible *value* of other religious particularisms, without trying to subsume them all into some grand religiously neutral theory. Heim argues that pluralism is actually crypto-inclusivist, in that it claims to believe in many goals but actually believes in only one – namely, "reality-centeredness" in the case of John Hick, liberation from social oppression for Paul Knitter, and universal faith and rationality for Wilfred Cantwell Smith.

The parallelist way of thinking allows for the possibility that different religions may be deeply and genuinely different, offering their adherents competing goals that, however good each may be, are profoundly incompatible. That is why the title of Heim's book is so significant: *Salvations* – in the plural. Against the pluralist insistence that all religions ultimately lead to the same salvation, Heim argues that we must acknowledge and respect each religion's own distinctive understanding of what salvation actually is. "Christians can consistently recognize that some traditions encompass religious ends which are real states of human transformation, distinct from that Christians seek." Christian theology should therefore consistently recognize that there are (or can be) many different religious goals, and hence many different salvations.

This position raises a number of questions. Its fundamental approach could be described as a "plurality of absolutes." All religions are to be recognized as being completely right in their own terms. But how can this be? Can all be right? Heim's argument, in effect, is that these claims are justified, epistemically speaking, even if they may be mistaken. This conclusion reflects a postmodern reaction against the modernist insistence on a single standard of justification for beliefs. The religions develop their own standards of determining what justifies a belief, and their beliefs are justified by their own standards. It is an argument that is not without its problems. However, it certainly moves us away from the modernist assumptions that underlie pluralism. It remains to be seen how this new approach will be evaluated in the coming years.

The debate over the Christian understanding of the relation of Christianity to other religious traditions will continue for some considerable time, fueled by the rise of multiculturalism in western society. The four options outlined above are likely to continue to be represented in Christian writing on the matter for some time to come.

Our attention now turns to the final aspect of Christian theology, traditionally known as "the last things," or, more technically, as *eschatology*.

QUESTIONS FOR CHAPTER 17

1   How would you define a "religion"?
2   Why was Dietrich Bonhoeffer so attracted to the idea of a "religionless Christianity"?
3   Do all religions lead to God?
4   How helpful and persuasive do you find Karl Rahner's idea of an "anonymous Christian"?
5   Why have ideas such as the resurrection and divinity of Christ proved to be such a hindrance to interfaith dialogue? Is there a case for their elimination, in order to make such a dialogue more fruitful?
6   What are the strengths and weaknesses of the "parallelist" approach?

18

The Last Things: The Christian Hope

In earlier discussions of the resurrection and the doctrine of salvation, we touched upon aspects of "eschatology" – that is, the Christian understanding of the "last things." The term "eschatology," which came into general use in the twentieth century, derives from the Greek term *ta eschata*, "the last things," and relates to such matters as the Christian expectations of resurrection and judgment. In the concluding chapter of this work, we shall deal with this subject in more detail.

Several major aspects of this topic have already been covered elsewhere in this volume. In particular, the following discussions should be noted:

1   The debate over the resurrection of Jesus Christ and its theological implications (pp. 320–5).
2   The rediscovery of the eschatological aspect of the New Testament concept of the "kingdom of God" in the late nineteenth century (pp. 313–14).
3   The eschatological dimensions of the Christian doctrine of salvation (pp. 329–30).

In the broadest sense of the term, "eschatology" is "discourse about the end." The "end" in question may refer to an individual's existence, or to the closing of the present age. A characteristic Christian belief, of decisive importance in this context, is that time is linear, not cyclical. History had a beginning; it will one day come to an end. "Eschatology" deals with a network of beliefs relating to the end of life and history, whether of an individual or of the world in general. It has unquestionably stimulated and contributed extensively to some of the most creative and fantastic movements within Christianity.

In recent years a distinction has been drawn between the two terms "eschatological" and "apocalyptic." In the past these terms had been regarded as meaning more or less the same thing. Since about 1980 there has been an increased awareness of the different meanings of the two terms, mainly resulting through the work of New Testament scholars such as Christopher Rowland. "Eschatology" continues to designate the branch of Christian theology concerned with the "last things," such as the resurrection from the dead, heaven, and hell. The term "apocalyptic" is now used to refer to a particular genre or type of literature, which generally has an interest in the "last things" but is not specifically identified by this interest. To make this difficult point clearer, we may explore the matter in more detail.

The term "apocalyptic" (deriving from the Greek word *apocalypsis*, meaning "unveiling," "disclosure," or "revelation") is now used to refer to a particular type of writing, found within sections of Judaism during the period extending from about two hundred years before Christ to about two hundred years after his coming. During this 400-year period, sections of Judaism produced writings which reflected a distinctive worldview and style of writing. Apocalyptic writings generally focus on the expectation of God's imminent intervention in the affairs of the world, in which God's people will be delivered and their enemies destroyed, with the present world-order being overthrown and replaced with a restored creation.

Particular emphasis is often placed on the role of visions and dreams, through which the writers learned of the secret plans of God. It will therefore be clear that while apocalyptic writings have an interest in the "last things," the term "apocalyptic" is better used to refer to a type of theology and a style of writing.

Developments in the Doctrine of the Last Things

It is generally thought that the most important developments relating to Christian understanding of the "last things" have taken place during the period since the Enlightenment. In what follows, we shall briefly consider the New Testament foundations for eschatology, before moving on to consider their more recent interpretations.

The New Testament

The New Testament is saturated with the belief that something new has happened in the history of humanity, in and through the life and death of Jesus Christ, and above all through his resurrection from the dead. The theme of hope predominates, even in the face of death. In view of the importance of the New Testament material to the shaping of Christian thinking on eschatology, we shall consider some of its leading themes. The two sources of outstanding importance are generally agreed to be the preaching of Jesus himself, and the writings of Paul. We shall consider each of these in what follows.

The dominant theme in the preaching of Jesus is the coming of the kingdom of God. This phrase is rare in contemporary Jewish writings, and is widely regarded as one of the most distinctive aspects of the preaching of Jesus. This term, or closely related ideas, occurs some 70 times in the Synoptic Gospels. The use of the word "kingdom" in this context is potentially misleading. Although this English word has been used regularly since the sixteenth century to translate the Greek term *basileia*, the term "kingship" is more appropriate. The term "kingdom" suggests a definite geographical region which is being ruled, whereas the Greek term refers primarily to the act of ruling itself. In New Testament scholarship, the term "the kingly rule of God" has often been used to make this point clear.

The term has strongly eschatological associations in the preaching of Jesus. Although many nineteenth-century liberal writers, such as A. B. Ritschl, attempted to interpret it in terms of a present set of moral values, it is clear that the term has both present and future associations. The kingdom is something which is "drawing near" (Mark 1: 15), yet which still belongs in its fullness to the future. The Lord's Prayer, which remains of central importance to individual and corporate Christian prayer and worship, includes reference to the future coming of the kingdom (Matthew 6: 10).

At the Last Supper, Jesus spoke to his disciples of a future occasion when they would drink wine in the kingdom of God (Mark 14:

25). The general consensus among New Testament scholars is that there is a tension between the "now" and the "not yet" in relation to the kingdom of God, similar to that envisaged by the parable of the growing mustard seed (Mark 4: 30–2). The term "inaugurated eschatology" has become widely used to refer to the relation of the present inauguration and future fulfillment of the kingdom.

Paul's eschatology also shows a tension between the "now" and the "not yet." This is articulated in terms of a number of key images, which may be summarized as follows:

1 The presence of a "new age." At several points Paul emphasizes that the coming of Christ inaugurates a new era or "age" (Greek: *aionos*). Although this new age – which Paul designates a "new creation" (2 Corinthians 5: 17) – has yet to be fulfilled, its presence can already be experienced. For this reason, Paul can refer to the "end of the ages" in Christ (1 Corinthians 10: 11). The position which Paul opposes in the early chapters of 1 Corinthians clearly corresponds to a realized eschatology, in which each and every aspect of the age to come has been fulfilled in the present. It seems that Paul's opponents at Corinth were teaching that the final age was now present, and all the benefits of eternity were to be had in the here and now. For Paul, there is an element of postponement: the ultimate transformation of the world is yet to come, but may be confidently awaited.

2 The resurrection of Jesus is seen by Paul as an eschatological event, which affirms that the "new age" really has been inaugurated. Although this does not exhaust the meaning of Christ's resurrection (which has significant soteriological implications: see p. 350), Paul clearly sees Christ's resurrection as an event which enables believers to live in the knowledge that death – a dominant feature of the "present age" – has been overcome.

3 Paul looks forward to the future coming of Jesus Christ in judgment at the end of time, confirming the new life of believers and their triumph over sin and death. A number of images are used to refer to this, including "the day of the Lord." At one point (1 Corinthians 16: 22) Paul uses an Aramaic term, *maranatha* (literally, "Come, our Lord!") as an expression of the Christian hope. The Greek term *parousia* is often used to refer to the future coming of Christ (e.g., 1 Corinthians 15: 23; 2 Thessalonians 2: 1, 8–9). For Paul, there is an intimate connection between the final coming of Christ and the execution of final judgment.

4 A major theme of Paul's eschatology is the coming of the Holy Spirit. This theme, which builds on a long-standing aspect of Jewish expectations, sees the gift of the Spirit as a confirmation that the new age has dawned in Christ. One of the most significant aspects of Paul's thought at this point is his interpretation of the gift of the Spirit to believers as an *arrabon* (2 Corinthians 1: 22, 5: 5). This unusual word has the basic sense of a "guarantee" or "pledge," affirming that the believer may rest assured of ultimate salvation on account of the present possession of the Spirit. Although salvation remains something which will be consummated in the future, the believer may have present assurance of this future event through the indwelling of the Spirit.

It will therefore be clear that the eschatology of the New Testament is complex. However, a leading theme is that something which happened in the past has inaugurated something new, which will reach its final consummation in the future. The Christian believer is thus caught up in the tension between the "now" and the "not yet." How this tension is to be understood and articulated is a subject of considerable interest in its own right and will be considered at points in this present chapter. Our attention now turns to the development of eschatological themes in the later Christian tradition.

Early Christianity and Roman beliefs about reunion after death

The human longing for consolation in the face of death may be traced back to classical times. Perhaps the most distressing aspect of death is that of *separation* – being forcibly, and it might seem irreversibly cut off from close friends and relatives, never to see them again. Classic mourning rites and funeral ornaments point to the sense of desolation which traditionally accompanied the death of a significant other. The Hellenistic world had become accustomed to the Hades myth, which portrayed Charon as ferrying the dead across the river Styx to the underworld for the fee of one obol – a coin which was placed in the mouth of a dead person for this purpose. Once on the other side, the dead person took part in a family reunion.

This basic belief undergirds two of Cicero's more important works, the dialogue on *On Old Age* and perhaps more importantly the final section of *De Republica* known as "Scipio's Dream." In this latter work, Cicero portrays Scipio meeting prominent Roman citizens in paradise, who take advantage of the occasion to lecture him on political ethics. Yet the work takes on a new tone as Cicero describes Scipio's reunion with his father: "I now saw my dead father, Paulus, approaching, and I burst into tears. My father put his arms around me and kissed me, urging me not to weep."

This classic scenario of a family reunion in the world to come had a significant impact on the style and subject-matter of the Christian writings of the era, even if they ultimately rested on rather different theological foundations. Cyprian of Carthage, a martyr-bishop of the third century, tried to encourage his fellow Christians in the face of suffering and death at times of persecution by holding before them a vision of heaven, in which they would see the martyrs and apostles, face to face. More than that; they would be reunited with those who they loved and cherished. Heaven is here seen as the "native land" of Christians, from which they have been exiled during their time on earth. The hope of return to their native land, there to be reunited with those who they knew and loved, was held out as a powerful consolation in times of trial and suffering.

> We regard paradise as our native land [*Patriam nostram paradisum computamus*] [...] Many of our dear ones await us there, and a dense crowd of parents, brothers, children, is longing for us, already assured of their own safety, and still longing for our salvation. What gladness there will be for them and for us when we enter their presence and share their embrace!

Cyprian himself was martyred for his faith in 258, presumably consoled by precisely the ideas with which he sought to console others.

The motif is also found in Ambrose of Milan's funeral eulogy for the emperor Theodosius, who died in Milan in January 395. Theodosius had earlier had a serious altercation with Ambrose as a result of his decision in 390 to order the slaughter of seven thousand citizens of Thessalonica to avenge the murder of the Roman governor Butheric. Ambrose, having consulted with his fellow bishops, informed Theodosius that he must do severe public penance before being allowed again to receive the sacraments. Theodosius eventually stripped himself of every sign of royalty and publicly repented of his sin. In his funeral oration, Ambrose asked his listeners to imagine the scene in heaven, in which Theodosius embraces his wife Flaccila and his daughter Pulcheria, before being reunited with his father and his predecessor as a Christian Roman emperor, Constantine.

Augustine: the two cities

One of the most influential reworkings of the corporate dimension of the eschatological ideas of the New Testament is that of Augustine of Hippo, found in his *City of God*. This work was written in a context which could easily be described as "apocalyptic" – the destruction of the great city of Rome, and the collapse of the Roman Empire. A central theme of the work is the relation between two cities – the "city of God" and the "secular city" or "the city of the world." The complexities of the Christian life, especially its political aspects, are due to the dialectic between these two cities.

Believers live "in this intermediate period" separating the incarnation of Christ from his final return in glory. The church is to be seen as in exile in the "city of the world." It is in the world, yet not of the world. There is a strong eschatological tension between the present reality, in which the church is exiled in the world, and somehow obliged to maintain its distinctive ethos while surrounded by disbelief, and the future hope, in which the church will be delivered from the world, and finally allowed to share in the glory of God. It will be clear that Augustine has no time for the Donatist idea of the church as a body of saints (pp. 394–6). For Augustine, the church shares in the fallen character of the world and therefore includes the pure and the impure, saints and sinners. Only at the last day will this tension finally be resolved.

Yet alongside this corporate understanding of eschatology, Augustine shows an awareness of the individualist dimensions of the Christian hope. This is especially clear in his discussion of the tension between what human nature presently is and what it finally will be. Believers are saved, purified, and perfected – yet in hope (*in spe*) but not in reality (*in re*). Salvation is something that is inaugurated in the life of the believer, but which will only find its completion at the end of history. This idea is developed by Martin Luther, as noted earlier (pp. 373–4).

Augustine is thus able to offer Christians hope, as they contemplate the sinful nature of their lives, and wonder how this is to be reconciled with the Gospel imperatives to be holy, like God. For Augustine, believers are able to reach out in hope, beyond their present condition. This is not a spurious or invented hope, but a sure and certain hope which is grounded in the resurrection of Christ.

Augustine is aware of the fact that the word "end" has two meanings. The "end" can mean "either the ceasing to be of what was, or the perfecting of what was begun." Eternal life is to be seen as the state in which our love of God, begun in this life, is finally brought to its completion and consummation, through union with the object of that love. Eternal life is the "reward that makes perfect," to which the Christian has looked forward throughout the life of faith.

Joachim of Fiore: the three ages

Augustine had proposed a relatively simple schematization of Christian history, which treated the period of the church as that era separating the coming (or "advent") and returning (or "second coming") of Christ. However, this failed to satisfy his later interpreters. Joachim of Fiore (c.1132–1202) developed a more speculative approach to history, with a strongly eschatological orientation, loosely based upon the doctrine of the Trinity. Joachim became a monk in the Benedictine monastery of Corazzo and was elected its abbot in 1177. He did not find this position to his liking and was eventually given permission to found his own congregations in the Sila mountains.

According to Joachim, universal history could be divided into three ages or eras:

1   The age of the Father, which corresponds to the Old Testament dispensation. Joachim referred to this as the *ordo conjugatorum*, in which humanity lived under the law until the end of the period of the Old Testament.
2   The age of the Son, which corresponds to the New Testament dispensation, including the church. Joachim designated this period as the *ordo clericorum*.
3   The age of the Spirit, which would witness the rise of new religious movements, leading to the reform and renewal of the church, and the final establishment of peace and unity on earth.

What gave Joachim's views a particular urgency was the precise dating of these periods. Each age, he argued, consisted of 42 generations of 30 years each. As a result, the "age of the Son" was due to end in 1260, to be followed immediately by the radical new "age of the Spirit." In this may be seen anticipated many of the millenarian movements of our own day.

Joachim's ideas caused consternation at the time, especially as the year 1260 approached. His views were condemned by the Fourth Lateran Council in 1215, and described as "conjectural" by Thomas Aquinas. In 1255 – only five years before Joachim's new era of the Spirit was due to dawn – his prophecies were censured as completely erroneous by a papal theo-logical commission. Yet others were more favorably disposed towards Joachim. Dislike of the highly institutional nature of the church led many to welcome Joachim's vision of a new "age of the Spirit," and the advent of the "spiritual church" in its place.

Dante Alighieri: the *Divine Comedy*

Among those who had a high regard for Joachim, we may note the Tuscan poet Dante Alighieri (1265–1321), who assigned him a place in paradise. Dante, based in the city of Florence, wrote the *Divine Comedy* in order to give poetic expression to the Christian hope and make comments on the life of both the church and city of Florence of his own day. The poem is set in the year 1300, and describes how Dante is led into the depths of the earth by the pagan Roman poet Virgil, who will act as his guide through hell and purgatory.

The work is an important representation of the medieval worldview, in which the souls of the departed were understood to pass through a series of purifying and cleansing processes, before being enabled to catch a glimpse of the vision of God – the ultimate goal of the Christian life. Its importance for our purposes in this section is its vivid depiction of the spiritual geography of the last things.

The *Divine Comedy* takes the form of three major interconnected poems, respectively entitled *Inferno* ("Hell"), *Purgatorio* ("Purgatory"), and *Paradiso* ("Paradise"). The work makes substantial use of the leading themes of Christian theology and spirituality, while at the same time including comment on contemporary political and social events. The poem describes a journey which takes place in Holy Week 1300 – before Dante's exile from Florence. From the substantial number of clues in the text, it can be worked out that the journey begins at nightfall on Good Friday. After entering Hell, Dante journeys downwards for an entire day, before beginning his ascent towards Purgatory. After climbing Mount Purgatory, Dante rises further until he eventually enters into the presence of God.

Throughout the journey, Dante is accompanied by guides. The first guide is Virgil, the great Roman poet who wrote the *Aeneid*. It is widely thought that Dante uses Virgil as a symbol of classic learning and human reason. As they draw close to the peak of Mount Purgatory, Virgil falls behind and Dante finds himself in the company of Beatrice (thought to be based on Beatrice Portinari, the idealized object of Dante's courtly love, who had died in 1290), who leads him through the outer circles of heaven. Finally, he is joined by Bernard of Clairvaux, who leads Dante into the presence of God.

The structure of the poem is immensely intricate, and it can be read at a number of levels. It can, for example, be read as a commentary on medieval Italian politics, particularly the intricacies of Florentine politics over the period 1300–4; or it can be seen as a poetic guide to Christian beliefs concerning the afterlife. More fundamentally, it can be read as a journey of self-discovery and spiritual enlightenment, in which the poet finally discovers and encounters his heart's desire.

The work is also an important witness to the use of literary application of the allegorical interpretation of the Bible. In his letter to Cangrande della Scala, Dante sets out the interpretative scheme that governs his work, which he compares to the nature of the Bible itself.

> The sense of this work is not simple, rather it may be called polysemic [*immo dici potest polysemos*], that is, having many senses. The first sense is that which comes from the letter; the second is that which is signified by the letter. And the first is called the literal, the second allegorical or moral or anagogical. To clarify this approach, consider these words: "When

Israel went out from Egypt, the house of Jacob from a people of strange language, Judah became God's sanctuary, Israel his dominion" (Psalm 114: 1–2). If we view this literally [*ad literam*], it refers to the exit of the children of Israel from Egypt at the time of Moses; if we view it as an allegory, it means the redemption achieved by Christ; if we see it according to its moral sense, it means the conversion of the soul from the struggle and misery of sin to the status of grace; in its anagogical sense, it refers to the blessed soul breaking free from the slavery of corruption to the freedom of eternal glory.

Dante's portrayal of the geography of hell is especially interesting, as he conceives of hell as consisting of a group of concentric circles – the perfect shape, according to ancient geometry. The "nine circles of hell" are as follows.

Level	Name
1	Limbo
2	The Lustful
3	The Gluttonous
4	The Avaricious
5	The Wrathful
6	Heretics
7	The Violent
8	The Fraudulent
9	The Treacherous

Dante portrays himself as descending through successive levels of hell, encountering various individuals who are condemned to its various regions. One of the most interesting aspects of Dante scholarship is to work out why Dante consigns various people to different fates – often reflecting aspects of papal and Florentine politics of the period. For example, "limbo" is seen as a kind of "ante-hell," in which no pain is experienced and which is illuminated by a "hemisphere of light" corresponding to the light of human reason. Dante populates this region with virtuous non-Christians, particularly pagan philosophers such as Aristotle (who is clearly *the* philosopher for Dante), Seneca, Euclid, and Virgil. Beyond this lies the second circle of hell, to which Dante consigns all those who have "made reason slave to appetite." Dante includes Achilles, Cleopatra, Helen of Troy, and Tristan (a hero of many medieval romances) among the inhabitants of this region.

Dante's *Divine Comedy* helped establish medieval perceptions of hell to no small extent. It is perhaps worth noting that Dante's vision represents a very substantial (and rather speculative!) elaboration on the very little biblical material which we possess on this matter. Dante knew that eschatological speculation made for excellent reading, and enlivened his text with comments on the city and church politics of his time. The work deserves close reading, both as a work of literature and as a witness to the medieval vision of the world.

Hope in the face of death: Jeremy Taylor

There is an important link between Christian theology and Christian living which it is too easy to overlook. The fact that this textbook has concentrated on academic issues of theology means that it has not always been possible to bring out clearly the close and natural connections between the beliefs that Christians hold and the way in which they live (and die). In the present section we shall consider a major theologian of the seventeenth century, who was concerned to explore the relationship between the Christian belief in resurrection and eternal life and the spirituality of the individual Christian believer.

Jeremy Taylor (1609–67) is widely regarded as one of the finest spiritual writers of the seventeenth century. He is often referred to as a "Caroline Divine," meaning a religious writer of the Church of England who was active during the reigns of Charles I and Charles II. Taylor supported the Royalist cause during the English Civil War of the seventeenth century, and was thus out of favor during the period of the Puritan Commonwealth. He was imprisoned for part of the period of the Commonwealth; after his release, he spent the remaining years of the Protectorate living in Wales, serving as chaplain to Richard Vaughan, earl of Carbery.

It was during this period that Taylor wrote the works for which he is best known, including *The Rules and Exercises of Holy Living* (1650) and *The Rules and Exercises of Holy Dying* (1651). This latter work was published in the year of his wife's death. These works are perhaps rather better known in their abbreviated forms of *Holy Living* and *Holy Dying*, and were often printed together in a single volume.

"It is a great art to die well," commented Taylor; the work to which these words are prefaced aims to set out the means by which a Christian can die with dignity and peace. One of the chief means by which Taylor believes that Christians can deal with the fear of death is to contemplate the hope of what lies beyond death:

> If thou wilt be fearless of death endeavour to be in love with the felicities of saints and angels, and be once persuaded to believe that there is a condition of living better than this; that there are creatures more noble than we; that above there is a country better than ours; that the inhabitants know more and know better, and are in places of rest and desire; and first learn to value it, and then learn to purchase it, and death cannot be a formidable thing, which lets us into so much joy and so much felicity. And, indeed, who would not think his condition mended if he passed from conversing with dull tyrants and enemies of learning, to converse with Homer and Plato, with Socrates and Cicero, with Plutarch and Fabricius? So the heathens speculated, but we consider higher. "The

dead that die in the Lord" shall converse with St. Paul, and all the college of the apostles, and all the saints and martyrs, with all the good men whose memory we preserve in honour, with excellent kings and holy bishops, and with the great Shepherd and Bishop of our souls, Jesus Christ, and with God himself.

We can see here a clear statement of the impact of Christian beliefs about heaven on Christian living. Taylor clearly believes that the contemplation of the Christian hope serves as a solace and balm to those who fear the end of life, by reminding them that something more wonderful awaits them beyond.

The Enlightenment: eschatology as superstition

The intensely rationalist atmosphere of the Enlightenment (pp. 67–70) led to criticism of the Christian doctrine of the last things as ignorant superstition, devoid of any real basis in life. Particular criticism was directed against the idea of hell. The strongly utilitarian outlook of the later Enlightenment resulted in a growing belief that eternal punishment served no useful purpose. Feuerbach argued that the idea of "heaven" or "eternal life" was simply a projection of a human longing after immortality, without any objective basis.

A more sustained critique of the Christian doctrine of hope was found in the writings of Karl Marx (pp. 72–3). Marx argued that religion in general sought to comfort those undergoing suffering in the present through persuading them of the joy of an afterlife. By doing so, it distracted them from the task of transforming the present world so that suffering could be eliminated. In many ways, Marxism may be regarded as a secularized Christian eschatology, with "the revolution" as a secularized counterpart to "heaven."

Related developments can be discerned within nineteenth-century liberalism (pp. 83–4). The idea of a cataclysmic end of history was set to one side, in favor of a doctrine of hope which was grounded in the gradual evolution of humanity toward moral and societal perfection. The Darwinian theory of natural selection, as expressed in popular versions of the theory of evolution, seemed to point to human history, like all of human life, moving upward toward higher and more sophisticated forms. Eschatology came to be relegated to the status of a theological curiosity. The notion of the "kingdom of God," shorn of its New Testament apocalyptic associations, was viewed (for example, by Albrecht Ritschl) as a static realm of moral values, toward which society was steadily advancing through a process of continuous evolution.

The twentieth century: the rediscovery of eschatology

The Enlightenment approach was largely discredited by two developments. In the first place, in the closing decade of the nineteenth century Johannes Weiss and Albert Schweitzer rediscovered the apocalyptic character of the preaching of Jesus, and argued forcefully that the "kingdom of God" was an eschatological notion (pp. 313–14). Jesus was to be seen not as the moral educator of humanity, but as the proclaimer of the imminent coming of the eschatological kingdom of God. This new emphasis proved to be of decisive importance in bringing about the recovery of eschatology in the twentieth century.

It must be stressed that not all New Testament scholars have agreed with the findings of Weiss and Schweitzer. For example, the British New Testament scholar Charles H. Dodd (1884–1973) argued that Jesus's preaching of the kingdom of God was not futurist, looking forward to something which had yet to happen, but was "realized" – that is, it had already happened. In his *Apostolic Preaching and its Development* (1936), Dodd argued that the "last things" have actually happened in the ministry of Jesus. What the Old Testament prophets regarded as future (such as the coming of the "Day of the Lord") has been fulfilled or realized in the life, death, and resurrection of Jesus Christ.

Dodd points out how Jesus himself declares that the "kingdom of God is at hand." The kingdom of God is not something in the distant future; it has already come upon people (Matthew 12: 28). The future does not lie ahead, in the distance – it has already happened, in the coming of Jesus.

Critics of this approach argued that Dodd had overstated his case. For example, it was suggested that the Greek original of the statement "the kingdom of God is at hand" more probably means "the kingdom of God is nearer now than it was earlier." In other words, the kingdom has not yet arrived; but it is closer than it was before. In some of his later writings, Dodd appears to have responded to this criticism. He began to write about the kingdom having "begun" rather than "arrived," and of "initiation" rather than of "realization." In other words, Dodd conceded that the "last things" in all their totality had yet to happen, even if they had begun to take place.

Three general positions are widely encountered within twentieth-century Christian discussion of the eschatology of the New Testament, as follows. It should be noted that it is the second of the three positions, here described as "inaugurated," which commands the greatest support within New Testament scholarship.

1 *Futurist*: The kingdom of God is something which remains in the future, and will intervene disruptively in the midst of human history (Weiss).

2 *Inaugurated*: The kingdom of God has begun to exercise its influence within human history, although its full realization and fulfillment lie in the future.

3 *Realized*: The kingdom of God has already been realized in the coming of Jesus (Dodd).

The second development which we need to consider concerns a general collapse in confidence in human civilization as a means of bringing the kingdom of God to fulfillment. World War I was an especially traumatic episode in this respect. The Holocaust, the development of nuclear weapons and the threat of nuclear war, and the continuing threat of the destruction of the environment through human exploitation of its resources, have all raised doubts concerning the credibility of the vision of liberal humanist forms of Christianity.

But what was to be done with the idea of eschatology? One approach, which attracted considerable attention during the 1950s and early 1960s, was due to the Marburg New Testament scholar Rudolf Bultmann. We will consider this in what follows.

Rudolf Bultmann: the demythologization of eschatology

Bultmann's controversial program of "demythologization" (p. 322) proved to be especially significant in relation to beliefs concerning the end of history. Bultmann argued that such beliefs were "myths," which required to be interpreted existentially. The New Testament relates "stories" concerning remote and inaccessible times and places (such as "in the beginning" or "in heaven"), and involving supernatural agents or events. Bultmann declares that these stories possess an underlying existential meaning, which can be perceived and appropriated by a suitable process of interpretation.

Perhaps the most important of these is the eschatological myth of the imminent end of the world through direct divine intervention, leading to judgment and subsequent reward or retribution. This insight is of central importance to our narrative, in that it allows Bultmann to deal with Schweitzer's demonstration of the "thoroughgoing eschatological conditioning" of the New Testament by a comprehensive process of demythologization. For Bultmann, this "myth," and others like it, may be reinterpreted existentially.

Thus, in the case of the eschatological myth, the recognition that history has not, in fact, come to an end does not necessarily invalidate the myth: interpreted existentially, the "myth" refers to the here and now of human existence – the fact that human beings must face the reality of their own death, and are thus forced to make existential decisions. The "judgment" in question is not some future event of *divine* judgment, to take place at the end of the world, but the present event of *our own judgment of ourselves*, based upon our knowledge of what God has done in Christ.

Bultmann argues that precisely this sort of demythologizing may be found in the fourth Gospel, written toward the end of the first century, when the early eschatological expectations of the Christian community were fading. "Judgment" is interpreted by Bultmann to refer to the moment of existential crisis, as human beings are confronted with the divine *kerygma* addressed to them. The "realized eschatology" of the fourth Gospel arises through the fact that the redactor of the Gospel has realized that the *parousia* is not some future event, but one which has already taken place, in the confrontation of the believer with the *kerygma*:

> To the "Now" of the coming of the Revealer, there corresponds exactly the "Now" of the proclamation of the word as an historical

fact, the "Now" of the present, of the moment. [...] This "Now" of being addressed at a specific moment is the eschatological "Now," because in it the decision is made between life and death. It is the hour which is coming, and, in being addressed, now is. [...] Therefore it is not true that the *parousia*, expected by others as an event occurring in time, is now denied or transformed by John into a process within the soul, an experience. Rather, John opens the reader's eyes: the *parousia* has already occurred!

Bultmann thus regards the fourth Gospel as partially reinterpreting the eschatological myth in terms of its significance for human existence. Christ is not a past phenomenon, but the ever-present word of God, expressing not a general truth, but a concrete proclamation addressed to us, demanding an existential decision on our part. For Bultmann, the eschatological process became an event in the history of the world, and becomes an event once more in contemporary Christian proclamation.

But such approaches failed to satisfy many critics, who felt that Bultmann had abandoned too many of the central features of the Christian doctrine of hope. For example, Bultmann's notion of eschatology is purely individualist; it is clear that the biblical notion is corporate. Another approach began to emerge within the later 1960s, which seemed to many to offer far more than Bultmann's truncated version of hope.

Jürgen Moltmann: the theology of hope

Jürgen Moltmann's *Theology of Hope* created a considerable impact on its publication in Germany in 1964. Moltmann here draws on the insights of Ernst Bloch's remarkable work, *Philosophy of Hope*. Bloch's neo-Marxist analysis of human experience is based on the belief that all human culture is moved by a passionate hope for the future that transcends all the alienation of the present. Bloch saw himself as standing in direct line to the biblical idea of revolutionary apocalyptic hope. Where Bultmann sought to make eschatology acceptable through demythologization, Bloch defended it by pointing to the vigorous social critique and prophetic vision of social transformation which accompanied the ideas in their original scriptural contexts. Both in Europe and North America, the 1960s saw the outburst of optimism concerning the future of humanity. Everything seemed so hopeful.

Against this background of a secular vision of hope, often grounded in a Marxist ideology, Moltmann argued the need for the rediscovery of the corporate Christian conception of hope, as a central motivating factor in the life and thought of the individual and the church. Eschatology needed to be rescued from its position as "a harmless little chapter at the conclusion of a Christian dogmatics" (Karl Barth) and given pride of place. Moltmann argues that eschatology is of central importance to Christian thinking.

Moltmann's attitude of orientation toward the future, defined and informed by the promises of God, is summarized in a slogan: *spes quaerens intellectum – spero, ut intellegam* ("hope seeking understanding – I hope, in order that I may understand"). Each of these phrases represents a significant modification of the viewpoint of Anselm of Canterbury, who emphasized the importance of faith, and was summarized in the slogans: *fides quaerens intellectum* and *credo, ut intellegam* ("faith seeking understanding" and "I believe, in order that I may understand": see p. 34). For Moltmann, Christian theology provides a vision of hope through the transforming work of God, which stands in sharp contrast to secular ideas of hope and social transformation.

If it is hope that maintains and upholds faith and keeps it moving on, if it is hope that draws the believer into the life of love, then it will also be hope that is the mobilizing and driving force of faith's thinking, of its knowledge of and reflections on human nature, history, and society. Faith hopes in order to know what it believes. Hence all its knowledge will be an anticipatory, fragmentary knowledge forming a prelude to the promised future, and as such is committed to hope. [. . .] The Christian hope is directed towards a *novum ultimum*, towards a new creation of all things by the God of the resurrection of Jesus Christ. It thereby opens a future outlook that embraces all things, including also death, and into this it can and must also take the limited hopes of a renewal of life, stimulating them, relativizing them, giving them direction.

For Moltmann, the "hope" in question is not individual, existential, or private; it is the public hope of the whole of the creation, as it awaits the renewing work of the "God of hope." It is therefore imperative that Christianity rediscovers its eschatology and realizes its enormous importance to a world which is longing for hope, and seeking that hope outside the Christian tradition. Only by rediscovering its own theology of hope can the church hope to gain a hearing in a secular culture.

Helmut Thielicke: ethics and eschatology

One of the most important modern discussions of the theological importance of eschatology is due to the German Lutheran writer Helmut Thielicke (1908–86). In his massive *Theological Ethics* (1958–64) Thielicke set out to explore the theological foundations of Christian ethics. Underlying Thielicke's approach to ethics is his dissatisfaction with the classical Lutheran approach to ethics, which speaks of "two kingdoms" or "two realms" of ethics.

For Thielicke, this approach failed to take eschatology seriously. Throughout the three volumes of his work, he emphasizes "the eschatological character of Christian ethics." By this he means that Christian ethics must take seriously the New Testament affirmation that the believer and the church exist in a tension between the present age (Thielicke uses the term "aeon") and the age to come. Both are simultaneously present to the believer, and Christian ethics must recognize the tension between the reality of the present age and the hope of the future age. These two aeons "run concurrently"; both are present to faith. The present age is passing away; the future age is only dawning, and has yet to break in fully. However, its future presence must already have an impact on Christian ethical thinking.

> Ethics has its place therefore precisely in the field of tension between the old and the new aeons, not in the old alone, nor in the new alone. [...] The problem of ethics lies in the fact that the two aeons run concurrently during the "last time" that is, the time between the Ascension and the Last Day. [...] This means that in the strict sense the problem of ethics is a *theological* problem. For it is posed by the interrelation of the two aeons.

For Thielicke, approaches to ethics which were based purely on secular criteria (such as Kantianism) would inevitably be judged to be deficient from a Christian perspective, on account of their failure to appreciate the eschatology of ethics. While it is probably fair to argue that it remains unclear exactly how Thielicke's emphasis on eschatology affects practical ethical decision making, it is clear that his analysis has reminded ethicists and theologians alike of the importance of this once-neglected aspect of the Christian faith.

Dispensationalism: the structures of eschatology

Dispensationalism is a movement which achieved considerable influence in twentieth-century North American evangelicalism, particularly during the period 1920–70. The term takes its name from its understanding of a series of "dispensations" (from the Greek term *oikonomia*) in the history of salvation. The origins of the movement lie in England with John Nelson Darby (1800–82). However, the movement became of particular significance in the United States under the influence of C. I. Scofield (1843–1921), whose *Scofield Reference Bible* (1909) became a milestone in dispensationalist thought.

The most distinctive feature of dispensationalism is its periodization of history. Scofield divided the history of salvation into seven periods or "dispensations," each of which represents a distinct covenant between God and God's people. These are:

1 Innocence, between creation and the Fall.
2 Conscience, between the Fall and Noah's flood.
3 Human government, from the flood to the call of Abraham.
4 Promise, from Abraham to Moses.
5 Law, from Moses to the death of Christ.
6 The church, from the resurrection to the present.
7 The millennium

While other schemes of dispensations have been put forward within dispensationalism, Scofield's is widely regarded as the most influential.

One of classic dispensationalism's most significant features is its interpretation of the term "Israel." For dispensationalists such as Scofield and Charles C. Ryrie (born 1925), the term

"Israel" always designates the earthly Jewish people, and never represents the Christian church. Israel and the church are two totally distinct entities, each with its own history and destiny. "Israel" refers to an earthly people whose hope focuses on an earthly kingdom; "the church" refers to a heavenly people whose destiny lies beyond this world.

Dispensationalists have thus had a particular interest in the modern history of the nation of Israel (founded in 1948), seeing in this development the fulfillment of dispensationalist understandings of the Old Testament. It should be noted that more recent dispensationalist writers have tended to soften this distinction between Israel and the church.

Two central and characteristic notions within dispensationalism are those of "the rapture" and "the tribulation." The former concerns the believer's expectation of being "caught up in the clouds" to meet Christ at the time of his return (1 Thessalonians 4: 15–17). The latter is grounded in the prophetic visions of the Book of Daniel (Daniel 9: 24–7) and is understood as a seven-year period of divine judgment upon the world. Dispensationalist writers remain divided as to whether the rapture is to be understood as *pretribulational* (in which believers are enabled to escape the pain of the tribulation) or *post-tribulational* (in which believers must endure the tribulation, in the assurance that they will subsequently be united with Christ).

The Last Things

In the remainder of this chapter we shall consider aspects of Christian teaching concerning the "last things." It should be noted that there is some reluctance to deal with some of these issues in many theological circles. One

reason for this was put forward by Erasmus in the early sixteenth century. Commenting on the enthusiasm with which certain Paris theologians wrote about hell, Erasmus remarked that they had evidently been there themselves!

Hell

Interest in hell reached a climax during the Middle Ages, with artists of the period taking, one assumes, a certain delight in portraying the righteous watching sinners being tormented by burning and other means of torture. The most graphic portrayal of the medieval view of hell is that of Dante, in the first of the three books of his *Divine Comedy*. Dante portrays hell as nine circles at the center of the earth, within which Satan dwells. On the gate to hell, Dante notices the inscription "Abandon hope, all ye who enter here!"

The first circle of hell is populated by those who have died without being baptized, and virtuous pagans. (This circle corresponds to the idea of "limbo" noted earlier at pp. 470–1.) Dante declares that it is this circle which was visited by Christ during his "descent into hell" between the time of the crucifixion and the resurrection. There is no torment of any kind in this circle. As Dante advances further into hell, he discovers those who are guilty of increasingly serious sins. The second circle is populated by the lustful, the third by the gluttonous, the fourth by the miserly, and the fifth by the wrathful. These circles, taken together, constitute "upper hell." At no point does Dante refer to fire in this part of hell. Dante then draws upon Greco-Roman mythology in suggesting that the River Styx divides "upper hell" from "lower hell." Now we encounter fire for the first time. The sixth circle is populated by heretics, the seventh by the violent, the eighth by fraudsters (including several popes), and the ninth by traitors.

This static medieval view of hell was unquestionably of major influence at the time, and continues to be of importance into the modern period. It may be found clearly stated in Jonathan Edwards's famous sermon "Sinners in the Hands of an Angry God," preached on July 8, 1741:

> It would be dreadful to suffer this fierceness and wrath of Almighty God for one moment; but you must suffer it for all eternity. There will be no end to this exquisite horrible misery. [. . .] You will know that you must wear out long ages, millions of millions of ages, in wrestling and conflicting with this almighty merciless vengeance.

However, the very idea of hell has been subjected to increasing criticisms, of which the following should be noted.

1   Its existence is seen as a contradiction of the Christian assertion of the final victory of God over evil. This criticism is especially associated with the patristic writer Origen, whose doctrine of universal restoration ultimately rests upon an affirmation of the final and total triumph of God over evil. In the modern period, the philosopher Leibniz identified this consideration as a major difficulty with the doctrine of hell:

> It seems strange that, even in the great future of eternity, evil must triumph over good, under the supreme authority of the one who is the sovereign good. After all, there will be many who are called, and yet few who are chosen or saved.

2   The notion of vindictive justice seemed un-Christian to many writers, especially in the light of many New Testament passages speaking of the compassion of God. A number of writers, especially during the nineteenth century, found it difficult to reconcile the idea of a loving God with the notion of the continuing vindictive or retributive punishment of sinners. The main difficulty was that there seemed to be no point to the suffering of the condemned.

While answers may be given to these objections, there has been a perceptible loss of interest in the idea of hell in both popular and more academic Christian circles. Evangelistic preaching now seems to concentrate upon the positive affirmation of the love of God, rather than on the negative implications of the rejection of that love. One response to this within evangelical circles has been the development of a doctrine of conditional immortality, to which we may now turn.

Since the early 1980s, a growing internal debate has developed within evangelicalism concerning a network of eschatological issues, centering on the issue of immortality. Responding to criticisms of the doctrine of hell made during the modern period, a number of evangelical scholars have developed the doctrine of "conditional immortality." An example of this may be found in Philip Edgcumbe Hughes's *The True Image* (1989). Hughes argues that humanity has been created with the *potential* for immortality:

> Immortality or deathlessness is not inherent in the constitution of humanity as a corporeal–spiritual creature; though, formed in the image of God, the potential was there. That potential, which was forfeited through sin, has been restored and actualized through Christ.

Hughes argues that the essence of salvation is the actualization of the potential for immortality, which is conditional upon a response to the gospel. Those who do not respond do not enter into immortality. It therefore follows that no division is necessary between the good and the evil, the believing and the unbelieving, after death. Augustine asserted that "after the resurrection, when the final universal judgment has been completed, there will be two kingdoms, each with its own distinct boundaries, the one Christ's, the other the devil's." Hughes argues that there will only be one. "When Christ fills all in all [...] how is it conceivable that there can be a section or realm of creation that does not belong to this fullness, and by its very presence contradicts it?"

This trend toward "conditionalism" or "conditional immortality" has met with considerable resistance within evangelicalism, with distinguished writers such as James I. Packer opposing it on the grounds of logical inconsistency and a lack of adequate scriptural foundation. It is a debate which is set to continue and perhaps extend further into the Christian community.

Purgatory

One of the major differences between Protestant and Roman Catholic understandings of the "last things" relates to the question of purgatory. Purgatory is perhaps best understood as an intermediate stage, in which those who have died in a state of grace are given an opportunity to purge themselves of the guilt of their sins before finally entering heaven. The idea does not have explicit scriptural warrant, although a passage in 2 Maccabees 12: 39–46 (regarded as apocryphal, and hence as lacking in authority, by Protestant writers) speaks of Judas Maccabeus making "propitiation for those who had died, in order that they might be released from their sin."

The idea was developed during the patristic period. Clement of Alexandria and Origen both taught that those who had died without time to perform works of penance would be "purified through fire" in the next life. The practice

of praying for the dead – which became widespread in the eastern church in the first four centuries – exercised a major impact upon theological development, and provides an excellent case study of the manner in which liturgy influences theology. What was the point of praying for the dead, it was asked, if those prayers could not alter the state in which they existed? Similar views are found in Augustine, who taught the need for purification from the sins of the present life, before entering the joys of the next.

While the practice of praying for the dead appears to have become well established by the fourth century, the explicit formulation of a notion of "purgatory" seems to date from two centuries later, in the writings of Gregory the Great. In his exposition of Matthew 12: 32, dating from 593 or 594, Gregory picks up the idea of sins which can be forgiven "in the age to come." He interprets this in terms of a future age in which sins that have not been forgiven on earth may be forgiven subsequently. Note especially the reference to the "purifying fire" (*purgatorius ignis*), which became incorporated into most medieval accounts of purgatory, and from which the term "purgatory" derives:

> As for certain lesser faults, we must believe that, before the final judgment, there is a purifying fire, for he who is the truth declares that "whoever utters blasphemy against the Holy Spirit will not be pardoned either in this age, or in the age which is to come" (Matthew 12: 32). From this statement, it is to be understood that certain offences can be forgiven in this age, whereas certain others will be forgiven in the age which is to come.

The theme of a fire which purifies – as opposed to a fire which punishes – is developed further in Catherine of Genoa's *Treatise on Purgatory*, which probably dates from around the year 1490:

Because the souls in purgatory are without the guilt of sin, there is no obstacle between them and God except their pain, which holds them back so that they cannot reach perfection through this instinct. They can also see that this instinct is held back by a need for righteousness. For this reason, a fierce fire comes into being, which is like that of Hell, with the exception of guilt. This is what makes evil the wills of those who are condemned to Hell, on whom God does not bestow his goodness; they therefore remain in their evil wills, and opposed to the will of God.

The idea of purgatory was rejected by the reformers during the sixteenth century. Two major lines of criticism were directed against it. First, it was held to lack any substantial scriptural foundations. Second, it was inconsistent with the doctrine of justification by faith, which declared that an individual could be put "right with God" through faith, thus establishing a relationship which obviated the need for purgatory. Having dispensed with the idea of purgatory, the reformers saw no pressing reason to retain the practice of prayer for the dead, which was henceforth omitted from Protestant liturgies. Both the concept of purgatory and the practice of praying for the dead continue to find acceptance within Roman Catholicism.

The millennium

The early Christian discussion of heaven tended to focus on a related, yet not identical idea – the millennium, or restored earthly kingdom lasting for a period of one thousand years, intervening between the coming of Christ and the establishment of a totally new cosmic order. This idea, which is based partly on a passage in the Book of Revelation (Revelation 20: 2–5), had considerable appeal to early Christian writers. An excellent example is provided by Irenaeus. The idea of a worldly millennium is, for Irenaeus, confirmed by a number of considerations, especially Christ's promise at the Last Supper to drink wine again with his disciples. How can this happen, he asks, if they are disembodied spirits? The reference to the future drinking of wine is a sure indication that there will be a kingdom of God established upon earth before the final judgment. Perhaps the clearest statement of the idea can be found in the writings of Tertullian.

> For we also hold that a kingdom has been promised to us on earth, but before heaven: but in another state than this, as being after the resurrection. This will last for a thousand years, in a city of God's own making, the Jerusalem which has been brought down from heaven which the Apostle also designates as "our mother from above" (Galatians 4: 26). When he proclaims that "our *politeuma*" that is, citizenship, "is in heaven" (Philippians 3: 20), he is surely referring to a heavenly city. [...] We affirm that this is the city established by God for the reception of the saints at the resurrection, and for their refreshment with an abundance of all blessings, spiritual blessings to be sure, in compensation for the blessings we have despised or lost in this age. For indeed it is right and worthy of God that his servants should also rejoice in the place where they suffered hardship for his name. This is the purpose of that kingdom, which will last a thousand years, during which period the saints will rise sooner or later, according to their merit. When the resurrection of the saints is completed, the destruction of the world and the conflagration of judgment will be effected; we shall be "changed in a moment" into the angelic substance, by the "putting on of incorruption" (1 Corinthians 15: 52–3), and we shall be transferred to the heavenly kingdom.

For Tertullian, the millennium was to be a period in which the righteous could be compensated for the suffering which they had endured for their faith, before their final transference to heaven itself.

However, opposition to the idea of a millennium began to grow. For example, Hippolytus argued that the reference to a period of a thousand years should not be understood as a literal prediction of the chronological duration of an earthly kingdom, but as an allegorical indication of the grandeur of the heavenly kingdom. As a result, the theme of the resurrection soon came to be of greater importance to patristic writers.

Yet in more recent years, the concept of the millennium has come to play a major role in popular Protestant theology and preaching. In what follows, we shall outline the three main positions readers are likely to encounter, along with some of their representatives.

Amillennialism

As we noted above, most writers did not regard the millennium as playing a significant role in Christian expectations for the future. This position was typical of Christian thinking for more or less 1,500 years since about 400. With the establishment of a stable Christian region in western Europe and beyond, interest in eschatology generally diminished. Although writers such as Joachim of Fiore occasionally excited interest in the issue, relatively few mainstream theologians engaged with these issues in any detail. For example, the Protestant Reformation saw surprisingly little discussion of eschatological issues. Hardly any mainline Protestant reformer wrote a commentary on the Book of Revelation. While there are exceptions, the concept of the millennium played virtually no role for most Christian writers.

However, the rise of positions that place considerable emphasis on the importance of the millennium has led to this position being named "amillennial," to distinguish it from two alternative positions, to which we now turn.

Premillennialism

This viewpoint, which is associated with (but not limited to) dispensationalism, holds that the figure known as "the Antichrist" will appear on earth, ushering in a seven-year period of suffering known as "the Tribulation." As noted above, this was the predominant view in the early church up to about 400. On this account of the end-times, this great period of destruction, war, and disaster on earth will be ended by God defeating evil at the battle of Armageddon. After this, Christ will return to earth to rule for a period of a thousand years (the millennium itself), during which the forces of evil will finally be conquered. This is often accompanied by a belief in the "pretribulation Rapture," which holds that Christians will be taken up from earth prior to a time of tribulation and the Second Coming. It is important to appreciate that premillennialism offers a strongly pessimistic view of the world, believing that things are deteriorating on earth and will go on doing so until God brings history to an end. Readers wanting to get a better understanding of this approach are recommended to read the best-selling "Left Behind" novels, written by Tim LaHaye and Jerry Jenkins, which reflect this viewpoint.

Postmillennialism

This viewpoint rose to prominence within American Protestantism during the nineteenth century. It holds that the return of Christ will occur at the close of a long period (not necessarily lasting one thousand years) of righteousness and peace, commonly called the millennium. Leading conservative Protestant theologians, such as the Princeton academics Charles Hodge (1797–1878) and Benjamin B. Warfield (1851–1921), took the view that God was bringing about his purposes through steady human progress over evil, progressively leading to a Christianized world. Postmillennialism sees the church as playing a major role in transforming whole social structures before the Second Coming, and endeavoring to bring about a "Golden Age" of peace and prosperity with great advances in education, the arts, sciences, and medicine. Where premillennialism is generally pessimistic in its outlook, postmillennialism is much more optimistic. Its critics argue that its credibility was severely damaged by the suffering and damage of World Wars I and II, both of which increased the appeal of premillennialism, especially in North America.

Heaven

The Christian conception of heaven is essentially that of the eschatological realization of the presence and power of God, and the final elimination of sin. The most helpful way of considering it is to regard it as a consummation of the Christian doctrine of salvation, in which the presence, penalty, and power of sin have all been finally eliminated, and the total presence of God in individuals and the community of faith has been achieved (see pp. 329–30).

It should be noted that the New Testament parables of heaven are strongly communal in nature; for example, heaven is portrayed as a banquet, as a wedding feast, or as a city – the new Jerusalem. Individualist interpretations of heaven or eternal life can also be argued to be inadequate, on account of the Christian understanding of God as Trinity. Eternal life is thus not a projection of an individual human existence, but is rather to be seen as sharing, with the redeemed community as a whole, in the community of a loving God.

The term "heaven" is used frequently in the Pauline writings of the New Testament. Although it is natural to think of heaven as a future entity, Paul's thinking appears to embrace both a future reality and a spiritual sphere or realm which coexists with the material world of space and time. Thus "heaven" is referred to both as the future home of the believer (2 Corinthians 5: 1–2; Philippians 3: 20) and as the present dwelling-place of Jesus Christ from which he will come in final judgment (Romans 10: 6; 1 Thessalonians 1: 10, 4: 16).

One of Paul's most significant statements concerning heaven focuses on the notion of believers being "citizens of heaven" (Philippians 3: 20) and in some way sharing in the life of heaven in the present. The tension between the "now" and the "not yet" (see pp. 465–7) is evident in Paul's statements concerning heaven, making it very difficult to sustain the simple idea of heaven as something which will not come into being until the future, or which cannot be experienced in the present.

Particularly in the Greek-speaking church, speculation focused on the nature of the resurrection body. What kind of body would believers possess when they were finally raised from the dead? The emphasis on the millennium had diverted attention away from this question, in that it had focused on the physical restoration of believers in an earthly realm, in which they retained human bodies. Yet the focus now shifted to the resurrection itself, with Origen soon being established as a leading thinker on this issue.

Origen found himself obliged to defend the doctrine of the resurrection against two rival teachings, each of which seemed to him to be perversions of the Christian faith. On the one hand, some writers had argued that the resurrection was simply a reconstitution of the human body, including all of its physical aspects and functions, on the last day. On the other, Gnostic critics of Christianity argued that anything material was evil, and thus rejected any understanding of the resurrection which included reference to physical elements. For Origen, it was clear that the resurrection body was a purely spiritual entity. Instead of having physical aspects suitable to life on earth, the resurrection body is adapted to the spiritual life of heaven. In part, this reflected his Platonist presuppositions, most notably the Platonic doctrine of the immortality of the soul.

> By the command of God the body which was earthly and animal will be replaced by a spiritual body, such as may be able to dwell in heaven; even on those who have been of lower worth, even of contemptible, almost negligible merit, the glory and worth of the body will be bestowed in proportion to the deserts of the life and soul of each.

However, Origen also insisted that the resurrection body possessed the same "form" (Greek: *eidos*) as the earthly body. The resurrection thus involved a spiritual transformation without loss of individual identity. However, the approach adopted by Origen seemed to many to involve the radical separation of body and soul. This dualism had its origins in Greek philosophy, rather than in Scripture.

According to some of his later critics, Origen's Platonism also shows itself in another aspect of his teaching concerning the resurrection body. In the sixth century, the Roman emperor Justinian criticized Origen for teaching that the resurrection body was spherical. In his dialogue *Timaeus*, Plato had argued that the sphere was the perfect shape, and it is thus possible that Origen may have included this

belief in his teaching. However, there is no explicit mention of this notion in any of Origen's known writings.

This type of approach is found in a modified version in the writings of Methodius of Olympus, one of Origen's more severe critics. Methodius argued that Origen could not really speak of "the resurrection of the body," for the simple reason that it was not the body that was raised, but some elusive "form." In his dialogue with Aglaophon, dating from around 300, Methodius offers another approach, which retains an emphasis on the physical reality of the future resurrection of the body, based on the analogy of the melting down and recasting of a metal statue.

> So it seems that it is as if some skilled artificer had made a noble image, cast in gold or other material, which was beautifully proportioned in all its features; then the artificer suddenly notices that the image had been defaced by some envious person, who could not endure its beauty, and so decided to ruin it for the sake of the pointless pleasure of satisfying his jealousy. So the craftsman decides to recast this noble image. Now notice, most wise Aglaophon, that if he wants to ensure that this image, on which he has expended so much effort, care, and work, will be totally free from any defect, he will be obliged to melt it down, and restore it to its former condition. [. . .] Now it seems to me that God's plan was much the same as this human example. [. . .] God dissolved humanity once more into its original materials, so that it could be remodeled in such a way that all its defects could be eliminated and disappear. Now the melting down of a statue corresponds to the death and dissolution of the human body, and the remolding of the material to the resurrection after death.

Origen's approach was also criticized by Augustine, who interpreted Paul's statements concerning the spiritual nature of the resurrection body in terms of submission to the Spirit, rather than a purely spiritual body.

So what does the resurrection body look like? What will people look like in heaven? If someone dies at the age of 60, will they appear in the streets of the New Jerusalem looking like a 60-year-old? And if someone dies at the age of 10, will they appear as a child? This issue caused the spilling of much theological ink, especially during the Middle Ages. By the end of the thirteenth century, an emerging consensus can be discerned. As each person reaches their peak of perfection around the age of 30, they will be resurrected as they would have appeared at that time – even if they never lived to reach that age. The New Jerusalem will thus be populated by men and women as they would appear at the age of 30, but with every blemish removed. Since Christ was aged about thirty at the time of his death, this is to be regarded as a perfect age – and is hence the apparent age of those raised to glory in heaven. Peter Lombard (c.1100–60) discusses the matter in a manner typical of his age:

> A boy who dies immediately after being born will be resurrected in that form which he would have had if he had lived to the age of thirty years, hindered by no defect of his body. So it can be seen that this substance, which is so small in birth, becomes so great in the resurrection, on account of its being multiplied in itself and of itself. From this, it can be seen that, even if he had lived, the substance would not have come from another source, but would have increased by itself, just as Adam's rib, from which the woman was made, and as the loaves were multiplied in the Gospels.

The subsequent Christian discussion on the resurrection body has attempted to explore the tension between physical and spiritual approaches to the issue. It must be said, however, that the debate is widely regarded as speculative and pointless. Other debates which are also viewed in this light include the question of whether there are relative grades or ranks among those in heaven. The fifth-century writer Theodoret of Cyrrhus argued that, since there were "many rooms in the Father's house" (John 14: 2), it followed that the relative status and privileges of those in heaven were determined by their achievements during their lives. This doctrine of "status by merit" was continued in the writings of Ambrose, and echoed in medieval theology.

At the time of the Reformation this doctrine came into disrepute, partly due to the Protestant dislike of the idea of "merit" in general. However, the notion of various degrees of blessedness seems to have lingered on in the Puritan devotional writings of the late sixteenth and early seventeenth centuries. Thus in 1589 William Fulke recognized a variation in degrees of glory in heaven, but put this down to God's gracious ordering of things, rather than any merits on the part of those specially favored:

> As the stars differ in glory, not according to their merits, but according to God's gifts in their creation; so the bodies of the saints shall differ in glory, not according to their merits, but according to God's free gift in the resurrection.

One aspect of the Christian expectation of heaven merits especial attention in closing this work: the beatific vision. The Christian is finally granted a full vision of the God who has up to this point been known only in part. This vision of God in the full splendor of the divine majesty has been a constant theme of much Christian theology, especially during the Middle Ages. Dante's *Divine Comedy* concludes with the poet finally capturing a glimpse of God: "the love which moves the sun and the other stars." The anticipation of the wonder and glory of this vision was seen as a powerful incentive to keep going in the Christian life. As John Donne put it four centuries later: "No man ever saw God and lived. And yet, I shall not live till I see God; and when I have seen him, I shall never die."

Christian theology can never fully capture that vision of God. But it can at least challenge us to think more deeply about God, and cause us to get excited about its themes. Perhaps it might even whet our appetites for what is yet to come – surely a fitting note on which to end this basic introduction to its themes.

QUESTIONS FOR CHAPTER 18

1 Explore the way in which one of the following ideas is used in the New Testament: kingdom of God; heaven; resurrection; eternal life. You will find it helpful to use a biblical concordance in undertaking this project.

2 Give a brief summary of the way in which either Rudolf Bultmann or Wolfhart Pan-

nenberg interpreted the resurrection. (You will need to turn back to chapter 12 to find some of the material you require for this answer.)

3 Study the following list of terms encountered in this chapter: age of the spirit; demythologization; the rapture; the tribulation; the two cities. With which of the following writers or movements would you associate each of them: Augustine of Hippo; Rudolf Bultmann; dispensationalism; Joachim of Fiore? (Note that two of the terms are linked with one of the writers or movements.)

4 Why is it increasingly unfashionable to speak of hell in many (but not all) Christian circles today?

5 Will everyone go to heaven? (To answer this question, you will need to draw on some of the material presented in chapter 13.)

6 Does the Christian hope relate to the present or to the future?

A Glossary of Theological Terms

What follows is a brief discussion of a series of technical terms that the reader is likely to encounter in the course of reading texts which relate to Christian theology. Many of them occur in the present work.

adoptionism The heretical view that Jesus was "adopted" as the Son of God at some point during his ministry (usually his baptism), as opposed to the orthodox teaching that Jesus was Son of God by nature from the moment of his conception.

aggiornamento The process of renewing the church, which was particularly associated with Pope John XXIII and the Second Vatican Council (1962–5). The Italian word can be translated as "a bringing up to date" or "renewal," and refers to the process of theological, spiritual, and institutional renewal and updating which resulted from the work of this council.

Alexandrian School A patristic school of thought, especially associated with the city of Alexandria in Egypt, noted for its Christology (which placed emphasis upon the divinity of Christ) and its method of biblical interpretation (which employed allegorical methods of exegesis). A rival approach in both areas was associated with Antioch.

allegory An understanding of how biblical texts are to be interpreted which sees certain biblical images as possessing deeper, spiritual meanings, which can be uncovered by their interpreters.

Anabaptism A term derived from the Greek word for "rebaptizer," and used to refer to the radical wing of the sixteenth-century Reformation, based on thinkers such as Menno Simons or Balthasar Hubmaier.

analogy of being (*analogia entis*) The theory, especially associated with Thomas Aquinas, that there exists a correspondence or analogy between the created order and God, as a result of the divine creatorship. The idea gives theoretical justification to the practice of drawing conclusions from the known objects and relationships of the natural order concerning God.

analogy of faith (*analogia fidei*) The theory, especially associated with Karl Barth, which holds that any correspondence between the created order and God is only established on the basis of the self-revelation of God.

anthropomorphism The tendency to ascribe human features (such as hands or arms) or other human characteristics to God.

Antiochene School A patristic school of thought, especially associated with the city of Antioch in modern-day Turkey, noted for its Christology (which placed emphasis upon the humanity of Christ) and its method of biblical interpretation (which employed literal methods of exegesis). A rival approach in both areas was associated with Alexandria.

anti-Pelagian writings The writings of Augustine relating to the Pelagian controversy, in which he defended his views on grace and justification. See "Pelagianism."

Apocalyptic A type of writing or religious outlook in general which focuses on the last things and the end of the world, often taking the form of visions with complex symbolism. The second half of the book of Daniel (Old Testament) and Revelation (New Testament) are examples of this type of writing.

apologetics The area of Christian theology which focuses on the defense of the Christian faith, particularly through the rational justification of Christian belief and doctrines.

apophatic A term used to refer to a particular style of theology, which stressed that God cannot be known in terms of human categories. "Apophatic" (which derives from the Greek *apophasis*, "negation" or "denial") approaches to theology are especially associated with the monastic tradition of the Eastern Orthodox church.

Apophthegmata The term used to refer to the collections of monastic writings often known as the "Sayings of the Desert Fathers." The writings often take the form of brief and pointed sayings, reflecting the concise and practical guidance typical of these writers.

apostolic era The period of the Christian church, regarded as definitive by many, bounded by the resurrection of Jesus Christ (c.AD 35) and the death of the last apostle (c.AD 90?). The ideas and practices of this period were widely regarded as normative, at least in some sense or to some degree, in many church circles.

appropriation A term relating to the doctrine of the Trinity, which affirms that while all three persons are active in all the outward actions of the Trinity, it is appropriate to think of those actions as being the particular work of one of the persons. Thus it is appropriate to think of creation as the work of the Father, or redemption as the work of the Son, despite the fact that all three persons are present and active in both these works.

Arianism A major early Christological heresy, which treated Jesus Christ as the supreme of God's creatures, and denied his divine status. The Arian controversy was of major importance in the development of Christology during the fourth century.

asceticism A term used to refer to the wide variety of forms of self-discipline used by Christians to deepen their knowledge of and commitment to God. The term derives from the Greek term *askesis* ("discipline").

atonement An English term originally coined in 1526 by William Tyndale to translate the Latin term *reconciliatio*. It has since come to have the developed meaning of "the work of Christ" or "the benefits of Christ gained for believers by his death and resurrection."

Barthian An adjective used to describe the theological outlook of the Swiss theologian Karl Barth (1886–1968), and noted chiefly for its emphasis upon the priority of revelation and its focus upon Jesus Christ. The terms "neo-Orthodoxy" and "dialectical theology" are also used in this connection.

beatific vision A term used, especially in Roman Catholic theology, to refer to the full vision of God, which is allowed only to the elect after death. However, some writers, including Thomas Aquinas, taught that certain favored individuals – such as Moses and Paul – were allowed this vision in the present life.

Beatitudes, the A term used to describe the eight promises of blessing found in the opening section of the Sermon on the Mount (Matthew 5: 3–11). Examples include "Blessed are the pure in heart, for they shall see God" and "Blessed are the peacemakers, for they shall be called children of God."

Calvinism An ambiguous term, used with two quite distinct meanings. First, it refers to the religious ideas of religious bodies (such as the Reformed church) and individuals (such as Theodore Beza) who were profoundly influenced by John Calvin, or by documents written by him. Second, it refers to the religious ideas of

John Calvin himself. Although the first sense is by far the more common, there is a growing recognition that the term is misleading.

Cappadocian fathers A term used to refer collectively to three major Greek-speaking writers of the patristic period: Basil of Caesarea, Gregory of Nazianzen, and Gregory of Nyssa, all of whom date from the late fourth century. "Cappadocia" designates an area in Asia Minor (modern-day Turkey), in which these writers were based.

Cartesianism The philosophical outlook especially associated with René Descartes (1596–1650), particularly in relation to its emphasis on the separation of the knower from the known, and its insistence that the existence of the individual thinking self is the proper starting point for philosophical reflection.

catechism A popular manual of Christian doctrine, usually in the form of question and answer, intended for religious instruction.

catharsis The process of cleansing or purification by which the individual is freed from obstacles to spiritual growth and development.

catholic An adjective which is used both to refer to the universality of the church in space and time, and also to a particular church body (sometime also known as the Roman Catholic Church) which lays emphasis upon this point.

Chalcedonian definition The formal declaration at the Council of Chalcedon that Jesus Christ was to be regarded as having two natures, one human and one divine.

charisma, charismatic A set of terms especially associated with the gifts of the Holy Spirit. In medieval theology, the term "charisma" is used to designate a spiritual gift, conferred upon individuals by the grace of God. Since the early twentieth century, the term "charismatic" has come to refer to styles of theology and worship which place particular emphasis upon the immediate presence and experience of the Holy Spirit.

Charismatic Movement A form of Christianity which places particular emphasis upon the personal experience of the Holy Spirit in the life of the individual and community, often associated with various "charismatic" phenomena, such as speaking in tongues.

Christology The section of Christian theology dealing with the identity of Jesus Christ, particularly the question of the relation of his human and divine natures.

circumincession See *perichoresis*.

conciliarism An understanding of ecclesiastical or theological authority which places an emphasis on the role of ecumenical councils.

confession Although the term refers primarily to the admission to sin, it acquired a rather different technical sense in the sixteenth century – that of a document which embodies the principles of faith of a Protestant church, such as the Lutheran Augsburg Confession (1530), which embodies the ideas of early Lutheranism, and the Reformed First Helvetic Confession (1536).

consubstantial A Latin term, deriving from the Greek term *homoousios*, literally meaning "of the same substance." The term is used to affirm the full divinity of Jesus Christ, particularly in opposition to Arianism.

consubstantiation A term used to refer to the theory of the real presence, especially associated with Martin Luther, which holds that the substance of the eucharistic bread and wine are given together with the substance of the body and blood of Christ.

contemplation A form of prayer, distinguished from meditation, in which the individual avoids or minimizes the use of words or images in order to experience the presence of God directly.

creed A formal definition or summary of the Christian faith, held in common by all Christians. The most important are those generally known as the "Apostles' Creed" and the "Nicene Creed."

dark night of the soul A phrase especially associated with John of the Cross, referring to the manner in which the soul is drawn closer to God. John distinguishes an "active" night (in which the believer actively works to draw nearer to God) and a "passive" night, in which God is active and the believer passive.

Deism A term used to refer to the views of a group of English writers, especially during the seventeenth century, the rationalism of which anticipated many of the ideas of the Enlightenment. The term is often used to refer to a view of God which recognizes the divine creatorship, yet which rejects the notion of a continuing divine involvement with the world.

detachment The cultivation of a habit of mind in which the individual aims to abandon dependence upon worldly objects, passions, or concerns. This is not intended to imply that these worldly things are evil; rather, the point being made is that they have the ability to enslave individuals if they are not approached with the right attitude. Detachment is about fostering a sense of independence from the world, so that it may be enjoyed without becoming a barrier between the individual and God.

Devotio Moderna A school of thought which developed in the Netherlands in the fourteenth century, and is especially associated with Geert Groote (1340–84) and Thomas à Kempis (1380–1471), which placed an emphasis on the imitation of the humanity of Christ. The *Imitation of Christ* is the best-known work emanating from this school.

dialectical theology A term used to refer to the early views of the Swiss theologian Karl Barth (1886–1968), which emphasized the tensions, paradoxes, and contradictions in the relationship between God and humanity and the absolute gulf fixed between the human and the divine.

Docetism An early Christological heresy, which treated Jesus Christ as a purely divine being who only had the "appearance" of being human.

Donatism A movement, centering upon Roman north Africa in the fourth century, which developed a rigid view of the church and sacraments.

doxology A form of praise, usually especially associated with formal Christian worship. A "doxological" approach to theology stresses the importance of praise and worship in theological reflection.

Ebionitism An early Christological heresy, which treated Jesus Christ as a purely human figure, although recognizing that he was endowed with particular charismatic gifts which distinguished him from other humans.

ecclesiology The section of Christian theology dealing with the theory of the church.

Enlightenment, the A term used since the nineteenth century to refer to the emphasis upon human reason and autonomy, characteristic of much of western European and North American thought during the eighteenth century.

eschatology The section of Christian theology dealing with the "last things," especially the ideas of resurrection, hell, the Last Judgment, and eternal life.

Eucharist The term used in the present volume to refer to the sacrament variously known as "the mass," "the Lord's Supper," and "holy communion."

evangelical A term initially used to refer to reforming movements, especially in Germany and Switzerland, in the 1510s and 1520s, but now used of a movement, especially in English-language theology, which places especial emphasis upon the supreme authority of Scripture and the atoning death of Christ.

exegesis The science of textual interpretation, usually referring specifically to the Bible. The term "biblical exegesis" basically means "the process of interpreting the Bible." The specific techniques employed in the exegesis of Scripture are usually referred to as "hermeneutics."

exemplarism A particular approach to the atonement, which stresses the moral or religious example set to believers by Jesus Christ.

fathers An alternative term for "patristic writers."

fideism An understanding of Christian theology which refuses to accept the need for (or sometimes the possibility of) criticism or evaluation from sources outside the Christian faith itself.

filioque A Latin phrase, literally meaning "and from the Son," found in western versions of the Nicene Creed. On this view, the Holy Spirit originates and proceeds from both the Father and the Son, rather than (as in the Eastern church) from the Father alone. The phrase had its origins at the third council of Toledo (589). By the ninth century, it was regularly in use within the western church. After the 1054 schism, it became one of the major theological points of difference between the Orthodox and Catholic churches, and a subject of intense debate and polemic on both sides.

Five Ways, The A standard term for the five "arguments for the existence of God" associated with Thomas Aquinas.

Fourth Gospel A term used to refer to the Gospel according to John. The term highlights the distinctive literary and theological character of this gospel, which sets it apart from the common structures of the first three gospels, usually known as the "Synoptic Gospels."

fundamentalism A form of American Protestant Christianity, originating in America, which lays especial emphasis upon the authority of an inerrant Bible.

hermeneutics The principles underlying the interpretation, or exegesis, of a text, particularly of Scripture, and particularly in relation to its present-day application.

Hesychasm A tradition, especially associated with the eastern church, which places considerable emphasis upon the idea of "inner quietness" (Greek: *hēsychia*) as a means of achieving a vision of God. It is particularly associated with writers such as Simeon the New Theologian and Gregory Palamas.

historical Jesus A term used, especially during the nineteenth century, to refer to the historical person of Jesus of Nazareth, as opposed to the Christian interpretation of that person, especially as presented in the New Testament and the creeds.

historico-critical method An approach to historical texts, including the Bible, which argues that their proper meaning must be determined on the basis of the specific historical conditions under which they were written.

history of religions school The approach to religious history, and Christian origins in particular, which treats Old and New Testament developments as responses to encounters with other religions, such as Gnosticism.

homoousion A Greek term, literally meaning "of the same substance," which came to be used extensively during the fourth century to designate the mainline Christological belief that Jesus Christ was of the same substance as God. The term was polemical, being directed against the Arian view that Christ was "of similar substance (*homoiousios*)" to God. See also "consubstantial."

humanism In the strict sense of the word, an intellectual movement linked with the European Renaissance. At the heart of the movement lay, not (as the modern sense of the word might suggest) a set of secular or secularizing ideas, but a new interest in the cultural achievements of antiquity. These were seen as a major resource for the renewal of European culture and Christianity during the period of the Renaissance.

hypostatic union The doctrine of the union of divine and human natures in Jesus Christ, without confusion of their respective substances.

icons Sacred pictures, particularly of Jesus, which play a significant role in Orthodox spirituality as "windows for the divine."

ideology A group of beliefs and values, usually secular, which govern the actions and outlooks of a society or group of people.

Ignatian spirituality A loose term used to refer to the approach to spirituality associated with Ignatius Loyola (1491–1556), based on his *Spiritual Exercises*.

incarnation A term used to refer to the assumption of human nature by God, in the person of Jesus Christ. The term "incarnationalism" is often used to refer to theological approaches which lay especial emphasis upon God becoming human.

justification by faith, doctrine of The section of Christian theology dealing with how the individual sinner is able to enter into fellowship with God. The doctrine was to prove to be of major significance at the time of the Reformation.

kenoticism A form of Christology which lays emphasis upon Christ's "laying aside" of certain divine attributes in the incarnation, or his "emptying himself" of at least some divine attributes, especially omniscience or omnipotence.

kerygma A term used, especially by Rudolf Bultmann (1884–1976) and his followers, to refer to the essential message or proclamation of the New Testament concerning the significance of Jesus Christ.

liberal Protestantism A movement, especially associated with nineteenth-century Germany, which stressed the continuity between religion and culture, flourishing between the time of F. D. E. Schleiermacher and Paul Tillich.

liberation theology Although this term designates any theological movement laying emphasis upon the liberating impact of the gospel, the term has come to refer to a movement which developed in Latin America in the late 1960s, which stressed the role of political action and orientated itself towards the goal of political liberation from poverty and oppression.

liturgy The written text and set forms of public services, especially of the Eucharist. In the Greek Orthodox church, the word "liturgy" often means "the (liturgy of the) Eucharist."

logos A Greek term meaning "word," which played a crucial role in the development of patristic Christology. Jesus Christ was recognized as the "word of God"; the question concerned the implications of this recognition, and especially the way in which the divine "logos" in Jesus Christ related to his human nature.

Lutheranism The religious ideas associated with Martin Luther, particularly as expressed in the Lesser Catechism (1529) and the Augsburg Confession (1530).

Manicheism A strongly fatalist position associated with the Manichees, to which Augustine of Hippo attached himself during his early period. A distinction is drawn between two different divinities, one of which is regarded as evil, and the other good. Evil is thus seen as the direct result of the influence of the evil god.

meditation A form of prayer, distinguished from contemplation, in which the mind uses images (such as those provided by Scripture) as a means for focusing on God.

Middle English literature Literature produced in the English language from the Norman invasion of 1066 to c.1485.

modalism A trinitarian heresy, which treats the three persons of the Trinity as different "modes" of the Godhead. A typical modalist approach is to regard God as active as Father in creation, as Son in redemption, and as Spirit in sanctification.

monophysitism The doctrine that there is only one nature in Christ, which is divine (from the Greek words *monos*, "only one," and *physis*, "nature"). This view differed from the orthodox view, upheld by the Council of Chalcedon (451), that Christ had two natures, one divine and one human.

mysticism A multifaceted term, which can bear a variety of meanings. In its most importance sense, the terms refers to the union with God which is seen as the ultimate goal of the Christian life. This union is not to be thought of in rational or intellectual terms, but more in terms of a direct consciousness or experience of God.

neo-Orthodoxy A term used to designate the general position of Karl Barth (1886–1968), especially the manner in which he drew upon the theological concerns of the period of Reformed Orthodoxy.

Old English literature The English literature of the period from 750 until the time of the invasion of the Normans in 1066.

ontological argument A term used to refer to the type of argument for the existence of God especially associated with the scholastic theologian Anselm of Canterbury. It claims that as God is greater than any other being that is conceivable, God must be greater than any being who exists only as an idea, so God must necessarily exist in reality.

orthodoxy A term used in a number of senses, of which the following are the most important:

orthodoxy in the sense of "right belief," as opposed to heresy; Orthodoxy in the sense of the forms of Christianity which are dominant in Russia and Greece; Orthodoxy in the sense of a movement within Protestantism, especially in the late sixteenth and early seventeenth century, which laid emphasis upon the need for doctrinal definition.

parousia A Greek term, which literally means "coming" or "arrival," used to refer to the second coming of Christ. The notion of the *parousia* is an important aspect of Christian understandings of the "last things."

patripassianism A theological heresy, which arose during the third century, associated with writers such as Noetus, Praxeas, and Sabellius, focusing on the belief that the Father suffered as the Son. In other words, the suffering of Christ on the cross is to be regarded as the suffering of the Father. According to these writers, the only distinction within the Godhead was a succession of modes or operations, so that Father, Son, and Spirit were just different modes of being, or expressions, of the same basic divine entity.

patristic An adjective used to refer to the first centuries in the history of the church, following the writing of the New Testament (the "patristic period"), or thinkers writing during this period (the "patristic writers"). For many writers, the period thus designated seems to be c.100–451 (in other words, the period between the completion of the last of the New Testament writings and the landmark Council of Chalcedon).

Pelagianism An understanding of how humans are able to merit their salvation which is diametrically opposed to that of Augustine of Hippo, placing considerable emphasis upon the role of human works and playing down the idea of divine grace.

perichoresis A term relating to the doctrine of the Trinity, often also referred to by the Latin term *circumincessio*. The basic notion is that all three persons of the Trinity mutually share in the life of the others, so that none is isolated or detached from the actions of the others.

Philokalia A Greek term (literally meaning "a love of that which is beautiful"), which is generally used to refer to two anthologies of Greek spiritual works: extracts from the works of Origen, or the collection of writings assembled by Macarius of Corinth and Nicodemus of the Holy Mountain in the eighteenth century.

Pietism An approach to Christianity, especially associated with German writers in the seventeenth century, which places an emphasis upon the personal appropriation of faith, and the need for holiness in Christian living. The movement is perhaps best known within the English-language world in the form of Methodism.

postliberalism A theological movement, especially associated with Duke University and Yale Divinity School in the 1980s, which criticized the liberal reliance upon human experience, and reclaimed the notion of community tradition as a controlling influence in theology.

postmodernism A cultural development, starting in the late twentieth century, which resulted from the general collapse in confidence of the universal rational principles of the Enlightenment. It is characterized by a rejection of absolutes and of objective and rational attempts to define reality.

praxis A Greek term, literally meaning "action," adopted by Karl Marx to emphasize the importance of action in relation to thinking. This emphasis on "praxis" has had considerable impact within Latin American liberation theology.

Protestantism A term used in the aftermath of the Diet of Speyer (1529) to designate those who "protested" against the practices and beliefs of the Roman Catholic church. Prior to 1529, such individuals and groups had referred to themselves as "evangelicals."

Quadriga The Latin term used to refer to the "fourfold" interpretation of Scripture according to its literal, allegorical, tropological moral, and analogical senses.

radical Reformation A term used with increasing frequency to refer to the Anabaptist movement – in other words, the wing of the

Reformation which went beyond what Luther and Zwingli envisaged, particularly in relation to the doctrine of the church.

Reformed A term used to refer to a tradition of theology which draws inspiration from the writings of John Calvin (1510–64) and his successors. The term is now generally used in preference to "Calvinist."

Sabellianism An early trinitarian heresy, which treated the three persons of the Trinity as different historical manifestations of the one God. It is generally regarded as a form of modalism.

sacrament A church service or rite which was held to have been instituted by Jesus Christ himself. Although Roman Catholic theology and church practice recognize seven such sacraments (baptism, confirmation, Eucharist, marriage, ordination, penance, and unction), Protestant theologians generally argue that only two (baptism and Eucharist) were to be found in the New Testament itself.

schism A deliberate break with the unity of the church, condemned vigorously by influential writers of the early church, such as Cyprian and Augustine.

scholasticism A particular approach to Christian theology, associated especially with the Middle Ages, which lays emphasis upon the rational justification and systematic presentation of Christian theology.

Scripture principle The theory, especially associated with Reformed theologians, that the practices and beliefs of the church should be grounded in Scripture. Nothing that could not be demonstrated to be grounded in Scripture could be regarded as binding upon the believer. The phrase *sola scriptura*, "by Scripture alone," summarizes this principle.

Socinianism A form of Christian heterodoxy especially associated with the Italian writer Socinus (Fausto Paolo Sozzini, 1539–1604). Although Socinus was noted for his specific criticisms of the doctrine of the Trinity and the incarnation, the term "Socinian" has come to refer particularly to the idea that Christ's death on the cross did not have any supernatural or transcendent implications. On

this view, Christ died as an outstanding moral example, to encourage humanity to avoid sin, not to make satisfaction for human sin.

soteriology The section of Christian theology dealing with the doctrine of salvation (Greek: *sotēria*).

Synoptic Gospels A term used to refer to the first three gospels (Matthew, Mark, and Luke). The term (derived from the Greek word *synopsis*, "summary") refers to the way in which the three gospels can be seen as providing similar "summaries" of the life, death, and resurrection of Jesus Christ.

Synoptic problem The scholarly question of how the three Synoptic Gospels relate to each other. Perhaps the most common approach to the relation of the three Synoptic Gospels is the "two source" theory, which claims that Matthew and Luke used Mark as a source, while also drawing upon a second source (usually known as "Q"). Other possibilities exist: for example, the Grisebach hypothesis, which treats Matthew as having been written first, followed by Luke and then Mark.

theodicy A term coined by the German philosopher Gottfried Wilhelm Leibnitz (1646–1716) to refer to a theoretical justification of the goodness of God in the face of the presence of evil in the world.

theopaschitism A disputed teaching, regarded by some as a heresy, which arose during the sixth century, associated with writers such as John Maxentius and the slogan "one of the Trinity was crucified." The formula can be interpreted in a perfectly orthodox sense and was defended as such by Leontius of Byzantium. However, it was regarded as potentially misleading and confusing by more cautious writers, including Pope Hormisdas (died 523), and the formula gradually fell into disuse.

theotokos Literally, "the bearer of God." A Greek term used to refer to Mary, the mother of Jesus Christ, with the intention of reinforcing the central insight of the doctrine of the incarnation – that is, that Jesus Christ is none other than God. The term was extensively used by writers of the eastern church, especially around the time of the Nestorian controversy, to articulate both the divinity of Christ and the reality of the incarnation.

transubstantiation The doctrine according to which the bread and the wine are transformed into the body and blood of Christ in the Eucharist, while retaining their outward appearance.

Trinity The distinctively Christian doctrine of God, which reflects the complexity of the Christian experience of God as Father, Son, and Holy Spirit. The doctrine is usually summarized in maxims such as "three persons, one God."

two natures, doctrine of A term generally used to refer to the doctrine of the two natures, human and divine, of Jesus Christ. Related terms include "Chalcedonian definition" and "hypostatic union."

typology A way of interpreting the Bible which sees certain Old Testament figures and events as anticipating aspects of the gospel. Thus Noah's ark is seen as a "type" (Greek *typos*, "figure") of the church.

Vulgate The Latin translation of the Bible, largely deriving from Jerome, upon which medieval theology was largely based.

Zwinglianism The term is used generally to refer to the thought of Huldrych Zwingli, but is often used to refer specifically to his views on the sacraments, especially on the "real presence" (which for Zwingli was more of a "real absence").

Sources of Citations

N ote that a figure in bold type against a reading indicates that the reading can be studied in greater depth in the companion volume to this Introduction: Alister E. McGrath, *The Christian Theology Reader* 3rd edn (Oxford/ Malden, MA: Blackwell Publishers, 2006). Thus **[2.7]** refers to the seventh reading in chapter 2 of the collection, entitled "Cyril of Jerusalem on the Role of Creeds." Note that unless otherwise indicated, all translations are my own.

Introduction

p. 3
Karl Barth, *Die protestantische Theologie im 19. Jahrhundert* (Zurich: Evangelischer Verlag, 1952), p. 3.

Chapter 1

p. 15
H. Denzinger (ed.), *Enchiridion Symbolorum*, 39 edn (Freiburg im Breisgau: Herder, 2001), §30; 36. **[1.6]**

p. 15
H. Denzinger (ed.), *Enchiridion Symbolorum*, 39 edn (Freiburg im Breisgau: Herder, 2001), §§125; 62–4. **[1.5]**

Chapter 2

p. 32
John of Damascus, *contra imaginum calumniatores* I, 16. **[4.20]**

Chapter 3

pp. 52–3
Jacques Benigne Bossuet, *Première Instruction pastorale* xxvii; cited in O. Chadwick, *From Bossuet to Newman. The Idea of Doctrinal Development* (Cambridge, UK: Cambridge University Press, 1957), p. 17.

p. 61
Martin Luther, *Lesser Catechism*; in D. *Martin Luthers Werke: Kritische Gesamtausgabe*, vol. 30, part 1 (Weimar: Böhlaus, 1910), 255–7. **[8.20]**

Chapter 4

p. 92

Statement of the National Committee of Black Churchmen; in Gayraud S. Wilmore and James Cone (eds.), *Black Theology: A Documentary History 1966–1971*, vol.1 (Maryknoll, NY: Orbis Books, 1993), pp. 101–2.

Chapter 5

p. 110

Thomas Merton, *Seeds of Contemplation* (Wheathampstead, UK: Anthony Clarke, 1972), pp. 197–8.

p. 115

Friedrich Schleiermacher, *The Christian Faith*, translated by M. R. Mackintosh and J. S. Stewart (Edinburgh: T&T Clark, 1928), pp. 98–9. **[4.27]**

pp. 118–19

Augustine of Hippo, *de doctrina Christiana*, II.xl.60–61. **[1.4]**

Chapter 6

p. 127

Second Vatican Council, *Nostra Aetate*, 28 October 1965, §4. **[9.7]**

p. 131

Augustine, *de utilitate credendi* III, 9. **[2.8]**

p. 132

Bernard of Clairvaux, *Sermones super Cantico Canticorum* XL.vi.2. **[2.11]**

p. 132–3

Martin Luther, *Dictata super Psalterium*, preface; in *D. Martin Luthers Werke: Kritische Gesamtausgabe*, vol. 3, ed. G. Kawerau (Weimar: Böhlau, 1885), 11. **[2.15]**

p. 135

Catechism of the Catholic Church (Collegeville, MN: The Liturgical Press, 1994), paras 101–8.

p. 136

Irenaeus, *adversus haereses* II.ii.1–iv.1. **[2.2]**

p. 137

Vincent of Lérins, *Commonitorium* II, 1–3. **[2.10]**

p. 137

Johann Adam Möhler, *Symbolism: or Exposition of the Doctrinal Differences between Catholics and Protestants* (New York: Dunigan, 1844), pp. 351–2 (translation modified at points). **[2.33]**

pp. 137–8

Catechism of the Catholic Church (Collegeville, MN: The Liturgical Press, 1994), paras 74–82.

p. 138

John Meyendorff, *Living Tradition: Orthodox Witness in the Contemporary World* (Crestwood, NY: St Vladimir's Seminar Press, 1978), 8. **[2.47]**

p. 139

Council of Trent, Session IV; in H. Denzinger (ed.), *Enchiridion Symbolorum* 39 edn (Freiburg im Breisgau: Herder, 2001), §1501; 496. **[2.19]**

p. 140

Michael Polanyi, *Personal Knowledge* (London: Routledge & Kegan Paul, 1958), p. 269.

p. 144

Iris Murdoch, *The Sovereignty of Good* (London: Routledge & Kegan Paul, 1970), p. 80.

p. 145

Alasdair MacIntyre, *Whose Justice? Which Rationality?* (Notre Dame, IN: University of Notre Dame, 1988), p. 6.

p. 150

C. S. Lewis, "The Weight of Glory"; in *Screwtape Proposes a Toast* (London: Collins, 1965), pp. 97–8.

Chapter 7

p. 155

James I. Packer, *God Has Spoken*, 2nd edn (London: Hodder & Stoughton, 1979), p. 82.

p. 155

First Vatican Council, Constitution on the Catholic Faith, chapter 3; in H. Denzinger (ed.), *Enchiridion*

Symbolorum, 39 edn (Freiburg im Breisgau: Herder, 2001), §3011, 816.

p. 160

Thomas Aquinas, *Summa contra Gentiles*, II.2.2–4.

p. 161

First Vatican Council, Dogmatic Constitution on the Catholic Faith, 2; in H. Denzinger (ed.), *Enchiridion Symbolorum*, 39 edn (Freiburg im Breisgau: Herder, 2001), §3004; 813.

p. 162

John Calvin, *Institutes* I.iii.1–2. **[2.17]**

p. 162

Jean Bodin, *Universae naturae theatrum* (Frankfurt, 1597), p. 10.

p. 163

Gallic Confession of Faith (1559), article 2.

p. 163

Belgic Confession of Faith (1561), article 2. **[2.21]**

p. 164

Sir Thomas Browne, *Religio Medici* (London, 1642), I. 16. **[2.27]**

p. 164

John Polkinghorne, *Science and Creation: The Search for Understanding* (London: SPCK, 1988), p. 20.

p. 165

Jonathan Edwards, *The Images of Divine Things*, ed. Perry Miller (New Haven, CT: Yale University Press, 1948), p. 134. **[2.31]**

p. 167

Thomas F. Torrance, "The Problem of Natural Theology in the Thought of Karl Barth." *Religious Studies* 6 (1970), pp. 121–35.

Chapter 8

---

pp. 176–7

Clement of Alexandria, *Stromateis*, V.iii.16.

p. 178

Cited in P. A. Schilpp, *The Philosophy of Rudolph Carnap* (LaSalle, IL: Open Court, 1963), p. 8.

p. 179

Karl R. Popper, *Conjectures and Refutations: The Growth of Scientific Knowledge* (London: Routledge & Kegan Paul, 1963), p. 281.

p. 180

John Polkinghorne, *One World: The Interaction of Science and Theology* (Princeton, NJ: Princeton University Press, 1986), p. 47.

p. 183

Martin Luther, *The Liberty of a Christian* (1520); in *D. Martin Luthers Werke: Kritische Gesamtausgabe*, vol. 7 (Weimar: Böhlaus, 1897), 25–6. **[6.33]**

p. 184

Ludwig Wittgenstein, *Culture and Value*, ed. G. H. von Wright, translated by Peter Winch (Oxford: Blackwell Publishers, 1980), pp. 82–6. **[1.26]**

p. 185

Anselm of Canterbury, *Proslogion*, 3. **[1.7]**

pp. 185–6

Gaunilo, *Responsio Anselmi*, 6. **[1.8]**

p. 186

Immanuel Kant, *Kritik der reinen Vernunft*, 2 vols. (Frankfurt am Main: Suhrkamp Verlag, 2000), vol. 2, pp. 533–4. **[1.19]**

p. 188

Thomas Aquinas, *Summa Theologiae*, Ia q. 2 a. 3.

p. 190

William Lane Craig, *The Kalam Cosmological Argument* (London: Macmillan, 1979), p. 149.

pp. 191, 192

William Paley, *Works*, 6 vols (London: Rivington, 1830), vol. 4, 16; 34–5. **[2.32]**

p. 193

Basil of Caesarea, *Epistle* 234.

p. 197

Sallie McFague, *Models of God: Theology for an Ecological Nuclear Age* (Philadelphia: Fortress Press, 1987), pp. 32–4. **[1.30]**

p. 197

Ian G. Barbour, *Myths, Models and Paradigms: The Nature of Scientific and Religious Language* (New York: Harper & Row, 1974), p. 15.

Chapter 9

---

p. 204

Mary Hayter, *The New Eve in Christ* London: SPCK, 1987), pp. 87–92. **[6.55]**

p. 204

Wolfhart Pannenberg, *Systematic Theology*, translated by Geoffrey W. Bromiley. (Grand Rapids, MI: Eerdmans, 1991), pp. 260–1.

p. 204

Sallie McFague, *Models of God: Theology or an Ecological Nuclear Age* (Philadelphia: Fortress Press, 1987), pp. 122–3.

p. 204

Catechism of the Catholic Church (Collegeville, MN: The Liturgical Press, 1994), para 239.

p. 205

Julian of Norwich, *Revelations of Divine Love*, trans. Clifton Wolters (London: Penguin Books, 1958), pp. 151, 174. **[3.26]**

p. 207

C. C. J. Webb, *God and Personality* (London: Allen & Unwin, 1919), pp. 74–5.

p. 207

Spinoza, *Ethics*, V, 17. **[3.30]**

pp. 208–9

Martin Buber, *I and Thou* (New York: Charles Scribner's Sons, 1958), p. 61.

p. 211

Anselm of Canterbury, *Proslogion*, 8. **[3.21]**

p. 213

Jürgen Moltmann, *The Crucified God* (London: SCM Press, 1974), p. 222.

pp. 214, 215

Charles Wesley, "And Can It Be?"; in John Wesley and Charles Wesley, *Hymns and Sacred Poems* (London: William Strahan, 1739), pp. 117–19. The hymn was originally entitled "Free Grace." **[5.23]**

p. 215

William Hamilton, "The Death of God Theology," *Christian Scholar* 48 (1965), pp. 27–48; citation at pp. 31, 41, 45.

p. 217

C. S. Lewis, *The Problem of Pain* (London: Fontana, 1967), pp. 14, 16.

p. 217

Thomas Aquinas, *Summa Theologiae*, Ia, q. 25, a. 3. **[3.24]**

p. 219

Dietrich Bonhoeffer, letter to Eberhard Bethge, dated July 16, 1944; in Dietrich Bonhoeffer, *Letters and Papers from Prison*, ed. E. Bethge,

translated by Reginald Fuller (New York: Macmillan, 1971), pp. 359–61. **[1.28]**

p. 225

Synod of Toledo (400), Canons 1, 9; in H. Denzinger (ed.), *Enchiridion Symbolorum*, 39 edn (Freiburg im Breisgau: Herder, 2001), §191, 199; 97.

p. 231

Irenaeus, *Demonstration of the Apostolic Preaching*, 12. **[3.2]**

p. 238

Basil of Caesarea, *de spiritu sancto*, IX, 23. **[3.10]**

p. 239

Gregory of Nazianzus, *Oratio theologica*, V, 26 (= *Oratio* XXXI, 26). **[3.11]**

pp. 239–40

Augustine, *de Trinitate*, XV.xvii.27–xviii.32. **[3.15]**

p. 241

Martin Bucer, *Commentary on the Gospels* (Basel, 1536), p. 85.

p. 241

Gallic Confession, 1559, article 4. **[2.20]**

p. 241

John Calvin, *Institutes*, III.ii.7. **[1.13]**

p. 242

Cyril of Alexandria, *in Joannis evangelium*, XVI, 20. **[3.17]**

p. 242

Martin Bucer, *Commentary on the Gospels* (Basel, 1536), p. 124.

Chapter 10

p. 245

Charles Gore, *The Incarnation of the Son of God* (London: John Murray, 1922), pp. 105–6.

pp. 245, 246

J. R. Illingworth, *Personality Human and Divine* (London: Macmillan, 1899), pp. 66–8.

p. 247

Irenaeus, *Demonstration of the Apostolic Preaching*, 6. **[3.3]**

p. 252

Charles Wesley, *Gloria Patri, or Hymns on the Trinity* (London: Strahan, 1746), No. 7.

p. 255

Epiphanius of Constantia, *Panarion*, lxii, 1. **[3.16]**

p. 256

Gregory of Nyssa, *Ad Ablabium: quod non sint tres dei*. In: Werner W. Jaeger, Hermann Langerbeck, and Heinrich Dörrie (eds), *Gregorii Nysseni Opera*, 3 vols (Leiden: E.J. Brill, 1996), vol. 3/1, pp. 37–52. **[3.9]**

pp. 256–7

Eleventh Council of Toledo, *Symbolum fidei de Trinitate et Incarnatione* 10–14; in H. Denzinger (ed.), *Enchiridion Symbolorum*, 39 edn (Freiburg im Breisgau: Herder, 2001), §§522–8; 242–3. **[3.20]**

p. 262

Karl Rahner, *The Trinity* (London: Burns & Oates, 1970), pp. 22, 82–3, 99–100.

p. 266

Jürgen Moltmann, "The Reconciling Power of the Trinity in the Life of the Church and the World"; in *The Reconciling Power of the Trinity: Report of the study consultation of the Conference of European Churches* (Geneva: The report of the study consultation of the Conference of European Churches, 1983), pp. 53–4.

p. 268

Catherine Mowry LaCugna, *God for Us: The Trinity and Christian Life* (San Francisco: HarperSanFrancisco, 1991), p. ix.

pp. 269, 70

Augustine, *de Trinitate*, XV.xvii.27–xviii.32. **[3.15]**

p. 270

Eleventh Council of Toledo, *Symbolum fidei de Trinitate et Incarnatione* 10–14; in H. Denzinger (ed.), *Enchiridion Symbolorum*, 39 edn (Freiburg im Breisgau: Herder, 2001), §§522–8; 242–3. **[3.20]**

Chapter 11

---

p. 275

Karl Barth, *Church Dogmatics*, 14 vols, edited and translated by G. W. Bromiley and T. F. Torrance (Edinburgh: T&T Clark, 1936–75), II/2, pp. 52–3.

p. 276

James Denney, *The Christian Doctrine of Reconciliation* (London: Hodder & Stoughton, 1917), pp. 245–6.

p. 283

Justin Martyr, *Apologia*, II.x.2–3. **[1.1]**

p. 284

Athanasius, *contra Arianos*, I, 5.

p. 286

Cyril of Alexandria, Letter IV, 3–5 (Second Letter to Nestorius). **[4.14]**

p. 287

Gregory of Nazianzus, Letter 101. **[4.10]**

p. 288

Nestorius, according to Cyril of Alexandria; in Fragment 49; Friedrich Loofs, *Nestoriana: Die Fragmente des Nestorius* (Halle, 1905), p. 280.

p. 289

Theodore of Mopsuestia, *Catechetical Homily* 8.13–14, as translated by Alphonse Mingana. *Woodbrooke Studies: Christian Documents in Syriac, Arabic, and Garshuni*. Cambridge, UK: Heffer, 1933, 89–90, with slight alteration for clarity. **[4.11]**

p. 292

Thomas Aquinas, *Summa Theologiae* IIIa q.1 a.3. **[4.22]**

p. 293

Wolfhart Pannenberg, *Jesus – God and Man*, translated by Lewis L. Wilkins and Duane A. Priebe (Philadelphia: Westminster Press, 1968), pp. 38–9. **[5.32]**

p. 293

Charles Gore, "Our Lord's Human Example," *Church Quarterly Review* 16 (1883), pp. 282–313; extract at p. 298. **[5.26]**

p. 294

Maurice F. Wiles, *The Making of Christian Doctrine* (Cambridge, UK: Cambridge University Press, 1967), p. 106.

p. 295

Irenaeus, *adversus haereses*, V.ii.1–2.

p. 295

Simeon the New Theologian, *Hymns of Divine Love*, 7. **[5.12]**

p. 295

John of Damascus, *contra imaginum calumniatores* I, 16. **[4.20]**

p. 298

Wolfhart Pannenberg, *Jesus – God and Man*, translated by Lewis L. Wilkins and Duane A. Priebe (Philadelphia: Westminster Press, 1968), pp. 69, 129–30.

Chapter 12

p. 309

G. E. Lessing, "Über den Beweis des Geistes und der Kraft"; in *Gotthold Ephraim Lessings sämtlichen Schriften*, vol. 13, ed. Karl Lachmann (Berlin: Göschen'sche Verlagshandlung, 1897), p. 6.

pp. 311–12

Albert Schweitzer, *The Quest of the Historical Jesus*, 3rd edn, translated by W. Montgomery (London: A. & C. Black, 1954), p. 17.

p. 315

Martin Kähler, *The So-Called Historical Jesus and the Historic, Biblical Christ*, translated by Carl E. Braaten (Philadelphia: Fortress Press, 1964), p. 43. **[4.29]**

p. 316

Rudolf Bultmann, "The Significance of the Historical Jesus for the Theology of Paul"; in *Faith and Understanding*, ed. R. W. Funk (London: SCM Press, 1966), pp. 220–46; extract at p. 241.

p. 320

G. E. Lessing, "Über den Beweis des Geistes und der Kraft"; in *Gotthold Ephraim Lessings sämtlichen Schriften*, vol. 13, ed. Karl Lachmann (Berlin: Goschen'sche Verlagshandlung, 1897), pp. 4–8. **[4.26]**

p. 321

D. F. Strauss, *The Life of Jesus*, ed. Peter C. Hodgson, translated by George Eliot (Philadelphia: Fortress Press, 1972), p. 758.

p. 322

Rudolf Bultmann, "New Testament and Mythology"; in H. W. Bartsch (ed.), *Kerygma and Myth*, 2nd edn (London: SPCK, 1964), p. 42.

p. 323

Wolfhart Pannenberg, "Redemptive Event and History"; in *Basic Questions in Theology*, vol. 1, trans-

lated by George Kehm (London: SCM Press, 1970), pp. 15–80; extract at p. 15.

Chapter 13

p. 328

Irenaeus, *adversus haereses*, V.i.1.

p. 328

John Macquarrie, *Principles of Christian Theology*, 2nd edn (London: SCM Press, 1977), p. 269.

p. 331

Athanasius, *contra Arianos*, II, 9.

p. 331

Athanasius, *Epistolae Festales*, vii.

pp. 331–2

Augustine, *de civitate Dei*, X, 20.

p. 332

Hugh of St Victor, *de sacramentis*, I.viii.6–7; 10 **[5.15]**

p. 332

François Turrettini, *Institutio theologiae elencticae*, topic 14, q. 5; in *Institutio theologiae elencticae*, 3 vols (Rome: Trajecti, 1734), vol. 2, pp. 424–7. **[4.25]**

p. 332

John Pearson, *Exposition of the Creed* (London, 1659), p. 348.

p. 333

Joseph Butler, *The Analogy of Religion*; in *Works*, vol. 1 (Oxford: Oxford University Press, 1897), p. 221.

p. 333

Horace Bushnell, *The Vicarious Sacrifice* (New York: Charles Scribner, 1866), p. 91.

p. 335

Rufinus of Aquileia, *Expositio Symboli*, 14. **[5.7]**

p. 335

Fulbert of Chartres, "Chorus novae Ierusalem"; in F. I. E. Raby (ed.), *Oxford Book of Medieval Latin Verse* (Oxford: Clarendon Press, 1959), p. 179.

p. 335

William Langland, *Piers the Ploughman*, trans. J. F. Goodridge (London: Penguin Books, 1959), pp. 226–7.

p. 336

Gustaf Aulén, *Christus Victor: An Historical Study of the Three Main Types of the Idea of the Atonement* (London: SPCK, 1931), pp. 17–22. **[5.29]**

p. 337

Paul Fiddes, *Past Event and Present Salvation* (London: Darton, Longman and Todd, 1989), p. 136.

p. 339

Thomas Aquinas, *Summa Theologiae*, IIIa, q. 48, a. 2. **[5.17]**

p. 340

E. P. Sanders, *Paul and Palestinian Judaism* (London: SCM Press, 1977), pp. 467–8.

p. 342

P. T. Forsyth, *The Justification of God* (London: Duckworth, 1916), p. 136.

pp. 342, 343

Karl Barth, *Church Dogmatics*, 14 vols, edited and translated by G. W. Bromiley and T. F. Torrance (Edinburgh: T&T Clark, 1936–75), IV/1, pp. 222–3, 296.

p. 343

J. I. Packer, "What did the Cross Achieve? The Logic of Penal Substitution," *Tyndale Bulletin* 25 (1974), pp. 3–45; extract taken from pp. 16–22. **[5.33]**

p. 343

Clement of Alexandria, *Quis Dives Salvetur*, 37. **[5.3]**

p. 344

Peter Abelard, *Expositio in Epistolam ad Romanos*, 2. **[5.14]**

p. 344

Juana de la Cruz, *Libro de Conorte*, fol. 451v; as cited in Ronald E. Surtz, *The Guitar of God: Gender, Power, and Authority in the Visionary World of Mother Juana de la Cruz (1481–1534)* (Philadelphia: University of Philadelphia Press, 1990), p. 42.

p. 346

Friedrich Schleiermacher, *The Christian Faith*, translated by M. R. Mackintosh and J. S. Stewart (Edinburgh: T&T Clark, 1928), pp. 429–31. **[5.24]**

p. 347

Hastings Rashdall, *The Idea of Atonement in Christian Theology* (London: Macmillan, 1920), p. 463.

p. 349

René Girard, *I See Satan Fall Like Lightning* (Maryknoll, NY: Orbis Books, 2001), pp. 154–6.

p. 351

Vladimir Lossky, "Redemption and Deification"; in *In the Image and Likeness of God*, translated by John Erickson and Thomas Bird (New York: St Vladimir's Seminary Press, 1974), pp. 97–8. **[5.30]**

p. 352

Charles Wesley, "And Can It Be?"; in John Wesley and Charles Wesley, *Hymns and Sacred Poems* (London: William Strahan, 1739), 117–19. The hymn was originally entitled "Free Grace." **[5.23]**

p. 356

Charles Wesley, "Where Shall My Wondering Soul Begin?"; *United Methodist Hymnal* (Nashville, TN: Abingdon Press, 1989), No. 342.

p. 356

Fanny J. Crosby [Van Alstyne], "Blessed Assurance"; *United Methodist Hymnal* (Nashville, TN: Abingdon Press, 1989), No. 369.

Chapter 14

pp. 360–1

Tertullian, *de baptismo*, 5. **[6.4]**

p. 361

Origen, *de principiis*, III.iv.1. **[6.5]**

p. 361

Lactantius, *Divinae Institutiones*, VI, 10–11. **[6.7]**

p. 364

Pelagius, *Letter to Demetrias*, 16. **[6.16]**

p. 366

Augustine, *de natura et gratia*, iii, 3–iv, 4. **[6.13]**

p. 367

Details as set out in the Letter of Faustus of Rhegium to Lucidus (473); in *Corpus Scriptorum Ecclesiasticorum Latinorum*, vol. 20, ed. A. Engelbrecht (Vienna: Tempsky, 1891), pp. 165–6.

p. 370

Thomas Aquinas, *Summa Theologiae*, IaIIae, q. 110, a. 1. **[6.26]**

pp. 372–3

Martin Luther, Preface to the Latin Works (1545); in *D. Martin Luthers Werke: Kritische Gesamtausgabe*, vol. 54 (Weimar: Böhlau, 1938), pp. 185–6. **[6.32]**

p. 375
Martin Luther, Lectures on Romans (1515–16), in *D. Martin Luthers Werke: Kritische Gesamtausgabe*, vol. 56 (Weimar: Böhlau, 1938), pp. 269, 272. **[6.34]**

pp. 376–7
John Calvin, *Institutes*, III.xi.2, 23. **[6.38]**

p. 378
Council of Trent, Session VI, chapter 4; in H. Denzinger (ed.), *Enchiridion Symbolorum*, 39 edn (Freiburg im Breisgau: Herder, 2001), §1524; 504. **[6.39]**

p. 378
Council of Trent, Session VI, chapter 7; in H. Denzinger (ed.), *Enchiridion Symbolorum*, 39 edn (Freiburg im Breisgau: Herder, 2001), §1529; 506.

p. 381
Augustine, *de dono perseverantiae*, XIV, 35.

p. 384
Remonstrant Articles 1–2.

p. 384
Charles Wesley, "Would Jesus Have the Sinner Die?"; Text in F. Whaling (ed.), *John and Charles Wesley: Selected Writings and Hymns* (London: SPCK, 1981), p. 183.

p. 385
Karl Barth, *Church Dogmatics*, 14 vols, edited and translated by G. W. Bromiley and T. F. Torrance (Edinburgh: T&T Clark, 1936–75), II/2, p. 166. **[6.51]**

p. 385
Emil Brunner, *The Christian Doctrine of God: Dogmatics*, vol. 1, translated by Olive Wyon (London: Lutterworth Press, 1949), pp. 346–51. **[6.52]**

p. 386
Max Weber, *The Protestant Ethic and the Spirit of Capitalism*, translated by Talcott Parsons (London: Allen & Unwin, 1930), p. 91.

p. 387
Charles Darwin, *The Descent of Man*, 2nd edn (London: John Murray, 1882), p. 619.

Chapter 15

---

p. 397
Martin Luther, *On the Councils and the Church* (1539); in *D. Martin Luthers Werke: Kritische*

Gesamtausgabe, vol. 50 (Weimar: Böhlau, 1914), pp. 628–30. **[7.12]**

p. 400
John Calvin, *Institutes*, IV.i.1.

p. 400
Sebastian Frank, letter to John Campanus (1531); in B. Becker, "Fragment van Francks latijnse brief aan Campanus," *Nederlands Archief voor Kerkgeschiedenis* 46 (1964–5), pp. 197–205. **[7.15]**

p. 401
Menno Simons, *Complete Writings*, ed. John C. Wenger (Scottdale, PA: Herald Press, 1956), p. 300.

p. 401
Schleitheim Confession (1527), article 6.

p. 401
Schleitheim Confession (1527), article 2.

p. 403
Henri de Lubac, *Catholicism* (London: Burns & Oates, 1950), p. 29.

p. 404
John Calvin, *Institutes*, IV.i.9–10. **[7.17]**

p. 404
Karl Barth, *Dogmatics in Outline*, translated by G. T. Thomson (London: SCM Press, 1949), 143.

p. 405
Rudolf Bultmann, *Jesus Christ and Mythology* (London: SCM Press, 1959), pp. 82–3.

p. 405
Leonardo Boff, *Ecclesiogenesis: The Base Communities Reinvent the Church*, translated by Robert R. Barr (Maryknoll, NY: Orbis Books, 1986), p. 11. **[7.28]**

p. 408
Second Vatican Council, *Nostra Aetate*, October 28, 1965; in *Vatican II: Conciliar and Postconciliar Documents*, ed. Austin Flannery, OP (Northport, NY: Costello Publishing; Dublin: Dominican Publications, 1975), pp. 738–42.

p. 409
Cyprian of Carthage, *de catholicae ecclesiae unitate*, 5–7. **[7.3]**

p. 411
Hans Küng, *The Church*, translated by Ray and Rosaleen Ockenden (London: Search Press, 1978), pp. 273–4.

p. 411

Louis Weil, "The Gospel in Anglicanism"; in S. Sykes and J. Booty (eds), *The Study of Anglicanism* (London: SPCK, 1988), p. 75.

p. 414

Cyril of Jerusalem, *Catechetical Lecture* XVIII, 23, 26. **[7.4]**

p. 415

Thomas Aquinas, *In symbolum Apostolorum*, 9. **[7.9]**

p. 415

Hans Küng, *The Church*, translated by Ray and Rosaleen Ockenden (London: Search Press, 1978), p. 303.

pp. 416–17

H. B. Swete, *The Holy Catholic Church: The Communion of Saints, A Study in the Apostles' Creed* (London: Macmillan, 1915), pp. 44–8. **[7.23]**

Chapter 16

---

p. 421

Hugh of St Victor, *de sacramentis*, IX, 2. **[8.14]**

p. 422

Bonaventure, *In IV Sent.*, preface; in *Opera Theologica selecta*, 5 vols (Quaracchi: Editiones S. Bonaventurae, 1934–64), vol. 1, p. 15.

p. 422

Peter Lombard, *Sententiarum libri quatuor*, IV.i.4; ii.1. **[8.15]**

p. 423

Martin Luther, *The Babylonian Captivity of the Church* (1520); in *D. Martin Luthers Werke: Kritische Ausgabe*, vol. 6 (Weimar: Böhlau, 1888), pp. 509–12, 513–14. **[8.17]**

pp. 423–4

Council of Trent, Session VII, Canon 1; in H. Denzinger (ed.), *Enchiridion Symbolorum*, 39 edn (Freiburg im Breisgau: Herder, 2001), §1601, 522–3.

p. 424

Petilian, Letter to Augustine (402); in Augustine, *contra litteras Petiliani*, III.lii.64; in *Corpus Scriptorum Ecclesiasticorum Latinorum*, vol. 52, ed. M. Petschenig (Vienna: Tempsky, 1909), pp. 462–3.

p. 425

Innocent III, *de sacro altaris mysterio*, iii, 6.

p. 425

The Thirty-Nine Articles, article 26.

p. 426

Peter of Aquila, *In IV Sent.* IV, dist. I, q. 1, c. 1.

p. 426

Peter Martyr Vermigli, *Loci Communes* (London, 1583), IV.ix.ll.

p. 427

Council of Trent, Session VII, Canon 6; in H. Denzinger (ed.), *Enchiridion Symbolorum*, 39 edn (Freiburg im Breisgau: Herder, 2001), §1606, 523.

p. 427

Philip Melanchthon, *Loci Communes* (1521); in *Melanchthons Werke in Auswahl*, ed. H. Engelland (Gütersloh: Bertelsmann Verlag, 1953), vol. 2, pp. 140–4. **[8.21]**

p. 428

Second Vatican Council, *Sacrosanctum Concilium*, December 4, 1963, in *Vatican II: Conciliar and Postconciliar Documents*, ed. Austin Flannery, OP (Northport, NY: Costello Publishing; Dublin: Dominican Publications, 1975), p. 20.

pp. 428–9

Martin Luther, *Ein Sermon von dem Hochwirdigen Sacrament*, 5–8; in *Luther's Works*, vol. 35 (Philadelphia: Muhlenberg Press, 1960), pp. 51–2.

p. 429

Huldrych Zwingli, *On Baptism*; in *Corpus Reformatorum: Huldreich Zwinglis sämtliche Werke*, vol. 91 (Leipzig: Heinsius, 1927), pp. 217–18. **[8.24]**

p. 430

Martin Luther, *The Babylonian Captivity of the Church* (1520); in *D. Martin Luthers Werke: Kritische Ausgabe*, vol. 6 (Weimar: Böhlau, 1888), pp. 513–14. **[8.19]**

p. 432

Theodore of Mopsuestia, *Catechetical Homily* 15.20; in *Katechetische Homilien*, ed. Peter Bruns, 2 vols. (Freiburg: Herder, 1994–5), vol. 1, p. 404.

pp. 433–4

Cyril of Jerusalem, *Fourth Address on the Mysteries*, 2–6. **[8.5]**

p. 434

John of Damascus, *de fide orthodoxa*, IV, 13. **[8.9]**

p. 434

Paschasius Radbertus, *De corpore et sanguine Christi*, III.l; III.4; IV.I. **[8.10]**

p. 434

Ratranmus, *De corpore et sanguine Christi*, 2, 9–11, 16. **[8.11]**

p. 435

Candidus of Fulda, *de passione domini*, 5. **[8.12]**

p. 436

Fourth Lateran Council, cap. 1; in H. Denzinger (ed.), *Enchiridion Symbolorum*, 39 edn (Freiburg im Breisgau: Herder, 2001), §802; 358.

p. 439

Edward Schillebeeckx, *The Eucharist* (London: Sheed & Ward, 1968), p. 137.

p. 439

Edward Schillebeeckx, *The Eucharist* (London: Sheed & Ward, 1968), p. 131.

p. 439

Paul VI, *Mysterium Fidei*, 46.

p. 440

Huldrych Zwingli, *On the Lord's Supper* (1526); in *Corpus Reformatorum: Huldreich Zwinglis sämtliche Werke*, vol. 91 (Leipzig: Heinsius, 1927), pp. 796–800. **[8.23]**

Chapter 17

---

p. 447

Anthony Giddens, *Sociology* (Oxford: Polity Press, 1989), p. 452.

p. 450

Ludwig Feuerbach, *The Essence of Christianity*; in *Gesammelte Werke*, ed. W. Schuffenhauer, vol. 5 (Berlin: Akademie Verlag, 1973), pp. 46–7. **[9.2]**

p. 456

John B. Cobb, Jr., "Beyond Pluralism"; in G. D'Costa (ed.), *Christian Uniqueness Reconsidered: The Myth of a Pluralistic Theology of Religions* (Maryknoll, NY: Orbis, 1990), pp. 81–95; extract at pp. 81–4. **[9.11]**

p. 458

Lesslie Newbigin, *The Gospel in a Pluralist Society* (Grand Rapids, MI: Eerdmans, 1989), pp. 168–70. **[9.12]**

p. 459

Second Vatican Council, *Nostra Aetate*, October 28, 1965; in *Vatican II: Conciliar and Postconciliar Documents*, ed. Austin Flannery, OP (Northport, NY: Costello Publishing; Dublin: Dominican Publications, 1975), pp. 738–42. **[9.7]**

p. 460

Clark H. Pinnock, *A Wideness in God's Mercy: The Finality of Jesus Christ in a World of Religions* (Grand Rapids, MI: Zondervan, 1992), p. 157.

p. 460

John Hick, *The Second Christianity* (London: SCM Press, 1983), pp. 82–3.

p. 461

John Hick, *The Second Christianity* (London: SCM Press, 1983), pp. 84–5.

Chapter 18

---

p. 467

Cyprian, *de mortalitate*, 26.

p. 470

Dante Alighieri, *Epistula* XIII, 7; in Dante Alighieri, *Epistola a Cangrande, a cura di Enzo Cecchini* (Florence: Giunti, 1995), p. 35. Note that several scholars, including Bruno Nardi, dispute the authenticity of this letter.

pp. 471–2

Jeremy Taylor, *The Rules and Exercises of Holy Dying* (London, 1651), section 8, 1. **[10.16]**

p. 474

Rudolf Bultmann, "The Eschatology of the Gospel of John"; in *Faith and Understanding*, ed. R. W. Funk (London: SCM Press, 1966), pp. 165–83; extract at p. 175.

p. 475

Jürgen Moltmann, *Theology of Hope: On the Grounds and Implications of a Christian Eschatology*, translated by James W. Leitch (London: SCM Press; New York: Harper & Row, 1968), pp. 32–6.

p. 476

Helmut Thielicke, *Theological Ethics*, 3 vols, ed. and translated William H. Lazareth (Grand Rapids, MI: Eerdmans, 1978), vol. 1, 43–4.

p. 478

Jonathan Edwards, "Sinners in the Hands of an Angry God"; in *The Works of President Edwards*, ed. S. B. Wright, 10 vols (New Haven, CT: Yale University Press, 1929–30), vol. 7, 163–77. **[10.17]**

p. 478

Gottfried Wilhelm Leibniz, *Essais de Theodicée* (Amsterdam, 1734), part 1, 82.

p. 478

Philip E. Hughes, *The True Image: The Origin and Destiny of Man in Christ* (Grand Rapids, MI: Eerdmans, 1989), 404–7. **[10.24]**

p. 479

Gregory the Great, *Dialogia* IV.xli.3. **[10.11]**

p. 480

Catherine of Genoa, *Treatise on Purgatory*, iii, v. **[10.14]**

p. 480

Tertullian, *adversus Marcionem*, III.xxiv.3–6. **[10.4]**

p. 483

Origen, *de principiis*, II.x.3. **[10.5]**

p. 483

Methodius of Olympus, *de resurrectione*, I.xlii.l–xliii.4. **[10.6]**

p. 484

Peter Lombard, *Sententiarum libri quatuor* II.xxx.15. **[10.12]**

p. 484

William Fulke, *The Text of the New Testament* (London, 1589), p. 300 (English modernized).

Index

Note: Page references in **bold** type indicate Glossary entries, while those in *italics* indicate maps and diagrams.

Index compiled by Meg Davies (Registered Indexer of the Society of Indexers)